1 MONTH OF
FREE
READING

at

www.ForgottenBooks.com

By purchasing this book you are
eligible for one month membership to
ForgottenBooks.com, giving you
unlimited access to our entire
collection of over 1,000,000 titles via
our web site and mobile apps.

To claim your free month visit:
www.forgottenbooks.com/free920541

ISBN 978-0-265-99453-5
PIBN 10920541

091-213

QUARTERLY REPORT ON SELECTED RESEARCH PROJECTS
OF THE AGRICULTURAL RESEARCH SERVICE
U.S. Department of Agriculture
April 1 to June 30, 1984

INSECT AND WEED CONTROL RESEARCH

A SPRAY-ON BIRTH CONTROL FOR COCKROACHES called hydropene is the latest chemical weapon to battle this pest. Manufactured by a commercial firm, hydropene was found in tests to prevent the birth of cockroach offspring. ARS reports that a single spraying throughout a 100-unit apartment complex in Gainesville, Florida, had cut the roach population 95 percent eight months later.

A COOPERATIVE RESEARCH AGREEMENT was signed with Brazil in April to find new biological weapons to control the imported red fire ant, which now infests 230 million acres in nine Southern states.

ONE PROMISING CONTROL FOR FIRE ANTS is a synthetic hormone that mimics the pest's juvenile hormone. Researchers baited ant colonies with soybean oil and corn grit laced with tiny amounts of hormone. Worker ants carried the lethal bait into the colonies, where the food was regurgitated and fed to the queen and to immature ants. Under the hormone's influence, immature ants developed into drones instead of workers. Without workers to gather food and tend the broods, the fire ant colonies soon crumbled and eventually disappeared. A chemical company is now manufacturing the hormone.

INSECT NEUROCHEMISTRY is a science that studies the insect's brain and nervous system to learn what causes behavior. If the chemistry in the brain that dictates behavior can be disrupted, the resulting false signals can halt molting, upset mating, realign hormones or prompt other fatal reactions. Current research is trying to interrupt the production of sex attractants in the corn earworm moth...Isolate hormones in the housefly to learn what effect they have on specific cells in the fly's body...Isolate hormones in the stable fly that control the insect's muscle contractions. As research unlocks the intricacies of the insect brain, this scientific work will lead to a new class of safer insecticides which alter the behavior of insect pests without harming other living things.

VIRUS LETHAL TO A WHOLE CLAN OF INSECT PESTS, including cotton budworms and bollworms, can be sprayed on cotton plants and will kill caterpillars soon after they attack the boll. After death, a caterpillar corpse disintegrates when touched, releasing billions more virus particles that are deadly to live caterpillars nearby. The developer of the virus reports that "the potential for biological control agents has scarcely been tapped."

A FIRST-OF-ITS-KIND PROCESS for encapsulating biological or chemical herbicides in water-absorbent gels made from algae has been developed by ARS scientists. The gels contain the herbicides for controlled release. Although still too expensive for commercial use, the process will be useful to researchers attempting to solve weed-control problems.

A CHEMICAL SCENT MAY SOON ATTRACT armies of "friendly" spined soldier bugs to a single field, where they can feed on a wide variety of crop-destroying insects.

The soldier bugs feed on insect larvae, so pests are killed at the stage when
they inflict the most damage to crops. After the pests are destroyed, the
scent, called a pheromone, could be used to lure the soldier bugs to another
field to feed on more insects, while any pests remaining in the first field are
mopped up with pesticides.

TESTS SHOW THAT COCKROACHES and mosquitoes are in fact not repelled by
ultrasonic gadgets commonly sold through the mail, nor do they keep the
mosquitoes from biting. The U.S. Postal Service asked ARS scientists to check
the effectiveness of these products.

NEW GUIDELINES FOR MATCHING application rates of commonly used herbicides to
soil properties will help farmers adjust amounts of chemicals to soil changes
resulting from changes in tillage practices.

CROP RESEARCH

APPLYING INFINITESIMAL AMOUNTS of the hormone brassinolide to young plants
speeds up growth and maturation of several fruits and vegetables by as much as 2
to 4 weeks. In research trials, the steroid increased potato yields 24 percent;
radish and lettuce yields, 15 to 30 percent, and bean and pepper yields, 6 to 7
percent. It also proved effective on soybeans. Once commercial companies
develop large-scale methods for synthesizing brassinosteroids, their use could
become commonplace.

APPLICATION OF A CHEMICAL BIOREGULATOR known as DCPTA to young soybean plants
causes significant increases in oil and protein content of the soybean. In
trials in California, soybean yields also increased by as much as one third.

COTTON PLANTS THAT NEED LESS WATER may result from genes borrowed from a
drought-resistant cotton plant found growing wild in Mexico. The plant has a
root system that carries more water up through the plant to leaf surfaces, and
its leaf pores have a better mechanism for regulating the intake of airborne
carbon and release of water.

A NEW CARROT known as 'A Plus' is a superior source of Vitamin A, packing 60
percent more carotene than varieties now on the market. The carrot also has
good flavor. Several companies have begun limited production of the seed.

"SWEET SANDWICH" IS A NEW ONION that, unlike other onions, becomes milder in
flavor while in storage at low temperatures. In commercial and home garden
trials in New York State, the sweet onion outproduced 15 other varieties at
1,615 bushels per acre.

IMPORTANT PLANT BREEDING LINES have been released to public and private
researchers...Three new kinds of soybeans, all noncommercial, have been
developed by ARS and North Carolina State scientists. Breeders can use these
germplasm lines to improve insect and nematode resistance in soybean cultivars
being designed for use by farmers. They also can improve yields...Five
sunflower germplasm sources with resistance to all four North American races of

rust have been released for use in sunflower breeding and hybrid seed programs
by ARS and the North Dakota Agricultural Experiment Station...Three new kinds of
sweet potatoes have been developed by ARS and university researchers in Texas
and South Carolina...Eight new groups of winter-hardy alfalfa germplasm have
been released by ARS and cooperating state agricultural experiment stations.
All groups have desired multiple disease and insect resistance.

INVESTMENTS IN RESEARCH on wheat breeding by ARS and Purdue University have paid
off by increasing wheat production in soft red winter wheat-growing regions by
over 1 billion bushels since 1946.

GROUND WAS BROKEN MAY 19 for the new South Central Agricultural Research
Laboratory, at Lane, Oklahoma. When completed, the laboratory will focus on
production, harvesting, and marketing systems for horticultural crops important
to the South Central region.

ANIMAL RESEARCH

A NEW BLOOD TEST proved over 90 percent accurate in detecting trichinosis in
live pigs. A result of biotechnology research, the test delivers a higher level
of accuracy than achieved before without slaughtering the animal.

RED BLOOD CELLS ENCAPSULATE DRUGS in a new slow-release system for prolonging
the effectiveness of drugs in animals. Encapsulating a drug can potentially
lower the required dosage and target it selectively to specific organs where it
is needed. Animal systems are models for the human system.

A GOAT VIRUS DISCOVERY could shed light on the cause of rheumatoid arthritis in
humans. Caprine arthritis-encephalitis (CAE) virus is the only virus proven to
cause cnronic arthritis in mammals. Now that the goat disease has been
identified, it is being studied as an animal model for the human ailment.

LIVER SAMPLING FOR BIOPSY has been developed that permits removing large liver
samples from live animals with little loss of blood. The procedure may find
application in human medicine--possibly to stop bleeding of persons with livers
damaged in serious accidents.

SKIN CANCER GROWTH IS INHIBITED by the use of an insect growth regulator, used
routinely to control agricultural pests. In tests, diflubenzuron stopped the
growth of malignant melanoma and skin carcinoma tumors in mice and reduced tumor
size as much as 22 percent in one day.

RESTRICTING FEED DURING PREGNANCY affects progeny. Pigs from gilts in
early-restricted diets had less backfat, less fat around the kidneys, smaller
fat cells, and larger trimmed hams and loins than adequately fed gilts.

EARLY WARNING SIGNAL FOR ACUTE KIDNEY DYSFUNCTION can be obtained from the blood
of sheep and swine. Animal red blood cells are interconnected by "bridges,"
which give advanced warning of kidney damage. The research raises the question
of whether humans may exhibit these "bridges" at the onset of kidney failure, as
well as during the progression of the disease. If proven applicable, these
findings may be used as a quick diagnostic tool for early detection of diseased
kidneys in humans.

NARROWLEAF SUMPWEED has been identified as almost certainly the cause of spring cattle abortions along the Eastern Seaboard from Nova Scotia to Texas. Although scientists have not yet demonstrated the cause-and-effect relationship between sumpweed and bovine abortions, they have shown that the weed causes changes in the reproductive systems of cattle. Livestock producers will benefit greatly by taking preventive measures.

RESOURCE AND ENVIRONMENTAL RESEARCH

STATE-OF-THE-ART TECHNOLOGIES--from computers to lasers to solar power--are being linked together to deliver automatically just enough water to thirsty plants. A fully equipped moving trickle-irrigation system also can apply herbicides, fertilizers, and mulch to plants as needed. Growers will be able to stretch the use of water, including slightly saline water, for irrigation.

"PAIRED-ROW" PLANTING, a new way of managing no-till small grains, when combined with deep banding of fertilizers, increases early growth of wheat and offers new possibilities for more efficient use of fertilizers and better control of weeds.

SLOT MULCHING VIRTUALLY HALTED SOIL EROSION in tests on winter wheat fields in the Palouse, exploiting the region's exceptionally abundant crop residues. The emerging conservation system relies on packing crop residues into slots dug 4 inches wide, 10 inches deep, and spaced 12 to 24 feet apart across the field's contour. The system enables runoff water to penetrate into frozen soil rather than washing it away. Residues keep the slot open and insulated throughout the region's typical freezing and thawing cycles.

A MOBILE UNIT THAT DETOXIFIES PESTICIDE WASTES on site simplifies the problems of safe disposal in remote areas where transportation is difficult or expensive. It combines use of high-energy ultraviolet light and oxygen to partially biodegrade such pesticides as 2,4-D, atrazine, and paraquat before the waste goes into disposal tanks. Much of the nation's groundwater that is contaminated by pesticide residues stems from a serious lack of disposal technology on farms, which typically rely on unlined pits to handle wastes.

A MOBILE SOIL-SAMPLING MACHINE has been developed that can extract in half a minute soil cores of various diameters and depths. Previous samplers took 10 minutes per core. Cores are used for soil chemical analysis, soil mapping, water content determination, root analysis, and other purposes.

A NEW WATER-MANAGEMENT STRATEGY has been developed so brackish water can be used to irrigate certain crops grown in rotation when they are in a tolerant stage. At other times and for sensitive crops in rotation, normal quality water is used. This strategy permits substantial conservation of valuable and limited water resources through re-use of waste water. Cyclic use of brackish water prevents the soil from becoming saline while permitting, over time, substitution of brackish water for better quality water for certain irrigations.

HUMAN NUTRITION RESEARCH

ZINC DEFICIENCY RETARDS BRAIN DEVELOPMENT in offspring of laboratory rats. Research showed that the hippocampus area of the brain of the zinc-deficient offspring was underdeveloped and low in zinc. This area of the brain normally has high concentrations of zinc, a trace mineral essential for the formation of nucleic acids and protein. Research implication: It might be prudent for pregnant women to consume foods rich in zinc, including oysters, the single best source, along with wheat germ, nuts, beef, turkey, and cheese.

FIRST ROOM-SIZE HUMAN METABOLIC CHAMBER has been built in Beltsville to monitor heat produced in the body during normal living. The unit will help explain why some people gain weight on diets that have little or no effect on other people. The chamber, called a calorimeter, also will be used to check the accuracy of existing calorie tables. Many of these tables are based on experiments that were conducted over 90 years ago.

DIET LOWERS CHOLESTEROL IN OLYMPIC ATHLETES when exercise would not hold down blood lipid levels. Research concludes that physically active people, who eat diets high in saturated fats, cannot rely solely on exercise to hold down their cholesterol levels. Switching athletes to a diet with three times more unsaturated than saturated fat lowered their cholesterol levels to normal.

A MORE PRECISE TECHNIQUE FOR MEASURING VITAMIN D and its 11 metabolites in the blood, milk and tissues has been discovered. The new technique replaces bioassay methods which are laborious and imprecise. Imbalances in vitamin D are implicated in rickets and osteomalacia, and other diseases affecting humans.

COMMERCIAL APPLICATION OF RESEARCH

GLASS REINFORCED COTTON CANVAS is being evaluated as a tent fabric with improved strength and flame retardant properties. Samples of the fabric have been sent to industry and commercial organizations in response to requests.

THE U.S. NAVY AND COTTON INDUSTRIES are working with ARS to develop fabric for cotton, flame retardant, easy-care garments for shipboard enlisted personnel. This research meets a need that became apparent when the British Navy encountered new weaponry in the Falkland Islands action.

SARA LEE'S RETAIL FOOD TECHNOLOGY DEPARTMENT expressed interest in an experimental evaluation of computer-formulated corn blends. They believe the program may have application in some of their food products.

NEW CLOTH which absorbs and releases four times more heat than ordinary fabric is of interest to Levi Straus. Another application of this material may be in building insulation and solar heated greenhouses.

A NEW SEWER SYSTEM will be put to practical use in eastern Ohio--the first area in the nation to construct a variable-grade gravity sewer (VGS). The VGS system cuts costs 40 - 50 percent, is virtually maintenance-free, compatible with existing sewer systems, and suitable for new urban developments as well as sparsely populated rural areas.

A NEW TEST to determine the shelf life of ground meats has been developed using commercially available equipment. The procedure, which measures lactic acid content, cuts testing time from 5 or 6 days to 1 hour.

#

QUARTERLY REPORT ON SELECTED RESEARCH PROJECTS
OF THE AGRICULTURAL RESEARCH SERVICE
U.S. Department of Agriculture
July 1 to September 30, 1984

INSECT AND WEED CONTROL RESEARCH

TINY SOUTH AMERICAN WASPS ATTACK THE COLORADO POTATO BEETLE, top destroyer of U.S. potato, tomato, and eggplant crops. A 3-year test by USDA researchers cooperating with three states (MD, VA, NJ) showed the pinhead-size wasp controlled 60 to 80 percent of beetles by laying eggs inside these pests' eggs. Chemicals to control these pests cost more than $120 million yearly, and beetles are developing resistance to them. Uncontrolled, beetles can cause 100 percent losses. Wasps are less expensive and more effective than chemicals and are environmentally safe.
Beltsville Agricultural Research Center, MD

NEW PARASITE MAY HELP CONTROL GYPSY MOTHS. Future gypsy moth outbreaks will be better controlled by an arsenal of biological weapons developed by Agricultural Research Service scientists to make these pests sick, sterile, or sought after by parasites. More than half of all gypsy moths, a serious pest of forest and backyard trees, are killed by a buildup of beneficial foreign parasites. All of the parasites were introduced by ARS researchers.
Newark, DE

A NEW CLASS OF DELAYED-ACTION INSECTICIDES has been found to have potential against fire ants and other insect pests, including cockroaches, houseflies, and mosquito larvae. One toxicant group--sulfonamide analogues--was particularly promising against fire ants.
Gainesville, FL

GRASSHOPPERS' EATING HABITS COULD BACKFIRE ON THEM. Scientists in Montana are screening range plants to find those that grasshoppers least prefer. Their objective: to control these voracious pests by limiting their food supply, at the same time preserving fragile western rangeland.
Bozeman, MT

PLANTING SMALL GRAINS IN SOYBEANS CAN SUPPRESS WEEDS that compete with them. To hold down weed growth while the soybean crop is getting started, USDA scientists planted 48 varieties of winter small grains with soybeans in spring. They want to find out which grains injured the crop least, which most effectively suppressed weeds, and which were most tolerant of herbicides. While small grains hold down weed growth, herbicide treatment may still be necessary.
St. Paul, MN

DIPPING MAY NOT BE NECESSARY TO CONTROL SCABIES. Cattle infected with the parasite may now be injected with low doses of a miticide rather than undergo dipping--a costly, potentially hazardous, and wasteful practice. Researchers found that low doses of avermectin eradicate mites in 7 days and also control intestinal parasites.
Kerrville, TX

- more -

BY MARKING SCREWWORM SPERM, SCIENTISTS CAN STUDY the mating habits of sterile and fertile screwworms in the field. A dye, acridine orange, fed to adults or larvae, stains all reproductive tissues without adversely affecting the insect's survival, longevity, or behavior. Marked males that mate with unmarked females transfer sperm that fluoresce under ultraviolet light. Eliminating screwworms would save the U.S. livestock industry over $350 million each year.
Chiapas, Mexico

PLOWING MAY SPREAD RATHER THAN CONTROL WILD MUSTARD, a serious weed pest in spring-seeded small grains in Minnesota and the Dakotas. USDA scientists, investigating the best time and method of eradicating the weeds, say the tiny seeds enter cracks in dry soil and move down below the plow layer (the depth reached by cultivation) or are carried belowground by soil organisms.
St. Paul, MN

IDENTIFICATION OF TWO TICKS MAY LEAD TO BETTER CONTROL OF CATTLE FEVER. Researchers now can readily identify two almost identical tick species that cause the disease. Proper identification will help in developing new bio-controls that rely on sterilizing male ticks through hybrid breeding. Each year, ticks cost the cattle industry over $560 million in losses.
Mission/Kerrville, TX

SEEDS OF WEEDS LIKE VELVETLEAF ARE SPREADING IN THE UNITED STATES because of a toxin they contain that makes them immune to decomposition by soil micro-organisms. Once these seeds germinate, however, they are susceptible to microbial attack. ARS scientists are gaining a better understanding of how soil microorganisms can be utilized to keep these weed pests controlled biologically by overcoming early seed immunity.
Columbia, MO

A HAND-HELD SNIFFING "GUN" THAT CHECKS FOR HIDDEN FRUIT in luggage of travelers entering the United States has been developed by federal researchers. The gun could help prevent accidental infestations of pests such as the medfly in California and Florida. In a 2-day test before the opening of the Olympic Games, the device was used to check 90 pieces of luggage at the Los Angeles airport. Illicit agricultural materials were detected in 15 percent of the luggage.
Eastern Research Center, Philadelphia, PA

EMERGENCY FUNDS ARE BEING USED TO CONTROL LYGUS BUGS that damaged more than 50 percent of the Nation's pea and lentil crops last year, causing an unexpected loss of $5 million. ARS recently signed a cooperative agreement with the University of Idaho to furnish emergency funds for research to develop controls for these damaging pests. Pea and lentil exports total about $70 million a year.
Yakima, WA

CROP RESEARCH

A PLANT GENE EXPRESSION CENTER at Albany, CA, will speed genetic engineering of crops to help meet tomorrow's food and fiber needs. It is a cooperative project of ARS, the University of California at Berkeley, and the California State

Experiment Station. Annual federal funding of $4 million will be matched by industry and various public institutions. A director and 10 senior scientists will form the core of the center.
Berkeley, CA

TREATING AND PELLETIZING GUAYULE SEEDS increases their germination rate, giving them a better chance of developing into rubber trees. Guayule, a natural source of latex rubber, has trouble germinating when seeds are planted directly in semi-arid fields. Treating seeds with polyethylene glycol, a fungicide, a plant-growth hormone, and other chemicals, and then encasing them in a sand gelatin pellet, increases their chances of surviving from 2 to 50 percent and permits sowing them directly in production fields. Growing guayule in the United States could reduce our trade deficit. Last year over 770,000 tons of natural rubber, worth about $800 million, were imported.
Beltsville Agricultural Research Center, MD

HARVESTING SOYBEANS USING ROTARY DISKS could trim losses of the nation's top export crop by $246 million annually. Rotary disks cut off the stalks and help "airlift" beans that break free so a larger percentage of them land in the harvesting machine instead of on the ground.
Urbana, IL

AGRICULTURAL RESEARCH CAN PAY BIG DIVIDENDS. Every person-year of scientific research to improve cultivars of soft red winter wheat has resulted in increased yields worth $4.5 million. Wheat breeding by Agricultural Research Service-Purdue University teams has returned $2.8 billion in increased yields since 1921. The ARS-Purdue cultivars are sought for their resistance to Hessian fly and other pests and diseases and are used worldwide as parents by other breeders. Now ARS is seeking to learn the chemical basis of resistance to Hessian fly.
West Lafayette, IN

MUCH OF THE NATION'S PLANT RESOURCES--over 600,000 samples--has been computerized to make them accessible to any scientist with a computer and a telephone. The Germplasm Resources Information Network (GRIN), an electronic seed/plant catalogue, is now on line. The product of 7 years of planning, GRIN will serve public and private researchers as well as curators of germplasm (plant gene) collections. GRIN can quickly locate combinations of plant genes needed to develop crops that can better cope with diseases, insects, harsh climates, and poor soil.
Beltsville Agricultural Research Center, MD

THE NATIONAL ARBORETUM'S NATIONAL COUNTRY GARDEN shows novices how to overcome problems with shade, space, and water and soil in growing vegetables and flowers wherever people live and under almost any conditions. The food is grown on vertical walls and in hanging baskets, old tires, even egg cartons. The 3-acre garden project was funded by over 100 gardening organizations and commercial firms. Food harvested from the garden will be donated to community kitchens.
National Arboretum, Washington, DC

- more -

Quarterly Report - p. 4

THE TRACE MINERAL NICKEL IS NECESSARY for normal nitrogen metabolism in plants. This is the first new element shown to be essential to plants since chlorine was added to the list in 1954.
Beltsville Agricultural Research Center, MD

A SUPERIOR FORAGE GRASS CALLED "TIFTON 78" has been developed by USDA and University of Georgia researchers. The new variety is a bermudagrass that establishes itself faster than Coastal bermudagrass. It spreads faster, starts earlier in spring, is taller and, like Coastal bermudagrass, is immune to rust.
Tifton, GA

CHRISTMAS TREES CAN BE GROWN IN SEMI-ARID DESERTS using runoff water "harvested" from adjacent land treated to prevent infiltration. Quetta pines and Arizona cypress were tested at Camp Verde, AZ, and methods were found to bring trees to marketable size in 3 to 4 years.
Phoenix, AZ

SCIENTISTS AND COMPUTERS ARE GOING UNDERGROUND to probe the secrets of how roots gather and carry water to aboveground parts of thirsty plants. What they learn in the tangled world of roots will someday help dryland farmers program their microcomputers to make quick management decisions to assure the highest possible yields.
Pendleton, OR

EMBRYO CULTURES ARE BEING USED TO CROSS two members of the cantaloupe family that are resistant to a nematode that severely damages this crop each year. Technology developed from crossing the African horned cucumber and the West India gherkin will be used to transfer this resistance to cantaloupes.
Charleston, SC

ARS SEEKS SCIENTISTS JUST STARTING THEIR CAREERS to staff 26 projects to help broaden support for basic research. Research fellowships totaling $910,000 should encourage scientific talent and help advance scientific techniques, especially in molecular biology and other biotechnologies.
Washington, DC

ANIMAL RESEARCH

NEW LIGHT ON HOW BOVINE VIRAL DIARRHEA, the most prevalent viral disease of cattle, is transmitted from cows to young calves could save ranchers several million dollars annually. BVD, also known as viral one-two, infects at least 80 percent of cattle herds. Experiments confirmed that a persistent infection, hidden in apparently healthy animals, makes them susceptible to a second more serious attack of the same virus that kills by attacking the animal's lymphoid centers. If ranchers can identify persistently infected cows before the second infection, they can slaughter animals before they are reinfected.
National Animal Disease Center, Ames, IA

EWES NEED NOT BE SLAUGHTERED AFTER A SINGLE ABORTION because the cause may not be inherited. Sheep abortions in 16 flocks in five states have been traced for the first time to a microscopic parasite. This parasite carries a disease,

- more -

called toxoplasmosis, that causes ewes to abort. Once infected, ewes will not abort again even if reinfected. An estimated one-third to one-half of U.S. adult sheep carry the organism that the animal's immune system keeps under control. Reproductive diseases in sheep and goats cost about $50 million in losses annually.
Beltsville Agricultural Research Center, MD

AN EXPERIMENTAL VACCINE MADE UP OF DEAD BOVINE BRUCELLOSIS bacilli has been developed at the National Animal Disease Center. A specific contagious disease of cattle, swine, sheep, and goats, brucellosis outbreaks in unvaccinated dairy herds will cause abortions and reduce milk yields by 20 percent. Several laboratories have developed sophisticated tests that are highly sensitive and can detect bacteria-infected animals better than conventional tests.
National Animal Disease Center, Ames, IA

CROSSBREEDING BENEFITS ARE EXTENDED TO SMALL HERDS. For the first time, small herds can benefit from complex crossbreeding systems previously limited to large herds. USDA geneticists have developed a technique that makes it practical to genetically match production traits in cattle with climate and available locally grown feeds. The new technique should help the 80 percent of U.S. farmers and ranchers with herds of 50 or fewer cows that currently use rotational crossbreeding--a practice that is difficult and inefficient with small herds.
U.S. Meat Animal Research Center, Clay Center, NE

VIROIDS, A NEW CLASS OF DISEASE-CAUSING PARTICLES, could give scientists a clue to causes of many still puzzling diseases. The discovery of these extremely small infectious particles by an ARS scientist has spurred new directions for research into many diseases of animals and plants. Viroids may also open a new path for research into diseases like some human cancers, infectious hepatitis, and multiple sclerosis, whose cause have eluded scientists.
Beltsville Agricultural Research Center, MD

MEMBRANE RESEARCH ATTRACTED OVER 300 OF THE WORLD'S LEADING SCIENTISTS to Beltsville recently to discuss the latest findings. Fluid, film-like membranes, a molecule or two thick, control the essential chemistry and physics of every living cell. Membranes keep all life forms alive and well. Thanks to high-powered instruments and enlightened understanding of the molecules of living things, scientists are now finding that membranes could hold the key to solving many problems in medicine, nutrition, and agriculture.
Beltsville Agricultural Research Center, MD

COMPUTERS CAN HELP DAIRY FARMERS MONITOR THEIR COWS' HEALTH in barn and pasture. Scientists are monitoring milk production and temperature to help spot mastitis infections and to tell them when cows are in estrus. Hopes are that the system can be used to help dairy farmers direct their attention to cows needing special attention before serious problems develop.
Urbana, IL

FEDERAL RESEARCHERS HAVE JOINED FORCES WITH INDUSTRY AND BREEDERS to improve the genetic quality of the nation's beef cattle. Their purpose: to improve the efficiency of beef production. Their efforts have already paid off in the form of a national sire evaluation program for at least 12 breeds of cattle,

- more -

providing much-needed information to breeders for improving their herds.
U.S. Meat Animal Research Center, Clay Center, NE

THE GREAT PYRENEES MAKE EXCELLENT GUARD DOGS for livestock on rangelands. The U.S. Sheep Experiment Station evaluated three breeds for their ability to protect grazing sheep from predators under both fenced pasture and open range conditions. Eighty percent of the dogs were judged successful.
Dubois, ID

RESOURCES AND ENVIRONMENTAL RESEARCH

EVIDENCE ACCUMULATES ON THE VALUE of leaving residues on fields to slow soil erosion. Even covering 30 percent of the surface of many soils can result in 60 to 70 percent less erosion than on soils with no residue cover. Other recent findings: soils on a 2.5-percent slope eroded 18 times more under plow disk tillage than under no-till. In soybean fields, soil losses on 2 percent slopes that have been fall-plowed or chiseled were three times as great as from no-till.
National Soil Erosion Laboratory, West Lafayette, IN

SEVERE EROSION CAN CUT SOYBEAN YIELDS BY 50 PERCENT. A 2-year study, done with USDA'S Soil Conservation Service, showed that 24 farms in the Southern Piedmont, GA, with normally high-yielding, good loamy soil experienced these heavy yield losses where most of the original top soil was lost.
Watkinsville, GA

A FOG-COLLECTING MACHINE MOUNTED ON A TRUCK is being used to analyze air samples for microscopic particles, like pesticides, wood smoke, dust, and other pollutants. The aim is to find out how pesticides and other organic chemicals cycle in the environment.
Beltsville Agricultural Research Center, MD

SOYBEANS LEAVE SOIL MORE SUSCEPTIBLE TO EROSION than corn, a 7-year ARS study in Iowa shows. Soil losses when corn followed soybeans averaged 4.3 tons per acre from spring plowing to spring plowing. Soil losses when corn followed corn were 3.1 tons per acre; losses when soybeans followed corn were 2.9 tons per acre.
Iowa State Research Center, Beaconsfield

LOW QUALITY WATER SUPPLIES can be used successfully to establish grass after surface mining in the northern Great Plains where natural precipitation is limited.
Mandan, ND

A NEW INSTRUMENT SIMULTANEOUSLY MEASURES WATER CONTENT AND SALINITY. Developed by ARS, it replaces two used in the past for the same purpose, speeds data collection, and reduces costs for land managers and research scientists.
Riverside, CA

HUMAN NUTRITION RESEARCH

INCREASED POTASSIUM INTAKE LOWERS BLOOD PRESSURE in men by increasing the level of sodium excreted. Although potassium and high blood pressure or hypertension have been linked for over two decades, USDA scientists have found an inverse

relationship between increased potassium intake and hypertension, a major health problem in the United States.
Human Nutrition Research Center, Beltsville, MD

VANADIUM MAY INFLUENCE CHOLESTEROL LEVELS as well as several biochemical processes involving other trace minerals like copper and iron, amino acids, and a blood protein. USDA scientists at the Human Nutrition Research Center, Fargo, ND, found high blood levels of cholesterol in rats fed diets high in vanadium and low in copper, or low in amounts of both minerals. In studies of the need for and roles of trace minerals in human diets, rats and chicks have proven reliable models.
Grand Forks Human Nutrition Center, ND

MOTHERS OF PREMATURE BABIES PRODUCE MILK THAT IS EASIER TO DIGEST and more suitable for developing the newborn infant's brain and nervous system than milk of mothers who deliver full-term infants. These findings are important in understanding the nutritional requirements of the premature infant and for proper handling of milk in human milk banks.
Beltsville Agricultural Research Center, MD/Eastern Research Center, Philadelphia, PA

AN EXCESS OF VITAMINS AND MINERALS CAN BE AS HARMFUL to human health as too little. Overdoses of many vitamins can force human metabolism to work overtime to rebalance, federal nutritionists find. Megadoses of iron, zinc, copper, and folic acid may cause more problems than they cure. The surest way to a nutritional balance for most adults is to eat balanced diets containing a variety of foods.
Human Nutrition Research Center, Beltsville, MD

TOO LITTLE COPPER AND CHROMIUM are present in the diets of many Americans, researchers find. Dietary copper helps keep serum cholesterol levels in check; chromium helps regulate blood sugar levels in many people. Copper is found in organ meats, not as popular with many Americans as they used to be. Chromium is found in whole wheat and mushrooms, among other foods.
Human Nutrition Research Center, Beltsville, MD

LOWER-SALT RECIPES FOR PROCESSED MEATS AND BAKED GOODS have been developed by ARS scientists. A 2-year study showed that the amount of table salt in hot dogs and corned beef and other processed meats can be reduced by 20 to 25 percent and that in bread‐ by 50 percent—without sacrificing flavor or texture or reducing their shelf-life.
Eastern Research Center, Philadelphia, PA

GERMINATING SORGHUM SPROUTS AT HOME CAN BE DANGEROUS because of the risk of cyanide poisioning. Less than 4 ounces of sorghum seeds, germinated at the right temperature, can produce enough cyanide to be fatal if eaten in one meal.
Eastern Research Center, Philadelphia, PA

SHELL-LESS TURKEY EGGS MAY UNLOCK THE SECRETS OF EMBRYONIC LIFE in animals and humans. Scientists at Beltsville have developed a new technique that keeps embryos alive outside their shells almost until hatching time. The technique could help expedite research to see how early nutrition relates to human ailments, possibly even to birth defects.
Beltsville Agricultural Research Center, MD

- more -

NEW COMPUTER METHOD PROBES WHAT HAPPENS TO HYDROGENATED VEGETABLE OIL during matabolism. The computer measures natural fatty acids, labeled fatty acids, and fatty acids formed during digestion, all in the blood.
Northern Research Center, Peoria, IL

A 12-STORY BUILDING TO HOUSE USDA'S CHILDREN'S NUTRITION RESEARCH CENTER in Houston, TX, will be built with a $49 million supplemental appropriation approved in August. The Center is the only USDA research facility to focus exclusively on the nutrient needs and status of pregnant and lactating women and of infants from conception to adolescence. Established in 1979, the Center will continue to be operated under a cooperative agreement between Baylor College of Medicine and the Agricultural Research Service.
Children's Nutrition Research Center, Houston, TX

COMMERCIAL APPLICATION OF RESEARCH/POSTHARVEST TECHNOLOGY

THE FIRST BACTERIA FOUND TO CONTROL BROWN ROT, the world's most pernicious disease of stone fruits like peaches and apricots, could replace chemicals in controlling the fungus. The first biocontrol developed to check a postharvest disease produces an antibiotic that is safer, more effective, and longer lasting than chemicals. Normally, harvested fruit is sprayed with a fungicide that loses its punch within 2 weeks, allowing the fungus to take over.
Kearneysville, WV/Byron, GA

USDA SCIENTISTS HAVE PRODUCED THE IDEAL COTTON PLANT—one with toxic gossypol in its leaves and stems but none in its seeds. Gossypol protects the plant from insects but also makes seed oil and meal unfit for use as food for humans or as feed for nonruminant animals. The new plants have the toxin in the right places, which saves time and money by eliminating the need to remove it from seed oil and meal after harvest.
Stuttgart, AR

CAMPBELL'S SOUP IS EVALUATING DEFATTED SOY FLOUR produced by USDA scientists at Peoria by extracting oil from soy flakes with supercritical carbon dioxide. The company earlier evaluated laboratory samples of the flour for flavor and physical properties. So far, the flour is not commercially available.
Northern Research Center, Peoria, IL

THE PROTEIN CONTENT OF RICE FLOUR WAS INCREASED from 8 to 25 percent by digesting some of the starch with an enzyme. The creamy white powder dissolves readily in water and can be used for gruels, puddings, and snack foods. A single serving of the flour can meet many of the vitamin and protein needs of 1- to 3-year-old children—an important discovery for less developed countries depending almost entirely on vegetable sources of protein. Food safety tests will be conducted before the product is marketed.
Western Research Center, Berkeley, CA

- more -

A NEW OVERSEAS OFFICE TO COORDINATE THE EXCHANGE OF AGRICULTURAL TECHNOLOGIES was established in the Netherlands. The coordinator's mission is to monitor the latest foreign technological developments--especially in biotechnology and genetic engineering--and to assess their impact on American agriculture. The new overseas office fulfills the department's congressional mandate to improve cooperation and communications with Europe's agricultural research community and its foreign cooperators.
Washington, DC

A TASK FORCE OF COTTON INDUSTRY AND USDA RESEARCHERS toured ARS cotton research facilities at Stoneville, MS, and New Orleans to establish closer working relationships among federal, state, and private researchers.
Stoneville, MS/Southern Research Center, New Orleans

INSECT-PRODUCED DUST INCREASES THE POTENTIAL FOR GRAIN DUST EXPLOSIONS by adding to the existing dust load at grain-handling facilities. Lesser grain borers and rice weevils, the main dust producers, are also the most damaging insects of stored grains.
Manhattan, KS

# # #

QUARTERLY REPORT ON SELECTED RESEARCH PROJECTS
OF THE AGRICULTURAL RESEARCH SERVICE
U.S. Department of Agriculture
October 1 to December 31, 1984

INSECT AND WEED CONTROL RESEARCH

A FUNGUS THAT DESTROYS GYPSY MOTHS IN JAPAN will be lab- and field-tested by ARS scientists at Ithaca, N.Y. The fungus could serve as another biological weapon against the insect pest's American cousins.
Insect Pathology Research Unit, Ithaca, N.Y.
R. S. Soper, Jr., insect pathologist, (607) 257-2030.

TO HOLD THE LINE ON THE SPREAD OF A PARASITIC MITE of bees that threatens the $180 million U.S. honey bee industry, an ARS entomologist from Laramie, Wyo., has been temporarily assigned to Weslaco, Tex., to cooperate with Mexican and Canadian scientists on controlling the pest.
Fruit Protection and Production Research, Weslaco, Tex.
W. Wilson, entomologist, (512) 986-3159.

AVERMECTIN, A NATURAL PRODUCT derived from soil microorganisms, has proved effective in lab and field studies against the red imported fire ant. It also shows promise in controlling boll weevils, bollworm, and tobacco budworm. The chemical will soon be commercially available.
Insects Affecting Man and Animals Laboratory, Gainesville, Fla.
D. F. Williams, entomologist, (904) 373-6701.

BETTER CONTROL OF LEAFY SPURGE IS NOW POSSIBLE by combining herbicides, plant growth regulators, and new application techniques that increase herbicidal effectiveness. The new system reduces the amount of chemicals needed for control, cuts costs per acre, and lowers environmental risks. Leafy spurge is a noxious, perennial weed that has damaged 3 million acres of U.S. pasture and rangeland, causing annual losses of about $20 million.
North Dakota, Montana, and Wyoming Experiment Stations
W. Shaw, national program leader, weed science, (301) 344-3301.

STINGLESS WASPS FROM EUROPE SAVED FARMERS $29 MILLION throughout the East and Midwest over the past nine years by protecting alfalfa fields from a costly pest called the alfalfa blotch leafminer, also an immigrant from Europe. Since first released, the wasps have overtaken and killed fast-spreading leafminer populations from the Canadian Maritime Provinces to Virginia and west to Michigan. Last year, the buildup of wasps was sufficient to prevent damage estimated at $13 million to alfalfa crops in 10 of the states. Alfalfa is nutritionally the leading feed crop of livestock and is grown on more than 26 million acres nationwide.
Beneficial Insects Research Laboratory, Newark, Del.
R. M. Hendrickson, entomologist, (302) 731-7330.

EVIDENCE THAT DWARF BUNT DISEASE of wheat could not cause an epidemic in Chinese winter wheat is presented in an ARS research report. The evidence should help U.S. wheat growers convince China that it should lift a quarantine on wheat grown in the Pacific Northwest.
Forage Seed and Cereal Research, Corvallis, Oreg.
E. J. Trione, chemist, (503) 754-3451.

ARS Quarterly Report - p. 2

INSECT AND WEED CONTROL RESEARCH (continued)

MINERAL AND VEGETABLE OILS PLUS SEX PHEROMONES can effectively trap and
suffocate grain weevils as well as flour, warehouse, and sawtoothed grain
beetles. The new traps will enable food-processing plants and warehouses to
quickly monitor the migration and buildup of beetles and to use less pesticide
and to help remedy environmental safety problems of bakeries and warehouses in
controlling pests.
Bee Management and Entomology Research, Madison, Wis.
W. E. Burkholder, entomologist, (608) 262-1732.

THE EUROPEAN ASPARAGUS WEEVIL can now be curbed with a two-pronged attack.
First, the huge stands of wild asparagus the weevils feed on should be
eliminated. Then fall tillage combined with pesticide spraying should kill at
least 90 percent of overwintering insects.
Insect Ecology and Behavior Research, Yakima, Wash.
E. Halfhill, entomologist, (509) 575-5974.

LYGUS BUGS THAT COST $54 MILLION A YEAR IN CROP LOSSES and control costs in
California alone can now be studied without seasonal interruption. A new mass-
rearing procedure and artificial diet allows these pests to be studied
year-round without relying on their natural food, fields of green bean pods.
Biological Control of Insects Research, Tucson, Ariz.
H. Graham, entomologist, (602) 629-6220.

TWO TOXINS FROM CROP RESIDUES ARE CUTTING YIELDS OF WHEAT AND BARLEY grown under
no-till. Acetic and butyric acids, formed in decaying straw and chaff left from
the previous crop, are the culprits. Studies are now underway to see if moving
the straw and chaff and seeding crops in one operation would control toxins and
at the same time save fuel costs.
Land Management and Water Conservation, Pullman, Wash.
L. Elliott, microbiologist, (509) 335-1551.

AFRICANIZED BEES CONTINUE THEIR NORTHWARD MARCH and are now in Central America.
Besides threatening American agriculture by reducing native bee pollination and
honey production, the bees would cause a $54 million loss to the beekeeping
industry if they spread to Savanah, Ga. as projected. Moreover, recent research
indicates the bees can overwinter as far north as New York City, which could
double or triple estimated losses. ARS scientists are currently investigating
various ways to deal with the problem, like breeding more gentle and productive
Africanized bees and learning how to better manage domestic honeybees. (A new
ARS film has just been released—Killer Bee Countdown.)
Bee Breeding and Stock Center Laboratory, Baton Rouge, La.
T. Rinderer, geneticist, (504) 766-6064.

A NEW SEX LURE ISOLATED FROM MALE RICE WEEVILS attracts grain weevils. Called
an "aggregation pheromone," it lures both sexes of rice, maize, and granary
weevils to traps for monitoring and control. Previously, few effective
attractants had been found for grain weevils
Bee Management and Entomology Research, Madison, Wis.
W. E. Burkholder, entomologist, (608) 262-3795.

INSECT AND WEED CONTROL RESEARCH (continued)

COLOR AERIAL PHOTOGRAPHY IS BEING USED TO DETECT infestations of camphorweed, a troublesome weed increasing its hold on south Texas rangelands. The weed produces a profusion of bright yellow flowers in the fall, when photographs can help researchers pinpoint infested areas, monitor the weed's spread, and delineate areas needing control measures.
Remote Sensing Research, Weslaco, Tex.
J. H. Everitt, range scientist, (512) 968-5533.

GAS CHROMOTOGRAPHY HAS RESOLVED A CONTROVERSY over the number of species of imported fire ants by comparing the venom from both red and black ants. Analysis of alkaloid patterns in ants' venom as well as the fact that the ants can intermate prove there is only one species—a finding that will help facilitate their control.
Insects Affecting Man and Animals Research Laboratory, Gainesville, Fla.
C. Lofgren, entomologist, (904) 737-6701.

PREEMERGENCE SPRAYING IS THE KEY TO HOLDING DOWN JIMSONWEED IN SOYBEANS. A four-year study showed that, when the weed was allowed to grow with soybeans, yields were reduced 23 percent as compared with only a 3 percent decrease when weeds emerged four weeks later than soybeans. Keeping soybeans free of several other weeds will also increase yields.
Soybean Protection Research, Urbana, Ill.
E. Stoller, plant physiologist, (217) 333-1277.

RED FLOUR BEETLES MAY SOON SUCCUMB TO MALATHION, thanks to isolation of the specific gene that provides resistance to this most commonly used insecticide for stored grain. By modifying the specific genes in the insect that resist insecticides, scientists may be able to develop an improved strategy with insecticide control. The red flour beetle's resistance has intensified in the last 15 years throughout the Midwest and Southeast, especially in Alabama, Florida, and Georgia.
U.S. Grain Marketing Research Laboratory, Manhattan, Kans.
R. Beeman, entomologist, (913) 539-9141.

TEN PERCENT HIGHER RICE YIELDS AND LOWER WEED CONTROL COSTS have boosted net profits of rice growers in the South by $25 million a year. New integrated weed management systems—that include fewer fertilizer and disease control applications and better water management—have increased yields and eliminated the need for two herbicide applications on 500,000 acres of rice.
ARS Research Production and Weed Control Research, Stuttgart, Ark.,
W. Shaw, national program leader, weed science, (301) 344-3301/Roy Smith, agronomist, (501) 673-2661.

NATURAL ALLELOCHEMICALS ARE AN EXCITING NEW WAY TO CONTROL WEEDS. Some weeds manufacture and exude chemicals through their roots and stems that injure other species growing nearby. One such plant, spikerush, exudes several chemicals harmful to aquatic weeds. These allelopathic chemicals have been identified, and progress is being made in synthesizing them. Allelochemistry offers many new approaches to selective weed control.
Western Regional Research Center, Oakland/Davis, Calif.
W. Shaw, national program leader, weed science, (301) 344-3301.

INSECT AND WEED CONTROL RESEARCH (continued)

FENOXYCARB APPLIED TO STORED WHEAT successfully controlled the rice weevil, lesser grain borer, confused flour beetle, and Indianmeal moth for two months without lowering the grain's germination. It appears to be an excellent pesticide candidate for protecting stored grain.
U.S. Grain Marketing Research Laboratory, Manhattan, Kans.
R. Beeman, entomologist, (913) 776-2710.

FENITROTHION, AN INSECTICIDE, shows promise for protecting stored peanuts. For years, malathion and synthesized pyrethrins have been the only two insecticides approved for use on stored oilseeds, but insect resistance to malathion and the uncertain supply of pyrethrins has spurred the search for substitutes. Like malathion, fenitrothion degraded after one year yet was more effective than malathion at all standard treatment rates.
Stored-Product Insects Research and Development Laboratory, Savannah, Ga.
L. Redlinger, entomologist, (912) 233-7981.

FOLIC ACID AND RIBOFLAVIN, both B-vitamins, may help protect a virus from breaking down during biological warfare against gypsy moths. Normally, the virus breaks down under the ultraviolet rays of the sun; the B-vitamins act as sunscreens for the virus in the same way that they protect human beings from sunburn.
Gypsy Moth Rearing Research, Otis, Mass.
M. Shapiro, entomologist, (617) 563-9303.

HONORS FOR 1984 ARS SCIENTIST OF THE YEAR went to James H. Tumlinson III for heading a team of USDA researchers that identified and synthesized the pheromones of several major insect pests. These chemicals are now being used commercially to lure insects into traps or to confuse them so they fail to mate.
Insect Attractants, Behavior, and Basic Biology Research Laboratory, Gainesville, Fla.
J. H. Tumlinson, chemist, (904) 373-6701

CROP RESEARCH

SINGLE CELLS FROM POTATO PLANTS that are difficult to cross are being fused to overcome major barriers to breeding better potatoes. The research is aimed at fusing cells from South American species with cultivated U.S. lines to capture genes that transmit such traits as disease resistance into domestic potatoes. New potato plants bred by cell fusion are generally bigger and stronger than either parent and are resistant to potato leaf roll virus, qualities needed by the $1.7 billion U.S. potato industry.
Plant Disease Resistance Research, Madison, Wis.
J. P. Helgeson, plant physiologist, (603) 262-1541.

RESISTANCE TO COLD, DROUGHT, NEMATODES, AND DISEASE is being bred into orange trees using Australian and Chinese relatives of citrus. Also promising is an Australian citrus relative whose fruit takes only one-third as long to mature as orange trees.
U.S. Horticultural Research Laboratory, Orlando, Fla.
H. Barrett, geneticist, (305) 898-6791.

CROP RESEARCH (continued)

FRUIT TREES CAN BE AUTOMATICALLY PRUNED—a year ahead—by applying a chemical called paclobutrazol to soil at the base of apple and other orchard trees. Branches automatically grow "pruned" the next year, letting in more fruit-producing light and eliminating insect hiding places. The technology could revolutionize how fruit is grown in the future.
Production, Harvesting, and Handling of Tree Fruits Research, Wenatchee, Wash.
M. Williams, plant physiologist, (509) 662-4317.

TO IMPROVE HONEY BEE HEALTH, drones are being bred to do a better job of removing dead and dying bees from the hive, lessening the chance of a disease like chalkbrood spreading through bee colonies. Chalkbrood is a fungus disease that can kill up to 50 percent of bee colonies. Bees annually produce honey and beeswax worth $140 million.
Carl Hayden Bee Research Center, Tucson, Ariz.
M. A. Gilliam, microbiologist, Honey Bee Nutrition Research, (602) 629-6347.

SPEEDY IDENTIFICATION OF THE NEW CANKER DISEASE OF CITRUS was possible because of research already underway at Beltsville on new methods for rapid and accurate disease diagnosis. The sophisticated test identified the disease not only as canker but also as a new strain of the bacterium, information that was so thorough and conclusive that eradication steps were initiated in Florida without delay. The same test also identified a bacterium that caused a new but similar disease found in Mexico. Its quick identification allowed USDA's Animal and Plant Health Inspection Service to make appropriate regulatory decisions to prevent entry into the United States.
Fruit Laboratory, Beltsville, Md.
E. Civerolo, plant pathologist, (301) 344-3569.

NEW PLANTING TECHNIQUE TRIGGERS FAST PEACH GROWTH. Planting young peach trees in killed sod can increase their growth by up to 45 percent in new orchards so that a sizable crop may be harvested in three years. Other kinds of fruit trees may also grow faster planted in killed grass.
Appalachian Fruit Research Station, Kearneysville, W. Va.
W. Welker, soil scientist, (304) 725-3451.

'GUARD,' THE ONLY HARD RED SPRING WHEAT with resistance to Hessian fly, was grown on 20,000 acres in South Dakota in 1984. Next year's planting is expected to reach 250,000 acres. 'Guard,' bred by ARS and South Dakota State University scientists and released in 1983, is also a high producer.
Plant Science and Entomology Research, Manhattan, Kans.
J. Hatchett, entomologist, (915) 532-5861.

TO STEER HONEY BEES AWAY FROM PESTICIDE-TREATED CROPS, scientists are looking at selective breeding among ways to develop bees that zero in on targeted pollens. Honey bees will not naturally respond to dietary conditioning, a tactic that works on other insects. Bees move pollen to fertilize crops worth nearly $19 billion annually.
Honey Bee Pesticides/Diseases Research, Laramie, Wyo.
A. Stoner, entomologist, (307) 766-2281.

CROP RESEARCH (continued)

ARTIFICIAL WINDSTORMS REVEAL PLANT CELLS ARE LOST IN WINDSTORMS. A wind tunnel in Manhattan, Kans., is providing new evidence that cells of young plants—as well as the soil—are literally blown away in windstorms that sweep across Great Plains farmlands. Farming practices that slow wind speed to 15 miles an hour at ground level will protect both soil and such crops as sorghums, soybeans, and wheat.
Wind Erosion Research, Manhattan, Kans.
D. V. Armbrust, soil scientist, (913) 776-2716.

INCREASING THE CALCIUM CONTENT OF PEARS AND APPLES can cure fruit of disorders that occur during growth and storage, like green stain, alfalfa greening, freckle pit, and cork spot. It also increases by 10 percent the calcium available for human nutrition from eating fruit.
Production, Harvesting, and Handling of Tree Fruits Research, Wenatchee, Wash.
J. T. Raese, plant physiologist, (509) 662-4317.

TAN SPOT, A DISEASE THAT CUTS YIELDS OF SUSCEPTIBLE SOYBEAN varieties by as much as 18 percent in about 84 percent of fields in southwestern Iowa, left unscathed such new varieties as 'Amsoy 17,' 'Beeson,' and 'Harcor'—all bred by ARS scientists to resist the disease.
Cereal and Soybean Improvement Research, Ames, Iowa.
Joh Dunleavy, plant pathologist, (515) 294-3122.

ZINC DEFICIENCIES CAN STUNT BEAN, POTATO, AND SWEET CORN GROWTH, but the problem can be solved by crop rotation. Beans not fertilized with zinc grew normally when planted after corn but absorbed 12 times as much zinc as when grown after sugarbeets or fallow. Why beans take up more zinc following corn is now under study.
Snake River Conservation Research Center, Kimberly, Idaho.
G. Leggett, soil scientist, (208) 423-5582.

FERTILIZING RANGELANDS with about 200 pounds per acre of ammonium nitrate consistently increased soil water use, tripled or quadrupled grass yields, and boosted protein content of grasses by 9 percent or more in a 9-year study.
Soil and Water Conservation Research, Lincoln, Nebr./Forage, Range, and Shelterbelt Research, Mandan, N. Dak.
J. Power, soil scientist, (402) 472-1484.

ETHREL, A PLANT GROWTH REGULATOR that prevents sugarcane from flowering, passed three years of tests and was recently approved by the U.S. Environmental Protection Agency for large-scale use on sugar plantations. Flowering decreases sugarcane yields by as much as 30 percent. Other benefits observed with ethrel have been extra growth and higher sugar yields.
Sugarcane Production Research, Aiea, Hawaii.
P. H. Moore, plant physiologist, (808) 487-0561.

PYTHIUM ROOT ROT SAPS WHEAT YIELDS in the Pacific Northwest by 15 to 20 percent, but the disease had gone unobserved because it stunts wheat plants uniformly. The identification of 10 species of Pythium is an essential first step toward its eventual control.
Wheat Breeding and Production Laboratory, Pullman, Wash.
J. R. Cook, plant pathologist, (509) 335-3722.

CROP RESEARCH (continued)

A SINGLE APPLICATION OF PHOSPHORUS in 1967 has maintained wheat yields at higher
levels on phosphorus-deficient soils in Montana after 10 crops in 17 years. The
single application of 80 pounds per acre, without nitrogen, increased yields
each crop year by 15 percent over those on untreated land. By adding nitrogen,
just 40 pounds per acre each crop year, increased yields 32 percent. Estimated
net return per acre: $19 more than the cost of fertilizing. About 20 million
acres in the Northern Great Plains are phosphorus-deficient.
Central Great Plains Research Center, Akron, Colo.
A. Halvorson, soil scientist, (303) 345-2259.

TWO NEW SOYBEAN VARIETIES resistant to soybean cyst nematode have been released
for commercial production. Their resistance, combined with early maturity, will
extend production 150 miles farther north to cyst-infested fields of the central
Midwest. Soybean cyst nematode costs growers about $150 million annually.
Another resistant variety, 'Epps,' has been released for the South.
Soybean Breeding and Production Research, Urbana, Ill./ Nematology Research,
Jackson, Tenn.
R. L. Bernard, geneticist, (217) 333-6459/L. D. Young, plant pathologist,
(901) 424-1643.

MONOCLONAL ANTIBODIES—DIAGNOSTIC TOOLS DEVELOPED IN MEDICAL RESEARCH—are
helping scientists identify the best Rhizobium strains to fix nitrogen and spur
forage production in poor, acidic soils. Scientists will then try to exploit
superior Rhizobium-innoculated crops to increase yields in poor soils.
Appalachian Soil and Water Research, Beckley, W. Va.
S. E. Wright, microbiologist, (304) 252-6426.

SEED OF 'HYCREST,' the first interspecific hybrid of crested wheatgrass, has
been released to breeders. Well adapted to intermountain rangelands, 'Hycrest'
grows well under semiarid conditions, is an excellent seed producer, and is as
well accepted by grazing animals as other crested wheatgrass. It is expected to
make a major impact toward revitalizing rangeland in the sagebrush ecosystem.
Forage and Range Research Laboratory, Logan, Utah
K. H. Asay, geneticist, (801) 750-3066.

COMPUTERIZED ESTIMATES OF WHEAT AND CORN YIELDS have become increasingly
accurate and valuable in global crop-production forecasts. In recent tests,
data from 25 sites spread around the world were punched into computerized models
of corn and wheat production. The computer simulations were accurate most of
the time and are now being evaluated for use by USDA's Foreign Agricultural
Service in parts of Asia and Europe.
Hydrology Laboratory, Beltsville, Md.
J. Ritchie, soil scientist, (301) 344-3490.

THREE ELMS OF DIFFERING SHAPES with resistance to Dutch elm disease are now
available to the public from nurseries. 'Dynasty,' a strong, vase-shaped tree,
is the first major cultivar of Chinese elm to be introduced into the U.S.
'Homestead' and 'Pioneer' elms, while resistant, lack the American elm's classic
vase-shape. However, both are highly tolerant of such urban stresses as air
pollution.
National Arboretum, Washington, D.C./Delaware, Ohio Nursery Crops Research,
Delaware, Ohio.
F. S. Santamour/A. M. Townsend, plant geneticists, (202) 475-4864.

CROP RESEARCH (continued)

FLUID DRILLING is a new technique for planting seeds by suspending them in a protective gel that carries them into the soil. The method, which also works for very young seedlings, may prove cheaper than using transplants to provide wildlife with food and cover on ranges, forests, and mined lands.
High Plains Grasslands Research Station, Cheyenne, Wyo.
D. T. Booth, range scientist, (307) 778-2220.

SEVERAL VARIETIES OF FOREIGN AND DOMESTIC VEGETABLES have proved promising candidates for cash crops on small U.S. farms. Those that adapt well and enjoy good consumer acceptance include the edible peapod, seedless watermelon, mung bean, and greenhouse cucumber.
U.S. Vegetable Laboratory, Charleston, S.C.
E. V. Wann, plant geneticist, (803) 556-0840

BEEF PRODUCERS CAN BEAT THE GRASS SHORTAGES that generally come in July and August. By planting seed mixtures that combine warm-season grasses, such as switchgrass and bluestem, with cool-season grasses, farmer can be assured that forage will be available during late summer.
Forage Plant-Soil-Climate Interactions Research, University Park, Pa.,
G. Jung, agronomist, (814) 237-7638.

THE REMOTE SENSING POTENTIAL OF LASER SYSTEMS for detecting crop stress has been demonstrated by ARS scientists. Corn deficient in iron, nitrogen, potassium, and phosphorus and soybeans deficient in boron, phosphorus, sulfur, calcium, magnesium, or potassium can be clearly differentiated from well-fertilized plants. Early stress detection should help improve crop production and commodity forecasting.
Field Crops Laboratory, Beltsville, Md.
J. E. McMurtrey III, agronomist, (301) 344-2646.

ANIMAL RESEARCH

ADDING A SMALL AMOUNT OF YEAST TO CALVES' FEED can help them regain appetites lost to stress from weaning or transportation. Not eating adequately makes calves susceptible to viral and bacterial infections. Just 1 to 2 percent yeast added to calves' poststress diet increased their appetites and ability to convert feed to nutrients. They gained weight more rapidly than calves not fed yeast.
Livestock and Forage Research, El Reno, Okla.
W. A. Phillips, animal nutritionist, (405) 262-5291.

CROSSBRED COWS LIVED 1.4 YEARS LONGER IN THE HERD and were more fertile than purebred cows in studies conducted in the 1960's and 1970's, according to analysis completed in 1984. Angus, Shorthorn, and Hereford cows lived an average of 8.4 years in herd; reciprocal crosses of these breeds averaged 9.7 years and had offspring that were 14 percent heavier than purebred calves.
University of Nebraska, Lincoln, Nebr.
L. Cundiff, geneticist, (402) 762-3241.

FINNRACE, AN IMPORTED BREED OF SHEEP, can greatly increase lamb production over domestic breeds. Ewes with 1/4 to 1/2 Finnrace blood produced 18 and 29 percent more lambs, respectively, than their Rambouillet, Targhee, and Columbia counterparts when flock-mated to Suffolk rams. The higher production was sustained throughout a typical productive lifetime of 7 years.
U.S. Sheep Experiment Station, Dubois, Idaho.
C. Parker, animal physiologist, (208) 374-5306.

ANIMAL RESEARCH (continued)

A COMMON WEED IS A PRIME SUSPECT IN CATTLE ABORTIONS occuring during the spring
in Louisiana and Texas. Laboratory studies must still confirm the field
findings: narrowleaf sumpweed caused abortions in rabbits, and cattle aborted
after grazing on land harboring the weed in the two states. The weed, which
also grows in Arkansas and Oklahoma, may be most toxic during its early seedling
stage when it grows rapidly.
Veterinary Toxicology and Entomology Research, College Station, Tex./Texas A&M
University.
L. D. Rowe, veterinary medical officer, (713) 260-9342.

A COMPUTER MODEL OF A DAIRY FORAGE SYSTEM can be used to evaluate new technology
and management strategies on farms feeding alfalfa and corn. The model
estimates factors such as crop yield, production costs, and net return. It can
also assess the impact of new forage conservation methods under a wide range of
conditions.
Fruit and Vegetable Harvesting Research, East Lansing, Mich.
C. A. Rotz, agricultural engineer, (517) 353-1758.

GERM-FREE PIGS AND CALVES begin life in a special "delivery room" in Ames, Iowa,
to make sure they have a clean bill of health in research seeking to overcome
diseases such as dysentery and diarrhea. The first germfree animal was born at
Ames in 1973; since then, about 100 pigs and 24 calves a year have been
delivered germ-free and the delivery has widened to other animals—from ducks
and turkeys to mice, rats, and guinea pigs.
National Animal Disease Center, Ames, Iowa.
P. Matthews/S. Whipp, veterinary medical officers, (515) 239-8200.

A NOTORIOUS WEED, QUACKGRASS, MAY GET A NEW REPUTATION as one of the most
nutritious and palatable grasses for livestock. Utilizing its aggressive
spreading by breeding it with bluebunch wheatgrass, which is drought resistant,
ARS scientists bred a new hybrid that, besides satisfying livestock appetites,
is a good candidate for controlling erosion on meadows and pastures in northern
states and also seems well adapted to saline sites in states like Montana. It
is expected to be available commercially within two years.
Forage and Range Research, Logan, Utah.
K. H. Asay, plant geneticist, (801) 750-3069.

INTRODUCING BENEFICIAL GENES into livestock may someday depend on a scientist's
ability to view nuclei in embryos shortly after fertilization. Centrifuging cow
and pig embryos at more than 15,000 times gravity caused the sedimentation of
dense materials in the ova and allowed for the first time the visualization of
cell nuclei. Further, the embryos were undamaged by the treatment, and healthy
pigs have been born when centrifuged embryos injected with genes were
transferred into surrogate mothers.
Reproduction Laboratory, Beltsville, Md.
R. Wall, animal physiologist, (301) 344-2362.

RESOURCES AND ENVIRONMENTAL RESEARCH

NO-TILL WITH SURFACE RESIDUES MAY BE FEASIBLE ON THE STEEPEST CORN-BELT SOILS.
Chisel plowing, paraplowing, and no plowing were tested for the first time on
slopes as steep as 18 percent at Coshocton, Ohio. The purpose of the six-year
conservation tillage study: to evaluate yields of corn and soybeans as well as
fertility; disease; pests; machinery; and losses of water, soil, and chemicals
on steep watersheds.
ARS North Appalachian Experimental Watershed, Coshocton/Ohio Agricultural
Research and Development Center, Wooster, Ohio.
C. Amerman, hydrologic engineer, (614) 545-6349.

STRIPMINE SPOILS CAN BE RETURNED TO PRODUCTIVE LAND by revegetating them with
two forages—thickspike wheatgrass and fourwing saltbush. Both grasses have
passed preliminary tests by germinating well in salt solutions similar to those
of soil and mining spoil in the Northern Great Plains. Also, fourwing saltbush,
a weed which grows on millions of acres from western North and South Dakota and
Kansas to eastern Oregon and Washington, was found to fill a very important void
in cattle diets by providing them with more protein, phosphorus, and carotene
than most range grasses, especially in winter.
Irrigation, Drainage, and Salinity Research, Mandan, N. Dak./
Agricultural/Surface-Mined Hydrology Research, Fort Collins, Colo.
R. Ries, range scientist, (701) 663-6448.

PLANT DAMAGE FROM DROUGHT IS SHARPLY INCREASED when plants are also exposed to
air pollution. A Beltsville team of hydrologists and plant physiologists found
that soybean yields were much lower when plants were subjected to a one-two
punch of drought plus air pollution than were the combined yield decreases of
soybeans exposed to each stress separately.
Plant Stress Laboratory, Beltsville, Md.
E. H. Lee, plant physiologist, (301) 344-3143.

ESTIMATING THE COST OF SOIL EROSION is difficult because all parts of a field do
not erode uniformly. Much of the soil from one part of a field is often
deposited on another when it rains. Results of a new cooperative agreement
between ARS and Purdue University to study field variability should make future
estimates of the erosion costs much more accurate.
National Soil Erosion Laboratory, West Lafayette, Ind.
H. Barrows, soil scientist, (317) 494-8685.

WIND EROSION, A SEVERE PROBLEM ON COARSE-TEXTURED SEMIARID SOILS, can be
controlled using the right combination of residue management, proper tillage,
and wind barriers. Dryland crop yields may be increased by covering the soils
with vegetative mulches to increase needed organic matter or by deep tillage
every two or three years to increase water infiltration.
Wind Erosion and New Crops Research, Lubbock, Tex.
D. Fryrear, agricultural engineer, (915) 263-0293.

NO-TILL IS A VIABLE ALTERNATIVE TO CONVENTIONAL TILLAGE for swelling heavy clay
soils like those of the Blackland Prairie of Texas. A four-year study comparing
the effects of tillage on soil properties and on wheat, grain sorghum, and
cotton yields showed both systems gave the same yields with no adverse effect on
these highly erodible soils.
Soil and Water Resources, Temple, Tex.
J. E. Morrison, agricultural engineer, (817) 774-1201.

RESOURCES AND ENVIRONMENTAL RESEARCH (continued)

LEAVING CROP RESIDUES ON THE SURFACE OF SOILS in the Southern Great Plains and using conservation tillage increased soil water during fallow, which in turn increased yields of subsequent crops. Conserving water from rainfall saves water needed for irrigation, which along with higher yields, makes an economic crop production system that also saves precious dwindling groundwater supplies in the Ogallala Aquifer.
Conservation and Production Research Laboratory, Bushland, Tex.
P. Unger, soil scientist, (806) 735-6738.

SPACE SHUTTLE RADAR MEASURED MOISTURE BENEATH GROWING CROPS as the U.S. Challenger passed 140 miles above farms near Fresno, Calif. Highly specialized radar measured water in soil down to six inches below the surface. Although it may be a decade before such a system is in widespread use, it should eventually be possible to produce daily soil moisture maps to guide farmer decisions.
Hydrology Laboratory, Beltsville, Md.
T. Engman, hydrologist, (301) 344-3490.

A NEW TREE FOR WINDBREAKS HAS BEEN RELEASED in the Central and Northern Great Plains. Oahe, a hackberry tree with a better rate of survival and growth than common varieties, is suited to well-drained soil in farmstead plantings for controlling soil erosion. It may replace the popular Siberian elm, which is dying from herbicides, disease, and winterkill.
Forage, Range, and Shelterbelt Research, Mandan, N. Dak.
R. Cunningham, plant geneticist, (701) 663-6448.

ARS HAS DEVELOPED A NEW TECHNIQUE for monitoring residues of the pesticide atrazine that can detect parts per trillion. The technique can be applied to a dozen other herbicides and will prove invaluable for tracing pesticides in water, soil, food, and feed.
Central Great Plains Research Station, Akron, Colo.
B. Dunbar, (303) 345-2259.

RUNOFF AND SOIL LOSSES WERE SIGNIFICANTLY LOWERED by winter cover crops and reduced tillage during a six-year study of grain corn and silage corn grown on Missouri claypan soil. Average annual values for crop or management factors derived from soil losses and rainfall data ranged from 11 to 57 percent of currently accepted values.
Watershed Research, Columbia, Mo.
R. Wendt, soil scientist, (314) 875-5331.

COFARM, A COMPUTER MODEL for efficient soil and crop management, can be used by farmers and researchers for organizing and storing data for individual fields, soils, and crops. COFARM can simulate the effects of different management practices and help farmers make decisions on fertilizing, tillage, drainage, residue management, and similar activities.
Soil and Water Management Research, St. Paul, Minn.
M. J. Shaffer, soil scientist, (612) 373-1444.

RESOURCES AND ENVIRONMENTAL RESEARCH (continued)

NO-TILL SOYBEANS GROWN ON CLAY BLACKLAND PRAIRIE SOILS in Mississippi reduced erosion but also reduced yields and net returns. ARS scientists have found a possible link between surface residue and stem canker disease of soybeans. Double-cropped wheat and soybeans, on the other hand, proved an excellent conservation system that is much more profitable than any of the one-crop soybean systems evaluated.
Corn Protection Research Laboratory, Mississippi State, Miss.
J. O. Sanford, agronomist, (601) 325-2350.

AN EXPERIMENTAL NO-TILL DRILL for planting small grains is the first such machine able to place fertilizer—in liquid or solid form and in any combination—either with the seed or "banded" below the seed. Crops planted with the no-till drill in paired rows proved more vigorous than conventionally seeded and fertilized rows planted the same day.
Land Management and Water Conservation Research, Pullman, Wash.
L. Elliott, microbiologist, (509) 335-1551.

SUBSURFACE DRAINAGE SYSTEMS CAN AID SOIL CONSERVATION in low-lying areas of the South with high water tables and high rainfall. High water tables increase runoff, soil erosion, and plant nutrient losses—especially during the rainy months in winter and spring—and inhibit crop production and mobility of farm machinery. Draining some of this groundwater can alleviate the problem.
Soil and Water Management Research, Baton Rouge, La.
C. Carter, agricultural engineer, (606) 258-2683.

SOIL EROSION WAS REDUCED 70 PERCENT UNDER CONSERVATION TILLAGE as compared with conventional tillage during 11 years of testing in Mississippi. Tests also showed that conservation tillage increased cotton seed yield and decreased runoff.
USDA Sedimentation Laboratory, Oxford, Miss.
C. Mutchler, hydrologic engineer, (601) 234-4121.

WIND-GENERATED ELECTRICITY FOR PUMPING irrigation water in the Great Plains can reduce the amount of electricity purchased while maintaining the farmer's ability to provide crops with water at critical growth stages. In trials, two wind turbines provided 77 percent of the energy consumed by a center pivot and irrigation pump and also provided some excess power each month.
Wind Powered Irrigation Research, Bushland, Tex.
R. N. Clark, agricultural engineer, (806) 378-5734.

HUMAN NUTRITION RESEARCH

TOO MUCH SALT AND NOT ENOUGH POTASSIUM IN U.S. DIETS may be increasing the chances of Americans getting high blood pressure. Results of a year-long study of 28 men and women show they are eating nearly double the amount of sodium in relation to potassium when a safe and adequate intake should be reversed—0.6 sodium to 1.0 potassium.
Vitamin and Mineral Nutrition Laboratory, Human Nutrition Research Center, Beltsville, Md.
Jim Smith, chemist, (301) 344-2417.

HUMAN NUTRITION RESEARCH (continued)

VITAMIN B$_6$ RELIEVES THE SYMPTOMS OF SICKLE CELL ANEMIA, an inherited blood disease affecting about 50,000 black Americans. Working with a physician at Columbia University, New York, ARS scientists found that patients given two 50-mg doses of the vitamin daily had less frequent and severe attacks of the disease.
Vitamin and Mineral Nutrition Laboratory, Human Nutrition Research Center, Beltsville, Md.
R. Reynolds, chemist, (301) 344-2459.

A HIGHER RATIO OF POLYUNSATURATED FATS IN DIETS can help lower blood pressure. Hypertension—chronic high blood pressure—increases the risk of heart attack and stroke and affects one out of every five Americans over the age of 25. By increasing their intake of polyunsaturated fats by 6 to 7 percent, 40-to 60-year-old men and women with normal or slightly high blood pressure lowered their blood pressure, regardless of their saturated fat intake.
Western Regional Research Center, Berkeley, Calif.
J. Iocono, director, (415) 556-9699.

CHOLESTEROL INHIBITORS HAVE BEEN ISOLATED AND IDENTIFIED in barley and oats. When these fractions were fed to chickens at concentrations of 25 parts per million, levels of cholesterol-bearing, low-density lipoproteins in chickens' blood plasma decreased by 40 percent, as compared with those of chickens fed a control diet of mainly corn. The inhibitors may someday be added to human foods to decrease the risk of heart disease.
Cereal Crops Research Unit, Madison, Wis.
D. Peterson, horticulturalist, (608) 262-3355.

SYNTHETIC SUGAR USED TO TREAT LIVER DISEASE can be made at less expense from whey, a cheesemaking byproduct. The new process could lower the cost of making lactulose and make it available for a wide range of food and drug uses and as a noncaloric sweetener. Lactulose is used to treat adverse brain effects from advanced liver disease, known as portal systemic encephalopathy or hepatic coma, which, if left unchecked, can lead to coma and death.
Food Chemistry Research, Eastern Regional Research Center, Phildelphia, Pa.
K. Hicks, chemist, (215) 233-6458.

BRAN ABSORBS MINERALS as it passes through the human digestive tract. Excessive amounts of wheat bran can remove enough calcium from the GI tract to cause a negative calcium balance. Dry-milled corn bran has been shown to bind more calcium, copper, iron, and zinc than it contained before it was ingested.
Cereal and Food Biochemical Research, Northern Regional Research Center, Peoria, Ill.
F. A. Dintzis, chemist, (360) 671-4011.

AN ELECTRONIC EGG MAY HELP LOWER BREAKAGE losses by detecting the forces being exerted against the shells of real eggs during mechanized grading and packing. About seven percent of U.S. eggs crack during the largely automated journey from hen to market. If egg breakage could be reduced by just one percent, about $20 million yearly could be saved, provided half of these could be salvaged and used for other purposes.
Food Protection and Processing Research, Richard B. Russell Agricultural Research Center, Athens, Ga.
J. A. Dickens, engineer, (404) 546-3132.

HUMAN NUTRITION RESEARCH (continued)

BITTERNESS IN CITRUS JUICES CAN BE REMOVED by passing them through a column packed with immobolized bacterial cells. A key step was isolating the bacteria able to metabolize limonoids which cause the bitterness. Commercial development of this simple debittering process could save the California citrus industry alone about $8 million. It should be available commercially in three to five years.
Fruit and Vegetable Research, Pasadena, Calif.
S. Hasegawa, chemist, (213) 681-7294

COMMERCIALIZATION OF A NEW PROCESS to produce partially defatted almonds may open new markets for the U.S. crop. In the process, almonds are pressed to remove 55 percent of the oil, expanded in hot water containing dextrose, and then salted and roasted in hot oil. After roasting, the nuts still contain 45 percent less oil than the unprocessed almonds.
Food Products Research, Southern Regional Research Center, New Orleans, La.
J. Pominski, chemical engineer, (504) 589-7012.

STRAWBERRIES PRODUCE A COMPOUND that can be formulated into a fumigant against aphids on lettuce and thrips on strawberries. The compound—ethyl formate—can be used as a fumigant on packaged lettuce and strawberries in a partial vacuum. It leaves no residue and also destroys insect pests on dried fruits. If approved as a fumigant, ethyl formate could aid the U.S. export of lettuce and strawberries to countries with restrictions on residue levels of fumigants.
Horticultural Crops Research, Fresno, Calif.
J. M. Harvey, plant pathologist, (209) 487-5334.

BRAN SPAGHETTI SCORES HIGHER IN PROTEIN AND MINERALS. Dietary fiber in spaghetti is increased threefold if 10 percent bran is added in making pasta. Bran also increases by about 40 percent protein, iron, calcium, manganese, phosphorus, and zinc in the spaghetti, which is inherently low in sodium, fats, and simple carbohydrates and contains a high level of complex carbohydrates.
Hard Red Spring and Durum Wheat Quality Laboratory, Fargo, N.D.
V. L. Youngs, food technologist, (701) 237-7728.

COMMERCIAL APPLICATION OF RESEARCH/POSTHARVEST TECHNOLOGY

APPLE PROCESSORS AND EXPORTERS NO LONGER NEED TO DIP FRUIT IN CHEMICALS to control storage scald, an unsightly brown surface skin condition. Virtually scald-free fruit can be had by just storing it in a controlled environment of 1 percent oxygen and 1 percent carbon dioxide.
Production, Harvesting, and Handling of Tree Fruits Research, Wenatchee, Wash.
K. Olsen, plant physiologist, (509) 662-4317.

IRRADIATING APPLES TO CONTROL CODLING MOTHS is being tested as an alternative to fumigation. Apples are being irradiated at low levels for different time periods and at varying doses when insects are in the young, middle-aged, and mature larval stages.
Crops Protection Research, Yakima, Wash.
A. Burditt, entomologist, (509) 575-5956.

COMMERCIAL APPLICATION OF RESEARCH/POSTHARVEST TECHNOLOGY (continued)

A NEW HYBRID DIESEL FUEL, made from crude vegetable oil, will be engine-tested as an alternative fuel for farm tractors. Developed by a new process that converts the vegetable oil to diesel fuel without altering its chemical structure, the new fuel remains clear, stable, and usable at low temperatures, is free of corrosive emulsifiers, and can be blended with other fuels on farms.
Exploratory Organic Reactions Research, Northern Regional Research Center, Peoria, Ill.
A. Schwab, chemist, (309) 685-4011.

FABRIC FINISHES LIKE DURABLE PRESS can now by improved because of a more direct method of analyzing tiny, individual particles on cotton fibers. The new method uses advanced technology (scanning electron microscopy and energy dispersive x-ray analysis) instead of the customary mechanical means or solvents to remove particles for further study.
Fiber and Yarn Technology Research, Southern Regional Research Center, New Orleans, La.
G. Louis, textile engineer, (504) 589-7586.

X-RAY ANALYSIS OF GRAIN KERNELS CAN DETECT HIDDEN INSECTS and tell whether larvae are dead or alive. Video film enlargement of x-ray scans reveals insect eggs and pupae that are too small for currently available detectors. Such image analysis may someday be computerized to automatically count the number of insects in a sample, a technique that will help to improve inspection standards and procedures.
Engineering Research, Western Regional Research Center, Albany, Calif.
T. Schatzki, chemist, (415) 486-3701.

UNPALATABLE FLAVORS IN GRAINS CAN BE REMOVED with a treatment that inactivates two enzymes responsible for the off-flavor. Treated common cereal grains retain their germ, remain rich in protein, vitamins, and minerals, and can be milled into shelf-stable, high-fat flour, whose texture and properties equal those of fresh or degerminated flours.
Field Crops Postharvest Research, Northern Regional Research Center, Peoria, Ill.
G. Bookwalter, food technologist, (309) 685-4011.

A MILD COTTON-CURING PROCESS THAT ADDS DURABLE PRESS QUALITIES to fabrics without using formaldehyde or its derivatives has attracted the interest of several major companies. The process has become attractive because of anticipated tightening of regulations by the U.S. Environmental Protection Agency that could eliminate certain formaldehyde uses because of potential cancer concerns.
Polymer Products Research, Southern Regional Research Center, New Orleans, La.
C. Welch, chemist, (504) 589-7062.

A FAST, NONDESTRUCTIVE METHOD for measuring the concentration of individual simple sugars—like glucose, fructose, and sucrose—in aqueous solutions has been developed using optical radiation in the near infrared region. The method has potential value as a quality-control procedure in food processing.
Quality Evaluation Research, Richard B. Russell Agricultural Research Center, Athens, Ga.
F. Meredith, chemist, (404) 546-3156.

COMMERCIAL APPLICATION OF RESEARCH/POSTHARVEST TECHNOLOGY (continued)

COTTON BATTING TREATED WITH BORIC ACID was better protected against smoldering in ARS tests than the foam presently used by furniture manufacturers. Peak surface temperatures also were lower for batting than for foam.
Special Products Research, Southern Regional Research Center, New Orleans, La.
D. J. Donaldson, chemist, (504) 589-7561.

NEWLY DISCOVERED GENES OPEN WAY TO LONGER SHELF LIFE for soybean oil products. Breeding the new genes into soybean varieties would help curb off-flavors and objectionable odors caused by the breakdown of unsaturated fatty acids. Soybean oil is used in margarines, salad dressings, and cooking oil.
Plant Science Research, West Lafayette, Ind.
J. R. Wilcox, geneticist, (317) 494-4772.

# # #

QUARTERLY REPORT ON SELECTED RESEARCH PROJECTS
OF THE AGRICULTURAL RESEARCH SERVICE
U.S. Department of Agriculture
January 1 to March 31, 1985

CONSERVATION AND NATURAL RESOURCES RESEARCH

GROUND WATER POLLUTION caused by applying dissolved chemicals at the surface
can occur much more quickly than previously suspected. New research
indicates that water moves down through wet soils twice as fast as predicted
by theoretical models. In drier soils, the rate is 4-5 times faster than
previously thought. Some chemicals, however, may break down on the way.
U.S. Water Conservation Lab., Phoenix, AZ
Herman Bouwer, (602) 261-4356

COLD SOILS CAN REDUCE the amounts of zinc and other trace minerals that
people get in their diets. New studies show plant roots do not penetrate
deeply enough into chilled soils to absorb sufficient minerals. One solution
to the problem could be boosting the zinc and phosphorus content of
fertilizers for spring and fall applications, perhaps with special fertilizer
formulas tailored to climatic conditions in each ecological zone.
U.S. Plant, Soil, and Nutrition Lab., Ithaca, NY
David Grunes, (607) 256-3003

A ONE-TIME APPLICATION of a soluble chemical can affect ground water for
several years. When potassium bromide, a tracer, was applied at a rate often
used for nitrogen fertilizer on two 3-acre-pasture watersheds, ground water
samples from springs supplied by the watersheds showed peak bromide
concentrations 21 to 24 months after application. After 45 months, there
still was no meaningful decrease.
North Appalachian Exp. Watershed Res. Lab., Coshocton, OH
Lloyd B. Owens, (614) 545-6349

SOIL EROSION REDUCES FERTILITY, even in the deep loess soils of the Palouse
in the Pacific Northwest. An ARS soil scientist finds that, about 15 inches
deep, the soils become calcareous. As soil washes away, reduced levels of
organic matter cause nitrogen to drop, and phosphorus levels 6-12 inches deep
are half again lower than in the top 6 inches of soil. Eroded soils also
store less moisture.
Soil Mgt. and Water Quality Research Lab., Kimberly, ID
Truman W. Massee, (208) 423-5582

SORDAN, A FORAGE HYBRID OF SORGHUM AND SUDANGRASS, may have the ability to
reclaim unproductive, salt-bound soils. An ARS scientist has discovered that
the roots of Sordan give off more than twice as much carbon dioxide as most
other plants. In moist soils, the high CO_2 levels lower the pH enough to
dissolve the lime in the soil. The dissolved lime, in turn, replaces
unwanted sodium attached to the clay, and the sodium can then be leached out
by irrigation. Expensive applications of gypsum would be unnecessary.
Testing the theory, a rancher planted Sordan on a totally unproductive salt-
bound field and subsequently harvested 20 tons of forage per acre. Tests
continue of this promising hybrid.
Snake River Conservation Research Center, Kimberly, ID

CROP PRODUCTION AND PROTECTION RESEARCH

IN AN EFFORT TO LOCATE specific sugarbeet genes, ARS scientists have discovered that establishing gene locations on chromosomes can be done much more quickly, efficiently, and precisely by using trisomic plants--those having a specific extra chromosome. They have now developed all nine possible trisomic types of sugarbeets and described them, paving the way for precise genetic engineering.
Crops Res. Lab., Fort Collins, CO
Richard J. Hecker, (303) 482-7717

A ONE-MINUTE TEST for rubber, resin, and moisture content of guayule, a shrub native to the southwestern United States, has been developed to replace the current slow, tedious process. Guayule is being studied as a potential source of domestic rubber. The new analysis method uses near-infrared reflectance spectroscopy with computer assistance.
Northern Regional Research Center, Peoria, IL
G. E. Hamerstrand, (309) 685-4011, Ext. 536

WHILE LITTLE BLUESTEM IS COMMON on tallgrass prairies, it is less palatable to cattle than other dominant tallgrasses. ARS scientists in Oklahoma have found that prescribed burning fails to stimulate the growth of little bluestem as it does such preferred grasses as big bluestem and indiangrass. This means that fire can be used to produce a more favorable composition of grass species on prairie grazing lands.
Range and Pasture Research Unit, Woodward, OK
Phillip L. Sims, (405) 256-7449

THE "GREENHOUSE EFFECT" of carbon dioxide may not be all bad. A number of scientists have predicted that rising levels of CO_2 in the atmosphere will eventually raise global temperatures enough to melt polar ice caps, cause sea levels to rise, and ultimately flood coastal cities. But not all scientists agree. An ARS physicist points out that actual temperature increases to date in the extreme northern latitudes are substantially below the projections of pessimistic climate modelers. He also observes that predicted higher CO_2 levels, while having no detrimental effect on people or animals, would significantly improve plant productivity by increasing photosynthetic activity, as laboratory tests have shown.
Soil, Plant and Atmosphere Systems Lab., Phoenix, AZ
Sherwood Idso, (602) 261-4356

A NEW BREEDING TECHNIQUE that makes use of early flowering lettuce plants can cut in half the time needed to develop disease-resistant varieties. Early flowering plants are commercially useless, since they skip the vegetative stage, but an ARS scientist has found that he can use the early flowering genes to carry more desirable genes. He was able, for example, to insert genes for mosaic resistance into a non-resistant lettuce variety in 375 days, compared to 750 days using normal lettuce. He believes the technique can be applied to other plants with early flowering varieties, including peas, soybeans, beans, spring wheat, rice, and sugarbeets.
U.S. Agricultural Research Sta., Salinas, CA
E. J. Ryder, (408) 443-2253

CROP PRODUCTION AND PROTECTION RESEARCH (continued)

WEEDS THAT SURVIVE herbicide spraying can be mopped up with a new tractor
attachment called a rotary herbicide wiper. A spinning disk wipes (instead
of sprays) a herbicide directly onto weeds growing beneath the crops. The
method avoids herbicide drift and increases operator safety.
Appalachian Fruit Research Station, Kearneysville, WV
William Welker, Jr., (304) 725-3451

THE MYSTERY OF STUNTED SEEDLINGS and uneven stands in tree nurseries has been
solved by ARS scientists in Oregon, who have shown that inoculation with
certain fungi enhances growth of at least 4 species of conifers--Western red
cedar, incense cedar, coast redwood, and giant sequoia. Conifer seedlings
were treated with 3 species of vesicular-arbuscular mycorrhizal (VAM) fungi,
which had inadvertently been killed during routine soil fumigation in the
greenhouse. Treatment not only increased biomass, but it also enhanced
seedling uniformity and size in all 4 species. Fumigants are now recommended
that will leave unharmed the VAM fungi occurring naturally in the soil.
Horticultural Crops Research Unit, Corvallis, OR
Robert G. Linderman, (503) 757-4544

MOLECULAR BIOCHEMICAL TECHNIQUES have determined that chloroplast DNA in
soybeans is inherited only from the female parent. Chloroplast DNA is the
site that contains the information for photosynthesis. This research has
academic significance in understanding the evolutionary history of the
cultivated soybean and practical application in breeding programs where it is
necessary to transfer desirable traits from wild species.
Cereal & Soybean Improvement Res., Ames, Iowa 50011
Reid Palmer, (515) 294-7378

THE TARNISHED PLANT BUG, until recently considered but a minor pest of cotton
in the Mid-South, is now known to cause considerable damage during the bug's
peak months of May and June. In tests in 1981-83, ARS researchers applied
aldicarb, a systemic insecticide, to cotton at planting. As a result, they
realized yield increases of as much as 20 percent. In 1984, several foliar
insecticides applied weekly in June successfully controlled plant bug
populations, while uncontrolled populations reduced yields as much as 40
percent and delayed harvest 2 weeks. Environmental hazards were kept to a
minimum during applications. Meanwhile, researchers have found a mite that
is a parasite and predator of the plant bug.
Southern Field Crop Insect Mgt. Lab., Stoneville, MS
E. G. King, (601) 686-2231

CROP PRODUCTION AND PROTECTION RESEARCH (continued)

GETTING THE BEST RESULTS from pesticides sprayed on plants depends on keeping the droplets on the leaves. An ARS researcher uses high-speed motion pictures to show that large portions of droplets sprayed on some plants rebound as many as six times after impact. He is currently testing droplet velocity, droplet size, electrostatic charge, and surfactants, as a first step in improving pesticide applications.
Agricultural Eng. Res. Lab., Wooster, OH
Donald L. Reichard, (216) 264-1021

BEAN RUST, A MAJOR FUNGUS DISEASE of snap and dry beans, was controlled biologically in tests under field conditions. Frequent application of Bacillus subtilis, a bacterium culture previously used to control bean rust under greenhouse conditions, may provide an environmentally desirable alternative to costly fungicides. Future research will seek to identify and purify the B. subtilis inhibitor and possibly modify its chemical structure to improve its stability in the environment.
Plant Pathology Lab., Beltsville, MD
C. Jacyn Baker, (301) 344-3486

AN INSECTICIDE developed from an extract of the tropical neem tree controls leafminer flies, a major insect pest of flower and vegetable crops. Produced by a commercial firm, the insecticide is the first pest control product to result from extensive ARS research demonstrating that neem tree compounds can be developed to control dozens of agricultural pests. The insecticide awaits EPA registration.
Biologically Active Natural Products Lab., Beltsville, MD
Martin Jacobson, (301) 344-2025

IN A NEW AUTOMATED PLANT CULTURE SYSTEM, plants develop twice as fast as with a manual system. Within the system, a microcomputer controls medium input and extraction in a sterile environment. Cultures were found to survive for record-breaking intervals without detriment using the automated system. The new system has promise for commercial application.
Fruit and Vegetable Chemistry Lab., Pasadena, CA 91106
Brent Tisserat, (818) 796-0239

TRICKLE IRRIGATION IS MUCH MORE EFFICIENT on cotton than is furrow irrigation when the objective is maximum lint yields and when water supplies are limited, according to the latest experiments with the traveling trickle irrigation system. The laser-directed machine also has helped demonstrate that low-cost saline water can be used to irrigate some crops because the water applied does not touch the plants.
Water Management Res. Lab., Fresno, CA
Claude Phene, (209) 291-3611

CROP PRODUCTION AND PROTECTION RESEARCH (continued)

'MARSHALL', A HARD RED SPRING WHEAT variety released in 1982 by ARS and the
Minnesota Agricultural Experiment Station, has taken over 57 percent of that
State's hard red spring wheat acreage. 'Era,' the former leader, dropped
from 64 percent of the acreage in 1979 to 16 percent in 1984. Both varieties
are semi-dwarf types. 'Marshall' has more protein than 'Era,' matures 2 days
earlier, and stands up well against the elements.
Plant Science Res. Lab., St. Paul, MN
Robert H. Busch, (612) 373-1370

MEDFLY THREAT TO U.S. ORCHARDS MAY BE LESSENED when a way is found to
synthesize a natural plant chemical. Scientists are about a year away from
reproducing an ingredient in the oil of angelica plants, a powerful
attractant to Mediterranean fruit flies. The lure lasted four times longer
in field tests than the attractant currently used in traps to detect new
invasions of the dangerous pest.
Biological Active Natural Products Lab., Beltsville, MD
Martin Jacobson, (301) 344-2025

USDA-DEVELOPED PECAN CULTIVARS TOOK TOP HONORS recently at an international
large pecan show. Released several years ago, 'Wichita,' 'Sioux,' 'Choctaw,'
and 'Cheyenne' are growing yearly in popularity. 'Wichita' is the most
widely propagated cultivar here and abroad. 'Cheyenne' is most recommended
for planting throughout the United States because of its good shelling
qualities. Each year's pecan crop is worth about $162 million, the third
largest nut crop.
Pecan Genetics and Improvement Research, Brownwood, TX
Richard Hunter, (915) 646-0593

STIMULATING APPLE TREE GROWTH INCREASES BRANCHING. Spraying 8-year-old trees
with AVG (aminoethoxyvinlyglycine) right after harvest increased threefold
the number of branches. This growth helps to build more quickly a fruit
tree's framework. AVG has no apparent adverse side effects but is still in
the experimental stage.
Tree Fruit Research, Wenatchee, WA
Eric A. Curry, (509) 662-4317

APPLYING PLANT GROWTH REGULATORS to soil beneath fruit trees could reduce
excessive vegetation and improve fruit quality. Commercial application of
this technique to several fruits, including apples, pears, sweet cherries,
peaches, nectarines, and plums, should hasten fruit production and make it
more consistent. Soil-applied growth regulators penetrate trees better and
improve insect and disease control, require fewer applications, and reduce
labor costs from hand pruning.
Tree Fruit Research, Wenatchee, WA
Max W. Williams, (509) 662-4317

CROP PRODUCTION AND PROTECTION RESEARCH (continued)

A NEWLY DISCOVERED MOVABLE ELEMENT IN SOYBEAN GENES may speed up genetic
engineering of crop plants. Scientists have found that molecules called Tgml
in soybean genes resemble those of "jumping" genes found earlier in corn and
snapdragons. This similarity suggests that this and other movable elements
may be appropriate for transferring genetic traits, like disease resistance
and high nutritional value, to plants that cannot be bred by traditional
means.
Plant Molecular Genetics Lab., Beltsville, MD
Lila Vodkin, (301) 344-3308

FUTURE "SOIL WARS" WILL ENLIST THE HELP OF BENEFICIAL ORGANISMS to battle
soilborne fungi and bacteria that each year cause over $4 billion in U.S crop
losses from disease. Over the past 3 years, research has accelerated in
finding ways to pack fungus-fighting organisms in gel pellets or powders for
farmers to spray onto their fields or drop into seed furrows. Several U.S
patents are pending or have been granted with industries' cooperation.
Agency scientists predict that the first commercial "battlefield" will be
against highly-destructive seedling diseases of horticultural crops.
Soilborne Diseases Lab., Beltsville, MD
George Papavizas, (301) 344-3682

THE FIRST PLANT WITH NATURAL RESISTANCE TO SEVERAL VIRUSES has been found by
agency scientists searching for plants immune to only one virus. If they can
find a way to transfer this virus-resistance to cultivated species of
potatoes and tomatoes, commercial producers of these crops could save more
than $200 per acre a year. Growing hybrids with built-in resistance to
potato leafroll, tomato yellow top, and beet curly top would be more
effective and less expensive and would not harm the environment.
Vegetable Crops Production, Prosser, WA
Peter E. Thomas, (509) 786-3454

FUNGUS IS IMPLICATED FOR FIRST TIME IN WHEAT AND BARLEY disease in the
Pacific Northwest. Discovery of Rhizoctonia bare patch in no-till and
reduced tillage fields--the first reported case of this fungus-caused disease
in the United States--is important because of the increasing trend toward
conservation tillage.
Wheat Breeding and Production, Pullman, WA
David Weller, (509) 335-6210

POTATO GROWERS CAN SAVE $60 per acre in fertilizer cost by better balancing
irrigation water and nitrogen applied to optimize potato yields on sandy
soils. Several years of research in Washington showed that farmers have been
applying too much water, and thereby moving fertilizer out of the reach of
plants--so they had to apply more fertilizer than was actually needed by the
potatoes.
Soil and Water Management, Prosser, WA
David A. Lauer, (509) 786-3454

CROP PRODUCTION AND PROTECTION RESEARCH (continued)

SHADE AND FLOWERING TREES WITH TOUGHER WOOD can be bred now that scientists
have found ways to select, within 1 year, young trees that resist decay
caused by injury. Research confirms that trees inherit the ability to
manufacture chemicals that "box in" wounded wood, thus preventing further
decay. Decay seldom kills trees, but decayed trees occasionally fall on
people and cause much property damage each year.
U.S. National Arboretum, Washington, DC
Frank Santamour, (202) 475-4850

THOUSANDS OF CEREAL GRAINS BEING GROWN in field nurseries will undergo a
battery of tests aimed at cataloging their characteristics for inclusion in
the National Small Grain Collection. For positive identification and botanic
classification, such qualities as early maturity, short stalk, and high
yielding are being determined as well as resistance to diseases, insects, and
drought, extreme temperatures, and end-product use (like milling, baking,
malting, and cooking). All these findings will significantly enhance the
collection's value to plant breeders and other researchers worldwide who
depend on the collection for seed and germplasm to develop new and better
varieties of grains.
Germplasm Resources Lab., Beltsville, MD
Leland W. Briggle, (301) 344-3713

ANIMAL PRODUCTION AND PROTECTION RESEARCH

FEED COST FOR FINISHING BEEF CATTLE CAN BE REDUCED by 25 cents per pound
if the animals have grazed wheat forage before the finishing period. Tests
showed that cattle grazing wheat forage, a feed source high in nonprotein
nitrogen, gained more weight faster than they did on other feeds during the
early part of the 200-day fattening period before they were slaughtered.
Livestock and Forage Res. Lab., El Reno, OK
William Phillips, (405) 262-5291

TESTS WERE "ENCOURAGING" of a genetically-engineered antigen that could
become a key to developing a vaccine against coccidiosis, an intestinal
disease of poultry that costs the industry $300 million a year. ARS
researchers worked with Genex Corp. to develop the antigen, which conferred
the first protection ever obtained against any species of coccidia by any
method other than inducing actual infection. Work with Genex will continue
to turn the antigen into a vaccine.
Animal Parasitology Institute, Beltsville, MD
Harry Danforth, (301) 344-2427

USING A SIMPLE NEW PROGRAM, a small, inexpensive computer can regulate the
environment of a poultry house, maintaining temperature and humidity within a
narrow range. Until now, a skilled operator was required to make adjustments
to control the environment in broiler houses, especially during periods of
changing weather.
Poultry Mechanization Res. Lab., Miss. State, MS
Floyd N. Reece, (601) 323-1964

ANIMAL PRODUCTION AND PROTECTION (continued)

CALF DEATHS, which cost U.S. beef producers more than $300 million annually, could be cut in half through improved management, according to ARS animal researchers. Records show that nearly 70 percent of calf losses occur at calving or during the first 72 hours after birth, with the major causes of death delayed or difficult births. This not only reduces the calf crop but also reduces the pregnancy rate the following year. One week after birth, the leading cause of calf death was disease, including pneumonia and scours.
Fort Keogh Livestock and Range Res. Sta., Miles City, MT
Robert A. Bellows, (406) 282-4970

PLASTIC BEEHIVE COVERS costing about $5 each helped honeybee colonies survive Wisconsin winters on 20% less honey than colonies consumed in uncovered hives. The ARS-designed covers, which should last from 5-10 years, are made from translucent white plastic.
Bee Mgt. and Entomology Res. Lab., Madison, WI
Eric H. Erickson, Jr., (608) 262-1732

NOT DIET ALONE, but an interaction between genetic makeup and diet, has been found to affect the cardiovascular system of pigs—eventually. A diet loaded with fat and cholesterol had no deleterious effects on either genetically fat or genetically lean pigs that were slaughtered at 6 months. After 16 months, however, lean pigs had more aorta surface with fat accumulations than did genetically obese pigs. Besides having implications on how diet and genetic makeup interact to increase pork production, the study may have implications for humans, since pigs are being used more and more as models in an attempt to resolve dietary and cardiovascular problems in man.
U.S. Meat Animal Research Center, Clay Center, NE
Wilson Pond, (402) 762-3241

TWO PRESSURIZED SPRAYS available commercially proved effective in protecting people from a tiny tick, Ixodes dammini, that transmits Lyme disease. First diagnosed 10 years ago in Old Lyme, Conn., the disease leaves many human victims with sore, swollen joints and, in some cases, heart disorders. In ARS tests in a tick-infested area in Massachusetts, a 0.5% permethrin spray applied to the exterior surface of military pants and jacket provided complete protection against attack by all life stages of the tick. Applications of 20% and 30% deet, a common insect repellent, provided 86% and 92% protection, respectively. Lyme disease is now the most common tick-borne disease in the United States.
Insects Affecting Man and Animals Res. Lab., Gainesville, FL
Carl E. Schreck, (904) 374-5968

ANIMAL PRODUCTION AND PROTECTION RESEARCH (continued)

MODIFYING ANIMAL DIETS by adding high levels of high-fiber foodstuffs in order to reduce costs was found to have some adverse effects upon sows during gestation. Reproductive performance was not affected by the addition of up to 95 percent alfalfa meal, except that the weaning weights in pigs was reduced. There was a significant reduction, however, in the sow's ability to digest fiber components at 100 days of gestation. That would suggest problems with under-nutrition, particularly with respect to energy, could occur during late gestation in sows fed high levels of high-fiber diets.
Nonruminant Animal Nutrition Lab., Beltsville, MD
Corlette Calvert, (301) 344-2222

A ROUGHENED PLASTIC LOOP helps cows fight off mastitis, the most serious disease of dairy cows, causing estimated losses of over $1 billion yearly. Cows with the new loop, inserted harmlessly into udders, experienced a 75% reduction in severe mastitis. The roughened surfaces of the loops attract disease-fighting white blood cells in the udder and are far more effective than loops with smooth surfaces that were tested several years ago.
Milk Secretion and Mastitis Lab., Beltsville, MD
Max J. Paape, (301) 344-2303

SHEEP UDDER DISEASE WAS ISOLATED FOR THE FIRST TIME in about 5 to 10 percent of range ewes in some Oregon and Idaho flocks. Microscopic lesions, characteristic of the virus-caused "firm udder disease," lower ewes' milk production so they must be culled, since they cannot produce enough milk for lambs. Ewes inoculated with the virus, however, failed to exhibit the classical symptoms of the disease. Research is continuing, but findings so far are a crucial first step in eventually controlling the disease.
Animal Disease Research, Pullman, WA
Scott Adams, (509) 335-6022

A VACCINE CONTAINING KILLED BLUETONGUE VIRUS that has been irradiated protects sheep from the disease when given in two sequential doses. Further research is under way to determine the optimal dose of radiation needed to inactivate the virus and stabilize the vaccine for storage as well as the optimal dose needed to immunize sheep. The new vaccines are safer to livestock than those that use live virus. They protect sheep against two of the five strains of the disease. Bluetongue costs farmers more than $30 million annually in losses.
Animal Disease Research Center, Plum Island, NY
Charles H. Campbell, (516) 323-2500

SYSTEMIC INSECTICIDE REDUCES EFFECTS OF BLUETONGUE disease of sheep. A single treatment with famphur, an experimental insecticide, can be applied while routinely handling animals before bluetongue season in fall. Famphur cannot prevent infection of bluetongue virus, but treated sheep show no symptoms of the disease—mouth sores, lameness, and abortions. The virus is spread by biting gnats.
Arthropod-borne Animal Disease Research, Denver, CO
Frederick R. Holbrook, (303) 234-2474

A POISON PLANT MAY CAUSE LAMB LOSSES OF 50 PERCENT in the Pacific Northwest when grazed by pregnant ewes. The toxic weed, called false hellebore, has been known to cause deformities in lambs. Now agency scientists suspect the plant may cause ewes to abort or lambs to die right after birth, depending on when during their pregnancy ewes eat the plant. Sheep deaths from eating poisonous plants cost ranchers over $10 million annually.
Poisonous Plant Res. Lab., Logan, UT
Richard F. Keeler, (801) 752-2941

CATTLE POISONED BY EATING TOXIC PLANTS for a short period may get sick and die many months later. Cattle fed three plants containing a chemical called pyrrolizidine alkaloids showed no immediate signs of poisoning; however, many months later they developed the classical symptoms and soon died. The discovery helps to explain why cattle sometimes are unproductive or die from undiagnosed causes.
Poisonous Plant Res. Lab., Logan, UT
A. Earl Johnson, (801) 752-2941

CROP UTILIZATION & POST-HARVEST TECHNOLOGY RESEARCH

ENZYMES IN CEREAL GRAINS are inactivated by heating so that they can be milled into flavor-stable, high-fat flours with texture and functional properties equal to those of fresh or degerminated flours. The process, for which a patent is being sought, inactivates peroxidase and lipase enzymes in corn, wheat, oats, rice, sorghum, millet, barley and rye. It retains natural oxidants and the germ, which is rich in nutrients.   .
Field Crops Post-Harvest Research, Peoria, IL
George N. Bookwalter, (309) 685-4011, Ext. 419

A QUICK AND EASY WAY TO MEASURE SALT IN HAMS and other processed meats has been developed by agency scientists. The new instrument has been developed to measure sodium chloride content by reflecting near-infrared light off these meats. Food processors and meat inspectors may use the new method to help keep down salt levels.
Instrumentation Lab., Beltsville, MD
Karl H. Norris, (301) 344-3650

A NEW PROCESS prevents free fatty acid formation on rice bran during storage. This opens up a new source of edible oils in rice-growing countries where domestic edible oil is in short supply. Without this process, the high level of free fatty acid formation in unstabilized rice bran makes extraction of edible oil too costly. India has signed a contract with the United States for use of the process.
Western Regional Research Center, Albany, CA
Robert Sayre, (415) 486-3821

CROP UTILIZATION & POST-HARVEST TECHNOLOGY RESEARCH (continued)

CRACKED EGGS that now escape detection in packing plants can be discovered
quickly by running them through a staining machine designed by an ARS
engineer. The machine sprays eggs with a stain, then washes them off.
Hairline cracks show up in blue. Cracked eggs can still be used in shelled-
egg industries.
Russell Agricultural Research Center, Athens, GA
James A. Dickens, (404) 546-3531

FERMENTATION OF CORN dry-milled fractions to ethanol yields distillers'
grains that are potentially superior to corn distillers' grains. The byproducts from the fermentation of corn grits and flours contain more protein
but less fat and fiber than contained in corn distillers' grains. Lower
fiber content may be desirable in baby foods. Lower fat content may offer
better taste and more stability in storage.
Northern Regional Research Center, Peoria, IL
Y. Victor Wu, (309) 685-4011, Ext. 328

DRY-MATTER AND SWEETNESS OF ONIONS are measured with a new instrument that
uses spectrophotometry, a process that exploits the interaction of chemicals
and light. The instrument can separate onions high in dry-matter from those
low in dry-matter, permitting the low-dry-matter onions, which spoil more
quickly, to be marketed first. The "onion meter" can also screen onions for
desired qualities for breeding purposes.
Quality Evaluation Res. Lab., Athens, GA
Gerald Dull, (404) 546-3320

BITTERNESS IN GRAPEFRUIT JUICE and the juice of navel oranges can be greatly
reduced and the flavor improved by a process that relies on polymers made
from simple sugars. The sugars are used as packing in a column through which
whole juice is passed.
Citrus and Subtropical Products Lab., Winter Haven, FL
Robert Berry and Philip Shaw, (813) 293-4133

A NEW SUNFLOWER SYNTHETIC (a diverse collection of seeds selected for one
common characteristic) that is high in oleic acid has been released
cooperatively by ARS and North Dakota State University to breeders and
industry. High oleic sunflower hybrids may be derived from this material in
the future. Sunflower oil high in oleic acid can be heated to a higher
temperature without smoking, frying food, like potato chips, faster. The oil
also can be used longer.
Oilseeds Res. Lab., Fargo, ND
Jerry F. Miller, (701) 237-7728

A PRIVATE FIRM, the Mycogen Corporation of San Diego, CA, has applied for an
exclusive license to develop, manufacture, and market the ARS-invented
Mycoherbicide Pelletizing Process. The system can be used in applying
microbial-based pesticides.
Southern Weed Science Lab., Stoneville, MS
Wm. Connick, Lynn Walker, Paul Quimby, Jr., (601) 686-2311

CROP UTILIZATION & POST-HARVEST TECHNOLOGY RESEARCH (continued)

SOFTNESS WITH INNER STRENGTH is the idea behind a new way of blending fabrics developed by ARS scientists. The material, called "filament-core," combines the best qualities of cotton and polyester in a new way. Instead of combining short, chopped strands of cotton and polyester, cotton fibers are wrapped completely around a continuous filament of polyester. The fabric has the feel of 100% cotton with the strength and durability of polyester. Several commercial companies have expressed interest in the process.
Special Products Lab., New Orleans, LA
Robert Harper, (504) 589-7561

HUMAN NUTRITION RESEARCH

FOLIC ACID CONTENT OF FOODS can be assayed in half the time it used to take-- and with less chance of human error--with an automated, computerized technique recently developed by ARS. Folic acid, a B-complex vitamin, is used in the treatment of nutritional anemias and of sprue, a chronic deficiency disease.
Western Regional Research Center, Albany, CA
Pamela M. Keagy, (415) 486-3193

LARGE DOSES OF FOLIC ACID CAN BE HARMFUL to pregnant women and to persons on zinc-deficient diets. A nutrition study showed that too much folic acid, an ingredient in vitamins, increased the incidence of maternal infection, fetal distress, and other complications. Males need only about 200 micrograms of folic acid a day, rather than the 400 micrograms currently listed as the recommended daily allowance. Either amount can be safely consumed by eating foods, like liver, beans, nuts and green leafy vegetables that are rich in natural folic acid.
Grand Forks Human Nutrition Research Center, Grand Forks, ND
David B. Milne, (701) 775-8353

NEW PORTABLE METHOD TO MEASURE TOTAL BODY FAT is faster and more accurate than measuring skinfold--the most commonly used method. Called infrared interactance, the method uses near-infrared light to estimate the percentage of body fat in humans. Scientists are testing this easy and harmless method for use by physicians, dietitians, athletes, and agencies involved in Third World development.
Energy and Protein Nutrition Lab., Beltsville, MD
Joan M. Conway, (301) 344-2977

A ONE-YEAR STUDY OF PEOPLE'S EATING HABITS, the first of its kind, raises new questions about how nutritional values have been traditionally measured. For example, when trained subjects were asked to record their food intakes, they repeatedly reduced the amount they normally ate by about 18 percent. The 12-month study monitored the intake of calories and 19 nutrients by 28 men and women in the Washington area. Typically, nutritional studies last only a few weeks.
Human Nutrition Research Center, Beltsville, MD
Dr. Walter Mertz, (301) 344-2157

HUMAN NUTRITION RESEARCH (continued)

YOGURT MAY HELP ALLEVIATE GASTROINTESTINAL INFECTIONS when the fermented milk is eaten by people whose vitamin and mineral levels are normal. Scientists are looking into this milk product's remarkable effects. Expanding the market for yogurt will help use surplus milk as well as provide a major source of calories and protein for the world's poor and undernourished, who are most susceptible to intestinal infections.
Protein Nutrition Lab., Beltsville, MD
Anthony D. Hitchins, (301) 344-2331

EXPERT SYSTEMS RESEARCH

A NEW COMPUTER PROGRAM will help provide increased protection for soil in the grain-farming region of the Pacific Northwest. Using air temperature records of prior years, the model estimates for farmers the latest possible fall seeding date that will provide enough crop cover to keep down soil losses from erosion.
Columbia Plateau Conservation Res. Center, Pendleton, OR
Ronald W. Rickman, (503) 276-2811

GLYCIM, A COMPUTER MODEL, simulates soybean growth under a variety of conditions. It summarizes what is known about the physical and physiological processes involved in the movement of water, carbon, nitrogen, oxygen, and other materials in the plant, soil, and atmosphere. It also predicts the number and size of organs on the plants, their response to their environment, and final yield.
Crop Science Research Lab., Mississippi State, MS
Basil Adcock, (601) 325-2311

Qua

 Agricultural
Research
Service

CONSERVATION AND NATURAL RESOURCES RESEARCH

A Search is Underway for bacteria to
help degrade and clean up pesticides and
other unwanted chemicals in the
environment. Now the technology exists
to clone the genes in bacteria that can
do this task. Once cloned, these genes
could be transferred to other
microorganisms to create a whole class
of superdegraders.
Pesticide Degradation Laboratory,
Beltsville, MD
Jeffrey Karns, (301) 344-2493.

Runoff and Soil Losses from corn grown
on a Missouri claypan soil under no-
till, conventional tillage, and reduced
tillage were compared during a 6-year
study. As expected, soil losses and
runoff were least on no-till, followed
by reduced and conventional tillage.
Winter cover crops planted with no-till
reduced both soil and water losses still
more. The study also disclosed that
crop management factors affect erosion
and runoff under natural farming
conditions more than would be predicted
by the Universal Soil Loss Equation
(USLE). The USLE is currently being
modified by ARS researchers at West
Lafayette, IN.
Watershed Research, Columbia, MO
Robert C. Wendt (314) 875-5331

Increasing the Amount of plant residues
left on the soil surface makes no-till
corn and soybeans use more native soil
nitrogen. In a dryland experiment in
eastern Nebraska, uptake of fertilizer
nitrogen applied at planting also
increased with increased quantity of
residues, as did recovery of fertilizer
nitrogen applied in earlier years. For
corn, very little nitrogen immobilized
in corn residues from the previous
year's crop was used, but the new crop
of soybeans took up almost all nitrogen
in the previous year's residues.

Soil and Water Conservation Research
Laboratory, Lincoln, NE
James F. Power, (402) 472-1484

Protecting Groundwater from pesticides
will be enhanced by revision of an ARS
computer model called CREAMS (short for
Chemicals, Runoff and Erosion from
Agricultural Management Systems). The
model can predict pesticides and farm-
management practices that may contaminate groundwater. Such predictions
along with identification of potential
problems will lead to alternative
pesticide use and management practices
for high-risk areas. CREAMS may also
pinpoint safe uses for pesticides that
should be limited to certain situations,
such as clay soils high above
groundwater supplies.
Environmental Quality Research, Tifton,
GA
Ralph A. Leonard, (912) 386-3514

CROP PRODUCTION AND PROTECTION RESEARCH

The Best Combination of beneficial
insects and insecticides is being sought
to control cotton pests. One of the
most promising beneficial insects is a
wasp, Microplitis croceipes, that is a
parasite of bollworms and tobacco
budworms. Each year, these two pests
destroy more than 1 billion dollars in
U.S. row crops. Studies show the
beneficial wasp can survive several new
insecticides used in cottonfields. In
some tests, enough wasps survived to
parasitize and kill half the remaining
cotton pests, saving about 40 percent of
the crop. In closely related research,
scientists have perfected a way to tag
wasps, making it possible to track them
in the wild and so devise more efficient
ways to use them as biocontrol agents.
This successful biological control
research has sparked related studies at
Gainesville, FL; Tifton, GA; Columbia,
MO; and College Station, TX.
Southern Field Crop Insect Management
Laboratory, Stoneville, MS
Edgar G. King, (601) 686-2311

Lowering Moisture by Freeze-Drying seeds markedly improved the storage life of onion, pepper, and parsley seeds at warm temperatures. Studies showed that air-drying followed by freeze-drying lengthened seed storability and viability in marketing channels. This makes seeds easier to transport in tropical areas, lowers energy cost for air-conditioning, and preserves germplasm better by reducing the need to grow new plants to get new seeds.
Seed Research Laboratory, Beltsville, MD
Lowell W. Woodstock, (301) 344-2491

Plants Tolerant to Drought or salty soil are closer to being engineered genetically. A new method has been developed to remove chromosomes from one plant cell, inject them into another, with genes in the inserted chromosomes functioning properly.
Florist and Nursery Crops Laboratory, Beltsville, MD
Robert Griesbach, (301) 344-3574

The Discovery that a fungus of berries mimics flowers to "spread" itself could help scientists control mummy-berry disease. It is caused by the Monilinia fungus and can cut blueberry yields by 80 percent. Now scientists know that the disease survives by "tricking" bees into spreading it. Fungal spores, after they infect blueberry leaves, cause the leaves to reflect ultraviolet light and give off the scent of sugars—both characteristics of flowers. A bee flies by, picks up the signals, and, reacting to the leaf as if it were a flower, stops to feed on sugars. When it goes to the next "real" blueberry flower, the bee brings with it—on its tongue and legs—the spores of the fungus to infect the flower, thereby perpetuating the disease. This phenomenon, called floral mimicry, has been unknown until now.
Beneficial Insect Introduction Laboratory/Mycology Laboratory, Beltsville, MD
Suzanne Batra, (301) 344-2384/Lekh Batra, (301) 344-2317

Pecans Can Be Grown more easily and cheaply with an experimental growth regulator, scientists have found. Paclobutrazol, now used on apple and other fruit trees, makes pecan trees into semidwarf trees without decreasing the number of pecans they produce. The smaller trees will save farmers money because they require less equipment for maintenance and are easier to prune, spray, and harvest.
Southeastern Fruit and Tree Nut Research Laboratory, Byron, GA
J. Wendell Snow, (912) 956-5656

Female Caribbean Fruit Flies choose their mates from courtship calls sung by males. Females prefer larger males whose song gives away their size—the larger the male, the shorter the interval between the tones in his mating call. Scientists believe that larger males are healthier and therefore sing a more vigorous song, which becomes constant and louder during mating. The volume during mating alerts females to the size of their mates. A male perceived to be too small will be rejected by the female. Knowing what kind of males the females find attractive will help scientists release stronger sterile males into the wild, resulting in a smaller fruit fly population.
Insect Attractants, Behavior, and Basic Biology Research Laboratory, Gainesville, FL
John Sivinski, (904) 947-7726

A Method for Growing better citrus fruit has been developed. Using gamma radiation, scientists can almost eliminate seeds from some of the tastiest but "seediest" varieties of citrus fruit. The 'Duncan' white grapefruit, the 'Pineapple' orange and the 'Foster' red grapefruit get high marks for flavor, aroma, color, juiciness, and size. But they also have too many seeds to be sold as fresh fruit. By irradiating seeds of these fruits before planting, citrus farmers can grow trees that yield commercially seedless fruit (fruits with fewer than 10 seeds) with excellent taste.
U.S. Horticultural Research Laboratory, Orlando, FL
C. Jack Hearn, (305) 898-6791

Control of Golden Nematodes, or
eelworms, may be possible by
synthesizing the chemicals in potato
roots that trigger the hatching of this
pest's eggs. Eggs may lie dormant in
the soil for years until the chemicals,
called exudate, ooze out of potato
roots. By applying synthesized exudate
to unplanted fields, farmers could
"trick" eggs into hatching, starve the
young worms, and reduce crop losses,
which can reach 10 percent. Research to
develop the synthetic hatching signals
continues.
Nematode Research, Ithaca, NY
Bill Brodie, (607) 256-3106

Scientists Identified Immunity to the
tomato ringspot virus in 13 varieties of
strawberries when they tested the 52
most popular natives in the United
States. Knowing which ones show
immunity will help breeders develop
varieties that resist the damaging
disease altogether.
Horticultural Crops Research, Corvallis,
OR
Richard H. Converse, (503) 754-3451/
Francis Lawrence, (503) 757-4623

A Method to Detect dwarf bunt disease in
wheat may help U.S. exports. China and
other countries are trying to prevent
the disease from crossing their borders,
and the new test will quickly and easily
identify disease-free grain. Using a
special microscope, scientists check for
fluorescence at certain spots on the
fungus spores--spots that identify the
disease because they are distinctive to
dwarf bunt fungus.
Forage Seed and Cereal Research Unit,
Corvallis, OR
Virginia O. Stockwell, (503) 754-3451

Control of the Colorado Potato Beetle
may be possible with a fungus, Beauveria
bassiana. When scientists sprayed the
fungus on potato plots, the treated
plots yielded 9,800 pounds per acre, 5.5
times more marketable potatoes than did
untreated ones.
Yakima Agricultural Research Laboratory,
Yakima, WA
K. Duane Biever, (509) 575-5963

Double-Cropped Soybeans planted in wheat
straw are sometimes stunted and
chlorotic when grown in heavy-textured
soils of the Mississippi Delta. Burning
the straw gets rid of chlorosis, but
burning also eliminates the soil
conservation benefits of leaving residue
on the ground. In their search for the
cause of the chlorosis, which may
involve a chemical released when wheat
straw decomposes, scientists have found
that drilling 25 pounds of nitrogen per
acre beside young soybean plants
overcomes the chlorosis.
Crop Science Research Laboratory,
Mississippi State, MS
Joe Sanford and Jim Hairston, (601) 325-
2085

A Newly Discovered Variety of gamagrass,
a tall, coarse grass valuable for
forage, has one or two genes that allow
it to produce 20 times more seed than
other gamagrasses. Since the plant is a
wild relative of corn, the genes may
enable plant breeders to produce higher
yielding varieties of corn.
Southern Plains Range Research Station,
Woodward, OK
Chester L. Dewald, (405) 256-7449

Farmers May One Day Control rootworm
with less pesticide spraying now that
seven odors given off by the roots of
corn plants have been identified. The
odors help rootworms locate their target
and so help farmers estimate just how
many worms are present before any
chemicals are applied. Odors might also
be changed or other compounds added to
the soil to "confuse" worms.
Biocommunications Chemistry Research
Unit, Albany, CA
Ron Buttery, (415) 486-3322

Most Early Deaths of melon seedlings
from heat stress--a nationwide problem--
can be stopped with two preplanting
procedures. First, farmers should wait
until the first true leaf is more than
10 days old before they transplant.
Second, they could "heat-condition"
seedlings with true leaves by warming
them at 35 degrees C for at least 2
hours before transplanting.
Agricultural Products Quality Research,
Weslaco, TX
Gene Lester, (512) 968-7546

Fungi That Provide a biological link between soil and plant by carrying minerals and water via tiny threads into roots are also known to convey herbicides. The fungi penetrate roots, living with the plant in a symbiotic relationship called mycorrhizae. For the first time, they have been shown to affect a plant's absorption of atrazine by enhancing the amount of intake by a plant. Scientists may someday exploit this phenomenon by using mycorrhizae to boost herbicide uptake by weeds, thereby cutting the amount needed.
Soil and Water Conservation Research, Lincoln, NE
Jim Ellis, (402) 472-1514

A Quick Test to detect pesticide residues in bees has been developed. The test, which identifies presence and levels of pesticide chemicals called organophosphates, is easier to conduct than previous ones and takes less time. Honey bees, which help produce 30 percent of our food, have been dying in large numbers, and 60 percent of the deaths are due to organophosphate poisoning. Knowing how these organophosphates affect the bees will help scientists make responsible recommendations for their use.
Honey Bee Pesticides/Disease Research, Laramie, WY
Jack Harvey, (307) 766-3381

Extracts of the Neem Tree are effective insecticides for more than 80 major insect pests. Leafminer flies, cockroaches, and the Colorado potato beetle are among the many pests controlled by extracts from the tropical tree. Now ARS scientists have found that neem will provide safe and relatively cheap control for the sweetpotato whitefly. This pest, which has developed resistance to many insecticides, cost farmers of vegetables, melons, and field crops over 100 million dollars in retail sales in 1981 alone.
Boyden Fruit and Vegetable Insect Research Unit, Riverside, CA
Donald L. Coudriet, (714) 787-3828

Sunflowers, Black Walnuts, and sorghum are among the many plants that produce chemicals from their root systems that inhibit the growth of other plants, including weeds. Recent laboratory tests have shown that populations of such serious weed pests as velvetleaf, pigweed, and lambsquarters decline sharply when planted alongside germinating sorghum. Current research on these allelopathic chemicals, which include a broad class of compounds called phenolics, could lead to (1) breeding crops with increased ability to manufacture these substances and (2) synthesizing the chemicals to produce herbicides that can be used without risk to the environment.
Eastern Regional Research Center, Philadelphia, PA
Donald Bills, (215) 233-6580

ANIMAL PRODUCTION AND PROTECTION RESEARCH

Livestock Producers may someday be able to choose male or female offspring, thanks to a technique that has been developed to sort out the X and Y sperm in animals. The technique uses a laser beam to separate chromosomes sexually and should dramatically shorten the time required for genetic improvements.
Reproduction Laboratory, Beltsville, MD
Larry Johnson, (301) 344-2809

Safer Chemicals to kill imported fire ants are on the way. Two new products containing compounds tested by ARS-- carbamate and avermectin--are expected on the market by yearend. Both break down quickly in the environment. ARS has also discovered a group of compounds--fluorinated sulfonamides-- that will kill fire ants over a longer time. Ants bring the poisoned bait back to their nests and share it with others through communal feeding. These promising insecticides are being tested in laboratory and field.
Insects Affecting Man and Animals Research Laboratory, Gainesville, FL
Robert K. Vander Meer, (904) 737-6701, Ext. 356

4

A First Step toward a vaccine to protect cattle from the larvae of the common cattle grub promises to give yearlings the same level of resistance to the pest that older cattle get from actual exposure to natural infestations. Once cattle are exposed to the parasitic fly, their immune systems develop resistance to the pest by producing antibodies. Scientists are trying to isolate the protein that causes this antibody response. Once isolated, the protein could then be cloned, using bacteria and recombinant DNA techniques to make a vaccine. Presently, cattle are treated with pesticides--an expensive, time-consuming method that can leave cattle sick while it is working.
Biting Fly and Cattle Grub Research, Kerrville, TX
John H. Pruett, Jr., (512) 257-3566

About One Percent of newborn pigs have birth defects, with one-quarter of them traced to genetic or environmental origins. To assist swine producers in determining whether a defect is caused by either culprit, scientists have put together a fact sheet that describes 25 genetic abnormalities and prescribes procedures known to reduce their incidence. Copies can be purchased from Purdue University Cooperative Extension Service, West Lafayette, IN. If the frequency of pigs born with birth defects could be decreased to one half, producers could increase their income by 50 million dollars.
Roman L. Hruska U.S. Meat Animal Research Center, Clay Center, NE
Lawrence D. Young, (402) 762-3241

Yearling Bulls from first-calf dams may have testes that are less developed than those of bulls from older dams. Young bulls with large testes may produce more sperm, reach puberty sooner, and be better breeders. Studies show that beef breeders should also consider differences among breeds and heritabilities, as well as the relationships between testes size and age and body weight, in selective breeding programs.
Roman L. Hruska U.S. Meat Animal Research Center, Clay Center, NE
Donald D. Lunstra, (402) 762-3241

Measurement of Growth and development of testes of eight breeds of boars indicated that those of Large White and Landrace were larger. Selecting boars within breeds with larger testes may result in genetic increases in growth rate and animals with thicker backfat. Correlations between testicular development and growth rate were greater for older than for younger boars. Such research could help pork producers select boars with increased fertility, which may produce daughters with increased reproductive ability.
Roman L. Hruska U.S. Meat Animal Research Center, Clay Center, NE
Lawrence D. Young, (402) 762-3241

To Reduce Loss of sheep to coyotes, scientists are testing attractants to lure the predators away from flocks. The lures are derived from rancid food and coyote urine, and one lure has been patented by ARS. Negotiations are underway for exclusive public licensing to an interested manufacturer.
Biocommunication Chemistry Research Unit, Albany, CA
Roy Teranishi, (415) 486-3161

To Cut Feed Cost for cows by as much as 60 percent, farmers can use alfalfa cubes as a protein supplement. Traditional supplements, cottonseed meal and soybean meal, are typically far more expensive, and alfalfa helps cows maintain weight and condition just as well as the other supplements do.
Fort Keogh Livestock and Range Research Laboratory, Miles City, MT
Don Adams, (406) 232-4970

A Reduction in the annual 150 million dollar loss to farmers because of ruminant parasite diseases may now be possible. Scientists have found a feeding stimulant that makes nematodes, grown in the lab, ingest four to five times the amount of anthelmintic (antiworm) drug they normally do. If worms could be tricked into eating greater amounts of the drug inside animals, farmers would need less to control these diseases.
Regional Parasite Research Laboratory, Auburn, AL
Leon Bone, (205) 887-3741

CROP UTILIZATION AND POSTHARVEST TECHNOLOGY RESEARCH

Repellents for German Cockroaches were 100-percent effective for up to a month in keeping the notorious pests out of places where they live and breed--boxes, ovens, and cabinets. Agency scientists who synthesized the repellents are seeking three patents for a number of compounds that are related to the well-known biting-insect repellent, deet. They are also lab-testing the new repellents against other, outdoor cockroaches.
Insects Affecting Man and Animals Laboratory, Gainesville, FL
Richard S. Patterson, (904) 374-5910

New Corn-Grinding System saves energy and boosts poultry productivity. By using rollermills instead of hammermills to grind corn for chicken feed, poultry producers can lower their energy cost by 15 percent for grinding and significantly increase by 5 percent broiler weight gains during the first 3 weeks of growth. Grinding is the second largest user of energy in feed preparation for poultry.
Poultry Mechanization Research, Mississippi State, MS
Floyd N. Reece, (601) 323-2230

Seeds Can Be Safely Stored in ammonia-refrigerated warehouses without risk of accidental leakage affecting germination. Ammonia is known to be toxic to germinating seeds, but its effect on dry seeds was previously unknown. For the first time, studies show that after a leak, gas levels encountered by soybean, corn, and peanut seeds stored in a warehouse are unlikely to injure them. This is good news for the American seed industry, which uses this method to store large numbers of seeds.
Seed Research Laboratory, Beltsville, MD
Lowell W. Woodstock, (301) 344-2491

To Maximize Profits and minimize fiber damage for each bale of cotton, a computer model of the ginning system was used to develop the best ginning recommendations. Results of the computer run showed that a processor would have only four possible processing sequences for optimal cleaning and drying of bales. This knowledge will allow a ginner to select one of these four sequences after estimating initial amounts of foreign matter and moisture in the cotton. Such systems, if used, could net cotton growers an estimated $20 more per bale--about 6 percent of its value.
U.S. Cotton Ginning Laboratory, Stoneville, MS
W. Stanley Anthony, (601) 686-2385

Hydrochilling, A New Method of quickly lowering temperatures of freshly slaughtered carcasses, could save time, money, refrigerater space, and energy. Spraying packaged meat with a safe refrigerant at 15°F cools the meat three to five times faster than conventional methods that take 24 hours or longer--using air to cool hot carcasses. This allows meat to be chilled, packaged, and shipped the same day the animal is slaughtered. Hydrochilling, along with quick handling and processing, like vacuum packaging, could make it practical to export fresh variety meats, such as livers, hearts, kidneys, and tongues, and so help expand lucrative U.S. markets in Europe for these products by increasing their shelf life 2 to 2-1/2 times.
Meat Processing and Marketing Research, College Station, TX
Raymond A. Stermer, (409) 260-9248

A Computer Program to help engineers plan and alter complex food processing systems is being developed at the Eastern Research Center. A complete potato-flake pilot plant, built when dehydrated mashed potatoes were first developed at the lab in the 1950's, recently went back into operation to provide prototype data for the computer simulation program. The simulator can already be used to "try out" a seemingly endless variety of modifications to potato-flake processing plants, with the aim of lowering costs or improving product quality. The simulator will eventually be able to answer technical questions about the design of many different kinds of food-processing systems.

Eastern Research Center, Philadelphia, PA
Michael J. Kozempel, (215) 233-6588
Raymond A. Stermer, (409) 260-9248

Losses Between Harvest and consumer may be eliminated with a computer program for producers and processors. For example, scientists analyzed data on the number of potatoes lost and the amount of energy used at each step in the production of french fries, potato chips, and so on. By accounting for the energy each step required, they were able to assess more accurately the most profitable use for the crop. The program can be used to make similar analyses for other food products.

East Grand Forks, MN
Lewis A. Schaper, (218) 783-0344

Raw Materials for Plastics, resins, and other products can be taken from sumac, a common American shrub. In particular, one group of chemicals found in sumac--polyphenols--can be used in several areas of industry. In addition to forming plastic, polyphenols can help make slow-release drugs, pesticides, and solvents. The chemicals, acting as molecular "glue," help slow down release of substances into the environment. Several polyphenols also contain tannins, which combine with hides to form leather. Farmers could grow, cut, and bale the sumac shrub should further research confirm these preliminary results.

Germplasm Resources Laboratory, Beltsville, MD
T. Austin Campbell, (301) 344-3638

Lipase Enzymes, giant molecules that are generated by some living things to degrade the fats and oils they ingest, also have the ability to alter certain fats and oils in the laboratory, transforming one kind of fat into another. In one series of experiments, beef tallow, a surplus item in the United States, was changed by the catalytic action of a lipase enzyme into cocoa butter. Today an ARS biochemist hopes to produce and isolate large quantities of a lipase enzyme from fungi, using modern techniques of genetic engineering. Lipase enzymes may hold the key to transforming fats and oils that are plentiful into other oils that are currently scarce or expensive.

Eastern Research Center, Philadelphia, PA
Phil Sonnet and Michael J. Haas, (215) 233-6412

New Top Coatings for Leather can be applied in a variety of colors more quickly and with less energy cost than with conventional methods, which require the slow evaporation of solvents in coatings in 100-foot-long drying ovens. Now, instead of evaporating, the solvents react chemically and become part of the coating, avoiding air pollution and waste of chemicals. The reaction occurs in seconds when the coated leather is exposed to electron beams or to ultraviolet light. The new coatings produce leather with excellent physical properties, including improved abrasion resistance.

Eastern Research Center, Philadelphia, PA
David C. Bailey, (215) 233-6515

HUMAN NUTRITION RESEARCH

A Newly Discovered Defective Gene could prove invaluable in identifying people genetically predisposed to develop coronary heart disease. This could lead to preventative diets for high-risk individuals. The gene codes for a major protein component of high-density lipoproteins (HDL)--the "good" lipoproteins that move cholesterol out of artery walls. The gene abnormality was identified in about 60 percent of subjects with genetic HDL deficiency, 33 percent of patients with premature coronary artery disease, and 4 percent of normal subjects.

USDA Human Nutrition Research Center on Aging at Tufts University, Boston, MA
Ernst Schaefer, (617) 956-0393

A Mother's Milk, depending on where she lives, can protect her baby from locally prevalent harmful bacteria. It is not clear, however, whether infants acquire immunity to these bacteria passively from her milk or whether unidentified agents or conditions in the milk trigger their immune systems. Studies underway to answer this question will use stable isotopes in mother's milk fed to infants to trace the exact source of this necessary immunity. Results may also shed light on why children of malnourished mothers don't grow as fast as those whose mothers are well nourished.
USDA Children's Nutrition Research Center at Baylor College of Medicine, Houston, TX
Cutberto Garza, (713) 799-6004

Taurine, An Amino Acid common to mammals, has no demonstrated function, but in some species, its deficiency can lead to loss of sight. Whether taurine is essential to humans is not known, but recently, it has been added to baby formulas as a precaution against possible deficiencies. Now, for the first time, direct evidence of taurine biosynthesis in man has been obtained using a heavy isotope of oxygen ($_{18}$O) as a tracer. After subjects breathed pure $_{18}$O, taurine containing the tracer appeared in the urine. Studies are underway to determine whether infants, too, can make adequate amounts of taurine or whether this ability appears during maturation.
USDA Children's Nutrition Research Center at Baylor College of Medicine, Houston, TX
Peter D. Klein, (713) 799-6000

A 6-Month Study on Folic Acid, part of the vitamin B complex, indicates that healthy males need only 200 micrograms per day--or half the Recommended Dietary Allowance (RDA). This amount can be ingested through normal dietary intake. The study also showed that supplements of folic acid can interfere with the absorption of zinc if the amount of this essential mineral in the diet is marginal--about one-fourth the RDA of 15 milligrams. However, supplements of

folic acid do not significantly affect the absorption of iron or copper.
Grand Forks Human Nutrition Research Center, Grand Forks, ND
David Milne, (701) 795-8424

Low-Fat Diets, accompanied by an increase in polyunsaturated fats, may stimulate kidneys to eliminate excess sodium and potassium, thereby lowering a person's blood pressure, studies show. This new information may indicate why blood pressure drops when people alter their intake of fat, as well as point to new ideas about ways to prevent hypertension with proper diet.
Western Human Nutrition Research Center, San Francisco, CA
Jack Iacono, (415) 556-9697

People on High-Fiber Diets should increase their intake of calcium and magnesium to maintain proper balance of these minerals, a human study disclosed. But 40 grams of fiber per day did not interfere with the balance of zinc, copper, manganese, or iron when the carbohydrate source was starch. When starch was replaced with sugars (primarily sucrose and fructose), however, the absorption of copper and manganese decreased, indicating that sugars can interfere with the bioavailability of certain minerals.
Beltsville Human Nutrition Research Center, Beltsville, MD
Sheldon Reiser, (301) 344-2396

Adequate Dietary Copper prevented blood clots in the heart and other serious cardiovascular damage in mice on a high-fat diet. Such diets were found to induce severe damage to the heart and vessels 20 years ago, leading to current concern over the fat content of human diets. The addition of copper to high-fat diets prevented the severe damage attributed to fat in the earlier studies.
Grand Forks Human Nutrition Research Center, Grand Forks, ND
Leslie Klevay, (701) 775-8353

High Sugar Intake may increase the risk for adult-onset diabetes in the 15 percent of the U.S. population

genetically predisposed to sugar sensitivity. Sugar-sensitive people, many of whom are unaware of it, show higher-than-normal levels of serum insulin and triglicerides. An inbred line of rats having many of the same metabolic characteristics as sugar-sensitive people is being used to study adult-onset diabetes, the most common type of diabetes. Sugar was five times more effective than starch in inducing diabetes in these rats.
Beltsville Human Nutrition Research Center, Beltsville, MD
Otho E. Michaelis, (301) 344-2093

Total Body Fat can now be estimated by a quick and easy method that uses short wavelengths of infrared light to read fat at key spots on the body. The method, called IRI for infrared interactance, could lead to portable machines for doctors' offices, hospitals, sports teams, and even the public to keep tabs on physical fitness. Tests show IRI is faster, easier, and more accurate than skinfold measurements--the most common method used today. IRI also compared favorably with the accepted standards for estimating body fat, which are time consuming and restricted to the laboratory.
Beltsville Human Nutrition Research Center, Beltsville, MD
Joan Conway, (301) 344-2977

Carbohydrate Intolerance, a serious type of malnutrition in very young infants worldwide, is characterized by continuous weight loss followed by chronic diarrhea aggravated by carbohydrates in the diet. These infants are unable to absorb even simple sugars through their gastrointestinal tract and will die if not treated. Studies on hospitalized infants with carbohydrate intolerance and less severe forms of diarrhea suggest that chronic malnutrition, combined with a rotavirus infection, contributes to the development of carbohydrate intolerance.
USDA Children's Nutrition Research Center at Baylor College of Medicine, Houston, TX
Veda Nichols, (713) 799-6179

Certain Foods Block Zinc Uptake. Phytate, a natural substance found in large quantities in whole-grain products, green beans, potatoes, and other common foods, may inhibit the body's ability to absorb zinc, an essential nutrient. In a 2-month study, young men with diets high in phytate absorbed only one-half as much zinc as when they were put on diets free of phytate. The results suggest that high levels of phytate in the diet could lead to zinc deficiency, even for individuals who take the Recommended Dietary Allowance of 15 milligrams of zinc each day.
Western Human Nutrition Research Center, San Francisco, CA
Judith Turnland, (415) 486-3487

EXPERT SYSTEMS RESEARCH

The ARS National Soil Erosion Lab is working with five State experiment stations--in Iowa, Missouri, Illinois, Indiana, and Ohio--on a Computerized Production System. Within the next 2 years, modules in the system will be available to Midwestern farmers for use in their own personal computers. Objective of the expert system will be to help farmers take steps to assure adequate return on their investment, while conserving and protecting soil and water at the same time.
National Soil Erosion Lab, West Lafayette, IN
Harold Barrows, (317) 494-8673

New-Wave Computers expertly reduce and recognize patterns from a welter of information available on cotton plants. These computers can handle several knowledge systems or models to analyze computer data swiftly and efficiently. Such systems will enable cotton growers to increase the growth and productivity of their crops by choosing the best possible management system. Part of the system is already online for farmers to access with personal computers. With the help of the Cotton Foundation and the support of industry, a prototype test of on-farm crop simulation is already underway. Within a year, farmers will be checking out various combinations of management options that

help avoid nitrogen and water stress,
advise which pesticide to apply and
when, and determine when to harvest
their crop. When completed, COMAX (Crop
Management Expert Systems), which was
developed by ARS in cooperation with
Clemson and Mississippi State
Universities, will help growers better
manage the Nation's 14 million acres of
cotton and shave annual crop losses by
10 percent or $500 million.
The Robey Wentworth Harned Lab,
Mississippi State, MS
Donald N. Baker, (601) 323-2230

Agricultural
Research
Service

CONTENTS

HUMAN NUTRITION

Postponing cataracts through diet may be
within sight. Sunlight and oxygen
damage the unique light-transmitting
proteins of the eye's lens. The damaged
proteins clump together, clouding the
lens. As people age, the enzymes that
apparently clear away the damaged
proteins become less effective, and
cataracts form. Research shows that
vitamin C and other "antioxidants" can
protect the lens proteins from damage,
while magnesium and manganese greatly
enhance the ability of certain enzymes
to dispose of the damaged proteins.
These findings may lead to dietary
recommendations that retard formation of
cataracts.
Human Nutrition Research Center on Aging
at Tufts University, Boston, MA
Allen Taylor, (617) 956-0371

Chromium is far more important than once
suspected in maintaining glucose and fat
(lipid) metabolism. Long-term
deficiency can lead to adult-onset
diabetes and cardiovascular disease.
Recent chemical analyses show that most
American diets are low in chromium.
Nonprocessed foods--fresh fruits,
vegetables, meat, and whole wheat
products—provide ample chromium.
Scientists found that runners excrete
large amounts of chromium on days they
exercise, indicating a need for high-
chromium foods for this group. Also,
diets high in simple sugars (glucose,
fructose, and sucrose) cause people to
lose chromium compared with diets high

in complex carbohydrates (starchy foods
and vegetables).
Vitamin and Mineral Nutrition
Laboratory, Beltsville, MD
Richard A. Anderson, (301) 344-2091

Zinc and copper uptake may be enhanced
during pregnancy, according to a recent
study. When fed similar diets, pregnant
women tended to absorb slightly more
zinc and significantly more copper than
nonpregnant women. The findings suggest
that the special zinc Recommended
Dietary Allowance for pregnant women--
which is significantly higher than the
RDA for other women—may need to be
adjusted. And the change in copper
absorption during pregnancy should be
taken into account when setting the
allowance for copper.
Western Human Nutrition Research Center,
San Francisco, CA
Judith R. Turnland, (415) 486-3487

Guar bars reduced the severity of adult-
onset diabetes in both men and women
after a 6-month study. Five guar bars a
day, eaten before meals, also helped the
diabetics reduce their intake of taboo
foods. The granola-type bars were made
with 12% guar gum, a high-fiber gelling
agent common in many processed foods.
Although the bars supply three to four
times more fiber than the average U.S.
diet, they do not interfere with the
uptake of iron, calcium, zinc,
magnesium, manganese, or copper, as some
other fibers can.
Carbohydrate Nutrition Laboratory,
Beltsville, MD
Kay Behall, (301) 344-2396

Elderly people may need more vitamin E
than the current RDA of 30 international
units a day, studies with aging rats
show. Certain areas of aging rats'
brains lost some of this essential
vitamin even when their diets contained the
amount considered adequate for all rats.

In another study, high doses (10 times adequate) of vitamin E improved the immune response of aging mice to a level comparable to that of young mice. Research is now underway to determine if high doses of vitamin E can improve older people's immune systems.
Human Nutrition Research Center on Aging at Tufts University, Boston, MA
Jeffrey Blumberg, (617) 956-0300

Thermogenesis literally means the generation of heat. Scientists use the term to describe the energy used by the human body to process food. ARS scientists are studying thermogenesis in human subjects because the amount of energy required to digest food seems to vary from person to person.
Thermogenesis also varies at different periods of weight loss, possibly because the body becomes more efficient at processing food. This may explain why it becomes so hard to lose those "last few pounds" when dieting.
Western Human Nutrition Research Center, San Francisco, CA
Herman Johnson, (415) 556-9699

Body-fat monitoring is gaining popularity in health clubs as Americans become obsessed with leanness. Some people may, in fact, be harming themselves by reducing too much, shedding necessary fat stores. Women, for example, can become infertile at excessively low body-fat levels. Generally, men should have a 10 to 20% body fat content, women 20 to 30%, with 15% considered the norm for both. ARS scientists are testing the accuracy of several popular new methods for measuring body fat.
Energy and Protein Nutrition Research, Beltsville, MD
Joan Conway, (301) 344-2977

Many elderly people could suffer from severe anemia similar to pernicious anemia if they take broad-spectrum antibiotics. These drugs kill off necessary intestinal bacteria that produce folic acid and supply the needed amount of this essential vitamin. About 20% of senior citizens studied can't secrete enough acid to allow for the absorption of folic acid obtained from food. Normally, intestinal bacteria would produce enough folic acid to make up for the deficiency. Antibiotics complicate matters by destroying bacteria.
Human Nutrition Research Center on Aging at Tufts University, Boston, MA
Robert Russell, (617) 956-0300

Mounting evidence for selenium requirements is based partly on recent studies at the Beltsville Human Nutrition Research Center. To maintain a balance of this essential mineral, both men and women need a daily intake of about 0.5 micrograms per pound of body weight (or 50 micrograms for a 100-pound person). The good news is that North Americans are already getting adequate selenium. Beef, bread, eggs, chicken, and pork provide about half the dietary intake of this mineral, which is involved in protecting cell membranes against damage.
Vitamin and Mineral Nutrition Laboratory, Beltsville, MD
Orville A. Levander, (301) 344-2504

A moderate vitamin C supplement does not interfere with vitamin B_6 or B_{12} metabolism. Earlier studies had suggested that high levels of vitamin C might destroy B_{12} and cause excess urinary output of B_6. However, volunteers in a recent study consumed 600 milligrams of vitamin C in their diets each day—the amount in a normal diet—plus one supplementary vitamin C tablet. There was no significant change in blood levels of either B_6 or B_{12} or in urinary excretion of B_6. The volunteers' intake was about ten times the RDA for vitamin C.
Western Human Nutrition Research Center, San Francisco, CA
Robert A. Jacob, (415) 556-3531

A quick and accurate method for measuring vitamin C in the blood can be used to monitor blood levels and detect changes long before an actual deficiency occurs. Until now, the most common methods didn't distinguish between actual vitamin C (ascorbic acid) and a closely related compound (isoascorbic acid). Because isoascorbic acid doesn't produce the same benefits as the vitamin

itself, results of tnese analyses were misleading. The new procedure not only solves that problem, it can also detect much smaller amounts of the vitamin.
Western Human Nutrition Research Center, San Francisco, CA
Stanley T. Omaye, (415) 556-0060

Does chronic obesity affect a person's use of dietary minerals? Doctors have reported that some obese children and adolescents have low blood levels of iron and zinc. To study this phenomenon, scientists turned to laboratory animals. Obese rats showed significantly lower levels of zinc, iron, copper, and manganese in their tissues than their lean littermates. Studies are underway to determine how chronic obesity alters tissue concentrations of these minerals and if a marginal intake of minerals affects obese animals more severely than lean animals.
Vitamin and Mineral Nutrition Laboratory, Beltsville, MD
Mark Failla, (301) 344-2022

Dietary boron increased growth rates and decreased incidences of rickets in laboratory chicks fed diets low in an active form of vitamin D. Additional findings from the experiment on interactions of dietary boron, calcium, magnesium, and vitamin D$_3$ suggest a metabolic role for boron, possibly involving the parathyroid gland. If findings from the studies on animal models lead to establishing a role for boron in human nutrition, assessment of the levels of boron in U.S. diets might have to be made.
Grand Forks Human Nutrition Research Center, Grand Forks, ND
Forrest H. Nielsen, (701) 795-8456

NEW & IMPROVED PRODUCTS AND PROCESSES

Africanized or "killer" bees can be distinguished from domestic honey bees with a fast, accurate test involving simple measurements of wings and other body parts. The ARS-developed system can be taught quickly to state and local technicians.
Bee Breeding and Stock Center Laboratory, Baton Rouge, LA
Thomas Rinderer, (504) 766-6064

Cold damage in some fresh produce can be gauged by measuring light emitted from fruits and vegetables that contain chlorophyll. A scientist has developed a rapid method for measuring the delayed light emission from produce to indicate the extent of any chilling injury. Damage from keeping fruit too cold for too long could previously be measured only by cutting open the fruit. The method will also detect other kinds of produce stress.
Horticultural Crops Quality Laboratory, Beltsville, MD
Judith Abbott, (301) 344-3128

Fresh pigskins can be processed into leather a new way without curing. The ARS-developed process, which eliminates salt curing and the attendant water pollution, can help the U.S. leather industry make its products more competitive with imported leather products. Eliminating the curing step also improves grease and nonhide-protein recovery.
Eastern Research Center, Philadelphia, PA
William J. Hopkins, (215) 233-6435

Corn treated with the insecticide ethylene dibromide (EDB), after being stored for 180 days, contained only 16 parts per billion of the chemical--far below the Environmental Protection Agency guideline of 900 ppb in grain. Processing corn into flakes, grits, meal, etc., further reduced EDB levels, as did extracting and refining oil from the crop. Knowing how much EDB remains after storage will help scientists make recommendations for safe use of crops treated with the compound, which causes cancer and genetic defects in laboratory rats.
Northern Research Center, Peoria, IL
G. T. Bookwalter (309), 685-4419

A biological control agent of grasshoppers can be produced more cheaply than ever, making it an

inexpensive, natural alternative to chemicals. Nosema locustae, which kills grasshoppers by destroying egg-producing tissues, is made by inoculating hoppers with the microbe. The new, three-step plan cuts today's production cost by 50 to 70% and should provide industry with a way to produce the biocontrol easily and inexpensively.
Rangeland Insect Laboratory,
Bozeman, MT
J. E. Handy, (406) 994-3344

An instrument that identifies the strongest insect attractants has been developed. Knowing which chemicals most effectively lure insect pests will help scientists develop effective biological controls. The new instrument, called the dual choice olfactometer, offers insects two natural lures—a chemical attractant taken from a pest's favorite plant and a sex pheromone, for example. Whichever chemical lures the insects will be the best candidate for synthesis of a natural control. The olfactometer works similarly for repellants.
Boll Weevil Research Laboratory,
Mississippi State, MS
Joseph C. Dickens, (601) 323-2230

Electronic marketing of baled hay, a crop worth $10.7 billion yearly, may be practical with vans equipped to analyze within minutes hay quality on site. Such analyses typically require a week, with samples mailed to labs. The vans, equipped with near infrared reflectance spectroscopy (NIRS) technology pioneered at Beltsville, MD, analyze hay at farms and auctions for protein and minerals. In Wisconsin alone, hay auctions using NIRS analysis have increased from 40 to 92 in the last 2 years.
Plant Science Research, St. Paul, MN
Gordon Marten, (612) 373-1679

Lawsuits or disputes about the identity of patented plants may be settled with a manual which explains how to compare electronic "fingerprints." Three-dimensional scanning electron micrograph (SEM) images of a leaf hair or pore of a known cultivar can easily be compared with that of the contested cultivar, since specimens are magnified up to 75,000 times for examination on a TV screen. (Cultivars are plant varieties that are cultivated rather than occurring naturally.) Research for the manual was partly funded by the industry on behalf of plant patent owners seeking a more reliable way to identify plants than "expert opinion." About 3,500 plant patents have been granted, most of them for plants sold by nurseries and greenhouses, a $5 billion a year business.
Nursery Crops Research Laboratory,
Delaware, OH
Charles Krause, (604) 363-1129

New procedures developed by ARS and USDA's Forest Service will lower the cost of manufacturing the powerful synthetic sex attractant that effectively controls the carpenterworm, a destructive pest of southern hardwood forests. The new procedure removes the chemical structures that had inhibited the effectiveness of the attractant.
Insect Attractants, Behavior, and Basic Biology Research Laboratory,
Gainesville, FL
R. E. Doolittle, (904) 374-5723

A simple nondestructive flotation technique that requires only water, sugar, and salt, can select wheat seeds containing the most protein. Beginning with high-yielding kernels, a breeder can skim off the top 1% for protein content by adjusting the solution. The technique is an especially useful tool for wheat breeders in developing countries where laboratory facilities are limited or nonexistent.
Wheat Research Laboratory, Lincoln, NE
C. James Peterson, (402) 472-5191

Insects in stored foods may be detected by the sound of their chewing, using a stethoscope attached to an amplifier. Such detection may make it possible to export commodities without fumigation—saving millions of dollars worth of U.S. trade in certain fruits.
Insect Biophysics Research,
Gainesville, FL
J. C. Webb, (904) 373-6701

Mosquitoes can be better controlled using a new class of insecticides—synthetic pyrethroids—that mimic the

4

more expensive but very effective insecticide pyrethrin, which is made from chrysanthemums. Of seven pyrethroids evaluated, cyfluthrin proved the most effective. Using less pyrethoid overall gives more effective control than the commonly used malathion, to which many mosquito species have developed resistance. Insects Affecting Man and Animals Research Laboratory, Gainesville, FL D. L. Kline, (904) 374-5933

Better quality cotton fiber as well as lower energy costs, noise, and air-pollution levels are possible with the first combination cotton gin/lint cleaner. The new design combines a gin stand and two lint cleaners into a single unit, and would replace the air-transport machinery currently used. Southwestern Cotton Ginning Research Laboratory, Mesilla Park, NM S. E. Hughs, (505) 526-6381

Moving air intake vents in cotton gins from the bottom to the top of the gin where hot air collects can save operators 15% of the overall cost of drying cotton or as much as 75% of the cost of secondary drying. Cropping Systems Research Laboratory, Lubbock, TX Weldon Laird, (806) 762-7413

To detect and intercept infestations of foreign khapra beetles at the southern border of the United States, federal agents are using an inexpensive trap developed by ARS to control insects in stored products. USDA's Animal and Plant Health Inspection Service recently purchased 2,200 cardboard traps that capitalize on the insect's propensity for hiding in cracks. They employ a food attractant and sex pheromone to lure the pest to the trap's center, where it suffocates in a reservoir of mineral and vegetable oils. This technology--now being used by grain storage and mill managers worldwide-- quickly monitors insect migration and buildup. Such early detection should curtail accidental introductions of the foreign pest, thus avoiding large-scale chemical fumigation and treatments. Each year such insects damage or destroy

roughly 5 to 10% of U.S. stored products. Stored-Products and Household Insects Laboratory, Madison, WI Wendell E. Burkholder, (608) 262-1732

Woolens treated with pyrethroid insecticides to protect against moths and beetles can be stored safely for longer than the 6-month time now claimed on the labels of these products. Tests show that the treatments will protect woolen fabrics stored in the dark for as long as 6 years. Stored-Product Insects Research and Development Laboratory, Savannah, GA Roy E. Bry, (912) 233-7981

Holes made by cattle grubs in hides sold for leather significantly lower their value. A vaccine is being sought that relies on the animal's own immune system to fight off the hole-boring parasite. So far, a crude vaccine has been developed that makes young cattle as resistant to the pest as older cattle become naturally. Once scientists have isolated the antigen that prompts infected animals to build immunity to the grub, they can develop a pure and effective vaccine by cloning the protein antigen. Such a vaccine could save consumers and the cattle industry about $600 million yearly. U.S. Livestock Insect Laboratory, Kerrville, TX John Pruett, (512) 257-3566

More cheddar cheese can be produced in less time, at less cost, with no additional equipment with a new ARS process. Using commercial starter cultures for making cheddar, the new method cuts processing time by as much as 30% by eliminating the traditional ripening step. Eastern Research Center, Philadelphia, PA J. F. Flanagan; Virginia Holsinger, (205) 233-6516

Nature's own insecticides, like toxic bacteria, may not withstand insect pests, as previously assumed. After only four generations of exposure, the Indianmeal moth, a major common grain pest, can become resistant to

Bacillus thuringiensis or BT, the most widely used biological insecticide. Previous attempts to breed insects resistant to BT were unsuccessful because they relied on inbred laboratory strains of insects, while in this study wild strains were used. Fortunately, this potential problem has been identified before grain-storage operators suffered economic losses. Followup studies will examine how resistance to the bacterium develops and how BT works to control insects.
U.S. Grain Marketing Research Laboratory, Manhattan, KS
William McGaughey, (913) 776-2705

SOIL, WATER, AND AIR

Farmers running short of irrigation water in the Southern High Plains (parts of Texas, Oklahoma, New Mexico) can adopt a dryland farming system that will hold down soil erosion while providing adequate water for crop production. The system calls for a 3-year rotation of wheat-sorghum-fallow combined with either stubble mulch tillage or no-till. Residue from earlier crops protects the soil from hard rains and runoff. In field tests, annual soil losses during the wheat sequence were less than half a ton per acre with either stubble mulching or no-till. Even during the fallow sequence, losses were well below levels injurious to the soil, and losses under no-till were practically nil.
Conservation and Production Research Laboratory, Bushland, TX
O. R. Jones, (806) 378-5738

Free labor from soil microbes can best be exploited when pore space in soil filled with water stays near 60%. At that point, aerobic (oxygen-needing) microbes are most active, as gauged by the amount of carbon dioxide they give off from breathing. Bacteria and fungi work hard to unlock nitrogen and other nutrients in soil organic matter, making them available to plant roots for uptake. However, above 80% water-filled pore space, aerobic microbes slow down

and their opposites, anaerobic microbes, thrive. These anaerobes waste plant-available nitrogen—from organic matter or fertilizer—by releasing it into the air as gas. Tests of the pore-space concept on both plowed and unplowed plots in four states show it to be a reliable and simple way to measure soil microbe activity.
Soil and Water Conservation Research, Lincoln, NE
John Doran, (402) 472-1510

Costs are drastically reduced for ARS-designed stream stabilization structures used by the Soil Conservation Service and the U.S. Army Corps of Engineers. The "low drop" grade control structures use rocks and steel sheets, rather than concrete, to break the force of what were once destructive waterfalls. Stilling basins downstream quiet streams before they can flow on—and provide excellent fish habitat.
USDA Sedimentation Laboratory, Oxford, MS
W. Campbell Little, (601) 234-4121

Subsoil compaction from wheel traffic of heavy harvest and transport equipment can extend as deep as 2 feet or more if the soil is wet at the time of traffic. Studies in Minnesota show that this compaction has persisted for at least 4 years in spite of annual soil freezing and has reduced corn yields up to 27% and soybean yields up to 19%. Part of the decrease for corn was caused by reduced nitrogen uptake from denitrification and restricted root growth. Compaction does not affect corn and soybeans the same way.
North Central Soil Conservation Laboratory, Morris, MN
Ward Voorhees, (612) 589-3411

Preventing fungus diseases in no-till acreage is the aim of ARS plant pathologists in Frederick, MD. Special greenhouse facilities there simulate the high humidity of the South, where crop residues can become breeding grounds for fungal plant diseases. Researchers are developing crop management practices, such as planting earlier maturing varieties and crop rotation, to reduce the spread of disease. These practices

may also encourage farmers to apply more no-till and low-till systems to reduce soil erosion.
Plant Disease Research, Frederick, MD
Frances Latterell, (301) 935-2632

Ground-penetrating radar can zero in on deeply hidden water channels that can carry pollutants from beneath a crop's root zone into an aquifer. Such radar is a kind of surveyor's tool for charting topographic maps underground—rather than on its surface. By mapping rebounding radar echoes, scientists can pinpoint those soil layers that water won't penetrate that correspond to aboveground slopes, ridges, and valleys. Such watertight layers may form channels. Radar mapping, especially of porous layers such as limestone and sandstone, can lead to better ways of tracing or predicting routes traveled by leachable pesticides or fertilizers if they move downward and sideways into aquifers. Groundwater supplies about half of the nation's drinking water.
Environmental Quality Research, Tifton, GA
Ralph Leonard, (912) 386-3462

Planting more native warm-season grasses in pastures in the Corn Belt and Northeast can mean more beef per acre—enough to pay some farmers with sloping, eroding acres to switch from growing row crops to feeding cattle. Grasses that do best in hot summer months include Indiangrass, switchgrass, and big bluestem. Warm-season pastures can supplement pastures planted with cool-season grasses, like bromegrass, tall fescue, and orchardgrass. Taken together, the pastures can carry more cattle and provide nutritious forage for 230 to 240 days. ARS scientists also report potential for further genetic improvement of warm-season grasses. Switchgrass, for example, has already been made more digestible, resulting in substantial increases in beef production.
Forage and Range Research Unit, Lincoln, NE
Kenneth P. Vogel, (402) 472-1564

A test based on rabbit blood serum can detect pesticides in soil, water, food, and other materials. This simple, inexpensive test could help government and private agencies monitor pesticides rapidly and accurately. With the help of special equipment, 96 samples can be analyzed in seconds. A totally automated system could analyze 2,000 samples a day.
Central Great Plains Research Station, Akron, CO
Bohn D. Dunbar, (303) 345-2259

Two new herbicides are acceptable alternatives to 2,4,5-T to control honey mesquite (Prosopis glandulosa), which now infests more than 90 million acres of rangeland in the southwestern United States. Triclopyr, now on the market, is slightly better at controlling mesquite than 2,4,5-T, and clopyralid, which is not yet registered by EPA, is superior to all presently known herbicides.
Grassland Protection Research Unit, College Station, TX
Rodney W. Bovey, (409) 260-9238

Several natural insect enemies of mesquite found in Argentina are promising candidates for introduction to the United States and could save the livestock industry $200-500 million. Using the insects as biological controls could greatly reduce the number of mesquite plants, which lower grass production, cause erosion, and waste soil water in the southwestern U.S.
Grassland, Soil and Water Research Laboratory, Temple, TX
Culver J. DeLoach, (817) 774-1201

CROP PRODUCTION AND PROTECTION

Plants grow 2 to 4 times faster with a new automated and computerized tissue culture system than with traditional tissue culture techniques. With the old method, plants had to be transferred regularly to new liquid solutions of nutrients (agar). The new system, which is inexpensive to build, drains off the

old solution every 2 hours to pump in a fresh supply while leaving plants undisturbed. Commercial growers and researchers can use the system to produce sturdy, fast-growing plantlets of citrus, carrots, orchids, date palms, and many other species.
Fruit and Vegetable Chemistry Laboratory, Pasadena, CA
Brent Tisserat, (213) 681-7294

A few surviving American elm trees in one Ohio town appear naturally resistant to Dutch elm disease. Cuttings from these trees are promising even after direct inoculations with the Dutch elm fungus. If found to be resistant, these few trees may become the genetic foundation for re-establising the American Elm. Meanwhile, the U.S. National Arboretum recently released two new elm varieties, 'Homestead' and 'Pioneer', both resistant to Dutch elm disease.
Nursery Crops Research, Delaware, OH/ U.S. National Arboretum, Washington, DC
Lawrence R. Schreiber, (614) 363-1129/ A. M. Townsend, (202) 475-4847

A half-inch long fly, so obscure it has no common name, is a promising weapon against insect larvae that annually devour billions of dollars worth of food, feed, and fiber crops. Preliminary tests showed the tiny fly, Archytas mamoratus, in its maggot or larval stage suppressed corn earworms and fall armyworms by invading the bodies of these pests, preventing them from developing into moths. In their worm stage, these pests cost the United States an estimated $1 billion yearly in destroyed cotton, corn, soybeans, and other crops, plus the cost of controlling them.
Insect Biology and Population Management Research, Tifton, GA
Harry Gross, (912) 382-6904

Potatoes for export as frozen french fries are being grown in Thailand as a substitute for opium poppies. Over the past 4 years, ARS has encouraged the Thais to switch to Russet Burbank potatoes that an American firm there is trying to introduce as french fries to nearby fast-food chains throughout Asia.

Such alternative crops have reduced by half the area where poppies were once grown for opium export. Thanks to ARS cooperation with Thai scientists, local farmers are growing more profitable alternative crops, forsaking the illicit trade in poppies, some of which reaches the United States.
Narcotics Substitution Project, Chiang Mai, Thailand
Jack Bond, (9011 6653 245888)

The number of hairs on the underside of beach strawberry (Fragaria chiloensis) leaves has something to do with repelling black vine and possibly other weevils. Having found heavy hairs on the underside of the leaves of a particularly resistant plant, scientists removed the hairs and the plant lost its resistance. Since 1974, when pesticides effective against weevils were banned, weevil destruction of plants has been on the rise.
Horticultural Crops Research Laboratory, Corvallis, OR
Robert P. Doss, (503) 757-4544

The seven-spotted lady beetle, a voracious predator of some 200 species of aphids that destroy valuable crops like peas and other legumes, was at one time found only in the marshlands of New Jersey. Scientists collected thousands of these beneficial beetles and distributed them widely throughout afflicted Eastern areas. Decendants of these beetles now protect a large range of Eastern-grown crops, including alfalfa, cereals, and corn, and are frequently the dominant lady beetle in these crops. The project proved so successful that USDA's Animal and Plant Health Inspection Service is considering funding a program to further distribute the predator throughout the Western United States.
Beneficial Insects Introduction Research, Newark, DE
Richard Dysart, (302) 731-7330

Rust, a serious disease of many kinds of beans in the East and Midwest, can be controlled by spraying leaves with a natural bacterium. In some test plots, the bacterium (Bacillus subtilis) almost completely controlled the leaf disease—

results that so impressed the chemical industry that several companies expressed interest in commercializing this, the most advanced technology for biocontrol of a foliar plant disease. Rust can cost the bean industry up to $250 million a year.
Plant Pathology Laboratory, Beltsville, MD
Rennie Stavely, (301) 344-3577

A newly found nitrogen-fixing bacterium may improve the productivity of soybeans. Mutants from a strain of Rhizobium japonicum, a rhizobium that makes nodules (the small knots on legume roots that house the bacterium) change the amino acid tryptophan into growth-stimulating hormones. Since the mutants can still fix nitrogen and nodulate soybeans, researchers want to find out whether plants with bacteria nodules are benefited.
Northern Research Center, Peoria, IL
Tsuneo Kaneshiro,
(309) 685-4011, ext 243

Using mycorrhizae to control insects could reduce insecticide use and yield losses by 20%. Mycorrhizae are a beneficial association of fungi and plant roots. The mycorrhizae may fight off leaf-chewing pests such as corn earworm and fall armyworm. Laboratory tests suggest that the mycorrhizae change the nutrient makeup in the leaves of soybean plants and thus deprive worms of sufficiently nourishing food.
Plant Physiology and Chemistry, Albany, CA
Raymond S. Pacovsky, (415) 486-3321

New breeding lines of soybeans that lack the protein that inhibits trypsin—an important digestive enzyme—could save as much as fifty cents per bushel for beans used as feed for chickens and swine. Normally the protein in raw beans inhibits the production of trypsin in the pancreas, and the bean can be effectively digested only when crushed and cooked. Beans from the new breeding lines require less processing to inactivate the inhibitor.
Soybean Germplasm Collection, Urbana, IL
Richard L. Bernard, (217) 333-4639

New disease-resistant grape rootstock is ready for release in California. The rootstock, developed cooperatively by ARS and the University of California-Davis, is resistant to the grape fan leaf virus and to the nematode which spreads it. Growers in California have tried unsuccessfully for 25 years to wipe out the nematode with soil fumigants. The fan leaf virus causes annual losses of nearly $25 million in the state's Napa Valley and Lodi areas.
Crops Pathology Research, Davis, CA
Austin Goheen, (916) 752-6896

Cut flowers may last three times as long by adding a new chemical called AOAA to vase water. AOAA inhibits the plant's ability to produce ethylene, an aging hormone. AOAA must still be approved by FDA before it can be marketed.
Horticultural Crops Quality Research, Beltsville, MD
Chien Wang, (301) 344-3128

Major pests of pecans in the South and Southwest can be controlled with little or no pesticide. Field tests of a new ARS biological control system has kept one of Georgia's largest pecan orchards practically free of insect pests—in part of the orchard without using any chemicals at all. The grower relied on lady beetles and lacewings, two natural predators of pecan aphids and mites. To encourage reproduction of these beneficial insects, all 1,700 acres of his orchard were planted in vetch and arrowleaf clover. During the first half of the 1985 growing season, the grower saved thousands of dollars in spraying costs. In late July, the appearance of one aphid species prompted him to spray all but 30 acres, but control by insects alone in the unsprayed section was at least as effective as on acres with sprayed trees.
Southeastern Tree and Nut Research Laboratory, Byron, GA
Lewis Tedders, (912) 956-5656

Discovery of the specific protein that causes sucrose to accumulate in plant cells could lead to genetically engineered crops with higher yields. Sucrose is an important factor in

regulating and determining plant growth and yield.
Plant Biochemistry and Bioregulation Laboratory, Logan, UT
Donald P. Briskin, (801) 750-3059

A beneficial insect, Bonnetia comta, can effectively parasitize black cutworm—a worm that infests and kills corn—but it arrives too late in the season under natural conditions to prevent damage. Large numbers of the larva, however, can easily be collected, stored, and placed around corn seedlings infested with black cutworm where they parasitize the cutworm and reduce damage to the corn.
Corn Insects Research Laboratory, Ankeny, IA.
Leslie C. Lewis; Joan E. Cossentine, (515) 964-6664

An improved method for growing tomato pollen in test tubes could improve the productivity of tomato plants. The method changes the ratio of nutrients in the agar the pollen is usually grown in. It can help scientists quickly find tomatoes that are tolerant to heat and could be used to find tolerance to other natural stresses, such as salt.
Biocommunication Chemistry Research, Albany, CA
Merle L. Weaver, (415) 486-3380

Peanut harvesting and grading can be improved using a new "impact blaster" and fiber optics—a reflected light detector. The "impact blaster" is beginning to replace time-consuming hand scraping of peanut pods to find out when peanuts are mature enough to harvest. And using fiber optics may eventually replace the less accurate visual method now used to find pods that are of better quality.
Southern Agriculture Energy Center, Tifton, GA
E. Jay Williams and Gordon E. Monroe, (912) 386-3348

New herbicides that can tell the difference between weeds and crops may eventually be developed from chemicals found in the fungus Alternaria. The microbial peptides—a chain of amino acids—can regulate growth and cause yellowing and death in sensitive weeds, such as johnsongrass (a serious pest of U.S. row crops), but not in corn and some other crops.
Southern Research Center, New Orleans, LA.
J. Vince Edwards; Alan R. Lax, (504) 589-7591; 7593

Some trees can be protected from the air pollutant ozone by treating them with ethylenediurea (EDU)—an antioxidant chemical that reduces foliage damage. By injecting EDU into small stems of trees such as red maple, honeylocust, pin oak and sweetgum, rather than spraying it on the soil, the dosage can be regulated and the chemical can travel directly to where it is needed.
Nursery Crops Research, Delaware, OH
Bruce R. Roberts, (614) 363-1129

A unique research facility in Frederick, MD, allows ARS scientists to study foreign crop pathogens under the strictest quarantine conditions. When the U.S. Army abandoned its biological warfare research in 1970, ARS personnel took over the facility, which was designed for studying pathogens in isolation. Here ARS researchers plan defense strategies to deal with the potential invasion of a host of foreign crop diseases.
Plant Disease Research, Frederick, MD
William Dowler, (301) 663-7344

Membranes in plant cells, like those in animal cells, have ion channels that convey messages, scientists have discovered. The tube-shaped proteins control vital cell processes by shuttling ions into or out of a cell. Now scientists can look for chemicals that open or block the channels, possibly leading to compounds that increase growth and yield in crops or, in the case of weeds, stop growth.
Weed Science Laboratory, Beltsville, MD
Charles F. Mischke, (301) 344-3388

Using a growth regulator, scientists increased tolerance to stress in soybeans, snap beans, and apple seedlings. In laboratory tests, paclobutrazol protected these crops against injury after they were exposed to air pollution in the form of sulfur

dioxide, freezing, and heat stresses.
These and other stress factors,
including drought, can devastate a crop.
Scientists hope the growth regulator can
be made into a spray or put into the
soil to protect these environmentally
sensitive crops.
Plant Stress Laboratory, Beltsville, MD
Edward H. Lee, (301) 344-4528

A device to improve fuel efficiency and
equipment performance in farm tractors
has been developed. It automatically
keeps an engine within 6 revolutions per
minute of a given setting, despite
changes in load conditions. Farmers
usually have their engines at full
throttle—a practice that is unnecessary
and fuel—inefficient if the tractor is
pulling a light load or no load. Now,
they can set it at one speed, and, if,
for example, the load becomes lighter,
the engine will burn less fuel. By
using the exact amount of fuel necessary
at all times, farmers could save fuel
and money.
Field Crops Mechanization Research Unit,
Stoneville, MS
Lowrey A. Smith, (601) 686-9311

Sorghum growers do not need insecticides
to control first-generation European
corn borers, research shows. Farmers
have traditionally applied insecticides
at the beginning of a season because
second-generation borers can devastate
sorghum crops. But all of the 208
sorghum lines tested by ARS resisted
leaf feeding by first-generation larvae.
Although some larvae lived for a short
time on leaves, the damage was not
economically significant. Research
continues to breed resistance to second-
generation borers as well.
Corn Insects Research Unit, Ankeny, IA
Wilbur D. Guthrie, (515) 964-6664

Since decreasing alfalfa's drying time
reduces loss of both crop and crop
quality, scientists have devised a
method that hastens drying time.
Applying a solution containing potassium
and sodium carbonates at mowing time is
the cheapest way to make first crop
alfalfa dry quickly, with less solution
necessary at subsequent cuttings. The
solution has also been shown to make hay

more digestible and tasty to livestock,
so animals may eat more and get more
nutritional benefit from it.
Agricultural Engineering Department,
East Lansing, MI
Clarence Rotz, (517) 353-1758

A new insecticide sprayer that will save
farmers money and reduce pollution has
been designed by ARS engineers. The new
sprayer catches, in a collector box,
insecticide that was sprayed off-target
and recirculates it. In field tests,
the sprayer cut the amount of
insecticides applied on sweet corn by
over 30%, yet provided as much
protection as traditional
nonrecirculating sprayers. The sprayer
could also be used for other crops that
are planted in rows and spaced apart.
Pesticide Application Technology Unit,
Wooster, OH
D. L. Reichard, (216) 263-3869

Producers of hybrid cottonseed should
rely on honey bees rather than native
wild bees for pollination. Cottons used
to make hybrid seeds, if pollinated by
an adequate number of honey bees,
yielded as much seed as nonhybrids. Two
fields without honey bees, on the other
hand, produced 79% and 91% fewer seeds
than did fields with honey bees.
Studies also show that distributing bee
colonies on three sides of a field
instead of one side only results in more
seed production.
Carl Hayden Bee Research Center,
Tucson, AZ
Gerald M. Loper, (602) 629-6140

Hydrilla, a fast-growing aquatic weed,
may be controlled by exposing it to low-
level lighting for one hour at night.
The light interrupts the critical
periods of darkness necessary for the
plant to form tubers, the bulblike roots
needed for hydrilla to reproduce. The
control technique, which has worked in
laboratory tests, is being tried in the
Potomac River near Washington, D.C., in
cooperation with the U.S. Army Corp of
Engineers.
Aquatic Weeds Control Research
Laboratory, Davis, CA
Lars W. J. Anderson, (916) 752-6260

ANIMAL PRODUCTION AND PROTECTION

A new method chemically couples foot-and-mouth disease virus and red blood cells. These viral-red blood cell combinations can be seen with the unaided eye and could be used to develop tests for foot-and-mouth disease virus and antibodies. Such tests would be ideal in countries that lack complex technical equipment required for current testing methods. The coupling methods could also be used to attach foot-and-mouth disease virus to other biological agents to develop more potent vaccines.
Plum Island Animal Disease Center, Greenport, NY
Richard C. Knudsen, (516) 323-2500

Certain strains of infectious bronchitis of chickens can now be controlled by vaccinating chicken embryos. This could save the poultry industry millions of dollars in labor, since present infectious bronchitis vaccines have to be injected into hatched chicks. Scientists modified a common strain of virus so that it would work in chicken embryos.
Poultry Research Laboratory, East Lansing, MI
Jagdev M. Sharma, (517) 337-6828

A new variant of Marek's disease virus that does not produce the tumors characteristic of the disease has been discovered. Next, scientists hope to isolate the genes responsible for producing tumors. By eliminating the tumor-causing gene, they expect to produce a new vaccine to combat the disease, which costs an estimated $156 million yearly in losses to farmers. Such knowledge could possibly lead to basic information about how viruses cause tumors in human cancer.
Regional Poultry Research Laboratory, East Lansing, MI
Robert F. Silva, (517) 337-6828

A recent survey of 3,000 cattle in 66 herds showed that about 1% of all cattle are carriers of the virus of bovine viral diarrhea (BVD), a leading cause of economic loss to the cattle industry. This large number of cattle that continuously carry and spread BVD to other herd members is a threat to the cattle industry. It is important that simple, efficient tests be developed so that these carriers be removed from cattle herds.
National Animal Disease Center, Ames, IA
Steven R. Bolin, (515) 239-8372

Two traits linked to the same gene on a sex-determining chromosome in chickens could have a far-reaching effect on the poultry industry. One such trait is growing feathers slowly, used to sex chicks at hatching. In most egg-laying strains, slow-feathering has been associated with decreased egg production, which in turn has been related to an increased occurrence of infectious leukosis viruses. In recent studies, scientists found that fast-feathering siblings did not produce a unique leukosis virus that was produced by slow-feathering chicks. This indicates that the leukosis virus is inherited only with the slow-feathering gene. Infection with this unique leukosis virus may lead to broad susceptibility to other leukosis viruses. Other research may lead to ways to prevent infectious avian leukosis.
Regional Poultry Research Laboratory, East Lansing, MI
Larry D. Bacon, (517) 337-6828

Genes from avian leukosis virus appear to have been successfully inserted into the reproductive cells of chickens for the first time. The researchers are now evaluating the chickens and their offspring to confirm the results. If successful, this technique opens the way to the use of a viral vector, or carrier, to insert other desirable genes—such as ones that control faster growth and disease resistance—into chickens. One more generation is needed to determine the stability of the inserted gene.
Regional Poultry Laboratory, East Lansing, MI
Lyman B. Crittenden, (517) 337-6828

Reproductive efficiency can be improved and costs reduced by altering the rearing and management system for gilts and boars. One study showed that young female pigs must be raised in groups of three or more to reach puberty earlier. No increase in sexual development problems was noted in groups as large as 27. Another study showed that young boars housed in groups of three performed twice as many successful matings as their individually penned counterparts.
Meat Animal Research Center, Clay Center, NE
Robert R. Oltjen, (402) 762-3241

For the first time, an identical copy of a gene from one species has been inserted into the fertilized egg of a food-producing animal and found to function. The gene is a replica of one found in humans that controls growth hormone. It was injected into fertilized pigs' eggs and proved active in a small percentage of these animals. The new technique may lead to the production of superior animals and new knowledge of genetic resistance to disease.
Reproduction Laboratory, Beltsville, MD
Vernon Pursel, (301) 344-2814

Researchers and producers have worked together to solve livestock reproduction problems nationally. Their cooperation, for example, has helped make turkey stud farms a success. Other achievements, such as more efficient scheduling of swine births and sheep-breeding seasons and controlling bovine brucellosis, may now be possible. Integrated Reproduction Management is a cooperative research effort of ARS, land-grant universities, industry groups, farmers, and USDA's Cooperative State Research Service and Extension Service to reduce livestock industry losses.
Beltsville Agricultural Research Center, Beltsville, MD
Roger J. Gerrits, (301) 344-3066
Daryl King, (301) 344-2774

Poor sexual performance in male pigs costs pork producers an estimated $2.5 million a year. ARS scientists are working to devise evaluation schemes to predict sexual drive in boars so that unfit ones go to market instead of gobbling up expensive feed without ever siring piglets. Hormones in unborn, growing and adult males may provide clues as to why up to 25% of males selected as breeding stock turn out to be sexually inadequate. Environment and penning arrangements also affect sexual performance.
U.S. Meat Animal Research Center, Clay Center, NE
J. Joe Ford, (402) 762-3241

Texel, a breed of white-faced sheep native to the Netherlands, is valued for its high yield of lean meat. These sheep will be bred for the first time in the United States by ARS researchers. The Texel breed may be an excellent source of lean meat for producers to use, either straight-bred or crossed with domestic breeds. The sheep, imported from Finland and Denmark, will be in quarantine in Nebraska for 5 years. Thirty-one lambs have been born to ewes that were pregnant when they were brought to the United States.
Meat Animal Research Center, Clay Center, NE
Robert Oltjen, (402) 782-3241

Ear tags treated with the insecticide fenvalerate can almost completely control the biting fly, Culicoides variipennis, that transmits bluetongue disease to cattle, sheep, and goats. The insecticide was effective within a week after treating just one ear tag per animal. The tags can be used as part of a more complex pest control program. Tags are attached in the early or midsummer but are removed at the end of the season to prevent flies from developing resistance to the insecticide.
Arthropod-borne Animal Diseases Research, Denver, CO
Fred Holbrook, (303) 236-9354

A blood test for diagnosing progressive pneumonia, a disease that can affect up to 50% of U.S. sheep, can help ranchers select breeder sheep resistant to the disease. The disease is fatal once the animals become sick, but a low percentage of the animals actually show

13

the signs of the disease—weight loss, difficult breathing, and listlessness. Tests showed that Columbia sheep are more resistant to the virus than Border Leicester.
National Animal Disease Center, Ames, IA
Randall C. Cutlip, (515) 239-8544

A new way to extract and separate plasmid DNA is the first reliable method for differentiating strains of the bacterium (Moraxella bovis) that causes pinkeye in cattle. The genetic markers of the 200 strains that were identified could be valuable in tracing the spread of the infection. Vaccines could be improved since the strains may correlate with virulence and resistance.
National Animal Disease Center, Ames, IA
Timothy J. McDonald, (515) 239-8200

Mosquito parasites, found to live inside microcrustaceans (small relatives of crawfish and crabs), may soon be bred and released in swamps and lakes. The discovery that the parasites live in microcrustaceans was made in Australia in a collaborative project with the ARS Gulf Coast Mosquito Research Laboratory in Louisiana. The parasites produce infectious spores that are released into the water, to be eaten by mosquito larvae. Some larvae become diseased and die before they can emerge as biting adults.
Gulf Coast Mosquito Research Laboratory, Lake Charles, LA
Tokuo Fukuda, (318) 433-0696

Antibiotics in milk may someday be detected by the dairy industry with a simple test developed by ARS. Concerns that some dairy cattle are illegally treated with chloramphenicol (CAP) led to this experimental test, which costs only about 25 cents in materials and detects CAP in a milk sample. This test is just one of many developed by ARS to measure drugs in milk, urine, blood, tissue residues, and animal feeds.
Eastern Research Center, Philadelphia, PA
Daniel P. Schwartz, (215) 233-6473

The yellow-fever mosquito transmits a virus disease called dengue that is currently in the Caribbean and Central America and now threatens the United States. However, another mosquito that harms neither man nor animals successfully provided biological control. An ARS pilot project proved so successful that the New Orleans mosquito control agency is rearing and releasing this predator to complement chemical treatments. Combined chemical and biological control was more effective than either method alone, wiping out 98% of the pests.
Mosquito Biology Research, Gainesville, FL
Dave Dame, (904) 374-5930

Resistance to viral infections may result from studying the Major Histocompatiblity Complex (MHC) in swine genes. MHC genes regulate the immune system, determining if an animal will be resistant to disease. Scientists hope eventually to clone MHC genes and use embryo modification techniques to produce new strains of animals with the MHC genes associated with resistance. This may help prevent viral infections in pigs.
Helminthic Diseases Research, Beltsville, MD
Joan Lunney, (301) 344-1768

Selenium-deficient diets in goats impair the ability of certain white blood cells to produce chemicals that control some of the body's defenses. This may lower the resistance of livestock to infections. Since livestock diets are often moderately deficient in selenium, this could have serious consequences for our meat supply. Scientists are seeking ways to remedy such deficiencies.
Parasite Research Laboratory, Auburn, AL
P. H. Klesius, (205) 887-3741

A system for growing winter and summer annual forages to complement native range in the Southern Plains was found to increase beef production 100%. There was also a fourfold decrease in cost of production per pound of additional gain. Calculations show that these forage

14

systems have resulted in a 30% increase in land-use efficiency.
Range and Pasture Research,
Woodward, OK
Phillip L. Sims, (405) 256-7449

To combat Edwardsiella, a disease that costs the U.S. catfish industry $1.5 million annually, scientists have produced monoclonal antibodies that can be used to diagnose the condition. They hope also to use the antibodies in the development of a vaccine against this serious bacterial pathogen.
Regional Parasite Research Laboratory,
Auburn, AL
Phillip Klesius, (205) 826-4382

To ensure that chickens are adequately protected against disease, laboratories that do serum analyses after vaccination may need standard protocols to aid in the performance of these tests. ARS scientists conducted a study, using Newcastle disease as a model, in which identical serum samples were analyzed by 15 different labs. Some labs reported that the serum had very high concentrations of a Newcastle antibody, which would indicate good protection, while others showed very low levels, the sign of an unprotected chicken. To improve accuracy and reliability, scientists recommend that officials standardize procedure in analysis labs and begin a certification program.
Southeast Poultry Research Laboratory,
Athens, GA
C. W. Beard, (404) 546-3434

An optimum plan has been devised for using a preventative drug against babesiosis—a parasitic disease of cows and sheep. Babesiosis limits American exports to tropical countries where it is endemic, because the disease can kill 80% of the imported nonimmune animals. In lab tests, a carefully prescribed dose of the drug Imidocarb allows only mild infections upon contact with the disease, with solid immunity resulting. However, if too much of the drug is given, the animals fail to develop a natural immunity and are fully susceptible. Too little of the drug allows the infection to kill the animal. Knowing exactly how much of the drug

animals need will increase exports by enabling ranchers to ship immune livestock to foreign countries.
Hemoparasitic Diseases Research Unit,
Pullman, WA
K. L. Kuttler, (509) 335-9665

More useful and efficient strains of Bacillus thuringiensis or BT, an economically important natural bacterium for insect control, may now be possible using recombinant DNA technology. First, however, the bacterium's cell wall had to be removed before the genetically engineered DNA could be added to the cell. Agency scientists identified and used commercially available enzymes for removing the walls. The next step is finding out how to induce bacterial cells to produce new cell walls. This research will facilitate development of improved industrial processes for producing, monitoring, and maintaining quality control of this valuable biological insecticide.
U.S. Livestock Insect Laboratory,
Kerrville, TX
Kevin Temeyer, (512) 257-3566

To reduce use and dependence on chemical nematocides for controlling roundworms in goats and other ruminants, new toxins from the bacterium Bacillus thuringiensis (BT) known to be lethal to this nematode are being investigated. So far, scientists have found the BT toxin acts like an ovicide, destroying the worm's eggs and developing larvae at its communicable stage. Each year, roundworms cause an estimated 5 to 10% loss in animal production from weight loss and death. This research may be extended to biological control of plant parasitic nematodes, like the soybean cyst nematode.
Parasite Research Laboratory,
Auburn, AL
Leon Bone, (202) 826-4382

15

"EXPERT" INFORMATION SYSTEMS

Costs and potential hazards of controlling weeds in irrigated crops will be lessened using models that predict the impact of agricultural chemicals on the environment. For example, predictions concerning the effect of soil-applied herbicides on weed population and groundwater contamination considers a welter of information—the current crop value, the herbicide cost, the amount applied, the cost of applying it, and the seed count and weed populations under alternative conditions—before recommending what action to take. Another model does similar crystal-balling for postemergence herbicides—first considering the actual weed population before recommending action. Scientists hope to minimize the use of herbicides while optimizing the value of the crop. Sugarbeet Production Research, Fort Collins, CO
Ed Schweizer, (303) 482-7717

Three weather stations that cover 80% of Virginia's peanut-growing area give farmers facts needed to make fungicide-spraying decisions to control Cercospora leaf spot disease. The stations are part of Virginia's Agro-Environmental Monitoring System, a cooperative venture between ARS and Virginia Polytechnic Institute and the State University at Blacksburg, VA. The Virginia researchers have joined a recently formed national network of peanut researchers to develop an overall peanut-growth model to help farmers with other decisions such as when to apply other pesticides and when to irrigate. Peanut Production, Diseases, and Harvesting Research Unit, Suffolk, VA
James L. Steele, (804) 657-6403

Infrared aerial photography may help save Rio Grande Valley cotton growers millions of dollars. Now inspectors can easily and cheaply detect cotton stalks harboring larvae of cotton's most serious pest, the boll weevil. By destroying stalks after harvest, weevils cannot overwinter to reproduce and cause heavy infestations in nearby fields the following season. In tests, farmers produced record yields with less pesticide, saving $25 to $30 million in one year. Decreasing the number of pesticide applications, which had averaged 10 per farmer, also helped spare beneficial insects that control Heliothis, another cotton pest. Subtropical Crop Insects Research Unit, Weslaco, TX
K. R. Summy, (512) 968-3159

Qua

QUARTERLY REPORT
ON SELECTED RESEARCH PROJECTS
OF THE AGRICULTURAL RESEARCH SERVICE
U.S. DEPARTMENT OF AGRICULTURE
October 1 to December 31, 1985

Agricultural
Research
Service

CONTENTS

HUMAN NUTRITION

Trends in the average American diet will
be easier to spot with a new computerized
system expected to be ready in 1986. The
system's components—an electronic scale,
bar code reader, and portable computer—
are streamlined to fit in the kitchens of
families who volunteer for food intake
studies. Current methods for determining
food intake, such as the "food diary" or
the "24-hour recall," are inaccurate,
tedious, and expensive by contrast.
Savings in time and money, plus expected
gains in accuracy, will make the new
system one of the first major advances in
determining dietary patterns in more than
40 years.
Western Human Nutrition Research Center,
San Francisco, CA
M. J. Kretsch, (415) 556-6231

Trained athletes don't suffer from sore
muscles because their bodies are already
geared up to repair muscle damage quickly, recent studies suggest. It now
appears that individual muscle fibers
tear apart at a "weak link" when con-
tracted muscles are being lengthened, as
in lowering a weight or walking down-
stairs. In sedentary people, the body
responds to this damage as it would to an
infection—by producing large amounts of
the polypeptide interleukin-1. People
who exercise regularly, however, maintain
high blood levels of this polypeptide,
which apparently triggers the repair
process.
Human Nutrition Research Center on Aging
at Tufts University, Boston, MA
William J. Evans, (617) 956-0333

People can maintain muscle quality
throughout life with regular exercise,
even though muscle mass inevitably declines with age. Men and women over 60
who underwent a moderate program of
aerobic training had a 16% to 20% increase in functional capacity—a measurement that reflects the ability of skeletal muscles to use oxygen. As people
age, their ability to repair damaged
muscle fibers diminishes, resulting in
the progressive loss of muscle mass. But
current strength-training studies with
men are showing that older people can
increase the size of remaining muscle and
decrease associated fat.
Human Nutrition Research Center on Aging
at Tufts University, Boston, MA
William J. Evans, (617) 956-0333

Several fat-soluble vitamins can now be
measured quickly, accurately, and at the
same time from blood plasma samples as
small as one-half milliliter. Clinicians
or researchers can use the new high-
performance liquid chromatographic method
to separate and measure vitamin E, vitamin A, and other carotenoids. Nutritional assessment of these vitamins may be
important in light of their reported
roles in reducing cancer risk.
Grand Forks Human Nutrition Research
Center, Grand Forks, ND
David B. Milne, (701) 795-8424

Breast-fed infants may be getting double
protection against infections. Recent
studies indicate that breast milk not
only contains infection-fighting factors,
it may also contain unidentified substances that stimulate the infant's immune
system to produce its own protective
factors. The low rate of clinical and
subclinical infections seen in exclusively breast-fed infants may partly explain
why they are able to use the energy and
nitrogen in their diets more efficiently

than do infants whose diets include standard infant formulas.
Children's Nutrition Research Center at Baylor College of Medicine, Houston, TX
Cutberto Garza, (713) 699-6004

A high-fat intake--40% to 45% of total calories--increases risk of colorectal cancer, according to an intensive study of vegetarians and nonvegetarians living in the same geographical area. The typical American diet is about 40% fat calories. The study substantiated results of animal studies as well as mounting epidemiological evidence linking fat intake to colorectal cancer. It also confirmed that the presence of certain sterols and bile acids in the stool are good indicators for risk of this type of cancer.
Lipid Nutrition Lab, Human Nutrition Research Center, Beltsville, MD
Padmanabhan P. Nair, (301) 344-2583

Barley extracts may provide a natural way to alter the ratio of serum cholesterols and thereby reduce risk of heart disease and stroke from atherosclerosis. In studies with chickens, rats, and pigs, diets containing barley flour reduced the "bad" LDL-cholesterol up to 53% but did not significantly reduce the protective HDL-cholesterol. The active components were identified as a complex alcohol similar to vitamin E and a rare plant triglyceride. When added to chicken feed in minute amounts, the extracts also inhibited the liver enzyme that controls the animal's own synthesis of cholesterol.
Cereal Crops Research, Madison, WI
David Peterson, (608) 262-4482

NEW & IMPROVED PRODUCTS AND PROCESSES

Cotton fibers were grown in a laboratory test tube directly from cells without growing any other part of the plant. Research at Texas Tech University demonstrated that, for the first time, an agricultural commodity could be grown in a test tube from plant tissue suspended in a nutrient solution. When the gene chemistry of this growth is fully understood, the knowledge may be applied to improve the genetics of the cotton plant

to produce longer and stronger cotton fiber. The work was partially financed by ARS as part of a project to improve fiber quality.
Cropping Systems Research Lab, Lubbock, TX
Jerry E. Quisenberry, (806) 746-6101

Tallow or beef fat can now be converted into water, fatty acids, and glycerin at low temperatures using a class of enzymes or proteins called lipases. Such technology could replace the currently used high-temperature method, reducing energy costs and preserving some of the fat's natural qualities. This is the first time enzymes and membranes have been used together to produce fatty acids. Adoption of the new technology is a milestone to the billion-dollar-a-year fatty acid industry, which produces many industrial and household products.
Eastern Research Center, Philadelphia, PA
Dennis J. O'Brien, (215) 233-6601

A long-sought-after chemical has been found that stimulates plants to simultaneously increase nutrients and yields for the first time. Made from two commercially available compounds, the plant bioregulator, called DCPT, appears to work by increasing the flow and use of photosynthetic carbon in many crops tested, including cotton, soybeans, alfalfa, bushbeans, guayule, and lemon. The increased productivity per unit of input could benefit producers of many major commodities.
Fruit & Vegetable Chemistry Research Lab, Pasadena, CA
Henry Yokoyama, (213) 681-7294

Citrus canker on fruit can be controlled by dipping the fruit in chlorine. Studies show that bacteria that cause citrus canker can survive on the surface of untreated citrus fruit for 24 hours at room temperature; in contrast, a 2-minute dip in 250-ppm chlorine and water killed the bacteria immediately. Chlorine-treated fruit can be shipped from areas contaminated with the canker without risk of spreading the surface bacteria. Last year, several million dollars in oranges were not exported

because of the canker problem and had to be used for juice.
Horticultural Crops Quality Lab, Beltsville, MD
Harold Moline, (301) 344-3128

Contamination of edible peanuts by natural toxins last year cost farmers, processors, and manufacturers $18.7 million to ensure that only the safest and most healthful peanuts reached the marketplace. Research has shown that when peanuts were water-stressed for 30 days before harvesting, they were contaminated by aflatoxins caused by the mold Aspergillus flavus; on the other hand, just 20 days of stress caused no contamination. This knowledge will help peanut growers more accurately predict when their crop might be contaminated so they will irrigate crops to prevent contamination and losses.
National Peanut Research Lab, Dawson, GA
Dick Cole, (912) 995-4441

A new type of filament-wrapped cotton yarn, named for its X-shaped structure, is stronger and can be stretched longer than conventionally wrapped yarns. Based on the Chinese finger puzzle where the more you pull, the tighter it gets, the X-wrap yarn twists to hold fibers close to the core. With this added protection, the yarn will not ball as much. Scientists have also invented a new device for making the X-wrap yarn.
Southern Research Center, New Orleans, LA
Gain L. Louis, (504) 589-7044

A gene that codes for a major wheat protein that determines flour quality has been cloned and its DNA sequence, or genetic code, determined. The availability of a pure form of this gene, called alpha-gliadin, and the knowledge of the information contained in its genetic code will permit bioengineering wheat flour protein at the molecular level. This is significant progress in developing ways to improve the baking quality of wheat flour that will benefit both consumers and producers.
Western Research Lab, Albany, CA
Frank C. Greene, (415) 486-3739

A portable meter suitable for use at supermarkets analyzes carbohydrates, carotene, and other constituents of papayas, onions, potatoes, cantaloups, and other produce. So far, the light-meter technology, called spectrophotometry, can measure sweetness in onions using near infrared light and carotene in papayas using visible light. Besides aiding consumers, such technology could also help plant breeders, growers, and packers screen large quantities of produce quickly.
Field & Horticultural Crops Research, Athens, GA
Gerald Dull, (404) 546-3320

Hamburger can now be tested faster, more cheaply, and more simply to determine how long the meat will retain its freshness until it is finally sold in supermarkets or used in fast-food restaurants. Originally designed to help buyers for the federal school lunch program, the patented test uses high-performance liquid chromatography to measure the lactic acid in meats. It takes about 1 hour as compared with 9 days for other techniques.
Engineering & Food Sciences Research, Albany, CA
A. Douglas King, (415) 486-3252

White blood cells needed to develop better vaccines and improve disease immunity in animals can now be collected continuously and in quantity from research animals. A small hollow plastic sphere, easily implanted under the animal's skin, has membrane-covered holes that only white blood cells can enter. Cells are flushed from the sphere and through an outlet tube with a syringe and saline solution. This technology is preferable to frequent bleeding of animals or sacrificing them to obtain an adequate supply of these cells. Also, cell biologists, immunologists, and other researchers will have purer cells that don't require processing to be isolated from whole blood.
Parasite Research Lab, Auburn, AL
Phil Klesius, (205) 826-4382

Cotton workers could be aided by two new tests based on a theory that microorganisms in cotton dust cause byssino-

sis, or brown lung disease. One quick test finds the level of micro-organisms on cotton bales by measuring the pH, or chemical acidity, of the bales. The other test can identify a large number of bacteria from numerous air samples, without testing each one individually, by simulating how the bacteria-laden dust settles in the passageways of workers' lungs.
Soil Microbial Systems, Beltsville, MD
Paul B. Marsh/Marion Simpson, (301) 344-3068

A microwave vacuum can dry rice efficiently without changing its cooking and eating qualities. At present, grain processors generally use fossil fuels to power the air-driers that remove water from rice so it can be milled and stored. But future fuel shortages or price increases could force processors to turn to alternative fuel sources, like an economical system powered by electricity.
Southern Research Center, New Orleans, LA
James I. Wadsworth, (504) 589-7012

Nigeria is planning to build a processing plant that will convert yam tubers, a major part of the diet of 100 million Nigerians, into edible, pre-cooked, dehydrated flakes. To eliminate storage problems that result in the loss of staple protein in yams, the plant will use the successful sweet potato-to-flake process developed by ARS researchers in 1962. The process has potential use for cassava, coco yam, white and sweet potato tubers, thus helping alleviate hunger in western Africa.
Southern Research Center, New Orleans, LA
Kenneth M. Decossas, (504) 589-7025

Acrylic plastics could be made from readily available renewable agricultural commodities instead of petroleum. The bacterium Klebsiella pnuemoniae can ferment up to 84% glycerol, a common byproduct of animal and vegetable fat processing, which eventually oxidizes into acrylic acid. Scientists have yet to determine if this process is economically feasible. Presently, acrylic is worth about 60 cents per pound, and billions of pounds are used annually to produce synthetic polymers such as plastics.
Northern Research Center, Peoria, IL
Patricia J. Sliniger, (309) 685-4011, Ext. 286

Processors of salad dressings that contain soybean oil may have new methods to permit longer use after opening. Exposure to oxygen causes soybean oils to become rancid. ARS researchers have found alternatives to hydrogenation, an expensive process used to make oils more stable. Using an antioxidant in the oil, or adding citric acid to inactivate the iron in the dressing, which hastens deterioration, or packaging it in a nitrogen atmosphere may be economical substitutes for hydrogenating the oil.
Northern Research Center, Peoria, IL
Timothy L. Mounts, (309) 685-4011, Ext. 555

Multicolored cloth can now be produced in a shorter time using cotton yarns treated with a new finish. By weaving undyed yarns that either absorb or resist a dye, a weaver can create a particular pattern, then dye the whole fabric to get a multicolored effect. Previously, to make a pattern, yarns had to be dyed beforehand and woven alternately to change the color of the fabric.
Southern Research Center, New Orleans, LA
Robert J. Harper, Jr., (504) 589-7063

SOIL, WATER, & AIR

ARS researchers have developed a workable reduced-tillage system for growing furrow-irrigated grain sorghum in the southern High Plains that may also prove successful with irrigated corn. The system increases the space between plant rows from the usual 10 inches to 30 inches and water furrow spacing from 40 to 60 inches. Grain yields using the wide-bed reduced-tillage system were 5% higher than with conventional tillage, and costs were reduced $3.50 per acre. Production efficiency was increased by lowering costs, time, and energy.
Soil & Crop Management Research Lab, Bushland, TX
Ronald R. Allen, (806) 378-5738

New ARS tests show that ozone levels that occur in the South reduce lint and seed yields of Stoneville-213 cotton by 11%. Earlier tests showed that the air pollutant reduces the yields of California-grown cotton by about 15% each year. Data on the response of field-grown cotton to various levels of ozone in the air will be used by the Environmental Protection Agency to set air-quality standards.
Air-Quality Plant Growth & Development Research Lab, Raleigh, NC
Allen S. Heagle, (919) 737-3311

The thriving poultry industry of the southern Piedmont gets rid of large amounts of broiler litter as fertilizer for forage crops, like Coastal bermudagrass. Interseeding the bermudagrass with annual rye increases the yields of high-quality forage by 32% to 35%, thus increasing nitrogen recovery in usable forage, while reducing both nitrogen concentrations and losses in bermudagrass pastures. This benefits both livestock feeders and the broiler industry.
Forage/Livestock Management Systems Research Lab, Watkinsville, GA
Stanley L. Wilkinson (404) 769-5631

Before reclamation laws were passed, bentonite miners left behind large tracts of barren mine spoils in Wyoming, Montana, and South Dakota. Mixing sawdust and other sawmill wastes, along with nitrogen fertilizer, into the spoil promotes the growth of perennial grasses and livestock forage. As a result of this research, 6,000 acres of abandoned bentonite-mined lands in Wyoming were recently scheduled for reclamation.
Mined Land Reclamation/Water Conservation Research Lab, Cheyenne, WY
Gerald Schuman, (307) 778-2220, ext. 2433

Conventional furrow irrigation for dry bean production in the West often wastes water and causes severe soil erosion, since fields are typically irrigated until the entire surface is wet. By irrigating only long enough for the water to reach the end of the furrow and then planting the bean seed in the bottom of the furrow a few days later, the quantity of water applied for preplanting was reduced 60%. Further, by limiting irrigation to the furrows where the beans were growing, total water applied was reduced 42% without affecting yields.
Soil Management and Water Quality Lab, Kimberly, ID
Robert D. Berg, (208) 423-5582

In the East, small cattle herds (100 head or fewer) are often fed in confinement in small or unpaved lots. Runoff water from the lots transports wastes and other pollutants into downstream waters. A newly designed system for measuring the amount and quality of the runoff revealed that quality was improved when the runoff water was forced through a shallow settling basin and into a tile-drained infiltration bed. The work provides action agencies with useful technology for controlling the quality of runoff from small feedlots.
North Appalachian Experimental Watershed Research Lab, Coshocton, OH
William M. Edwards, (614) 545-6349

A $100,000 ARS project to develop economical and reliable methods for mapping soils affected by salt accumulation has been funded by USDA's Soil Conservation Service. Scientists will employ new instruments that are fast and easy to use and that provide reliable data on a large scale. Salt accumulation is a potential danger on all irrigated cropland; in California alone, up to 1 million acres are starting to show damage.
U.S. Salinity Lab, Riverside, CA
James Rhodes, (714) 683-0170

A collapsible fabric dam that controls water levels of both a stream and its adjacent groundwater table may help overcome seasonal droughts in agricultural fields of mid-Atlantic states. Water pumped from behind such a dam supplied eight center-pivots, four volume guns, and one subirrigation system. Moreover, the raised water table sustained crop growth on nonirrigated parts of the 2,000-acre study area. Raising the water table also reduced the amount of subsurface drainage, thus reducing entry of nitrates into stream water by 50%.
Coastal Plains Soil & Water Conservation Center, Florence, SC
Coy W. Doty, (803) 669-5203

A cutback in erosion from 25 down to 0.002 tons per acre annually was achieved on a southern Piedmont watershed in 10 years with conservation tillage and balanced double cropping. Moreover, annual surface runoff was lowered from 18% to 0.5% of precipitation. Researchers gradually converted the 6.7-acre watershed--with slopes averaging 4%--from soybean monocropping to wheat/soybean double cropping, balancing erosion-prone row crops with closely spaced small grains. They changed rotations in response to weed problems, yield decreases, and nitrogen costs, most recently by drilling crimson clover into crop residues.
Southern Piedmont Conservation Research Center, Watkinsville, GA
George W. Langdale, (404) 769-5631

Atmospheric nitrogen is banked in the soil by soybeans in the southeastern Coastal Plain, whether grown by conventional or conservation tillage systems. Depending on seasonal rainfall, 15 to 125 lb per acre of nitrogen fixed from the atmosphere are made available for subsequent crops. This differs from the Midwest, where soybeans are often net consumers of soil nitrogen. Researchers advise managing the bonus nitrogen to avoid pollution by leaching or runoff. Effective practices include timely seeding of small grains, strip cropping, or maintaining a good cover of crop residues.
Coastal Plains Soil & Water Conservation Center, Florence, SC
Patrick G. Hunt, (803) 669-5203

Large worm holes may be significant channels for the rapid movement of fertilizers and pesticides through a crop's root zone into groundwater. Water colored with a dye and sprinkled onto a no-till cornfield in Ohio quickly drained through larger worm holes called macropores. The field, in no-till corn for 22 years, has excellent infiltration. In the past 5 years, runoff totaled 0.5 inches. No-till systems effectively control erosion and runoff. But agricultural chemicals may bypass the soil's fine pores and drain through macropores. Results from this research will be used

to develop equations that predict such movement out of the root zone under no-till fields.
North Appalachian Experimental Watershed, Coshocton, OH
William M. Edwards, (614) 545-6349

Nitrate levels in groundwater were reduced about one-third in field experiments when ammonium-nitrogen fertilizer was treated with nitrapyrin, a bacterial growth inhibitor. The action of soil bacteria on ammonium produces nitrate, which leaches readily through soil into groundwater. High nitrate levels in drinking water are considered an objectionable pollutant.
North Appalachian Experimental Watershed, Coshocton, OH
L. B. Owens, (614) 545-6349

A modified method for predicting soil loss also includes the amount of soil deposited on a field from elsewhere in the calculation as well as the amount of soil lost to erosion. Recent studies on contoured land, similar to fields in the Corn Belt, show that more erosion results from slopes of short length and shallow grade than from steep long slopes. This theory contrasts with previous methods that use soil erosion as the only criterion for estimating average annual loss.
National Soil Erosion Research Lab, West Lafayette, IN 47907
L. Darrell Norton, (317) 494-8682

CROP PRODUCTION & PROTECTION

Primitive, nearly extinct races of peanuts--some descendants of plants grown by early man--have been collected from the coast of Peru. These late-maturing forms may have genes for tolerance to drought and heat that may improve our current commercial peanut varieties. Also collected were the nitrogen-fixing bacteria growing on the peanuts. They will be evaluated for their efficiency in converting atmospheric nitrogen to the form needed by plants.
Plant Science Research Lab, Stillwater, OK
Don Banks, (405) 624-4124

Alfalfa losses each year from disease and insects amount to about 40% of the annual $6 billion crop. Alfalfa germplasm, called KS189, was released this year with built-in protection against five major diseases and three major insects of this important forage. This new alfalfa was developed from an introduction from India and demonstrates the value of having diverse sources available for developing improved germplasm.
Plant Science & Entomology Research, Manhattan, KS
Edgar Sorensen, (913) 539-6101

Leaves of a cold-hardened citrus hybrid may contain substances that will help plant breeders and geneticists develop more cold-tolerant citrus varieties. Hybrid leaves contain fatty acids that are part of a larger molecule called triacylglycerol (triglycerides) similar to those found in a hardy species but different from those in a less hardy species. These substances may play a vital role in keeping leaf membranes fluid during freezing. Last year's freeze cost Florida citrus growers $253 million in losses.
Citrus & Subtropical Product Lab, Winter Haven, FL
Harold Nordby/George Yelenosky, (813) 293-4133/(305) 898-6791

The vulnerability of the entire U.S. sunflower crop to diseases has been lessened by broadening the genetic base for hybrid sunflowers. Until now, such hybrids have been produced for seed from a single source of cytoplasmic male sterility (CMS). CMS permits controlled breeding by allowing the desirable characteristics in sunflower genes to be more easily identified and more quickly incorporated into commercial hybrids. Such controlled-breeding ability will help commercial seed producers develop high-volume, low-cost hybrid seeds that are less vulnerable to diseases that otherwise could wipe out the $400 million seed industry that exports 80% of its yearly crop.
Oilseed Research Project, Fargo, ND
Jerry Miller, (701) 237-8155

The oil-producing enzymes (proteins) in the cells of soybeans have been located. Structures called plastids within the cells of seeds have been shown to form oil--a mechanism that differs from that in animals. Finding the location of the proteins that govern oil synthesis increases the likelihood of improving soybean oil production through plant breeding. U.S. soybean oil production is a $1 billion-a-year industry.
Soybean & Nitrogen Fixation Research, Raleigh, NC
Richard Wilson, (919) 737-3267

Screening peach and other fruit trees for improved disease resistance will be three times faster using tissue culture instead of conventional breeding. In one procedure, specimens of callus (soft tissue that forms over a wound from any plant part) from immature embryos from various types of peach trees were treated with a toxin from the bacterial leaf spot pathogen. Most specimens died immediately; those that survived were given heavier and heavier doses of the toxin until the most resistant types were found. These survivors will be cloned, grown to tree size, and field-tested for resistance. This technology may also help produce superior plants that are cold tolerant as well as disease resistant and avoid a disastrous crop loss like the one that destroyed the $350 million peach crop in the East this year.
Tissue Culture & Molecular Biology, Beltsville, MD
Freddi Hammerschlag, (301) 344-2752

Sorghum, an important food and feed crop, may now be improved faster using new techniques of biotechnology. A simple and easily reproducible method has been developed to isolate, culture, and sustain cell divisions of protoplasts (single cells without walls). The protoplast permits the insertion and expression of foreign genes into sorghum. Such technology will enable scientists to use tissue culture to reproduce cells and to form callus, giving breeders the tools to make rapid improvements in the crop.
Plant Science, Gainesville, FL
Prem Chourey, (904) 392-7237

The best barley for malting and brewing can now be distinguished from less suitable varieties currently used for feed. Protein extracts from the grain can be used to quickly identify its variety using electrophoresis (a technique that sorts out protein molecules on the basis of size). This "fingerprinting" ensures that all the grain is the same variety and of uniform high quality and will prevent problems for brewers. About half of the nation's barley crop is used to brew beer.
Cereal Crops Research, Madison, WI
David M. Peterson, (608) 262-4482

A fungicide can now effectively control chalkbrood--primary pest of leafcutter bee larvae. The bee is a major pollinator of alfalfa grown for seed in the Northwest. In field tests, scientists reduced the incidence of the disease by nearly 50% in bee domiciles dusted with the fungicide captan with no adverse affect on the bees or their larvae.
Pollinating Insect Biology Lab, Logan, UT
Frank D. Parker, (801) 750-2525

A new switchgrass variety, Trailblazer, accounts for a 35% increase in beef production per acre as compared with Pathfinder, a widely used commercial variety. The increased weight gain was brought about by only a 6% improvement in digestibility. Trailblazer was released in 1984, and certified seed will be commercially available in 1986. Primarily grown in the Central Plains and Corn Belt, the new grass or other improved warm-season grasses can be used to reseed about one-third the acreage in these areas.
Forage & Range Research, Lincoln, NE
Kenneth P. Vogel, (402) 472-1564

A natural chemical derived from leaves of the wild tomato may protect stored wheat from weevils. The chemical effectively repels and inhibits the growth of granary, rice, and maize weevils, without being toxic to humans or animals. A derivative was found to be more potent than the natural compound and might prove useful as a control for insect pests that

have become resistant to currently approved chemical insecticides.
U.S. Grain Marketing Research Lab, Manhattan, KS
Karl J. Kramer, (913) 776-2767

An experimental variety of alfalfa that doesn't overwinter can produce about 60% more nitrogen during the fall of the seeding year than overwintering varieties commonly grown in the northern United States. The new alfalfa produces just as large a summer hay crop as traditional alfalfas. It fixes nitrogen in the autumn during the time when winter-dormant varieties are busy storing carbohydrates for overwinter survival. It is intended for use in rotations requiring only 1 year of alfalfa.
Plant Science Research, St. Paul, MN
Donald K. Barnes, (612) 373-0865

The 850,000-specimen National Fungus - Collection, the largest collection in the United States, is now being computerized. Anyone interested can have easy access to information about occurrence and distribution of the 270,000 specimens of rusts, smuts, and polypores--wood decay fungi-- already in the computer data base. The information could be used to correctly identify a fungus, for example, for a physician treating a victim of mushroom poisoning or for agricultural scientists trying to control fungal diseases of plants and animals.
Mycology Lab, Beltsville, MD
David A. Farr, (301) 344-2274

A new test can pick out types of white clover resistant to allelopathic chemicals--which inhibit the growth of other plants--produced by tall fescue. The chemical gives the fescue a competitive edge in pastures. The test, more accurate than previous ones, could be used to select resistant white clovers that are easier to establish and maintain in tall fescue pastures.
Crop Science Research Lab, Mississippi State, MS
Gary A. Pederson, (601) 325-2726

For the first time, crimson clover has been regenerated in the laboratory using a tissue culture technique called somatic embryogenesis. This technique could

regenerate thousands of plants from single cells by forming an embryo plant that eventually germinates into an adult plant. It may be the first step towards using tissue culture to produce improved forage legumes, such as arrowleaf, kura, white, and crimson clover species, with higher yields or improved resistance to disease.
Crop Science Research Lab, Mississippi State, MS
Gary A. Pederson, (601) 325-2726

Applying water often, up to once a day, can help shallow-rooted citrus trees grow better and produce more fruit in the sandy flatwood soils typical of south Florida. Currently, the trees are usually watered from irrigation furrows every 2 weeks, but this infrequent watering schedule cannot maintain adequate soil moisture during dry, warm spring months. With too little irrigation, water content of the soil near the roots is rapidly exhausted, thus severely reducing plant photosynthesis.
Plant Stress & Protection Research, Gainesville, FL
L. Hartwell Allen, Jr., (904) 392-6180

Germplasm of nitrogen-fixing legumes, some introduced from countries in Asia, Africa, and South America, is being developed to tolerate the semiarid conditions in the intermountain area of the western United States. Studies of the legumes thus far have helped in improving seed production and adaptation and have increased information about the problems of the millions of acres of grasses that get less than 12 inches of precipitation annually. Presently, no legumes, except those that are toxic to livestock, are well adapted to low rainfall areas.
Forage & Range Research, Logan, UT
Melvin D. Rumbaugh, (801) 750-3067

A sex pheromone from a parasitic worm of soybean roots has been isolated and purified for the first time. This cyst nematode destroys soybean crops, costing farmers losses of over $400 million a year. Scientists hope to use the pheromone to develop an environmentally safe control for the pest. This approach will lead to new strategies for controlling

other plant nematodes that cause an estimated $6 billion damage annually to U.S. crops.
Nematology Lab, Beltsville, MD
Robin Huettel, (301) 344-3081

Researchers have found effective traps for the northern corn rootworm beetle, a pest of about 70 million U.S. acres of field and sweet corn. The best traps so far are yellow, baited with a sticky mixture of eugenol--a food lure that attracts Japanese beetles--and placed outside of cornfields at heights from ground level up to 10 inches. This is the first report of a pure chemical, not a pheromone, attracting the pest. The goal of capturing the beetle is to gain reliable data about the distribution and density of infestations and estimates of future populations.
Japanese Beetle Research, Wooster, OH
Thyril L. Ladd, Jr., (216) 263-3898

Bacteria called fluorescent pseudomonads that live on wheat roots can help protect the plants from Pythium root rot, a serious fungal wheat disease. Wheat yields may be increased as much as 26% when these beneficial bacteria are applied to wheat seed. This is especially significant since chemical treatment against Pythium is often ineffective and no known varieties of wheat are resistant to this root disease.
Root Disease & Biological Control Research, Pullman, WA
David M. Weller/R. J. Cook, (509) 335-6210

The pigment glands of some strains of cultivated cotton produce natural chemicals that may improve the insect defenses of the fiber crop. Researchers at ARS and Texas A&M evaluated chemical variations and effects on insects of terpenes--chemicals that repel or attract insects--from 30 cotton lines, including wild Australian cotton. Then they developed a "gene package" that may be bred commercially to control insect pests.
Cotton Pathology Research, College Station, TX
Alois A. Bell, (713) 260-9232

Procedures to synthesize strigol, an unusually active seed germinator, may help to better protect crops from plant pests. To see whether parasitic plant pests that require a host plant to live can be coaxed into "suicidal germination," ARS and cooperating researchers are testing several precursors (simple molecules formed as strigol is synthesized) and analogs (chemicals close in structure to strigol). The "suicide" comes when strigol and related chemicals "lie" to weeds such as witchweed and branched broomrape, causing them to germinate and sprout earlier than their host plants and thus starve to death.
Crop Protection Research, New Orleans, LA
Armand Pepperman, (504) 589-7564

For the first time, crop scientists have proposed creating a chronology—a history of sequential events—to explain how specific weeds affect a crop at different times in its life cycle. This idea stemmed from new findings that a reduction in yield of soybeans early in the growing season is a direct effect of weeds shading the beans. Later yield losses may come from further competition for light, water, or nutrients, as well as allelopaths—the chemicals plants use against other plants to maintain their dominance. All these aspects would be included in the chronology and could result in better methods to manage weeds and increase yields.
Crop Production Research, Columbia, MO
Richard J. Aldrich, (314) 882-2405

Farmers and homeowners may one day prevent weeds from sprouting. The top 6 inches of each acre of cultivated land harbors tens of millions of dormant weed seeds. Methyl isothiocyanate (MIT), the active ingredient in several all-purpose pesticides, directly kills weed seeds; most herbicides kill only the 5% to 10% of these seeds that emerge each year. When methods are developed for dispersing MIT evenly throughout the soil, the "seedicide" could practically eliminate pesky weeds.
Weed Science Lab, Beltsville, MD
John Teasdale, (301) 344-3504

A newly discovered mite may help control the spotted sunflower stem weevil, a pest of over 3 million acres of sunflowers grown in North and South Dakota and Minnesota. This tiny pyemotid mite engorges itself on the weevil's blood and can survive cold conditions, be kept dormant for more than a year, and live under water for days. It may be economically feasible to transport the submerged and engorged mass-reared mites and release them with one well-timed application in sunflower fields, thus controlling the stem weevil for 1 or more years without harming humans or other flora and fauna. Field tests must be run to determine if these mites can be released in time to significantly affect the sunflower stem weevil population.
Metabolism & Radiation Research Lab, Fargo, ND
John Reinecke/Sharon Grugel/John Barker, (601) 323-2230

A new strain of the fungus Colletotrichum coccodes, found in Minnesota, kills eastern black nightshade, a serious midwestern weed problem, especially in soybeans. The fungus does not infect potatoes and tomatoes, plants related to the nightshade. It can kill young weeds but needs 16 hours or more of 100% humidity to cause infection. With more research, the fungus may be successful for field application.
Weed Research Lab, St. Paul, MN
Robert N. Andersen, (612) 373-0877

New methods for crop and weed management could result from laboratory studies of Palmer amaranth, a weed common to the Southwest. Volatiles--easily evaporated organic compounds--from residues of the weed drastically reduce seed germination in onions by about 65% and in tomatoes and carrots by about 25%. Current research may help farmers decide when to safely plant onions and carrots in soils that contain amaranth residues, since they eventually stop giving off the yield-reducing volatiles.
Crop Protection Chemistry, New Orleans, LA
William J. Connick, Jr., (504) 589-7553

A parasitic mite could add to the growing arsenal of biological control defenses to control pests on apples. The mite, Callidosoma metzi, was found feeding on adult male tufted apple bud moths. This major pest of apples destroys about 15% of the apple crop at harvest in the Shenandoah Valley of Virginia and neighboring states. About 29% of the moths collected each had from 1 to 13 immature mites. Besides helping to control moths, this mite at later stages may also attack small insects and other mites that destroy this valuable crop.
Appalachian Fruit Research,
Kearneysville, WV
Mark Brown, (304) 725-3451

Cotton plants may soon be bred to be resistant to the boll weevil. Two new germplasm lines, already released to commercial plant breeders, are the first to be grown from primitive races of cotton that naturally repel the weevil. The new lines produce half the lint that commonly grown cotton does but have good flowering and fiber-producing characteristics, as well as built-in resistance to the boll weevil. Breeders can use the lines to develop superior cottons that can be grown with fewer, if any, insecticide applications.
Crop Science Research Lab, Mississippi State, MS
Jack C. McCarty, (601) 323-2230

Hairs on the leaves of a wild strawberry plant may offer a new defense against one of the fruit's worst insect enemies on the west coast. Hairs on the underside of leaves of beach strawberry, Fragaria chiloensis, repels black vine weevils that are tough to control with currently registered pesticides. Such resistance may be a genetic trait that can be transferred to commercial varieties. It could save 20% of this major strawberry-producing area's $40 million annual crop.
Horticultural Crops Research, Corvallis, OR
Robert Doss, (503) 757-4544

ANIMAL PRODUCTION & PROTECTION

Planting winter and summer annual forages dramatically increased the efficiency of native range in Oklahoma by markedly improving red meat production and net returns. Use in a forage-cow/calf production increased land-use efficiency 30%, improved beef production 100%, and decreased the production cost per pound of additional gain by 75%. Results were similar for an integrated forage-livestock production system: beef production was increased from 44 to 185 lb per acre, while land requirements were reduced from 8 to 2 acres per yearling steer.
Range & Pasture Research Lab, Woodward, OK
Phillip L. Sims, (405) 256-7449

The bloody range wars between cattlemen and sheepmen may have been based on a misconception, according to ARS scientists. In recent tests, sheep and cattle grazed the same range harmoniously with a net increase in pounds of meat to land used over exclusive grazing by a single species. That's because cattle prefer grass and just a few forbs; sheep, on the other hand, prefer forbs with a little grass. Further, the sheep improve grass production for the cattle by keeping the brush down.
Jornada Experimental Range, Las Cruces, NM
Dean M. Anderson/Clarence V. Hulet, (505) 646-5190

An organ culture system has been developed for short-term maintenance of intestinal sections from piglets. This will allow easier study of diseases associated with the intestine, such as porcine coronavirus, transmissible gastroenteritis virus, and a porcine herpes virus--pseudorabies virus. The organ cultures lend themselves to disease studies in which subtle cellular changes or sequential changes in intestinal tissues are difficult to observe in host animals. Apparently, this is the first time non-embryonic intestinal sections of either animals or humans have been maintained in test tubes for more than 3 hours without

11

marked decay. Intestinal sections remain viable for 5 days with this system.
National Animal Disease Center, Ames, IA
Phletus P. Williams, (515) 239-8398

Yellowjackets are highly beneficial predators of pests like caterpillars and flies, besides bothering humans at picnics. Researchers have found that a synthetic chemical attractant that was developed to better manage the beneficial spined soldier bug also works for yellowjackets. Since the chemical can summon females within short distances, homeowners may be able to use the lure to catch yellowjacket queens in the spring or trap workers that become a nuisance.
Insect & Nematode Hormone Lab,
Beltsville, MD
Jeffrey Aldrich, (301) 344-2631

Beef cattle given daily injections of bovine growth hormone converted more of their feed to muscle protein and less of it to fat. Scientists are researching exactly how the growth hormone changes the metabolism of cattle and feel that these preliminary experiments can lead to more efficient methods of meat production. The hormone is harmless to humans.
Roman L. Hruska U.S. Meat Animal Research Center, Clay Center, NE
Joan H. Eisemann, (402) 762-3241

Lethal genes may be used in the future to control mosquitoes. Scientists have described genetic techniques to introduce six recessive, lethal, mutant genes into mosquitoes. The recessive genes act like time bombs; when the mosquitoes reproduce, the offspring inheriting these lethal genes die before they can lay eggs.
Insects Affecting Man & Animals Research Lab, Gainesville, FL
Jack A. Seawright, (904) 374-5940

A potentially dangerous parasite of sheep has been identified for the first time in North America. Until now, Nematodirus battus was thought to be limited to the British Isles and a small area in Europe, where it is a significant parasite of lambs. Now that the parasite has been newly found in western Oregon's Willamette Valley, ARS scientists are working

with Animal and Plant Health Inspection Service and state researchers trying to determine the parasite's potential threat to the sheep industry.
Biosystematic Parasitology Lab,
Beltsville, MD
J. R. Lichtenfels, (301) 344-2444

A new shipping fever vaccine reduces losses in beef cattle that cost the industry millions of dollars annually. An active vaccine against one type of bacterium, Pasteurella haemolytica, that causes the pneumonia was effective in protecting cattle after two vaccinations. The vaccine needs to be refined before it can be released for commercial use.
Conservation & Production Research Lab,
Bushland, TX
Charles W. Purdy, (806) 378-5764

Implanted temperature-sensing devices may help keep future dairy cows healthy and tell farmers when to breed them. The devices send 1,024 temperature readings a day via radio to a computer. A change in temperature can indicate onset of an illness or other physiological changes such as the beginning of the estrous cycle. Installing such a system on a farm could save dairy farmers substantial sums by preventing lost milking time due to illness and by minimizing missed "heats."
Milk Secretion & Mastitis Lab,
Beltsville, MD
Alan Marc Lefcourt, (301) 344-2541

A new method has been found to protect dairy cattle from milk fever, a disease that costs the dairy industry about $150 million a year. Milk fever occurs shortly after calving; affected cows experience low blood calcium and paralysis. Intravenous infusion of a small amount of synthetic bovine parathyroid hormone a few days before and after calving prevented the disease. Commercial methods to produce the hormone and a suitable means for farmers to administer it to cows are being developed.
National Animal Disease Center, Ames, IA
Ronald Horst, (515) 239-8312

Avian influenza virus has been isolated from eggs of naturally infected chickens for the first time. Researchers can use

12

this information to prevent the spread of this virus via eggs shipped for eating or hatching. Scientists from ARS and USDA's Animal and Plant Health Inspection Service collaborated on this research.
Southeast Poultry Research Lab, Athens, GA
Max Brugh, (404) 546-3433

A new oral vaccine prevents diarrhea in baby pigs. Nursing piglets fall victim to an often fatal bacterial diarrhea caused by the bacterium E. coli. Oral vaccination of the mother before the first and second lactations stimulated antibodies in the milk that protected the baby pigs. Current vaccination procedures protect the pigs for only the first few days after birth.
National Animal Disease Center, Ames, IA
Harley W. Moon, (515) 239-8253

Heartwater is a serious blood disease of cattle that originated in Africa and has spread to the Caribbean. Scientists fear that this tickborne disease will spread to the United States. A new rapid experimental test has been developed for heartwater that may help keep infected animals from being imported into the United States. It may also help quickly detect any outbreaks of the disease.
Plum Island Animal Disease Center, Greenport, NY
Linda Logan, (516) 323-2500

Beef cows selected for twinning rate could significantly cut meat producers' costs. Two-thirds of the feed cost for beef production go for feeding reproducing females. A study has shown that twinning rate can be increased by about 8% by selecting for twinning those daughters born to mothers that have had three or more sets of twins.
Roman L. Hruska U.S. Meat Animal Research Center, Clay Center, NE
Keith Gregory, (402) 762-3241

White blood cells from cattle have been successfully fused with mouse cells to produce hybrid cells. These new fused cells produce pure bovine antibodies that resemble those that protect cattle from disease. The ability to produce large quantities of pure antibody in culture will allow scientists to determine how these antibodies function. This knowl-
13

edge may lead to improved methods for protecting animals against disease.
Milk Secretion & Mastitis Lab, Beltsville, MD
Albert J. Guidry, (301) 344-2285

New markers that allow scientists to identify fat-prone pigs even before they are born may lead to leaner hams and pork chops. One marker, lipoprotein lipase (LPL), is an enzyme that controls the movement of fat molecules from the bloodstream to fatty tissues. Obese pigs have high LPL levels that they pass on to their offspring. However, low blood levels of swine growth hormone (SGH) signals this tendency toward obesity. Since pigs' cardiovascular and digestive systems resemble those in humans, such markers in humans may someday help streamline diets of infants genetically prone to be fat.
Animal Physiology Research Lab, Athens, GA
Gary Hausman, (404) 546-3584

A newly discovered organ in the stable fly, the largest found thus far in any fly species, could lead to new methods of controlling this serious livestock pest. The neurohemal organ, located next to the fly's heart, controls other organs by releasing hormones either directly on the organ, as an ordinary nerve would do, or at a distance by releasing them into the fly's body cavity. These neurohormones affect the heart and may regulate other vital physiological functions, such as the fly's biting behavior, reproduction, and growth—activities scientists some day hope to be better able to control.
Veterinary Toxicology & Entomology Research Lab, College Station, TX
Shirlee M. Meola/Benjamin Cook, (409) 260-9339

"EXPERT" INFORMATION SYSTEMS

A new computer model can save research time in developing cotton plants resistant to tobacco budworm, a major insect pest in the United States. The model tests the cotton plant's response to feeding by the insect larvae. When compared with 2 years of actual field data, it accurately predicted the yield and maturity of cotton artificially infested with budworm larvae. Scientists

expect to further improve the model and use it to examine other simulated genetic changes before breeding the plant in order to develop additional resistant cotton germplasm.
Crop Science Research Lab, Mississippi State, MS
Johnie N. Jenkins, (601) 323-2230

CREAMS is a mathematical model for evaluating the effects of various farm management practices on nonpoint-source pollutant loads at the edge of fields. Now Chemicals, Runoff, and Erosion from Agricultural Management Systems has been modified to calculate potential chemical loadings to groundwater. In tests, the model produced good results when compared with observed data on sandy soils in the Golden Sands area of central Wisconsin. The model will also be used in a groundwater research project, carried out cooperatively with the U.S. Geological Survey, to simulate root-zone loadings of agricultural chemicals.
Environmental Quality Research Lab, Tifton, GA
Ralph A. Leonard/W. G. Knisel (912) 386-3462

The first version of a new method for predicting soil losses from the action of water is scheduled for release in April 1989. Known as the USDA Water Erosion Prediction Project, it will replace the Universal Soil Loss Equation, developed by ARS and its cooperators 25 years ago and now in wide use throughout the world. Scientists expect to improve soil erosion prediction methods using modern computer technology and concepts based on fundamental erosion processes.
National Soil Erosion Research Lab, West Lafayette, IN
G. R. Foster, (317) 494-7748

Nitrate leaching to groundwater can be controlled with information from an updated and expanded computer model called Nitrogen-Tillage-Residue Management. The model predicts the best nitrogen fertilizer practices for producing high crop yields, while protecting the environment from excess nitrate leaching. The model is also a valuable research tool. Results of tests that would take several years with standard field-plot techniques can be calculated in a few weeks using the model.
Soil & Water Research Management, St. Paul, MN
M. J. Shaffer (612) 373-1444

A peanut growth simulation model will help farmers with crop management decisions such as when to apply pesticides and when to irrigate. The model is a cooperative project of ARS and the Virginia Polytechnic Institute. Weather stations already provide farmers with information to make fungicide applications to control Cercospora leaf spot disease. Full use of the model throughout peanut-growing areas should help farmers reduce costs without increasing the risk of disease, pests, or drought.
National Peanut Research Lab, Dawson, GA
Jim Davidson, (912) 995-4481

Basic physical and physiological processes involved in the movement of water, carbon, nitrogen, oxygen, and other materials in the soybean plant, soil, and atmosphere have been accounted for in a new simulation model. The model enables a user to predict the number and size of plant organs formed in response to environment and management factors. Ultimately, farmers will be able to use the information to select the best management practices for growing soybeans.
Crop Simulations Research, Mississippi State, MS
Donald L. Baker, (601) 323-2230

QUARTERLY REPORT
OF SELECTED RESEARCH PROJECTS
OF THE AGRICULTURAL RESEARCH SERVICE
U.S. DEPARTMENT OF AGRICULTURE
January 1 to March 31, 1986

Agricultural
Research
Service

CONTENTS

Human Nutrition

Poor nutrition and too much exposure to the sun contribute far more than aging, to dry, wrinkled skin. Using a "model" epidermis grown in culture dishes from human skin cells, scientists can separate the effects of aging, nutrients, and ultraviolet radiation on skin and then learn how they interact. One study showed that beta carotene—the compound that gives carrots their color—can protect skin cells against a moderate sunburn dose of ultraviolet radiation. This research has also turned up a growth stimulant that is 50 times more potent on skin cells than a previously known epidermal growth factor.
Human Nutrition Research Center on Aging at Tufts, Boston, MA
Barbara Gilchrest, (617) 956-0372

Vitamin B$_6$ may spell relief for asthmatics. Chemical analyses by ARS researchers showed that people with bronchial asthma have abnormally low levels of the vitamin in their blood. In a preliminary study at Columbia University-affiliated hospitals, 15 adult bronchial asthma sufferers reported dramatic decreases in both the duration and severity of attacks when they received daily supplements of 100 milligrams of vitamin B$_6$—50 times the Recommended Dietary Allowance. A larger collaborative study with Scripps University in California is now underway.
Vitamin and Mineral Nutrition Lab, Beltsville, MD
Robert D. Reynolds, (301) 344-2459

Megadoses of vitamin B$_6$ should not be recommended to reduce blood clotting in humans as some reports have suggested. A study involving 12 healthy men showed that 100 milligrams of B$_6$ (50 times the Recommended Dietary Allowance) had no effect on the clotting of blood platelets even though blood levels of the vitamin increased significantly.
Lipid Nutrition Lab, Beltsville, MD
Norberta Schoene, (301) 344-2388

Originally designed to measure the fat content of pigs, TOBEC (Total Body Electrical Conductivity) is being adapted to measure body fat painlessly and precisely in people of all sizes and ages. The body's fat-to-lean ratio is often a much more accurate indicator of health and fitness than the more commonly used height-and-weight tables. TOBEC uses an electromagnetic field to measure the amount of water in a subject's body, which is then used to calculate the amount of fat. The standard technique for measuring fat—underwater weighing—is inconvenient and inappropriate for very young or elderly patients. TOBEC doesn't present these problems and is now being calibrated to match the accuracy of underwater weighing.
Western Human Nutrition Research Center, San Francisco, CA
Marta Van Loan, (415) 556-5729

TOBEC will soon help scientists determine how much of the important nutrients are needed for the optimum lean-to-fat ratio in infants as they grow. Scientists have adapted TOBEC (Total Body Electrical Conductivity) into a baby-sized version of the instrument in order to study the body composition of infants under different diets. The system is as accurate or better than current methods for estimating body composition and has the advantages of being rapid, safe, simple, and noninvasive to the body.
Children's Nutrition Research Center, Houston, TX
Marta Fiorotto, (713) 799-6013

The type of carbohydrate we eat is important in controlling risk factors for heart disease and diabetes. A high-sugar diet elevated blood insulin and glucose in human volunteers when compared with a high-starch diet—even though both diets contained less fat, salt, and cholesterol and more fiber as recommended in the dietary guidelines. High blood insulin has been linked to heart disease and adult-onset (type II) diabetes; and diabetics, who already have high blood glucose, are in a high-risk category for heart disease.

Carbohydrate Nutrition Lab,
Beltsville, MD
Sheldon Reiser, (301) 344-2396

Premature coronary artery disease is the leading cause of death among diabetics. Tissue culture studies are shedding light on why diabetics are so prone to develop the disease. Using cultured human liver cells, scientists found that glucose significantly inhibits the breakdown of low-density lipoproteins (LDLs)—the major carriers of cholesterol in the blood. LDLs deposit cholesterol in artery walls, leading eventually to atherosclerosis. The excess amount of glucose in the blood of diabetics apparently serves to increase this "bad cholesterol" in the blood by interfering with the breakdown of LDLs in the liver.

USDA Human Nutrition Research Center on Aging at Tufts, Boston, MA
Ernst J. Schaefer, (617) 956-0393

An assumption that people and laboratory animals with adult-onset (type II) diabetes absorb more zinc through their intestines than nondiabetics is not valid. Rats with experimentally induced diabetes and control rats consuming equivalent amounts of zinc absorbed the same amount of dietary zinc. But the diabetic rats excreted less of the mineral in their feces because less zinc from body stores entered the intestines. About 30% of people over age 65 suffer from diabetes or some form of glucose intolerance.

Grand Forks Human Nutrition Research Center, Grand Forks, ND
Forrest H. Nielsen, (701) 795-8353

What substances in foods influence the body's use of essential trace elements? Answers to that question will come faster now that a method has been developed for measuring the absorption and retention of several trace elements simultaneously in laboratory animals. Using a multichannel analyzer, scientists can measure the energy emitted from radioactive isotopes of copper, iron, and zinc, but the technique can be adapted for use with isotopes of other essential trace elements.

Grand Forks Human Nutrition Research Center,
Grand Forks, ND
Henry C. Lukaski, (701) 795-8429

After menopause, too little calcium in the diet could contribute to rapid loss of bone mineral in the spine, according to a study of 100 healthy postmenopausal women. The 25% of women in the study with the lowest calcium intake—less than half the Recommended Dietary Allowance—lost spine bone at an annual rate of 7% compared with 1% for the group as a whole. The RDA for calcium is 800 milligrams.

USDA Human Nutrition Research Center on Aging at Tufts, Boston, MA
Bess Dawson-Hughes, (617) 956-0415

Women can retard serious bone loss after menopause by building a larger bone mass through proper diet and weight bearing exercise, such as walking and running. But women athletes who have ceased menstruating (amenorrheic) due to intense physical training may be at greater risk for osteoporosis in later life. In a study of young female runners, the amenorrheic group had significantly less bone mineral in the spine than did the normally menstruating group, despite the fact that both groups reported a calcium intake above the Recommended Dietary Allowance. Low levels of circulating estrogens in the amenorrheic women apparently hampers their use of calcium.

USDA Human Nutrition Research Center on Aging at Tufts, Boston, MA
Elizabeth C. Fisher, (617) 956-0333

Taking calcium supplements at mealtime may affect a person's absorption of trace minerals in the food. Less than half the radioactive iron added to a breakfast drink was absorbed when the subjects took 500 milligrams of calcium (62% of RDA) during the meal. However, zinc absorption was not changed. Calcium carbonate reduced absorption of the iron tracer as much as a form of calcium phosphate did, indicating that the calcium alone hampered absorption, not the phosphate. Tests are now underway to determine if calcium supplements reduce iron uptake from foods. Nutrition Research Center on Aging at Tufts, Boston, MA
Bess Dawson-Hughes, (617) 956-0415

Most of the world's people shun the best dietary source of calcium and high-quality protein because their bodies no longer produce enough of the enzyme needed to digest milk sugar (lactose). A recent study shows that digestion markedly improves when "lactose intolerant" people consume yogurt or specially prepared sweet acidophilus milk. Both products contain bacteria that produce the missing enzyme, but in commercial sweet acidophilus milk, the enzyme remains inside the organism during digestion. Now, a simple method has been developed for rupturing these bacteria by high-frequency sound waves which release the enzyme into the milk. Energy & Protein Nutrition Lab, Beltsville, MD
Frank E. McDonough, (301) 344-4351

New & Improved Products

Young bulls will provide about 5% more meat than steers do for the same price. Research showed that young bulls gain weight faster and more efficiently than steers. The meat has the same cooking quality as meat from steers, but less fat. The main drawback to consumer acceptance is that steer meat has more marbling than bull meat, which researchers say is not the most important part of meat quality anyway. Scientists are looking for ways, including genetic improvement, to produce leaner meat at less cost with the flavor, juices, and other qualities necessary for consumer acceptance. Livestock & Range Research Lab, Miles City, MT
Joseph J. Urick, (406) 232-4970

In their search for aflatoxin-resistant corn, scientists have found an unlikely ally—the maize weevil. This pest, which attacks field corn and stored grain, is being used experimentally to spread the aflatoxin-producing fungus Aspergillus flavus in test corn. In corn being tested for resistance, the weevil did a better job of spreading the fungus than currently used methods of infection. As a result, scientists can better control contamination so as to more accurately tell which types of corn are more resistant to aflatoxin. Crop Production Research, Columbia, MO
B. Dean Barry, (314) 875-5342

A sobriety test for "drunk" peanuts has been developed by ARS scientists. When peanuts are subjected to extreme hot or cold temperatures before they are cured, they produce alcohol and related compounds that cause a bitter taste. Taste tests have been relied on up to now to detect this, but now agency researchers have found a quicker, more effective way. Peanuts are ground up in a blender, a sensor detects the alcohol vapor from the peanuts, and a special meter measures it—much like a breath test for drunk drivers. The method is being field-tested in three of the top peanut-producing states—Georgia, Texas, and North Carolina—and the results are promising. Market Quality and Handling Research, Raleigh, NC
James W. Dickens/Harold E. Pattee (919) 737-3101

A waste byproduct in the manufacture of corn sweeteners has the unusual ability, after simple chemical treatment, to remove the major sources of bitterness in grapefruit juice and navel orange juice. The product is called cyclodextrin polymer, and its donut-shaped molecules actually trap the bitterness molecules inside their holes, where they are held by a weak chemical bond. Later, the

bonds can be loosened with a chemical wash and the bitterness molecules removed. The cyclodextrin, which is unchanged by the process, is subject to Food and Drug Administration approval before it can be used commercially. Citrus & Subtropical Products Lab, Winterhaven, FL
Philip E. Shaw, (813) 293-4133

Mushrooms can now be explosion-puff dried by a government-patented process, stored for over a year, then restored with high flavor and texture for cooking. The process has the potential of expanding mushroom exports and U.S. sales. Conventional drying methods that can leave mushrooms too chewy, and with off-flavors, have been unacceptable to the U.S. mushroom industry. The puff dried mushroom is also an appealing snack or crouton—light, crunchy with concentrated flavor.
Eastern Research Center, Philadelphia, PA
John F. Sullivan, (215) 233-6588

Sour rot—the most pernicious destroyer of tomatoes after ripening—can be controlled by a chemical known to check sour rot in citrus. Sour rot is caused by Geotrichum candidum, a pathogen that also attacks harvested carrots, cucumbers, and peaches and makes them decay. Dipping tomatoes in the experimental fungicide guazatine takes only 20 to 30 seconds, yet cuts the incidence of sour rot to about 5% compared to 50% in untreated tomatoes. Fungicide treatment would benefit growers, shippers, and retailers as well as consumers of fruits and vegetables.
Fruit & Vegetable Harvesting Research, East Lansing, MI
Clyde L. Burton, (517) 353-5185

Seven U.S. companies are pilot-testing a new enclosed tank for fermenting and storing pickled cucumbers that may revolutionize the pickle industry. The tank will allow processors to use less salt in brining and can improve the quality of pickles for consumers with more control over fermentation. Inside the tank, pickles are fermented in an oxygen-free environment. Processors now use open-air tanks kept outdoors, where possible contamination from rainwater and other foreign material requires more salt in brine solution. Lower salt concentration means less water pollution from used brine. ARS, North Carolina State University, and Pickle Packers International are cooperating in the project. Scientists are also developing improved bacterial cultures-to use in the tanks and are studying the safety and quality of brined cucumbers at low salt concentrations.
Food Science Research, Raleigh, NC
Henry P. Fleming, (919) 737-2979

Robot-like food tasters are helping food processors maintain the quality of packaged products containing beef, pork, poultry, fish, milk, fruit, nuts, vegetables, oils, syrups, gravies, and other foods. Researchers developed a technique for trapping and testing flavor volatiles, easily evaporated organic compounds, on the production line. That means processors could replace substandard ingredients during processing instead of waiting to test the end product, thus reducing waste. Similar methods are being developed to track the browning of sugars and amino acids that occur during baking, meatpacking, and the processing of cereals and candies.
Southern Research Center, New Orleans, LA
John R. Vercellotti, (504) 589-7073

Berberine, an antimalarial drug formed in cells of a plant called heavenly bamboo plant, might someday be produced more efficiently by keeping mass colonies of these cells alive in laboratory cultures. So far, ARS scientists have succeeded in establishing vigorously growing cell colonies of heavenly bamboo in liquid culture. The next steps would be to determine what conditions will induce the cells to produce larger amounts of berberine and then to get the cells to excrete more of the berberine into their liquid surroundings instead of storing it in special compartments. The goal is to establish cell colonies that would produce a continuous supply of berberine without killing them to extract the compound.
Western Research Center, Albany, CA
Betty K. Ishida, (415) 486-3486

Warmed-over meat flavors can now be precisely described, using special terms developed by a panel of meat industry experts and federal researchers. Grainy, fishy, cardboard, metallic, and painty are among the 15 descriptive words. They are based on panel evaluations of the taste of meats affected by various cooking, storage, and reheating procedures. Scientists are investigating the chemical causes of the warmed-over flavor; answers could help industry modify the handling, processing, and storage of cooked meats to prevent undesirable tastes and odors.
Southern Research Center,
New Orleans, LA
Allen J. St. Angelo, (504) 589-7073

If stored potatoes are about to spoil, a computer signals an early warning. Spoilage even within large storage bins can be forecast. That's because potatoes and diseases produce gases that are measured by a gas chromatograph, and ARS researchers put the computer to work to analyze the data along with air movement and bin temperatures. Such a forecasting system may also be suited to monitor gases from other commodities that can perish in storage. It can also be designed to control fans in storage areas and remove concentrations of gases that enhance disease risk.
Red River Valley Potato Research Lab,
East Grand Forks, MN
Jerry L. Varns/Lewis A. Schaper, (218) 773-2473

A cucumber that stays sweet while it fights off insects and plant diseases has been developed by ARS and University of Nebraska scientists. County Fair 83 is ideal for home gardens and suited for both salads and homemade pickles. Differing in size and color from standard commercial processing varieties, the cucumber does not become bitter even under severe stress caused by plant disease, drought, or inadequate soil nutrients.
Vegetable & Forage Research, Madison, WI
Clinton E. Peterson, (608) 262-1830

A new seed thresher, developed by ARS engineers, removes stubborn fuzz, stickers, and hairs from seeds of expensive flowers and oilseed crops. Because these appendages can clog planting machines, processors often have to remove them by hand, a costly process. The thresher has a swiftly rotating nylon filament—similar to the kind used in certain weed-cutting machines—that whips the unwanted appendages off the seeds without injuring the delicate embryos they contain.
National Forage Seed Production Research Center, Corvallis, OR
Arnold G. Berlage, (503) 757-4815

Crop residues can be treated chemically to improve their ability to remove oil from emulsions in waste water, common in metal plating and other industries. Straw from small grains, along with cornstalks, cobs, and husks, when soaked with fatty quaternary ammonium salts, can, for example, remove machine oil from water. The treatment causes the fibers to swell and separate in water, providing maximum surface area for soaking up oil. A patent for the treatment has been applied for.
Northern Research Center,
Peoria, IL, George F. Fanta
(309) 685-4011, Ext. 335

Three commercial firms are using a new chemical process developed by an ARS biochemist for converting undigestible and often wasted crop residues into high-quality feed for cattle. The process, which uses a solution of hydrogen peroxide to dissolve plant lignin enough to make the residue digestible to cattle, is being patented by USDA and licensed on a "partially exclusive" basis through the Department of Commerce.
Northern Research Center, Peoria, IL
J. Michael Gould, (309) 685-4011

A rapid new process has been developed for identifying the 21 major components that contribute to the flavor and aroma of single-strength orange juice. The process, which can be duplicated by the citrus industry, involves a combination of low temperature distillation and direct injection of the distillates into a gas chromatograph, an extremely sensitive instrument for identifying different chemicals. This analysis will provide processors with the data they

need to bring the flavor of processed
orange juice closer to that of freshly
squeezed juice. It could also enable
industry to identify the source of off-
flavors in juice and to take steps to
correct or modify them.
Citrus & Subtropical Products Lab,
Winterhaven, FL
Manuel Moshonas, (813) 293-4133

Sugarbeet pollen for making exact copies
of hybrid sugarbeets is now possible,
thanks to a new and inexpensive way of
storing this valuable genetic resource to
preserve it. The pollen is collected
from growing plants, dehydrated to 12%
moisture or less, and then stored in
liquid nitrogen at -196°C. Pollen stored
this way for 1 year fertilized male
sterile flowers as well as fresh pollen.
The scientists say they have every reason
to believe that pollen could be stored
for 10 or 20 years by this method.
Crops Research Lab, Fort Collins, CO
Richard J. Hecker, (303) 482-7717

Gift boxes of muskmelon fruit will last
up to 40 days—instead of the typical 14
days—if a new packaging technique is
used. Mature, ripe muskmelon can command
premium prices if they are given an
antifungal treatment, thoroughly dried,
wrapped with shrink-film, and stored
under refrigeration at 4°C. This
virtually eliminates water loss (from
transpiration) during storage, a major
factor affecting the fruit's shelf life.
Subtropical Agricultural Research Lab,
Weslaco, TX
G.E. Lester, (512) 565-2423

Consumers should get better quality
fruits and vegetables from new packaging
materials made from polyvinylchloride
(PVC). Other advantages include a more
stable supply during an extended
marketing season and enhanced potential
for exports. PVC packaging captures
carbon dioxide that most fruits and
vegetables give off and maintains the
carbon dioxide at the optimum level to
preserve them. In all tests, the quality
of products packaged in PVC bags was
higher than the quality of products
packaged in materials that lose carbon

dioxide. One company is already testing
the PVC bags on a commercial scale.
Horticultural Crops Research Lab,
Fresno, CA
Roger Rij, (209) 487-5334

Soil, Water, & Air

Large volumes of the insecticide
coumaphos, generated by dipping
operations to detick cattle at the U.S.-
Mexican border can be degraded by a
simple two-step treatment. Part of the
insecticide is broken down with
pesticide-eating bacteria; the remainder
is treated with ultraviolet light and
ozone. The two-step treatment may be the
answer to cleaning up other waste
pesticides on farms.
Pesticide Degradation Lab,
Beltsville, MD
Jeffrey Karns, (301) 344-2493

Artificial light may deter pondweed from
reproducing and reduce its chances of
clogging reservoirs, ponds, and canals.
Greenhouse studies show that both
American and sago pondweed need 12 to 14
hours of darkness to form reproductive
tubers, or winter buds. Tuber formation
might be disrupted by shining lights on
the plants at night to deprive them of
darkness. This technique cut tuber
formation by 50% in a recent small-scale
experiment with another aquatic pest,
hydrilla, in the Potomac River. Like
pondweed, hydrilla can clog reservoirs,
farm ponds, and irrigation canals.
Aquatic Weeds Control Lab, Davis, CA
David F. Spencer, (916) 752-6260

Air pollutants, including ozone and acid
rain, are costing farmers from $1 to $5
billion in crop losses each year. Ozone
may be an even more pervasive problem
than acid rain, according to ARS
research. Ozone is created by a
photochemical reaction involving sunlight
and automobile or industrial exhaust that
contains nitrogen oxides and
hydrocarbons. In open-field chambers and
in greenhouses, scientists have found
that ozone pollution causes plants to die
prematurely and discolor. It is absorbed
into plant leaves, causing death of cells

and reducing food production. The ARS field studies are part of the National Crop Loss Assessment Network, which is assessing the effects of ozone on crop productivity for various crops at five sites across the country.
Air-Quality-Plant Growth & Development Research, Raleigh, NC
Walter W. Heck, (919) 737-3311

The same beneficial fungi that provide some plants with extra nutrients may also help prevent soil erosion. In greenhouse tests, soil growing onions colonized with mycorrhizae was better aggregated, more porous, and more permeable to water, and thus less prone to erosion than uncolonized soil. Besides stimulating overall plant growth and enhancing development of a strong root system, mycorrhizae can also help keep soil in place. Mycorrhizae work well with associated microorganisms to produce compounds which bind soil particles (silt, clay, and sand) that might otherwise be blown or washed away.
Western Research Center, Albany, CA
Richard S. Thomas, (415) 486-3289

Advances in surge irrigation and furrow diking for the Southern Great Plains are benefiting farmers and agribusiness. Guidelines for the new technology, worked out by ARS scientists, are enabling farmers to curb water use and cut fuel costs for pumping. Interest in the new technology has so far resulted in the opening of 10 firms that make and sell valves and related equipment. In addition, over 2 million acres were furrow-diked last year. Six firms are now manufacturing furrow-diking equipment.
Conservation and Production Research Lab, Bushland, TX
Bobby A. Stewart, (806) 378-5724

Leveling cropland with laser-controlled equipment to spread irrigation water evenly may eventually be used in areas with higher than normal rainfall without risking crop damage from too much water. Previously, the method was considered suitable only for areas, like the southwestern United States, that have low rainfall and flat topography. The new study takes into account factors such as precipitation patterns, irrigation strategies, crops grown, soil types, natural drainage through the soil profile, inundation time, and storm season and frequency.
U.S. Water Conservation Lab, Phoenix, AZ
Allen R. Dedrick, (602) 261-4356

Placing nitrogen fertilizer deeper than 6 inches can make more of it available to the plant. In a field study on plants that had been tilled 1 and 4 years by each of three tillage methods, the activity of nitrifying bacteria, which convert the ammonium form to the nitrate form that plants can use, was greatest in the 6- to 12-inch layer. Deeper placement also bypasses the zone of greatest activity of denitrifying bacteria that, under wet conditions, convert the nitrate back to nitrogen gas, allowing it to escape to the atmosphere. These studies provide new data for mathematical models that predict crop fertilizer needs.
North Central Soil Conservation Research Lab, Morris, MN
W.H. Caskey, (612) 589-3411

Some small grains can be planted earlier in the spring in northern states when soil is insulated by snow trapped in crop residues left from reduced tillage. Warmer soil means less frost penetration; frost disappears 10 to 30 days earlier in the spring. In a 3-year study, averaged data showed that frost disappeared first and more snow was trapped on no-till fields than on fields where fall plow and chisel plow practices were used.
North Central Soil Conservation Research Lab, Morris, MN
G.R. Benoit, (612) 589-3411

Soil plowed with knife-like "paraplows" has better water infiltration generally throughout the growing season, compared with other types of plowing. The paraplow loosens soil and lets water soak in, while maintaining crop residue on the soil surface and preventing the soil from sealing and crusting. Increased soil water infiltration, together with the residue cover, reduces runoff and erosion hazards. Paraplowing had better infiltration than moldboard plowing, disking, or chisel plowing. Those types

of plowing either turn over the soil completely or loosen it more than the paraplow, which was introduced into the United States about 5 years ago from England.
Soil & Water Conservation Research, Ames, IA
D.C. Erbach, (515) 294-5723

Heavy farm machinery can inadvertently cause root rot diseases in beans and peas. Diseased roots have great difficulty penetrating layers of compacted soil. These restricted, infected roots lack sufficient nutrients and water because they cannot expand in the soil. Soil compaction can be reduced before seeding by chisel plowing just deep enough into the soil to break up hard tillage pans.
Vegetable Crops Production Research, Prosser, WA
John M. Kraft, (509) 786-3454

A chemical that protects shade trees from ozone damage has been tested successfully on 2-year-old seedlings. ARS scientists used an antioxidant chemical called ethylenediurea to protect leaves of honeylocust, red maple, pin oak, and sweet gum. The chemical works best when injected directly into the tree stem; it increases enzyme and membrane activity in leaf cells where photosynthesis takes place. Ozone, an air pollutant created when sunlight reacts with automobile and industrial exhausts, damages trees and makes them more vulnerable to attack from insects and disease.
Nursery Crops Research Lab, Delaware, OH
Bruce R. Roberts, (614) 363-1129

Crop Production & Protection

Five little-known perennial grasses could be milled for whole-grain flour, adding much-needed diversity to the world's supply of staple grains. The protein and nutrient contents of the grasses—Luna pubescent wheatgrass, Oahe intermediate wheatgrass, agrotricum W-21, Tualatin tall oatgrass, and Michael's rye--compare favorably with the world's most widely planted cereal crops. Further, because grasses need not be replanted yearly like

annual cereal crops, they could be grown on erosion-prone soils and reduce tillage. More research is needed to determine these grasses' potential growth and yield before they can be developed as key cereal grains.
Western Research Center, Albany, CA
Grace D. Hanners, (415) 486-3623

A new hybrid called Johnstone fescue, developed in Kentucky, combines fescue's long life and resistance to stress with the palatability of ryegrass. The result: cattle grazing the new hybrid gained 30% to 50% more weight (about 0.9 kg) than cattle grazing Ky 31 tall fescue. Through a special agreement between ARS and the Kentucky Agricultural Experiment Station, a quantity of seed has been made available by license to a Kentucky seed company for commercial production.
Grass & Turf Research, Lexington, KY
Jim Leggett/Robert Buckner
(606) 257-3146

Proat, a new high-protein oat variety, produced more protein per acre than any other variety in 5 years of tests in Minnesota. Released by ARS and the Minnesota Agricultural Experiment Station, Proat resisted crown rust and smut in Minnesota and Wisconsin tests. Proat's high protein yield may make it especially useful to dairy farmers who feed oats to cows; oat millers should also find it acceptable because of its high bushel weight.
Plant Genetics Research, St. Paul, MN
Howard W. Rines, (612) 373-0879

Tomato yields were 17% higher when phosphorus fertilizers were applied by a subsurface drip irrigation instead of surface drip irrigation. The subsurface system, 18 inches deep, placed the fertilizer in the plant's root zone, which extends 5 or 6 feet below the surface when plants are irrigated. But phosphorus applied by the surface system penetrated no deeper than 21.6 inches. More precise fertilizer placement is needed to maximize efficiency of major innovations in water management.
Water Management Research, Fresno, CA
Claude J. Phene, (209) 251-0437

Waiting too long to plant winter wheat can cost farmers dearly. Recent tests show that farmers in the southern Piedmont region of Georgia and the Carolinas can improve wheat yields and boost net returns (by as much as $40 million for the region) if they plant during the last 2 weeks of October. Later plantings (between November 1 and Christmas Day) reduce yields by 1.2% a day. However, to get high yields by planting early, farmers must use wheat cultivars resistant to the Hessian fly. Southern Piedmont Conservation Research Center, Watkinsville, GA
James E. Box, Jr., (404) 769-5631

Natural chemicals in a rangeland plant may be used to control a notorious weed, leafy spurge, that infests western land. For the first time, scientists have identified three chemicals in a plant called "small everlasting" that make it toxic to the weed. In lab studies, the three chemicals in small everlasting kept leafy spurge seeds from germinating and spurge seedlings from developing. Current chemical controls, used in the upper Great Plains, are expensive and have not succeeded in eradicating the weed.
Western Research Center, Albany, CA
Gary D. Manners, (415) 486-3250

Death of mimosa seedlings, previously attributed to fusarium wilt, was shown to be due instead to a combination of the wilt fungus and root-knot nematodes. New screening methods to select superior mimosa varieties that resist both pests may solve a puzzle of why plants previously selected for resistance to wilt died anyway, seemingly because of the wilt fungus.
U.S. National Arboretum, Washington, DC
F. S. Santamour, (202) 475-4850

Eighty new strains of Bacillus thuringiensis (BT) have been discovered by a new isolating method that is both simple and rapid. The bacteria are now marketed in products that control certain crop-eating caterpillars, but scientists worldwide want to increase the number of pests that BT could control. The method is a long sought breakthrough to

distinguish among closely related strains of the bacteria and thus opens the way to possible farm and garden use of BT for control of many more insect pests. Insect Pathology Lab, Beltsville, MD
Russell Travers, (301) 344-4331

Phosphorus-deficient apple trees improved when fertilized with phosphorus—results that run counter to claims that the practice is uneconomical. Apple trees in phosphorus-deficient soils thrived when given mono-ammonium phosphate, MAP. The fertilized trees had increased shoot growth, fruit size, and yield compared with trees receiving no phosphorus fertilizer or only nitrogen fertilizer. In most cases, the quality of the trees also improved. The tests were conducted on Delicious apple trees that had been bearing for 15 years. Improvements from using MAP are already apparent in some commercial orchards.
Tree Fruit Research Lab, Wenatchee, WA
J. Thomas Raese, (509) 662-4317

Using chemical fallow to control weeds makes it feasible and economical to crop land 2 years out of 3 in the central Great Plains. Traditionally, such lands are cropped every other year to allow the soil to store water during the fallow year for the next crop. Using atrazine, either in a single or split application at 2.5 to 3 pounds per acre, controlled weeds from after wheat harvest through the following corn-cropping season. Corn grain yields ranged from 50 to 100 bushels per acre, demonstrating the feasibility of a winter wheat/corn/fallow rotation.
Central Great Plains Research Station, Akron, CO
R.L. Anderson, (303) 345-2259

A soilborne fungus can help soybeans survive a lack of water. The fungus (vesicular arbuscular mycorrhizae (VAM)), causes infected soybean plants to increase hormone production. Hormones stimulate hairs to grow on the plant's roots, making the root system larger and extending it further into the soil. That, in turn, helps the plants take in more water and better utilize nutrients in the soil. In VAM-infected soybeans,

9

yields were 50% higher than in noninfected soybeans.
Soil & Water Conservation Research, Lincoln, NE
James R. Ellis, (402) 472-1511

A distant relative of corn is being used in extensive crossbreeding experiments to improve its resistance to disease and drought. A new procedure for crossing eastern gamagrass with corn produces a higher percentage of hybrid kernels that germinated than did previous crosses. Sterility of crosses, however, remains a problem. Some commercial corn lines crossed more easily than others with eastern gamagrass. In other research, at Woodward, OK, a variety of gamagrass was discovered that produces 20 times more seed than other gamagrasses.
Cereal Genetics Research, Columbia, MO
Jack B. Beckett, (314) 882-8214

Nitrogen management is the key to controlling Fusarium root rot, a disease that cuts wheat yields on more than 100,000 acres in the Pacific Northwest. ARS scientists found that farmers can prevent wheat plants from being stressed for water—the cause of the disease—by applying 10 to 25 pounds per acre less nitrogen. This allows wheat to best use available water. Besides helping wheat farmers increase their yields by about 10 bushels per acre and saving wasted fertilizer, this research should head off root rot disease that would have plagued over 1 million acres of wheat had the problem been left unchecked.
Wheat Breeding & Production, Pullman, WA
R. James Cook, (509) 335-1116

The most costly factor in breeding programs to improve soybeans is identifying the high-yielding cultivars. Two years of screening tests on exotic soybean germplasm showed that the highest yielding lines were those whose bean pod took the longest time to fill. This knowledge may be helpful in identifying natural variability among types of soybeans and could make easier development of higher yielding soybeans to boost yields of this major export crop.
Soybean Breeding Unit, Urbana, IL
R.L. Nelson, (217) 333-7279

Today's field corn hybrids grown under conventionally tilled systems are fighting off armyworm infestation by compensating for or outgrowing the defoliation damage caused by the insect. In tests with armyworm larvae of various ages and densities, corn plants sustained 50% defoliation yet produced yields equal to those of undamaged plants. Results of 2 years of tests suggest that armyworm defoliation may not warrant insecticide treatment under conventionally tilled systems.
Corn Insects Research Unit, Ankeny, IA
W.B. Showers, (515) 964-6664

Corn stalk rot is now commonly linked to Fusarium moniliforme, a fungus that attacks stressed plants. In a 2-year test, six Corn-Belt adapted hybrids were analyzed for Diplodis maydis (once considered the most common cause of corn stalk rot) and F. moniliforme. Test results indicate that breeders have done a good job of developing corn resistant to D. maydis. Future breeding programs should stress F. moniliforme resistance.
Plant Introduction Station, Ames, IA
R.L. Clark, (515) 294-3255

Plants have a natural, genetically controlled chemical defense mechanism that studies show can ward off diseases. By producing natural chemicals known as sesquiterpenoids, some varieties of cotton can mount an impressive defense against the destructive verticillium fungus. Lab and greenhouse tests showed for the first time that cotton plants, resistant to verticillium wilt disease, produced four times more sesquiterpenoids than susceptible cottons. Such findings should help geneticists and molecular biologists to select for and incorporate resistance genes into commercial cottons to reduce verticillium-related losses and to decrease the need for fungicides.
Western Research Center, Albany, CA
Nabil A. Garas, (415) 486-3650

A waxy plant is a healthy plant. Research shows that the more natural wax there is on the leaves of alfalfa plants, the healthier the plant. Wax increases a plant's resistance to drought and reduces damage by insects and some herbicides—it may also reduce the risk of bloat in

10

cattle grazing alfalfa. Another study showed that the amount of wax on plant leaves is a trait that can easily be passed on from one plant to another by breeding.
Forage and Range Research, Logan, UT
Melvin D. Rumbaugh, (801) 750-3077

Extra protection against the destructive pink bollworm and other cotton insects may come from cotton plants with deeply divided leaves like those of the okra plant. Some okra-leaf cottons sustained 30% less pink bollworm damage and yielded 7% more cotton than normal-leaf cotton plants. Okra-leaf cottons may contain specific chemicals or have tougher boll walls that discourage insect feeding. This insect resistance and yield advantage may be incorporated into commercial normal-leaf cotton varieties.
Western Cotton Research Lab, Phoenix, AZ
F. Douglas Wilson, (602) 261-3524

Some muskmelons will germinate and grow better than others when subjected to mild water stress after planting. This knowledge can help producers achieve more uniform stands and improve per-acre yields. It can also reduce energy costs for pumping water in irrigated areas, such as the Lower Rio Grande Valley.
Subtropical Agricultural Research Lab, Weslaco, TX
James R. Dunlap, (512) 968-5438

Seeds planted in moist soil often crack open, leaking amino acids, proteins, and sugars into the surrounding soil. Disease-causing fungi—nourished by the leaking seeds—begin to grow and infect the young seedlings. Leakage is a big problem in grain and some legume crops such as peas, beans, and soybeans because plants never completely recover. A researcher developed a meter to measure the cracking point of seeds so he could begin breeding crops that produce crack-resistant seeds.
Grain & Legume Genetics & Physiology Research, Pullman, WA
Stephen C. Spaeth, (509) 335-9521

Injecting apple and pear tree trunks with an iron compound can correct chlorosis, an iron deficiency that causes poor fruit quality and yield. After several years of study, researchers found that the most effective method of reducing chlorosis for the longest time (3 to 4 years) is by injecting the trunks in the spring and fall with ferrous sulfate, an iron compound. The disease, which growers recognize by the yellow color of the leaves, often occurs in trees grown in high-calcium, poorly drained soils.
Tree Fruit Research Lab, Wenatchee, WA
J. Thomas Raese, (509) 662-4317

Special cell structures in the ovaries of plum flowers may protect this delicate part of the plant from freezing. Studies suggest that similar arrangements of cells may be bred into peaches and other flowering, frost-prone crops to protect them against freezing. Certain spring-flowering fruit trees, such as peaches, are vulnerable to late frosts that kill off the flowers so no fruit can be produced.
Snake River Conservation Research Center, Kimberly, ID
John W. Cary, (208) 432-5582

English walnut and a closely related species—wingnut—have been crossbred for the first time. The new hybrid is resistant to two major enemies of walnuts—a soil fungus (phytophthora) and microscopic worms (nematodes)—and may provide a new rootstock for walnuts. Since the new hybrid doesn't occur in nature, scientists used a sophisticated technique known as somatic embryogenesis to create it. The technique involves nurturing dissected embryos in a special nutrient gel. Wingnut is native to northern China.
Crops Pathology & Genetics Research, Davis, CA
Gale H. McGranahan, (916) 752-2460

Lygus bugs may find life more hazardous as they eat—and damage—plants ranging from cotton to fruits, vegetables, and seed crops like alfalfa. Scientists have figured out how to raise millions of these pests for research aimed at finding parasitic enemies that devour them or their eggs. What makes this possible are a new artificial diet and an insect nursery where scientists maintain a year-round supply of the pests. Previously, lack of an artificial diet had hampered

11

researchers because it was almost impossible to maintain an adequate supply of lygus bugs during seasons when their natural foods were in short supply. Biological Control of Insects Lab, Tucson, AZ
Harry M. Graham, (602) 629-6220

Reducing the number of chromosomes in sugarcane may help scientists to improve the species through genetic engineering. The 110 to 120 chromosomes in commercial varieties of sugarcane make it difficult, if not impossible, to study inheritance or to use genetic engineering to produce superior plants. But researchers have produced sturdy plants with only 32 chromosomes, using a tissue culture technique known as anther culture and a wild relative of sugarcane. The next step is to reduce the number to 16 and finally to 8—a workable number for engineering improved plants.
Sugarcane Physiology Lab, Aiea, HI
Paul H. Moore (808) 487-5561

A little stress isn't always a bad thing for plants. Studies show that a plant will overcome or succumb to a stress depending on its "living conditions" before that stress. For example, 2 days of moderately severe drought prepared coleus and poinsettia plants to survive in air heavily polluted with sulfur dioxide; however, severe drought increased chilling injury when coleus plants were later exposed to 5°C temperatures. This research is expected to yield general principles that will help growers cut their losses and aid breeders in developing varieties with broad tolerance to stresses.
Plant Stress Lab, Beltsville, MD
Donald T. Krizek, (301) 344-3143

An accessible and easy-to-use-system for cataloguing new plant germplasm has reached the half-million entry mark. Using a computer terminal and a telephone, scientists can tap into the Germplasm Resources Information Network (GRIN) and have available much of the nation's plant resources to develop cultivated crops that are sturdier or more productive. Each plant or seed assigned a PI number becomes a part of the GRIN database. Plant Introduction

(PI) number 500,000 is Purplestraw wheat, a commercial wheat grown in the southeastern United States valuable as parent material to develop other cultivated wheat varieties.
Germplasm Introduction and Evaluation Lab, Beltsville, MD
George White, (301) 344-2431

Animal Production & Protection

Senepol, a breed of beef cattle that is relatively new to the United States, shows promise in Florida trials as a desirable addition to breeding programs in coastal areas from the Carolinas to Texas. The placid red cattle were originally bred on St. Croix in the U.S. Virgin Islands, where they adapted well to the tropical environment, including hungry cattle ticks and hot weather. This adaptation is also evident in central Florida's subtropical Bahai grass country, where Senepol-Angus crosses have calved without assistance, proved good milk producers, and gained weight well. Their meat grades somewhat higher than that of Brahman-Angus crosses.
Beef Cattle Research Station, Brooksville, FL
Will T. Butts, (904) 796-3385

Rams respond sexually to short days and long nights. By changing ram's day-night pattern, scientists may be able to mate sheep more often than in the typical fall breeding season. Scientists are perfecting lab techniques to determine seasonal differences in ram sperm fertility. Once they have perfected this technology, producers will have improved methods of picking rams to breed at a particular time. This flexibility in picking rams' breeding seasons will give producers the option of mating sheep at other seasons. This could make lamb meat available year round—an advantage for consumers and producers alike.
U.S. Sheep Experiment Station, Dubois, ID
James Fitzgerald, (208) 374-5306

12

Having piglets born at the farmer's and sow's convenience, rather than leaving the date and time of birth to chance, may soon be a reality. Usually, about one out of four piglets die before weaning--many could be saved if an attendant were present to assist sows at delivery. In recent tests, an experimental hormone was used to prevent early unscheduled births; later, another commercially available hormone was given to pregnant sows to induce birth during normal farm working hours. If the annual average number of piglets weaned could be increased from 13 to 18 per sow, pork production could be increased at lower cost to farmer and consumer.
Reproduction Lab, Beltsville, MD
H.D. Gutherie, (301) 344-2820

Pigs don't "pig out," despite popular misconceptions. To increase weight gain of livestock, pigs were force fed a semiliquid diet of 20% more food than they would normally consume. Compared with litter mates who were not force fed but given all the feed they wanted, force-fed pigs gained 40% more weight--with the amount of preferred lean tissue distinctly improved. The goal: to establish what would happen if a strain of pigs could be bred that would eat more feed. Once feed intake is increased, each increment of feed intake above normal would improve the efficiency of animal growth.
Roman L. Hruska U.S. Meat Animal Research Center, Clay Center, NE
Jerome C. Pekas, (402) 762-3241

Six-day old chicks placed on a diet to maintain their weight for 6 more days had 25% less abdominal fat at market age (8 weeks) than chicks fed normal diets. They also gained weight using less feed than chicks that were not on the diet. On day 12 after birth, they were placed on a normal diet designed to put on weight as quickly as possible. A commercial system producing leaner chickens at less cost would also save the poultry industry more than $500 million yearly loss to fat and provide the consumer with leaner and cheaper chicken.
Nonruminant Animal Nutrition Lab, Beltsville, MD
Robert W. Rosebrough, (301) 344-2866

Unlocking the energy stored in forage crops for livestock will result in efficient dairy and beef production. Forage crops and feed grain have almost identical amounts of stored energy; however, forage crops are less digestible. Scientists believe that cinnamic acids may be part of a complex of chemicals that limit forage crops' digestibility. Tests are continuing to pinpoint the other chemicals involved.
Roman L. Hruska U.S. Meat Animal Research Center, Clay Center, NE
Hans J. Jung, (402) 762-3241

Monitoring the sexual preferences of female ticks could help control these pests in biological control programs. Cattle infested with ticks do not gain weight efficiently, causing ranchers large financial losses. To reduce tick populations, scientists have proposed releasing large numbers of sterile male ticks to mate with wild females. However, the success of such programs depends on how well sterile male hybrids compete with wild males for the sexual favors of females. In mating tests, one group of sterile males was twice as successful as another group at competing for wild females. Research is continuing to explain the differences in competitiveness between the two hybrid types.
Cattle Fever Tick Research Lab, Mission, TX
Ronald D. Davey, (512) 585-6788

Not all animals browse alike on rugged terrain, and ranchers should consider that when managing grazing land. Studies showed that cattle avoid terrain with more than 20% slopes, wild horses avoid 30% slopes, and deer, 40% slopes when the grazing site included other land with less grade. Bighorn sheep moved freely over terrain with slopes up to 80%.
Squaw Butte Experiment Station, Burns, OR
David Ganskopp, (503) 573-2064

Livestock producers could save an estimated $63 million a year in one state alone by planting Mozark, a new variety of a fungus-free fescue. Pasture trials of the tall grass increased daily weight gains for calves and yearlings 30%

compared with those grazing pastures with the fungus. Small amounts of the seed, developed cooperatively by ARS and the University of Missouri, will be released to growers this fall. The rest will be used to increase supplies in anticipation of a big demand. Other varieties of fungus-free fescue are being evaluated in Missouri and other states.
Dairy Forage Research Center, Madison, WI
Fred Martz, (314) 875-5354

A radio transmitter has been designed to monitor the activity within a cow's first stomach or rumen—without having to restrain the animal or connect it to wires or tubes. The transmitter measures changes in pressure caused by muscle contraction of the rumen and could prove an invaluable research tool for monitoring this organ's unique activity in feeding trials. Encased in a capsule small enough to be placed in the rumen through a stomach tube, the transmitter works well for up to 2 months and can be made from inexpensive, commercially available parts.
National Animal Disease Center, Ames, IA
Joseph L. Riley, (515) 239-8356

Changes in animals' body temperatures can be remotely sensed by a temperature telemetry transmitter. Designed so that it can be surgically implanted, the transmitter pulses at an interval that is converted to a temperature reading on a chart recorder. Easy to build from standard parts, it provides animal research with a simple yet reliable way to track the temperature effects on animals of various diseases.
National Animal Disease Center, Ames, IA
Joseph L. Riley, (515) 239-8356

Poultry producers who cool their broiler houses in summer must avoid exposing their birds to heat, especially when catching, transporting, and holding broilers for the processing plant. Evaporative cooling helps broilers gain more weight with less mortality, compared with flocks raised under a conventional cooling system. But losses because of heat prostration can quickly outweigh these economic advantages when broilers

are removed from the cool environment where they have been acclimated.
South-Central Poultry Research Lab, Mississippi State, MS
James W. Deaton, (601) 323-2230

A method for predicting obesity in pigs may lead to slimmer humans as well as leaner pigs. Scientists have, for the first time, devised a method to detect lipoprotein lipase (LPL) in pig fetuses. This enzyme controls the movement of fat molecules from the bloodstream to the fatty tissues. The "marker enzyme" may one day be used to help streamline diets for people genetically prone to obesity.
Nonruminant Animal Nutrition Lab, Beltsville, MD
Robert W. Rosebrough, (301) 344-2866

Lifespans of insects can be lengthened or shortened by periodically resetting their biological clocks, a series of studies show. Face flies lived longer than normal if their "day" was extended an extra 6 hours by artificial light about every sixth day. But when the 6 hours of extra daylight occurred about every third or ninth day, the flies died much earlier than normal. Studies with coddling moths produced similar results. Livestock Insects Lab, Beltsville, MD
Dora K. Hayes, (301) 344-2474

A tiny parasite as small as the head of a pin can be used to control house flies. The microparasite Spalangia endius used as part of an integrated pest management program was very efficient in controlling house flies on over a 100-square-mile area that included seven different poultry farms in the Southeast. Such an effective biocontrol can be used economically to keep this noxious pest in check.
Insects Affecting Man and Animals Research Lab, Gainesville, FL
Richard S. Patterson, (904) 374-5910

Cat fleas have been shown for the first time to be resistant to insecticides, which may be the major reason they are so difficult to control. Now, scientists have developed five new insect-growth

regulators for cat flea control; one is commercially available.
Insects Affecting Man and Animals Research Lab, Gainesville, FL
Richard S. Patterson, (904) 374-5910

Cockroach populations have been consistently underestimated by scientists. A recent survey of 550 low-income apartments in the Gainesville area showed each apartment housed an incredible 20,000 roaches. This information emphasizes the need for new and better control technologies and strategies that employ an integrated, multiple approach to killing this tough insect, which has survived much longer than man.
Insects Affecting Man and Animals Lab, Gainesville, FL
Richard S. Patterson, (904) 374-5910

Conventional ways to control insects often become ineffective because insects develop resistance to the chemicals, but another generation of insecticides is on the way. Four insect neuropeptides— "messengers" that regulate vital internal functions—have been isolated, doubling the known number of these natural bioregulators. Using the cockroach as a model, researchers have also created chemical duplicates of the peptides, a step that could eventually give consumers a new arsenal of pest-specific insecticides.
Veterinary Toxicology and Entomology Research Lab, College Station, TX
Mark Holman, (409) 260-9372

"Expert" Information Systems

Corn farmers could increase their net income by using a new computer model for weed control that ARS scientists began testing last year. Scientists are still fine-tuning the system, which tells the farmer when to apply herbicides and how much he should use. The computer model is also expected to help protect the environment by reducing herbicide application. The model, based on biological and economic considerations, takes into account weed seeds in the soil, weed populations, weed control

responses, grain yield, herbicide cost, and grain price. In the new system, herbicides are applied only when the model indicates they will yield a positive return.
Crops Research Lab, Fort Collins, CO
Edward E. Schweizer, (303) 482-7717

Nutrient deficiencies and incipient stresses to plants, such as drought, air pollution, disease, and insect damage, may be sensed remotely. ARS cooperated with NASA (the National Aeronautics and Space Administration) in developing the technology that exposes plant leaves to nitrogen or helium-neon laser and then measures the glow—the wavelengths and intensities of the light emitted from them. So far, four wavelengths look promising for measuring discrete physiological differences in plant status like those caused by plant stress and nutritional status.
Field Crops Lab, Beltsville, MD
James E. McMurtrey, III, (301) 344-3616

Farmers can save soil and reduce sediment by maintaining crop residues on the soil. ARS researchers figure how much residue should be left by using a mathematical equation they developed. That equation, put into a computer, helps researchers predict soil erosion for different soils, crops, and climates. Field tests confirm that as corn residues were increased—from 0 to 6 tons an acre—runoff and erosion were reduced.
Soil and Water Conservation Research, Lincoln, NE
J.E. Gilley, (402) 472-2975

Quarterly Report
of Selected Research Projects

United States
Department of
Agriculture

 Agricultural
Research
Service

April 1 to June 30, 1986

CONTENTS

Human Nutrition

Starch occurs naturally in two forms--amalose and amalopectin--but each has a remarkably different effect on diagnostic warning signs for diabetes. In a pilot study with 24 nondiabetic men and women, crackers specially made with a high amalose content elicited only a slight rise in blood glucose and insulin, but the crackers high in amalopectin caused a rise nearly as great as a high-sucrose (table sugar) confection. The findings suggest that high-amalose foods may help diabetics or borderline diabetics regulate their blood sugar. Results of a longer study will be available later this year.
Carbohydrate Nutrition Lab, Beltsville, MD
Kay Behall, (301) 344-2385

Muscle damage caused by prolonged, intensive exercise may take up to 12 weeks to repair--much longer than previously thought. The discovery was made using an electron microscope to compare leg muscle tissue from 40 marathon runners after a race with equivalent tissue from 12 nonrunners. The study also showed that constant injury and reinjury in older runners or in veteran runners can lead to the loss of muscle tissue, which is replaced by connective and scar tissues. The findings indicate that great care should be taken to fully recover from exercise-induced muscle injury.
USDA Human Nutrition Research Center on Aging at Tufts, Boston, MA
William J. Evans, (617) 956-0333

The ability to metabolize blood alcohol--a function that involves zinc--may be a more sensitive indicator of adequate zinc in the body than measurements of circulating zinc, according to a 6-month study. Five women on a decreasing zinc intake consumed a screwdriver (orange juice and vodka) for breakfast periodically throughout the study. After 4 months on a diet containing only one-sixth the Recommended Dietary Allowance of zinc for women, their ability to clear alcohol from the blood was significantly impaired, even though standard blood tests for zinc level did not show a zinc deficiency. After 1 month of zinc supplementation, the condition was corrected.
Grand Forks Human Nutrition Research Center, Grand Forks, ND
David B. Milne, (701) 795-8424

Vitamin D deficiency among the elderly, especially those living in northern climates, may be an unrecognized epidemic. Deficiency leads to softening of the bones, compounding the bone loss due to osteoporosis and increasing the chance of fractures of the hip and spine. In a recent study, 40% of patients entering a Boston hospital with fractured hips had little or no vitamin D in their blood. Decreased milk consumption is the major cause of age-related vitamin D deficiency, followed by decreased exposure to the sun.
Human Nutrition Research Center on Aging
Boston, MA
Michael Holick, (617) 956-0345

Vitamin C may reduce risk of coronary heart disease. A recent nutrition survey of 680 men and women over age 60 substantiates evidence that the vitamin can increase HDL-cholesterol in the blood. Often called the "good cholesterol," HDL-cholesterol prevents clogging of arteries. Levels began rising with a vitamin C intake twice the Recommended Dietary Allowance of 120 milligrams--and increased proportionately with vitamin

intake. However, the effect diminished with age and stopped altogether after age 80.
Human Nutrition Research Center on Aging Boston, MA
Paul F. Jacques, (617) 956-0314

Selenium might soon be measured more easily and less expensively than ever before. A new analytical method, based on the intensity of blue color formed when selenium reacts with specific chemicals, can detect several different forms of the mineral, including selenium-containing proteins. In trace amounts, this essential element protects body cells against damage, but slightly larger amounts can be toxic. Early results show the new method is as sensitive as existing ones.
Western Human Nutrition Research Center, San Francisco, CA
Chris Hawkes, (415) 556-0131

People who live in regions of the world with selenium-poor soils--Scandinavia, New Zealand, and China--can get this essential trace element by applying it to crops, according to a study with rats. In cooperation with Finnish scientists, ARS scientists compared the bioavailability of selenium from wheat grown with selenium-enriched fertilizers and from U.S-grown wheat, where soil selenium is adequate. There was no difference.
Beltsville Human Nutrition Research Center, Beltsville, MD
Orville Levander, (301) 344-2504

Formula-fed and breast-fed infants consume about the same amount of energy (calories) at 1 month of age. But by 4 months, formula-fed babies consume significantly higher amounts of energy than breast-fed infants. Nevertheless, breast-fed infants gain weight about as fast as those on formulas, apparently because they are able to use the protein and energy in mothers' milk more efficiently or because of a difference in body composition. These findings will help scientists adjust existing recommendations for formulas, some of which are based only on theoretical estimates of needed energy.
Children's Nutrition Research Center, Houston, TX
Corinne M. Montandon, (713) 799-6181/
Nancy F. Butte, (713) 799-5794
2

Soluble fiber--the portion of fiber that dissolves in water--has been credited with lowering cholesterol and improving glucose tolérance. But determining just how much soluble fiber is in a given food is difficult because of its complicated chemical composition. But methods for measuring soluble fiber in cereals, for instance, may not be appropriate for fruits. A recent review of current laboratory procedures led to the suggestion that each major fiber-containing food group have its own specific method of measurement. This approach may increase the accuracy of the amounts and types of fiber listed for foods.
Western Research Center, Albany, CA
Alfred C. Olson, (415) 486-3692

A tabletop robot is helping chemists assess the vitamin content of foods commonly eaten in the United States. The 2-foot-tall mechanical assistant takes over much of the tedious work of sample preparation, allowing chemists to double their daily analyses with more accuracy. Some of the nutrient values in USDA's food tables are calculated or inferred from measurements of other foods, not of the actual foods. Also, the U.S. diet has changed from agricultural commodities to processed foods, which can alter the types and amounts of vitamins. The robot is speeding this essential work.
Nutrient Composition Lab, Beltsville, MD
Darla Higgs, (301) 344-2370

New & Improved Products

If Marie Antoinette lived today, she might say, "Let them eat cornstalks." A new process turns wheat straw, cornstalks, and other heretofore inedible plant parts into a no-calorie, high-fiber product that can replace up to 50% of the flour in baked goods and other foods. The additive doesn't change taste, texture, or baking qualities. In fact, the mixture of hemicellulose and cellulose fibers actually makes foods moister. The substance is made by treating straw and stalks with hydrogen peroxide, which washes out the lignin, or woody portions of the plant, permitting humans to ingest the remaining fibers.
Northern Research Center, Peoria, IL
J. Michael Gould, (309) 685-4011, Ext. 318.

Millions of pounds of vegetables and fruits fail to survive the trip from farms to consumers who live in the New York City market area. In a series of 3-year studies of each of 30 major produce crops, plant pathologists traced heavy losses to disease organisms or to mechanical damage inflicted by improper handling. Losses were especially heavy for lettuce (34 million pounds annually), tomatoes, peaches, and citrus. There were first-time reports of diseases attacking other than original host crops. The scientists investigated what happened to produce, not only as it moved from farms through terminal markets to food chain stores, but also while it was in home refrigerators awaiting consumption. Obtaining such information is a necessary first step for more effective disease control on farms and in marketing channels and to better packaging and handling of produce at wholesale and retail markets.
Horticultural Crops Quality Research, New Brunswick, NJ
Michael Ceponis, (201) 932-9881

Three ARS-patented compounds show promise in fighting staph infections. While looking for natural preservatives for foods, cosmetics, lubricants, paints, and other products, researchers found that derivatives of one-third of the tested new compounds synthesized from glycolic acid and fatty acids from cottonseed oil inhibit microbial growth of staph. This discovery takes on increased significance because new, virulent strains of Staphylococcus aureus, first noticed in an Australian hospital, are unaffected by most antibiotics.
Southern Research Center, New Orleans
August V. Bailey/Gene Sumrell, (504) 589-7058

Unshelled walnuts can be sold to Japan for the first time, now that scientists have found a way to keep the nuts free of the codling moth. The new process uses safe, yet higher-than-normal doses of the regular walnut fumigant, methyl bromide, under vacuum pressure. Higher doses are needed to kill moths living in nuts at harvest time; at that stage, the pests are twice as resistant to the fumigant. Vacuum pressure helps the fumigant penetrate the tough walnut shell. Because of the new process, Japan recently lifted its import ban on unshelled walnuts from the United States. Japan had quarantined the walnuts because it does not have the codling moth and was afraid the nuts would carry the moth into the country.
Horticultural Crops Research Lab, Fresno, CA
Patrick V. Vail, (209) 487-5310.

One way to maintain the quality of U.S. grain in storage is to make sure it's free of toxins that are poisonous to animals and humans. Scientists, who are studying fungi to see what triggers them to produce these toxins, have found chemical inhibitors that stop production of trichothecene toxin--one of the most harmful toxins in the world. The discovery may help scientists find environmentally safe inhibitors for specific toxins that contaminate U.S. grain.
Northern Research Center, Peoria, IL
Anne E. Desjardins, (309) 685-4011 Ext. 378

New thermal fabrics that warm you when you're cold and cool you when you're hot were developed by ARS scientists a few years ago. Now an improved process to treat fabrics overcomes an earlier problem where the fabric treatment could not withstand laundering or exposure to moisture. Polyethylene glycols are durably bound to fabric and absorb and store heat when surrounding temperatures rise and then release heat when temperatures fall. Eventually, the treatment could be used on building insulation, draperies, packaging materials, and aerospace and military applications.
Southern Research Center, New Orleans, LA
Tyrone L. Vigo, (504) 589-7529

Seed oil rich in epoxy acid of value to industry can be harvested from the East African vernonia plant. The epoxy acid can be used in chemical coatings, plastics, and adhesives. The African plants are the first vernonia species known to mature all of its seed at once so that a complete crop can be harvested. Vernonia is a possible new crop for drier parts of Hawaii and Puerto Rico, and it may be

adapted to southern parts of California, Arizona, and Texas.
Germplasm Introduction and Evaluation Lab, Beltsville, MD
Robert E. Perdue, Jr., (301) 344-2431

Lowering U.S. need to import rapeseed oil is a possible benefit from two new varieties of crambe. BelAnn and BelEnzian crambe could produce two crops per season on 22,000 acres. The new crop, being further tested in an ARS pilot project in Iowa, could replace imported rapeseed as the source of erucic acid for plastics, nylon, and high-temperature lubricants.
Germplasm Quality and Evaluation Lab, Beltsville, MD
T. Austin Campbell, (301) 344-2720

Fresh fruits and vegetables shipped in a new and improved refrigerated van will stay crisp and fresh longer. Because the van--known as the Advanced Design Perishables Trailer--provides far better air circulation than conventional refrigerated vans, produce should arrive at its destination no more than 4 to 8° warmer than when it left, according to ARS marketing specialists. Its exclusive design features allow better circulation underneath the load and provide more uniform chilling of the sides. The van has been extensively tested using long-distance shipments of lettuce, melons, grapes, oranges, and other fresh fruits and vegetables.
European Marketing Research Center
Rotterdam, The Netherlands
Tom Hinsch, 011-31-10-765-535

Puff-drying of mushrooms could solve two problems of the processed foods industry. Besides saving 40% of the energy required in conventional food-drying systems, this process allows the mushrooms to be stored indefinitely. Extended storage would allow growers to retain part of their crop to extend sales. Uncooked, the mushrooms can be eaten as a tasty, nutritious, low-calorie snack; cooked in boiling water they retain their flavor and texture. Mushrooms processed this way are tasty and inexpensive to produce. Puff-drying is also an alternative to canning, where solids, vitamins, and amino acids are lost, and to freeze-drying which is very expensive.
Eastern Research Center, Philadelphia, PA
John Sullivan/Michael Kozempel, (215) 233-6588

Lawn furniture coverings, tents, tarpaulins, and other outdoor and industrial fabrics can be improved by combining cotton with high-tenacity artificial fibers, such as glass and Kevlar. The blended fabrics are lighter, stronger, more durable to weathering, and more flame-resistant than standard all-cotton fabrics.
Southern Research Center, New Orleans
George F. Ruppenicker, (504) 589-7023

Matching the right weave with the right finish can make for stronger outdoor cotton fabrics, such as tents and awnings. All-cotton fabrics, finished with a flame-retardant treatment, can be made more durable and tear-resistant with advanced "open" weaves--like those found in baskets. Previously, tightly-woven cotton could not stand up to a large amount of chemical finish.
Southern Research Center, New Orleans
Robert J. Harper, Jr., (504) 589-7029

A nutritious, high-energy flour can be made from mesquite bean pods, using a new process developed by ARS scientists. By using standard food-processing techniques, dried pods of mesquite, a prolific range pest, are converted into high-protein, sweet-tasting flour and a gum that can be used as a natural thickening additive. Scientists found mesquite gum to be better than the guar gum U.S. processors import to thicken ice cream, salad dressings, puddings, and other foods. Taste tests proved crackers and tortilla chips made with mesquite flour preferable to those made only with conventional flours. Scientists in Chile and Mexico cooperated in the mesquite pod research, which was partially funded by the Agency for International Development. A firm in Chihuahua, Mexico, is using the process to produce various food items.
Western Research Center, Albany, CA
Robert Becker, (415) 486-3623

A prototype electronic apple is helping researchers study damage to fruit as it bumps along the marketing chain from tree to consumer. The "apple" measures blows to fruit; it senses temperature, humidity, and light and sends the data to a computer for analysis. Its ability to locate points where damage occurs along the handling system will help engineers improve equipment and handling procedures to reduce bruising and decay in apples and other fruits, including oranges, cherries, blueberries, and tomatoes.
Fruit and Vegetable Harvesting Research, East Lansing, MI
Bernard R. Tennes, (517) 353-5203

Soil, Water, & Air

Global greenhouse effects predicted during the next century could substantially improve the ability of plants to use water efficiently. ARS experts say carbon dioxide in the Earth's atmosphere may double during the next century, producing conditions that will dramatically boost plant growth and crop production. Cotton grown in greenhouses with double the amount of carbon dioxide in the air produced much higher yields using the same amount of water as cotton grown under normal conditions. Besides agriculture, this increased water-use efficiency of plants will have major implications for other important water users--like cities with parklands and businesses with landscaped areas.
Arid Zone Crop Production Research, Phoenix, AZ
Bruce A. Kimball, (602) 261-4356

Natural fertilizing of soybeans by soil bacteria could be stepped up with genes from rare types of soybeans. Scientists screened 1,300 types of soybean plants and found 13 with genes that develop a symbiotic relationship only with superior strains of nitrogen-fixing bacteria.
Nitrogen Fixation and Soybean Genetics Lab, Beltsville, MD
Perry B. Cregan, (301) 344-3070

Yields of winter wheat planted into heavy soybean residue were reduced by as much as 29% when it was planted in rotation with soybeans. ARS and Purdue University scientists, who did the research as part of a special USDA project, believe that the cause is toxic chemicals from rapidly decaying soybean stems, leaves, and hulls that reduce seed germination rates, delay emergence, reduce tillering, and stunt plant growth. The answer: lessen the toxic effects by spreading soybean residue evenly on the soil surface before planting wheat and by disking in residue just below the surface.
Plant Science Research, West Lafayette, IN
T.S. Abney, (317) 494-4650

A staggered grid system of soil sampling is as reliable as the standard method but requires 40% fewer samples. By using the new system, construction workers, farmers, ranchers, and other land managers can achieve great savings in time and labor spent on collecting soil samples.
Soil and Water Management Research, St. Paul, MN
Dennis Linden, (612) 373-1444

Crop yields increase--and so does farm income--with the amount of residue left on the surface of the soil, according to results of a 4-year study in eastern Nebraska. But when residue is removed, yields decline. The dryland field study compared the effects on production of continuous no-till corn and soybeans of leaving the previous crop's residues on the soil. During the 4 years, an average of 42, 53, 59, and 63 bushels of corn per acre and 25, 30, 33, and 35 bushels of soybeans per acre were produced annually on the 0%, 50%, 100%, and 150% residues, respectively. Critical factors in producing the higher yields were increases in available water and decreased stress from high temperatures. Lower yields also mean reduced residues, so removing the same percentage of residues each year results in a downward spiral of yields.
Soil and Water Conservation Research, Lincoln, NE
Wallace W. Wilhelm, (303) 491-1989

Seeding rates for two native prairie grasses--big bluestem and switchgrass-- can be sharply reduced by applying the herbicide atrazine before plants emerge. In the past, recommended seeding rates have been 6-12 lb/acre for big bluestem and 3-6 lb/acre for switchgrass. With

the atrazine treatment, the lower rates—previously considered minimums—resulted in excellent stands. Since seed of these grasses—which are used for pasture, range, and conservation plantings—costs from $6 to $12 per pound, potential savings in seed costs in the conservation reserve program are substantial. The prairie grasses grow well in Nebraska, Kansas, South Dakota, and parts of Iowa and Missouri.
Forage and Range Research Unit, Lincoln, NE
Kenneth P. Vogel, (402) 472-1564

Salty water drained from fields can be reused to irrigate salt-tolerant crops, saving high-quality water for drinking and minimizing the need to build expensive systems to dispose of leftover salt-laden drainage water. When applied through a surface drip-irrigation system, recycled water produced cotton yields that compared well with cotton furrow-irrigated with unsalty water. Similar systems could be used with other salt-tolerant crops like asparagus, date palms, and sugarbeets.
Water Management Research, Fresno, CA
James E. Ayars, (209) 251-0437

Crop Production & Protection

Elm trees have been grown for the first time from leaf cells. The achievement is a step toward developing an American elm tree resistant to Dutch elm disease. The next step will be to fuse protoplasts, or stripped-down leaf cells, from a disease-resistant elm species to those of a disease-susceptible American elm. From thousands of fused protoplasts regenerated into shoots, a few with disease resistance may show potential for developing into trees with typical American elm grandeur.
Nursery Crops Research Lab, Delaware, OH
S.C. Domir, (614) 363-1129

One of the nation's worst weed pests, Russian thistle, may be curbed chemically. The pest readily infests fields, putting down deep roots that rob moisture from crops. For example, under ideal moisture conditions in the Pacific Northwest, the thistle can cut spring wheat yields by 55%. Tests show that fall spraying of chlorsulfuron plus a surface-active agent will provide year-long control, reducing thistle numbers by 90%. Such effective residual chemical control also saves money and soil. Wheat growers can skip at least three cultivations needed to uproot emerging thistle plants. Without these cultivations, wheat stubble can stand intact over the winter and protect soil from erosion.
Nonirrigated Agriculture Weed Science Research, Pullman, WA
Frank L. Young, (509) 335-1551

Seven mold-eating fungi may eventually join other biological controls in combating expensive corn diseases like stalk rot, which costs U.S. corn producers about $1.2 billion a year. In their search for new, higher yielding plants, breeders may have overlooked the presence of these naturally occurring fungi. Now they are screening corn tissue to find genotypes that support fungus growth. This will help breeders create new corn lines that encourage development of beneficial fungi that devour various disease organisms before they damage plants.
Cereal and Soybean Improvement Research, Ames, IA
Nader G. Vakili, (515) 294-8412

Tiny electrical probes can detect how insects find and home in on scents of ripening fruit or other crops. The probes are inserted into the antennae of the Mediterranean fruit fly, the cotton boll weevil, and other agricultural pests and record electroantennograms that alert scientists when the insect detects a specific odor. These recordings could help researchers devise ways to disrupt the insects' ability to find potential mates by chemical communication. Scientists may also be able to confuse the insects' response to fruit odors and distract them from finding egg-laying sites in susceptible crops.
Tropical Fruit and Vegetable Research Lab, Hilo, HI/Boll Weevil Research Lab, Mississippi State, MS/Western Research Center, Albany, CA
Eric B. Jang, (808) 959-9138/Joseph C. Dickens, (601) 323-2230/Douglas M. Light, (415) 486-3862

6

Sunflowers are more likely to hold their heads up for harvesting if their stalks have been dwarfed by a herbicide intended to kill wild oats. Normal-height plants tend to topple during windy weather, especially when the heads become heavy with ripening seeds. But the herbicide difenzoquat temporarily slows cell division in young sunflower stalks. When sprayed with the difenzoquat, sunflower seedlings grew only two-thirds as tall as untreated plants but matured normally otherwise. This is yet another example of an agricultural chemical initially used as a herbicide also demonstrating growth-regulating properties.
Metabolism and Radiation Research Lab, Fargo, ND
Jeffrey C. Suttle, (701) 237-5771

Leaving straw, stalks, and leaves on the soil after harvest is a good way to protect next year's wheat crop from greenbugs, tiny pests which feed on growing wheat and other grains. The greenbug, a kind of aphid, is attracted to dark areas like bare soil and green crops, so the light-colored crop residues are an effective camouflage. Scientists are also working on a better way to avoid the greenbug menace--finding wheat varieties which can withstand attacks. So far, two of the wheat lines being studied show some tolerance to greenbug feeding.
Wheat and Other Cereal Crops Research, Stillwater, OK
Robert L. Burton, (405) 624-4231

Blueberries, a $45-million-a-year U.S. crop, are now healthier because an easy-to-use test can detect a major disease-causing virus. The test makes it easier to identify blueberry red ringspot virus in raw sap from the leaves and bark of highbush blueberry plants. Previous tests took 2 to 3 days, were not as sensitive, and could be performed only in the late summer. The new test takes 1 day, is highly sensitive, and allows the virus to be identified in dormant blueberry stock or during the growing season. Until now, nursery operators had no practical way of knowing if this disease-causing virus was present in a symptomless stock of blueberries--a lack of information that sometimes caused considerable crop loss. Elimination of the virus is expected to result in symptomless fruit and a possible 10% to 20% increase in crop yield.
Horticultural Crops Research Lab, Corvallis, OR
Richard H. Converse, (503) 757-4819

Two new rice varieties have been developed by ARS researchers and cooperators in Louisiana, Mississippi, and Texas. The Rexmont has characteristics needed by the food-processing industry for quick cooking and soupmaking. Gulfmont matures a few days earlier than Lemont, a popular variety released by ARS and the cooperating states a few years ago. Both of these long-grain semidwarf varieties resist being flattened to the ground after high winds.
Rice Research, Beaumont, TX
Charles N. Bollich, (409) 752-2741

Baking horticultural crop plants can produce virus-free stock for nursery operators and breeders. Scientists have found that growing plants in a chamber at a constant 100° F slows down the spread of any viruses present and speeds plant growth. Researchers can then snip off new plant growth before any virus develops and make it available to nursery operators. Virus-free plant material is essential for nursery operators to propagate healthy stock and is needed by breeders to develop new plant varieties. While the heat treatments are hard on some plants, a slight increase in carbon dioxide inside the growth chamber helps plants tolerate the hothouse better.
Horticultural Crops Research Lab, Corvallis, OR
Richard H. Converse, (503) 757-4819

A powerful sex lure produced by an insect of California vineyards has for the last 4 years enticed male moths to experimental traps and away from grape leaves. Wormlike larvae of the grapeleaf skeletonizer quickly reduce grape leaves to skeletons. Now the sex lure, which so far has been synthesized only in ARS laboratories, has been patented and is available to commercial manufacturers. Entomologists use the traps to sample skeletonizer populations and to decide when and where to apply insecticides. Someday, however, the traps and lures

might be used on a larger scale to decrease the number of skeletonizers, particularly if the insects become resistant to pesticides currently in use.
Horticultural Crops Research Lab, Fresno, CA
Edwin L. Soderstrom, (209) 487-5310

Identifying the hormonal trigger that enables cotton plants to survive drought and other stresses by shedding their bolls may lead to ways of curbing yield losses. Cotton plants often shed most of their bolls when severely stressed. Bolls contain the cells that develop into cotton fibers. Researchers found that stress upsets a delicate balance of hormones that regulate the enzymes that cause shedding. Exploiting this knowledge would result in guidelines for growers to prevent damaging levels of stress. Promising management practices might include adjustments in irrigation and nitrogen fertilization and in optimum spacing of plants.
Western Cotton Research Lab, Phoenix, AZ
Gene Guinn, (602) 261-3524

Honey bees slack off on their job of pollinating hybrid cotton plants. New hybrids yielding 25% more cotton than self-pollinating commercial varieties come from a cross between yellow-flowered Pima and white-flowered upland cottons. For some reason, honey bees, which are dependable pollinators for some crops, often avoid flowering cotton plants. They tend to stick to either the yellow or the white--whichever they try first-- not a mixture. Besides this single-color preference, bees may dislike cotton pollen simply because its shape differs slightly from that of pollen in most other crops. The bee's meticulous taste means four times as many honey bees are needed to produce hybrids of Pima-upland cotton seed as are needed for commercial varieties. Once the cause of the bees' reticence is understood and overcome, insect labor will speed the development of still higher quality, higher yielding hybrid cottons.
Carl Hayden Bee Research Center, Tucson, AZ
Gerald M. Loper, (602) 629-6140

A staggered planting pattern for corn, in which seeds are planted alternately 3.5 inches on either side of an imaginary centerline, can increase yields of certain corn varietiesfrom 2% to 8%. The pattern, called precision twin-row planting, gives plants a competitive edge in absorbing available light, water, and fertilizer nutrients over corn planted in single rows.
Coastal Plains Research Center, Florence, SC
Doug L. Karlen, (803) 669-5203

Don't waste your money! That's the advice for farmers who use polymeric polyhydroxy acid (PPA), a water-soluble adjuvant, or additive, alleged to enhance the performance of herbicides sprayed on weeds like cockleburs, pigweeds, and johnsongrass. Although other surface-active agents boost performance of common herbicides, tests show that PPA is not cost effective.
Southern Weed Science Lab, Stoneville, MS
Chester G. McWhorter, (601) 686-2311

Pecan weevils, a major pest of pecans, can be detected in orchards cost effectively with cone-shaped traps placed in the lowest crotch of the trees. These traps are less expensive and easier to monitor than the common cone-emergence trap, which is placed on the ground, where it disrupts various management and harvesting activities. Once weevils are detected by the traps, which they can enter easily but cannot leave, they can be eliminated with insecticides.
Southeastern Fruit and Tree Nut Research Lab, Byron, GA
Jerry A. Payne, (912) 956-5656

Big-eyed bugs, which are used to control several insect pests of crops like tobacco budworm and corn earworm (also known as cotton bollworm and tomato fruitworm), can now be raised in larger numbers by feeding them an artificial diet. The new hamburger-based diet combines several important human foods whose nutritional values closely match this beneficial bug's natural diet. The substitute food is cheap and readily available, and the bugs willingly switch from it to their

natural diets when they are released in the wild.
Biological Control of Insects Lab, Tucson, AZ
Allen C. Cohen, (602) 629-6220

Soft white spring wheat with genetic resistance to the Hessian fly and powdery mildew has been developed and registered by ARS and Idaho researchers. Seeds of the new breeding line, known as PI 468960, are now available to wheat breeders for further crop development.
Cereal and Vegetable Crop Production, Aberdeen, ID
Donald W. Sunderman, (208) 397-4181

Hard red winter wheat that withstands attacks of the Hessian fly has been developed by ARS and Kansas State University researchers. A single dominant gene found in a wild wheat collected in Iran in the 1950's is effective against all known strains of the fly, the most destructive wheat pest worldwide. This is only the second fly-resistant gene transferred directly from a wild species to cultivated wheat.
Plant Science and Entomology Research, Manhattan, KS
J.H. Hatchett/T.S. Cox, (913) 532-6154

The zigzag flight of insects may be far from random. ARS studies suggest that flight patterns may be systematic, purposeful ways to pick up odors that can lead an insect to its prey. One species of wasp, for example, that lays its eggs in a crop-eating caterpillar, flies predictable routes to catch a whiff of its target on air currents. These odors differ, depending on what sort of plant the caterpillar is eating at the time, and consequently affect the wasp's ability to locate it. The aim of the research is to help cut crop losses by finding ways to make parasitic insects even more efficient hunters of destructive insect pests.
Insect Biology and Population Management Lab, Tifton, GA
W. Joe Lewis/M.A. Keller, (912) 382-6904

Tomatoes and potatoes taste better and often are larger when grown in soil that incorporates certain decomposing waste products, such as wine-grape residues,

according to tests conducted by ARS and a cooperator. The humic substances in the residue, which are organic acids derived from humus, promote root growth, providing an opportunity for beneficial soil micro-organisms called mycorrhizae to colonize the plant more easily. Many of these additives are already available commercially.
Horticultural Crops Research Lab, Corvallis, OR
Robert G. Linderman, (503) 757-4544

Produce growers and nursery operators can safely rid their soil of plant pathogens and weed seeds without harming beneficial soil micro-organisms at about one-fifth of today's costs. ARS has found that the fumigant metham sodium, which is sold under several trade names, can be applied for about $200 an acre and is safer, as effective, and cheaper than the current fumigant, methyl bromide, which is applied for about $1,000 an acre and kills beneficial soil micro-organisms. Scientists are now developing economical ways of treating potting soil mixes with metham sodium to rid them of pathogens and weed seeds.
Horticultural Crops Research Lab, Corvallis, OR
Robert G. Linderman, (503) 757-4544

A new insecticide, Avermectin B1, is toxic to the striped cucumber beetle which spreads bacterial wilt among cucumbers, melons, and related crops. Beetles die after walking on dried residues of the chemical or from ingesting it, and less-than-lethal doses of Avermectin B1 disrupt the beetle's ability to produce viable eggs. Certain beneficial nematodes also control the cucumber beetle, and trickle irrigation is an ideal way to deliver the nematodes to their host. Trickle irrigation--along with black plastic mulch--provides the humid environment in which nematodes thrive. Using nematodes to control beetles avoids the cost of expensive chemical insecticides and resulting risk of killing honey bees.
ARS Asian Parasite Lab, Seoul, Korea
D.K. Reed, (02) 963-6561

9

Only time will tell if virus-free plant material can survive unchanged for as long as a century, despite any disasters that might be caused by nature or people. Scientists have designed a 100-year experiment to see if strawberry plant germplasm can be safely stored at minus 385° F. Growing tips of the plant--the size of a pinhead--were dropped into vials of antifreeze solution, placed in a freezing chamber, and gradually reduced to -40° F. Then the tips were plunged in liquid nitrogen at -385° F. Periodically over the next 100 years, scientists will grow the tips into whole plants and check them for possible mutation.
National Clonal Germplasm Repository, Corvallis, OR
Harry B. Lagerstedt, (503) 757-4448

The first Russet potato with resistance to the golden nematode, a potentially serious pest of potatoes worldwide, has been bred in an ARS lab. For 40 years, agricultural officials have recognized the golden nematode as a threat to U.S. potato crops and contained it--with quarantines, local controls, and inspections--to parts of New York, where it was first found in this country. Called NemaRus, the new potato can be grown for high yields in northeastern states and Florida and in mid-Altantic states under irrigation. It also is resistant to widespread virus diseases and to fusarium tuber rot, a serious disease of stored potatoes.
Vegetable Lab, Beltsville, MD
Raymon E. Webb, (301) 344-3380

A gift of 30 bonsai plants from the Lingnan School of Penjing, in Hong Kong, to the people of the United States of America is being prepared for display at the U.S. National Arboretum. The classic plants, called penjing in Chinese, will be added to 53 specimens already in the National Bonsai Collection. The product of a natural art form developed in the Orient, bonsai are dwarf trees or shrubs planted in trays and kept small by pruning both tops and roots. Some bonsai live for centuries.
U.S. National Arboretum, Washington, DC
Robert F. Drechsler, (202) 475-4818

Plants tissue-cultured in test tubes are not necessarily free of two of the smallest known disease-causing organisms: viruses and viroids. To detect these organisms, the RNA from a known virus or viroid is used to make a strand of complementary DNA, or cDNA. Scientists use the strand to recognize viral or viroid RNA in a plant tissue extract. The cDNA and RNA of related or identical viruses and viroids will automatically link together. The technique has already been used to detect and compare viruses in fruit and bulb crops and to check seed potatoes for the potato spindle tuber viroid.
Florist and Nursery Crops Lab, Beltsville, MD
Roger H. Lawson/Ramon L. Jordan/John Hammond, (301) 344-3244

Soaking seeds to get them off to a fast start may actually do more harm than good, ARS scientists have found. When a seed is planted, it takes up water from the soil, allowing the plant to expand and grow. But if the seed is soaked or the ground is too wet, the seed takes up water too quickly, and its protective cover cracks, leaving the young seedling vulnerable to disease-causing soil fungi. One way to reduce seed damage, still in the experimental stage, is to coat seeds with a waxy compound that slows water uptake and prevents fracturing.
Grain and Legume Genetics and Physiology Research Lab, Pullman, WA
Stephen C. Spaeth, (509) 335-9521

A mere breeze can sometimes force pesticides sprayed by jet-propelled systems into missing their targets. Researchers are currently studying computer simulations of windblown pesticide sprays, as well as performing wind tunnel experiments, to determine exactly how pesticides get diverted by the wind. One problem is that the movement of the spraying machinery itself can account for misdirected spray. A prototype has been developed for a system which may provide the solution--nozzles attached to lifting mechanisms that can rise to treetop levels. Researchers are hoping for success in developing wind-resistant

spraying mechanisms and procedures to reduce costly pesticide waste.
Ohio Agricultural Research and Development Center, Wooster, OH
Robert D. Fox, (216) 263-3871

Animal Production & Protection

A new process for isolating pure hemoglobin--the iron-containing portion of blood--may be useful in veterinary and human medicine. In about 5 hours, the two-step filtering process recovers about 90% of the hemoglobin from one-half liter of packed red blood cells. The technique may be used for any animal blood. It produces an ultrapure protein, which may be a safe alternative for use in artificial blood cells for both animal and human blood transfusions.
Veterinary Toxicology and Entomology Lab, College Station, TX
John R. DeLoach, (409) 260-9484

The "Asian tiger mosquito" (Aedes albopictus), which may carry painful dengue fever and encephalitis, has invaded parts of Texas, Louisiana, Mississippi, and Tennessee. ARS scientists tested a predator mosquito that may control the "Asian tiger" but is harmless to people, domestic animals, and wildlife and they are collaborating with the New Orleans Mosquito Control District in breeding it. Use of the predator is likely to be as effective against the "Asian tiger" as it was earlier against the yellowfever mosquito (Aedes aegypti) because of similarities in breeding habitat. Because they are cold-tolerant, the "Asian tiger" may survive in northern parts of the country. ARS is continuing to investigate improved chemical and biological control technologies.
Mosquito Biology Research, Gainesville, FL
Dave Dame, (904) 374-5930

Plasma cholesterol, a major risk factor in heart disease, is influenced by genetics. A group of 318 five-month-old swine, consisting of four different breeds--including some crossbred animals--were studied. Results showed that levels of both cholesterol and triglycerides in their blood plasma were inherited and independent of body weight and

depth of backfat. Scientists believe that they can use the pig as a model to study the relationship between diet and genetics and human heart disease.
Roman L. Hruska U.S. Meat Animal Research Center, Clay Center, NE
Wilson G. Pond, (402) 762-3241

White blood cells may be a key to better understanding and controlling brucellosis, a serious disease of cattle. For the first time, two chemicals have been found that suppress bovine white blood cells, known as neutrophils. These chemicals allow Brucella bacteria to live inside the neutrophils, where they are relatively safe from antibodies and antibiotics. Scientists believe that if they can neutralize the effects of these chemicals, the cow's own immune system might be able to control brucella infections. This might also work with other difficult-to-treat bacterial infections.
National Animal Disease Center, Ames, IA
Peter C. Canning, (515) 239-8219

A new drought-resistant wheatgrass for western rangelands yields 25% more livestock feed. Such hybrids seldom occur naturally in the wheat family because the endosperm--the starch portion of the seed that nourishes the hybrid embryo--fails to develop. A team of scientists is using genetic engineering techniques to rescue the embryo. They artificially feed the embryo in agar, a plant gelatin containing nutrients, until it germinates and grows into a seedling. If the new plant is sterile--having only half the number of chromosomes it needs to reproduce--it can be treated with a chemical called colchicine, which doubles its chromosome number. The same strategy can be applied to other range grasses and even to new wheat varieties.
Crops Research Lab, Logan, UT
Richard Wang, (801) 750-3222

A previously unsuspected chemical has been found that may play an important role in liver poisoning of humans and livestock by pyrrolizidine alkaloids--natural chemicals found in hundreds of plants. The new findings challenge previous theory in toxicology and veterinary medicine which attributed the pois-

11

oning exclusively to compounds known as pyrroles. Pyrrolizidine alkaloids kill horses, cattle, pigs, and other livestock by causing cumulative and irreversible damage to the liver. The new information should help veterinary researchers develop an antidote.
Western Research Center, Albany, CA
William F. Haddon, (415) 486-3693

A hybrid sorghum tested in Puerto Rico shows promise as a new source of forage for livestock producers in the Tropics. Researchers crossed Millo Blanco, a sorghum variety that doesn't flower and is sensitive to day length, with Greenleaf, a sudangrass variety insensitive to day length. The resulting hybrid produce excellent yields and has good levels of crude protein and digestibility for livestock use.
Tropical Agriculture Research Station, Mayaguez, PR
Antonio Sotomayor-Rios, (809) 834-2435

A culture of cells of the common household cockroach provides a model system to develop more effective insecticides. The self-reproducing cells secrete chitin--a unique substance found in the exoskeleton, or outer shell, of insects. Some of the most selective insecticides available are compounds that inhibit the synthesis of chitin; insects can't molt, so they die. Chemical companies can use the cell lines to test new chemicals easily for their potential as insecticides.
Insect Physiology and Metabolism Research, Fargo, ND
Edwin P. Marks, (701) 237-5771, Ext. 473

A perennial alfalfa has been discovered that resists its two most destructive pests--the alfalfa weevil and potato leafhopper. Glandular hairs of the alfalfa secrete a sticky, nontoxic substance that traps the larvae and nymphs as they emerge from the eggs laid on the stem of the plant. The alfalfa also resists downy mildew, rust, and summer black stem. Scientists hope to breed these traits into an improved forage for livestock.
Plant Science and Entomology Research, Manhattan, KS
Edgar L. Sorenson, (913) 532-7247

Dairy farmers can now find out when cows are in heat and add up to $300 per cow per year to farm profits. The first electronic device to detect heat, or estrus, is over 90% accurate in preliminary tests. The estrus detector is a joint U.S.-Israeli research project aimed at pinpointing a cow's fertile period for breeding. Artificial insemination, the primary means of breeding dairy cows, fails about half the time because farmers misjudge their cows' estrous periods.
Animal Reproduction Lab, Beltsville, MD
Gregory S. Lewis, (301) 344-2798

Goats in Hawaii can eat Leucaena, a plant which is poisonous to most domestic cattle, and suffer no ill effects. Scientists have discovered that the goats' stomachs contain a bacterium which protects them from the toxic substance. While tests of cattle in Texas and Iowa indicate that they don't have this natural protection, studies have shown that the beneficial bacterium can be transplanted from one animal to the other. In Australia, steers with Leucaena-poisoning symptoms--loss of hair, goiter, and ulcers of the esophagus--recovered soon after they were fed mixtures of bacteria from food digesting in the stomachs of Hawaiian goats. Senepol cattle, a Virgin Island breed, can digest Leucaena.
National Animal Disease Center, Ames, IA
Milton J. Allison, (515) 239-8373

Getting cattle and sheep on rangeland to graze together, despite their inclination to stand apart, may help ranchers save lambs from coyotes and cut the costs of fencing. Research shows such mingling occurs after "bonding," a process that involves an initial penning and feeding of 45-day-old lambs with yearling heifers for 30 days. Thereafter, new lambs can be added to bonded groups out on the range. Cattle protect bonded lambs by intimidating and threatening approaching predators. In tests this year, researchers have lost no bonded lambs to coyotes. Without bonding, losses in one small flock of sheep were 50% in 2 weeks. Because bonded lambs stay close to cattle, both species can be confined with a few strands of barbed wire. By contrast, an electric fence to confine and protect

sheep can cost upwards of $2,500 a mile.
Jornada Experimental Range, Las Cruces,
NM
Dean M. Anderson/Clarence V. Hulet, (505)
646-5190

Stable flies, pests that inflict painful
bites on people and animals, could be
better controlled now that scientists
have found out how far they travel.
Research shows that these flies, which
infest beaches and reduce revenues from
tourism in coastal New Jersey and Florida, will hitch a ride on storm currents,
traveling at least 135 miles. Sometimes
called dog flies, they migrate from
agricultural areas toward the beaches,
following weather patterns. Officials
now realize that reduction in number of
stable flies can best be achieved with
areawide control measures.
Insects Affecting Man and Animals
Research Lab, Gainesville, FL
Jerome A. Hogsette, (904) 769-0210

Stable flies are also serious pests of
animals in dairy barns and feedlots. In
these restricted areas, the flies can be
virtually eliminated using calcium cyana-
mide, a nitrogen fertilizer. The compound was 100% effective in killing
stable fly larvae in manure. No objectionable residue remains after treatment,
and the nitrogen-fortified manure can be
sold to help cover the cost of materials
and labor.
U.S. Livestock Insect Lab, Kerrville, TX
F.W. Chamberlain, (512) 257-3566

Control of large roaches will be cheaper
and safer, now that an entomologist has
determined exactly where the critters
live. Typically, pesticides are sprayed
around the perimeters of an infested
home. But research has determined that
these roaches--often called water bugs or
palmetto bugs--actually set up housekeeping in tree holes, the canopies of palm
trees, and certain kinds of mulch. They
only migrate to people's homes when their
own quarters become too cramped. The
best way to control the pests, therefore,
is to place toxic bait or spray near
these key outdoor areas, which eliminates

unnecessary pesticides around the home.
Tests show this approach works.
Insects Affecting Man and Animals
Research Lab, Gainesville, FL
Richard J. Brenner, (904) 374-5937

Only two-thirds of beef cattle matings
result in pregnancy. Scientists now
believe the major cause is that immature
eggs fail to develop after fertilization.
Studies are being conducted to examine
factors that influence healthy egg production. This should lead to information
that can be used to improve cattle pregnancy rates by ranchers or cattle producers especially those using artificial
insemination and embryo transfer techniques. The information will also help
scientists better understand the biology
and genetics of eggs and early embryos to
make meat production more efficient.
Fort Keogh Livestock and Range Research
Lab, Miles City, MT
Robert B. Staigmiller, (406) 232-4970

Cattle grazing fescue grass infected with
endophytes, a toxin-producing fungus,
produce less milk and meat than normal
and often die. The disease can now be
detected more quickly--in 3 weeks instead
of 8. Plant tissues suspected of containing endophytes are first treated with
fungicides that control unwanted fungi
while allowing the endophyte fungus to
grow and be detected. The fungus,
Acremonium endophyte, infects about 35
million acres of tall fescue grass in the
southern United States.
National Forage Seed Production Center,
Corvallis, OR
Ronald E. Welty, (503) 757-4824

Several kinds of wasp, called seed chalcids, damage forage crops by laying their
eggs inside developing seeds of clover
and alfalfa. When the wasp larvae hatch,
they eat the seeds. Heavy infestations
of chalcids can destroy up to half a
forage crop, and insecticides are ineffective against them. Now ARS researchers have identified the plant odors
that attract the wasps--an important
first step in developing compounds that
will impair the seed chalcid's ability to
recognize its host plants.
National Forage Seed Production Center,
Corvallis, OR
James A. Kamm, (503) 757-4824

13

Brassica forages are fast growing, high
yielding, and very nutritious for livestock. Farmers and ranchers often have
difficulty establishing good stands,
especially in the southern Great Plains,
where it may be too dry or too cool for
the seeds to germinate. Recent tests
show that the problem can be overcome by
treating seeds with polyethylene glycol
(PEG) before spring planting. PEG helps
carry out the metabolic process up to the
germination point and speeds up germination once the seed is planted.
Forage and Livestock Research Lab, El
Reno, OK
Srinivas C. Rao, (405) 262-5291

Fat cells in animal fetuses are being
studied as a new approach to producing
leaner meat. Training high-powered
microscopes on pig fetuses, scientists
can determine the size and number of fat
cells, which may predetermine the amounts
of fat in meat products. The fetus is
taken from sows to study the mechanism
that regulates formation of fat cells,
which appear in the second half of the
114-day gestation period. Scientists who
hope to control fat in meat animals must
first identify how genetics, nutrition,
and hormone levels influence fat composition and development.
Richard B. Russell Agricultural Research
Center, Athens, GA
Dennis Campion, (404) 546-3226

The protein content of soybeans--already
the major source of supplemental protein
in animal diets--is getting a boost with
the help of 12 new germplasm lines developed by ARS researchers. The new beans
are about half protein, up to 10% more
than in commonly grown soybeans.
Soybean and Nitrogen Fixation Research,
Raleigh, NC
Thomas E. Carter, Jr., (919) 737-3267

"Expert" Information Systems

A watershed model (SWAM) simulates the
movement of water, sediment, and chemicals through a small watershed with mixed
land use. It tracks water and pollutants
through fields, channels, reservoirs, and
into ground water. SWAM, short for Small
Watershed Model, was developed by ARS to
help planners and employees of action
agencies like the Soil Conservation
Service assess the significance of non-
point source water pollution and to help
them evaluate alternative management
practices for controlling runoff. Since
SWAM is a state-of-the-art simulation
model, it will also help researchers
develop scale models for larger
watersheds.
Hydro-Ecosystems Group, Fort Collins, CO
E.H. Seely, (303) 221-0578

Custom-made weather predictions, thanks
to a new computer program, may soon help
farmers plan planting dates and other
tasks around the farm. In a demonstration program for South Dakota, a computer
uses weather data from 20 weather stations and considers current and historical weather conditions, including
precipitation, maximum and minimum temperatures, and solar radiation. The
program can make the information farm-
specific because it lets the user delete
data from nearby stations that are wetter
or drier than the farm. The manual
explaining the technical aspects of the
program, expected to be available in
about a year, will permit others to
develop similar programs for their
states. Such information could also be
useful to urban planners.
Aridland Watershed Management Research
Unit, Tucson, AZ
David A. Woolhiser, (602) 629-6381

ROOTSIMU is a computer model that predicts soybean root growth by simulating
water movement and water uptake under
various weather conditions. Because the
model uses small time increments, it can
simulate short- and long-term changes in
rates of crop growth. It can also illus-
trate differences between irrigated and

14

nonirrigated plants. Scientists can obtain software for the model in such scientific computer languages as FORTRAN, CSMP, and ACSL.
Crop Management Systems Research, Urbana, IL
Morris G. Huck, (217) 333-4370

Swine breeders will soon be able to improve production efficiency with the help of a computer program called the Swine Testing and Genetic Evaluation System (STAGES). It enables breeders of purebreds and prospective buyers of breeding stock to compare various genetic traits among animals in a herd. In a few years, with more data, comparisons may be made across herds. The National Association of Swine Records, the National Pork Producers Council, and USDA's Extension Service helped fund the work that was carried out by ARS and Purdue University researchers.
Roman L. Hruska U.S. Meat Animal Research Center, Clay Center, NE
Dewey L. Harris, (402) 762-3241

Qua

Quarterly Report
of Selected Research Projects

United States
Department of
Agriculture

 Agricultural
Research
Service

July 1 to September 30, 1986

CONTENTS

New & Improved Products

Starch from surplus corn may be the key
ingredient for the first biodegradable
plastic mulch. Starch-plastic films could
replace plastic mulches currently in use,
which are made only from petroleum-based
chemicals. The black film protects tomatoes and other high-value crops from weeds
and drought, extend the growing season by
warming the soil earlier in the spring,
and help farmers produce an earlier crop
at a good price. Although the starch-
plastic film costs a little more to produce and market than the pure plastic, its
ability to biodegrade offsets the expense
of having to dispose of it--about $100 an
acre--and it doesn't harm the environment.
A successful pilot run has been completed
by a commercial manufacturing firm.
(PATENT)
Northern Research Center, Peoria, IL
Felix H. Otey/William M. Doane, (309) 685-
4011, Ext. 356

Note: A scientist familiar with each
research project is listed for further
information. If the scientist is
unavailable, other scientists at the
same telephone number may be equally
familiar with the work.

Items marked with the word PATENT are
being patented by ARS. For more
information contact Ann Whitehead,
National Patent Program, Bldg. 005,
Rm. 401, Beltsville Agricultural
Research Center, Beltsville, MD 20705,
(301) 344-2786.

Citrus fruits use a weapon of their own to
fight fruit flies, and scientists hope to
make the ammunition last longer. The
flies do their worst damage as the peel
softens during ripening. Oils in the
peels can kill off the eggs and larvae,
scientists have found. But oil content
drops as the peel ripens making the fruit
more susceptible to attack. In tests to
slow the peel's aging, scientists in
Florida, Israel, and Peru sprayed gibberellic acid--a natural plant hormone--on
orange and grapefruit trees before the
fruits changed from green to their ripe
color. This made the peel more resistant
to the insects, but did not affect ripening. The hormone may become part of a new
strategy to combat fruit flies.
Insect Attractants, Behavior, and Basic
Biology Research Lab, Gainesville, FL
Patrick D. Greany, (904) 374-5763

Vegetable oil from soybeans tastes rancid
if reused or stored in sunlight. Reducing
the off-flavor, caused by a fatty acid, is
costly. Scientists using traditional
plant breeding have cut the linolenic acid
content from 9% to 3%. As a step to
eliminating this fatty acid, they are
using genetic engineering to examine an
oil-making enzyme in soybeans. When they
discover how the enzyme works, they may be
able to regulate oil and linolenic acid
content. That research could lead to new
soybeans whose oil is suited to specific
cooking and industrial uses. Soybeans are
the leading world source of edible vegetable oils; producing and processing them
is a multibillion-dollar industry in the
United States.
Soybean and Nitrogen Fixation Research,
Raleigh, NC
Richard F. Wilson, (919) 737-3267

Moths and beetles that attack peanuts in
warehouses are usually repelled by pesticides, but they are rapidly developing
resistance to malathion and other chemicals. So scientists are trying a new
approach--tiny parasitic wasps and predators that prey on moths and beetles. In

one study, two parasites, Trichogramma and Bracon, used together reduced the Indian meal moth by 85% and the almond moth by 98%. These are the two major insect pests of stored peanuts in Georgia. If commercial tests are successful, the parasites and predators may provide a natural, nonchemical way to protect stored peanuts.
Stored Product Insects Research and Development Lab, Savannah, GA
John H. Brower, (912) 233-7981

With record farm surpluses, the conversion of crops into medicines, clothing, acrylic plastics, and paints may be an idea whose time has come. Someday, bacteria may play a role in turning surplus corn, soybeans, and other crops into synthetic polymers* for making plastics and other industrial products. ARS has patented the most promising of five tested strains of a bacterium (Klebsiella pneumoniae) that changed up to 84% of glycerol--a soybean byproduct--into a chemical used to make polymers. The strain worked almost three times faster than other known strains. Currently, industry uses petroleum to produce polymers. A future rise in oil prices could make surplus U.S. crops a good alternative source for making polymers. (Reported in the Dec. 1985 Quarterly.) (PATENT)
Northern Research Center, Peoria, IL
Patricia J. Slininger, (309) 685-4011, Ext. 286
*Giant molecules formed by the union of smaller molecules.

Contraband foods and plants in luggage from abroad can be spotted by an experimental video and X-ray system. The United States bans these foods and plants because they may contain foreign insects or diseases not found here that could wipe out our crops or livestock. The system can help USDA inspectors at airports quickly screen luggage of arriving passengers for illegal meats, fruits, vegetables, and other foods and plants. The patented experimental system uses a combination of X-ray, computer, and video to detect food-shaped objects in luggage. The system can scan one bag about every 3 seconds, alerting inspectors to those bags that need to be hand-searched and eliminating the need to hand-search hundreds of other bags free

of illegal items. In tests at San Francisco International Airport, the equipment has detected oranges, fresh mangoes hidden in tin cans, cookies with an illegal meat filling, partly cooked duck eggs, and similar contraband. (PATENT)
Western Research Center, Albany, CA
Thomas F. Schatzki, (415) 486-3407

Kidney dialysis machines may one day rely on surplus starch from the Nation's store of nearly 15 billion bushels of corn. These life-saving machines separate toxic substances from blood. A new ARS patented method to convert a gelatin starch-plastic blend into a semipermeable membrane could replace cellulose or petroleum-based synthetic polymers. These membranes can filter large particles out of solutions and have medical, industrial, and research uses. More research is needed to determine the method's capabilities. Starch would come from crops such as corn, wheat, rice, and tapioca. (PATENT)
Northern Research Center, Peoria, IL
Felix H. Otey, (309) 685-4011, Ext. 356

Cleaner cotton means more money for producers and fewer problems for processors. ARS scientists and a firm in North Carolina came up with a way to clean cotton lint, and the textile industry is already using it. The method uses a multicylinder design with carding components that disentangle and align the cotton fibers without damaging them. Conventional, gin-type lint cleaners have only one cylinder and no carding components. In tests, the new cleaner removed more dirt and dust from cotton lint than three stages of conventional cleaning. It improves lint's market value for the producer and reduces dust problems for the processor. Researchers are now looking at ways to increase the capacity of the new cleaner. (PATENT)
Cotton Ginning Research, Lubbock, TX
Roy V. Baker, (806) 746-5353

Spoilage in liquid eggs, used in baked goods, custards, and other products, can be detected more quickly and objectively with new chemical tests. Food inspectors now rely on odor or bacteriological tests. Agency scientists are using liquid and gas chromatography to analyze eggs for two chemical substances present at higher

levels in spoiled liquid eggs. The tests will be especially helpful when eggs are just beginning to spoil and odor may not be present. If further research confirms the preliminary findings, inspectors with the USDA's Agricultural Marketing Service may be able to use the methods for on-the-spot tests.
Food Flavor Quality Research, Southern Research Center, New Orleans, LA
Mona L. Brown/Cletus E. Morris, (504) 589-7514

Grapefruit and orange juices from early season, unripened fruit, often give consumers more "pucker" than they bargained for. That astringence, as well as a bitter or sour taste, is due to several groups of compounds that scientists found in high levels in the juices. Processors can remove most of these flavor-damaging compounds by using a centrifuge to separate most of the pulp from the liquid. Juice from about 500,000 tons of early-season grapefruit and 900,000 tons of early oranges could be improved by this procedure. Several citrus processors have already adopted it. (PATENT)
Citrus and Subtropical Products Lab, Winter Haven, FL
James H. Tatum, (813) 293-4133

Beef carcasses can be cleaned more quickly and efficiently with a patented automated system that cleans them as they move down the packinghouse line. A high-pressure shower of vinegar and water kills more than 90% of the aerobic bacteria on the meat. Unlike chlorine solutions the industry uses now, the new system also slows down spoilage during refrigeration. Recently tested in an Illinois packinghouse, the vinegar shower could save meatpackers $30 million a year and could better control organisms that cause food poisoning. (PATENT)
Bioengineering Research, Columbia, MO
Maynard E. Anderson, (314) 875-5355

What odor and flavor essences make the perfect tasting apple? To answer this question, researchers are using gas cbromatography to measure minute levels of volatile compounds—down to parts per billion. These compounds, which can change the flavor of fruit, are affected by weather and horticultural practices.

Scientists hope to use data from these measurements to advise growers on how to best manage their orchards—prune, irrigate, and fertilize them—to improve apple flavor.
Tree Fruit Research Lab, Wenatchee, WA
Stephen Drake, (509) 662-4317

Fermented sweetpotatoes show promise as a commercial source of ethyl alcohol and a high-protein residue. Adding a commercial enzyme to a mix of potatoes and water yields 8% by weight of alcohol after fermentation. The fuel grade alcohol can be used in pharmaceutical or industrial chemicals or as a liquid fuel, and the residue may be a high protein food for people or animals. The sweetpotato is a promising crop for energy production because it continues to grow bigger during its long growing season. An acre of tubers can yield 1,000 gallons of alcohol, compared with 250 to 300 gallons per acre for corn.
Plant Proteins Research, Northern Research Center, Peoria, IL
Y. Victor Wu, (309) 685-4011, Ext. 328

Vegetable oil bottlers can borrow the bright orange and yellow coloring in fruits and vegetables to keep the oil from developing off-flavor when exposed to light. Only a few drops (5 to 10 parts per million) of the natural coloring, beta carotene, reduces off-flavor of soybean oil in clear bottles without affecting its color. Besides improving the flavor, beta carotene adds vitamin A. It can also be used to preserve the flavor of fat-containing foods like potato chips.
Vegetable Oil Research, Northern Research Center, Peoria, IL
Kathleen A. Warner, (309) 685-4011

Domestic sugarbeet processors, nearly all of them, now use a safer test to find out how much sugar is in the beets. Sugar content is the basis for setting the price processors pay to beet growers. Until 5 years ago, the industry used lead for sugar testing, but environmental concern prompted ARS scientists to develop a reliable test that uses aluminum instead. Now, processors can quickly determine sucrose content by adding aluminum to beet juice samples. To uncover other secrets of the sugarbeet, scientists often make

several analyses of the same sample. But, adding a metal--lead or aluminum--can make further analyses impossible, so scientists are developing a new sucrose test that would not rely on a metal.
Sugarbeet Research, Fort Collins, CO
Susan S. Martin, (303) 482-7717

The "bugging" of apples may one day help detect wormy apples in commercial packing lines. Scientists have developed a device that eavesdrops on codling moth larvae as they eat or move about inside an apple. Consumers rarely find these worms in apples, but scientists plan to develop a system that can screen out any "bad apples" that may have slipped past regular insect control methods. Now the scientists are trying to filter out background noise--such as conveyor belts--so they can listen in on many apples at once and even detect motionless larvae.
Insect Ecology and Pest Management Research, Yakima, WA
Harold H. Toba, (509) 575-5981

Sugarcane's sugar content can be measured faster with near infrared spectroscopy. In this process, used for years to analyze chemicals, a special meter shines an invisible light on sugarcane to reveal how much sucrose, a sugar, is in the cane. Using the new 5-minute analysis, sugar manufacturers can know almost immediately how much to pay farmers for their sugarcane. Scientists are working with Louisiana State University and a commercial firm to develop a less expensive sugar meter which will help the sugarcane industry automate sugar mills.
Composition and Properties Research, Southern Research Center, New Orleans, LA
Alfred D. French, (504) 589-7500

Crispness in apples and other fruits is due in part to pectin, a substance in plant cell walls that helps strengthen them. Little is known about the changes in pectin during fruit ripening, but scientists can now measure changes in the polyuronides--the building blocks of pectin--within intact plant cell walls. They believe that, like a zipper, the polyuronides bind together with metals the plant uses as nutrients. The shape of these building blocks can alter as temperature and water levels change in the

plant. The new technique should help scientists understand the role polyuronides play in the softening process in certain fruit.
Plant Science Research, Eastern Research Center, Philadelphia, PA
Peter L. Irwin, (215) 233-6420

Bales of cotton usually contain debris--leaves, broken and immature seeds, and bark. The cotton industry needs a better method to determine how much debris is present when cotton is graded for marketing. Scientists believe they have found this method--shining near infrared light on samples taken from a cotton bale. The light reflects differently on the debris, and these differences are recorded on a computer printout. A bale can be analyzed in less than 30 seconds--more precisely than current methods of visual inspection. If further tests are successful, USDA's Agricultural Marketing Service and the cotton industry could use this method to select the best way to clean cotton.
Cotton Quality Research Station, Clemson, SC
Robert A. Taylor (803) 656-2488

Flashing lights and sounds can tell how strong textiles are. Using light and sound, researchers have indirectly measured the tensile strength of textiles--the cloth fibers' resistance to being pulled lengthwise--without damaging them. In the procedure, lights of certain infrared wavelengths flash off and on more than 100 times per second at a cotton sample in a sealed chamber. Cotton fibers emit sounds that indicate how much strength they have lost through aging or abuse. Fibers artificially aged and weakened by heating at 190°C emitted sounds similar to those produced by 800-year-old fibers from archaeological sites in the Southwest.
Plant Polymer Research, Northern Research Center, Peoria, IL
J. Michael Gould, (309) 685-4011, Ext. 318

Apples resist softening better during storage when treated with salts. After picking Delicious apples, scientists treated them with one of three salts--calcium, magnesium, or strontium. They found that after 5 months of storage, calcium chloride was most effective in

4

reducing decay and maintaining fruit firmness and overall quality. Commercial apple growers are beginning to use this salt to reduce damage to apples after they are picked. An estimated 30% of fruit is damaged by softening and other problems during storage.
Horticultural Crops Quality Lab, Beltsville, MD
William S. Conway, (301) 344-3128

Crop Production & Protection

A "sex change" may turn a wild cousin of corn into a new grain crop. Male flowers of one type of eastern gamagrass, which grows mainly in the Southeast and Mexico, have changed spontaneously to female and begun producing seed, increasing seed production by about 2,500%. Scientists believe the change results from a mutation—one gene or group of genes being replaced by another. They believe the "new" genes are actually old ones that had long been dormant. With the increased number of seeds, and a higher protein content than corn, this cousin of corn could become a nutritious grain crop for both humans and animals. The new type of gamagrass would first have to be bred for even higher seed production. So far, scientists have produced varieties yielding twice as many seeds as the first new type they studied.
Southern Plains Range Research Station, Woodward, OK
Chester Dewald, (405) 256-7449

A fungus that safely controls sicklepod—a weed that costs soybean farmers about $4 million each year—is being developed commercially. Sprayed on experimental soybean fields, Alternaria cassiae infects and kills 98% of sicklepod, which mostly affects soybeans in the Southeast. Researchers say that the best time to apply the fungus is when the weed is still a seedling, because mature sicklepod resists the fungus. One application per season is usually enough, because sicklepod seedlings that sprout later are shadowed by adult soybean plants and can't compete for nutrients, water, and sunlight. (PATENT)
Southern Weed Science Lab, Stoneville, MS
C. Boyette, (601) 686-2311

Roadside plants, two wasps, and a mite could help prevent the tarnished plant bug from entering cottonfields and destroying as much as 40% of the crop. The bug prefers other plants, but will venture into cottonfields if food is scarce. Establishing roadside plants like daisies near cottonfields provides the hungry bug with enough preferred food to distract it from the cotton. Research continues to determine what roadside plants will best keep the pest satisfied. Also, the wasps and mite could keep the bug from proliferating. One wasp, Anaphes ovijentatus, is a parasite of the bug's eggs, while immature stages of the mite Lasioerythraeus johnstoni and the wasp Peristenus stygicus are parasites of immature plant bugs. Later stages of the mite also eat older bugs.
Southern Field Crop Insect Management Lab, Stoneville, MS
O.P. Young/G.L. Snodgrass, (601) 686-2311
Biological Control of Insects Lab, Tucson, AZ
H.M. Graham, (602) 629-6220

Genetic traits of wheat and rice, the two most important foods globally, will be preserved for the future because seed samples from foreign countries are being stored at the National Seed Storage Laboratory. If presently used varieties are attacked by a new disease or insect, scientists would have available the germplasm to breed new traits into the two grains. Last year the lab accepted more than 2,000 wheat samples from Mexico; this year it will get another 2,000. Rice from the Philippines and sugarcane from Barbados will also arrive later this year.
National Seed Storage Lab, Fort Collins, CO
Dorris C. Clark, (303) 484-0402

Liquid nitrogen could be used to store more than two-thirds of the seed stored in temperature- and humidity-controlled rooms for one quarter of the current cost. Seeds are regrown periodically to replenish the stored samples that are beginning to lose the ability to germinate. Cryopreservation storage in liquid nitrogen at about -320°F extends the life of seed samples and reduces the number of times a seed type must be regrown. Regrowing seed is costly and risky since drought, insects, or diseases could kill

the only remaining supply. The National Seed Storage Laboratory now preserves seed of 34 major crops in liquid nitrogen vats. Scientists will test 1% of the 2,150 samples each year to ensure that germination never dips below 85%.
National Seed Storage Lab, Fort Collins, CO
Phillip C. Stanwood, (303) 484-0402

Corn plants can be tricked by a chemical into using less water early in the growing season. Then, just as ears are forming, plants make up for early deprivation by using more water. This practice increased yields by 15% at a test site where the normal precipitation, only 15 inches a year, is supplemented by 4 inches of irrigation water. Scientists applied a chemical growth regulator—a type of antigibberellin—to seed just before planting. This stunted growth for about 60 days so plants would leave some of the scarce water in the soil. After the chemical wore off, the plants resumed normal growth and used the water they shunned earlier.
Central Great Plains Research Station, Akron, CO
David C. Nielsen, (303) 345-2259

A protein discovered in soybean seeds, by telling scientists more about how bacteria fix nitrogen in plant roots, may eventually increase the efficiency of producing the bean. Scientists who purified the protein and described its molecular properties found that a plant-growth hormone called indoleacetic acid increases the protein's capacity to bind with sugars on the surface of the bacterium Rhizobium japonicum. These findings provide insights on how the bacterium and plant roots enable the plant to begin fixing nitrogen from the air, thus making its own nitrogen fertilizer. (PATENT)
Microbial Properties Research, Northern Research Center, Peoria, IL
Morey E. Slodki/Tsuneo Kaneshiro, (309) 685-4011, Exts. 246/243

The potato chip industry—a $3 billion annual business growing at the rate of 8% each year—prefers fresh, high quality potatoes to long-term stored ones. Researchers are developing a new, round white potato that can be grown in the South and resists two widespread diseases, southern bacterial wilt and bacterial soft rot. The new variety is expected to extend the early spring and summer harvest seasons, improve yields, and decrease production costs by about 20% to 25%, particularly in the Southeast. It may also give the South increased opportunity to meet the growing demand for chips. About 12% of total U.S. potato production goes into potato chips.
Vegetable Lab, Beltsville, MD
Raymon E. Webb, (301) 344-3380

A fungus that protects crops from disease may soon be available in a preparation that farmers can apply to the soil whenever necessary. Talaromyces flavus is a soilborne fungus that suppresses verticillium wilt, a costly disease of potatoes, cotton, eggplants, and other crops. But farmers can't rely on natural outbreaks of the fungus to occur at the right time. Technology has now been developed for mass-producing this beneficial fungus and packaging it in nutrients that give it a shelf life of several months or more. (PATENT)
Soilborne Disease Lab, Beltsville, MD
George C. Papavizas, (301) 344-3682

Range grass seed may soon be treated chemically to sprout within days rather than weeks after seeding. Scientists are looking at this and other ways to cut the germination time. In many areas in the West, the soil surface dries quickly after a rain and over 90% of the seeds die just after they begin to sprout roots. In greenhouse tests, scientists used chemicals to cut normal germination time of seeds from 7 days to about 24 hours. They are also studying the use of a gel to help protect seeds that have already sprouted from damage during planting for possible use in reclaiming ranges in the arid West.
High Plains Grasslands Research Station, Cheyenne, WY
Dennis M. Mueller, (307) 772-2433

Pecan trees can be grown with no change in nut yield or quality at lower cost and without harming the environment by using integrated pest management (IPM). In a yearlong study comparing IPM with conventional pest controls, scientists treated pecan trees only when plant tissues were

susceptible to disease or when insect populations exceeded certain limits. Under conventional control, insecticides and fungicides were applied routinely regardless of whether diseases or insects were present. Under IPM, pecan trees received three fewer insecticide and three fewer fungicide applications.
Southeastern Fruit and Tree Nut Research Lab, Byron, GA
Dennis Ring, (912) 956-5656

The sex scent--or pheromone--from the male papaya fruit fly has been synthesized and will be used as the first environmentally safe lure for females. This pest costs farmers in Florida and Texas $2,000 per acre each year in chemical insecticides. Male flies put out the pheromone when they are waiting to mate on a papaya. The scientists will place the synthetic phero-mone on a fake papaya covered with a sticky substance to trap females.   In lab tests, the phony papaya proved to have the right size, shape, and colors and will next be tested outdoors.
Insect Attractants, Behavior, and Basic Biology Research Lab, Gainesville, FL
Peter J. Landolt, (904) 374-5756

Potato-damaging insects may be eluding farmers in dry areas of Washington, Ore-gon, and Idaho. Researchers trying to control the Colorado potato beetle have found that the pest--thought to hibernate underground for only a year before emerg-ing to feast on potatoes--can stay under-ground up to 5 years. Scientists would like to force the insects to emerge so they can be destroyed. One way might be to irrigate growers' fields at specific times early in the season. Also, para-sites, such as the fungus Beauvaria bas-siana, and beneficial nematodes can help control the beetle.
Insect Ecology and Pest Management Re-search, Yakima, WA
Duane Biever, (509) 575-5877

Velvetleaf, one of most vexing weeds in American fields, fails to germinate when exposed to a chemical extracted from a wild plant called Eryngium paniculatum found in Uruguay. Velvetleaf is a major problem for soybean growers not wanting to endanger their crop by using pesticides. Lab tests have proven successful with this

natural plant extract; the next step is field testing.
Bioactive Constituents Lab, Northern Research Center, Peoria, IL
Gayland F. Spencer, (309) 685-4011, Ext. 347

Sugarbeets are now nearly four times more resistant to a root rot caused by a soil fungus, Rhizoctonia, than they were 20 years ago. This disease kills only about 4% of sugarbeets annually, although for some growers it can wipe out the entire crop. Last year, an ARS breeding line of resistant plants had 98% of its beets rated "harvestable," compared with 27% in the best commercial variety. Breeders will combine this disease resistance with other desirable traits, such as increased sugar yield, to provide new commercial varieties.
Sugarbeet Research, Fort Collins, CO
Richard J. Hecker, (303) 482-7717

A new sweetpotato that really isn't sweet can be used in place of white potatoes and can be readily grown in tropical regions where potato production has been difficult and costly. The new sweetpotato, as yet unnamed, was developed in Puerto Rico from multiple crosses of low-sweetness varie-ties. Compared with other sweetpotatoes, it contains only small amounts of beta amylase--the enzyme that converts starch to malt sugar during cooking. Several lines of this sweetpotato have now been developed, and their germplasm will soon be available to plant breeders.
Tropical Agriculture Research Station, Mayaguez, PR
Franklin W. Martin, (809) 834-2435

Worms in apples can be effectively killed with methyl bromide without affecting the fruit's quality. Test results are impor-tant to apple growers because they could lead to a certification process that uses methyl bromide to fumigate apples and other fruit exported to Japan. The Japa-nese don't buy American apples now for fear of importing the destructive codling moth in its larval stage. Experts believe Japan--where apples sell for nearly $1 apiece--represents a vast, untapped market for American fruit exports.
Tree Fruit Research Lab, Wenatchee, WA
Stephen Drake, (509) 662-4317

"The bends" injure divers who rise too quickly to the surface. Now the phenomenon that causes this problem is helping scientists understand how plants interact with disease-causing organisms. The bends occur when nitrogen in the blood expands as air pressure decreases. To simulate these conditions, scientists place plant tissues in a pressurized nitrogen gas chamber. When they remove the tissue, the gas in the cells expands and breaks them open, separating the fibrous cell walls. The new process is helping scientists learn how bacteria and fungi attack cells and why these pests harm certain plants and not others in cases of potato blight and other disease infections. Until now, it has been difficult to purify biologically active cell walls quickly for scientific research.
Plant Science Research, Eastern Research Center, Philadelphia, PA
Gerald Nagahashi/Thomas S. Seibles, (215) 233-6427

A 1-day test can identify different types of greenbugs. Learning quickly which kinds of greenbugs are present helps farmers know which resistant crop varieties to plant. Greenbugs are aphids that feed on wheat, sorghum, other crops, and grasses. Until now, identifying the differences has taken months of rearing and observing the insects. The new test is based on variations in the insects' enzymes that show their preference for host plants. Researchers are continuing to refine the test.
Sorghum Research, Lincoln, NE
S. Dean Kindler, (402) 471-5267

Cantaloups have been bred to resist downy and powdery mildew--diseases that cost farmers millions of dollars in fungicides each year. Developed jointly by ARS and Israeli researchers, the new cantaloup seeds have been distributed to commercial breeders and should be available to farmers in a few years. Future work with cantaloup includes developing one that requires little or no chemicals in its cultivation and researching soilborne diseases that affect it.
Vegetable Lab, Charleston, SC
Claude E. Thomas, (803) 556-0840

Apple breeders have produced new apple germplasm with resistance to disease and insects. One type of apple resists apple scab, the plum curculio weevil, and the European red mite; two others resist apple scab and the codling moth. Once plants are bred from the resistant germplasm, growers will be able to grow the juicy, tart-to-sweet apples at less cost and with less pesticide use, and they will lower the chance of pests developing resistance to pesticides.
Insect Control Research, West Lafayette, IN
Hilary F. Goonewardene (317) 494-4607

A hormone in the corn earworm has been isolated that could help control this major pest of corn and cotton. The H-AKH hormone regulates essential fats and probably regulates sugars that energize the worm. Scientists will study the hormone's structure to find and clone genes that control its production. Altering these genes would upset the insect's development.
Livestock Insects Lab, Beltsville, MD
Howard Jaffe, (301) 344-2474

Virus-free apple trees are being propagated commercially from tissue cultures, thereby cutting from 3 years to 5 months the time it takes to produce plantable trees. With tissue culture, apple shoots are grown from tissue to plantlets and then rooted in small slugs of a nutrient medium. Gala, a new apple variety, this year became the first to be commercially propagated from tissue culture and marketed. ARS scientists perfected the micropropagation technology and tested it for 7 years before it was commercialized.
Fruit Lab, Beltsville, MD
Richard H. Zimmerman, (301) 344-4647

Geneticists have discovered an unusual gene in a wild Argentine potato species, Solanum commersonii. Because of this gene, the 24 chromosomes in this wild potato can duplicate themselves to match the 48 found in common commercial potatoes. This gene is highly sought after because potato breeders can use it to breed commercial potato varieties with all of their parental traits. This would transfer intact such desired characteristics as resistance to disease, insects,

and frost. It could also result in increased yields of 10% to 30%.
Vegetable Research, Madison, WI
Robert E. Hanneman, Jr., (608) 262-1399

A tall fescue strain having a gene for larger leaves can help suppress weeds and thus reduce the need for herbicides and tillage on this forage grass. Compared with a strain lacking this gene, the strain having it produced up to 73% more forage and allowed 24% fewer velvetleaf plants, a major weed. Without competition from weeds, both strains produced equal amounts of forage. Plant breeders can also select for this high leaf-area trait in breeding programs for other crops with weed problems.
North Central Soil Research Lab,
Morris, MN
Frank Forcella, (612) 589-3411

Tuskegee crape-myrtle is the first of a colorful new wave of these belles of the southern landscape. It and other varieties on the way are hybrids that for the first time resist mildew. Tuskegee has dark pink blossoms and mottled-gray bark. By 1988, at least 13 more hybrid crape-myrtles will be released to commercial nurseries from Maryland south to Florida and west to California. ARS conducts the only crape-myrtle breeding program in the world.
U.S. National Arboretum, Washington, DC
Donald R. Egolf, (202) 475-4862

Animal Production & Protection

Miniature swine, three selected lines of them, are helping scientists determine the genetic basis for parasite and disease resistance in livestock. These inbred swine have different versions of a gene complex called the major histocompatibility complex (MHC), which regulates an animal's immune system. Understanding how MHC works could lead not only to breeding disease-resistant livestock but also to designing superior vaccines against animal viruses or parasites.
Helminthic Diseases Lab, Beltsville, MD
Joan Lunney, (301) 344-1768

ARS and University of Florida entomologists are conducting a crash investigation of the Asian cockroach, a superpest that probably invaded the United States at the Port of Tampa. What they have found so far is bad news for the householder. The roach breeds outside in litter and lawns and, worse yet, can fly into homes, which it generally does during the hour after sundown. It resembles the German cockroach, which is unable to fly. Many insecticides that kill it are registered for use only in or near the home. Furthermore, scientists fear the roach will quickly develop resistance to these chemicals. Research is underway to develop effective controls for this new pest.
Insects Affecting Man and Animals Research Lab, Gainesville, FL
Richard Brenner, (904) 374-5937

Leaner chickens at the supermarket may become a reality, thanks to a new application of a physical principle discovered in the 17th century. The pycnometer measures the volume of air displaced by a chicken in a sphere; dividing the chicken's weight by its volume gives its density. Since lean chicken meat is denser than fat chicken meat, this harmless method will allow scientists to efficiently pick poultry with low fat for breeding experiments. Previously, chickens had to be killed or subjected to complicated tests to measure their density.
Poultry Research Lab, Georgetown, DE
Vernon A. Garwood, (302) 856-0046

A small beetle from Austria is the newest insect to join the ranks of those imported into the United States to attack leafy spurge. This weed pest has taken over more than 2-1/2 million acres of grazing land, mainly in the Western United States. The combination of control costs and losses in cattle production add up to $20 to $30 million each year for farmers and ranchers. This summer, scientists placed the beetles on spurge plants in a Wyoming test plot. They anticipate that the beetle, which feeds on spurge in Europe, will adapt and help halt the spread of spurge here. As an adult, the quarter-inch-long beetle eats spurge

leaves; in its larval stage it eats the weed's small roots.
Plant Protection Research, Western Research Center, Albany, CA
Robert W. Pemberton, (415) 486-3757

Ranchers could increase profits by about 50% if they provide cows and calves with complementary pastures--of crested wheatgrass, for example--along with native range grasses. Scientists have developed equations to calculate the best ratio of complementary pasture to rangeland--for example, 1 acre of crested wheatgrass to 4 or 5 acres of native range--for maximum profit in southeastern Wyoming. Crested wheatgrass starts growing earlier in the spring than native range grasses and provides livestock with needed nutrition. These pastures can last for 40 years on good land. The equations can also be used in other cattle-producing areas in the West by adapting them to other complementary forages.
High Plains Grasslands Research Station, Cheyenne, WY
Richard H. Hart, (307) 772-2433

Anaplasmosis is a blood disease of cattle and sheep that is spread by ticks. Each year it costs the U.S. beef industry alone $100 to $200 million. Researchers supported by Federal and State funds have developed a "subunit" vaccine containing a specific protein from the surface of the parasite that induces neutralizing antibodies. In laboratory tests, the new vaccine appears promising. A commercial vaccine may be only a few years away.
Animal Diseases Research Lab, Pullman, WA
John Gorham, (509) 335-7321

Anaplasmosis can be spread from the pregnant ewe to the fetus. It is not a widespread disease of sheep but can cause anemia and death. Scientists found that in 3 of 20 pregnant sheep with anaplasmosis, the disease crossed the ewe's placental barrier and infected lambs. This new information is important in diagnosing the disease. Previously, such transmission was only known to occur in cattle. Animal health personnel and sheep producers should be aware that new cases of sheep anaplasmosis may occur through the placenta without the presence of blood-feeding ticks or biting flies--

usually believed to be the main transmitters of the disease.
Animal Diseases Research, Caldwell, ID
Jerry L. Zaugg, (208) 454-8657

Frozen precooked chicken products such as TV dinners and pot pies sometimes have off-flavors when heated. These flavors are caused by chemical changes in the meat when it is cooked and stored. Scientists suspect that iron, present in low levels in poultry meat, may act as a catalyst to cause the off-flavors. They are studying different forms of iron found in cooked meat and are looking for ways to block iron from contributing to the off-flavors. With further research, they may be able to advise industry on how to improve the flavor of these chicken products.
Poultry Meat Quality and Safety Research, Athens, GA
Catharina Ang, (404) 546-3493

"Where does milk come from?" is a question asked not only by curious children but also by scientists. Researchers want to know how a cow's mammary gland cells actually produce milk. Several years ago, the scientists isolated the hormone prolactin--the switch that starts milk production in pregnant cows. They have now discovered that prolactin prepares the cow's mammary gland to produce milk by attaching to and changing the shape of a molecule on the surface of the gland's cells. Knowing how prolactin binds to this switch and stimulates mammary gland cells will help scientists better understand how cows and other mammals produce milk.
Milk Secretion and Mastitis Lab, Beltsville, MD
Anthony V. Capuco, (301) 344-1672

Dairy goat breeders now have access to a "computer mating" list that will enable them to match the best bucks with the best does. For 3 years, ARS has cooperated with the American Dairy Goat Association in publishing national evaluations and breeding lists of dairy goat bucks. The agency has now extended the procedures to include doe listings. The Nation's half million dairy goats, mostly on smaller family farms, produce milk on a more varied diet than cows require. Also, many people allergic to cow's milk can safely

10

consume goat's milk and cheeses. The new listings could help improve production for the dairy goat industry.
Animal Improvement Programs Lab, Beltsville, MD
George R. Wiggans, (301) 344-2334

An improved trichinosis test developed by ARS will be marketed by a commercial company. Swine trichinosis is caused by a parasitic worm and can be transmitted to humans in undercooked pork. The new blood test is about 96% accurate. Human incidence of this disease is low in the United States, but the test could boost export sales to countries that do not buy U.S. pork because of the potential presence of trichina in fresh pork. The test should also benefit foreign countries with high rates of swine trichinosis. (PATENT)
Helminthic Diseases Lab, Beltsville, MD
H. Ray Gamble, (301) 344-1770/Kenneth D. Murrell, (301) 344-2195

Chickens sometimes have bacteria in their intestines that don't harm them but can cause food poisoning in humans. Contamination can occur if during processing chicken meat comes into contact with these salmonella bacteria. Scientists are studying ways to keep the bacteria out of the chicken's gut before processing. In lab tests, day-old chicks that had no salmonella bacteria in their guts were treated with harmless fecal bacteria. Several days later they were exposed to salmonella. These chicks were 90% less susceptible to retaining the salmonella in their intestines--possibly because the harmless bacteria became attached to the intestine and made it more difficult for the salmonella to take hold. Scientists hope to conduct field tests to see if this procedure can be used commercially.
Poultry Meat Quality and Safety Research, Athens, GA
Leroy C. Blankenship, (404) 546-3478

Human Nutrition

A sweet tooth can undo the cardiovascular benefits of eating a little less fat, cholesterol, and salt and a little more fiber. Researchers found that men and women on this test diet had lower total cholesterol levels when complex carbohydrates supplied twice as many calories as sugars. But when the carbohydrate makeup was reversed--and sugars supplied twice as many calories as complex carbohydrates--circulating cholesterol increased, specifically, the form linked with atherosclerosis (hardening of the arteries).
Carbohydrate Nutrition Lab, Beltsville Human Nutrition Research Center, Beltsville, MD
Sheldon Reiser, (301) 344-2396

Makers of infant formulas are beginning to change the starch makeup in response to recent findings on the ability of infants to digest segments of this important energy source. A study of 1-month-olds showed that an enzyme secreted by their intestinal cells plays a larger role in digesting glucose polymers than previously thought. This enzyme works best on short chains of glucose, but infant formulas contain a substantial amount of longer chains. Although healthy infants can handle the longer chains, premature infants and those with gastrointestinal problems have difficulty. Companies are now putting more of the shorter polymers in infant formulas to make digestion easier for all infants.
Weaning Lab, Children's Nutrition Research Center, Houston, TX
Robert Shulman, (713) 799-6013

Bone building is a physiological balancing act among vitamins, minerals, and hormones. The body converts dietary vitamin D (calciferol) into its active form--a hormone that helps the body absorb calcium from food and grow bone. Researchers studied how the two forms of vitamin D interact with dietary zinc, using young female rats as models for menstruating women. Rats fed the active form of vitamin D had more bone growth than those fed the dietary form. But if zinc intake was five times greater than the amount considered adequate, it prevented the increased growth. Consuming excessive levels of zinc is ill advised.
Vitamin and Mineral Nutrition Lab, Beltsville Human Nutrition Research Center, Beltsville, MD
J. Cecil Smith, (301) 344-2022

Premature infants need more protein and minerals than mother's milk provides, so

11

hospitals feed them special formulas containing the extra nutrients. But these formulas lack infection-fighting substances found in breast milk. To retain this natural protection and provide adequate nutrients, researchers are concentrating protein and minerals from a "bank" of human breast milk and adding them to the premie's mother's milk. Early trials with premies indicate that fortified breast milk has the same nutritional value as special formulas and supports the same rate of growth. More than 200,000 premies are born each year.
Lactation Lab, Children's Nutrition Research Center, Houston, TX
Richard Schanler, (713) 799-6004

Two new synthetic sugars could find their way into future food products because of their potential health benefits. Researchers have developed methods to produce large amounts of maltulose and lactulose from agricultural byproducts like cornstarch and whey. In feeding studies, rats manufactured less fat from maltulose than from sucrose (table sugar). They could also digest 40% of their carbohydrates as maltulose without any gastrointestinal problems. Lactulose, on the other hand, is indigestible. But because it acidifies the colon—a condition which has several known health benefits and reportedly may reduce risk of colon cancer—lactulose could be used to sweeten gum or mints and thus be consumed in very small amounts. Both synthetic sugars are sweeter and more water soluble than their precursors—maltose and lactose—and are therefore more desirable for food processing.
Carbohydrate Nutrition Lab, Beltsville Human Nutrition Research Center, Beltsville, MD
Otho Michaelis, (301) 344-2093

How much zinc does the body actually absorb from different foods? Bioavailability is difficult to measure accurately, and recent efforts to standardize the measurements for zinc demonstrate how many conditions can affect the results. In studies with rats, the amount of zinc absorbed by rats depended not only on the type of food, but also on the amount of zinc in the meal and on the level of zinc the rats had become accustomed to eating.

Depending on these conditions, they absorbed zinc from chicken, milk, or peanut butter 20% to 40% better than from navy beans or soy flour. (PATENT)
Grand Forks Human Nutrition Research Center, Grand Forks, ND
Janet R. Makalko, (701) 795-8328

Analyzing trace elements in food, blood, or tissue samples takes only a few seconds with a precision instrument, but preparing the samples for analysis is a multistep job that requires much time and attention. A new method combines the heat and acid treatment of samples into one simple procedure that can free up as much as 90% of a technician's time and improve the accuracy of the analyses. Several trace elements can be determined at one time, using relatively inexpensive equipment already present in most labs involved in mineral analyses.
Vitamin and Mineral Nutrition Lab, Beltsville Human Nutrition Research Center, Beltsville, MD
Claude Veillon, (301) 344-2010

Fiber can sometimes interfere with the body's ability to absorb needed nutrients from foods. A recent study with rats showed that the particle size of the fiber may sometimes be the culprit. Coarsely ground wheat bran—like that found in some whole-grain breads and breakfast cereals—interacted with vitamin E in the intestine so that the vitamin was not as readily available. But finely ground wheat bran—like that in whole wheat flour—didn't interfere with the vitamin's availability. Unlike E, vitamin A availability was not affected by particle size.
Food Quality Research, Western Research Center, Albany, CA
Talwinder Kahlon, (415) 486-3305

A healthy cardiovascular system requires selenium. This trace element regulates the balance of prostaglandins—hormonelike substances, some of which are manufactured by blood platelets and blood vessel walls that, respectively, promote or inhibit blood clotting. Rats on a selenium-deficient diet produced more clot-promoting prostaglandins and fewer clot-inhibiting prostaglandins than rats given adequate selenium. Most North Americans

are already getting enough selenium in
their diets and should not need supplements. The safe and adequate intake is 50
to 200 micrograms per day.
Lipid Nutrition Lab, Beltsville Human
Nutrition Research Center, Beltsville, MD
Norberta Schoene, (301) 344-2388

Daycare costs many families as much as or
more than they spend for clothing or
health care, an analysis of consumer
expense statistics shows. In 1980-81,
nearly 60% of working couples with preschool children paid for child care which
averaged 6% of their total expenses.
Clothing and health care costs averaged 6%
and 4%, respectively. Married women with
preschoolers have been the fastest growing
segment in the work force. With the trend
expected to continue, the demand for child
care is likely to increase. Just under
half of the Nation's working single parents paid for preschool child care, which
averaged 10% of their total expenses.
This figure reflects both higher actual
costs of child care and lower incomes of
single parents. This information, along
with other research on the changing spending patterns of families, will be used by
the Joint Economic Committee of Congress
for a new report on the economic status
and choices of American families.
Family Economics Research, Hyattsville,
MD
Frankie N. Schwenk, (301) 436-8461

Blood platelets--the disk-shaped bodies
involved in blood clotting--are also very
sensitive indicators of a person's intake
of vitamin E (tocopherol). Researchers
developed this nutritional test using
rats, and a followup human study confirmed
that tocopherol levels in platelets
closely reflected dietary vitamin E
levels. The new test fills a void because
tocopherol in blood serum is no longer
considered an accurate index of the body's
vitamin E.
Lipid Nutrition Lab, Beltsville Human
Nutrition Research Center, Beltsville, MD
Joseph T. Judd, (301) 344-2014

Scientific Information Systems

A computer program that can cut irrigation
energy costs by about 15% in Colorado has
been upgraded for use in the Pacific
Northwest. First developed to schedule
irrigation on 2,200 acres that had 15
groundwater pumps, the program now controls water pumped from the Columbia River
and diverted through a maze of auxiliary
pumps and pipes to irrigate 12,000 acres
on the Oregon side of the river. Further
testing in the area will show the program's adaptability to other irrigation
systems.
Irrigation and Drainage Research, Fort
Collins, CO
Dale F. Heermann, (303) 491-8229

Major outbreaks of ticks, mosquitoes,
roaches, and other insects--and the diseases they transmit--may one day be de-
feated by State and local officials armed
with personal computers. Scientists are
developing computer models to predict an
insect's population growth and how best to
control it. So far, scientists have
completed a model for the Lone Star tick.
This biting pest infests public parks and
can carry Rocky Mountain spotted fever and
other diseases. The tick also causes
weight loss in calves. For 3 years the
model has accurately predicted population
trends in three infested areas, and testing continues. Scientists plan models for
cockroaches, fire ants, and cattle grubs.
They are already working on models for
ticks, mosquitoes, and diseases carried by
mosquitoes, such as malaria and yellow and
dengue fevers.
Insects Affecting Man and Animals Research
Lab, Gainesville, FL
Gary A. Mount, (904) 374-5900

Airborne video cameras can show farmers
and ranchers where the best grazing lands
are, and they can do so in minutes--a big
plus compared with the weeks it may take
to process data from satellites. ARS
scientists have found that separate black-
and-white video images, made at several
thousand feet through special (red and
near-infrared) filters, can be combined
into one picture that reveals how well
rangeland grasses are growing and how many
cattle they can support. The combined

13

image is so detailed that scientists can tell the grasses from the weeds and can spot drought, insect infestations, and other factors important to rangeland management.
Remote Sensing Lab, Weslaco, TX
James H. Everitt, (512) 968-5533

A computerized network that brings news about molecular biology and genetic engineering to biomedical researchers is now being used to improve crops and livestock as well. ARS has established a link with the commercial network, called Bionet, which establishes instant electronic communications so that the agency can share findings among research locations and among researchers in the medical world. The network will be especially helpful for scientists who investigate the molecular structures of various genes and the hereditary codes which the genes pass on to new cells.
Agricultural Systems Research Institute, Beltsville, MD
Patricia Laster, (301) 344-1845

Six priorities for information systems and models have been identified by ARS. Meeting these needs will make agriculture more profitable while protecting soil and water. The priorities are: (1) conservation-production systems for major physiographic regions, like the Corn Belt and Mississippi Delta; (2) remote sensing technologies to help USDA action agencies assess natural resources and inventory crops; (3) production marketing systems for increased exports of major farm commodities; (4) systems and models to assess and predict effects of farming practices on the environment—for example, on water quality; (5) systems and models for cutting production, processing, and marketing costs; and (6) "expert" systems—computer programs that mimic the thinking of human experts—to help farmers and action agencies make timely decisions.
National Program Staff, Beltsville, MD
C.R. Amerman, (301) 344-4034

Soil, Water & Air

Cyst nematodes dramatically reduce soybean yields on millions of acres, but conservation tillage systems can help farmers recoup their losses. In tests of strip-tillage and no-tillage systems, soybean yields were 39% higher than with conventional tillage. When rotated with corn, soybean yields were 28% higher under conservation tillage than under conventional tillage. The results show that nematodes thrive when soybeans are grown continuously and that conservation tillage retards nematode buildups.
Soil Plant Interaction Research Unit, National Soil Dynamics Lab, Auburn, AL
J.H. Edwards, (205) 826-4100

Energy bills of some farmers in the Central Great Plains fell by almost 40% when they lowered the water pressure in their center-pivot irrigation sprinklers. Lower pressure uses less energy for applying water on a smaller area. Farmers can avoid wasteful runoff and possible soil erosion by not plowing under crop residues, and by adopting minimum and no-tillage farming systems. Crop yields using a conservation farming strategy can be just as high as yields with conventional plowing.
Central Great Plains Research Station, Akron, CO
Rome H. Mickelson, (303) 345-2259

Ozone, not acid rain, is the most serious atmospheric pollutant in the United States in its effects on vegetation, reports an ARS scientist. Caused by a photochemical reaction of sunlight with auto and industrial exhausts, the ozone that damages crops is different from the beneficial ozone layer above the earth that filters out ultraviolet rays. In ARS tests, damaging ozone, which can be blown great distances, significantly reduced yields of cotton, corn, winter wheat, and soybeans. On the other hand, during the 10-15 years that acid rain effects on trees and plants have been studied, no cases of injury to vegetation have been caused by acid rain alone. While this may not be true world-wide, acid rain in the United States is probably not an important factor in forest decline, according to the ARS researcher. Air Quality Program, Raleigh, NC Walter W. Heck, (919) 737-3311

Nitrogen lost to the atmosphere from fertilizer can now be measured more accurately. That should eventually help farmers lower fertilizer costs. Today's farmers must guess at this nitrogen loss and apply more fertilizer according to their estimates. The trouble is that some years the amount lost is not as great as in others. Farmers end up spending money for unneeded fertilizer. Even when the excess remains in place for the next crop's use there is the added risk during wet years that the extra fertilizer could get washed into surface or groundwater supplies. Information about nitrogen loss will be used to develop improved guidelines for efficient fertilizer use by farmers. Soil-Plant-Nutrient Research, Fort Collins, CO Arvin R. Mosier, (303) 482-5733

Blue grama grass, a nutritious food for livestock, also protects soil against wind and water erosion. This grass could be even more effective at controlling erosion if bred 20% larger. Researchers found some native plants that grew wider than others in the same pasture and are trying to incorporate the trait in their breeding work. Past work has concentrated on improving the grass' poor sprouting record. These larger plants might be ideal parents for improving grasses in Wyoming, Colorado, and other Central Plains States. High Plains Grasslands Research Station, Cheyenne, WY Marilyn J. Samuel, (307) 772-2433

A new soil sampler more accurately measures soil water acidity (pH) than older devices. Accurate measurement is critical for maintaining safe water supplies because acidity affects how fast dissolved chemicals, nutrients, and metals move through soil. Earlier devices made the water sample appear less acidic than it was because they allowed dissolved carbon dioxide to escape from the sample. The ARS-developed sampler, which is multi-chambered to minimize carbon dioxide loss,

gives scientists readings just as quickly as the earlier devices from depths as much as 100 feet below the surface. U.S. Salinity Lab, Riverside, CA Donald L. Suarez, (714) 683-0170

Farm profitability can be increased by lowering input costs with a system that relies on crop rotations and multiple cropping, as well as animal manures and legume green manure crops that are plowed under to return nutrients to the soil. So far, studies at the Rodale Research Center, Kutztown, Pennsylvania, show that crop yields equal those from conventional farming techniques. The low-input system should also reduce soil erosion and groundwater pollution from fertilizers or pesticides. In addition, computer simulation models are being modified and tested for use with low-input cropping systems. U.S. Pasture Research Lab, University Park, PA Jerry Radke, (215) 683-6383

Wind reduces soil productivity in subhumid and semiarid agricultural regions by blowing away soil nutrients. To better understand this loss, scientists collected airborne dust samples at various heights above the soil surface and analyzed them for nutrient content. In all cases, the concentration of nutrients was greater in the windblown soil than in the surface soil. Continued erosion by wind will decrease availability of nutrients to plants, and eventually reduce the soil's ability to grow crops without adding expensive supplements. Wind Erosion and New Crops Research, Big Spring, TX Ted M. Zobeck/Donald W. Fryrear, (915) 263-0293

Qua

Quarterly Report
of Selected Research Projects

United States
Department of
Agriculture

 Agricultural
Research
Service

October 1 to December 31, 1986

CONTENTS

New & Improved Products

Herbicides encased in starch granules are safer and more efficient than conventional herbicides that are sometimes sprayed off target. Four companies now share an exclusive license to manufacture products from the ARS patented process that allows a starch matrix to release a herbicide slowly. The starch-based formulations protect the herbicide from water and are still effective after lying on the soil surface for months. They can be used with conservation tillage systems and can increase crop yields. (PATENT)
Insect and Weed Control Research, West Lafayette, IN
M.M. Schreiber/W. Doane, (317) 494-4556

Adding a popcornlike aroma to unscented American rice might sell more of this surplus commodity at home and overseas. Some of the world's rice crop has a

Note: One or more scientists familiar with each research project are listed for further information. If the scientists are unavailable, others at the same telephone number may also be familiar with the work.

Items marked with the word PATENT are being patented by ARS. For more information contact Ann Whitehead, National Patent Program, Bldg. 005, Rm. 401, Beltsville Agricultural Research Center, Beltsville, MD 20705,.
(301) 344-2786.

natural popcorn scent preferred by the people of many countries. The aroma is not found in most American varieties, which limits export sales. Scented rice varieties cost more, yield less, and may be harder to grow than fragrance-free rice. With further research and development, a fragrance-imparting chemical could soon be added to unscented domestic rice during milling. It was first isolated, identified, and synthesized in 1983 by ARS researchers. This enhancement of domestic rice could boost the current $665 million export market for U.S. rice, especially to the Middle East and Asia.
Food Quality Research, Western Research Center, Albany, CA
Ronald G. Buttery, (415) 486-3322

More aromatic raisins may result from a new variety of seedless muscat grape now being tested in California. Until this variety is ready for commercial release, muscat grapes will continue taking only a small share of the $650 million raisin market. Muscat grape seeds now have to be removed by machine--making the skins sticky--and the skins must then be oiled for packaging.
Horticultural Crops Research Lab, Fresno, CA
David W. Ramming, (209) 487-5334

Energy needed to convey and clean cotton fibers after they have been pulled from seed could be cut in half. The potential savings comes from a new machine--the first major redesign of a gin-processing system in about 25 years. Scientists combined two machines--the cotton gin and cotton lint cleaner--to achieve this energy savings and at the same time substantially reduce fiber damage, air pollution and floor space requirements in ginning mills.
Southwestern Cotton Ginning Lab, Mesilla Park, NM
S.E. Hughs/M.N. Gillum, (505) 526-6381

Explosion puffed blueberries are being
processed commercially by a Georgia company that has built a plant to use the
technology. ARS scientists introduced the
technology to the Georgia Blueberries
Association and evaluated berries before
and after processing to ensure their
quality. Originally developed by the ARS
Research Centers in Albany, Calif. and
Philadelphia, Pa. to dry fruits and vegetables, explosion puffing retains the
berries' natural flavor and texture and
allows them to be easily rehydrated. The
industry estimates that they will process
about 1-million pounds of berries annually. (PATENT)
Field and Horticultural Crops, Athens, GA
Gerald Dull, (404) 546-3320

Imported canned meats are tested here to
make sure they were cooked long enough and
at a high enough temperature to kill any
foreign viruses that might enter the food
chain and endanger U.S. livestock. Scientists can now tell to what temperature the
meat was heated by using two new tests
that detect changes in enzymes in fully
cooked meat. The new tests are quicker,
more sensitive and more accurate than
current ones. If further study confirms
these initial findings, the tests may be
used by USDA's Food Safety and Inspection
Service in regulating imported canned
meats.
Poultry Meat Quality and Safety Research,
Athens, GA
William E. Townsend/Carl E. Davis, (404)
546-3569

More than 90% of cherry peppers were
successfully separated from branches and
leaves when run through an experimental
trash removal machine. In the best
machine of several tested, peppers were
first fed through a pegged combing belt to
remove trash. They were then passed along
a counter-rotating roll bed, invented by a
farmer, which pulled off still more leaves
and branches.
ARS engineer at Michigan State University,
East Lansing, MI
Dale E. Marshall, (517) 353-5201

2

tifies a protein by the amino acids on its surface rather than by its size or chemical charge, which are used in more difficult and time-consuming methods. Combined with a new rapid technique to isolate corn proteins, RP-HPLC reveals the percentage of different proteins--a key to predicting how much of the nutritionally important amino acids lysine and tryptophan are in the proteins.
Plant Protein Research, Northern Research Center, Peoria, IL
J.W. Paulis/J.A. Bietz, (309) 685-4011, ext. 359

New wraps for individual fruits and vegetables help them stay fresh longer than current cling-type wraps or plastic bags. The new wraps shrink when heated and fit tightly around each fruit or vegetable, keeping moisture in and air out. In tests, polyethylene or copolymer wraps reduced shriveling and maintained freshness of cucumbers, eggplants, peppers and tomatoes for 3 weeks longer than current packaging. The new wraps, most effective where refrigeration is scarce or where the growing season is short, cost only an extra penny or two an item.
Horticultural Research Lab, Orlando, FL
Lawrence A. Risse, (305) 897-7326

A tasty, nutritious new food--a custard-like dessert--is made from nonfat dry milk, rice flour, and sugar mixed with food gums and a little vegetable oil. The instant product has no eggs and no cholesterol and is easily digested. The gums provide valuable fiber. A commercial food processor could make the product with artificial sweeteners for the calorie conscious and with lactase-treated nonfat dry milk for the lactose intolerant. (PATENT)
Food and Feed Research, Southern Research Center, New Orleans, LA
Ranjit S. Kadan, (504) 589-7088

An exceptional new strawberry, Lester, is now available to the home gardener. Very productive and resistant to rootrot, Lester ripens earlier, is more attractive and has a skin less susceptible to shipping damage than other midseason varie-

ties, making it more marketable. It is sweet with a good aroma. Resistant to leaf diseases and fruit rots, this strawberry is best adapted to the Mid-Atlantic area but has been grown from New England south to North Carolina and from Maryland west to Illinois.
Fruit Lab, Beltsville, MD
Gene L. Galletta, (301) 344-4652

A new iceberg lettuce resistant to big vein--a major disease of this crop--has been developed and given to seed companies. Named Pacific, the lettuce is suited for the Salinas and Imperial Valleys of California, where 40% of the nation's lettuce crop is grown and where big vein is the second-worst disease. Big vein causes an unattractive crisscrossing of white or pale yellow veins in lettuce leaves, can prevent normal lettuce heads from forming, or can delay growth. Of the three lettuces that ARS researchers have developed so far to counteract big vein, Pacific is the most resistant.
Vegetable Production Research Lab, U.S. Agricultural Research Station, Salinas, CA
E.J. Ryder, (408) 443-2253

New commercial uses continue to be found for "super slurper"--the ARS cornstarch product that can absorb 2,000 times its own weight in water. One firm now mixes super slurper into soil to retain more water and nutrients when growing vegetables and soybeans. Another began using it as an electrolyte (a nonmetallic electrical conductor) in batteries. Earlier commercial uses of super slurper since its development in 1975: in body powder, diapers and sanitary napkins and for medical, industrial, and other agricultural purposes. (PATENT)
Plant Polymer Research, Northern Research Center, Peoria, IL
William M. Doane, (309) 685-4011, ext. 556

An ARS-developed technique to steam pecans before shelling is being used commercially by a plant in Madill, Oklahoma. Compared with the existing practice, the new technique increases from 75% to 90% the number of unbroken half-kernels, reduces from 12

hours to 3 minutes the time it takes to do
the shelling and leaves nuts cleaner.
Field & Horticultural Crops, Athens, GA
William R. Forbus, (404) 546-3131

Brightly colored strains of a yeastlike
fungus, Aureobasidium pullulans, may
increase the value of surplus farm commodities as raw materials for industrial
chemicals. Scientists identified red,
yellow, orange and purple strains of the
fungus with enzymes that excel at breaking
the sugar xylose away from xylan, a component of brans milled from grains.
Abundant supplies of xylose, produced by
the enzymes, could be converted into ethyl
alcohol and a variety of other chemicals
used in making pharmaceuticals, pesticides, foam insulation and industrial
resins. Basic studies on gene regulation
of enzyme production may be useful in
making genes inserted into microorganisms
express their specific characteristics.
Fermentation Biochemistry, Northern
Research Center, Peoria, IL
T.D. Leathers/P. Bolen, (309) 685-4011,
ext. 377

New treatments are being developed to
control enzymatic browning in fresh or
lightly processed fruits and vegetables.
The research has taken on a new urgency
since sulfites were banned by the Food and
Drug Administration last July on raw
produce because a number of people with
asthma are allergic to the chemical. Safe
and promising replacements for sulfites
include combinations of stabilized reducing agents, chelating agents and enzymes
inhibitors. Several treatments are based
upon novel approaches to the problem of
browning.
Plant Science Research, Philadelphia, PA
Gerald M. Sapers, (215) 233-6417

Dill seed, lemon peel oil, and black
pepper contain compounds that act as
nature's own protection against insects.
Chemicals in dill seed oil repel confused
flour beetles, the most abundant and
injurious pest in flour mills in the
United States. A chemical in lemon peel
oil repels cowpea and rice weevils, two
other stored grain pests. And black

4

A sexy plant that probably has more hormones than it should will interest miners, ranchers and environmentalists. Indian ricegrass can revitalize barren, sandy land previously mined for copper, coal and other minerals. Highly endowed with the growth hormone giberellic acid, the plant grows well in sandy, disturbed soils without fertilizer or organic matter—two requirements for most reclamation projects. In fact, the sandier the soil, the better it grows. But it has rarely been planted successfully. After carefully reviewing 50 years of research on growing the plant, scientists found a small but important fact: When Indian ricegrass is planted 6 inches deep in the sand, it flourishes. Once a staple of Paiute Indians who boiled it to make a nourishing mush, Indian ricegrass is also a highly nutritious winter forage for livestock and wildlife.
Pasture and Range Management, Reno, NV
James A. Young, (702) 784-5607

Only 1% to 2% of herbicides and less than 0.2% of insecticides farmers apply on irrigated land run off unused. Runoff can be reduced even more by selecting alternative pesticides and application methods. To find out which pesticides and herbicides were most prone to escape from fields, scientists carefully measured runoff. This published information is now available to irrigators.
U.S. Salinity Lab, Riverside, CA
William F. Spencer, (714) 787-5145

Maple and ash trees help reduce air pollution. In growth chambers, both trees absorbed sulphur dioxide through microscopic pores, or stomates, in their leaves. Maple even converted the pollutant to nutrients and was more effective than the ash as an air filter for sulphur dioxide.
Nursery Crops Research Lab, Delaware, OH
Bruce R. Roberts, (614) 363-1129

Lichens—small plants composed of fungi and algae—may be an index of air quality. Scientists from ARS, Tel Aviv University, and Israel's Volcani Center discovered that tree lichens transplanted from a rural area to a smoggy city produced less of one hormone (indole-3-acetic acid) and 50% more of another (ethylene). Further research may lead to using lichens in monitoring air pollution. Scientists also want to know more about how lichens may affect trees, for example, by releasing hormones that stimulate tree growth.
Plant Hormone Lab, Beltsville, MD
Jerry D. Cohen, (301) 344-3632

Salt buildup in soil has plagued irrigators for nearly 4,000 years. Today, accurate mapping of salt-threatened areas should help avoid the devastation experienced by ancient farmers. At one time, determining areas of salt buildup was the hardest and most time-consuming task in mapping. Scientists have modified a commercially available long-range navigation system (LORAN) to speed research aimed at controlling soil salinity. The system is so accurate it can pinpoint salty areas within 15 feet of where scientists previously measured salinity. Now, with new computer programs, scientists will be able to monitor much larger areas accurately and at a lower cost than previously possible. Any trends toward increasing salinity can be identified and programs to abate salinity developed.
U.S. Salinity Lab, Riverside, CA
James D. Rhoades, (714) 683-0170

Alaskan farmers can now grow a healthy crop of barley, control weeds, and reduce soil erosion on 65,000 acres of newly cleared land in the Alaskan interior. In studying the potential of the new cropland, researchers found it deficient in nitrogen and prone to erosion. While no-till cropping will control erosion, it promotes unacceptable weed growth. Researchers suggest that to disrupt weeds, farmers lightly cultivate new fields before planting barley. Other techniques are under study.
Subarctic Agricultural Research,
Fairbanks, AK
Jeffery S. Conn, (907) 474-7614

Winterfat—a perennial shrub native to the western United States—is nutritious for livestock and wildlife and promises to be

ideal for reclaiming strip-mined areas and improving rangeland. Scientists discovered that thrashing the seeds, necessary to remove the tiny hairs that make planting difficult, damages about 25% of the delicate embryos. They are now coating unthrashed seeds with a gel that glues them to the soil surface and helps anchor seed hairs.
High Plains Grasslands Research Station, Cheyenne, WY
D. Terrance Booth, (307) 772-2434

Red clover cultivars have been identified that will tolerate toxic levels of aluminum and low-phosphorus soil. They should prove useful in the acid infertile soils of Appalachia, where hay yields are often less than 2 tons per acre. Besides enhancing pasture production, the new red clovers should reduce fertilizer costs and promote conservation of natural resources.
Appalachian Soil and Water Conservation Research Lab, Beckley, WV
V.C. Baligar, (304) 252-6426

Wildfires fueled by cheatgrass threaten millions of acres of dry, sandy western rangeland once thought to be fireproof. For the last 10 years, cheatgrass, which usually grows in less arid soil, has been invading and overrunning rangeland and fueling wildfires over entire rangelands that once fed livestock and wildlife. Scientists studying this problem believe there may be three reasons for this ecological disaster. The most dramatic is that cheatgrass genes have mutated, allowing the grass to thrive in its new environment. The way livestock is managed on rangeland and the effects of subtle changes in the climate are two other explanations.
Pasture and Range Management, Reno, NV
James A. Young, (702) 784-5607

Crop Production & Protection

New corn lines that resist fall armyworm and southern rust have been released to breeders, and southeastern farmers will benefit in two ways. Corn farmers could use less pesticide, and growers of winter crops like wheat could double crop--plant corn as a summer crop for grain or silage. Many growers can't do this now because of high pesticide costs to control armyworm. Commercial companies are crossbreeding the old and new lines for high yield as well as pest resistance.
Crop Science Research, Mississippi State, MS
Paul Williams, (601) 325-2311/Joe Sanford, (601) 325-2745

Old wheat seed--harvested 3 to 6 years ago--is more vulnerable to Pythium root rot than a current year's seed. This discovery is significant because many seed dealers hold onto their seed inventories for several years. Pythium is a soil fungus that begins its attack on wheat by infecting embryos during seed germination. Then it infects and destroys the roots and root hairs needed to take in water and nutrients. Thanks to this research, the seed industry is now literally cleaning house. One dealer disposed of $250,000 worth of seed last summer because of this finding. (PATENT)
Root Disease and Biological Control Research, Pullman, WA
R. James Cook, (509) 335-3722

Insect pests may become resistant to insecticides, but they are no match for natural biological controls. For example, a serious pest of cotton, called the tobacco budworm, has developed resistance to the insecticides permethrin and methomyl. In lab tests, however, resistant budworms were destroyed by natural organisms at least as often as nonresistant budworms. Both succumbed to a virus (Baculovirus heliothis), a bacterium (Bacillus thuringiensis), a fungus (Nomuraea rileyi) and a protozoan (Vairimorpha necatrix). The first two have been registered for use on cotton against Heliothis

pests. Researchers think it unlikely that resistance will develop to either the virus or the bacterium. The fungus and the protozoan are still experimental controls.
Biological Control of Insects Research Lab, Columbia, MO
Carlo M. Ignoffo, (314) 875-5361

Future U.S. wheat crops may be safer from the Hessian fly because researchers have found four new sources of genetic resistance in Moroccan durum wheats. Annual damage by the fly can be $100 million in the United States. In Morocco, it can destroy half the durum and bread wheat crop. Tests will determine whether the four sources are identical or different from each other. Researchers will then try to breed new resistance into U.S hard red winter wheats. Breeding resistant varieties is the only practical control for the fly; pesticides are costly and don't work well. ARS, university and Moroccan scientists are conducting the research.
Plant Science and Entomology Research, Manhattan, KS
J.H. Hatchett, (913) 532-6154

A long-standing sibling rivalry between white rice and a weedy variant of its own species, red rice, may soon come to an end. Until now, farmers have had no defense against the red rice weed, because herbicides that killed it also did in the crop itself. After 4 years of research, scientists are ready to release to commercial breeders a line of white rice that tolerates the herbicide alachlor, which kills red rice. The weed costs farmers over $1 million annually in Arkansas, where almost half of U.S. rice is produced. Not only does it reduce yields by stealing soil nutrients and using its height to compete for sunlight but its presence in white rice after harvest also reduces the market price.
Rice Production and Weed Control Research, Stuttgart, AR
Robert Dilday, (501) 673-2661

It is now possible to "vaccinate" an alfalfa plant against one race of a disease-causing fungus with spores of a closely related fungus to which the plant is already immune. The disease is anthracnose, a scourge of alfalfa that damages some $200 million in plants annually. One variety of alfalfa has been bred that is resistant to Race 1 of the anthracnose fungus but will succumb to Race 2 of the same species. If spores of Race 1 are sprayed on the plant, however, the plant responds with an immune reaction that also makes it immune to the Race 2 fungus. The discovery provides scientists with a new technique for studying how genetic resistance works in the alfalfa plant.
Germplasm Quality and Enhancement Lab, Beltsville, MD
Nichole O'Neill, (301) 344-3331

New bait to trap Caribbean fruit flies, which sometimes force growers to fumigate after harvest, may be around the corner; scientists have identified chemicals that attract the pests. Using a machine that works like an electrocardiograph, scientists tested antennae response to chemicals in odors produced by male flies. Having zeroed in on the chemicals that most excite the antennae of both sexes, scientists will try luring flies in the lab to verify the electroantennagrams.
Subtropical Crop Insects Research, Weslaco, TX
David Robacker, (512) 565-2647

Coating corn seed with a weed killer (EPTC) controls foxtail just as well as conventional spray that uses 200 times more herbicide. Only one-fourth of an ounce of EPTC (S-ethyl dipropyl carbamothioate) in a starch solution will coat an acre's worth of corn seeds. Foxtail can cut corn yields by as much as 70%.
Plant Polymer Research, Northern Research Center, Peoria, IL
Baruch S. Shasha, (309) 685-4011, ext. 310

Four colorful new crape myrtles resistant to powdery mildew disease have been released by ARS ornamental breeders to

cooperating wholesale nurseries. They will be the sole source of the new cultivars in 1986. All the new crape myrtles are semidwarfs, with colors ranging from white to medium pink and lavender. They are unusually cold-hardy. Powdery mildew is a persistent disease of crape myrtles, coating the leaves and preventing flowering. The frequent spraying necessary to control the disease is impractical for home gardeners. The new cultivars are Acoma, Hopi, Pecos and Zuni.
U.S. National Arboretum, Washington, D.C.
Donald R. Egolf, (202) 475-4862

Redesigned fruits and vegetables that look and taste better, pack more nutrition and stay fresh longer are emerging every month from ARS research. Improved versions of familiar staples include a carrot that is vitamin-packed (Beta III), a baking potato for the East that is drought resistant (Russette) and a mildew-resistant cantaloup. These new fruits and vegetables are being developed to resist diseases, insects and damage from cold; to breed more vitamins and minerals right into the food itself; and to get it to the table faster, partly to provide consumers with produce that is tastier, juicier and easier to eat.
National Program Staff, Beltsville, MD
Howard Brooks, (301) 344-3912

Tight husks help prevent a carcinogen called aflatoxin from forming on corn. Studies show that tight husks reduce infestations of European corn borers and corn earworms, whose feeding makes kernels susceptible to Aspergillus flavus--a fungus that can produce aflatoxin. For the Southeast, where some varieties have high yields but loose husks, breeders can reduce aflatoxin-infected corn by incorporating husk tightness into their breeding programs.
Crop Production Unit, Columbia, MO
Dean Barry, (314) 882-3486

Widespread tests with a "super carrot" in Nepal, Bangladesh, central Africa and elsewhere will reveal whether it can adapt to diverse climates and soils. The Beta III carrot, packing 10 times the carotene

of standard varieties native to those areas, could supply much more vitamin A. Lack of this vitamin in millions of children in developing countries often leads to blindness or death. Agency scientists in the United States are working with Beta III germplasm so breeders here can produce hybrids with improved flavor as well as high carotene levels.
Vegetable Crops Research, Madison, WI
C.E. Peterson, (608) 262-1830

Pesticides may become safer, more efficient and less expensive to use because of a new way to analyze fungicide particles on plants. Scientists can now track airborne fungicide using electron beam analysis--a combination of scanning electron microscopy and energy dispersive X-ray analysis. They can tell where the particles land and whether they may harm the plants. This technique, developed jointly by ARS and Ohio State University, will allow chemical companies to formulate more efficient compounds and permit nurseries to use less pesticide by targeting it more accurately.
Nursery Crops Research Lab, Delaware, OH
Charles R. Krause, (614) 363-1129

Vegetable pests can be controlled with the lowest recommended quantity of pesticide if it is applied in an oil formulation in water from a center-pivot irrigation system. In field tests in Georgia, insect pests of tomatoes, broccoli, cowpeas, peanuts, turnips, cabbage, spinach and collards were killed with commercial pesticides dissolved in either petroleum or once-refined soybean oil. The overhead sprinkler chemigation system also reduced costs of application and provided more efficient control of chemicals.
Insect Biology Management Systems Research, Tifton, GA
J.R. Young, (912) 382-6904

A unique form of the fungus Phytophthora infestans that causes potato late blight, a destructive disease of the tuber throughout the world, has been discovered in a collection of fungi from Mexico. The Mexican fungus is the only strain ever found to contain double-stranded RNA (dsRNA). This corroborates earlier find-

ings that the Mexican organism differs from all other strains ever examined. Detection of the dsRNA gives researchers a new way to compare strains of fungi from different locations to determine relatedness. It also provides a cytoplasmic marker that can be used to study the genetics of this important pathogen.
Foreign Disease-Weed Science Research, Frederick, MD
Paul W. Tooley, (301) 663-7344

A new bioregulator will soon allow fruit growers to plant more vigorous, disease-resistant rootstock in high-density orchards, with higher yields at lower cost. When scientists sprayed the growth regulator paclobutrazol on apple trees, they had fewer excess shoots, later bud development, more fruit setting and higher calcium levels than untreated trees. Working with industry, researchers expect the synthetic regulator to be commercially available in about a year.
Appalachian Fruit Research Station, Kearneysville, WV
Stephen S. Miller, (304) 725-3451

Stem sawfly, an insect that eats through the stems of small cereal grains, can topple up to 40% of the crop, making harvest difficult or impossible. Researchers recently released genetic material to wheat breeders that cuts this damage dramatically. The resistance to sawfly was incorporated into a broad base of genetic material adapted to the hard red wheat area of the northern plains. Breeders can pick the plant types best suited to their areas to produce commercial varieties.
Cereal Crop Improvement, Bozeman, MT
Allen F. Cook, (406) 994-5059

Small farmers can turn to European varieties of cucumbers as alternative crops. These "burpless" delicacies, prized for their thin skins, seedlessness, and taste that is less bitter than common varieties, can be grown in water bags or on fairly poor soil. Studies show that European varieties, most of which have qualities that could result in grades of U.S. No. 1 or better, could earn a farmer a profit of

$7,000 or more per acre in a good year. They must, however, be grown in a screen enclosure to keep out winds that can damage their thin skins and insects that might pollinate the cukes, ruining their seedlessness.
South Central Family Farms Research, Booneville, AR
D.J. Makus, (501) 675-3834

To transfer biocontrol technology, ARS scientists worked with Maryland officials to use European weevils to attack pesky Carduus thistles, also from Europe. The weevil can be used in many states to eat seeds of the thistles in pastures and highway plantings. In a 4-year cooperative study, the imported weevils controlled up to 95% of thistles at highway test sites in Maryland. The State's transportation department spends more than $200,000 a year to control the thistle with mowing and herbicides.
Beneficial Insects Lab, Beltsville, MD
John J. Drea, (301) 344-1791

The major pest of U.S. pecans can be lured into traps by a new attractant that mimics the insect's sex pheromone. Scientists developed the chemical as part of a control program designed to offset losses to the pecan industry estimated at $30 million a year. Pecan growers are already using traps baited with this pheromone early in the growing season to catch hickory shuckworms (Cydia caryana). The number of worms caught can be used to estimate the total infestation. With this method growers now have a better idea of how much pesticide to apply and when to apply it.
Yakima Agricultural Research Lab, Yakima, WA
Les M. McDonough, (509) 575-5970

Several different lines of male-sterile corn and sorghum have been identified, enabling breeders to produce new hybrid lines with greater genetic diversity and enhanced disease resistance. The new lines will help breeders avoid the risks inherent in uniformity of hybrids, which led to the appearance in 1970 of Southern corn leaf blight, which wiped out 15% of

9

the total U.S. corn crop. An ARS researcher also found that a single gene may be responsible for both male sterility and disease susceptibility in corn. All male-fertile, disease-resistant mutants in corn failed to possess this unique gene.
Plant Pathology Lab, Gainesville, FL
Daryl R. Pring, (904) 392-3631

Chinch bugs, pests of corn and sorghum in the Southeast, have the potential for severely damaging the South's 15 million acres of pasture planted in bermudagrass. The best control is to eliminate goosegrass, a common weed, from bermudagrass pastures. Entomologists have found that infestations of adult and nymph chinch bugs originate on goosegrass, the plant host that these bugs prefer. The weed has to be controlled with herbicides early in the spring, however, or the chinch bugs will migrate to bermudagrass when the goosegrass is killed.
Georgia Coastal Plain Experiment Station, Tifton, GA
Robert E. Lynch, (912) 382-6904

Using a new sampling method that saves up to 60% of labor costs, scientists can check fewer sterile insects each day to control infestations of the Mediterranean fruit fly or other devastating pests. Until now, up to tens of thousands of specially dyed sterile male flies had to be checked daily in field traps to make sure the ratio of sterilized to normal males was correct for control. Sterile males drastically reduce the population by mating with females, producing no live offspring. The new method allows sampling according to the level of accuracy needed at a particular stage in fruit fly eradication efforts.
Tropical Fruit and Vegetable Research Lab, Honolulu, HI
Donald O. McInnis, (808) 988-2158

Sweet potatoes can be planted from vine cuttings without suffering from all-too-common dehydration if growers take several simple steps: (1) hold cuttings for 2 days under humid conditions before planting, (2) stimulate rooting before transplanting, (3) keep leaves on cuttings and (4)

irrigate promptly after planting. In field tests, planting in the morning vs. evening had no measurable effect on dehydration.
Tropical Agricultural Research Station, Mayaguez, PR
F.W. Martin, (809) 834-2435

A Utah bee may benefit California crops used to feed livestock and valued at over $600 million. Preliminary results show that the emergence of wild but gentle Osmia sanrafaelae bees from their nests can be synchronized to coincide with early blooming of alfalfa and clover plants. The timing is perfect--the day before the plants blossom, scientists release the hibernating bees, transplanted from southeastern Utah to California, from cold-storage coolers. At present, these forage crops are mostly pollinated by honey bees. But potential problems with Africanized honey bees, expected to enter California from Mexico in about 3 years, are causing scientists to search for other pollinators. Africanized bee aggressiveness, as well as possible legislation against the use of honey bees in urban areas, prompted the study.
Pollinating Insect Biology, Logan, UT
Frank D. Parker, (801) 750-2525

An overlooked mite--too big for the microscope but too small to be seen with the naked eye--was found to cause leaf yellowing of zoysia, a popular lawn grass from the Orient. Scientists had thought that a virus was the culprit until they discovered the tiny, submarine-shaped mite (Eriophyes zoysiae) on and inside zoysia grass blades, sucking up the plant's juices. Now that they know what to look for, researchers can work with only mite-free plants in developing economical zoysia seed for lawns and ballfields. Most homeowners today plant zoysia in plugs, bits of sod that spread to make a rugged, drought-tolerant lawn.
Germplasm Quality and Enhancement Lab, Beltsville, MD
Nichole O'Neill, (301) 344-3331

A new way to identify strains of a plant virus based on comparative size of viral proteins is faster and more reliable than the old way--by observing symptoms of sick plants. Researchers used the improved method to isolate two of the five to seven viral proteins created by maize dwarf mosaic virus (also called sugarcane mosaic virus) in infected corn, sorghum, sugarcane and millet. The method allows researchers to follow a virus strain as aphids spread it within a field or from one geographic area to another. A time-saver for breeders, the method allows them to select for resistance to the major characteristics of the virus instead of wasting time with minor strain variations. Sorghum Research, Lincoln, NE
Stanley G. Jensen, (402) 472-6023

A new ARS manual on gnat-size flies will help shipping inspectors tighten security against foreign Agromyzidae flies that threaten U.S. crops. Many of the 4,000 or so Agromyzidae species, collectively called leaf miners, are major pests of 150 crops, including wheat, alfalfa, potatoes and chrysanthemums. In words and drawings, the book describes 531 species known to be in this country, including 43 not previously reported.
Systematic Entomology Lab, Beltsville, MD
Douglass R. Miller, (301) 344-3183

Picking the gypsy moth's brain revealed a scientific first--a hormone that controls growth and molting in this pest. The hormone, PTTH, could lead to a safer insecticide--perhaps through genetic engineering--that would affect only the gypsy moth. The pest causes millions of dollars in damage to the Nation's forests and shade trees each year. Isolating this hormone may lead to controlling the pest by genetic engineering.
Insect Reproduction Lab, Beltsville, MD
Edward P. Masler, (301) 344-1732/
Thomas J. Kelly, (301) 344-1787

Hard wheat kernels grind slower and louder than soft ones. Two new instruments make use of these characteristics in measuring the hardness or softness of wheat--a key to grading and pricing this major crop.

One machine measures the force needed to crush a kernel, while the other reads the sound pattern made by grinding. U.S. Federal Grain Inspection Service officials hope one of the machines will accurately distinguish hardness in new wheat varieties. Many come from crossbreeding traditional hard and soft wheats and are therefore difficult to judge by sight. Since wheats can get mixed during marketing, the hardness test should help U.S. sellers confirm their grain's quality and raise the quality of domestic flour and the value of wheat exports.
U.S. Grain Marketing Research, Manhattan, KS/Instrumentation Research Lab, Beltsville, MD
Charles R. Martin, (913) 539-9141/
Karl Norris, (301) 344-3650

Animal Production & Protection

ARS scientists have demonstrated for the first time that genes of avian leukosis virus can be inserted into the germ line of chickens and inherited for two generations. This is, in fact, the first time that genes of any kind have been artificially inserted into poultry gem lines. The work opens the door to new and exciting genetic research in poultry, since it demonstrates that retroviruses, of which the avian leukosis is one example, have the potential for use as vectors, or carriers, for the insertion of nonviral genes to enhance poultry disease resistance and productivity.
Regional Poultry Research Lab, East Lansing, MI
Lyman B. Crittenden, (517) 337-6828

Farmers could save more than $25 an acre by planting only 10 pounds of alfalfa per acre instead of the recommended 20. Planting tests showed that seeding alfalfa at 5, 10, 15, and 20 pounds per acre did not produce significantly different amounts of the forage. Agronomists do not recommend seeding 5 pounds, however, because it might not be enough under normal farming practices, but 10 pounds is plenty. Other tests showed that planting alfalfa in herbicide-killed stands of wheat, sorghum-sudan grasses and fescue

without cultivation may save farmers the
cost of seedbed preparation and reduce
soil erosion.
Dairy Production and Genetics Research
Lab, Lewisburg, TN
John R. Owen, (615) 359-1578

Every year about 7% of all calves born in
the United States die, raising production
costs for farmers and meat prices for
consumers. Scientists have found that
more than half this loss is due to difficult or delayed birth. While continuing
research to eliminate calving difficulties
and make natural birth less risky, they
have developed a new measure to reduce
calf deaths at birth. Pregnant females
are injected with a synthetic hormone that
causes 95% to calve within 48 hours. This
concentrates the delivery time so that
someone can be present to assist the
mother should she experience calving
difficulty. While calves are born 2 to 7
days earlier than normal and grow slightly
slower, more total beef is produced
because more calves live.
Fort Keogh Livestock and Range Research,
Miles City, MT
Robert A. Bellows, (406) 232-4970

Cowboys are electronically weight-watching
cattle in Montana. Scientists, who sometimes double as cowboys, hitch up computers and other technology to keep tabs on
cattle roaming the range. A portable
electronic system, that includes computers, microwaves, and a radio transmitter
to do the monitoring, is fast, easy, and
accurate and saves the time and labor of
rounding up and weighing cows on the
range. Such a system is now strictly used
for research, but when it becomes afford-
able to ranchers, it would allow them to
spot animals that are lagging behind
others in gaining weight. The findings
could also cut ranchers' operating costs
and help them supply better quality beef
to the consumer.
Fort Keogh Livestock and Range Research
Station, Miles City, MT
Pat Currie, (406) 232-4970

vital information for feeding trials.
Fort Keogh Livestock and Range Research,
Miles City, MT
Pat O. Currie, (406) 232-4970

Coccidiosis, a parasitic disease of poultry, costs the industry $100 million yearly for drugs to combat this disease in broiler flocks. Alternatives are needed to overcome emerging drug-resistant strains of the parasite and to stop the spiraling medication costs. One alternative would be to vaccinate birds to boost their natural immune systems. Now that scientists have found a way to clone in volume specific antibodies against many species of Coccidia, three genetic engineering companies will use these antibodies to identify and produce genetically engineered proteins or antigens--a first step in devising a commercial vaccine against the disease.
Protozoan Disease Lab, Beltsville, MD
Patricia C. Augustine, (301) 344-2428

Bagasse--the material that's left over after sugarcane is crushed--may prove a less expensive feed for shrimp farmers in Hawaii, who currently import feed. An experimental feed of carbohydrate, protein, fats and minerals added to pellets made from bagasse supplies nutrients for microscopic bacteria in shrimp ponds. Bacteria adhere to the pellets and proliferate as a low-cost feed for young shrimp. Cost of the bagasse-based feed is estimated at $100 a ton; the closest feed of equivalent quality for raising marketable shrimp is currently $300 to $450 a ton. What's more, a succulent, highly popular variety of shrimp grew faster in ponds supplied with the pelleted bagasse than they did when the traditional dried feedlot manure was added to the ponds. The study was conducted by ARS in conjunction with Hawaii's Oceanic Institute to improve marine shrimp farming.
Tropical Aquaculture Research,
Waimanalo, HI
Donald W. Freeman, (808) 259-7951

86/12

Young turkeys can now be protected against a highly contagious disease that can kill up to 20% of them. A new vaccine against hemorrhagic enteritis of turkeys has been prepared by propagating --in cell cultures outside the bird--the virus that causes the disease. The vaccine has been found effective and safe in field trials in Minnesota and North Carolina. Unlike currently used vaccines, which are prepared inside turkeys, the new vaccine protects birds without the risk of transmitting other viruses and should cost much less to prepare.
Poultry Research Lab, East Lansing, MI
Keyvan Nazerian, (517) 337-6828

Adding 5% fat to a diet fed to turkeys during 16 summer weeks resulted in an increase of 9.1 eggs laid per hen, even though the flock ate 2.1% less feed. In the commercial turkey industry, there is a recurring problem of decreased feed consumption followed by a drop in egg production during summer heat stress. The added fat increased the metabolizable energy of the turkeys, increasing egg output. Adding more than 5% fat, however, did not appear to be beneficial.
Avian Physiology Lab, Beltsville, MD
Edward J. Robel, (301) 344-2545

Feeding beef cattle a drug related to adrenaline increases carcass protein and decreases fat. In tests with four Hereford steers, blood flow rose an average 47% and uptake of alpha amino nitrogen--precursor of protein--rose 44% after 9 days of treatment with clenbuterol. Although the drug is not yet approved for commercial use in animals, its effects on protein and fat levels make it worth further study.
Nutrition Research, Clay Center, NE
Joan Eisemann, (402) 762-3241

A device that injects anhydrous ammonia and other liquid preservatives into hay while it's being baled could be a lifesaver for farmers and livestock alike. A syringe, powered by a tractor's hydraulic system, draws liquid preservative from a tank mounted on the back of a baler and injects precise amounts into the bale. The conventional method--spraying after baling--often puts too much ammonia on the hay; it also poses greater health risks

13

for farmers who improperly handle the
chemical and for cattle that consume hay
overtreated with the preservative.
(PATENT)
Dairy Forage Research, East Lansing, MI
C. Alan Rotz, (517) 353-1758

A biotechnology technique, similar to
tests that determine if humans have been
exposed to diseases, will tell scientists
if grasshoppers have been infected by
viruses. Scientists hope to control
grasshopper populations by spreading some
of these viruses more thoroughly than
nature does. Thus far they have developed
two monoclonal antibodies and one DNA-
probe to differentiate six entomopox
viruses that naturally infect and kill
only grasshoppers. It is not yet known
how many of the hundreds of grasshopper
species in the United States will succumb
to these viruses, but researchers are
working to find out. They are using
state-of-the-art laboratory techniques to
map genetic material in the viruses. They
hope to alter them genetically to make the
viruses lethal to more grasshoppers.
Rangeland Insect Lab, Bozeman, MT
John E. Henry, (406) 994-3344

Farmers with fescue pastures in Arkansas
and southern areas with similar climates
should make sure that their summer-grazing
cattle are at least three-eighths Brahman.
In recent tests in Arkansas, Brahman
cattle grazing on fescue outgained Angus
all summer long by an average of half a
pound a day. The Brahman may tolerate two
conditions that bother Angus: the sun's
heat and a fungus in fescue thought to
slow weight gains.
South Central Family Farms Research,
Booneville, AR
M. Brown, (501) 675-3834

A successful first step has been taken
toward a vaccine against an intestinal
worm that causes severe economic losses to
farmers in the Southeast. The nodular
worm, Oesophogostomum radiatum, feeds on a
cow's blood, causing anemia, weight loss,
and sometimes the death of calves. In
preliminary tests with two groups of cows,
one group was injected with extracts from

14

the worm grown in culture. Both groups
were then infected with live worms. Cows
that got the shot gained an average of 23
pounds over the next 10 weeks; cows without the shot lost 4 pounds.
Helminthic Diseases Lab, Beltsville, MD
Louis C. Gasbarre, (301) 344-2509

Vaccinating heifers a month before breeding may save dairy and beef cattle embryos
from death by a herpes virus. In tests
with heifers infected with the virus 1 or
2 weeks after pregnancy began, three-
fourths of embryos died within 35 days.
Infectious bovine rhinotracheitis can
occur naturally or from live-virus vaccines given too close to breeding. Embryo
deaths are often missed because ranchers
are unaware that cows are pregnant.
Immunopathology Research, National Animal
Disease Center, Ames, IA
Janice M. Miller, (515) 239-8273

Blood-typing chickens is an accurate way
to tell if the birds have resistance to
Marek's disease, a tumor produced by a
virus. Chickens with a B-21 blood type
are more resistant than chickens with
other blood types, although the degree of
improved resistance may vary from one
strain of chickens to another. The B-
complex genes also may be related to the
number of eggs chickens produce. Breeders
should identify the B-genes in their base
breeding lines and select for them to
obtain chickens that lay more eggs and
resist Marek's disease.
Avian Leukosis Research, East Lansing, MI
Larry D. Bacon, (517) 337-6828

Matching dairy cow forage to soil type can
lower a farmer's cost of producing milk
without increasing dairy surpluses. For
example, the forage bromegrass usually
costs more to produce than alfalfa and
yields less milk. On high acid soils,
however, the large amounts of lime necessary to grow alfalfa make bromegrass a
more economical forage choice. The finding was part of a larger study of the
impacts of various forages on production
costs, feed intake and milk production and
composition.
U.S. Dairy Forage Center, Madison, WI
Charles Kiddy, (608) 263-2030

Heifers have a 20% higher pregnancy rate if ranchers and farmers let them go into heat twice before breeding them during their third heat. To increase pregnancy rates in herds, researchers are testing feeding schemes that encourage early puberty so the cows reach the third heat cycle earlier in the breeding season. This would increase the number of pregnant heifers delivering calves earlier in the year, giving them more time to gain weight before winter.
Fort Keogh Livestock and Range Research, Miles City, MT
Robert B. Staigmiller, (406) 232-4970

Bitterbrush is sweet news for wildlife but is difficult to grow. The shrub is an important food for livestock and essential for deer living on western rangeland, where food can be sparse during the winter. Scientists discovered that bitterbrush seed can be planted in the spring—and avoid getting eaten by birds and rodents—if it gets 2 weeks of cold, moist conditions. Until now, ranchers and game wardens thought its seeds had to be sown in the fall to chill sufficiently to germinate.
Pasture and Range Management, Reno, NV
James A. Young, (702) 784-5607

Hormones that control digestion in humans may have a strong evolutionary link to a newly discovered natural chemical in the digestive system of the common cockroach. The cockroach chemical, which ARS scientists and their colleagues have named leucosulfakinin, is strikingly similar to two human hormones. In humans, one hormone controls production of hydrochloric acid in the stomach, while the other regulates the contractions of the gall bladder. The findings come from a study of chemicals that cockroaches produce in their bodies. These chemicals might become models for new insecticides that would kill cockroaches but be harmless to other life forms.
Western Research Center, Albany, CA
Ronald J. Nachman, (415) 486-3637

Ranchers grazing livestock on selenium-laden soils may be losing millions of dollars because of lowered production from their animals. One selenium-accumulating plant found on western ranges, Astragalus bisulcatus, is also a selenium indicator. It could be a natural warning sign to tell ranchers to keep livestock away. Although livestock normally won't eat the plant, its presence means palatable grasses growing in the area are probably high in selenium. Although usually not fatal, selenium may suppress the outward signs of the cow's fertile cycle, in turn delaying breeding.
Poisonous Plant Research Lab, Logan, UT
Lynn F. James, (801) 752-2941

Custom-built artificial viruses may lead to a stronger genetically engineered vaccine against foot-and-mouth disease in livestock. Scientists have now pieced together more parts of the disease-causing virus; the current genetically engineered vaccines stimulate immunity with only one part. The goal is a vaccine with all the genes of the virus that produce immunity—but without the genes that would allow the reconstructed virus to live or make animals sick. The disease causes severe economic losses in foreign countries, but an improved vaccine would cut both the risk and the cost of outbreaks here.
Plum Island Animal Disease Center, Greenport, NY
Douglas M. Moore, (516) 323-2500

Scientific Information Systems

Computerized eyes are capturing and analyzing visual images to help farmers curb soil erosion. The eyes are in the camera of an image analyzer that can scan photos and compute the number of wormholes in no-till-farmed soils or the percentage of crop residues left to protect a harvested field against erosion. The device can also analyze soil particles for size, shape and pore distribution pattern. With this information, scientists can better understand such phenomena as water infiltration or how crusts seal off soil pores and produce more surface runoff.
National Soil Erosion Lab, West Lafayette, IN
L. Darrell Norton, (317) 494-8682

Bacteria can now be "fingerprinted" much
more effectively. With a computer program
that singles out the unique protein pattern of a species, scientists identified
six species of Erwinia bacteria, some of
which cause slimy soft rot in harvested
vegetables. Once scientists learn more
about the role these proteins play, they
can genetically engineer the bacteria so
the organisms cannot produce disease. The
research may also lead to resistant vegetable varieties and other ways to control
soft rot.
Horticultural Crops Quality Lab,
Beltsville, MD
Harold E. Moline/William R. Hruschka,
(301) 344-3128

A computer program can come very close to
predicting the actual amount of stripe
rust disease that wheat will get. The
program, which can run on most personal
computers, is the first of several that
scientists hope to develop for cereal
crops. If the computer predicts that the
disease infestation will cause less damage
to wheat than the cost of control measures, farmers can ignore the disease and
still come out ahead. The only information farmers need enter into the computer
is weather data and flowering date of the
crop. The simplicity of the program lends
itself to predicting disease infestations
any place in the world.
Cereal Crop Improvement, Bozeman, MT
Albert L. Scharen, (406) 994-5158

To help farmers manage their pastures,
scientists cooperating with the University
of Kentucky have devised a plant growth
model to be incorporated into an expert
system for small farms. PASTURE, when
told how much a specific piece of land
will be fertilized, irrigated and grazed,
responds with how much dry matter (and of
what quality) will be produced. The
computer model has been validated and
works for bermudagrass and fescue; it will
be adapted to about 17 other types of
forages, including clovers.
South Central Family Farms Research,
Booneville, AR
Lance Tharel, (501) 675-3834

16

Water evaporation measured by airborne sensing systems came within 12% of ground-based data in recent tests over cotton, wheat and alfalfa fields. The tests were part of an irrigation management and water conservation study. Rapid measurements of water evaporation over entire farms could become critical in water conservation programs that depend on efficient irrigation scheduling.
U.S. Water Conservation Lab, Phoenix, AZ
Ray D. Jackson, (602) 261-4356

Heavy downpours during intense storms can be simulated with greater accuracy through a new procedure that analyzes highly erratic rainfall patterns on a minute-by-minute basis. A combination of rain gauge equipment and mathematical techniques enables researchers to include sudden and extreme variations in rainfall data in computer models that estimate the availability of soil water for crops. When fully developed, such models will play a significant role in water conservation and irrigation management.
Coastal Plains Soil and Water Conservation Research Center, Florence, SC
Edward J. Sadler, (803) 669-5203

The CAT-scan, a sophisticated tool in human diagnostic medicine, should help breeders select livestock of the future with just the right amount of fat to suit consumers. Standing for computer-assisted tomography, the CAT-scan permits geneticists to study cross-sectional images of animals constructed from X-ray data and to save for breeding those judged genetically superior.
Genetics and Breeding Research, Clay Center, NE
Kreg A. Leymaster, (402) 762-3241

Human Nutrition

New evidence suggests that partially hydrogenated vegetable oils in margarine and shortening do not increase the risk of heart disease. Hydrogenation, which makes solid fat from oils, converts up to 20% of unsaturated fats into trans isomers not found in natural vegetable oils. These isomers were thought to be only partially metabolized by the body as saturated fats. Analysis of organ tissue from human cadavers and biopsies of fat tissue, however, shows that the isomers are primarily used for energy and do not accumulate in cells enough to alter cell formation that could lead to elevated serum cholesterol and fat levels. The findings agree with results of human and animal metabolism studies.
Vegetable Oils Research, Northern Research Center, Peoria, IL
E.A. Emken, (309) 685-4011, ext. 280

How does atherosclerosis (hardening of the arteries) begin? Scientists are closer to answering that question after finding that cells in blood vessel walls can produce a substance that promotes clotting and turns normally smooth arterial walls into "fly paper" for white blood cells. The substance, interleukin-1, was thought to be produced only by certain white blood cells. But, using recombinant DNA techniques, scientists found that the cells lining blood vessels and the adjacent smooth muscle cells, begin producing interleukin-1 when irritated by toxins. The next question is whether dietary fats and cholesterol also trigger production of interleukin-1.
Human Nutrition Research Center on Aging, Boston, MA
Peter Libby, (617) 956-0393

Viva la différence! is getting a new translation as nutrition studies suggest it's the difference that keeps one sex long-lived. Most studies are done on male animals and men to eliminate the variable of hormone fluctuations, but scientists may be making a big mistake by generalizing from these studies for both sexes. Female rats, for example, survived copper

17

deficiency experiments that killed 40% to 70% of their male counterparts from ruptured hearts in 8 weeks. Female rats reportedly survive a year on such copper-deficient diets. This is the first scientific evidence that an animal's sex can protect against heart-related death.
Vitamin and Mineral Nutrition Lab, Beltsville Human Nutrition Research Center, Beltsville, MD
Meira Fields, (301) 344-2422

A low-calorie diet without exercise puts women at risk of losing lean tissue as well as fat, according to a strictly controlled study of moderately overweight young women. A no-exercise group ate 1,200 calories a day but lost no more fat than another group of women who consumed 1,800 calories a day but exercised actively. The 1,200 calorie group lost more total weight than the high-calorie group, but this was attributed to loss of body water and wasting muscle tissue. The findings stress that weight loss programs should be evaluated in terms of their effects on overall health and fitness of dieters.
Western Human Nutrition Research Center, San Francisco, CA
Amy Belko, (415) 556-5695

Another curse of aging, a rat study shows, is that it retards the ability to retrieve fats from storage for ready energy. But endurance exercise reverses this trend. Older rats that were subjected to 60 minutes on the treadmill each day were able to mobilize and burn more fat from their fat pads than the ones that ran or waddled for only 10 minutes. During exercise, the 60-minute group had higher levels of epinephrine--a stress hormone also known as adrenaline--which may have accounted for the increased capacity of their muscles to burn fat.
Human Nutrition Research Center on Aging, Boston, MA
Carol N. Meredith, (617) 956-0334

Extremely small amounts of certain poisons may actually be ingredients for a healthy diet. Studies with animals indicate that arsenic, for example, may play a role in

18

Vitamin A in the body could be measured more accurately, according to preliminary animal studies. An estimated one-third of the U.S. population, especially the poor, doesn't get enough vitamin A through eating liver, fresh milk, and fresh vegetables such as carrots and corn. The new test calls for injecting a vitamin A-like material, allowing 1 week for it to be stored in the liver, and then measuring the amount left in the blood. The test proved to be 75% accurate for determining how much vitamin A was in the liver of rats--making it the most accurate non-radioactive test so far. Longer-term studies with rats are now under way. A future experiment with humans is planned. Western Human Nutrition Research Center, San Francisco, CA
Betty J. Burri, (415) 556-6016

For the first time, scientists can "watch" the liver convert dietary sugars into a host of chemicals that transport hormones and nutrients, detoxify drugs, store the body's fuel and perform other essential functions. In the new technique, scientists feed isotope-labeled sugars to animals or humans, then flush the labeled products from the body with acetaminophen (the main ingredient in Tylenol and other analgesics) so they can be identified and measured. This is a rapid, accurate, harmless and painless way to study the chemistry behind conditions like diabetes and obesity, the inflammatory response to infection and, indirectly, the conversion of sugars to fats. Human Nutrition Research Center on Aging, Boston, MA
Marc K. Hellerstein, (617) 956-0402

Look for stable isotopes--nonradioactive variations of nature's elements--to cause their own explosion in nutrition research for children. Scientists are now using heavy forms of carbon, hydrogen and oxygen as tracers to determine if and how nutrients are digested, absorbed and used; to estimate infants' body fat or energy expenditure as they grow; and to track the body's synthesis and breakdown of its own chemicals. Stable isotopes are especially suited for infants and children because

they are harmless and the tests are quick, easy, painless and accurate. Children's Nutrition Research Center, Houston, TX
Peter Klein, (713) 799-6000

Calorie counters may be getting fewer calories in their diets than they think, according to preliminary findings. USDA food tables--the primary references for food composition--report calorie content in terms of energy the body can use. The method of calculating this figure was developed around the turn of the century, but the food supply has changed since then. Are the calculated numbers still accurate? In a recent study, 12 men consumed ordinary foods in a mixed diet for 12 weeks. Direct measurement of the available energy in the diet averaged 5 percent below the calculated values. The discrepancy will be tested further using a human calorimeter, a chamber that measures the heat from a person's metabolism of food. Energy and Protein Nutrition Lab, Beltsville Human Nutrition Research Center, Beltsville, MD
Carolyn Miles, (301) 344-2127

Vitamin K, essential for blood clotting, can now be detected in tiny amounts. The new method could lead to a Recommended Dietary Allowance and will help answer unresolved questions about clotting and bleeding disorders, such as how to balance vitamin K intake with anticlotting drugs. Because the new method is faster and far more sensitive than previous ones, its developers have already established normal fasting blood levels of the vitamin. These levels are about 1,000 times lower than those for vitamins A and E. Scientists will also be able to look at the body's absorption of the vitamin from foods and study its metabolism. Human Nutrition Research Center on Aging, Boston, MA
James A. Sadowski, (617) 956-0337/
Yacoob Haroon, (617) 956-0367

19

Calcium supplement sales are booming as
women try to protect themselves against
brittle bones, or osteoporosis. But it's
still not clear whether the pills are
effective over the long term. A 5-year
study of 360 women is now under way to
resolve the question for women past menopause. In a preliminary 7-month study,
postmenopausal women, whose daily calcium
intake from all sources was half or less
the Recommended Dietary Allowance, lost
spinal bone at a significantly greater
rate than women whose intake exceeded the
800-milligram RDA.
Human Nutrition Research Center on Aging,
Boston, MA
Bess Dawson-Hughes, (617) 956-0415

*U.S. GOVERNMENT PRINTING OFFICE:1986-180-916:40248/ARS

G.X.5
Qua

Quarterly Report
of Selected Research Projects

United States
Department of
Agriculture

 Agricultural
Research
Service

January 1 to March 31, 1987

CONTENTS

New & Improved Products

Taste panels agree that the flavor of salt-free cakes--white, yellow, spice, and devil's food--is as good or better than that of the typical bakery cake, which may contain as much as half a teaspoon of salt. Commercial bakers interested in capturing the salt-free market can avoid problems of low-salt or no-salt cakes--more shrinkage and less firmness--by altering the order in which they mix ingredients and possibly by changing the type of sugar used. People on a salt-free diet at home, of course, can continue to bake their own salt-free cakes from scratch.
Food Science Research, Eastern Research Center, Philadelphia, PA
Virginia H. Holsinger, (215) 233-6703

Note: One or more scientists familiar with each research project are listed for further information. If the scientists are unavailable, others at the same telephone number may also be familiar with the work.

Items marked with the word PATENT are being patented by ARS. For more information contact Ann Whitehead, National Patent Program, Bldg. 005, Rm. 401, Beltsville Agricultural Research Center, Beltsville, MD 20705, (301) 344-2786.

The Atlantic potato, an ARS-developed variety, makes chips with lower fat content than any other variety. After only 5 years of large-scale production, Atlantic is the third most popular chipping potato in North America. Usually, when potato chips are deep fried, fat replaces the water in raw chips. Atlantic chips, however, absorb less fat than other varieties because Atlantic has the lowest ratio of water to solid tissue. Potato chip makers prefer Atlantic because they get more chips per pound from varieties with a high proportion of solid tissue.
Vegetable Lab, Beltsville, MD
Raymon E. Webb, (301) 344-3380

Improving corn quality could boost exports, and two new methods quickly find the range in moisture content--a crucial sign of quality. Until now, only the average moisture of a load of corn could be measured. While that level might appear satisfactory, small amounts of too-moist corn can get moldy and damage the whole load. Similarly, overdried corn can break, leaving explosive dust or fragments more vulnerable to insects. One of the new methods works by examining how a single corn kernel and the water in it affect a surrounding electric field. The other method detects moisture extremes by measuring the electricity conducted by kernels passed through crushing rollers. If used commercially, either method should help improve corn quality.
Plant Structure and Composition Research, Athens, GA
Stuart O. Nelson, (404) 546-3101/
U.S. Grain Marketing Research Lab, Manhattan, KS
C.R. Martin, (913) 776-2730

Beer could taste better if barley breeders developed varieties with more of three essential enzymes. In beer-making, malt, or sprouted barley, is crushed or steeped into mash, from which a liquid called wort is extracted. ARS scientists have found that the three enzymes--a ribonuclease and two nucleases--speed up fermentation as yeast is added to the wort. They convert malt's genetic material to compounds called nucleobases. The enzyme action should also improve the flavor of the beer. Until now, nucleobases have not been considered in barley breeding; some varieties provide barely enough for good malting quality.
Cereal Crops Research, Madison, WI
Neville Prentice, (608) 262-4481

A two-step treatment can now rid apples of the pesky codling moth without damaging fruit quality. Cold storage kills the eggs, and fumigation with low levels of methyl bromide kills the larvae. When these treatments are approved by Japan, western U.S. apple growers will be able to net millions of dollars exporting apples there. Fruit known to host the codling moth has been banned, except for treated cherries and walnuts, because Japan is codling moth-free.
Yakima Agricultural Research Lab, Yakima, WA
Harold R. Moffitt, (509) 575-5960

Nonfat dry milk illegally adulterated with cheaper whey proteins will be easier to spot with a test to identify proteins in milk. Each type of milk protein moves to a different position on a special gel when an electric current is applied, allowing scientists to identify the pattern later. The test is a new use for a common lab procedure, gel electrophoresis. When nonfat dry milk is diluted with whey proteins, electrophoresis provides absolute evidence of adulteration. USDA's Agricultural Marketing Service may use the test to ensure that nonfat dry milk is not diluted with whey.
Food Science Research, Philadelphia, PA
Jay J. Basch/Edyth L. Malin,
(215) 233-6444

Using starch granules to encase a bacterium used for years as a biocontrol agent against many insect pests may make it more effective. In lab tests, all European corn borers that ate Bacillus thuringiensis (Bt) in a moist granular starch matrix died within a week; all borers on a Bt-free diet survived. For several months before the tests, the starch had protected the Bt from ultraviolet radiation--a wavelength of sunlight. Until now, the market for Bt and nearly all other insect-fighting microbes has been limited because they degrade rapidly in the natural environment. Encasing them in a starch bait solves that problem. The granules can be formulated simply and inexpensively. (PATENT)
Plant Polymer Research, Northern Research Center, Peoria, IL
Richard L. Dunkle, (309) 685-4011, Ext. 542

Citrus canker bacterial strains recently discovered in Florida may be native to the state and not brought in from other areas as previously thought. That is based on mapping the DNA, or genetic material, in 43 of the known canker strains from around the world. Scientists had assigned these strains to three groups, but the new Florida strains vary greatly and don't fall into any of these groups. Consequently, scientists now believe the strains may be Florida natives. The findings may help state and federal regulatory agencies in their efforts to control the spread of canker.
Fruit Lab, Horticultural Science Institute, Beltsville, MD
Edwin L. Civerolo/John S. Hartung,
(301) 344-3374

Irradiation could make ethyl alcohol more economical to produce. Treating corn or other cereal grains with gamma radiation eliminates the costly cooking of grain mash, necessary to rupture its molecular structure. Once this is done, the mash is turned into a jelly with the starch exposed for later enzyme action that converts it to a fermentable sugar.

Irradiation accomplishes the same thing as cooking by cleaving the starch molecules. In all experiments comparing heat gelatinization to irradiation, alcohol yield was about the same.
(PATENT)
Food and Feed Safety Research, Southern Research Center, New Orleans, LA
Youn W. Han, (504) 286-4228

Scientists interested in genetically engineering oilseed crops have synthesized a gene that carries the "blueprint" for a key protein required for producing plant oil. They placed the gene, assembled from 16 DNA fragments, into bacteria, which then made the protein in large amounts. Now, the action of this critical protein, heretofore produced only in small amounts by plants, can be studied more extensively.
(PATENT)
Seed Biosynthesis Research, Northern Research Center, Peoria, IL
P.D. Beremand, (309) 485-4011, Ext. 293

The growing blueberry industry can expect three new varieties this spring. All are early ripening highbush berries superior to present varieties. Although highbush blueberries are predominantly grown in the north where they receive adequate chilling in winter, Cooper and Gulf Coast have a low chilling requirement, making them ideal for southeastern growers. Duke, a northern highbush blueberry that combines plant vigor and high productivity with good fruit quality, grows well in the Mid- Atlantic area, westward to southern Michigan, and in western Oregon and Washington.
Small Fruits Research, Poplarville, MS
James M. Spiers, (601) 795-8751/
Fruit Lab, Horticultural Science Institute, Beltsville, MD
Arlen D. Draper, (301) 344-3571

Another blueberry type, called rabbiteye, may have greater potential as an export crop for farmers in the Southeast. One rabbiteye variety, Climax, holds up under shipping conditions for 2 to 3 weeks without significant disease or weight losses. That is based on lab studies and test shipments to the agency's lab in Rotterdam, The Netherlands. The studies also showed that Climax is better than another rabbiteye variety, Woodard, for long-distance shipping.
U.S. Horticultural Research Lab, Orlando, FL
William R. Miller, (305) 897-7325

Pollen makes many of us wheeze and sneeze, but most plants need it to propagate. Usually pollen lives only a few hours once it leaves the plant, but scientists can freeze or chill it to give it a longer life--a big plus for plant breeders. Scientists have now preserved pollen from pearl millet--a protein-rich grain--for more than 4 years to create a ready supply for breeding. Pearl millet tolerates drought better than most grain crops, including corn and wheat. Grown in India and Africa for human and animal consumption, millet is also a major livestock forage in the southern United States.
Forage and Turf Research Lab, Tifton, GA
Wayne W. Hanna, (912) 386-3353

Either of two chemicals newly added to Trimedlure (TML), the attractant in traps to detect the Mediterranean fruit fly, greatly improves the effectiveness of the lure under extremes of temperature. The additives reduce or eliminate unwelcome crystallization associated with Trimedlure during cool weather and extend the attractant's persistence when weather is hot.
(PATENT)
Insect Chemical Ecology Lab, Beltsville, MD
T.P. McGovern, (301) 344-2138

It looks like mayonnaise, but Govert, a mixture developed by ARS, isn't for sandwiches. Govert makes weed biocontrols out of disease-causing organisms that will not ordinarily infect

weeds unless there's dew in crop fields. Made of lecithin, wax, mineral oil, and water, it provides the moisture needed for Alternaria cassiae and other fungi to survive and develop on leaves. In lab tests, Govert helped A. cassiae infect and kill 88% of sicklepod plants without added moisture. (PATENT)
Southern Weed Science Lab,
Stoneville, MS
Chuck Quimby, (601) 686-2311

Crop Production & Protection

The corn rootworm, the target of more insecticides than any other pest of corn, can be controlled with at least 90% less of the insecticide carbaryl if mixed with new, environmentally safe baits. The baits include sex phero- mones, which attract the pest, and cucurbitacins--natural chemicals in certain wild gourds--which stimulate feeding. In preliminary tests, adult rootworms gorged themselves to death on carbaryl-poisoned bait. Farmers typi- cally apply about 1 pound per acre of carbaryl; only one-tenth to one- hundredth that amount is needed if it is applied with the bait, which does not appear to attract beneficial insects such as ladybirds and honey bees.
Crop and Entomology Research,
Brookings, SD
Gerald A. Sutter, (605) 693-3241

New natural enemies of weeds have been identified in laboratory tests: bacte- ria that attack weed seeds and seedlings but not crops. Some rhizobacteria make weed seeds rot in the ground, thwarting such natural defenses as a hard coat and toxic chemicals. They even destroy other bacteria that normally protect weed seeds from enemy fungi. Other rhizobacteria stymie the growth of weed seedlings, limit essential nutrients, or make weed roots susceptible to disease- causing microbes. In tests, rhizobacte- ria were effective against velvetleaf, morningglory, pigweed, and jimsonweed. Applied to the soil every few years, these microbes could replace herbicides.

Scientists are testing more than 500 strains of them for their potential as natural weed-seed herbicides for crop fields and gardens.
Crop Production Research, Columbia, MO
Robert J. Kremer, (314) 882-2405

Female insects that sterilize their sons--and produce female descendants that do the same--have been bred for the first time. By crossing tobacco bud- worms with a related species, scientists came up with hybrids that pass along a trait for male sterility. The trait could mean genetic control of a pest that devours millions of dollars worth of cotton, tobacco, and vegetables a year. Further, the budworm is also becoming resistant to the chemicals that best control it, the pyrethroids. In a test on St. Croix in the U.S. Virgin Islands, these "femmes fatales" with sterile sons reduced a natural popula- tion by 75%. The scientists are seeking the same kind of sterility in the boll- worm (corn earworm)--a closely related and even more serious crop pest.
Southern Field Crop Insects Lab,
Stoneville, MS
Edgar G. King, (601) 686-2311

Cotton growers in California's Imperial Valley will soon be using a farming technique aimed at cutting pesticide and water use. Because scientists have proven it possible, this year all grow- ers will follow a "short season" sched- ule. This new schedule starts when the soil is warm, uses irrigation, chemical termination of growth and defoliation of the plants, and an early harvest in early November. Then all crop residue must be plowed under to kill insects that normally live above ground. Insec- ticides to control pink bollworms and other insects will be sprayed only if their populations threaten to soar and cause economic losses. While the cotton yield may be less, total profit for growers should be greater because of reduced costs for water and insecti- cides. Studies show the short-season will greatly reduce the buildup of overwintering pink bollworms, cotton leafperforators, and whiteflies so that the potential number that survive and

infest the crop next year will drop dramatically. (PATENT)
Western Cotton Research Lab, Phoenix, AZ
Louis A. Bariola, (602) 261-3524

Farmers can field dry alfalfa quicker and avoid losing nutrients from the thick stems of first harvest by mechanical crushing, which reduces drying time by about 40%. Spraying a drying agent, potassium carbonate, reduces drying time another 10%. For the third and fourth harvests, mechanical crushing doesn't work, but spraying the drying agent reduces drying time 20% to 50%. Nutrient content is a major factor in the price a farmer can get for the hay. (PATENT)
Dairy Forage Research, East Lansing, MI
C. Alan Rotz, (517) 353-1758

Not all foreign insects that slip into the United States are bad news. Two species of wasp--one from Africa and one from South America--are newly reported as established in southern Florida. Both are predators of caterpillars that feed on plants and will augment beneficial native predators.
Systematic Entomology Lab, Washington, DC
Arnold S. Menke, (202) 382-1803

Plant growth inhibitors are of more than passing interest to electric utilities, who currently spend an estimated $800 million a year to prune trees mechanically under power lines. Orchardists also pay a big annual pruning bill. Now three chemicals show promise in controlling woody growth by inhibiting a tree's natural production of gibberellin, a growth stimulant. Two chemicals, flurprimidol and XE10-19, are experimental; a third, paclobutrazol, has so far been registered for use on shade trees but not fruit trees. In recent ARS tests, flurprimidol retarded the height of apple and shade trees by 35% to 50% without causing obvious foliage injury. The growth retardants may be applied by injection at the base of the trunk, although painting the bark

with the chemicals and spraying the root zone have also proven effective.
Foreign Disease-Weed Science Research, Frederick, MD
John P. Stenett, (301) 663-7132

Sunflowers inhibit the germination and growth of neighboring plant species, including many common weeds, by producing toxic chemicals, a phenomenon known as allelopathy. Furthermore, when sunflower stalks and leaf residue were disked into the soil after harvest, the next year's emergence of sunflowers was reduced by from 13% to as much as 45%. The allelochemicals from sunflower residues evidently interfere with the crop's own growth as well as with that of weeds.
Foreign Disease-Weed Science Research, Frederick, MD
G.R. Leather, (301) 663-7132

The herbicidal qualities of 31,000 chemical compounds evaluated from 1944 to 1976 are summarized in a new USDA publication, Technical Bulletin No. 1721. The results cover 2 dosage rates and 10 kinds of plant responses on 6 plant species. These evaluations should be useful to the chemical industry and others interested in herbicides.
Foreign Disease-Weed Science Research, Frederick, MD
Richard A. Creager, (301) 663-7132

Updated fertilization guidelines can enhance revegetation of Old World bluestems to protect eroded farmlands in the Conservation Reserve Program on the southern Great Plains. Research shows this perennial grass produces forage most efficiently from an April application of 60 pounds of nitrogen per acre. In related studies, Plains bluestem proved better adapted than other grass varieties to iron-deficient soils. An Old World bluestem variety especially bred for the region's iron-deficient soils will be released sometime this year.
Range and Pasture Research, Woodward, OK
William A. Berg, (405) 256-7449

Yams can be grown in Puerto Rico with cassava, another root crop, and yield more food than yams alone at lower cost per acre. A 2-year study shows that the woody cassava plants—which take the place of the wooden stakes and wire trellises—can yield 60% more tubers from the same plot. This intercropping system also provides more carbohydrates per acre by supplying two marketable crops.
Tropical Agricultural Research Station, Mayaguez, PR
Heber Irizary/Edmundo Rivera, (809) 834-2435

A new specialized form of a fungus that causes plant disease, discovered in Panama in 1985, is showing promise for biological control of a noxious weed threatening Hawaii. Introduced to Oahu from Central America in 1941, the weed Clidemia hirta is today the most serious weed pest in Oahu's rain forests and has spread to forests of other Hawaiian islands. Lab tests showed the fungus causes defoliation and dieback of the weed within 8 days after inoculation. Hawaii's State Board of Agriculture has granted permission for field testing, after extensive host range studies showed the fungus to be specific to Clidemia hirta. In tests in Oahu forests, the fungus has shown excellent potential as a biocontrol agent for this weed.
Foreign Disease-Weed Science Research, Frederick, MD
Frances M. Latterell, (301) 663-2632

Yellow starthistle, a range weed from Eurasia, might be controlled by a European weevil on the 8 million acres the thistle infests in California. ARS scientists first tested the seedhead weevil, Bangasternus orientalis, in Greece, Italy, and California. It attacks the thistle at bud stage or before seed set. Released in 1985 in three California counties, the weevil successfully colonized, overwintered, and became established to help control the yellow star. Additional releases are planned, along with continued evaluation of its ability to control the pest. Spreading dramatically from 1.2 million acres in 1958, the thistle is one of a dozen imported weeds for which scientists have sought natural enemies in Europe since the late 1950's.
Biological Control of Weeds Lab, Albany, CA
Donald M. Maddox, (415) 486-3625/
Biological Control of Weeds Lab, Rome, Italy
Paul H. Dunn, 648-0140

Florida beggarweed can be destroyed by a newly discovered fungus without hurting the weed's crop victims—peanuts and soybeans. Not only does beggarweed cut yields of peanuts 25% and soybeans 10%, it's so similar to the crops that most chemicals that control it damage the crops, too. In lab tests, the fungus, Colletotrichuum truncatum, controlled the weed but didn't harm 19 varieties of soybeans, 4 types of peanuts, or 74 other plant species, including crops that might be growing in neighboring fields. A commercial company is interested in developing C. truncatum as a safe alternative to chemicals.
(PATENT)
Coastal Plains Experiment Station, Tifton, GA
John Cardina, (912) 386-3351

Two weed controls that don't want to work together have been tricked into cooperating. In lab tests, the fungus Fusarium lateritium kills 20% to 30% of one of the most serious broadleaf weeds, velvetleaf; the chemical 2,4-DB kills 50% to 60%. Together they could provide total control of the weed in soybeans and corn except for one problem: the chemical kills the fungus. But scientists found that applying 2,4-DB first and then the fungus—even just seconds later—gives 100% control. They think the plant quickly "grabs" the tiny 2,4-DB molecules into its cells so that large fungus molecules never touch the lethal chemical. Scientists are developing a sprayer that will disperse the fungus from one end and 2,4-DB from the other.
Southern Weed Science Lab, Stoneville, MS
Doug Boyette, (601) 686-2311

6

Adding pectin to a test fungus, _Alternaria crassa_, increases the potency of the fungus and turns it into a control for three serious soybean weeds-- eastern black nightshade, hemp sesbania, and showy crotalaria. This marks the first time the host range of a bio-control agent has been expanded. Scientists think the pectin stimulates the fungus to produce extra pectin-destroying enzyme--enough to destroy a weed's cell walls and give the fungus quick entry. Scientists tried pectin with four biocontrol fungi, but A. crassa, now used to control jimsonweed, was the only one that got the extra push. Field tests are needed, but one firm has already shown interest in the mixture as the first multivictim bio-control agent for weeds. (PATENT)
Southern Weed Science Lab,
Stoneville, MS
Doug Boyette, (601) 686-2311

Add sweetpotato weevils to the growing list of pests that can be monitored and controlled by pheromones (chemical attractants). The major female-produced pheromone of the sweetpotato weevil has been isolated, identified, and success-fully synthesized. Identification was particularly difficult because the pheromone compound's chemical structure differs from that of all other known pheromones and is produced in minute amounts. In field tests, the synthetic pheromone attracted as many males to traps as did the natural scent. The synthetic pheromone offers farmers a sensitive lure to trap a devastating pest that is hard to see because the larvae feed underground and the adults feed at night. (PATENT)
Insect Chemistry Research,
Gainesville, FL
Robert R. Heath, (904) 374-5735

Commercial and wild tomato plants are providing scientists with valuable clues to how plants survive in salty water. Commercial tomatoes have a natural mechanism to block out some salt from water the plants take in. Their wild ancestors take salt in but concentrate it in older leaves. By storing salt in specific plant parts, wild plants can withstand saltier water than their modern cousins. To gain information that would lead to more salt-tolerant crops, scientists are now studying the two different survival mechanisms by comparing ATPases--plant enzymes--found in various parts throughout the plant and analyzing the cellular biology of tomatoes.
U.S. Salinity Lab, Riverside, CA
Michael C. Shannon, (714) 683-5733

An insect native to southern California devours up to 95% of the eggs laid by the beet leafhopper. Scientists are now closely studying the biology of the beneficial insect, _Anagrus giraulti_, to develop ways to mass-rear quantities of them in labs. Scientists would release enough of these insects to control leafhoppers and their relatives that threaten vegetables with curly top virus and citrus with stubborn disease. Several other members of this helpful insect species have been imported from Europe and South America in hopes of finding insects even better suited for leafhopper control. Each year, curly top destroys about $5 million worth of California vegetables like beans, tomatoes, and cucurbits despite a $1 million leafhopper control program. Stubborn disease annually ruins California and Arizona citrus worth about $15 million.
Boyden Entomology Lab, Riverside, CA
Dale E. Meyerdirk, (714) 351-6741

Guayule, a desert shrub that contains natural rubber, is extremely drought tolerant. Scientists had kept guayule alive on just 15 inches of water a year, but when the plants were irrigated, they quickly doubled their rubber yield. This finding could help U.S. strategies for growing guayule in case supplies of imported natural rubber are cut off. Guayule farmers could let plants subsist on scant rainfall, then irrigate just before harvest in late winter or early spring, when rubber content is at its peak.
U.S. Water Conservation Lab, Phoenix, AZ
Dale A. Bucks, (602) 261-4356

A snag in genetic engineering of oats has become a stepping stone for conventional breeding approaches for improved grain quality and yield. In tissue cultures of plant cells intended to receive new genes, chromosomes often break--causing unwanted genetic changes that weaken plants. But the breaks provide scientists opportunities for mapping genes according to heritable traits. Many unique lines of oats lacking particular chromosome segments can be developed to aid the mapping and to help in developing new varieties with predictable traits. This tactic has already been successful with chromosome-deficient lines of wheat.
Plant Science Research, St. Paul, MN
H.W. Rines, (612) 625-5220

A fungus that devastates several important crops brings about its own destruction. A protein secreted by a Phytophthora fungus triggers host plants to produce a chemical that poisons the fungus. Working first with tobacco tissue culture and with a species of the fungus that causes black shank disease, ARS scientists isolated the protein labeled Ppn 46e. When exposed to the protein, the tissue culture produced capsidiol, which sick plants make to inhibit the fungus. The scientists then proved that this fungus also produces the protein in living plants.
Plant Disease Resistance Research, Madison, WI
John P. Helgeson, (608) 262-0649

A pecan tree can tolerate from 10 to 50 yellow aphids (depending on the species) per leaf before it loses significant energy. By using this as a basis for estimating potential damage to a tree and spraying pesticides only when and where needed, the pecan industry could save about $20 million a year on pesticide use, reduce any environmental threats from these chemicals, increase nut production, and extend the time it takes the aphid to develop pesticide resistance. Aphids can rob a tree's energy significantly during a growing season, reducing nut production 20% to 80%.
Southeastern Fruit and Tree Nut Research Lab, Byron, GA
Bruce W. Wood, (912) 956-5656

Pecan seedlings grow more when inoculated with a fungus that allows the roots to absorb more mineral nutrition. The fungus, Pisolithus tinctorius, is a commercially available inoculum that has greatly increased growth and survival of forest trees inoculated in the nursery. This is the first time it has been used on pecan seedlings.
Southeastern Fruit and Tree Nut Research Lab, Byron, GA
Ronald R. Sharpe, (912) 956-5656

The key to biological control of verticillium wilt in maples may be a bacterium. Caused by a fungus, verticillium wilt is a sometimes fatal disease of maples. In tests, several strains of the bacterium Bacillus subtilis were injected into the tissue of potted Norway maples, inhibiting verticillium growth and significantly reducing the fungus infection. These strains occur naturally in the stem tissue of red, silver, and Norway maples.
Nursery Crops Research Lab, Delaware, OH
Lawrence Schreiber, (614) 363-1129

"Fingerprinting" a rose leaf can precisely identify varieties, thereby protecting plant patents for this $44 million-a-year industry. By magnifying a rose leaf 10,000 to 20,000 times with a scanning electron microscope, scientists found that stomata--natural, porelike openings--have different shapes, depending on the variety. Differences were also apparent in subsidiary cells around the stomata, glandular hairs, and wax arrangement on leaves. This fingerprinting technique can also be used to distinguish varieties of trees and other nursery plants.
Nursery Crops Research Lab, Delaware, OH
Charles Krause, (614) 363-1129

Southern Delite, a new sweetpotato variety, will help farmers lower their growing costs. The new variety, based on 7 years of tests, sprouts better and requires less chemical pesticides than other sweetpotatoes. When exposed to root-knot nematodes, Southern Delite had 28% higher yields than a leading variety called Centennial. The new sweetpotato, developed in cooperation with the South Carolina Agricultural Experiment Station, should be available to farmers on a limited basis in the spring of 1987. U.S. Vegetable Lab, Charleston, SC Alfred Jones, (803) 556-0840

Sunflower seed production and oil quality both improved in south Texas when nematodes, or roundworms, were kept in check. Farmers long have known the nematode is bad news for crops but hadn't realized how much it damaged sunflowers in the Lower Rio Grande Valley, where the crop was only recently established. Tests show fumigating soils against the nematode can be economically worthwhile for Valley sunflower growers. Subtropical Plant Research Lab, Weslaco, TX Charles M. Heald, (512) 968-7546

Pesticide use on cotton was cut in half by counting the number of pink bollworm eggs on plants as an indicator of when to spray rather than waiting to count the number of larvae. This technique could save a grower with 2,000 acres as much as $140,000 each year. Although growers must learn to identify eggs by sight, scientists who developed the technique say that once it's mastered, it's easy. Most growers use 12 to 16 insecticide applications per season in California, often on a weekly schedule, after the larvae are discovered inside cotton-producing bolls. The new egg monitoring calls for only five to eight applications. Western Cotton Research Lab, Phoenix, AZ William D. Hutchison, (602) 261-3524

Electron microscopy studies show that a virus that damages eastern U.S. strawberries contains the same kind of bullet-shaped virus particles as those found by Japanese scientists in their strawberries. Although latent C virus is known to be widespread and highly damaging to cultivated strawberries, little is known of its identity. Now that evidence has been found of the nature of this virus--which each year damages up to 17% of the total U.S. strawberry crop valued at over $70 million--scientists believe they can develop a rapid, accurate method to detect strawberry latent C virus disease. Horticultural Crops Research Lab, Corvallis, OR Richard H. Converse, (503) 757-4819

Oat plants tolerant to acid soil could produce more income for potato farmers. When new oat selections with acid tolerance are released, they could be ideal for rotating with potatoes, a crop that must be in acidic soil to avoid scab disease. Acid-tolerant oats could be planted after the potato harvest and would be a good livestock feed crop in the Northeast and Northwest, the country's chief potato-growing regions. Plant Stress Lab, Beltsville, MD Charles Foy, (301) 344-4522

Mushroom flies surprised scientists in the Northwest by showing up in force during field tests to identify natural attractants for clover seed chalcids. While few chalcids appeared, several species of Megaselia mushroom flies did. The flies were particularly attracted by 1-phenylethanol, a compound in red clover and other plants. Scientists think the attractants will also work well with species of Megaselia that are major pests of commercial mushrooms here and abroad. Currently, no potent natural attractant is known for these pests. Besides spreading mushroom diseases, the flies eat the mycelium, the threadlike structure within the growing medium that produces the fruiting part of a mushroom. Forage Seed and Cereal Research, Corvallis, OR James A. Kamm, (503) 757-4365

Pecan growers may soon have a quick, reliable, and inexpensive way to see if the pecan pollen they're about to use is dead or alive. It calls for pressure-treating a mix of boric acid, table sugar, calcium nitrate, and a culture medium such as agar. Then the mix is cooled in shallow plates and pollen is added. If fertile, a pollen grain will begin growing its pollen tube within a few hours. Male nuclei pass through this tube to enter the embryo sac. The new, do-it-yourself test could save time and money for growers who use artificial pollen.
Plant Physiology Research, Athens, GA
Ida E. Yates, (404) 546-3523/
Pecan Breeding Research Lab,
Brownwood, TX
Tommy Thompson, (915) 646-0594

Animal Production & Protection

Grass tetany, a serious, sometimes fatal, disease of cattle, may be curbed as a result of the discovery that potassium governs the movement of magnesium from soil into plants. Research shows that too much potassium inhibits movement of magnesium from roots to the leafy tops of grasses and cereal forages. Cattle lacking sufficient dietary magnesium may develop grass tetany. Fertilizers for forages should strike a balance of enough potassium to meet needs for plant growth, but not enough to block uptake of magnesium into forage plant tops.
U.S. Plant, Soil, and Nutrition Lab,
Ithaca, NY
David Grunes, (607) 255-5480

Newly discovered fungi play a large role in helping cows break down hard-to-digest grasses. A cow's rumen—part of its stomach—is full of bacteria, fungi, and other organisms that break down grasses and feeds. The previously unknown fungi are among those that help break down fibers that contain lignin, a woody substance that makes grass and other forages, like alfalfa, hard to

digest. Scientists say learning about the new fungi may lead to ways to improve cows' digestion.
Plant Structure and Composition Research, Athens, GA
Danny E. Akin, (404) 546-3482

Two shots with an experimental vaccine, prepared from a bacterial extract, in one test reduced by 35% illness and death of calves with bovine respiratory disease. The illness at some time afflicts 30% to 80% of feedlot calves. If further tests succeed, the vaccine could eliminate the $16 to $21 per calf feedlot operators now spend treating calves for the disease. Caused by a variety of bacterial and viral agents, the disease costs the operators more than $500 million annually in lost weight gains, death of calves, and treatments. Calves get the disease when weakened by illnesses and travel.
Conservation and Production Lab,
Bushland, TX
Charles W. Purdy, (806) 378-5764

Changing the sex of a female lamb to male before it's born can mean gaining an extra pound per week on 16% less feed. In the first study of its kind to improve growth in lambs, male sex hormone—testosterone—was injected into pregnant ewes 4 weeks after breeding. Female embryos in test ewes developed male-like genitals. The altered lambs were unable to reproduce.
U.S. Meat Animal Research Center,
Clay Center, NE
John Klindt, (402) 762-3241

Bacteria sometimes sabotage efforts to turn them into "factories" for producing commercial quantities of products such as insulin and human growth hormone. Scientists recently found that some types of the bacterium Bacillus subtilis rearrange the genetic material transplanted into them, thereby changing the expected product. Once they understand how the maverick bacteria do this, scientists may be able to tame them and

10

further advance the science of genetic engineering. (PATENT)
Livestock Insects Lab, Kerrville, TX
Kevin B. Temeyer, (512) 257-3566

Cattle with zebu blood lines probably survive protein deficiency during winter and drought periods in the South better than our traditional, English-derived breeds. Zebus are Asian natives that in the United States include the humpback Brahmans. In tests, cattle with one-half, one-quarter, and no zebu breeding were placed on feed rations low in protein. All lost similar amounts of body protein, but the zebu crossbreeds recovered much faster than the nonzebu, English counterparts. Zebus were first imported to the southern United States because of their tolerance to heat.
Forage and Livestock Research Lab, El Reno, OK
Samuel W. Coleman, (405) 262-5291

Future hybrid forages could have the wide adaptability of tall fescue and the high nutritional content of giant fescue, a wild European species. These grasses are close cousins that were crossed and chemically treated to produce fertile hybrids with the most desired qualities of each parent. Now new varieties can be developed from these hybrids by selecting for genetic stability through several generations. Such varieties should be nutritionally better for grazing than tall fescue in hot summer months.
Tobacco and Forage Research, Lexington, KY
Georgia C. Eizenga, (606) 257-3686

Test cattle digested switchgrass and flaccidgrass more completely than bermudagrass, enabling them to gain weight twice as fast. All three grasses are subtropical perennials, but switchgrass or flaccidgrass would be better alternatives as summer forage for southern beef cattle, especially yearlings.
Plant Science Lab, Raleigh NC
J.C. Burns, (919) 737-2657

Young calves fed barley and hay instead of cows' milk during drought gained about 2 pounds a day, compared to about 2 to 2-1/2 pounds per day gain on milk when the mother had plenty of forage to eat. When drought hit Montana ranges in 1984 and stunted plant growth, researchers removed hungry calves from their mothers and fed them barley. Other calves fed oats gained 25% less. Researchers speculate that feeding barley to young calves could become more popular even when range grasses are plentiful.
Fort Keogh Livestock and Range Research, Miles City, MT
Robert B. Staigmiller, (406) 232-4970

Fly maggots that infect dairy calves' bedding are suppressed by a compound ARS scientists found to inhibit fly development. In small hutches used to raise calves outdoors, the compound suppressed maggots and emergence of adult flies by 90%. As many as 50,000 maggots can develop in straw bedding and feces in the hutches. The importance of fly control grows as farm areas become urbanized. (PATENT)
Livestock Insects Lab, Beltsville, MD
Ed Schmidtmann/Richard Miller, (301) 344-2973

A bacterium that causes swine dysentery uses the pig's cholesterol to grow. Now scientists have discovered what Treponema hyodysenteriae bacteria do with the cholesterol: they convert it to a chemical called cholestanol and take it into cell membranes. This action may be involved in the bacteria's destruction of the pig's intestinal tissues.
National Animal Disease Center, Ames, IA
Thad B. Stanton, (515) 239-8288

■■■■■■■■■■
Soil, Water & Air

Wind erosion can be controlled by planting wheat in a checkerboard pattern of cross rows instead of the usual parallel lines. In field tests, crossplanted plots reduced by seven times the potential soil loss before wheat became dormant. That's because more ground is

11

covered with wheat plants than in parallel row planting. Potential sandblast damage was also reduced because closely planted rows kept soil particles from becoming airborne.
Cropping Systems Research Lab,
Big Spring, TX
J.D. Bilbro, (915) 263-0293

Nutrients are continuously being lost from farmland to water in runoff and erosion. To minimize this loss, scientists have developed a mathematical model that measures the amount of an essential element for crop growth--phosphorus--as it attaches to or detaches from sediment along its journey through small agricultural watersheds. The new model is designed for use by the USDA's Soil Conservation Service to help farmers develop the best plans to manage agricultural soil and decrease phosphorus loss and pollution of lakes and streams.
Soil Nitrogen and Environmental Chemistry Lab, Beltsville, MD
Harry M. Kunishi, (301) 344-3065

Fifteen times more soil from grazed-out wheatlands can be saved by no-till. Only 2 tons of soil per acre were lost with no-till, compared with 30 tons with conventional tillage. Farmers in the southern Great Plains typically let wheat mature for grain on their better land, allowing cattle to graze it out on more erodible land. Grazing out--grazing grain instead of harvesting it--is encouraged to help growers stay within the Federal wheat program's acreage diversion requirements.
Range and Pasture Research,
Woodward, OK
William A. Berg, (405) 256-7449

Major floods can be forecast in the intermountain area of the Northwest with the aid of a new database on soil frost, assembled for the years 1971 through 1984. Serious floods are often caused regionally by rain or snowmelt that runs off the land rapidly when the soil is frozen. The studies confirmed that frost penetrated the ground more deeply and more often at low elevations than at high because of the deeper snow cover at higher elevations. Land resource managers can use the information from the study to help predict flood occurrence and severity.
Northwest Watershed Research Center,
Boise, ID
C.L. Hanson, (208) 334-1363

Irrigators in the Northwest could reap more dollars, tests show, by plowing less and using crop rotations that can cut irrigation needs by 30% and erosion by 95%. Many farmers now make 15 tillage trips to grow 2 years of dry beans after 3 years of alfalfa. One alternative uses only two or three tillings--replacing the conventionally tilled beans with no-till wheat, barley, or corn and then minimum-till corn or beans. Scientists found the system could save $122 an acre--plus savings on nitrogen needs--compared with the same rotation grown with conventional tillage. Now researchers are beginning a cooperative project with a conservation district to help irrigators cut erosion through better tillage methods.
Soil and Water Management Research,
Kimberly, ID
David L. Carter, (208) 423-5582

If irrigators know the water level in their canals, they can accurately gauge water use and avoid waste. A new, simple-to-operate sensor has been developed to detect water depth in open irrigation canals. Until now, such sensors have been too costly for most agricultural uses and too inaccurate, hindering efforts to efficiently manage irrigation water. The new technique is up to 10 times more accurate than those currently available at the same or lower cost for equipment.
U.S. Water Conservation Lab, Phoenix, AZ
Allen R. Dedrick, (602) 261-4356

A simplified gate-control mechanism can provide constant waterflow in irrigation canals. Without accurate flow regulation, some fields get too much water; others, too little. Called a dual-acting, controlled-leak system, the new

mechanism uses a novel float device that can be easily fitted to most existing canals, eliminating costly electronic equipment and electricity. Fully electronic controls now used can be off by 5% to 10%; the new mechanism has an error rate of only 2%.
U.S. Water Conservation Lab, Phoenix, AZ
Albert J. Clemmens, (602) 261-4356

Scientific Information Systems

Sugarcane growers uncertain about the wisdom of planting only their single most productive variety on a large portion of their acreage may soon have a new computer program to help them decide. The program helps them weigh the risks and benefits of sticking with a given variety over a 20-year period. It takes into account commercial data as well as the predicted arrival of a new pest, potential drops in yield, and alternative allocations of cropland to different varieties.
Sugarcane Field Station,
Canal Point, FL
Barry Glaz, (305) 924-5227

Radar measurements of soil moisture made from aircraft or satellite may yet become valuable in agricultural planning. But first things first: mathematical models have to be developed that properly compensate for signal distortions due to vegetation and rough terrain. Data from 1984 space shuttle experiments are enabling researchers to determine how accurately (or inaccurately) some current models handle actual surface conditions—and to see how they can be improved.
Hydrology Lab, Agricultural Systems Research Institute, Beltsville, MD
Edwin T. Engman, (301) 344-3490

It's well known that growing several varieties is good health insurance for small grains and other crops having small, upright plants. Now computer-simulated disease epidemics show that crops sporting large amounts of foliage

(potato plants, for example) might also fare better during a major outbreak if several varieties are grown. Genetic variation could protect these crops against viral diseases spread by flying insects, as well as from disease-causing organisms from widely separated points.
Plant Science Research, Raleigh, NC
Kurt J. Leonard, (919) 737-2721

Herbicide residues decomposed by sunlight aren't likely to jeopardize the environment or food supply. Studies on the interaction of sunlight with herbicide chemicals have so far identified 45 photoproducts—22 of them previously unknown. All were less toxic than the compounds from which they came. Data from the studies will help scientists predict the environmental fate of new herbicides before field trials are begun.
Metabolism and Radiation Research Lab, Fargo, ND
Fred S. Tanaka, (701) 237-5771, Ext. 5468

Winter power failures can cripple farmsteads, but ARS has patented computerized controls for small windmills that provide backup electricity to homes. Computer adjustments make such windmills 29% to 47% more efficient. One sensor periodically samples output voltage while the controls increase voltage a step at a time. As output decreases, the computer lowers the voltage gradually to keep output as high as possible for the available wind. Another sensor measures windspeed so the control will turn off the turbine if there is too little or too much wind for safe, efficient operation. (PATENT)
Wind Powered Irrigation Research, Bushland, TX
R. Nolan Clark, (806) 378-5734

Soil nutrient losses can be predicted more accurately with new equations for use with existing computer models of soil erosion. Until now these models handled losses of nitrogen, carbon, and phosphorus only under a limited range of farming practices and soil conditions. The new equations can be adapted to a

13

far greater variety of conditions and can account for loss of potassium too. They also describe what happens to phosphorus, a major water pollutant, in terms of its bioavailability—its readiness to be taken up and metabolized by crops or aquatic weeds.
Water Quality and Watershed Research Lab, Durant, OK
Andrew N. Sharpley, (405) 924-5066

Wildfire hotspots on rangeland, such as smoldering logs, were clearly visible on black-and-white video images taken with an infrared camera on a low-flying aircraft. In recent trials, conventional video technology was used instead of the more complex and costly thermal scanning systems. Everything could be viewed live on a video monitor in the aircraft. Tests indicate that airborne video in the mid-infrared range could help detect dangerous hotspots before wind causes them to ignite other areas during wildfire mop-up operations.
Remote Sensing Research, Weslaco, TX
Paul R. Nixon, (512) 968-5533

County agricultural agents could help farmers find the best time to apply insecticides, thanks to a new mathematical model. The model is the basis for methods of sampling a pest population that describe the insect's distribution within a crop. With the model, the agents could develop numerical tables for determining precise levels of infestation on individual farms. Studies show that such an approach worked to control four species of cereal aphids on winter wheat in South Dakota.
Grain Insects Research Lab, Brookings, SD
Norman C. Elliott, (605) 693-5212

Estimating plant development using a new computer program will help wheat farmers improve scheduling of farm operations. Farmers entering maximum and minimum air temperatures into PLANTEMP can now predict how quickly their wheat will grow. Many decisions—such as when to apply herbicide or fertilizer—require knowing the stage of development of the wheat crop. Poorly timed applications can damage the crop or reduce the effectiveness of weed or disease controls.
Columbia Plateau Conservation Research Center, Pendleton, OR
Ronald W. Rickman, (503) 276-3811, Ext. 292

Human Nutrition

The role of vitamin C in preventing bleeding and inflamed gums—two early signs of gingivitis—has been confirmed in a closely controlled human study. Gingivitis is currently the major cause of tooth loss in U.S. adults over 40. When volunteers increased vitamin C intake from 5 mg to about 60 mg per day—the Recommended Dietary Allowance—their gums bled less and were less inflamed when probed. These symptoms were further reduced when vitamin C intake was increased to slightly more than 600 mg, or 10 times the RDA. The results confirmed findings by other researchers that vitamin C is needed to maintain healthy gums.
Biochemistry Research Lab, Western Human Nutrition Research Center, San Francisco, CA
Robert A. Jacob, (415) 556-3531

Contrary to some dietary advice, eating several small meals each day may not help burn up more calories than eating the same amount of food in only one or two large meals. A study showed that the rate at which the body uses calories in foods during digestion was essentially the same, whether volunteers ate two large meals or ate the same amount of food at several smaller meals. Although the smaller meals may have some physiological and psychological benefits for dieters, and may be a necessity for people with diabetes or other disorders, splitting the day's intake into smaller meals may not, by itself, boost the rate at which the body uses up calories.
Body Composition and Energy Metabolism Lab, Western Human Nutrition Research Center, San Francisco, CA
Amy Z. Belko, (415) 556-5695

14

A carrot a day may not prevent night blindness if protein or calorie intake is well below desirable levels. Young rats lost their ability to see in dim light when kept on diets very low in protein or somewhat low in protein and very low in calories, even though eye levels of vitamin A remained normal. A nutritionally complete diet restored night vision in both groups.
Human Nutrition Research Center on Aging at Tufts, Boston, MA
Robert M. Russell, (617) 556-3336

Sweet corn, harvested and consumed at the immature, "milky" stage, has a high level of nutritionally available niacin. Field corn, harvested at maturity, does not. As corn matures, researchers found, niacin is converted from digestible forms into forms that lab animals cannot digest. These findings may have implications for people, including many Latin Americans, who eat mainly cornmeal diets that contain low amounts of available niacin. A deficiency of this B-complex vitamin can increase the risk of pellagra. This disease is marked by dermatitis, inflammation of mucous membranes, and gastrointestinal disorders.
Plant Protein Research, Northern Research Center, Peoria, IL
Jerold A. Bietz, (309) 685-4011, Ext. 594

New equations are being developed to enable nutritionists to measure the ratio of body fat to lean for black Americans. Equations now in use were developed a number of years ago from a sample of white men and women, and a recent ARS study of 92 black men and women reveals that the old equations are poor predictors of body fat for black people. The new equations for black Americans can be used with three common methods for predicting fat-to-lean ratios: (1) measuring skinfold thickness at nine body sites, (2) measuring circumferences at similar sites, and (3) measuring body impedence by passing a harmless, painless electric current through the body. The resistance to the

current is proportional to the amount of lean tissue one has.
Energy and Protein Nutrition Lab, Beltsville Human Nutrition Research Center, Beltsville, MD
Joan M. Conway, (301) 344-2977

The way people walk may prove to be a clue to vitamin B6 deficiency, if preliminary results with lab rats hold true for humans. Lab rats who had been on a vitamin B6-deficient diet for only 9 days began to have problems with the way they moved their hind legs. Such "gait analysis" is sometimes used by toxicologists to screen pharmaceuticals. Vitamin B6, found in such foods as whole grain products and liver, is used in the body to manufacture niacin, amino acids that form proteins, and neurotransmitters--the natural chemicals that transmit messages in the nervous system. In the United States, females over age 15 and elderly men are the most likely to be deficient in this vitamin.
Nutrient Intake and Performance Lab, Western Human Nutrition Research Center, San Francisco, CA
Monica C. Schaeffer, (415) 556-5655

A potent hormone--the activated form of vitamin D--may be useful for treating the scaly, itchy skin disease known as psoriasis. Of 16 psoriasis patients who had not responded to other therapies, 12 had substantial or complete clearing of the unsightly patches of skin from topical applications or oral doses of the hormone. The preliminary findings are an important first step toward understanding and treating a disease that has baffled medical researchers.
Human Nutrition Research Center on Aging at Tufts, Boston, MA
Michael F. Holick, (617) 556-3176

The anticoagulant used to prepare blood plasma samples can affect the accuracy of chemical analysis--the most common method of assessing human health and nutritional status. In a comparison of two commonly used anticoagulants, citrate pulled fluid from blood cells,

15

diluting the plasma sample by about 10%, whereas heparin did not. This dilution accounted for a 10% error between plasma and serum concentrations in 13 clinical tests--including trace elements, vitamins, proteins, and lipids. (Plasma contains the clotting factor absent in serum.) The discrepancy between citrated plasma and serum analyses-- previously thought to be interchangeable data--must also be taken into account when comparing groups in large nutritional or epidemiological studies or in following the same individuals in long-term studies.

Vitamin and Mineral Nutrition Lab, Beltsville Human Nutrition Research Center, Beltsville, MD
J. Cecil Smith, (301) 344-2022

More evidence that gender influences the consequences of copper deficiency comes from a study of male and female rats. Copper deficiency reduced circulating iron in both sexes but had a greater effect on the males' hemoglobin and another clinical indicator of iron status, hematocrit. Giving rats excess iron improved these measurements in females but not in males. Similar differences occurred in the immune system. Copper deficiency depressed the activity of T lymphocytes--key players in the immune response--to a greater extent in the males.

Grand Forks Human Nutrition Research Center, Grand Forks, ND
Tim R. Kramer, (701) 795-8399

*U.S. Government Printing Office : 1987 -180-917/60191

Qua

Quarterly Report
of Selected Research Projects

United States
Department of
Agriculture

 Agricultural
Research
Service

April 1 to June 30, 1987

New & Improved Products

Sulfite alternatives may come from vitamin C derivatives and other compounds that, in lab studies, stopped or slowed browning of apple slices and juice for up to 48 hours. Last July, the Food and Drug Administration banned sulfites in raw fruits and vegetables. Preliminary results from an 18-month study show that dipping apple slices in either of two classes of compounds closely related to vitamin C—ascorbic acid-2-phosphates and ascorbic acid-6-fatty acid esters—was most effective. The compounds worked particularly well when mixed with cinnamic acid or an inorganic phosphate compound. Combinations with beta-cyclodextrin were effective in apple juice. Industry is interested in working with agency scientists to develop these

compounds for commercial use. (PATENT)
Plant Science Research, Eastern Regional Research Center, Philadelphia, PA
Kevin B. Hicks/Gerald M. Sapers,
(215) 233-6458/6417

U.S. Navy sailors are testing new cotton uniforms that are wrinkle-free as well as fire-resistant. Researchers treated denim fabrics with chemicals to achieve both qualities, and the fabrics were made into pants, chambray shirts, and khaki uniforms. Fire-resistant uniforms now issued to sailors are inconvenient because they need ironing. Firefighters and others who need fire-resistant, no-iron cotton uniforms could also benefit.
Textile Finishing Chemistry Research, Southern Regional Research Center, New Orleans, LA
Robert J. Harper, (504) 286-4567

New European-type hops, based on the Hallertauer mittelfrueh hop, prized for its Old World beer flavor and aroma, may be available to U.S. brewers by 1990. Over the past 20 years in Germany, the original hop has fallen victim to verticillium wilt, a fungal disease. Acreage dropped about 80%, and the hop virtually disappeared from world markets. As a result, many European hop growers were forced to switch to higher yielding, healthier varieties. Now, after 12 years of breeding and genetics research, an ARS plant geneticist has successfully crossed a genetically modified Hallertauer mittelfrueh with other European hops. U.S. hop growers will have a choice of three to five flavorful new selections that are high-yielding and disease-resistant. The new hop could bring growers in Oregon, Idaho, and Washington $15 million or more a year.
Horticultural Crops Research Lab, Corvallis, OR
Alfred Haunold, (503) 757-4424

Note: One or more scientists familiar with each research project are listed for further information. If the scientists are unavailable, others at the same telephone number may also be familiar with the work.

Items marked with the word PATENT are being patented by ARS. For more information contact Ann Whitehead, National Patent Program, Bldg. 005, Rm. 401, Beltsville Agricultural Research Center, Beltsville, MD 20705, (301) 344-2786.

Soybean meal has few competitors as an ingredient of high-protein feed. Soybean oil, however, a byproduct of meal production, must compete with many vegetable oils, often unsuccessfully, and large oil surpluses often restrict soybean meal production. Researchers in the past developed soybean varieties that produce more meal and less oil. Now they have identified the plant enzymes that regulate oil production and are trying to develop plants that can produce soybeans for either the protein or oil market by genetically controlling these enzymes in the seed.
Soybean and Nitrogen Fixation Research, Raleigh, NC
R.F. Wilson & J.W. Burton, (919) 737-3267
Soybean Protection Research, Urbana, IL
R.W. Rinne, (217) 333-1117

Processes for making biodegradable plastic, which were developed by ARS scientists, have been licensed to a firm that plans further research and development. The firm aims to have a plastic resin, containing 40% to 50% cornstarch, ready for commercial manufacture of trashcan liners within a year. The firm's goals also include making fast-food packaging and plastic mulches for gardens and high-value crops. (PATENT)
Northern Regional Research Center, Peoria, IL
Felix H. Otey, (309) 685-4011, Ext. 356

A new way to make apricot juice may boost the use of this fruit as an ingredient in soft drinks, other beverages, and foods. The simple and inexpensive method uses enzymes and porous, ceramic filters—both already used in food processing—to extract a thin, clear apricot juice from thick, pulpy concentrate. It could increase the retail value of this fruit by an additional $15 million. At present, apricots are either dried, frozen, canned, sold fresh, or pulverized to make apricot concentrate.
Food Processing and Conversion Lab, Western Regional Research Center, Albany, CA
Charles C. Huxsoll, (415) 486-3252

Sweetpotato french fries haven't yet hit the market, but industry is interested in studies showing that they retain their quality and beta carotene content after 1 year of frozen storage. Sweetpotatoes are an excellent source of beta carotene, which the human body converts to vitamin A. Small amounts of beta carotene would be lost during frying, but agency and North Carolina State University scientists found that it was unchanged in sweetpotato french fries after one year of storage at 0°F. There were no appreciable changes in flavor, texture, or appearance of the cooked fries. The study confirms that consumer acceptance of sweetpotato french fries wouldn't be hampered by short shelf life.
Food Science Research, Raleigh, NC
William M. Walter, Jr., (919) 737-2979

A hot water bath kills fruit flies in Haitian mangoes and makes the fruit safe for continued import into the United States. That will encourage trade under the Reagan administration's Caribbean Basin Initiative. Normally, Haitian mangoes are free of flies, but to kill strays the fruit is dipped in water at 115.5°F for 75 minutes. The fruit is undamaged, and in lab studies the treatment has killed more than 99.99% of the fruit flies infesting mangoes. USDA's Animal and Plant Health Inspection Service has approved the bath as an alternative to the chemical ethylene dibromide, which in October is scheduled to be banned for use on mangoes. Last year the United States imported about 90% of its mangoes, 16% from Haiti.
Subtropical Horticulture Research Station, Miami, FL
Jennifer L. Sharp, (305) 238-9321

The practicality of using Bacillus subtilis for postharvest control of brown rot in peaches was demonstrated in ARS pilot tests on two simulated packinghouse lines and in a real packinghouse in Georgia. Results indicated that the brown rot control could be used on a commercial scale. Another "good guy" micro-organism, Enterobacter cloacae, stopped the Rhizopus rot fungi for up to 5 days on 70% of the peaches tested.

During a 2-month experiment, a Pseudomonas bacterium in tandem with a yeastlike organism stopped any blue and gray molds from forming in Golden Delicious apples. ARS scientists have found other organisms that, in preliminary tests, control green and blue molds of citrus. If developed commercially, these biocontrol microbes could provide safe alternatives to chemical fungicides. (PATENTS)
Appalachian Fruit Research Station, Kearneysville, WV
Charles L. Wilson/Wojciech Janisiewicz, (304) 725-3451/
Southeastern Fruit and Tree Nut Research Lab, Byron, GA
P. Lawrence Pusey, (912) 956-5656

A new marketing strategy aims to stimulate commercial pickup of ARS research. A Technology Opportunity Package is being offered for sale to U.S. textile manufacturers to describe Polytherm. This chemical treatment makes fabrics adjust to hot and cold temperatures and could prove useful for building insulation, draperies, gloves, and clothing. The opportunity package is intended to encourage firms to make proposals for capitalizing on the research. The package includes a videotape, fabric samples, and technical papers describing how Polytherm fabrics are made. Companies can purchase it for $325 from NTIS, Springfield, VA 22161. Ask for the Polytherm Technology Package, Order No. PB87-181186/NAC. Firms have until September 1 to submit proposals. (PATENT)
Office of Cooperative Interactions, Beltsville, MD
Richard M. Parry, (301) 344-2734/
Textile Finishing Chemistry Research, Southern Regional Research Center, New Orleans, LA
Tyrone L. Vigo/Joseph Bruno, (504) 286-4487/4486

A new test, quicker and simpler than current ones, distinguishes from harmless strains a bacterium that can cause food poisoning. Scientists use a purple dye to identify a plasmid--genetic material outside the cell chromosome--that occurs only in virulent strains of Yersinia

enterocolitica bacteria. The test will help microbiologists study this pathogen and improve food safety for consumers. (PATENT)
Microbial Food Safety Research, Eastern Regional Research Center, Philadelphia, PA
Saumya Bhaduri, (215) 233-6521

Shade tree seedlings were healthier and more uniform in size after soil they were growing in was fumigated to kill pathogens. Of two popular fumigants tested--vapam and methyl bromide--vapam proved to be the most effective in eliminating disease-causing organisms. It can be applied as a liquid any time of the year and is safer, cheaper, and easier to use than methyl bromide.
Horticultural Crops Research Lab, Corvallis, OR
Robert G. Linderman, (503) 757-4544

Pecan growers in arid states such as Texas and Arizona could benefit from research showing that pecan pollen can be frozen by liquid nitrogen at -185°F for 21 months without losing its potency. These growers need a ready supply of stored pollen because they often have to artificially pollinate their trees. Freezing pollen with liquid nitrogen has been done with other plants, but this is the first time for pecans. Until now, pecan pollen could be preserved only a week at or above 41°F. If the research is developed commercially, growers could store pollen from late-blooming varieties to pollinate early blooming ones, or vice-versa, to increase productivity.
Plant Physiology Research, Richard B. Russell Center, Athens, GA
Ida E. Yates, (404) 546-3523

Strawberry fields forever? No, but a new variety, Lateglow, extends the season through June and well into July. Released by ARS and the Maryland Agricultural Experiment Station, Lateglow bears firm, sweet, juicy berries that are less susceptible to skin injury than most other varieties. Ideal for the northeastern and central United States where root diseases pose a problem, the new

berry resists red stele and verticillium wilt and withstands powdery mildew, leaf spot, and leaf scorch. Plants should be available to fruit growers this fall.
Fruit Lab, Horticultural Science Institute, Beltsville, MD
Gene J. Galletta, (301) 344-3571

Intestinal gas from eating lima beans could be greatly lowered by plant breeding. Scientists made the discovery while studying how bean plants react to high levels of ozone, an atmospheric gas. Chemical analysis of different types of lima beans in the ozone study showed that sugars in lima beans that induce gas formation vary greatly from one type to another. Levels of the sugars—nondigestible polysaccharides (NDP's)—are controlled by genes that may be shifted or eliminated through breeding. NDP's in limas and other beans cause formation of intestinal gas that makes beans less acceptable to some consumers.
Microbiology and Plant Pathology Lab, Beltsville, MD
Charles A. Thomas/Filmore I. Meredith, (301) 344-3354

Crop Production & Protection

Urban dwellers can now have garden-fresh tomatoes from window boxes or tiny pots. Planting tomatoes in 3-1/2-inch pots yields compact, space-saving plants and tomatoes that compare favorably in size and taste, if watered and fertilized frequently, to those grown in the garden. The plants are dwarfed because the limited amount of soil in the tiny pots forces the roots to become densely branched and matted. This reduces nutrient uptake, hormone content, and plant growth. In experiments with one variety—Better Bush—plants grown in 3-1/2-inch pots in one sense outyielded those grown in 11-inch pots, because nearly three times as many plants could be grown in the same space.
Plant Stress Lab, Beltsville, MD
Donald T. Krizek, (301) 344-3143

Red may be a tomato's favorite color, but a potato may be partial to blue. Using red plastic mulch instead of black caused a 20% jump in the yield of tomatoes during the first year of an experiment. The red mulch increased the amount of light reflected onto the plants from the long, or red, end of the visible spectrum and reduced the amount of blue and green. This made the tomato plants grow faster and taller. This summer, researchers are testing whether blue mulch, which intensifies the shorter wavelengths, will make potatoes yield more or better quality tubers.
Coastal Plains Soil and Water Conservation Research Center, Florence, SC
P.G. Hunt, (806) 669-5203

The nuclear polyhedrosis virus used in controlling the gypsy moth, may soon be produced at less cost. Normally, the virus is grown in fifth-stage larvae of the gypsy moth. In tests, fourth-stage larvae not only produced more virus per milligram of larva tissue, but also the virus they produced was more potent. Already, two companies have expressed interest in the new information.
Insect Pathology Lab, Beltsville, MD
Martin Shapiro, (301) 344-3864

What do European cornborers do after dark? Answer: They leave the cornfield and gather in adjacent grassy areas to drink dew and attract mates. The significance: Farmers can cut back on areas sprayed for the pest by as much as 85% by spraying only the grassy borders. Insect predators of corn borers also frequent the grass, but researchers found that the most effective ones survived when exposed to several insecticides that kill the corn borer. The best time to apply insecticides is at mating time, so that most of the female borers die before they can return to the cornfield to lay eggs. Researchers caution, however, that the procedure won't work in cornfields full of grassy weeds, since the borers will congregate there instead of in the field borders.
Corn Insects Research, Ankeny, IA
William B. Showers, Jr., (515) 964-6664

An inexpensive, practical way to control three important pests of potatoes in the Pacific Northwest, and to reduce pollution, is to combine several insecticides at planting time or soon after plants emerge. Research shows this approach works well against the green peach aphid, the Colorado potato beetle, and the Great Basin wireworm. Singly, none of the chemicals are effective against these three insects. But combinations of four insecticides--aldicarb, carbofuran, fonofos, and phorate--kill the insects on contact or by entering the root systems of plants the insects feed on. Sowing granules of insecticide combinations directly into the ground at the time of planting reduces the danger of pollution from aerial spraying. And applying a combination costs less than applying each chemical individually.
Crops Protection Research, Yakima, WA
Harold H. Toba, (509) 575-5981

Blackened areas may not form on the skin of peaches that have superficial skin injuries if the release of certain atoms in the peach is blocked. Experiments with California-grown peaches showed that cations--positively charged atoms--of metals such as iron, copper, and zinc can be blocked by the compound EDTA. Only brown spots remain on the injured skin. Normally, these cations interact with the natural pigment anthocyanin, turning areas near the skin injury from brown to black. Further analysis of the activity of cations in peaches might lead to new, natural means to interfere with these atoms and protect the soft fruit.
Horticultural Crops Research Lab,
Fresno, CA
Douglas J. Phillips, (209) 487-5334

Adding calcium to an insecticide slows its chemical breakdown long enough for it to control insects effectively. Scientists took their cue from farmers who add calcium compounds to insecticides to help them control bitter pit--a potentially serious storage disease of apples--as well as codling moths. The scientists made the discovery while evaluating the efficiency of various farm applications of the insecticide azinphosmethyl in the field. Azinphosmethyl kills codling moths on apples, is safe to use, and does not harm fruit. Without the added calcium, the chemical often breaks down before the end of the insect's 21-day life cycle.
Pesticide Residue and Insect Attractants Research, Yakima, WA
Jay C. Maitlen, (509) 575-5973

A guest that repays its host by killing it could one day save wheat farmers up to $375 million a year. The host is downy brome, or cheatgrass, one of the worst weed pests for dryland wheat farmers in the Great Plains and Northwest. The guest is a newly discovered species of Pseudomonas--a common soil micro-organism that colonizes root surfaces, lives off the roots' waste products, and then produces a poison that slows the weed's growth. It does not affect wheat. The new biocontrol agent provided excellent control of downy brome in the greenhouse and in preliminary field tests. Up to 2 years of field tests will be run to make sure the bacterium colonizes only cheatgrass. If it does, then farmers will have the green light to prepare batches of the organism, raising it inexpensively on wheat straw that can be spread on their fields.
Land Management and Water Conservation, Pullman, WA
Lloyd F. Elliott, (509) 335-1552

Lentils may be bred to ward off a serious virus spread by several aphid species in the Pacific Northwest, the major U.S. lentil-producing area. Scientists found two collections of lentil plants that resist infection by the pea enation virus, which deforms seeds and causes flowers and seed pods to drop off, severely lowering lentil quality and yield. In wet years, the disease can reduce yields as much as 50%. Seed from the two collections is now available for breeders. New lentil plants--capable of dramatically reducing the severity of the disease--could be available to growers in less than 4 years.
Grain and Legume Genetics and Physiology Research, Pullman, WA
Frederick J. Muehlbauer, (509) 335-9521

Neem tree extracts sprayed on white birch trees control leafminer, a damaging pest of birch, just as effectively as a toxic pesticide. Birch leafminer, Finusa pusilla, is one of the top two pests of ornamental and forest birches. Neem is a tropical tree used for centuries in Asia and Africa to repel insects from crops, homes, and livestock housing. ARS researchers have thus far shown that neem extracts can control 80 major agricultural pests. Birch is the first tree known to get protection from the extracts. Florist and Nursery Crops Lab, Beltsville, MD Hiram G. Larew, (301) 344-2268

Drought tolerance has been transferred between plants using microinjection. This new genetic engineering system opens vast opportunities to build new crops rapidly to withstand environmental stresses. Using a hair-thin glass needle, an ARS scientist microinjected 30 to 50 genes—making up a chromosome—from a wild, dry-weather petunia into single cells of a commercial petunia variety. Petunias grown from the cells proved more drought tolerant in greenhouse tests. Florist and Nursery Crops Lab, Beltsville, MD Robert J. Griesbach, (301) 344-3574

Kangaroo paw is a unique new crop from Australia for U.S. florists and nursery workers. Flowers of bright red, purple, green, or yellow form a single row along tall woolly spikes. An excellent cut flower for years in Australia, kangaroo paw has commercial potential as a potted plant in the United States. Dwarf types are suitable for patios in the South. ARS scientists, in cooperation with an Australian nursery and several U.S. universities, are evaluating kangaroo paw hybrids for large-scale field or greenhouse production. Florist and Nursery Crops Lab, Beltsville, MD Roger H. Lawson, (301) 344-3570

An antibiotic produced by bacteria found in the roots of wheat plants has proven to be highly effective against major root diseases of wheat and other cereal crops.

Scientists discovered the antibiotic, called P 2-79, after culturing a strain of the bacterium Pseudomonas fluorescens taken from the roots of wheat plants that survived "take all" root disease. P 2-79 inhibits all important classes of fungi and is particularly effective in low concentrations against take-all and two other root diseases, Pythium and Rhizoctonia solani. The antibiotic may become useful as a seed or soil treatment. (PATENT) Root Disease and Biological Control Research, Pullman, WA David M. Weller, (509) 335-6210

A pine pest that costs American and foreign timber harvesters millions of dollars annually could itself fall victim to a newly described mite. The pyemotid mite, discovered by scientists with USDA's Forest Service and the Canadian Department of Agriculture, parasitizes and weakens Douglas-fir moths. ARS scientists identified and described the mite as a potential biocontrol insect for the moths. Systematic Entomology Lab, Beltsville, MD Robert Smiley, (301) 344-3891

Gallatin, a new barley that outproduces currently grown varieties and has stiffer straw to hold it upright for easier harvest should be available to farmers by 1988. This variety is the result of 10 years of cooperative research involving ARS, Montana State University, and the University of Idaho. It is best adapted for dryland areas of the Pacific Northwest and the Northern Great Plains. Cereal Crops Improvement, Bozeman, MT Eugene A. Hockett, (406) 994-5158

A voracious predator of the azalea lace bug has been discovered in the Western Hemisphere. Scientists have found specimens of the predator, an insect native to Japan, in four locations in Maryland. Little is known about this insect, Stethoconus japonicus, except that it feeds only on the azalea lace bug. Scientists are beginning research to study its habits, biology, and effective-

ness as a biocontrol to help gardeners and commercial producers protect their azaleas.
Systematic Entomology Lab, Washington, DC
Thomas J. Henry, (202) 382-1780/
Florist and Nursery Crops Lab,
Beltsville, MD
John W. Neal, Jr., (301) 344-4559

A fungus from Japan has been experimentally released to kill gypsy moth caterpillars. ARS scientists injected fungal protoplasts into young caterpillars and let them climb into the forest canopy of the Shenandoah National Park near Front Royal, Virginia, to feed and breed. When the infected caterpillars died, the fungus emerged through them and released spores into the air, and three more stages of caterpillars were killed. Now scientists are checking to see if the fungus survived over the winter to reinfect this year's park population.
Insect Pathology Research, Ithaca, NY
Richard S. Soper, Jr., (607) 257-2030

Apache, the newest red-berried, disease-resistant pyracantha, reduces maintenance costs by eliminating the need for disease-control sprays. The compact shrub resists scab and fire blight and is well-suited for landscaping as a foundation plant, low hedge, or patio planter. It has glossy dark-green leaves, cream-white flowers in May, and shiny dark fruit that ripens in August and lasts until December.
U.S. National Arboretum, Washington, DC
Donald R. Egolf, (202) 475-4862

Shoshoni viburnum is a superior dwarf type of the popular landscape plant. Unlike most viburnums, which are too large for home gardens, Shoshoni is ideal for foundation plantings, rock gardens, borders, and low hedges. With unusual horizontal branching, it has masses of cream-white flowers in double rows, lots of red berries, and maroon fall leaves. Shoshoni is the 14th viburnum released from the National Arboretum, which has the only viburnum breeding program in the world.
U.S. National Arboretum, Washington, DC
Donald R. Egolf, (202) 475-4862

Leaf hairs on sugarcane are bad news for the sugarcane borer but could be good news for growers. Some growers spray pesticides two or three times a season to control the borer, one of the worst sugarcane pests. Leaf hairs make egg laying harder for the borer, act as roadblocks to larvae heading for shelter on the stalk, and sometimes force the larvae to "bail out" from sugarcane leaves. Breeders are trying to cross wild hairy varieties with commercial hairless ones to build in this natural defense against the borer.
Sugarcane Field Station, Canal Point, FL
Omelio Sosa, Jr., (305) 924-5227/2250

Genetic engineering to improve soybeans is a step closer now that scientists have been able to get roots to grow from soybean cells in lab dishes. The soybean's own genes for root and shoot development turn off in the lab for unknown reasons, so ARS researchers have enlisted a soil microbe, Agrobacterium tumefaciens, to insert root-formation genes into the soybean cell culture. Without the ability to grow whole plants from genetically improved soybean cells, genetic engineering is useless. Research continues on the next step: getting shoots to form on the rooted cells, making a whole plant.
Tissue Culture and Molecular Biology Lab, Beltsville, MD
Lowell D. Owens, (301) 344-4072

After 6 months in the Far East, an ARS plant explorer has returned with 200,000 seeds and cuttings from exotic flowering cherries. Plants from these sources will be selected and bred for ornamental cherries that can thrive in colder climates and in the heat of southern Florida, Texas, and California. Among the features of the cherries found overseas are roselike blossoms with as many as 50 petals.
U.S. National Arboretum, Washington, DC
Roland M. Jefferson, (202) 475-4854

A second year of ARS trials of integrated pest management for pecan orchards in the Southeast has proved successful, and pecan growers can now adopt techniques

used in the 2-year study. Researchers compared an IPM orchard with a conventionally managed orchard during 1985 and 1986. Pests managed included insects and other arthropods, diseases and weeds. Under IPM, profits were increased $30 to $50 per acre, pesticide loads were decreased, environmental pollution was lowered, and the risk of pests developing resistance to chemicals was reduced. IPM trees received three fewer applications of fungicide and insecticide in 1985 and two fewer fungicide and three fewer insecticide applications in 1986 than did the conventionally managed trees.
Southeastern Fruit and Nut Research Lab, Byron, GA
Jerry A. Payne, (912) 956-5656

Two gardening tricks were combined in experimental tomato plots in the South and increased yields nearly 40%. Aluminum foil placed flat on the ground under plants caused the sun's rays to bounce away from young seedlings during hot months of the fall growing season, preventing temperature stress. Then, when temperatures dropped, black plastic mulch absorbed heat and warmed the soil, making plants more productive.
U.S. Vegetable Lab, Charleston, SC
James M. Schalk, (803) 556-0840

Lygus bugs, which cause millions of dollars damage annually to such U.S. crops as alfalfa and cotton, have an immune system similar to that of humans. When certain parasitic insects lay eggs inside lygus bugs, blood cells surround the insect eggs and prevent them from hatching. This spares the lygus bugs from certain death, since the larvae would have eaten the insides of their hosts. Scientists continue seeking parasitic insects that lygus bugs won't or can't encapsulate. The pest costs farmers $54 million a year in California alone.
Biological Control of Insects Lab, Tucson, AZ
Jack W. Debolt, (602) 629-6220

Insulating peach tree trunks can reduce a tree's self-poisoning with cyanide. This poisoning, triggered by fluctuating

spring temperatures, occurs as part of peach tree short life (PTSL), a disease that costs southeastern peach growers about $27 million annually. As changing temperatures make plant tissue more permeable, prunasin--a compound thought to be a natural defense against insects and disease--breaks down and releases cyanide, which eventually kills the tree. Scientists will work with engineers to develop an inexpensive insulating material.
Southeastern Fruit and Tree Nut Research Lab, Byron, GA
Charles C. Reilly, (912) 956-5656

Soil, Water & Air

Fish with a hearty appetite for hydrilla, a notorious waterweed, have cleared up some 400 miles of Imperial Irrigation District canals in southern California. ARS and Irrigation District researchers cooperated in the experiment to see if the fish--known as triploid grass carp--could cut weed-cleaning costs. Within 1 year after the carp were stocked, the District spent only $50,000 for chemical and mechanical controls, as opposed to the earlier annual cost of about $250,000. The Irrigation District is now determining if the fish can control regrowth from hydrilla's roots and bulb-like tubers. Unlike other carp, triploid carp can't reproduce, so they don't pose the threat of crowding out native fish. Grass carp have been used successfully in China for hundreds of years to keep waterweeds in check.
Aquatic Weeds Control Research, Davis, CA
Lars W.J. Anderson, (916) 752-6260

Reclaimed strip mines in central Appalachia have potential as pasture to produce beef cattle. But the nutrient phosphorus, low in the region's soils, limits yields of both forage grasses and legumes that can be fed to cattle. A 4-year study showed that a mere 100 pounds of phosphorus per acre will maintain a tall fescue-red clover mixture on reclaimed soils and triple the number of animals the pasture can support. These findings could be applied to thousands of acres of

strip-mined land through five states in central Appalachia.
Appalachian Soil and Water Conservation Lab, Beckley, WV
Douglas Perry, (304) 252-6426

An underground "plow", designed to shatter shear planes or layers of impervious soil caused by subtilling fallowed fields in dryland wheat regions, should help conservation tillage farmers. Shear planes cut crop yields by blocking infiltration of water and forcing plant roots to grow sideways in search of openings. To eliminate shear planes, researchers developed a system of three V-shaped sweeps aligned horizontally. Each sweep is 5 feet wide and equipped with four steel shanks properly bent and twisted to shatter soil. In tests under several moisture conditions, soil the entire depth of the shanks was fractured and left highly porous. Moreover, treated soil was underlain by step-like corrugations that store water. When 60% of the soil pore spaces are filled with water, conditions are ideal for microbes that unlock nitrogen and other nutrients in organic matter, providing free fertilizer to the plants. The new V-sweep system, which keeps crop residues on the soil surface, can remedy problems related to conservation tillage. It can help conservation farmers who practice a kind of "tillage rotation" by periodically reverting to moldboard plowing to loosen soil compacted by field equipment or to disrupt the buildup of diseases or pests. (PATENT)
Soil and Water Conservation Research, Lincoln, NE
Lloyd N. Mielke, (402) 472-1516

Soil is routinely fumigated in nurseries to rid it of disease organisms. But what happens to beneficial organisms such as mycorrhizae--fungi that assist certain plants in their uptake of minerals and other functions? A pioneer lab experiment showed that fumigation was helpful in three ways: (1) Organisms that cause root diseases were effectively eliminated and did not reoccur until later in the season when the plants were stronger, (2) the mycorrhizae were at first suppressed

but later returned in greater numbers in fumigated soil than in nonfumigated, and (3) seed germination and plant size improved.
Horticultural Crops Research Lab, Corvallis, OR
Robert G. Linderman, (503) 757-4544

Crop yields worldwide could be 60% to 80% greater sometime near the middle of the next century, according to scientists who are studying the effect of increasing carbon dioxide in the air. They say previous estimates of a 30% yield increase are too low because calculations left out a projected increase in air temperature of 5°F to 10°F. Higher temperatures would considerably enhance the yield of plants growing in a high-CO_2 environment.
U.S. Water Conservation Lab, Phoenix, AZ
Sherwood B. Idso, (602) 261-4356

If a water shortage forced growers of plums and other fruits to rely on salty water for irrigation, they could probably get by for one season without a loss of fruit. But giving the trees salty water for three seasons in a row could reduce yields and could even kill the trees, according to results of a California study on Santa Rosa plums--this country's most widely planted commercial plum variety. Similar results are expected with plum relatives such as apricots, peaches, cherries, nectarines, and almonds.
Water Management Research Lab, Fresno, CA
Glenn J. Hoffman, (209) 487-5337

A new planter attachment applies fertilizer at just the right distance from wheat seeds and disturbs soil only about half as much as the best attachment now available. Fertilizer placed too close to seed can prevent it from sprouting. Farmers using conservation tillage can't spread fertilizer on the surface because micro-organisms that break down crop residue tie up the fertilizer and keep it from the roots of the next wheat crop. Newly designed blades attached to a planter will allow dryland wheat farmers in six states (Kansas, Nebraska, South

9

Dakota, Montana, Washington, and Oregon) to put fertilizer in close, but not too close, to the seed. (PATENT)
Columbia Plateau Conservation Research Center, Pendleton, OR
Dale Wilkins, (503) 276-3811

The Universal Soil Loss Equation—used to predict the amount of soil erosion caused by rain and snow—has been revised for steeply eroding slopes. Current prediction equations for erosion show extremely high rates for steeply sloping lands, worrying Soil Conservation Service personnel and others who use the equation. An analysis of erosion data by researchers has resulted in a new set of relationships for slope steepness to predict erosion. These new relationships will improve predictions for steep crop, range, and forest lands in the Pacific Northwest and lead to better identification of highly erodible land eligible for the Conservation Reserve Program.
Land Management and Water Conservation, Pullman, WA
Donald K. McCool, (509) 335-1552

Soybean yields on no-till sandy Coastal Plains soils can be increased if farmers plant beans using an in-row subsoiler. The subsoiler is a chisel that cuts a furrow 12 to 14 inches deep into the subsurface layer of the soil. This allows plant roots to grow through compacted soil layers to reach water. In studies of eight Alabama soils, ARS and Auburn University scientists found yields from no-till were comparable to or higher than those from conventionally tilled plots when an in-row subsoiler was used.
Soil-Plant Interactions Research, Auburn, AL
Charles B. Elkins, (205) 826-4100

Contrary to general recommendations, grasses on some arid lands in the Southwest should not be mowed or burned. Such practices create green, lush pastures for 2 to 3 months, but trials show that untouched areas actually provide more annual vegetation for grazing livestock and wildlife. Researchers who discovered this say mowing and burning big sacaton

grass in Arizona may be why this high forage producer covers only 5% of the area it did 100 years ago.
Arid Land Watershed Management Research, Tucson, AZ
Jerry R. Cox, (602) 629-6881

Five agronomic zones underlie a simple system for customizing conservation tillage technology developed by the STEEP project and speeding it to individual dryland wheat farms in the Pacific Northwest. STEEP, short for Solutions to Economic and Environmental Problems, is an 11-year-old cooperative effort that has researched ways to conserve water and soil in a region where sloping fields often have erosion rates exceeding 50 tons per acre. Cooperators in the project are ARS and the experiment stations of Washington, Oregon, and Idaho. To transfer STEEP-developed technology, the new agronomic zone system depends on only three elements: annual precipitation, growing degree days, and soil depth. Within zones where these elements are similar, growers could use standardized agronomic and conservation practices. Soil conservationists will soon design erosion control methods that are zone-specific. The agronomic zone system incorporates soils data from the Soil Conservation Service and 50 years of historical records from the National Weather Service.
Columbia Plateau Conservation Research Center, Pendleton, OR
Clyde L. Douglas, (503) 276-3811, Ext. 292

Animal Production & Protection

Six firms have obtained licenses to make and sell a patented ARS vaccine against a viral disease in turkeys. The vaccine is the first to be federally licensed for use against hemorrhagic enteritis, a disease caused by a virus that suppresses a turkey's immune system. In 1986 the disease was second only to salmonella as the most common intestinal disorder in turkeys. The new vaccine is safer than current vaccines and may protect turkeys from other diseases brought on by a weakened immune system. Its use could

lower production costs and lead to lower consumer prices. (PATENT)
Regional Poultry Research Lab,
East Lansing, MI
Keyvan Nazerian, (517) 337-6828

A beetle that destroys the Styrofoam insulation in chicken houses can be controlled with any of five experimental pesticides. During its larval stage, the lesser mealworm (Alphitobius diaperinus) feeds on spilled chicken feed. It is a problem in layer and broiler houses in climates cold enough to require heat and insulation, particularly in "high-rise" houses where feed and chicken litter sift down from cages high above the floor. As the beetle's larval stage ends, millions of mealworms climb out of the litter and bore into exposed Styrofoam panels to pupate, riddling the insulation with holes and rendering it useless. The new chemical controls can be mixed into chicken feed in amounts as low as 1 or 2 parts per million and either kill the larvae outright or prevent their maturing into beetles. More research, including tests by the Food and Drug Administration, will be necessary to make sure that residues, if any, in the chickens meet safety standards. (PATENT)
Livestock Insects Lab, Beltsville, MD
Richard W. Miller, (301) 344-2478

A chemical extracted from fire ant larvae may lead to baits laced with insecticide attractive only to this pest of cattle and humans. In tests, the chemical, which has not yet been identified, induced worker ants to pick up immature ants in the nest, move them about, and feed and groom them. The worker ants also carried into the nest baits treated with the chemical. Current commercial insecticidal baits, made with a soybean-oil-based attractant, are stolen by other ants. This not only reduces the effectiveness of the bait but also kills harmless or beneficial ant species.
Imported Fire Ant Research Lab,
Gainesville, FL
Clifford S. Lofgren, (904) 374-5920

Over the years, beef breeders have tended to select the largest, fastest growing bulls to pass on superior genetics to the next generation. Now, just as a Toy Poodle female might have trouble giving birth to puppies sired by a Great Dane, some beef cattle have calving difficulties that sometimes kill cow and calf. After 10 years of study, scientists have bred animals that produce 6-1/2% smaller calves at birth. After birth, they maintain satisfactory growth. This new generation of livestock produces 2% more live calves, needs 6% less assistance at birth, and weighs only 8% less at 6 months of age compared to herds where bull selection was based solely on size and weight.
Fort Keogh Livestock and Range Research, Miles City, MT
Joseph J. Urick, (406) 232-4970

Cough drops for bees? Not exactly--but the same menthol that soothes sore throats and makes breathing easier during head colds also helps honey bees with mites in their breathing tubes. In tests, menthol killed all the mites in infested colonies within 3 weeks. Colonies with the mite produced one-eighth the honey of healthy colonies in studies at the University of Georgia, so menthol could prevent serious losses to the $100- to $150-million-a-year honey industry.
Honey Bee Research, Weslaco, TX
William T. Wilson, (512) 968-3159

Ultrasound imaging, also known as the sonogram, is being used to monitor live fetuses inside pregnant sheep that have eaten poisonous locoweed plants. For the first time, scientists can see how locoweed harms the fetal heart by reducing heart rates, causing irregularity, and reducing the strength of contractions. They can also observe how the fetus and placenta grow and develop. Previously, mother and fetus had to be killed and autopsied to provide data on the effects of these plants. As with humans, the painless imaging technique involves aiming sound waves at an organ like the heart. The organ can be viewed on a TV monitor.
Poisonous Plant Research Lab, Logan, UT
Kip E. Panter, (801) 752-2941

Annual bromegrass is a problem plant that substantially reduces the amount of forage available for livestock grazing some western ranges. Scientists have demonstrated that commercially available herbicides destroyed at least 90% of this pest within the first year without harming nutritious grasses that cattle eat. Key to success was in careful timing and reducing application rates from amounts normally applied to commercial crops. Grass yields increased five-fold because these plants could use moisture previously consumed by bromegrass. Cost for one of the chemicals came to about $1.60 per acre, well within reason for land with severe annual brome infestations.
Fort Keogh Livestock and Range Research, Miles City, MT
Pat O. Currie, (406) 232-4970

After 70 years, some mysterious outbreaks of sunburn in southeast Texas cattle may have been solved. Other plants there that cause sunburn had been ruled out. With a test originally developed for people, scientists found the culprit—dead leaves from the giant rain-lily, mixed in with forage. Live leaves aren't a problem. The direct cause of the sunburn may be a chemical reaction, a bacterium, or a mold on the rain-lily's dead leaves. Scientists are now working on ways to control the plant, since cows will not nurse their calves when their udders are sunburned.
Pesticides and Other Chemicals Research, College Station, TX
Loyd D. Rowe, (409) 260-9369

Nine unique enzymes have been identified in Culicoides variipennis, an insect that spreads bluetongue disease among animals. Like police using fingerprint files, scientists are relying on unique enzyme patterns created with electrophoresis* to identify insect populations with the greatest potential for spreading bluetongue.
Arthropod-borne Animal Diseases Research Lab, Laramie, WY
Richard A. Nunamaker, (307) 776-6698
*A system that uses high voltage to separate proteins by their electrical charges.

Some insecticides highly toxic to crop-destroying insects kill fewer honey bees than less potent insecticides. Honey bees, which annually help pollinate $20 billion worth of crops in the United States, usually return to their hives after coming in contact with the synthetic pyrethroids. Scientists previously thought these pesticides contained some chemical that repelled bees. Findings now suggest that the potent pesticides sicken bees so quickly that they fly back to their hives before being exposed to lethal doses.
Carl Hayden Bee Research Center, Tucson, AZ
Gordon D. Waller, (602) 629-6709

Chicken and turkey hatcheries can use a new test to identify a virus with the jawbreaking name of reticuloendo-theliosis. The virus is suspected of costing the poultry industry millions of dollars annually by suppressing a bird's immune system, making it more susceptible to Marek's disease and other tumor-producing afflictions. Until now, the virus had been difficult to diagnose, and previous testing took up to 7 days. ARS researchers developed monoclonal antibodies that detect the virus in a simple test in less than 4 hours.
Regional Poultry Research Lab, East Lansing, MI
Lucy F. Lee, (517) 337-6828

Exotic zoo animals—as well as farm animals—might be saved by drugs that are identified as effective against two disease-causing bacteria. In lab tests, the effectiveness of drugs against Mycobacterium paratuberculosis and M. avium can be checked in only 3-1/2 days. In ruminants, M. paratuberculosis causes Johnes disease. The next step will be to test the drugs in infected animals, which either die or have to be destroyed.
National Animal Disease Center, Ames, IA
Ada Mae Lewis-Hintz, (515) 239-8377

Scientific Information Systems

Bats locate insect meals by sending out sound waves and waiting for echoes. A device that uses the same technique to count insects in crop fields--and another that uses infrared light--have been invented by an ARS scientist. The devices, along with ARS software in a personal computer, could one day tell farm managers when and when not to apply pesticides. They currently hire workers to do expensive manual counts. Commercial companies have expressed interest in the systems, which use pheromones to lure insects for counting. The sound wave system emits high-frequency sound waves and counts echoes bouncing off moths as they fly towards the attractive scent. The other device counts interruptions in an infrared light beam as moths fly into a trap. Pheromones of the 12 to 15 moth pests that cause most crop damage have been synthesized, so many farmers can benefit from these systems.
Subtropical Agricultural Research Lab, Weslaco, TX
Don E. Hendricks, (512) 565-2647

Juggling irrigation needs of southeastern farmers in dry years may be less complicated with a new computer model for managing water in watersheds drained by artificial channels. Most previous models looked at a single field or were designed for the arid Southwest. The new model was originally developed and tested--using data from moderately dry 1983 and moderately wet 1984--to predict how dams built in the channels would affect water levels and to help USDA's Soil Conservation Service select sites for new dams. But these channels are increasingly important sources of irrigation water, so the model could help manage water demand as well as supply.
Coastal Plains Soil and Water Conservation Research Center, Florence, SC
John E. Parsons, (803) 669-5203

Erosion prediction technology will soon become more accurate and versatile, yet be sufficiently user friendly to permit on-site calculations via lap computer.

This advance will come when WEPP (short for Water Erosion Prediction Project) replaces the 25-year-old Universal Soil Loss Equation, better known as USLE, in August 1989. USLE is based on a large mass of observations incorporated into a lumped model. By contrast, WEPP incorporates data on the actual mechanics of many separate erosion processes. For example, scientists at Lincoln, Nebraska, are studying the intricacies of overland waterflow, including how runoff is first dammed by crop residues, then released to find alternate flow routes. Other stations are conducting research on various processes. WEPP is a cooperative effort of ARS, Soil Conservation Service, Forest Service, and Bureau of Land Management.
Soil and Water Conservation Research, Lincoln, NE
John E. Gilley, (402) 472-2975/
National Soil Erosion Lab,
West Lafayette, IN
George R. Foster, (317) 494-7748

Almond nut yields can now be predicted with a computer program that takes into account honey bee activity, weather, and tree variety, so growers can manage their orchards better. Yields can drop from 1,000 pounds per acre to practically zero if honey bees fail to pollinate almond blossoms at just the right time. Researchers are now refining a program for apple orchards--another crop highly dependent on bee pollination.
Carl Hayden Bee Research Center, Tucson, AZ
Gloria D. Hoffman, (602) 629-6709

A hand-held device, constructed with about $25 worth of common electronic parts, locates honey bee hives that have lesser wax moths hiding inside. Undetected, these moths eat the honeycomb and can destroy entire bee hives. The device works up to 7 feet away by converting and amplifying a high-frequency sound--inaudible to humans--that moths emit to call their mates.
Carl Hayden Bee Research Center, Tucson, AZ
Hayward G. Spangler, (602) 629-6380

13

Frozen soils cause severe water runoff and soil erosion in northern U.S. croplands. A newly developed computer program predicts the depth and duration of frost in tilled soils with or without plant residue or snow cover. Over 2 years in development, and at least 2 years away from final application, the new model of the Simultaneous Heat And Water (SHAW) program will demonstrate the impact of soil temperature and freezing on various tillage and residue management systems. Growers will be able to use this information to find the best combination of tillage and residue management practices for minimizing runoff and erosion of frozen soils. Currently available empirical and computer-based methods are not sensitive or accurate enough to make these predictions.
Land Management and Water Conservation, Pullman, WA
Keith E. Saxton, (509) 335-2724

Applying nitrogen to corn only when most needed could get farmers more for their fertilizer dollar. A new mathematical technique applied to field data pinpoints the two growth peaks when corn need for N is greatest. The first peak occurs when plants set potential ear size and number of kernels; the second, when ears flesh out after tasseling. Side dressing with fertilizer just before these peaks would be more efficient and possibly less costly than fertilizing before planting.
Coastal Plains Soil and Water Conservation Research Center,
Florence, SC
Douglas L. Karlen, (803) 669-5203

Replacing the Wind Erosion Equation developed in the mid-60's with a more accurate computer prediction model is being aided by a new soil sampler. At least 75% of wind-eroded soil particles are blown no higher than 8 inches. The above-ground part of the sampler is an 8-inch-high, pie-shaped box attached to a wind vane that rotates to collect wind-blown soil. The sampler is used along with other older models that collect blowing soil up to 20 feet above ground.

Test results are being used to develop the computer model.
Wind Erosion, Conservation, and Production Systems Research, Big Spring, TX
Donald W. (Bill) Fryrear, (915) 263-0293

A module to predict how atmospheric increases in carbon dioxide stimulate the growth of wheat plants is being developed by ARS as a "plug in" component for a computer model called CO2WHEAT. The Department of Energy, contractor for this research, seeks accurate data on CO_2 and the greenhouse effect for its global climate model. It is known, for example, that higher concentrations of CO_2 trigger two important events: plants synthesize more carbon for plant growth, and changes occur in how stomates, or leaf pores, regulate water losses by transpiration. Information from the module may result in managing wheat crops to use water more effectively. An existing ARS model, PLANTEMP, which now predicts how temperature affects wheat's vegetative development, will be expanded. It will also predict how temperature affects wheat's vegetative growth or size, and the development and growth of a plant's reproductive organs or seed heads.
Columbia Plateau Conservation Research Center, Pendleton, OR
Ronald W. Rickman, (503) 276-3811

■■■■■■■■
Human Nutrition

Heart disease may be more prevalent in men than in women because of the small size of cholesterol-carrying particles in their blood. Low density lipoproteins (LDL's)--the major cholesterol-carrying particles--come in a range of sizes. The small, dense particles are thought to deposit the lion's share of cholesterol in artery walls--leading to atherosclerosis--because they can cross the arterial lining more readily. Men are much more likely than women to have small, dense LDL particles, according to analysis of plasma samples from 280 participants in the Framingham Offspring Study (children of people in the classic Framingham Study). Those in the study having the small particles also had higher levels of total cholesterol and

triglycerides and were generally older.
Human Nutrition Research Center on Aging
at Tufts, Boston, MA
Ernst Schaefer, (617) 556-3101

A simple breath test can now replace the
unpleasantness of swallowing a flexible
tube to detect a bacterium suspected of
playing a role in causing peptic ulcers.
The patient first drinks a glass of water
containing urea made with a harmless form
of heavy carbon. If the alleged culprit,
Campylobacter pylori, is lurking in the
stomach, it will quickly split the urea
into ammonia and heavy carbon dioxide,
which is exhaled in the breath. Tried on
26 people, the breath test was as accurate in detecting the bacterium as a
tissue biopsy taken through the tube. It
should help scientists understand how
ulcers form as well as design better
treatments. The research was supported
by the Veterans Administration, National
Institutes of Health, the Agricultural
Research Service, and Baylor College of
Medicine.
Children's Nutrition Research Center at
Baylor, Houston, TX
Peter D. Klein, (713) 799-6000

Breast-fed infants are satisfied with far
fewer calories than currently believed
adequate for normal growth. During their
first 6 months, nursing infants took in
20% fewer calories than the Recommended
Dietary Allowance for energy. This
suggests that the RDA, which is based on
20-year-old measurements of formula
intake and overestimates of breast milk
intake, needs to be revised. Today's
formulas are closer in composition to
mother's milk, but mother's milk is still
more finely tuned to infant requirements.
Children's Nutrition Research Center at
Baylor, Houston, TX
Janice E. Stuff, (713) 799-6178

Fish oil concentrates reduced vitamin E
levels in mice far more than did corn
oil. Mice getting diets containing 5%
fish oil needed 6 to 7 times more vitamin
E in their feed to maintain the same
plasma levels as mice on diets containing
5% corn oil. A similar finding with

rabbits was reported 46 years ago, but
was forgotten as people stopped taking
cod liver oil. A study is now looking
for this effect in human plasma. People
taking fish oil capsules should be aware
of the potential for vitamin E
deficiency.
Human Nutrition Research Center on Aging
at Tufts, Boston, MA
Simin N. Meydani, (617) 556-3129

Are polyunsaturated fats better than
saturated fats in suppressing the liver's
ability to produce additional fat? Some
scientists had speculated so. But a new
study of lab rats shows that both types
of fat are equal in slowing down the
animal liver's routine fat production.
The next step: to learn if the results
are true for humans.
Biochemistry Research Lab,
Western Human Nutrition Research Center,
San Francisco, CA
Gary J. Nelson, (415) 556-0899

A nutrition survey of nearly 700 elderly
Bostonians shows that large doses of
vitamin C do not reduce blood levels of
other vitamins or minerals, as reports
have suggested. Nearly all those survey-
ed got adequate vitamin C as reflected by
their blood levels. And many participants, particularly the women, took 10
times the Recommended Dietary Allowance
(600 milligrams) or more. The women who
had high blood levels of C also had
higher levels of vitamins B_2, E, and
folate (or folic acid), suggesting they
are aware of good nutritional practices.
Western Human Nutrition Research Center,
San Francisco, CA
Robert A. Jacob, (415) 556-3531

The body's ability to maintain adequate
mineral levels with a high-phytate diet
was borne out in a recent study.
Phytate--a constituent of bran--was
thought to block mineral absorption
dramatically. During half of a 1-month
study, 10 men consumed meals containing
about four times as much phytate as the
typical American diet. During the other
half, the phytate was removed. As expected, the men retained more iron, zinc,

15

copper, manganese, magnesium, and calcium when the phytate was missing. But, after an initial slump on the high-phytate diet, mineral levels improved, indicating the body compensates by absorbing more or by excreting less.
Vitamin and Mineral Nutrition Lab, Beltsville Human Nutrition Research Center, Beltsville, MD
Eugene R. Morris, (301) 344-2282

Age-related cataracts have now been linked to a person's vitamin status in a preliminary study. A scientist from the Brigham and Women's Hospital, Boston, teamed with ARS to evaluate the nutritional status of 78 people with cataracts and 35 without. Those with cataracts had lower plasma levels of vitamin D, carotenoids (beta carotene and its relatives), or possibly vitamin C. The cataracts were located in different areas of the lens depending on the nutrient. The findings seem consistent with lab studies showing that vitamin C may protect the eye's lens against age-related cataracts and provide the first evidence that carotenoids may do the same.
Human Nutriton Research Center on Aging at Tufts, Boston, MA
Paul F. Jacques, (617) 556-3322

West German studies on rats suggest that traces of lead are necessary for optimum growth and that deficiency impairs the oxygen-carrying capacity of the blood by altering iron metabolism. At the request of the Environmental Protection Agency, ARS scientists repeated some of these studies and concluded that lead is not essential for growth or iron metabolism. Although lead raises the oxygen-carrying capacity of young, slightly iron-deficient rats, it acts as an external agent, like a drug, rather than as an integral part of iron metabolism.
Grand Forks Human Nutrition Research Center, Grand Forks, ND
Eric O. Uthus, (701) 795-8382

16

Qua

Quarterly Report
of Selected Research Projects

United States
Department of
Agriculture

a2s Agricultural
Research
Service

July 1 to September 30, 1987

CONTENTS

New & Improved Products

A private company and ARS signed what is believed to be the first cooperative research agreement under a 1986 Federal law to speed up the transfer of government research from the lab to industry. North Carolina-based Embrex, Inc., and agency poultry scientists will work together in developing an egg-injected vaccine for coccidiosis, a chicken disease that costs the industry about $300 million a year. The research team will test potential vaccines that can be injected through eggshells into 17-day-old embryos. Embrex will use an egg-injection system it devised using a patented technology invented by agency scientists in East Lansing, Michigan. (PATENT)
Protozoan Diseases Lab, Beltsville, MD
Michael D. Ruff, (301) 344-2300

Note: One or more scientists familiar with each research project are listed for further information. If the scientists are unavailable, others at the same telephone number may also be familiar with the work.

Items marked with the word PATENT are being patented by ARS. For more information contact Ann Whitehead, National Patent Program, Bldg. 005, Rm. 401, Beltsville Agricultural Research Center, Beltsville, MD 20705, (301) 344-2786.

Two new small watermelons--sweeter, firmer, and crisper than other small, "icebox" types and most big ones--could be big sellers here and abroad. ARS test-shipped to Europe Mickylee and Minilee, two 5- to 12-pound melons developed in 1984 by the University of Florida. The melons need no refrigeration, and all 10 importers who saw them liked them better than other icebox types. Some would have ordered 20-ton container loads--if the melons had been available. Small European shops and street vendors don't want 25-pound monster melons, and per capita consumption in the United States has dropped, partly because families are smaller today. Extension workers in Florida are urging farmers to plant Mickylee and Minilee, which can be grown wherever regular watermelons can grow.
Export and Quality Improvement Research, Orlando, FL
Lawrence A. Risse, (305) 897-7326

More accurate detection of a bacterium that causes food poisoning is now possible. Scientists have developed a method for distinguishing between healthy and injured cells of Listeria monocytogenes, a bacterium that causes the food-poisoning disease listeriosis. The bacterium, which can grow in meats and dairy products, is killed by heating during cooking or pasteurization. But improper heating only injures the organism, which can then repair itself and multiply. Current tests sometimes fail to pinpoint these injured cells; the new test detects them and lets industry and regulatory agencies know the true level of contamination. In 1985, L. monocytogenes killed 47 people who ate tainted cheese in California. On September 1, USDA's Food Safety and Inspection Service officials began monitoring

the organism in cooked, ready-to-eat meat and poultry.
Microbial Food Safety, Eastern Regional Research Center, Philadelphia, PA
James L. Smith/Robert L. Buchanan, (215) 233-6620

Linear plasmids, genetic molecules found until now in only one yeast, could lead to new commercial yeasts and new, more efficient shuttles for moving genes from one micro-organism to another. Now scientists have discovered these strings of free-floating DNA in four non-commercial yeasts. Unlike the circular plasmids used by genetic engineers or the linear plasmids in many filamentous fungi, linear plasmids in the four yeasts are not surrounded by cell structure membranes that hamper getting DNA in or out of a cell.
Fermentation Biochemistry, Northern Regional Research Center, Peoria, IL
Paul L. Bolen, (309) 685-4011, ext. 272

Potato plants with a built-in insect repellent have come from cell-fusion experiments. ARS scientists discovered a few wild potato plants from South America with high levels of leptine, an insect-repelling toxin. In a petri dish they fused cells from the wild plants with cells from a commercial potato. Then they grew the fused cells into whole plants that had leptine in their leaves. The hybrid plants have built-in resistance to the Colorado potato beetle--a voracious pest that each year costs over $120 million to control.
Vegetable Lab, Beltsville, MD
Stephen L. Sinden/Kenneth L. Deahl, (301) 344-4507

A commercial mill for processing the fast-growing plant kenaf into pulp for papermaking is expected to be operational by mid-1990 in Texas. As part of a $1.4 million Kenaf Demonstration Project involving USDA and commercial groups, 83,000 copies of the Bakersfield Californian were printed on kenaf paper in July 1987, showing it could compete with paper from wood pulp in production costs and quality. In the 1960's and 1970's, ARS research in Peoria, Illinois, had demonstrated the technical feasibility of making paper from kenaf. Studies by plant scientists in Beltsville, Maryland, and Savannah, Georgia, also gave high marks to the plant as a potential pulp source to help supply the $58 billion U.S. paper industry. Kenaf could be grown in many parts of the country as an alternative crop.
Oil Chemical Research, Northern Regional Research Center, Peoria, IL
Marvin O. Bagby, (309) 685-4011, ext. 531

Future lawns will stay green year round and save mowing time. A new turf in the final stages of testing is a zoysia grass that will be sold as seed rather than as expensive zoysia plugs. This zoysia needs to be mowed only one third as often as other zoysias, grows sideways, spreads out to cover the ground, and tolerates drought. Lawns seeded with a mixture of zoysia and fescue grass seeds stay green year round. The zoysia seed in the mix keeps grass green in the summer, and in many locations, the fescue will keep it green all winter. An experimental mix of the two grasses is undergoing final tests. Scientists are evaluating new types of lawn grasses for disease resistance, vigor, smooth and even growth, cold or heat tolerance, rooting power, and blade width.
Germplasm Quality and Evaluation Lab, Beltsville, MD
Jack J. Murray, (301) 344-3655

Russet Burbank potatoes--used by most restaurants for making french fries and baked potatoes--may soon be replaced by less heat-sensitive varieties. The record-breaking summer temperatures of 1985 in western Idaho and eastern Oregon caused Russet Burbank potatoes to build up excessive amounts of sugar in their stem ends. French fries made from these potatoes can have dark, unappetizing areas that make them unacceptable for freezing or for use by fast food restaurants. As a result, in the 1986 growing season farmers lost 40% of their contracts; 12,000 fewer acres were planted to potatoes. ARS scientists screened their potato-breeding stock and found a

smoother skinned, heat-resistant line equal in all other respects to Russet Burbank. If the breeding experiments are successful, new heat-resistant potatoes could be available to growers in 3 years.
Cereal and Vegetable Crop Production, Aberdeen, ID
Joseph J. Pavek, (208) 397-4181

Putting peanut butter on TV and analyzing it with a computer is a better way for USDA inspectors to measure specks in peanut butter that can lower its quality. Now inspectors look for specks, usually the ground-up red skins of the nut, with the naked eye. A new experimental system, however, uses a video camera and a computer that divides pictures of peanut butter samples into about 245,000 tiny grids. The computer analyzes each grid based on 256 shades of gray from black to white. Specks appear black. The computer determines the percentage of the grids that represents specks, and the grade is based on this finding. Scientists are building a prototype system that will be tested in an USDA Agricultural Marketing Service field office in Georgia.
Market Quality and Handling Research, Raleigh, NC
Thomas B. Whitaker, (919) 737-3101

Florida orange juice producers and agency scientists are cooperating to improve the flavor of orange juice packaged in new sterile containers. These small plastic containers come with straws and have become popular for consumers. Heat-pasteurized juice is added after the containers are sterilized with a mild solution of hydrogen peroxide or other chemicals. But some companies stopped packaging orange juice this way because the juice starts losing its flavor after only two weeks of storage at room temperature. ARS scientists have detected changes in the oils and other juice chemicals that cause the flavor loss. This information will help the juice industry improve the quality of the products.
U.S. Citrus and Subtropical Products Lab, Winter Haven, FL
Manuel G. Moshonas, (813) 293-4133

Small-town businesses in Illinois and Idaho have been licensed to make new products using super slurper, an absorbent cornstarch material that agency scientists developed and patented in 1976. The Central Illinois Manufacturing Company, in Bement, now makes super slurper-based fuel filters that have helped boost its workforce from 25 to 100 over the last 4 years. And 18 months ago, Polysorb, Inc., of Smelterville, Idaho, began making medical and recreation cold packs and other products from super slurper in a new factory that was previously a closed-down bowling alley and recreation center. The company started with 30 workers and recently added 20 more, was in the black after the first year, and is considering a multimillion-dollar expansion so it can offer new super slurper products.
Plant Polymer Research, Northern Regional Research Center, Peoria, IL
William W. Doane, (309) 685-4011

More than $6 million of unshelled, American-grown walnuts have been sold in Japan in recent months, thanks to a safe and effective walnut fumigation technique developed by ARS researchers. Sales of the jumbo walnuts, packed in small cellophane or net bags, were twice what the U.S. walnut industry had predicted. In the past, unshelled walnuts from America couldn't be sold in Japan because of the threat of codling moth—a walnut pest. The improved technique uses the standard fumigant, methyl bromide, applied at safe, yet higher-than-normal, doses under vacuum pressure to ensure that any codling moth larvae living in the nuts are killed.
Horticultural Crops Research Lab, Fresno, CA
Patrick V. Vail, (209) 487-5334

Cotton growers in the Carolinas have cut insecticide use by 60% to 70% and are making about $77 more per acre thanks to a joint program to eradicate the boll weevil. The strategy: timed sprayings of malathion for two seasons and special traps—developed and patented by agency scientists—to catch strays and monitor weevil movements. The cooperative pro-

gram among USDA agencies, growers, and State agencies has boosted cotton production and brought eight new gins and numerous gin improvements worth about $12 million to North Carolina alone. This fall, weevil eradication is moving onto 375,000 acres of cotton in Georgia, Alabama, and north Florida. To battle the weevil in these States, a cotton growers' group expects to produce about one million of the traps over the next 2 years.
Boll Weevil Eradication Research, Raleigh, NC
Willard A. Dickerson, Jr., (919) 856-4780

To make U.S. soybean exports to Europe more competitive, increase the oil content, and decrease the damage from handling. That's the gist of a continuing survey of soybean exports, designed to evaluate U.S. grading standards and identify ways to improve handling. The survey gave mixed reviews to 1986 U.S. soybean exports compared with those from South America. Soybeans from Argentina were cleaner and had a lower percentage of broken hulls than U.S. soybeans, but U.S. soybeans contained more oil—making them worth 8.5 cents more per bushel—and less linolenic acid, which impairs flavor when it breaks down. Brazilian soybeans contained more oil than U.S. soybeans but had a lower value at the refinery mainly because of greater damage to kernels.
Vegetable Oil Research, Northern Regional Research Center, Peoria, IL
T.L. Mounts, (309) 485-4011, ext. 601

Small farmers are increasing their incomes with new pepper and strawberry varieties. One farmer in upstate New York is growing about 2 acres of the everbearing Tristar strawberry, which continues to produce fruit into mid-October. He hopes to make up to $20,000 an acre in profit this year, and says he can make about eight times more per acre with Tristar than he can with traditional varieties. Another small farmer in South Carolina is growing 15 acres of a hot pepper, Carolina Cayenne, which has resistance to the southern root knot

4

nematode. The new variety has saved him between $750 and $1,500 in nematode control costs, and he has bought equipment to dry the peppers and sell them to a company that uses them in sausage seasoning and in a batter mixture for Louisiana Cajun-style chicken.
Fruit Lab, Beltsville, MD
Gene Galletta, (301) 344-4652
U.S. Vegetable Lab, Charleston, SC
Richard L. Fery, (803) 556-0840

Protein-fortified soft drinks and soy-based coffee creamer are some products that could result from a new method for processing soy protein. The method makes the raw protein more soluble or blendable in foods than current processing methods and does so under lower temperatures. This eliminates the bitterness and off-flavors often caused by high-temperature processing. The new method also processes the protein three times faster than current methods and saves energy costs. Soy protein is now used in infant formulas, soy-based meat substitutes and other products. New uses for the protein could help lower the soybean surplus, estimated to be 500 million bushels this year.
Food Systems Research, Southern Regional Research Center, New Orleans, LA
Frederick F. Shih, (504) 286-4354

Crop Production & Protection

A continental caterpillar that eats the leaves of field bindweed—one of the worst problem weeds in the United States—has been imported to see if it will help control the plant. Scientists have released and are carefully monitoring the caterpillars in Texas and Oklahoma. Known as Tyta luctuosa, the insect is found in Eurasia and North Africa. Those used for the experiment in the two States were collected by the ARS lab in Rome, Italy. The caterpillar is the first insect ever approved for control of bindweed in the United States; other candidates had to be rejected because they also feed on sweetpotato, a bindweed relative.
Plant Protection Research, Western Regional Research Center, Albany, CA
Sara S. Rosenthal, (415) 486-3624

Lines of corn with consistently high rates of photosynthesis and consequently higher yields, have for the first time been bred successfully in a classical breeding program. Precise yield increases will be measured later this year, but the final season of a 7-year experiment left no doubt among Illinois researchers that they have bred corn that makes its food more efficiently. Quantifying exact increases in the photosynthetic rate will be impossible, however, because of annual climatic variations. Breeding crops for higher rates of photosynthesis is a goal that has eluded scientists for many years and may not be possible for most crops using standard breeding techniques. The experiment demonstrated that corn plants with higher photosynthetic capabilities are better able to make use of light at high intensities.
Crop Management Systems Research, Urbana, IL
Doyle B. Peters, (217) 333-6732

A virus disease called net necrosis causes patches of black to form on potatoes. The disease is caused by the potato leafroll virus, which is spread by aphids. Scientists have recently found that whether potatoes turn black depends on: (1) which strain of the virus is attacking the plant and (2) how early in the growing season a particular strain is carried to potato plants by aphids. Now scientists are matching virus strains with the aphid species that carry them. This information is needed to develop ways to help growers control the disease that costs U.S. potato farmers $124 million a year.
Insect Ecology and Pest Management Research, Yakima, WA
Duane Biever, (509) 575-5963

Pueblo, the newest pyracantha introduced by the U.S. National Arboretum, resists both fire blight and scab. Fire blight usually kills young pyracantha shoots, and scab defoliates the plant and disfigures the fruit. Pueblo's broad-spreading growth habit (it grows twice as wide as it grows tall) makes it ideal for barrier mass plantings for parks,

highways, commercial developments, and large estates. Like five other new low-maintenance pyracantha varieties introduced by the Arboretum, Pueblo sports cream-white flowers in May and profuse orange-red fruit from autumn to early winter.
U.S. National Arboretum, Washington, DC
Donald R. Egolf, (202) 475-4862

Chippewa and Huron are the first landscape viburnums to combine a heavy red fruiting deciduous species with an evergreen species. Both have a lush, heavy-textured, dark-green foliage; a massive, cream-white floral display in May; a brilliant red to purple autumn foliage from September to early December; and abundant, glossy red fruit from September until winter. These varieties may be used in the landscape as individual plants, or as a large, informal hedge.
U.S. National Arboretum, Washington, DC
Donald R. Egolf, (202) 475-4862

Euonymus trees and shrubs may soon be free of scale insects without chemical sprays. Euonymus scales that afflict these small evergreen shrubs and trees are white (male) and brown (female) insects with tough backs that help protect them from chemical sprays. Two beetles imported from the Asian Parasite Lab in Seoul, Korea, Chilocorus and Cybocephalus, devoured a heavy infestation of scales on the U.S. National Arboretum's euonymus specimens, saving the trees from the axe. Previously covered with a nearly solid dusting of white scales, the plants are now scale-free. Scientists are releasing the beetles in the area from Pennsylvania to Georgia and in Texas and Michigan.
Beneficial Insects Lab, Beltsville, MD
John J. Drea/Robert Carlson, (301) 344-1791/4450

Rhizobacteria on the roots of peanut plants help supply not only nitrogen, but also many other essential minerals. This finding could lead to healthier plants and more nutritious peanuts. Scientists field-tested Florunner peanuts inoculated with eight rhizobia strains. Compared to plants that were not inoculated, those

inoculated with a commercial strain of Bradyrhizobium had greatly increased levels of many nutrients in root nodules, including iron, phosphorus, boron, calcium, magnesium, zinc, copper, potassium, and manganese. Nutrient gains also appeared in the peanuts themselves. Scientists hope to discover just how rhizobia send these nutrients into plants. Similar tests are planned with soybeans.
Plant Stress Lab, Beltsville, MD
Robert K. Howell, (301) 344-4527

Resistant bread and durum wheats developed by Federal and State scientists prevented a severe stem rust epidemic—similar to those of the early 1950's—from occurring last year in the northern plains. Surveys showed that abundant rust on the southern susceptible wheats and possible overwintering of rust on northern winter wheats increased the severity of the disease by causing spore showers that were the earliest in 20 years in the spring wheat region. An estimated 90% of the wheat now grown in Minnesota, North Dakota, and Nebraska is resistant to stem rust.
Cereal Crops Research, Fargo, ND
James D. Miller, (701) 237-7068
Cereal Rust Lab, St. Paul, MN
Alan P. Roelfs, (612) 625-7295

Garbanzos, also known as chickpeas, succumbed to an epidemic this summer. A fungal disease called Ascochyta blight has left garbanzo fields in the Pacific Northwest looking scorched. If the disease is severe enough, it could halt garbanzo farming in this major growing area for at least a year or until growers can clean out their fields. Ascochyta rabiei fungus forms spores in cold, damp straw and other residues lying on the soil surface. ARS scientists, who discovered the disease in 1983, recently found it could be spread by splashing raindrops or when fungal spores carried by the wind "rain" infection on newly planted fields. A sunny, wet spring helped spread the disease this year, and yields dropped more than 50%. To control the fungus, scientists are working out a program of integrated pest management

that involves planting healthy seeds, treating seeds with fungicides, rotating garbanzos with other crops, deep plowing or burning residues, and breeding disease resistance into commercial garbanzo varieties.
Plant Germplasm Introduction and Testing, Pullman, WA
Walter J. Kaiser, Jr., (509) 335-1502

Young soybean plants need sunlight to grow; even 2 to 3 weeks in the shade can reduce branching. As early as 2 weeks after they emerge, shading of beans by weeds can reduce branching by 50%. Weeds filter out the red and blue wavelengths of the light spectrum but let the far-red pass through, preventing the soybeans from producing branches. According to ARS scientists, shading probably alters the balance of growth regulators in the plant. The next step: to try to use growth regulators to trick young soybeans into ignoring the weeds.
Crop Production Research, Columbia, MO
R.J. Aldrich, (314) 875-5357

Leaf-tying and leaf-rolling moths, serious pests of fruit trees and ornamental shrubs, can be distinguished from similar, harmless species by referring to a new publication series. "Moths of America North of Mexico" is being published by a private foundation licensed to use ARS research. Scientists have provided information for 130 volumes covering 15,000 moth species. The most recent in the series, fascicle 7.1, contains the 84 dichomeridime species that occur in the United States and includes identification aids for the major moth pests of the group.
Systematic Entomology Lab, Washington, DC
Ronald W. Hodges, (202) 382-1778

ARS scientists have won a major victory against a soilborne fungus that attacks tomatoes grown on ground beds. Germplasm is now available that resists tomato fruit rot caused by the fungus Rhizoctonia solani. Because of this disease, processing tomatoes, which are mechanically harvested, cannot be grown

6

in the Gulf Coast States. The disease-
resistant germplasm was developed by
crossing wild fruit lines tolerant of
fruit rot with modern, more productive
varieties.
Vegetable Lab, Beltsville, MD
Thomas H. Barksdale, (301) 344-3583

Shade tree seedlings were healthier and
more uniform in size when grown in soil
fumigated to kill pathogens with vapam
but not with methyl bromide. Both fumigants effectively eliminated pathogens--
disease-causing organisms--but vapam did
not kill beneficial fungi that work
symbiotically with plant roots (called
mycorrhizae); methyl bromide did.
Mycorrhizal fungi aid in plant uptake of
water and nutrients, and their presence
probably accounted for the better seedling growth after the vapam treatment.
Since vapam is safer, cheaper, and easier
to apply, its use could greatly benefit
nursery workers growing shade tree
seedlings.
Horticultural Crops Research Lab,
Corvallis, OR
Robert G. Linderman, (503) 757-4544

White lupine may be the forage to warm
the hearts of Maine farmers. Most forages find the growing season there too
short and too cold. ARS is developing
this cold-weather legume, originally from
the Middle East, to produce a high protein (34% to 40%) fodder or grain. By
planting this nitrogen-fixing legume for
a year, Maine farmers could expand the
normal 2-year rotation of potatoes and
oats to 3 years, decreasing soil erosion
and diversifying crops. Research continues to improve the legume's ability to
compete with weeds and its tendency to
stay green late into the harvesting
period.
New England Plant, Soil and Water Lab,
Orono, ME
William M. Clapham, (207) 581-3266

Road salt hurts some pines more than
others, so it pays to choose the right
species. In a 3-year study, 13 species
were subjected to a salt spray like that
kicked up by cars and trucks traveling

slushy roads. Salt builds up in plant
tissue and kills cells. Harmed least
were ponderosa pine, Austrian pine, and
Japanese black pine. Southwestern white
pine, the most salt-tolerant of the soft
pines studied, may be a good replacement
for the highly susceptible eastern white
pine in the Snow Belt. Ponderosa pine
worked best at keeping salt out of its
needles, making it an excellent candidate
for roadside tests.
U.S. National Arboretum, Washington, DC
A.M. Townsend, (202) 475-4824

A bluegrass variety, probably introduced
from Europe in the 1800's, has gotten out
of hand. Roughstalk bluegrass has become
a serious weed in perennial ryegrass
grown in western Oregon for seed. Valued
at $30 million a year, the ryegrass seed
is used to grow turf and livestock feed
throughout much of the central States.
As roughstalk bluegrass has invaded
ryegrass fields, it has forced growers to
take fields out of production sooner than
normal. ARS researchers recently found
that two herbicides--fenoxaprop and
dalapon--control established plants of
this weed without decreasing ryegrass
seed yield. If the use of either or both
of these products can be registered, seed
growers can look forward to higher
yields, fewer problems cleaning the seed,
and longer producing ryegrass fields.
Forage Seed and Cereal Research,
Corvallis, OR
George Mueller-Warrant, (503) 757-4502

Beneficial soil organisms that live with
soybeans can change the nutrients in the
living plant--and thus in the soy foods
we eat--in a way that chemical fertilizers can't. This finding might give
scientists an innovative, effective way
to improve soy products to increase
export markets for this surplus crop. An
ARS study has shown for the first time
that beans from soybean plants grown
along with certain soil organisms had
higher amounts of nutrients like zinc and
copper than beans picked from plants
grown with chemical fertilizers. The
helpful organisms--bacteria that furnish
nitrogen and mycorrhizal fungi that
provide other needed minerals--increased

both the quantity of soybean oil in the seeds and the ratio of polyunsaturated to saturated oils.
Plant Development Quality Research, Albany, CA
Raymond S. Pacovsky, (415) 486-3529

A 2-year test will screen and evaluate four insects--three beetles and a fly from Northern Europe--with the potential to control purple loosestrife, a weed from Europe. One of the two worst pests of U.S. wildlife areas, Lythrum salicaria has invaded hundreds of thousands of acres of northern American wetland, pastures, and rice fields. It has little or no food value for ruminants or wildlife and competes successfully with valuable native plants. Each year, it costs an estimated $150 million in agricultural losses, wildlife damage, and control measures. Unfortunately, it is an attractive plant and is sold by U.S. nurseries as an ornamental. Because of the extent of the infestation, treatment with herbicide is costly, inefficient, and hazardous. Besides doing basic research in the States to find the weed's weaknesses, ARS is cooperating to find controls with the U.S. Fish and Wildlife Service, Virginia Polytechnical Institute and State University, and the International Institute of Biological Control in Switzerland.
Beneficial Insects Lab, Beltsville, MD
John Drea/Stephen Hight,
(301) 344-1791/1125

A new drought-resistant lima bean will be released to seed companies in the near future. The new variety has large beans, and they stay green after maturity, two desirable market characteristics. Despite only three-quarters of an inch of rain and no irrigation, the new lima thrived. If the genes controlling its drought tolerance can be isolated, adding the ability to other crops, such as tomatoes and corn, might be possible through genetic engineering.
Microbiology and Plant Pathology Lab, Beltsville, MD
Charles A. Thomas, (301) 344-3354

Better liquid media for growing plant cells in the lab should save time and money for scientists trying to develop new crop varieties from bioengineered cells. New media have been developed that can keep cells healthy for months. Previously, growing cells in liquid culture--as a first step toward regenerating whole plants--has required transferring cells to fresh medium every 7 to 10 days. In a solid medium, cells form large clumps called callus and the medium still needs changing monthly. Unlike older media, the new ones have little agar (0.1% to 0.4%) and produce a slurry that does not have to be aerated by shaking. Tested on carrot, tobacco, soybean, and corn cells, the new media should work with any plant species.
Microbial/Plant Technology, Southern Regional Research Center, New Orleans, LA
Alice A. Christen/Donna M. Gibson, (504) 286-4264

Aflatoxin, a carcinogen, may be produced in corn by the fungus Aspergillus flavus. Now scientists have developed five corn lines that resist A. flavus. Current commercial varieties of field corn (which is fed to animals and used in corn products for people) have little if any known resistance to the mold, but the new lines averaged only 9% infected kernels, compared to 31% in susceptible lines. Three of the lines have been released to breeders, who can now incorporate the newly found trait with other good traits. Two more lines await release--probably within a year. Farmers, who have trouble selling corn with the mold, should welcome new resistant varieties.
Crop Science Research, Mississippi State, MS
Gene E. Scott, (601) 325-2736

One way to beat crop pests is make the crop itself resistant to them. Eight lines of cotton that tolerate the tobacco budworm--a major cotton pest--are being released to commercial breeders for further breeding. When the new lines and a commercial variety--Stoneville 213-- were infested with budworms in field tests, the new lines yielded up to 100% more cotton. Commercial breeders will

breed the new lines to incorporate the tolerance with existing desirable characteristics, a process that usually takes about 5 years.
Crop Science Research Lab,
Mississippi State, MS
Johnie Jenkins, (601) 323-2230

Midafternoon low humidity affects the growth of tomatoes. Tomato plants growing in test fields had extremely low photosynthesis rates in midafternoon. Scientists found that, unlike other plants, tomato leaf stomata (natural openings) do not close under low humidity that frequently occurs in midafternoon. The dry air reduces photosynthesis and growth. With these results, researchers will be able to identify new tomato lines that can better withstand low humidity.
Plant Photobiology Lab, Beltsville, MD
J.A. Bunce, (301) 344-3607

Beneficial fungi all look alike when they're living in plant roots. Scientists may have an easier time telling them apart with a technique that has been successful in identifying the fungus Glomus mosseae in sudangrass roots. By passing electrical current through a gel containing proteins that make up the fungus, they have pinpointed those specific to the fungus. Next they will attempt to produce antibodies that detect the proteins and thereby identify G. mosseae. Knowing what beneficial root fungi, called mycorrhizae, are present in plants is important to scientists trying to exploit them to improve crop production. More than 90% of the world's plants take up phosphorus and other nutrients through mycorrhizae.
Soil-Microbial Systems Lab,
Beltsville, MD
Patricia D. Millner, (301) 344-3214

Plants treated with a growth regulator may withstand water stress better. Drought can decrease fruit production and shorten tree life. When applied to apple seedlings, paclobutrazol reduced water loss and prevented the buildup of abscisic acid, a plant hormone that inhibits growth.
Fruit Lab, Beltsville, MD
S.Y. Wang, (301) 344-1776

Soil, Water & Air

An ingenious device readily converts several kinds of manual irrigation valves to automatic operation using compressed air controls. Automating irrigation this way makes it easier for farmers to improve efficiency. And because air pressure is needed to keep valves open, any electrical or equipment failure automatically closes the valves, preventing accidental releases of water common to nonpneumatic systems. The new device clamps to the top of an irrigation valve without necessitating any changes other than replacing the handle and threaded stem used to open and close the valve. When pressurized air enters the chamber at the top of the upper shaft, a diaphragm compresses a spring, raising the shaft and turning on the water. When the air is vented from the chamber, the spring pushes the shafts down and stops waterflow. (PATENT)
Irrigation and Drainage Research,
Grand Junction, CO
Clayton H. Gibson/Ronald E. Yoder,
(303) 243-5418

Trillions of raindrops fall on each acre of Corn Belt land each year, detaching and eroding soil particles. For the first time, scientists can measure pressures caused by the drops when they strike the earth. An instrument the size of a soil particle, only 1/25-inch in diameter, can measure these pressures without interfering with the action of the drop on the soil. Water dropped on the simulated soil particle from 45 feet, showed that drops exert much less pressure on soils than on hard materials such as steel. This new finding demonstrates that physical and chemical soil properties, such as clay content, may greatly affect the extent of erosion. This furthers understanding of soil erosion by rainfall. In the United States, rain erodes 3.2 billion tons of soil annually from crop and range land.
National Soil Erosion Research Lab,
West Lafayette, IN
Mark A. Nearing, (317) 494-8680

Conservation tillage practices that leave adequate crop residues on the soil surface can control wind erosion on sandy soils without decreasing the yield. That's good news for farmers who worry that yields will be less than those from conventionally plowed land. In a 3-year study, researchers compared the effects of conventional tillage and three conservation tillage systems--no-till and two forms of subsurface tillage, Paraplow and ro-till--on corn used to feed livestock. No benefit was found for conventional tillage. Grain yields were highest with the Paraplow.
Weeds, Soil, and Water Management Research, Prosser, WA
David E. Miller, (509) 786-3454

A powerful new seed planter that helps prevent soil erosion could lower costs of conservation tillage, putting it within reach of wheat farmers throughout the United States. An ARS engineer cooperated with a New Zealand scientist to develop the small, light planter, which uses less fuel and could cost farmers two-thirds less than current no-till drills. Unlike current no-till seed drills, the new planter drills through a thick bed of straw and other residues to deposit seed and fertilizer without disturbing the soil and exposing it to erosion. Another advantage is that it cuts a small, precise slot in the ground that is big enough to trap water in the seed zone and help seeds germinate. A Washington State company will build and test a full-scale prototype of the drill this fall.
Land Management and Water Conservation, Pullman, WA
Keith E. Saxton, (509) 335-2724

Birdsfoot trefoil and alfalfa could be a cheap source of nitrogen for growing reed canarygrass. Besides being able to fix nitrogen from the air (changing it into a form plants can use), legumes can transfer some of the nitrogen to grass, increasing productivity and reducing the need for fertilizers. A study of N transfer showed that more N gets transferred when more legume than grass is grown in the same plot, and N transfer

can take place laterally for more than 8 inches. The canarygrass got 68% of its N from the alfalfa (17% of the N the alfalfa fixed) and 79% from the birdsfoot trefoil (13% of the N the trefoil fixed). Both legumes also fixed 9% to 12% more N when they were grown with grass than when they were grown alone.
Plant Science Research, St. Paul, MN
Gary H. Heichel, (612) 625-6228

Peanut yields increased about 7% over 3 years when peanuts were trickle-irrigated with low-sodium water from shallow wells and decreased by 5% when they were sprinkler-irrigated from deep wells. Even peanuts that were not irrigated had somewhat higher yields than those that were sprinkler-irrigated. Trickle-irrigated plants yield more because the leaves are wetted less, which reduces leafspot and other foliar diseases. Water quality also affects yields. Deep well water in the mid-Atlantic coastal plain has too much sodium. Using deep well water for irrigating in this area can hurt crops unless care is taken to overcome problems related to high sodium.
Peanut Production, Diseases, and Harvesting Research, Suffolk, VA
Floyd J. Adamsen, (804) 657-6744

Even though growers in the arid West commonly surround underground plastic drainpipes with gravel, this practice may not enhance crop yields on irrigated farmlands. The finding may save growers and irrigation districts the cost of gravel or other materials used around drains (adds significantly to installation costs). Although gravel usually helps keep soil particles from getting into drainpipes and plugging them, with certain soils the problem apparently doesn't occur, so gravel isn't needed. A 10-year cooperative experiment in Egypt yielded this result, which researchers expect will apply to U.S. farmlands in California, Colorado, New Mexico, Texas, and Utah, where soil and irrigation practices resemble the Egyptian site. The experiment also provided additional evidence that properly installed underground pipes boost yields of crops such as cotton, rice, wheat, and clover year

after year by carrying away unused water that would otherwise saturate the soil and drown plant roots. Underground drainage also drastically reduces buildup of salt on irrigated farmlands.
Water Management Research Lab, Fresno, CA
Glenn J. Hoffman, (209) 251-0437

The most profitable way to grow soybeans in Tunica clay—a major soil in the Southeast—is to plant a single crop and irrigate, according to a 3-year study in Mississippi. Monocropping soybeans, in fact, produced higher returns than did any variation of irrigated double-cropping with wheat. Without irrigation, however, it was a different story. Returns were higher from double cropping, mainly because of profits from wheat. The comparisons were made under several tillage systems in standing stubble and burned stubble. Profits were highest from double-cropping in burned stubble with minimum tillage inputs. Tunica clay is representative of about 10 million acres in the alluvial plain of the Mississippi River.
Field Crops Mechanization,
Stoneville, MS
Richard A. Wesley, (601) 686-2311

Getting maximum soybean yields in another southern soil—Sharkey clay—calls for planting beans early and irrigating them from the time they start flowering until seeds are fully developed. Three years of field tests on fine-textured soils in central Mississippi showed that yields were highest for the earliest planting (mid-May rather than late May or early June) and the largest amount of water applied. Beans are most sensitive to water stress at the podfill stage. Also, applying the fungicide benomyl to the leaves of soybeans significantly increased yields under optimum irrigation but not enough to justify the cost. Planting date had no effect on yield of nonirrigated beans. About 6 million acres of soybeans are grown on these soils each year. Timely planting and proper irrigation can increase a soybean grower's profit by about $40 per acre.
Soybean Production Research,
Stoneville, MS
Larry Heatherly, (601) 686-9311

Animal Production & Protection

Mowing and baling hay the same day could save farmers' time and increase the crop's value. In field tests with a USDA prototype machine, researchers cut alfalfa in the morning and baled it in the afternoon—all in less than 6 hours. With conventional mower-conditioners, 2 to 4 days are needed to dry hay to the 20% moisture content needed for baling. The new machine shreds alfalfa immediately after it's mowed, forms the hay into thin, continuous mats, and lays the mats on the stubble to dry in the sun. The hay can then be harvested by conventional equipment. The time saved with the machine cuts down the chance of damage from rain and improves hay quality and digestibility.
U.S. Dairy Forage Research Center,
Madison, WI
Richard G. Koegel, (608) 263-5636

Ranchers' alert: Keep ewes away from the false hellebore plant until after day 33 of pregnancy. Severe birth defects in sheep grazing western rangelands are caused, in part, by a chemical in the false hellebore plant. Scientists who isolated and identified the compound, cyclopamine, found that pregnant ewes grazing the plant on day 14 after conception often gave birth to severely deformed "monkey-faced" lambs. If ewes eat the leaves 19 to 21 days after conception, cyclopamine can cause lambs to die before birth. Now under study is another compound in the leaves that when they're eaten by ewes during days 27 to 33 of pregnancy, may cause lambs to suffocate at birth from collapsed windpipes.
Poisonous Plant Research Lab, Logan, UT
Richard F. Keeler, (801) 752-2941

"Fat as a pig" may become an obsolete expression if USDA scientists have their way. In recent tests, pigs given daily injections of pig growth hormone grew 10% to 20% faster on 30% less feed. Chops from these pigs had 7.35% more meat and 28.62% less fat on the rim of the chop, although the fat ratio in the meat itself was unchanged. Before hormone therapy

11

can be used on farms, it must be approved by the Food and Drug Administration. Also, daily injections would be impractical; other delivery systems such as implants have to be developed. The tests are part of the ARS program to produce leaner meat while retaining the nutritional quality of meat products for consumers.
Nonruminant Animal Nutrition Lab, Beltsville, MD
Norman C. Steele, (301) 344-2222

Three to four percent more turkey eggs hatched when injected with a vitamin, biotin, in tests with 14,000 eggs. Turkey embryos are deficient in this vitamin essential to fat and protein metabolism. Low hatching rates--about 20% less than for chickens--cost the turkey industry about $70 million annually. Biotin deficiency is only a part of the turkey hatchability problem. Nevertheless, scientists estimate $500,000 in annual savings if the vitamin injection increases hatchability by only 1% of the 50 million eggs laid annually. The automated injection was given on the 25th day of the normal 28-day incubation period. (PATENT)
Avian Physiology Lab, Beltsville, MD
Edward Robel, Jr., (301) 344-2545

Cost of pork production may drop as a result of the recent discovery of two bacterial organisms in pigs' intestines similar to those in cows' rumen. Knowing how Bacteroides succinogenes and Ruminococcus flavefaciens increase in number and break down fiber may lead to feeding pigs grain byproducts and other high-fiber feeds instead of more expensive, low-fiber corn and soybeans.
U.S. Meat Animal Research Center, Clay Center, NE
Vince H. Varel/Wilson G. Pond, (402) 762-3241

Cicer milkvetch may become a popular livestock feed, on a par with its more famous legume cousin alfalfa. Although it produces only about 90% of the hay that alfalfa does, milkvetch on grazing land has several advantages over alfalfa.

Milkvetch doesn't bloat grazing livestock, isn't affected by insects and diseases that plague alfalfa, and is extremely winter hardy. Scientists say the best seeding technique is to plant alternate rows of milkvetch and smooth bromegrass using conventional equipment. Bromegrass grows faster and helps hold the milkvetch upright so livestock and wildlife can eat it.
Great Plains Systems Research, Fort Collins, CO
Charley E. Townsend, (303) 484-8777

Flatpea, a stress-tolerant perennial legume, has potential for use as hay or pasture in Appalachia. In this hilly region, slope angle and direction and soil shallowness and acidity can limit the amount of water available to plants and lower the productivity of other forage legumes. Also, when soil moisture is low, levels of some chemicals in drought-tolerant plants increase. Flatpea produces a chemical that is a nervous system toxin, but scientists have discovered that it is not elevated in leaves and stems of drought-stressed flatpea plants. They are now developing flatpea plants that contain lower levels of this chemical. Cultivating these plants could provide nutritious food for livestock and conserve natural resources at the same time. Flatpea's ability to use atmospheric nitrogen and live for 50 years or more can reduce the costs of nitrogen fertilization and plant reestablishment.
Appalachian Soil and Water Conservation Research Lab, Beckley, WV
Joyce G. Foster, (304) 252-6426

Inducing labor in cows allows producers to have medical help available in case of complications. In tests, cows gave birth an average of 36 hours after being injected with prostaglandins, along with another FDA-approved drug, dexamethasone. Inducing labor is most effective within 10 days of the calculated date of calving. It costs just $7 per animal, a worthwhile investment for improving calf survival rates, especially for those conceived by artificial insemination or embryo transfer.

U.S. Meat Animal Research Center, Clay Center, NE
Sherrill E. Echternkamp, (402) 762-3241, ext. 274

Livestock health officials can now determine quickly and easily if cattle are free of epizootic hemorrhagic disease (EHD). EHD doesn't kill livestock, but it does prevent exports to places that are disease-free. ARS researchers have developed ways to make monoclonal antibodies to EHD virus. These antibodies can be used in tests to differentiate between EHD and bluetongue—a viral disease so closely resembling EHD that experts have often had trouble telling the two infections apart. (PATENT)

Arthropod-borne Animal Diseases Research Lab, Laramie, WY
Thomas E. Walton, (307) 721-0304

Africanized bees now in South and Central America threaten people and animals with their obnoxious stinging behavior. They are headed toward the United States, but a natural tranquilizer discovered in ARS labs may reduce the threat. A native American bee called the fire bee emits a chemical to subdue domestic honey bees so they can steal their honey. Scientists hope the fire bee's tranquilizer, or something close to it, can be synthesized in the lab and used to calm the invaders if they come. They would also have to determine what amounts, if any, are safe for use near pets, livestock and people.

Honey Bee Breeding, Genetics, and Physiology Research Lab, Baton Rouge, LA
Tom Rinderer, (504) 766-6064

Hopelessly queenless describes the occasional bee colony that doesn't replace its dead queen like it's supposed to. Many beekeepers count on their worker bees to replace the essential queen quickly. When they don't, a beekeeper might want to supply one for them. In tests, hives left queenless for 3 weeks, had shorter-lived workers and 59% less honey production. The longer hives are queenless, the less productive workers

become, and the colony eventually dies out. Bees from these hives are not, however, more aggressive than those from normal hives, as was once thought.

Honey Bee Breeding, Genetics and Physiology Research, Baton Rouge, LA
John Harbo, (504) 766-6064

Poultry disease caused by mold contamination of feedstuffs may soon be eliminated by adding a substance to feed. Aflatoxins, natural poisons produced by molds, cost the poultry industry up to $100 million annually in bird deaths and reduced production. In recent ARS tests, feed treated with an anticaking compound (hydrated sodium calcium aluminosilicate) was experimentally contaminated with aflatoxins. Birds fed the mix had 50% to 100% fewer disease symptoms normally associated with aflatoxins. Apparently, the compound ties up the aflatoxins that then pass harmlessly through the birds' intestinal tract. The compound's aflatoxin-inactivating properties were discovered by scientists at Texas A&M University. Approval by the Food and Drug Administration is needed before the compound can be used to neutralize aflatoxins in feed.

Veterinary Toxicology and Entomology Research Lab, College Station, TX
Leon F. Kubena, (409) 260-9249

Lactating Jersey cows fed round bales of alfalfa-orchardgrass hay stored uncovered outside produced significantly less milk than those fed rectangular bales protected from the weather. Milk production was not affected by type of bale when the hay was stored inside. Farmers save the costly labor and time of producing and storing rectangular bales by making round bales, uncovered outside. To prevent loss of valuable nutrients, dairy producers using round-bales should either store them inside or, if outside, be sure they are off the ground and covered with plastic.

Dairy Experiment Station, Lewisburg, TN
H.D. Baxter/J.R. Owen, (615) 359-1578

Blood pressure can be lowered by consuming more linoleic acid—the main polyunsaturated fatty acid in safflower, corn, and soybean oils—according to new findings. Previous research found that elevated blood pressure could be lowered by reducing total fat calories and increasing the proportion of polyunsaturated to saturated fats. But subsequent studies indicated that the proportion of polyunsaturated to saturated fat was unimportant. It now appears that the total amount of linoleic acid in the diet, and not its proportion to saturated fat, is the determining factor. People would get the most benefit, however, from reducing total fat while increasing vegetable oils in their diets.
Lipid Nutrition Lab, Beltsville Human Nutrition Research Center,
Beltsville, MD
Joseph Judd, (301) 344-2014

How much calcium people get in their diet is important, especially since low intake may be associated with osteoporosis in elderly women. A study reported in the ARS Family Economics Review compared costs of different foods that provide equal amounts of calcium. It showed that among dairy products, milk generally provides the most calcium at the least cost. Other economical sources are tofu (soybean curd) processed with calcium sulfate and enriched or fortified breads. Calcium can also be obtained from dark green leafy vegetables, fish with edible bones, and some enriched or fortified cereals. About two-thirds of the U.S. population does consume their Recommended Dietary Allowance (RDA) for calcium.
Family Economics Research Group,
Hyattsville, MD
Dianne D. Odland, (301) 436-5194

Human skin cells may help people maintain adequate levels of the active form of thyroid hormone, which keeps the body's metabolism humming. When the thyroid gland secretes too little hormone, the body's primary system for converting the hormone to its active form fails, and a secondary system kicks in. If scientists could find a way to stimulate the secondary system, it might provide a more natural way to treat hypothyroidism. Trouble has been, until now they didn't know where it was located. ARS collaborated with a scientist at Tufts University and a visiting scientist from China to pinpoint one source of the necessary enzymes. These occur in the keratinocytes—the cells in the outer layer of skin.
Human Nutrition Research Center on Aging at Tufts, Boston, MA
Philip R. Gordon, (617) 556-3144

Bottle-fed babies might have fewer digestive problems if a natural protein in breast milk is added to infant formula. Lactoferrin was known to help infants absorb iron from mother's milk and protect them against intestinal infection. It now appears that the protein also speeds growth and development of the intestinal tract. Concentrated in human colostrum (the breast secretion preceding milk), the protein stimulates rapid division of cells that generate the intestinal lining. Cow milk- and soy-based formulas inhibit this cell division; lactoferrin restores it. Bottle-fed babies have more colic, diarrhea, and food intolerances than breast-fed babies, which may be caused by an immature digestive capacity. Studies of several newborn animals show that their digestive systems mature much faster—within a few days after birth—if they are suckled. A method for synthesizing lactoferrin by recombinant DNA is being developed elsewhere.
Children's Nutrition Research Center,
Houston, TX
Buford L. Nichols, (713) 799-6006

When Bugs Bunny says, "What's up, doc?" he isn't asking about his cholesterol level; the fiber in his diet keeps it low. Now scientists have pinpointed the chemical in carrots and other "rabbit foods" that lowers cholesterol. Calcium pectate—a salt of pectin found in plant cell walls—binds to and eliminates bile

acids, which the body normally reuses to digest fats. This forces the body to dip into its supply of cholesterol to make more bile acids. Calcium pectate also binds to free-floating fatty acids, reducing their concentration and thus may play a role in preventing colon cancer. Canadian studies suggest that free saturated fatty acids may be involved in promoting formation of tumors.
Macromolecular and Cell Structure Research, Eastern Regional Research Center, Philadelphia, PA
Peter Hoagland, (215) 233-6426

How much of a trace element is absorbed by the human body and how much is retained? A small, windowless room encased in 75 tons of steel is helping scientists answer such questions with a new degree of accuracy. With its 32 ultrasensitive gamma-ray detectors and unique computer program, this whole-body counter can detect harmless doses of radioactive isotopes in a person and distinguish them from background radiation. In fact, one dose emits less radioactivity than subjects would get during a study from their own naturally occurring radioactivity or from normal radiation in the environment.
Grand Forks Human Nutrition Research Center, Grand Forks, ND
Glenn I. Lykken, (701) 795-8418

Foods high in fiber may not interfere with the way the body absorbs and uses the B vitamin folate--an important finding now that Americans are being encouraged to add more high-fiber foods to their diet. Earlier studies by other researchers had suggested that fiber might adversely affect folate intake. The vitamin is needed for growth and reproduction and for preventing anemia. ARS and University of California at Berkeley researchers studied six volunteers who spent more than 5 weeks on a liquid diet, supplemented with portions of navy beans and wheat bran. Neither the beans nor bran altered the availability of the common (polyglutamate) form of folate; bran actually enhanced absorption of the less common (monoglutamate) form. The best sources of folate include whole wheat products,

nuts, liver, yeast, leafy vegetables, and legumes such as beans.
Food Quality Research, Western Regional Research Center, Albany, CA
Pamela M. Keagy, (415) 486-3193

Scientific Information Systems

Water evaporation from row-cropped soils in semi-arid regions can now be evaluated more easily. A computer simulation model called ENWATBAL, (short for combined energy and water balance), describes how the amounts of heat and water in a row crop continuously change. The model can predict as accurately as field measurements the use of soil water from a row-cropped field. In a 74-day experiment on cotton, the model showed that of the total water used by the crop, 30% evaporated from the soil surface, regardless of whether the crop was irrigated. The model can be used to evaluate the effects of different management practices, such as changing the spacing between rows, in semi-arid agriculture.
Plant Stress and Water Conservation Research, Lubbock, TX
Jerry L. Hatfield, (806) 746-5353

The flow of water across watersheds, whether in the mountains or on broad flood plains, can be simulated by a computer model. Called the Simulator for Water Resources in Rural Basins (SWRRB), the model is being used by the U.S. Environmental Protection Agency, USDA's Soil Conservation Service, the Bureau of Land Management, and the National Oceanic and Atmospheric Administration (NOAA). NOAA is using the model to predict sources of pollutants in the Nation's coastal waters and estuaries. The model has already been used as evidence in water rights disputes in New Mexico. ARS has proved the model works for about a dozen rural watersheds nationwide and most recently for the drainage area for the Dallas city water supply, its first use on an urban site.
Natural Resources System Research, Temple, TX
Jeffrey G. Arnold, (817) 774-1201

15

Remote sensing of radiation reflected from growing crops can be complicated by a change in the slope of the land on which they grow. Reflected radiation is the difference between the amount of radiation that hits the crop and what is absorbed by plants--a clue to crop health and yield. Scientists took ground-level measurements of wheat growing in central Italy to learn potential problems for satellite-collected data. They now believe satellite data from crops growing on uneven terrain can be corrected using topographical information, such as slope angle and length, stored in computers. U.S. Water Conservation Lab, Phoenix, AZ Paul J. Pinter, Jr. (602) 261-4356

Selenium, an important trace mineral in the human diet, draws increasing scientific interest--especially its possible role in cancer prevention. Unfortunately, data on selenium content in foods are spotty and uncertain. To help scientists and nutritionists deal with this problem, a computer program called an expert system evaluates published data on selenium content in foods. Called SELEX, the system can be used on most personal computers to objectively rate the quality of research that produced the data and the data's reliability. Model and Database Coordination Lab, Beltsville, MD Douglas W. Bigwood, (301) 344-1825

Weeds crowding out range grasses need to be spotted. But the sheer variety of weed species presents a confusing picture for anyone trying to assess range condition from aerial photographs or satellite images. Now scientists have determined the correct light wavelengths to make many weeds stand out on remotely sensed images based on the degree of leaf hairiness. On a color infrared photograph, for example, a densely hairy weed such as silverleaf sunflower and most other western range weeds stand out as light pink. Moderately hairy weeds such as bullnettle appear light red; hairless species such as prairie coneflower appear deep red. A transparent overlay made from the color infrared photograph could be superimposed on other overlays, such as soil maps. That would allow ranchers, wildlife specialists, and others to identify and pinpoint the location of specific weed infestations. USDA's Soil Conservation Service, with ARS help, will eventually have computer software and equipment that will generate such overlays at the push of a button. Remote Sensing Research, Weslaco, TX James H. Everitt, (512) 968-5533

Salmon breeding grounds and valuable topsoil in the Pacific Northwest can be protected by conservationists using a new computer program. The program simulates different tillage methods to show how each method keeps soil in place on the 500-square-mile Tuccannon River basin in eastern Washington. Severe soil erosion can muddy streams and rivers, killing steelhead and chinook salmon populations. Information from this study will apply to other spawning grounds that produce fish worth half a billion dollars annually in the Northwest. Hydro-Ecosystem Research, Fort Collins, CO Jurgen D. Garbrecht, (303) 221-0578

* U.S. GOVERNMENT PRINTING OFFICE: 1987-180-916:60146/ARS

Quarterly Report
of Selected Research Projects

United States
Department of
Agriculture

Agricultural
Research
Service

October 1 to December 31, 1987

CONTENTS

Insect & Weed Research

Editor's note: Biological control of insects, weeds, and other pests of crops and farm animals is 100 years old in 1988 and is growing in importance. It includes such environmentally safe approaches to pest control as importing natural pest enemies (predators and parasites); using insect and plant pathogens; breeding resistance to pests into crops and animals; finding natural pest repellents; and employing novel stratagems that turn a pest's own biology against it.

Biocontrol

A tiny predatory fly (Leucopis obscura), discovered in France by the ARS European Parasite Lab, is proving an effective

> Note: One or more scientists familiar with each research project are listed for further information. If the scientists are unavailable, others at the same telephone number may also be familiar with the work.
>
> Items marked with the word PATENT are being patented by ARS. For more information contact Ann Whitehead, National Patent Program, Bldg. 005, Rm. 401, Beltsville Agricultural Research Center, Beltsville, MD 20705, (301) 344-2786.

biological control for a destructive invader of Hawaii's pine forests. It is the European pine adelgid, an aphidlike pest, which causes die-back, chlorosis, and needle death in pines, and slows tree growth. After importing the Leucopis fly, culturing it, and releasing it on several of Hawaii's islands, entomologists there have concluded that the predator has reduced the population of the adelgid below economically significant levels. The biocontrol is doubly important because the adelgid could easily cross the Pacific and infest pines in the continental United States. Systematic Entomology Lab, Beltsville, MD
John Drea, (301) 344-1791

A weed-destroying fungus and several species of small beetles—all potential natural enemies of the notorious weed leafy spurge—are among the "finds" an ARS scientist has brought back from the vast grasslands of China's Inner Mongolia. It was the first expedition an American researcher has made to China expressly to gather natural enemies of weeds such as spurge, a plant that occurs in low population levels there but is growing out of control in America's northern Great Plains. Agency researchers will now determine if the fungus and beetles can be safely released in the United States to control spurge. These possible candidates are already well adapted to the harsh Mongolian climate—a promising indication that they may be able to survive the severe winters of America's Great Plains. Biological Control, Rangeland Insect Lab, Bozeman, MT
Robert W. Pemberton, (406) 994-4890 Foreign Disease—Weed Science Research, Frederick, MD
William L. Bruckart, (301) 663-7344

Three species of beneficial wasps that kill fruit flies such as the Mediterranean fruit fly can now be raised in the lab in quantities of 2 million or more a week. Wasps are then set free in fruit fly-infested areas as a natural control. They lay eggs in fly larvae, which provide food for their own larvae when they hatch. Until recently, researchers didn't know how to consistently produce enough female wasps to meet the ideal 1:1 ratio of females to males. The wasps are Biosteres tryoni, B. longicaudatus, and Opius fletcheri. ARS scientists discovered that a mated female wasp, who carries a reservoir of sperm, chooses whether to release this sperm to fertilize her eggs. Fertilized eggs produce females; unfertilized eggs produce males. They also discovered that the female wasp's choice is influenced by the size of the fruit fly larvae she parasitizes. Fruit Fly Biology and Control, Tropical Fruit and Vegetable Research Lab, Honolulu, HI
Tim T.Y. Wong, (808) 988-2158

New ways to control insects may develop from a chemical found in a wasp that is a parasite of caterpillars. When injected into many types of insects, the chemical stops them from molting so they can't mature. Extracted from the female Euplectrus plathypenae wasp, the chemical stopped growth in all butterflies and moths tested, including the bollworm, armyworm, and cabbage looper, and some beetles--asparagus beetle and common green lacewing. The next step: isolate and identify the chemical to determine its most effective uses.
Biological Control of Insects Research Lab, Columbia, MO
Thomas A. Coudron/Ben Puttler, (314) 875-5361

A chemical gum that repels ticks has been found in a sweet-smelling African shrub (Commiphora erythraea). The shrub, a relative of the myrrh plant, produces a gum that shows promise as a repellent to the three most prevalent U.S. ticks--American dog tick, lone star tick, and deer tick. The gum is actually toxic to the dog and lone star ticks. ARS tests,

conducted in cooperation with a visiting chemist from Tanzania, indicate that the purified active ingredient in the gum could be developed into an environmentally safe tick control. The dog tick is the primary transmitter of Rocky Mountain spotted fever, and the deer tick transmits Lyme disease to humans. The lone star tick is a pest of livestock and humans in southern states.
Livestock Insects Lab, Beltsville, MD
J.F. Carroll, (301) 344-4171
Insect Chemical Ecology Lab, Beltsville, MD
J.D. Warthen/A. Maradufu, (301) 344-2139

New attractants may help control borers that attack the roots and bark of peach and other stone-fruit trees. The attractant, or pheromone, was more than 90% effective in controlling the lesser peach tree borer and the peach tree borer in tests in commercial orchards in Georgia. When placed in a dispenser hung from the tree, the pheromone confuses male borers so that they are unable to locate females. A Japanese and an Australian company are working with agency scientists to develop the pheromone, which could help reduce the amount of chemical insecticides now used to control the pests. The pheromone has potential for use on some 80,000 acres of peach trees in Georgia, South Carolina, Michigan, and Pennsylvania.
Southeastern Fruit and Tree Nut Research Lab, Byron, GA
J. Wendell Snow, (912) 956-5656

Calling all fire ants: scientists have isolated the "recruitment pheromone"--a chemical attractant foraging ants use to enlist the aid of their nest mates. Previously, scientists had isolated a different pheromone--Z,E-a-farnesene-- that an ant deposits with her stinger to mark a trail from a food source to the nest. When she arrives at the nest, she tells her sisters via the recruitment pheromone that "soup's on." Ants then follow her trail back to the food. The recruitment pheromone, scientists have discovered, consists of the trail pheromone plus another compound, called a

2

homosesquiterpene. This is the first time scientists have shown that two types of fire ant behavior—recruitment and trail following—are controlled by different chemical combinations produced by the same gland. Isolation of the two chemicals may lead to new poisoned baits that only fire ants will eat. The pheromones can also be used to detect ant presence and to estimate populations.
Imported Fire Ant Research, Gainesville, FL
Robert K. Vander Meer, (904) 374-5918

A chameleon of the insect world—a mosquito in its youngest form—adapts to the color in its environment. The discovery, scientists hope, could allow them to genetically sterilize lab-reared insects to release into wild populations to compete with fertile mosquitoes as mates. In tests with Anopheles mosquitoes, larvae reared in white containers stayed a white-beige color. Those reared on black adapted by producing more pigment and eventually turned jet black. Scientists are checking to see if the ability is carried on a gene. If so, they hope to cut off the part of the gene that "turns on" pigment production, called the promoter, and find a sterility gene to attach it to. Larvae with the new gene could be raised in black containers to activate the sterility gene. Most sterilization techniques like radiation weaken mosquitoes and make them less competitive as mates, whereas this method would probably not weaken the insects.
Insects Affecting Man and Animals Research Lab, Gainesville, FL
Mark Benedict, (904) 374-5973

By increasing the amount of a natural chemical produced by some wild species of cotton, scientists could develop plants resistant to tobacco budworm, a serious pest of cotton. Experts have known that a chemical called gossypol, produced by glands in cotton, stunts the growth of budworm caterpillars when they eat the plant. Since smaller caterpillars eat fewer cotton leaves and are more prone to diseases and predators, scientists have bred the crop for high levels of gossypol. In recent studies with scientists from Texas A&M, a second compound, caryophyllene oxide, boosted the beneficial effects of gossypol enough to stunt caterpillar growth 50% or more than with gossypol alone. If this compound could be incorporated into commercial cotton lines, resistance could be improved without increasing the level of gossypol in the leaves and seeds, which can be harmful to humans and livestock when used for oil or feed.
Southern Crops Research Lab, College Station, TX
Robert Stipanovic, (409) 260-9233

Combinations of weapons appear to be the best answer to control the soybean cyst nematode (SCN), a tiny parasitic worm that attacks the root systems of soybeans. SCN can reduce yields by 10% to 80%. Since first discovered in this country, in North Carolina in 1954, SCN has spread west to Texas and north to Minnesota. In Illinois, ARS scientists have responded to the threat by developing several soybean varieties resistant to different races of the nematode. When these are planted as part of a system of crop rotations (modified for the Corn Belt from rotations first recommended in Mississippi), the SCN-resistant beans are helping keep SCN below threshold levels and are enabling farmers to increase yields, usually without resorting to nematocides. The rotations have been widely adopted by Illinois farmers during the 1980's and may well prove practical throughout the Corn Belt. In one typical rotation, a farmer who has experienced soybean losses from nematodes should plant a nonhost crop in the following year. The crop can be corn, sorghum, sunflower, alfalfa, or red clover. In year 2, the farmer plants an SCN-resistant soybean variety; in year 3, a nonhost crop again. In year 4, the farmer can once again plant a susceptible soybean variety if soil analysis shows that SCN populations are below threshold levels. Scientists find that when no host plant is available to the nematodes, between 50% and 90% of the population is eliminated each year by starvation and biocontrol organisms. They have also found that if an SCN-resistant soybean is

planted _every_ year, it will soon lead to high populations of a race of nematodes that can overcome the resistance.
Crop Protection Research, Urbana, IL
G.R. Noel/D.I. Edwards, (217) 333-0996

Other Pest Research

Like prompting a police officer on patrol to call for backup, squashing a yellowjacket might incite nearby yellowjackets into frenzied attack. ARS scientists found that the venom of southern yellowjacket wasps contains a chemical called the alarm pheromone. It signals nesting wasps at least 15 feet away that defense is needed. Smashing a wasp breaks its venom sac, releasing the pheromone into the air. The alarm summons guard wasps to come out and sting whoever or whatever gets in their way. Scientists found and synthesized the alarm pheromone—the first wasp pheromone isolated that is known to provoke attack.
Insect Attractants, Behavior, and Basic Biology Research Lab, Gainesville, FL
Peter J. Landolt/Robert R. Heath, (904) 374-5700

Mushrooms are being gobbled up by dark-winged fungus gnats, costing growers thousands of dollars annually in insecticides and reduced yields. Until now, the only way to rid the fungus of the insect pest was to treat a whole growing room with expensive insecticides; this often meant treating more than 110 tons of growing medium (compost). In lab studies, scientists infected compost with gnats. They found that the gnat maggots, as they move through their life cycle, prefer the top 2 inches of medium, then burrow down to lower levels. As they mature, however, they come back to the top 2 inches. The conclusion: it is more effective to apply pesticides only to the top 2 inches of the compost to kill the second generation of gnats, which are more destructive than their parents because there are more of them. Targeting treatment lowers the cost of applying insecticides.
Vegetable Lab, Horticultural Crops Institute, Beltsville, MD
William Cantelo, (301) 344-4557

4

Drown those flies! Flooding manure stored in pits with water can control up to 90% of immature stable and house flies. These filth flies cause livestock diseases and discomfort and reduced weight gain and efficiency. They also annoy people and have even led to nuisance suits against farmers. Chemical controls have had limited success and may cause environmental damage. But in recent experiments, 30-minute flooding of manure drowned 30% of the immature flies; 90% died when it was flooded for 4 hours or longer. After use, the water can be used as fertilizer. For best results, manure storage systems should be designed and managed for flooding.
Livestock Insects Research, Lincoln, NE
Conrad B. Gilbertson, (402) 437-5267

Insects, like chickens and reptiles, can safely store potentially poisonous by-products of growth inside their egg shells until they hatch. Scientists found that purines, nitrogenous compounds similar to those found in human urine, are concentrated in eggs as developing insect embryos produce and excrete them. Knowing this, people who rear beneficial insects that devour these eggs can avoid feeding times when purine concentration is greatest.
Biological Control of Insects Lab, Tucson, AZ
Allen C. Cohen, (602) 629-6220

To reduce the cost of controlling purple nutsedge—often called the world's worst weed—scientists have added inorganic salts to herbicides. The herbicides monosodium methane arsenate (MSMA) and glyphosate, currently used on the weed, offer unreliable and expensive control. By adding salts such as ammonium chloride, control levels increased by 30% to 50%, reducing the cost to control nutsedge in cotton and soybean fields.
Southern Weed Science Lab, Stoneville, MS
Chester McWhorter, (601) 686-2311

For the first time, scientists have found ways to raise worker bees from larvae inside the lab. Lab-reared workers are needed for research on honey bee brood diseases. The new technique calls for rearing larvae in beeswax cups under carefully controlled temperature and humidity and for feeding them a mixed diet of royal jelly, water, glucose, fructose, and yeast extract. Three quarters of the larvae so raised reached the adult stage and were normal size.
Beneficial Insects Lab, Logan, UT
J.N. Vandenberg, (801) 750-2524

Sightings of the worst honey bee pest known were recently confirmed in 10 states, and ARS promptly launched a research program to combat it. The varroa mite (Varroa jacobsoni) threatens the $30 to $50 million a year industry that sells bees to other countries because mite-free areas don't want the pest. The mite weakens bees and makes them far less efficient pollinators. To combat the pest, scientists are looking for fumigants, growth inhibitors, and biological control organisms.
Beneficial Insects Lab, Beltsville, MD
Hachiro Shimanuki, (301) 344-2205

Ultrasensitive equipment to detect sound can pick up the faint noises of wormlike, Oriental fruit fly larvae living and feeding inside papayas. ARS researchers in Hawaii are testing the equipment, developed by colleagues in Florida, to see if it can give scientists useful new clues about the habits of fruit flies and other destructive insect pests, while leaving the fruit intact. Also, with further development, the equipment might someday be reliable enough to supplement or perhaps even replace other methods for treating papayas intended for out-of-state sale. Such treatments are required to ensure that the fruit is free of oriental, melon, or Mediterranean fruit flies—among the most devastating pests of fruits and vegetables worldwide. But more work is needed: 15% of the time the equipment indicated that fruit was infested, when in fact it was not.
Tropical Fruit and Vegetable Research Lab, Hilo, HI
James D. Hansen, (808) 959-9138
Insect Attractants, Behavior, and Basic Biology Research Lab, Gainesville, FL
J.C. Webb, (904) 374-5740

What do diapers, body powder, fuel filters, and now tiny worms have in common? Super slurper! Made of cornstarch and holding 2,000 times its weight in water, it could one day help tiny soil-dwelling worms called nematodes kill a citrus pest. Citrus root weevils, which can destroy 20% to 30% of a grove, are easily killed by worms that penetrate their guts and release lethal bacteria. The problem: the worms die quickly if the soil dries out. But in field tests, super slurper saw the nematodes through serious water stress, and 60% of the weevils died. That's compared to 25% without the absorbent's help. Citrus growers could dip new tree roots into wormy super slurper before planting so their groves contain trees with weevil control attached right to their roots. For already infested groves, the scientists are looking into injecting the mixture into the soil near trees with a nozzle. Other ARS labs are testing the super slurper/nematodes combo on pests of corn and vegetables. (PATENT)
U.S. Horticultural Research, Orlando, FL
William Schroeder, (305) 897-7379

Have pity on your azalea bushes; don't wait until June to spray them for the azalea lace bug. New ARS studies show these leaf-feeding pests lay eggs in the fall that hatch in the first week of May—not in June, as was previously thought. Scientists say gardeners in the Mid-Atlantic states should spray just before Memorial Day to kill all the young bugs before they can reach adulthood and lay their own eggs. This will eliminate a gardener's lace bug problem. Most garden pest sprays will do the job. The findings also apply to another pesky bug, the andromeda lace bug, which only recently has developed a taste for azaleas.
Florist and Nursery Crops Lab, Beltsville, MD
John W. Neal, (301) 344-4559

Flixweed and tansy mustard may no longer rob wheat crops of water. If glyphosate, a common herbicide, is applied before mid-May on fallow land, studies show, these annual weeds die, saving up to 5 inches of water for the next wheat planting. Left to mature on fallow land, these two closely related weeds can use up nearly all water in the top 36 inches of soil.
Soil and Water Management Research, Sidney, MT
J. Kris Aase, (406) 482-2020

Cuphea--a relatively unknown but highly valuable oilseed plant--has an ally: a tiny bee half the size of the honey bee that pollinates the plant. Cuphea oil has potential for use in making soaps, detergents, and lubricants. Honey bees (Apis mellifera) want nothing to do with cuphea, possibly because of the sticky hairs that completely cover the plant. But scientists found that wild Osmia bruneri bees are less fussy. Preliminary tests show the gentle, nonstinging wild bees can be easily managed.
Pollinating Insect Biology Lab, Logan, UT
Vincent J. Tepedino, (801) 750-2559

A pesky fly no longer drives cattle to bury themselves in a lake up to their heads, say ranchers on Montana's Blackfoot Indian Reservation. A combination of sterile male flies and insecticides essentially cleared heel flies from a 300-square-mile area that includes part of the reservation and private ranches in southern Alberta. Heel flies, a worldwide pest of cattle, cost the U.S. livestock industry an estimated $680 million a year. When the bumblebee-like flies buzz cattle, the animals panic and run wildly until they hit a fence--or lake. This panic interferes with normal mating urges and can cause spontaneous abortions and other injuries. When cattle grubs hatch from eggs stuck to cattle's legs or bellies, there's more misery. The grubs burrow through the hide and start a six-to-eight month trip to the steer's upper back, where they cut breathing holes and spend up to three

more months in cysts before emerging. The holes cause a loss in value of hides sold for leather. Fluid build-up under cysts discolors prime cuts of meat.
U.S. Livestock Insects, Kerrville, TX
Sidney E. Kunz, (512) 257-3566

New & Improved Products

Fungi grown in the lab on processed wheat produce substances that may lead the way to a new generation of biodegradable, environmentally safe chemicals to control plant diseases. For example, lab studies show that cyclopenol, a chemical antibiotic produced by Penicillium cyclopium, is 95% effective in stopping the growth of a fungus that caused the terrible Irish potato blight in the 1840's. Another natural chemical, cyclopenin, also produced by P. cyclopium, stunts the growth of certain plants, makes chicks drowsy, and has potential as a tranquilizing drug. And in lab studies, 6-pentyl-pyrone, from the fungus Trichoderma viride, inhibited the growth of a fungus that produces aflatoxin, a potent carcinogen found in some crops under certain conditions. While findings are preliminary, chemical companies are interested in further research to develop these and other natural chemicals into commercial products.
Plant Physiology Research, Richard B. Russell Research Center, Athens, GA
Horace G. Cutler, (404) 546-3311

A major maker of french fries is using an ARS test that determines potato ripeness based on low sugar content. The best-tasting fries come from potatoes that reach full maturity just before harvest. (Maturity means the potatoes have thoroughly converted sugar into starch). Low-sugar potatoes also preserve their processing quality longer in storage. Potato breeders are using the sucrose test to speed up development of potato varieties with superior storage and processing quality. One large processor of potato chips is building a quality-

assurance facility near the ARS lab in Minnesota and will use the new test as well as other quality tests developed by the agency.
Potato Handling, Storage and Processing, Red River Valley Potato Research Lab, East Grand Forks, MN
Paul Orr, (218) 773-2473

Watermelons reaching the market early command the best prices, and researchers found that trickle irrigation and mulching tripled early-season yields on sandy soil in Indiana. By trapping the sun's heat to warm the soil, black polyethylene plastic mulch made the watermelons grow faster and begin ripening 2 weeks earlier. Drip hose and plastic mulch raised the production cost by $300 per acre, but this was offset by a yield increase estimated to be worth more than $1,000. More than 2,300 watermelons per acre grew from irrigated and mulched vines--almost twice the total season yield of non-irrigated, unmulched vines.
U.S. Vegetable Lab, Charleston, SC
Harbans S. Bhella, (803) 556-0840

Autumn Gold, a new iceberg lettuce that resists mosaic virus, may be on the market within a year. The lettuce is designed for December and January harvest in California and Arizona desert regions, where much of the nation's winter lettuce crop is produced. Resistance to mosaic virus is important because mosaic-infected lettuce is worthless: infected plants form small, distorted heads, with leaves that have an unhealthy "mosaic" pattern of dark and light green. Another Autumn Gold advantage: the lettuce doesn't bolt (go to seed too early). Bolting is a common, hot-weather problem with some other varieties planted for late fall or early winter harvest from desert farmlands.
Vegetable Production, U.S. Agricultural Research Station, Salinas, CA
Edward J. Ryder, (408) 443-2253

Orange juice imports, amounting to $400 million in 1987, can be significantly reduced by three new orange varieties introduced by ARS scientists in Florida. Florida has been unable to meet market demand for orange juice because its principal varieties, late-season Valencia and early season Hamlin, leave a market gap. The new Sunstar, Midsweet, and Gardner, which ripen in midseason, yield as well as and make a better grade of juice than current varieties. They also supply oranges for the fresh and processing markets.
U.S. Horticultural Research Lab, Orlando, FL
C. Jack Hearn, (305) 897-7339

A hand-held light meter that measures body fat is being produced by a Maryland company that based its design on technology developed by an ARS scientist. The scientist discovered that a person's percentage of body fat can be accurately measured using reflected infrared light from the bicep of the arm that the individual writes with. The light technology was originally developed for testing agricultural commodities. The company added a built-in computer that compares a person's weight, height, and sex with medically established values and produces a customized printout suggesting an individualized health and fitness plan.
Instrumentation Lab, Beltsville, MD
Karl H. Norris, (301) 344-3650

At least 10 peanut shelling companies are using a new machine that will improve peanut quality by removing more than 95% of broken shells, sticks, poor-quality peanuts, and other debris from unshelled peanuts before storage. One thousand pounds of peanuts can contain up to 30,000 pieces of field debris that harvesting machines scoop up. Screens used in shelling plants to remove this debris have a low cleaning capacity, often clog, and are only about 30% efficient. The new machine, manufactured by an Alabama company, uses 29 belts spaced so that debris falls through the spaces while peanuts move across the top of the machine. Peanut buyers and farmers are also buying the machine because it has a

high capacity that permits additional cleaning options on the farm and at buying points. About 300,000 tons of peanuts--20% of the U.S. crop--are now being cleaned using the new machine, and the percentage is expected to grow. Researchers estimate it saves about $5 per ton--a 20% savings in cleaning costs. The machine also has potential for cleaning soybeans, pecans, walnuts, and other crops.
National Peanut Research Lab, Dawson, GA James I. Davidson, Jr./
Paul D. Blankenship, (912) 995-4441

Postharvest decay of stored fruit caused by various fungi may be controlled safely by a chemical now used to bleach flour and wood pulp. Lab tests show chlorine dioxide is at least as effective as currently used sodium hypochlorite in reducing disease-causing fungi, but at much lower concentrations. Sodium hypochlorite (common household bleach) is added to water used to process most apples, cherries, and other tree fruit: it protects fruit from rot during long-term storage. But chlorine gas, produced by the sodium hypochlorite, is difficult to keep at an effective level. Chlorine dioxide, properly used, poses no problem. Scientists will next examine the use of chlorine dioxide to protect fruit from mold on commercial fruit-packing lines.
Tree Fruit Research Lab, Wenatchee, WA Rodney G. Roberts, (509) 662-4317

Preventing grain dust explosions with soybean oil could protect lives and properties. ARS scientists found that just 200 parts per million of soybean oil reduces airborne dust by 90%. After 1 year of storage, 200 to 800 ppm soy oil did not affect odor, germination, flammability, or handling properties of corn, wheat, and soybeans. Research findings may persuade grain elevator operators to spray soy oil on the commodities during handling to control airborne dust.
Although USDA's Federal Grain Inspection Service in early 1987 allowed soybean oil to be used on the three grains, many processors questioned its usefulness and its effect on quality. Since 1978, grain dust explosions have killed more than 13 people and injured 400 each year.
Vegetable Oil Research, Northern Regional Research Center, Peoria, IL
Timothy L. Mounts/Kathleen Warner, (309) 685-4011, ext. 555

Improving the milling quality of rice by only 3% to 4% could increase rice revenues by $21 to $28 million a year in Arkansas alone. Milling quality is primarily determined by the number of whole kernels of rice and the kernels that break during harvesting; farmers get paid more for whole kernels than broken ones. Growers in the Southern Rice Belt generally set their combine cylinder speed between 850 and 950 rpm. Slowing the speed of the combine cylinder from 1,000 to 600 rpm reduced the number of broken kernels by about 7% in 11 varieties. Unfortunately, the slower speed leaves too many kernels on the stalk to be economical. Growers may find that an intermediate speed of 700 to 800 rpm could provide a happy medium. Furthermore, several management practices, such as proper seedbed preparation and uniform seedling emergence, irrigation and drainage, and fertilization may minimize the effect of combine cylinder speed and moisture content of grain, which also affects rice's milling quality.
Rice Production and Weed Control Research Lab, Stuttgart, AR
Robert H. Dilday, (501) 673-2661

Before zein--a major class of corn protein--was replaced in the 1950's by cheaper petrochemicals in many industrial products such as inks and cork particle bindings, 15 million pounds were produced annually. But if petrochemical prices rise again, the zein market could pick up once more, especially now that researchers have a way to monitor how processing affects its quality and uniformity in corn hybrids. By using two types of a special analysis called electrophoresis, they found the protein more resilient to wet milling than they expected. Millers could use similar analyses to monitor zein quality, and scientists are using them to learn how corn plants store proteins. The research could lead to

corn with higher nutritional quality and less susceptibility to breakage and spoilage.
Plant Protein Research, Northern Regional Research Center, Peoria, IL
Curtis M. Wilson, (309) 685-4011, ext. 361

Apples in the 21st century could be picked by a mechanical apple harvester if an expected shortage in labor materializes. The rod-press harvester, attached to a tractor, gently pushes apples off trees pruned to grow along a T-shaped trellis. Apples drop through foam-lined decelerators that help break their fall and minimize damage. In field studies last year, 93% of Golden Delicious apples picked with the harvester met high-quality grades for fresh market sale. Earlier machine harvesters caused too much damage. Workers now pick fresh-market apples by hand, but new immigration laws and other factors are making it more difficult to find hand labor. (PATENT)
Appalachian Fruit Research Station, Kearneysville, WV
Donald L. Peterson, (304) 725-3451

Salmonella bacteria in poultry could be reduced by eliminating the organisms in the feed-manufacturing process. Current pellet-manufacturing machines use one-stage steam conditioners to add moisture and heat to the feed mixture to help form pellets. An experimental two-stage conditioner, built by ARS scientists, doubles the time of heat treatment without reducing the feed flow rate. In pilot trials, feed inoculated with Salmonellae was processed through the new conditioner. Results: while some of the organisms survived the first stage, all were eliminated at the end of the second stage. Three-fourths of U.S. poultry feed is pelleted.
Poultry Meat Quality and Safety, Richard B. Russell Research Center, Athens, GA
Albert D. Shackelford, (404) 546-3531

A Dallas-based company killed grain-eating insects in 25 million bushels of stored corn and sorghum in 1987 by safely fumigating the grain with carbon dioxide, a procedure developed by agency scientists. Grain in storage bunkers in Illinois, Idaho, Iowa, and Colorado was fumigated with carbon dioxide gas for 15 days. This killed virtually all the red flour beetles, foreign grain beetles, rice weevils, and other insects at a cost of one-half cent per bushel. This is comparable to the cost of treatment with conventional chemical fumigants such as phosphine.
Stored-Product Insects Research and Development Lab, Savannah, GA
Edward G. Jay, (912) 233-7981

Safflower seeds have a potentially valuable genetic trait—an incomplete hull—that could lead to higher yields of cooking oil. The trait is the result of a rare genetic recombination. The hull, or outer covering of the seed, is high in fiber but low in oil. Seeds only partially covered by their hull yield more oil than fully encased seeds. Partial-hull seeds contain 49% oil, and the hulls are dark; normal seeds have only 36% oil and are completely covered by a white hull. Safflower breeders who want to develop high-oil, partial-hull safflower varieties can quickly pick out the partial-hull seeds by their distinctive dark color.
U.S. Cotton Research Station, Shafter, CA
A. Lee Urie, (805) 746-6391

Hurricane Danny may have done millions of dollars in damage when it hit in 1985, but it has also provided information to save Louisiana sugarcane growers $1 million a year. After the hurricane, data was gathered on the brittleness and tendency to lodge, or fall over, of various sugarcane varieties. From this type of information, researchers developed standards by which to evaluate new sugarcane varieties for their ability to stand up well to mechanical harvesters. Lodged or broken sugarcane cannot be picked by the mechanical harvesters. Since hurricanes cannot be counted on every year to evaluate new varieties,

9

researchers also developed a hand-held device that measures brittleness. Six varieties, which had other desirable characteristics, have already been eliminated from consideration for release.
Sugarcane Research, Houma, LA
Hugh N. Fanguy, (504) 872-5042

A milk protein, casein, may help slow the growth of bacteria that can cause spoilage in food products. Computer predictions based on lab studies indicate that a mixture of the protein and calcium salt at 36°F will retard the growth of some types of food-poisoning bacteria, such as those that cause salmonellosis and the often-fatal botulism. Scientists say the protein and salt appear to use up water that these microbes need to grow. Food processors may be able to use this information to develop new products that last longer in storage and have minimal artificial preservatives.
Macromolecular and Cell Structure Research, Eastern Regional Research Center, Philadelphia, PA
Thomas F. Kumosinski, (215) 233-6475

Three new experimental soybean lines, developed by agency scientists, may improve the quality and nutritional content of soybean oil. The new lines, distributed to more than 30 companies for commercial development, contain only 3.5% linolenic acid, compared to 8% or 9% in current varieties. This acid can cause soybean oil to turn rancid. Last year processors spent $700 million to remove it from oil to prolong shelf life. The experimental soybeans may also have higher amounts of another fatty acid, linoleic acid, which is essential for proper body metabolism.
Soybean and Nitrogen Fixation Research, Raleigh, NC
Richard F. Wilson, (919) 737-3267

Crop Production & Protection

By measuring fragments of DNA, the basic hereditary material that makes up genes, researchers are now able to distinguish clearly and reliably between two look-alike species of sugarcane. Breeders who manage international collections of the world's sugarcane, such as the collections in Hawaii and Florida, should be able to use the approach to identify the two incoming plants and to doublecheck existing collections to make sure that older cane plants were identified correctly. Accurate identification of the two species, Saccharum barberi and S. sinense, is critical because they are among the six used today in producing hybridized, commercial sugarcane varieties. A technique known in biotechnology as "restriction fragment length polymorphism" showed that S. sinense has an additional fragment of DNA that's not found in S. barberi.
Sugarcane Physiology Lab, Aiea, HI
Paul H. Moore, (808) 487-5561
Department of Botany, University of Georgia, Athens, GA
Betty J. Wood, (404) 542-0281

City-tough, decorative trees in greater variety are possible by the 21st century thanks to the first scientific method to predict success of tree grafts. Previously, there was no reliable way to know if a stem from one tree could graft well to a root from another. This has limited the varieties of high-quality trees available to landscape planners. An ARS scientist found that each tree has unique enzymes for making lignin, the strengthening glue that binds the cell walls of woody plants. By matching similar sets of enzymes from different trees, nursery growers can, for the first time, predict if the stem and the root will grow into a solid graft. Grafted trees, unlike those grown from seeds, can be grown to market size 3 years sooner and tend to be more uniform in size and shape.
U.S. National Arboretum, Washington, DC
Frank S. Santamour, (202) 475-4864

10

Strawberries are sweet on the vine and the tongue, but so far only 1 variety of 10 tested survives well in the produce department. Strawberries are not usually bred for shelf life but rather for their size, yield, and taste. Of the 10 varieties tested under simulated retail conditions, 9 had more than 75% decay from fungal growth after 3 days. But after the same period, Cardinal strawberries had less than 10% decay. Preliminary investigations have begun to find out exactly what makes Cardinal more resistant to fungal decay. As a first step, a check is being made for correlation between the makeup of the cell wall (sugars and carbohydrates) and susceptibility to decay in the strawberry. For taste, Cardinal was rated a 4 out of 10, with 1 being the best.
South Central Agricultural Research Lab, Lane, OK
Benny D. Bruton, (405) 889-7395
Horticultural Crops Quality Lab, Beltsville, MD
William S. Conway/Kenneth C. Gross, (301) 344-3128

Potatoes and peppers prefer white. Spray-painting traditional straw mulch white increased yields of potatoes 25% compared to fields mulched with red-, blue-, and yellow-painted straw and no mulch. White-mulched fields also yielded more number-one quality potatoes—large, perfectly shaped ones that are sold as baking potatoes. Changing from black plastic mulch to white had a similar effect on bell pepper plants. With white mulch, peppers produced 8,365 pounds per acre compared to 6,990 pounds per acre with black plastic mulch.
Coastal Plains Soil and Water Conservation Research Center, Florence, SC
Patrick G. Hunt, (803) 669-5203

Peach growers could get a marketable crop a year earlier, thanks to peach trees that began life in a lab dish. Peach trees from small shoots raised by tissue-culture techniques bore 10 times more fruit in their second year than conventionally grafted trees. Normally, peach trees need 3 years to begin producing a cash crop. But 2-year-old tissue-cultured trees produced 285 peaches per tree, compared to 33 peaches on trees from standard stock. Eventually, the two types of trees will produce similar yields, but a sizable second-year crop would benefit the orchard grower's cash flow.
Tissue Culture and Molecular Genetics Lab, Beltsville, MD
Freddi Hammerschlag, (301) 344-4072

An obscure citrus fruit, Citrus ichangensis, that has very little of the natural, bitterness-causing compound limonin, may provide clues researchers can use to eliminate the compound in another citrus—the navel orange. Currently, bitterness caused by limonin costs California navel orange growers an estimated $6 to $8 million each year in lost juice sales. Apparently, the obscure fruit, instead of forming the bitter limonin, forms mostly a related but nonbitter substance, which ARS researchers discovered and named "ichangensin." With further study, molecular biologists might someday be able to isolate genes responsible for ichangensin production and insert them into navel oranges to reduce bitterness.
Fruit and Vegetable Chemistry Lab, Pasadena, CA
Shin Hasegawa/Raymond D. Bennett, (818) 796-0239

Crested wheatgrass varieties from the Middle East could benefit U.S. livestock producers by providing an extra $25 million a year in increased beef, mutton, and wool production. Seeds from these imported selections were found to have more vigorous seedlings and the plants to have broader, more numerous leaves than currently available crested wheatgrass on dry western rangelands. The reason for the greater vigor may be that the cells of these grasses have 42 chromosomes, while the cells of U.S. crested wheatgrasses contain either 14 or 28 chromosomes. Scientists will now try to develop new varieties from the introduced strains that are even better adapted to the West.
Forage and Range Research Lab, Logan, UT
Kay H. Asay, (801) 750-3069

Strawberry germplasm has been developed that is resistant to eastern and western North American races of the fungus that causes red stele disease. Red stele, which attacks the root, is one of the most destructive diseases of strawberries. It poses a threat even to resistant varieties, which are susceptible to exotic races. Several races of the disease fungus, Phytophora fragariae, exist from Maine to North Carolina and from California to Washington. Breeding new resistant varieties is the only practical and effective control.
Fruit Lab, Beltsville, MD
John L. Maas, (301) 344-4653

Screening the alfalfa gene pool should lead to finding parent genes for new aluminum-tolerant varieties that can grow well in acid soils. Increasing alfalfa's aluminum tolerance would particularly benefit farmers in the Southeast, where soils tend to be acid and have a high concentration of the mineral. Liming acid soil to counteract high aluminum levels succeeds as long as rainfall is adequate. But roots on non-aluminum-tolerant alfalfa varieties do not penetrate soil below the liming depth where they could draw moisture during drought.
Germplasm Quality and Enhancement Lab, Beltsville, MD
T. Austin Campbell, (301) 344-3638

Growing desirable, more nutritious shrubs that are more tolerant to drought and salty soil would increase the amount of feed for livestock and wildlife in the Southwest. So far scientists have discovered many differences among more than 300 native shrubs. They are identifying those that produce the most feed for animals and have the best traits for surviving the arid range environment. They plan to develop a breeding program to produce seed for use in renovating rangeland in Texas, New Mexico, and Arizona.
Jornada Experimental Range, Las Cruces, NM
Jerry R. Barrow, (505) 646-4842

Three new houseplants are being introduced to U.S. markets for the first time. The potted plants include a dwarf of the native American lisianthus, an evergreen member of the cypress family from Holland called Cupressus marf, and a Jerusalem cherry from Denmark. All are hardy and require little care. They are being introduced under a new-crops program with a mission to search for, test, and introduce new plants that have market potential for the floral and nursery industries. Each of the plants has been evaluated by ARS, industry, and university specialists for 3 to 5 years.
Florist and Nursery Crops Lab, Beltsville, MD
Mark Roh, (301) 344-1883

Minerva is the National Arboretum's newest rose of Sharon. The plant is a sterile triploid, breaking from traditional varieties which spread unwelcome seeds that germinate all over the lawn. It has lavender blooms for about 4 months or longer. Tolerant of air pollution and light frost, Minerva (Hibiscus syriacus) can be grown as a container plant or as an addition to parks, lawns, roadsides, or shopping malls.
U.S. National Arboretum, Washington, DC
Donald R. Egolf, (202) 475-4862

Unusual cold spells, as cold as -10°F, did not affect three new crape myrtles while older varieties died back or were killed. Biloxi, Miami, and Wichita are the first crape myrtles to combine mildew resistance, lush dark green leaves that change to autumn colors, bright flowers, and deep brown trunks. Besides mildew resistance, the hybrids also have sinuous mottled bark patterns and most are cold-tolerant from Baltimore, Maryland, southward. The crape myrtle is the most popular summer flowering small tree of southern states. The new varieties are among more than 20 recently developed hybrids.
U.S. National Arboretum, Washington, DC
Donald R. Egolf, (202) 475-4862

Cropland fertilization practices could become more efficient through ARS research based on recent findings by U.S. and Australian scientists that plants release ammonia gas into the atmosphere. Ammonia contains nitrogen, an essential plant nutrient supplied by fertilizers or fixed from the air by legumes. ARS growth-chamber studies showed that the more nitrogen fertilizer applied to wheat, the more ammonia the plants gave off. As much as 20% of the nitrogen in fertilizer could wind up being wasted as ammonia gas.
Crops Research Lab, Fort Collins, CO
Jack N. Morgan, (303) 491-8224

A crop of plump red tomatoes has yielded what is probably a new world's record of 100 tons an acre of field-grown tomatoes. Water and fertilizer were delivered to the root zone of the plants by thin plastic pipes buried in the soil. This irrigation system, known as subsurface drip irrigation, not only gave higher yields of cotton and cantaloupe crops—as well as tomatoes—on experimental plots, but also reduced leaching of salts into the underground water supply and eliminated costly loss of water to evaporation. The system also contributed to uniformly high-quality crops because below-surface pipes apply water and fertilizer more evenly from one end of the field to the other.
Water Management Research Lab, Fresno, CA
Claude J. Phene, (209) 453-3100

Soil, Water & Air

Microbes in soil produce a variety of chemical binding agents that increase a soil's mechanical strength (ability to withstand breaking up under loads) and improve its structure. One broad class of binders, a form of carbohydrates called polysaccharides, are produced in part when microbes decompose plant residues. The chemicals that result undergo further transformation by microbial activity to form more complex soil polysaccharides. It has been known that these compounds reduce a soil's erodibility by increasing its ability to clump in small aggregates. New research shows that these carbohydrates also increase a soil's strength and its mechanical resistance to the impact of raindrops. The finding helps show why residue management is so effective in protecting soil from water erosion, since the residues enhance microbial activity near the soil's surface. It also helps explain why soils high in organic matter (3% to 6%), which typically contain more microbes, are less erodible than soils low in organic matter. The bodies of microbes themselves have also been found to help glue soil particles together. ARS chemists in Peoria, Illinois, have come up with various test compounds derived from cornstarch that mimic the binding action of soil polysaccharides. Field tests will determine whether these new compounds, when sprayed on a soil's surface during seedbed preparation, can help reduce erosion during critical spring weeks in the Corn Belt, when rainfall can be intense and prolonged.
National Soil Erosion Lab,
West Lafayette, IN
Diane E. Stott, (317) 494-6657

Soil and water used to grow corn and other row crops in furrows in arid parts of the West can be conserved. Irrigation water flowing in these furrows may erode the soil, but farmers can leave plant residues in them to reduce erosion. However, the residues also reduce the speed at which water moves in the furrows, so more water soaks into the soil at the upper end of the furrow. Previous research has shown that furrow irrigation streams move just as fast when water is turned on and off for short periods as when it flows continuously. And intermittent or surge flow uses only about one-half as much water to wet the length of the furrow. ARS scientists have shown that if farmers leave plant residues in furrows and apply water in surges, they can reduce erosion and improve irrigation uniformity.
Weeds, Soil, and Water Management
Research, Prosser, WA
David E. Miller, (509) 786-2226

Sponges and bryozoans are good indicators of when a stream is getting too much sediment-laden runoff from farm fields. Bryozoans are minute invertebrate animals that form branching, mosslike colonies; they, along with sponges, live attached to vegetation and snags (dead trees) in streambeds. In aquarium experiments two species of bryozoans and one sponge species were killed by 4 days of exposure to as little as 600 parts per million of soil particles suspended in water. This information should help federal and state agencies monitor and alleviate the negative changes in water quality from runoff.
Sedimentation Lab, Oxford, MS
Charles N. Cooper, (601) 232-2900

Groundwater protection efforts advanced with recent refinements to GLEAMS, a computer model for tracking leachable agrichemicals that may percolate into aquifers, natural underground reservoirs. GLEAMS, short for Groundwater Loading Effects of Agricultural Management Systems, can predict the movement of 10 major pesticides under different weather conditions, even heavy rainstorms of once-in-50-years intensity. ARS researchers recently expanded GLEAMS to track the pesticides' breakdown products, or metabolites. They also simplified the system to make it more user-friendly. By plugging in data for local soil, weather, and crops, users can select management practices that best protect groundwater. One such practice is timing the dates of pesticide applications to periods of lower rainfall, thus reducing pesticide percolation and leaching. About 125 sets of GLEAMS software are already in use by USDA's Soil Conservation Service, state water quality groups, university scientists, pesticide manufacturers, and others.
Environmental Quality Research, Tifton, GA
Walter G. Knisel/Ralph A. Leonard, (912) 386-3462

To model pesticides in surface runoff from agricultural land, scientists must be able to predict the amount of pesticide washed from plants to soil by rain. Using a multi-intensity rainfall simulator to measure carbaryl (used to control cotton insects) washed from cotton plants, scientists found that the amount of rainfall was more important than its intensity. Thus, in developing models to measure pesticide washoff, rainfall intensity can be ignored during natural storms, when rainfall intensities vary within or between storms. This information will help modelers better predict washoff from plants and develop guidelines for respraying for pest control chemicals after rain or overhead irrigation.
Soil and Water Research, Baton Rouge, LA
Guye H. Willis, (504) 387-2783

Dark straw stubble left standing on Alaskan soils can warm them, thereby lengthening the short growing season in marginal subarctic agricultural areas. Scientists monitored stubble colored black or white to see how color affects temperatures and reflected solar radiation. On clear fall days, soil surface temperatures from black stubble were 10°F higher than those from white stubble. Solar radiation reflected from the black stubble was 5%; the white reflected 40%. These preliminary results indicate that breeding wheat, barley, or other cereal grains with dark-colored straw may hasten snow melt and raise soil temperatures, factors the scientists will study this spring.
Subarctic Agriculture Research, Fairbanks, AK
Brenton Sharratt, (907) 474-7187

A 2-year program to collect more accurate data on soil losses from the erosive action of water was begun by ARS scientists in the summer of 1987. Teams of soil erosion researchers are moving rain simulators and measuring devices to the sites of major cropland and rangeland soils across the United States to determine the erodibility of rangeland and cropland soils. Similar data are being collected by the Forest Service on forest

14

soils. Findings from the extensive field tests are critical in developing a more accurate method for calculating soil losses on different soil types, slopes, and land configurations under different range and crop conditions. Called the Water Erosion Prediction Project (WEPP), the new erosion model that emerges will replace the Universal Soil Loss Equation, a predictive formula in use since the early 1960's. The need for improved methods of estimating erosion intensified recently because of provisions of the 1985 Farm Bill (PL 99-198, the Food Security Act of 1985) requiring farmers to maintain low erosion rates on their land or risk losing eligibility for the benefits of many USDA farm programs. National Soil Erosion Lab, West Lafayette, IN John Laflen, (317) 494-8673

It doesn't begin to happen until the fifth year of no-till farming in the Corn Belt, but starting then, the condition of the topsoil reflects the impact of a greatly increased earthworm population, fed by crop residues left on the surface of the soil. Earthworm holes, in turn, sharply increase the water infiltration rate. This increased soil porosity is considered a plus by soil scientists, since it increases soil moisture and means less water runoff and soil erosion during rainstorms. After 21 years of growing no-till corn in watersheds at Coshocton, Ohio, scientists observed the following: large soil pores at the surface fell from 9% in year one to only about 2% in year 5, as the soil settled, or consolidated. During years 5, 6, 7, and 8, however, the number of large soil pores increased sharply, to nearly 12%, leveling off in the ninth year at a little over 12% and continuing through year 21, the most recent year. Infiltration on the no-till watersheds was greater than for any other tillage method observed. The soil in the area is a Rayne silt loam. National Soil Erosion Lab, West Lafayette, IN L.D. Norton, (317) 494-8682 North Appalachian Experimental Watershed Research, Coshocton, OH W.M. Edwards, (614) 545-6349

In irrigated fields in the West, earthworms can be good news and bad news. After several hours of furrow irrigation in the fine silty soils of southern Idaho, water often starts soaking into the soil too fast, failing to reach the end of the furrow. Cause of this "backing up," scientists have discovered, is accelerated water infiltration through earthworm holes. But earthworms also help crop growth by enabling roots to penetrate the soil more deeply, allowing plants to tap a larger reservoir of water and nutrients and withstand drought better. One answer to increasing infiltration during irrigation is to irrigate more frequently and for shorter periods. Another, perhaps more practical answer is to install automated systems like cablegation, which can ensure uniform top and bottom furrow wetting. National Program Leader for Soil/Atmosphere, Beltsville, MD W. Doral Kemper, (301) 344-4242

Animal Production & Protection

A new warm-season forage grass bred by agency scientists produced 36 more pounds of beef per acre than earlier varieties, based on a 4-year study with steers. This new variety, Tifton 78 bermudagrass, may be the best one developed in 50 years of breeding research, according to the research leader. In the study, Tifton 78 became established earlier and faster, started growth earlier, yielded up to 25% more hay, and was 7% more digestible than earlier varieties. It also produced a pound of beef gain with less than 5 cents of fertilizer, and despite the 1986 drought, it still produced 89% as much beef as in seasons with higher rainfall. Coastal Plain Experiment Station, Tifton, GA Glenn W. Burton, (912) 386-3353

Embryo transplants will help scientists overcome a big obstacle to breeding disease-resistant cattle--lack of cattle with the same immunity genes for use in research. Today those genes-- collectively called the major histo-

compatibility complex--can be studied in inbred rodents, where rapid reproduction allows relatively quick gene manipulation. Since the same approach in cattle would take 40 to 100 years, scientists are using embryo transfers instead. Fertilized embryos are removed from inbred cows, split to form identical twins, and implanted in surrogate mothers. Results so far include twin sisters and a bull from the same biological mother with the same histocompatibility complex on half of their chromosomes. When the sisters are bred to the bull, 25% of the offspring should have identical genes for immunity. Those offspring will be "pioneers" from which researchers can develop cattle with genetic resistance to diseases such as stomach worm, foot-and-mouth disease, and bluetongue.
Helminthic Diseases Lab, Beltsville, MD
Louis Gasbarre, (301) 344-2509

Moldy grain killed three whooping cranes at the U.S. Interior Department's breeding flock in Maryland in fall 1987. ARS microbiologist John L. Richard tested feed pellets for the Patuxent Wildlife Research Center and found a toxin commonly produced by Fusarium, a mold often found on grain crops. The toxin belongs to a group of compounds called trichothecenes, which are produced by several mold genera. The precise trichothecene involved is expected to be identified soon. Other trichothecenes had earlier been identified by ARS microbiologist Richard J. Cole as the cause of death of about 9,500 nonendangered, migrating sandhill cranes in West Texas and eastern New Mexico. The cranes died after eating mold-contaminated peanuts left after harvest on fields near their summer roosting areas. This fall's illness at Patuxent struck 80% of the captive flock of 293 cranes. Sixteen died: 3 adult whooping cranes and 1 Mississippi sandhill crane, both endangered species; and 12 Florida and greater sandhill cranes, nonendangered species used as foster parents for endangered cranes. As insurance against such disasters, Patuxent has a growing supply of frozen crane sperm. Thomas J. Sexton, ARS Distinguished Scientist of the Year for 1987, used his

16

expertise in preserving poultry semen to help Patuxent freeze crane sperm.
National Animal Disease Center, Ames, IA
John L. Richard, (515) 239-8263
National Peanut Research Lab, Dawson, GA
Richard J. Cole, (912) 995-4441
Avian Physiology Lab, Beltsville, MD
Thomas J. Sexton, (301) 344-2545

Lamb could be available all year, but that may involve resetting the biological clocks of sheep. Left to their own devices, sheep normally mate in the fall and produce lambs in the spring. The following fall, these lambs--now fattened to about 120 pounds--reach the market at about the same time. Scientists have shown that ewes have increased levels of the hormone melatonin, released by the body during the short days and long nights of winter, that "tell" them when to mate. Ewes receiving experimental implants of melatonin in the spring will breed then despite the lengthening days of summer, thus providing lamb at different times throughout the year.
U.S. Sheep Experiment Station,
Dubois, ID
John N. Stellflug, (208) 374-5306

The science of sex preselection--choosing male or female offspring in advance--is closer than ever. Unique technology, developed by ARS, gives 90% to 95% accurate predictions of whether bull, boar, or ram sperm cells would produce a male or a female upon fertilizing an egg. A laser-driven instrument sorts X chromosome-bearing (female) sperm from Y chromosome-bearing (male) sperm, based on differences in amounts of DNA in each. Dairy farmers could cut expenses by producing more heifer calves than bull calves. Beef and sheep farmers would benefit with more males, and swine farmers with more females for faster meat production. The experiments were conducted with sperm treated to remove tails and outer coverings. Although the treated and sex-sorted sperm remains viable when injected into mammalian eggs, scientists have now moved on to preliminary testing with intact sperm which would be suitable for artificial insemination.
Reproduction Lab, Beltsville, MD
Lawrence A. Johnson, (301) 344-2809

Scientists are mobilizing bacteria found in alfalfa fields to fight fungi that attack the crop. In lab and greenhouse tests, alfalfa had 70% less root rot and 50% less leaf spot when treated with Bacillus subtilis or an unknown species of Flavobacterium. A substance produced by the bacteria inactivates the fungi that cause these diseases, which cost farmers $400 million annually. The disease-fighting bacteria can be sprayed in liquid suspension or applied as a freeze-dried powder. Scientists are conducting field tests to see if the bacteria can successfully compete with other leaf micro-organisms. In the United States, alfalfa is grown on 28 million acres and is worth about $10 billion annually.
U.S. Regional Pasture Research Lab, University Park, PA
Kenneth T. Leath, (814) 863-0945

Continuous cattle grazing from spring to fall can produce the same beef gains as short-duration rotation grazing schemes—and at much lower cost to the rancher. In field tests of short-duration grazing, cattle were moved every few days from one pasture to another, for a total of eight pastures, a system that requires expensive fences to divide rangeland. The same number of cattle were allowed to graze in one undivided pasture all season long. Results were the same. Key to keeping weight gains high and protecting range from overgrazing, ARS scientists found, is not short-duration grazing but rather controlling stocking rate—the right number of animals for each pasture. An acceptable variation on continuous grazing calls for fencing the pasture into quarters and reserving a different quarter each year for September grazing only. This gives the fall quarter an opportunity to regain its vigor.
High Plains Grasslands Research Station, Cheyenne, WY
Richard H. Hart, (307) 772-2433

Advanced blood tests may help make millions of acres of western ranges safer for grazing animals. Pregnant cattle, sheep, and goats often abort after eating broom snakeweed plants. Now, isotopes of iodine added to samples of an animal's blood are helping scientists measure small but important changes in the levels of the reproductive hormones progesterone and estrogen, which are needed to maintain pregnancy. Results of this study will help the scientists determine why plants cause abortion, so ranchers and other livestock managers can take steps to protect their livestock.
Poisonous Plant Research Lab, Logan, UT
Kip E. Panter, (801) 752-2941

A virus once used in human smallpox vaccine may be enlisted to combat foot-and-mouth disease. A highly efficient immunizer, vaccinia virus will be genetically engineered to accept several genes from the foot-and-mouth disease virus that stimulate an animal's immune system. The genetically engineered virus will be used to make a safe, live-virus vaccine that contains only a noninfectious part of the foot-and-mouth disease virus. Researchers hope the new vaccine will have all the genes for the structural proteins of the virus. The original genetically engineered vaccine had only one gene for structural protein. The new work will be carried out cooperatively by ARS and a researcher from the State University of New York. Not present in the United States, the foot-and-mouth disease causes major economic losses worldwide. Cattle, sheep, goats, and swine from countries where it occurs cannot be imported into countries free of the disease. It causes blisters and sloughing in the mouth, nose, and feet of infected animals.
Molecular Biology Lab, Plum Island Animal Disease Research Center, Greenport, NY
Douglas M. Moore, (516) 323-2500

A better forage may have been found for subtropical Florida, where loss of forage quality in the late summer and fall cuts into cattle weight gains. In a test conducted by ARS and the University of Florida, steers grazing Rhizoma perennial peanuts (Arachis glabrata) gained weight 65% faster than those grazing bahiagrass. The latter, the major forage of Florida, is an early-season grass that loses its

digestibility and protein content after midsummer. _Rhizoma_ perennial peanuts (which generate no seed) produce high-quality forage until the first frost, contain high levels of protein, and are easily digestible. Once established, forage peanuts are hardy and relatively drought resistant.
Subtropical Agricultural Research Station, Brooksville, FL
E.L. Adams, (904) 796-3385

Adding a little fat to the diets of calves sent to feedlots might decrease losses from an often fatal respiratory disease. Shipping fever, caused by the stress of transportation, costs the beef industry $500 million annually in lost weight gains, deaths of calves, and treatments. In tests, however, weight gain and feed intake improved when 4% fat was added for 2 weeks to the diet of calves stressed by travel. Calves that already had the disease continued to have lower weight gain and higher mortality. Calves spend about 25 weeks in the feed-lot, so the 2 weeks of extra fat did not make them fatter at slaughter.
Conservation and Production Research Lab, Bushland, TX
N.A. Cole, (806) 378-5748

A quick, new test is being developed for leptospirosis, a disease that causes abortions and other reproductive failures in beef and dairy cows. The test will use genetic probes cloned from hardjo-bovis, a newly identified strain of _Leptospira_. It is the most common strain among cattle in the United States. Because diagnostic blood tests are not specific for this strain, researchers are testing cow urine. The bacteria live in the urinary tract and the disease spreads through infected urine. The probes would work by binding only to the disease organism to indicate its presence in a urine sample. Researchers will soon have a test ready for veterinary and diagnostic labs.
National Animal Disease Center, Ames, IA
Richard Zuerner, (515) 239-8200

Once rangeland has been damaged by severe droughts or overgrazing by cattle and sheep, the land will not naturally heal itself even if all grazing stops for 70 years. Instead of the range improving, less nutritious shrubs take over, replacing the more nutritious grasses and increasing soil erosion. When ranchers follow recommendations from scientists, however, the grasses return. For example, researchers found that a single 6-ounce application of tebuthiuron per acre killed brush and increased perennial grass production from an average 44 pounds per acre to 460 pounds annually.
Jornada Experimental Range,
Las Cruces, NM
Robert P. Gibbens, (505) 646-4842

A tissue culture cell line derived by an ARS scientist from the fall armyworm, a pest of corn and wheat, is playing a part in the development of a potential AIDS vaccine. Researchers at MicroGeneSys, a West Haven, Connecticut, based biotechnology company, selected a refinement of the armyworm cell line as the factory for a basic component of the vaccine. They did this primarily because insect cells have membranes similar to those of mammalian cells but cannot pick up mammalian viruses that might contaminate the vaccine. The cell line was first developed because scientists needed an in vitro system to study viruses with potential as biocontrols for insects that feed on crops. In addition, ARS scientists isolated the insect virus that MicroGeneSys is using as the "engine" inside the cell factory to produce the vaccine component. Food and Drug Administration officials recently approved the AIDS vaccine for clinical testing.
Insect Pathology Lab, Beltsville, MD
James L. Vaughn, (301) 344-3689
Horticultural Crops Research Lab, Fresno, CA
Patrick C. Vail, (209) 453-3002

Scientific Information Systems

Deciding which little piggy goes to market and which one stays home—to raise another litter—is simpler today for U.S. hog breeders, thanks to a new computer program. STAGES, for Swine Testing and Genetics Evaluation System, predicts the dollar value of specific genetic traits such as backfat thickness and body weight. It can also forecast production efficiency, feed conversion rate, litter size, litter weight weaned per sow, growth rate, and weaning and growth data for an entire herd, including individual animals and their parents within the herd. Designed for breeders of purebred seedstock hogs and for breeding stock customers, STAGES is now available through the eight U.S. breed associations. In the future, breeders with on-the-farm computers could access the program by phone and get a printout in minutes. STAGES was developed by ARS and researchers at Purdue University with support from the National Association of Swine Records, the National Pork Producers Council, and the USDA's Extension Service.
U.S. Meat Animal Research Center, Clay Center, NE
Dewey Harris, (402) 762-3241

Plant explorers could soon be running computer checks on which seeds and genes are needed most in America's germplasm collections. A computer program, being developed by ARS, uses artificial intelligence to help scientists evaluate the genetic diversity in existing collections, the relative danger of losing any particular germplasm, and the importance of replenishing it. The numerous criteria include a crop's dollar value, its geographical distribution and that of its wild relatives, its susceptibility to disease, and the long-term viability of its stored seeds. By using the program to help assign priorities, scientists can determine quickly which germplasm shortages are most critical so plant expeditions can be planned more effectively.
Germplasm Services Lab, Beltsville, MD
Alan A. Atchley, (301) 344-4423

Rangeland water losses to western juniper woodlands are being studied through use of a new computer model that simulates water consumption by these evergreen trees. Juniper acreage on mountain slopes in western states has doubled over the past 100 years and might be posing a serious threat to grassland production in some rangeland areas. Just one medium-sized tree, according to the computer model, can take up as much as 32 gallons of water per day from precipitation and snowmelt that would otherwise flow to rangelands below. Data from the studies could help ranchers and environmentalists work together on strategies for managing western juniper woodlands that affect several million acres of rangeland in Oregon, Idaho, Nevada, and California.
Range and Meadow Forage Management Research, Burns, OR
Raymond F. Angell, (503) 573-2064

French fries, potato flakes, hash browns, and other processed potato products might be produced more efficiently through use of a new computer model that predicts changes in texture in potatoes during heating. The model takes into account the entire cooking process to include gelatinization (absorption of water and swelling by starch granules) that occurs during the pre-cooking stage. When combined with data from other models in a computer simulation of potato processing, such information could help commercial processors reduce energy costs while achieving a more uniform and higher quality product.
Engineering Science, Eastern Regional Research Center, Philadelphia, PA
Michael F. Kozempel, (215) 233-6588

Valuable manganese deposits hidden beneath densely vegetated regions might be located through satellite measurements of leaf temperature. Preliminary greenhouse tests with two soybean varieties showed that leaf temperatures increased when soils had high levels of manganese, an element that helps to toughen steel alloys. The tests were performed in cooperation with the National Aeronautics and Space Administration, which often works with ARS to develop new remote-sensing techniques. At present, satel-

19

lite detection of minerals under heavy plant cover is based on visible and near-infrared light reflected from plants during limited time windows in spring and fall. The greenhouse tests suggest that shifting to thermal wavelengths could open these windows for most for the growing season and make surveys from space more effective in mineral exploration.
Plant Stress Lab, Beltsville, MD
Charles D. Foy, (301) 344-4522

Airborne lasers can detect tiny, short-lived gullies that are causing serious soil erosion on farms across the country. In recent tests, lasers beamed to the ground from low-flying aircraft revealed gullies as small as a foot wide and 6 inches deep. So far, such gullies--called "ephemeral" because they're erased by plowing only to reappear after the next rain--are not accounted for in national soil erosion estimates because of the time required to locate and measure them through conventional ground survey techniques. Laser measurements of ephemeral gullies taken from the air could fill that void, say scientists, once the computer programming needed to analyze the laser data is perfected.
Hydrology Lab, Agricultural Systems Research Institute, Beltsville, MD
Thomas J. Jackson, (301) 344-3811

Cornfields can be irrigated and fertilized by sprinklers on a computer schedule that reduces soil erosion and potential pollution of drinking water by nitrates. This is the first program that allows farmers to best schedule applications of nitrogen fertilizer, a source of groundwater-contaminating nitrates. The new routine, which uses the CERES-Maize model developed by scientists from ARS, Texas A&M, and Michigan State University, calculates how much water the soil can hold before it runs off or drains.
Weeds, Soils, and Water Management Research, Prosser, WA
Tom Hodges, (509) 786-3454

Dairy farmers could improve their cattle feed operations with a new computer model that simulates bacterial and fungal damage to alfalfa under a wide variety of storage conditions. Studies made with the model have already shown how bacteria and fungi can cause hay in silos to lose crude protein as well as dry matter. The model, which links with other models in a computer-simulated dairy farm, will help farmers predict the economic impact of different storage operations and develop alfalfa storage systems that minimize bulk and nutrient losses.
U.S. Dairy Forage Research Center, East Lansing, MI
Alan Rotz, (517) 353-1758

Computer "flash cards" can sharpen a farmer's eyesight for knowing when to spray pesticides to fight crop diseases. Gauging severity of a plant disease from diagrams or leaves of diseased plants is difficult even for the experienced farmer or scientist. However, by flashing pictures of diseased leaves, DISTRAIN trains the eye, in about an hour, to accurately assess severity of any one of eight wheat or barley diseases. Since farmers base their spraying schedules on disease severity, computer training can in the long run reduce unnecessary spraying and lower pesticide residues in the environment. Programs similar to DISTRAIN could be written for hundreds of diseases causing more than $12 billion in U.S. crop losses yearly. Farmers can run the programs on home, Extension office, or university computers.
Germplasm Quality and Enhancement Lab, Beltsville, MD
Jack Murray, (301) 344-3655

Small farmers now have help for state-of-the-art management for their grazing space with the computer program PASTURE. Although the program runs on a large computer, results and economic analysis from PASTURE are available to be used on any IBM-compatible personal computer. The program allows farmers to project effects of management decisions under many "what if?" conditions, such as pasture size, type of forage, weather, fertilizer practices, irrigation, and

rotation time between pastures. By running a number of scenarios, farmers can determine which decisions will save the most money and achieve the highest profit. PASTURE can be run for 18 common forages including bermudagrass, alfalfa, and fescue.
South Central Family Farms Research Center, Booneville, AR
Michael A. Brown, (501) 675-3834

Wheat farmers in the northern Great Plains now have a computer program to help them decide whether to apply phosphorus fertilizer, based on fertilizer costs and wheat market price. Many soils in the northern Plains are deficient in phosphorus; adding just the right amount of commercial fertilizer will overcome this deficiency. The program, called PHOSECON, for phosphorus economics, was originally designed to calculate the dollar return from applying phosphorus to spring wheat. PHOSECON also indicates how nitrogen increases the protein content and thus the value of the wheat, since growers are often paid according to how much protein their wheat contains. The program is available to farmers through the North Dakota State University Cooperative Extension Service.
Central Great Plains Research Station, Akron, CO
Ardell D. Halvorson, (303) 345-2259

Human Nutrition

The element boron, until now not considered an important nutrient, may be a key to preventing osteoporosis. Findings of a 6-month study of 12 postmenopausal women corroborate 6 years of animal studies indicating that boron is important in regulating the nutrients and hormones involved in bone building. After the women switched from a very low boron intake (one-fourth milligram per day) to an ample intake (3 mg), they lost 40% less calcium, one-third less magnesium, and slightly less phosphorus in their urine. More significantly, their blood levels of estrogen doubled, matching that of women on estrogen replacement

therapy--currently the only effective treatment for osteoporosis. Levels of testosterone, which the body converts to estrogen, more than doubled. The 3-mg boron supplement was equivalent to eating lots of fruits, green vegetables, nuts, and legumes. Followup studies are in progress or planned.
Grand Forks Human Nutrition Research Center, Grand Forks, ND
Forrest H. Nielsen, (701) 795-8456

A spoonful of sugar helps the medicine go down; it also helps the calcium get absorbed. Ten grams--about a teaspoonful--of glucose sugar taken with calcium can increase the body's uptake of this essential mineral by nearly 25%. At only 40 calories, that's one-quarter the amount of glucose previously reported to enhance calcium absorption. Glucose polymers, sold in drug stores under several brand names as calorie supplements, are as effective as glucose sugar. Both appear to work in postmenopausal women as well as in young women. Calcium is not absorbed very efficiently, particularly in older people. This research is looking for ways to maximize a person's own ability to absorb it.
Human Nutrition Research Center on Aging at Tufts, Boston, MA
Richard J. Wood, (617) 556-3185

A test for vitamin C that dentists sometimes use to check their patients' levels isn't reliable, according to results of a 3-1/2-month experiment by researchers from ARS and the University of California at San Francisco. Because vitamin C (ascorbic acid) is needed for healthy gums, patients with gum disease are often checked for vitamin C deficiency. The older test, the "lingual ascorbic acid test," which measures how long it takes for a drop of blue dye to lose its color when placed on the tongue, gave results that were unrelated to the volunteers' known vitamin C intake. ARS researchers are working on a replacement test that would be a simple, fast, and reliable check of vitamin C levels--and would not require taking blood or using any similarly invasive method.

Biochemistry Research, Western Human Nutrition Research Center, San Francisco, CA
Robert A. Jacob, (415) 556-3531

Breast milk alone provides adequate nourishment and keeps infants healthy even when the mother is somewhat under-nourished and harbors several infections. An ARS-financed study in Katmandu, Nepal, found the growth of 2- to 6-month old infants appropriate for their age (but at the lower end of normal for U.S. infants) despite their mothers' mild protein deficiencies and low energy reserves. Compared with U.S. infants, Nepalese infants had similar blood levels of calcium, magnesium, copper, and iron but their zinc and selenium levels were lower. None displayed medical problems, even though all the mothers had chronic hepatitis A infections, and 92% showed signs of intestinal parasites from con-taminated food and water. Older children who no longer got breast milk, however, were malnourished and sick.

Vitamin and Mineral Nutrition Lab, Beltsville Human Nutrition Research Center, Beltsville, MD
Robert D. Reynolds, (301) 344-2422
Phyllis B. Moser, University of Maryland, (301) 454-5371

There's hope for mothers of very pre-mature infants who can't seem to produce enough milk for their newborns--as long as the mothers don't smoke. Women who delivered 8 to 12 weeks before term were instructed to empty both breasts using an electric pump at least 5 times a day for a total of more than 100 minutes. Twenty-three (80%) of 30 nonsmoking mothers maintained an adequate supply of milk during the first month. But only 3 (27%) of 11 smoking mothers continued to produce enough milk. They averaged 18% less milk than the nonsmoking women the first 2 weeks after giving birth, and 40% less by the fourth week. Although mother's milk must be fortified with extra protein and minerals for low-birthweight infants, it is preferred over formula or donor milk because it enhances the infant's immunity to infections.

Children's Nutrition Research Center, Houston, TX
Judith M. Hopkinson, (713) 799-4834

Many people today may be suffering from a mild copper deficiency (less than 1 milligram per day) because they do not eat enough of the foods high in copper. Over the long run, that could be bad news for their hearts. In lab animals, copper deficiency has caused most of the risk factors for heart disease. Recent studies with eight men and eight women indicate that the earliest signs of copper deficiency occur after 3 or 4 months on a copper intake of 0.8 mg or less. Some people in the United States and other industrialized countries get only 0.8 mg through their diets but can remedy that by eating more copper-rich foods such as liver, oysters, chickpeas, nuts, and seeds. One study also showed that two copper-containing proteins are sensitive indicators of the onset of deficiency. The enzymatic activity of ceruloplasmin--found in the blood--and cytochrome-c-oxidase--found in all body cells--dropped even though standard indicators of body copper remained unchanged.

Grand Forks Human Nutrition Research Center, Grand Forks, ND
David B. Milne, (701) 795-8424

A mild copper deficiency has been shown for the first time to raise blood pres-sure, but only when the body is stressed. During a hand-grip test, eight healthy young women who got only 0.6 to 0.7 milligram of copper daily for 3 months had greater than normal increases in both systolic and diastolic pressures, with substantial increases in diastolic pres-sure. Isometric exercises normally result in smaller blood-pressure in-creases than those measured in the study. The women had no change in blood pressure while at rest or moving about, and the low copper intake did not affect heart rate. The recommended daily intake for copper is currently 2 to 3 mg, but most

Americans get only about half that amount.
Grand Forks Human Nutrition Research Center, Grand Forks, ND
Henry C. Lukaski, (701) 795-8429

Evidence that vitamin C may increase blood levels of the so-called "good" cholesterol has been corroborated in a survey of 238 elderly Chinese Americans, whose eating habits differ from the typical American diet. Scientists found the same correlation between blood levels of vitamin C and HDL-cholesterol that was noted in an earlier survey of nearly 700, mostly Caucasian, men and women over 60. The higher the vitamin C, the higher the "good" cholesterol. But the correlation was not found in smokers. They also had lower vitamin C blood levels. Because surveys are merely "snapshot" observations of populations, these findings are only circumstantial evidence. The scientists are now administering large daily doses of vitamin C (about 17 times RDA) to volunteer subjects to see if it, in fact, elevates HDL-cholesterol over the long term.
Human Nutrition Research Center on Aging at Tufts, Boston, MA
Gerald Dallal/Paul Jacques, (617) 556-3347/3322

Getting older doesn't have to mean getting weaker. In a 12-week strength training program, 12 healthy, untrained men ranging in age from 60 to 72 years disproved the notion that age itself causes a decline in muscle function. After training both legs on a thigh-knee machine, muscle size increased 15% and strength of the quadriceps increased 170%. There was also a significant increase in the turnover of actomyosin (a protein that allows the muscles to contract). Increased muscle strength could have a marked effect on the capacity of the elderly to lead independent lives.
Human Nutrition Research Center on Aging, Boston, MA
William J. Evans, (617) 556-3076

Muscle soreness not only signals damage to muscle cells, it also means the cells won't be refueled and ready for hard work until well after the soreness disappears. In a 45-minute bout of exercise, 5 sedentary men pushed their thigh muscles to the limit at the same time that their muscles were lengthening—what a runner experiences when going downhill. This eccentric component of exercise is what damages muscle cells. Ten days later, their affected muscles were still low in glycogen—the storage form of glucose that powers body cells. By contrast, muscle refueling occurs 1 to 2 days after concentric exercise, where they contract under force—as in running uphill. Because most exercise involves both components, people can't avoid eccentric exercise and shouldn't: it appears to trigger the improvement that comes with fitness. Those who have very sore muscles should ease back into training. Marathoners, in fact, may need up to 3 months before competing again, researchers say.
Human Nutrition Research Center on Aging at Tufts, Boston, MA
William Evans, (617) 556-3076

ᴏᴐ

Qua

Quarterly Report
of Selected Research Projects

United States
Department of
Agriculture

Agricultural
Research
Service

January 1 to March 31, 1988

CONTENTS

Insect & Weed Research

Biocontrol

Wasps are better at controlling the two
worst crop pests--tobacco budworm and
corn earworm--if they first learn what
odor to follow. Microplitis croceipes
wasps naturally parasitize the caterpillars but haven't done well when reared
in the lab and released into crop fields.
Scientists found one reason why and hope
to help wasps do better. When a wasp
first comes out of its cocoon, it encounters two chemicals found in caterpillar
feces. The first is instinctively recognized by the wasp as signaling the presence of a caterpillar. It is called the
host recognition cue and it tells the
wasp, "pay attention to the next chemical, because it is an airborne one that
will lead you right to caterpillars in
crop fields." By associating the two
scents, the wasp actually learns to trail
the second, airborne chemical to find a
caterpillar. Because this chemical
varies with what a caterpillar eats,
wasps learn to trail different odors, for
example, caterpillar feces odors that
result from eating cotton or corn, not
both. Since lab-raised wasps have
experienced only lab-raised caterpillars,
when they get to a field they look for--
but don't find--caterpillar feces odors
that result from eating artificial diets.
The scientists are now working to
reproduce the two natural chemicals.
With them, they could increase the wasp's
usefulness in three ways: expose lab
wasps to the feces chemical of
caterpillars eating the target crop, put
the chemicals all around crop fields to
keep wasps interested in searching for
hosts, and guide wasps to focus their
search on the most important part of a
crop (for example, the boll on a cotton
plant).
Insect Attractants, Behavior, and Basic
Biology Research Lab, Gainesville, FL
James H. Tumlinson, (904) 374-5730
Insect Biology and Population Management
Research Lab, Tifton, GA
W. Joe Lewis, (912) 382-6904

Note: One or more scientists familiar
with each research project are listed
for further information. If the
scientists are unavailable, others at
the same telephone number may also be
familiar with the work.

Items marked with the word PATENT are
being patented by ARS. For more
information contact Ann Whitehead,
National Patent Program, Bldg. 005, Rm.
401, Beltsville Agricultural Research
Center, Beltsville, MD 20705,
(301) 344-2786.

The day is not far off when apples will
no longer tempt the apple maggot. That's
the hope of ARS scientists working to
determine why an apple line they developed repels this maggot, named Rhagoletis
pomenella. Researchers determined that
the resistant apples produce chemicals
that result in the apple being unacceptable to the insect; their next step is to
transfer this resistance trait to new or
existing apple varieties. The result
could be maggot-free apples with less
need for pesticides. Currently, growers
apply three to five chemical sprays per
season to battle the maggot, long a
serious pest in the Northeast and Mid-

west east of the Mississippi River—and a recent arrival in the Pacific Northwest. Insect and Weed Control Research, West Lafayette, IN
Hilary F. Goonewardene, (317) 494-4607

A big-eyed bug can attack and consume a destructive pea aphid half its weight in less than an hour. Using piercing mouthparts and powerful enzymes, these pint-sized predators turn their prey into an easily digested slush. Scientists seeking ways to mass-rear the big-eyed bug say that it's appetite is comparable to a 150-pound man eating 75 pounds of beef stew in one hour. Finding a way to satisfy such an appetite in the lab had stymied researchers hoping to rear and release these predators to control crop-destroying insects. The most satisfying artificial diet, comprising beef, liver, and table sugar solution, is sealed in 1-inch-long packages of Parafilm; the big-eyed bugs penetrate the packages with their mouthparts to extract the nourishment. So far, predators reared on the diet retain the natural instinct to kill and eat their prey in the field, even after 40 generations of dining in the lab.
Biological Control of Insects Lab, Tucson, AZ
Allen C. Cohen, (602) 629-6220

Microscopic "caves" in the leaves of trees and shrubs such as coffee and gardenia may act as a natural defense against destructive insects. Known as leaf domatia, the structures shelter beneficial mites that fight off harmful insects and disease-causing fungi. Domatia can also take the form of tufts of short hairs in which the beneficial mites lay eggs and escape predators. ARS researchers found beneficial mites living in 26 of the 31 domatia-bearing plant species they studied, including holly, dogwood, ash, oak, viburnum, and custard apple. Plant geneticists may be able to breed domatia into new varieties of trees and shrubs. Or, domatia—already present in more than 1,000 tree and shrub species—could possibly be made larger or

more numerous.
Rangeland Insect Lab, Bozeman, MT
Robert W. Pemberton, (406) 994-4890
Plant Protection Research, Western Regional Research Center, Albany, CA
Charles E. Turner, (415) 559-5975

A new "odd couple"—an insect and a microbe—appear to work together as biological controls of European corn borer, the second worst U.S. corn pest. The green lacewing eats corn borer eggs and larvae, while the micro-organism, Nosema pyrausta, infects larvae, and subsequently borer eggs, with a fatal disease. The disease is deadly to most insects but—researchers discovered—is harmless to the lacewing. Instead, after the lacewing eats Nosema-infected borer eggs, it may spread borer disease to other areas of the field. Because most insecticides that kill the corn borer indirectly kill the micro-organism, researchers will try next to determine how farmers can maintain natural N. pyrausta populations with tilling practices, crop management, and less pesticide. In Iowa alone, the borer causes $112 million in losses to corn each year.
Corn Insects Research, Ankeny, IA
Leslie C. Lewis, (515) 964-6664

ARS is negotiating with a private firm to develop and license a newly found strain of virus that makes gypsy moths sick. The new strain of nuclear polyhedrosis virus discovered at Abington, Massachusetts, is more effective in disabling the pest in the caterpillar stage than other known strains. To mass-produce the virus, ARS scientists have developed a new lab culture of gypsy moth fat body cells, a rare achievement in insect science. The infected body cells are suspended in vats of rich nutrient liquid to reproduce. This allows for a more controlled production of the virus than traditional production in gypsy moth caterpillars.
Insect Pathology Lab, Beltsville, MD
Edward M. Dougherty, (301) 344-3692

The grape root borer is a serious threat to the eastern grape industry. The larval stage of this insect pest infests the root system of grapevines and can drastically reduce fruit yield and quality. The borer is difficult to control with pesticides because it lives inside the roots of the grapevine. ARS researchers have isolated and synthesized the sex pheromone produced by the borer to find partners at mating time. Preliminary test results indicate the synthesized version of the pheromone may become an important new control agent for the borer when used in high concentrations at mating time. The chemical confuses the insects, making it difficult for them to find mating partners. The researchers plan field trials this summer to try to control the grape root borer in vineyards in several states. (PATENT)
Insect Chemical Ecology Lab,
Beltsville, MD
Meyer Schwarz, (301) 344-2253/
Southeastern Fruit and Tree Nut Lab,
Byron, GA
J. Wendell Snow, (912) 956-5656

Houseflies are in trouble. They're under attack on some Maryland farms in a 4-year study to test nonchemical controls. The two main weapons: tiny parasitic wasps that kill fly pupae and traps that catch adults. The wasp, Muscidifurax raptor, lays eggs in housefly pupae. When the eggs hatch, the larvae eat fly pupae. The traps capture surviving adults. One trap is a white, pyramid-shaped model coated with a glue that nabs flies when they land. The other trap, now on the market, uses an agency-developed bait that sounds like the beginnings of a banana cake recipe: sugar, baking powder, brewer's yeast, and a chemical that smells like banana are the main ingredients. This trap cut housefly populations in half on six Maryland farms.
Livestock Insects Lab, Beltsville, MD
Richard Miller/Lawrence Pickens,
(301) 344-2478

Suntan lotion protects human skin from the sun's rays; dyes do the same for viruses so they survive five times longer than undyed viruses to kill insect pests. In field tests, dye-protected nuclear polyhedrosis viruses killed 90% of cabbage loopers and cabbage worms. Until now, they couldn't be used as a biological control, since they can't tolerate the sun on their own. An ARS scientist cooperated with Lim Technologies in Richmond, Virginia, to develop a potential product for farmers and a possible joint patent. ARS sent virus and protective dyes to Lim scientists, who mixed them in with their own encapsulation materials and sent them back. The ARS entomologist field-tested many formulations until he found that a green dye offers the best protection. The dye, the encapsulation material and, of course, the virus do not hurt the environment or other organisms. ARS scientists are now trying to find the insect cell line that will produce the most potent virus. When they do, private companies can pick up on that technology, as well.
Insect Pathology Lab, Beltsville, MD
George J. Tompkins, (301), 344-4325

Chinese peasants farming their land have used it for hundreds of years; now farmers here could use root bark powder from the Chinese bittersweet bush to cut losses from pests. In lab tests done with a cooperating scientist from China, the powder reduced the body weight of fall armyworm caterpillars 39% to 63%, depending on the dose. Scientists think the powder either repels caterpillars so they won't eat or somehow paralyzes their stomachs so they can't digest. Either way, the powder greatly reduces damage by the pests. The scientists have determined the chemical structure of one active component of the powder and named it celangulin. It could now be synthesized by chemical companies to make a safe antifeedant in crop fields. Research outside the agency has shown the powder has the same effect--in varying degrees--on many insects, including European corn borers, American cockroaches, migratory locusts and other grain and vegetable pests.
Insect Chemical Ecology Lab,
Beltsville, MD
Nobel Wakabayashi, (301) 344-1102

Other Insect Research

The first vaccine against parasitic cattle grubs should be ready for testing in a few months. Cattle grubs--heel fly larvae--are worldwide pests. Grubs damage hide and meat, and adult flies annoy cattle, interfering with feeding and reproduction. Total annual losses in the United States are estimated in the millions of dollars. Now under a technology transfer agreement, a California biotech firm, Codon, will genetically engineer Escherichia coli bacteria to mass-produce a natural protein isolated from grubs by ARS scientists. The protein triggers an immune response in cattle that is fatal to grubs. A vaccine made from this protein will give calves protection that their parents develop only after they have been infested for a year or more. Grubs live 6 to 8 months inside cattle before cutting breathing holes through the hide and eventually emerging as buzzing flies.
U.S. Livestock Insects Lab,
Kerrville, TX
John H. Pruett, Jr., (512) 257-3566

A special "soup kitchen" has turned out another lab growth medium for spiroplasmas, mysterious corkscrew- or wave-shaped bacteria that lack cell walls and live in many plants, insects, and ticks. By keeping spiroplasmas alive outside their hosts, ARS scientists can pursue ways to diagnose and control crop diseases caused by these microbes. The studies could lead to plants bred or genetically engineered to resist spiroplasmas, as well as to spiroplasmas bioengineered to attack specific insect pests such as Colorado potato beetles. The latest lab "soup," with 80 ingredients, is the first precisely defined for rabbit-tick spiroplasmas and is boosting studies of this microbe at other institutions.
Insect Pathology Lab, Beltsville, MD
Kevin Hackett, (301) 344-3086

A giant net has been built by ARS researchers to monitor the annual migration of pest insects from the Gulf Coast area north into the Corn Belt. In the spring, corn earworm and tobacco budworm moths migrate north by the billions to lay eggs in crops in the Midwest. Hatching larvae cause millions of dollars of damage to corn and other crops. Scientists in Texas designed a 50-square-foot, pyramid-shaped net to trap the vanguard of the migrating moths. Towed from a helicopter, the net enables researchers to sample large volumes of air quickly to determine the size and progress of advancing moth populations accurately. When correlated with radar-tracking systems, a predictive or early warning system might help midwestern farmers to schedule pest control operations.
Pest Management Research,
College Station, TX
Kenneth R. Beerwinkle, (409) 260-9364

To field-test their products, seed corn companies and insecticide makers need to establish uniform insect populations. A new ARS lab procedure to produce eggs of western corn rootworms is more economical and provides a more natural environment for the larvae than previous methods. From every 100 million rootworm eggs produced in the lab, researchers have reared about 53 million adults. Nearly all the adult females mated and produced viable eggs. By using this means of producing large numbers of high-quality eggs each year, private and government researchers could limit environmental variation in field plots from one year to the next. Insecticides and crop losses relating to corn rootworms cost U.S. farmers about a half billion dollars each year.
Crop and Entomology Research, Northern Grain Insects Research Lab,
Brookings, SD
Terry F. Branson, (605) 693-5208

New & Improved Products

A new cotton fiber promises to improve durable-press cotton's resistance to wear. The fiber, a rare crystalline form of cellulose derived from native cotton, is called Cellulose III. It is also permeable to dyes, pigments, and other

4

textile chemicals. To convert plain cotton cellulose to Cellulose III, lab technicians treat it with ammonia vapors at high temperatures and pressure until its crystalline structure changes. The changes in geometric configuration can be observed by X-ray diffraction. The new form of cellulose adds strength to durable-press cottons. Inexpensive lab techniques to produce these new crystalline substances are under study.
(PATENT)
Fiber Quality Research, Southern Regional Research Lab, New Orleans, LA
Timothy A. Calamari/Lawrence Yatsu, (504) 286-4265

Southern cotton growers can make more money by growing smooth-leaf cottons instead of varieties with hairy leaves, ARS research shows. Farmers once turned away from smooth-leaf cottons because they produced lower yields and were more susceptible to insects and diseases, but new varieties have overcome these problems. Researchers found that smooth-leaf cottons were graded higher and brought $2.50 more per bale than hairy-leaf varieties in 1985 to growers in Alabama, Arkansas, Louisiana, Mississippi, and Tennessee. About 12% of the 1985 crop was smooth-leaf cotton and the percentage is increasing.
U.S. Cotton Ginning Lab, Stoneville, MS
Samuel T. Rayburn, (601) 686-2385

Carbonated milk may become a nutritious alternative to soft drinks. Scientists have made two types of this carbonated drink--one mixed with filtered apricot juice and the other with artificial strawberry flavoring. The scientists bubbled carbon dioxide gas through a mixture of water, nonfat dry milk, juice or flavoring, and other ingredients. Refrigerated, the juice mixture stayed fresh 2 to 3 months; the flavored drink, up to 6 months. Commercial companies are interested in making such drinks, which would contain calcium and protein and create a new market for surplus nonfat dry milk. If these drinks were to capture 3% to 5% of the carbonated drink market, they could wipe out the powdered

milk surplus, estimated at 550 million pounds last year.
Food and Feed Processing Research, Southern Regional Research Center, New Orleans, LA
Ranjit S. Kadan, (504) 286-4332

A new diagnostic super-kit will quickly detect some of the world's most damaging viruses to plants and seeds in one test. Within a few months, Agdia, Inc., of Indiana will develop a prototype kit through a technology transfer agreement with ARS. The kit is based on ARS-developed monoclonal antibodies that react to a site on a protein molecule common to most, if not all, potyviruses. Named after potato virus Y, potyviruses affect many important crops including corn, soybeans, wheat, lettuce and other vegetables, and ornamentals such as tulips and Easter lilies. Seed-testing firms, nurseries, government agencies that quarantine plants, and farmers are among the kit's potential customers. So far, the kit can detect at least 30 potyviruses. Prior to this kit, there existed only tests for a single potyvirus, or a few closely related strains, and those have to be run one at a time.
Florist and Nursery Crops Lab, Beltsville, MD
Ramon L. Jordan, (301) 344-1646

Ordinary soap made from animal fats and lye is a safe and effective cleanser that biodegrades quickly. Without modification, however, it washes poorly in cold and hard water. ARS scientists have modified soap by blending it with other fat-derived surfactants, called lime soap-dispersing agents, to form new, highly effective household laundry detergents. These soap-based detergents contain no phosphates; are nontoxic to humans, domestic animals, wildlife, and algae; and biodegrade rapidly and completely. Normal waste treatment and disposal systems can easily digest them to harmless effluent. The new detergents work well in hard, soft, cold, and hot water. They equaled or outperformed the most effective household detergents on the U.S. market in various tests. Manu-

facturers abroad are making laundry detergents, dishwashing liquids, and toilet soaps using this technology. (PATENT)
Animal Biomaterial Research, Eastern Regional Research Center, Philadelphia, PA
Stephen Feairheller, (215) 489-6585

Invisible light waves are being tested to predict flour quality quickly and accurately. When ARS scientists scanned flour samples with near-infrared light, they found that the amount of light reflected at certain wavelengths is related to bread-baking properties. The volume of a loaf of bread, the single most important factor in determining flour quality for breadmaking, was predicted to within 4% of actual loaf size. Optimum mixing times and water absorption were also predicted accurately using near-infrared technology.
Wheat Genetics, Quality, and Physiology Lab, Pullman, WA
Gordon L. Rubenthaler, (509) 335-4055

Pickle makers may soon be getting help from yeasts now used to make beer, wine, and baked goods. Picklers have not previously used yeasts during fermentation because they form carbon dioxide, which can cause pickle bloating. But the industry has overcome this by using new ARS technology to purge the CO_2 during pickle processing. Agency scientists found several Saccharomyces yeasts that reduce the acidity of pickle brine by preventing fermenting bacteria from converting all the cucumber sugars into lactic acid, a major factor in pickle taste. Because processors would not have to add chemical buffers to reduce acidity, these yeasts can improve pickle quality and reduce costs.
Food Science Research, Raleigh, NC
Mark A. Daeschel, (919) 737-2979

Bread made from processed oat hulls is now available commercially through Pepperidge Farms. An ARS-developed process turns cereal grain hulls and brans and other heretofore undigestible plant parts into a no-calorie, high-fiber product that can replace up to half of the flour in baked goods and other foods. The additive does not change taste, texture, or baking qualities. In fact, the mixture of hemicellulose and cellulose fibers actually makes foods moister. The substance is made by treating oat hulls with hydrogen peroxide, which washes out the lignin, or woody portions of the plant, permitting humans to ingest the remaining fibers.
Plant Polymer Research, Northern Regional Research Center, Peoria, IL
J. Michael Gould, (309) 685-4011

The tropical neem tree that yields insecticidal chemicals also shows promise for controlling a major agricultural contaminant: aflatoxin. This toxin, produced by Aspergillus flavus and A. parasiticus fungi, can infect certain crops and make them unfit for consumption. Scientists found in lab studies that neem leaves, ground up or boiled in a solution, blocked more than 98% of the aflatoxin production by A. parasiticus. Scientists are planning greenhouse studies to see if the neem solution can be sprayed on crops to get the same result. If so, neem, long used in India and Africa as an insect repellant, toothpaste, and soap, may become a new biocontrol for aflatoxin.
Food and Feed Safety Research, Southern Regional Research Center, New Orleans, LA
Deepak Bhatnagar, (504) 286-4388

Country-style hams that are salted and dried should be cured at 75°F for 35 days or at 90°F for 11 days to ensure they are free of the organism that causes trichinosis in humans. That was a recommendation ARS made to USDA's Food Safety and Inspection Service to help FSIS establish regulatory guidelines for dry-curing country hams. The FSIS regulates ham curing to ensure that the processes used will inactivate trichinae. In a study of 93 artificially infected hams, ARS scientists found that trichinae remained

6

infective for up to 90 days in hams cured at 50°F.
Helminthic Diseases Lab, Beltsville, MD
H. Ray Gamble, (301) 344-1770

Improvements in harvesting machines and operations promise to keep cherry orchards alive and well in Michigan, where 98% of the state's tart cherry trees are mechanically harvested. Redesigned trunk shakers can save growers of tart cherries $25,000 to $30,000 per acre over the first 15 years of orchard life by sharply reducing trunk damage and premature tree deaths. Researchers now recommend using less force, fewer shakes, and soft rubber clamp pads that pocket the tree trunk like a softball glove. Studies show 70% of Michigan's tart cherry trees are damaged from currently used trunk shakers and clamp pads.
Fruit and Vegetable Harvesting Research, East Lansing, MI
Galen Brown, (517) 355-4720

Just off press is an extensive revision of Agricultural Handbook Number 155, Market Diseases of Beets, Chicory, Endive, Escarole, Globe Artichokes, Lettuce, Rhubarb, Spinach, and Sweet-potatoes. Containing descriptions and color illustrations of economically important postharvest diseases and disorders of these nine vegetables, the publication will be useful to inspectors, produce handlers, market specialists, and research workers.
Horticultural Crops Quality Lab, Beltsville, MD
Harold E. Moline, (301) 344-3128

![bar]

Crop Production & Protection

Wild lettuce from Turkey, Greece, Portugal, Israel, and other parts of the world naturally resists the virus that caused this winter's dramatic rise in iceberg lettuce prices. Among other approaches, ARS researchers are trying to cross these wild varieties with commercial lettuce to develop domestic resistant varieties adaptable to the desert climate of California and Arizona, where most of our winter lettuce crop is grown. ARS scientists were the first to discover and name lettuce infectious yellows virus, which is carried by the gnat-sized sweetpotato whitefly. At least a dozen kinds of weeds that border lettuce fields can harbor the whitefly and serve as a source of the virus. Top priority now is to find out which weeds whiteflies prefer and to encourage growers to get rid of them.
U.S. Agricultural Research Station, Salinas, CA
James D. McCreight/James E. Duffus, (408) 755-2800

Armed with important new information, fruit growers can take effective steps to prevent tree kills from a devastating soil-dwelling fungus Phytophthora megasperma. Until now, it was thought that the fungus was made up of many "strains," each of which could infect only one specific crop. Thus, in the past, a peach grower whose orchards were killed by the fungus might replant with cherry trees, mistakenly assuming that the fungus, although still present in the soil, couldn't harm the new trees. Now, evidence from ARS experiments with more than a dozen different orchard crops rules out the "strains" idea, and shows that the same Phytophthora megasperma that kills peaches is also capable of killing cherry, grape, apricot, apple, pear, kiwi, as well as many other crops. This finding prepares orchardists who have lost trees to the fungus to take steps to prevent recurrence. Many trees and rootstocks resist Phytophthora; a nonresistant apricot, for instance, can be grafted to a resistant plum rootstock. Research also shows that using sprinkler irrigation instead of flooding an orchard periodically from canals can minimize the severity of the disease and spread of the pathogen. Worldwide, Phytophthora species are among the most damaging pathogens of orchard crops, ornamentals, and other economically important plants.
Crops Pathology and Genetics Research, Davis, CA
S.R. Mircetich, (916) 752-1919

Growers irrigating two everbearing strawberries to offset summer heat last season report that they grossed a new high of $25,000 to $30,000 per acre by selling the berries at higher, out-of-season prices. And they expect the same results this year. The two berries, Tribute and Tristar, stay in season through October in the Northeast and Midwest, 4 months longer than spring-fruiting types. ARS introduced them in 1981 after genetically resetting the plants through breeding to bear fruit all summer and fall. The varieties are the best-tasting everbearers yet and are just as juicy as earlier types, making them ideal for both the fresh market and processed fruit products. They can be harvested in the summer and fall of the same year in which they are planted and are very winter hardy and resistant to diseases.
Fruit Lab, Beltsville, MD
Gene J. Galletta, (301) 344-3571

The genetic address of higher yielding corn is being mapped by tagging corn chromosomes with previously identified unique gene sequences. The tags are used to identify chromosomes that control yield and other traits, such as disease resistance and sturdiness. Researchers have already tagged several sequences on the chromosome that directly affect yield, allowing them to manipulate yield in either direction by selecting corn lines for the presence or absence of those gene sequences.
Plant Science Research Lab, Raleigh, NC
Charles W. Stuber, (919) 737-2289

New wax beans can fight off 33 races of bean rust disease. With less disease, these and other super-rust-resistant beans could lower farmers' need to spray pesticides and thus reduce pesticide residue in the environment. Rust, one of the most damaging bean leaf diseases, costs farmers up to $250 million yearly. The rust fungus, Uromyces appendiculatus, is a genetic quick-change artist that can develop new strains to attack bean varieties bred to resist certain races of it. So scientists are breeding resistance to more than 30 rust races into each common bean that rust can kill—snap, wax, pinto, navy, pink, black, red Mexican,

and great northern beans. Since 1984, ARS and the New Jersey and Florida state experiment stations have released 17 super-rust-resistant snap and wax beans to commercial breeders. Seed companies are cross-breeding to develop super-rust resistance into varieties available to the farmer.
Microbiology and Plant Pathology Lab, Beltsville, MD
Rennie Stavely, (301) 344-3600

Certain genes in wheat dictate the quality of flour used for breadmaking. ARS researchers and colleagues in England have worked out the intricate structure (nucleotide sequence) of two genes thought to be responsible for high-quality flour. These genes "tell" the wheat plant to manufacture special glutenin proteins usually found in superior flour. Knowing the exact sequence of the genes will help scientists improve the genetic makeup and thus the breadmaking quality of wheat varieties.
Plant Development-Productivity, Western Regional Research Center, Albany, CA
Frank C. Greene, (415) 559-5614

Virtually all commercial yellow dent corn grown in the United States traces its ancestry to two varieties, Reid Yellow Dent and Lancaster Sure Crop, developed about a century ago. Hoping to increase genetic diversity in Corn Belt hybrids, scientists made crosses from among 10 corn strains from temperate and tropical climates. Several crosses, which grew vigorously and outyielded their parents, could lead to many new genetically diverse hybrids. In related studies at about 30 locations, including three in the United States and Puerto Rico, ARS and Latin American scientists are identifying useful corn germplasm in the Latin American Maize Project. LAMP is administered by USDA and funded by Pioneer Hybrid, International.
Cereal and Soybean Improvement Research, Ames, IA
Linda M. Pollak, (515) 294-7831
National Program Staff, Beltsville, MD
Quentin Jones, ARS collaborator, (301) 344-1560

Now seedless grapes can have seedless parents. Grape breeders until now used a seeded female to produce seedless grapes, with a success rate of only about 10%. A new lab method accelerates the development of hybrid grape seedlings possessing the seedless trait. Even so-called seedless grapes have seeds in early stages of development, but they abort and disappear before maturity. By using the immature seed before abortion and growing it on tissue culture, a plant can be grown for use in hybrid breeding. Preliminary tests show a 35% to 70% successful seedless rate. This means about a 50% increase in plants producing seedless grapes.
Horticultural Crops Lab, Fresno, CA
Richard L. Emershad, (209) 487-5334

Why are American elm trees dying on the Washington, D.C., mall, the site of world-famous museums and monuments? ARS scientists and cooperating researchers have identified the culprit: a new genus of bacteria similar to the organism that causes Legionnaire's disease. The newly found bacteria don't infect people. Xylella is the first completely new genus of bacteria discovered and described since 1939. Besides attacking elms, the bacteria cause about a dozen plant diseases, including Pierce's disease of grapes, phony peach disease, and leaf scorches of almond, plum, sycamore, oak, maple, and mulberry. Researchers also came up with a way to grow Xylella in the lab. This achievement and identification of the organism will help scientists find controls for the diseases.
Plant Science Research, Eastern Regional Research Center, Philadelphia, PA
John M. Wells, (215) 233-6429

A lengthy process has begun to breed filbert trees resistant to a fatal disease—Eastern filbert blight. The disease of filberts, or hazelnuts, is spreading to more and more trees in the Pacific Northwest, the only area in the United States with commercial plantings of the nuts. ARS scientists have provided filbert breeders, including a team at Oregon State University, with seed, pollen, and grafting material of blight-resistant filbert strains, but breeding

new trees, testing them, and starting new orchards could take as many as 20 years. The blight is unknown in Europe and appears to have originated on our East Coast, where it has prevented growers from planting commercial filbert orchards.
National Clonal Germplasm Repository, Corvallis, OR
Joseph Postman, (503) 757-4448

The fledgling rice industry in Puerto Rico will benefit from the release of Rico 1, a new medium-grain rice developed and released by ARS scientists in cooperation with Texas A&M University and other researchers. With excellent yield, comparable to most available medium-grain varieties in the Southern United States, Rico 1 is well adapted to that region's climate as well as to Puerto Rico's. Foundation seed is available from the Texas Rice Improvement Association in Beaumont, which cooperated in the rice project.
Rice Research Lab, Beaumont, TX
Charles N. Bollich, (409) 752-2741

For the first time, wheat farmers in the Pacific Northwest have proof that burning their fields to rid them of residues could be doing them more harm than good. Many farmers feel residues reduce yields and fertilizer benefits and increase disease. Results of a 6-year study in a wheat/fallow farming system showed that burning straw and other residues left on fields after harvest does not increase yields, improve nitrogen fertilizer efficiency, or decrease the amount or severity of Cercosporella foot rot disease, as farmers thought. To the contrary, indiscriminate burning pollutes the air and leaves the soil unprotected and vulnerable to erosion. The dry, hilly Columbia Plateau region in parts of Oregon, Washington, and Idaho has some of the highest erosion rates in the United States.
Columbia Plateau Conservation Research Center, Pendleton, OR
Paul E. Rasmussen, (503) 276-3811

The best way to grow alfalfa from Virginia to Vermont is to plant in the early spring (early March in Pennsylvania), use a no-till drill, and spray herbicide to suppress grass competition. Field studies showed that while there was no yield difference between plantings made at the end of March and the end of May, slug and insect damage was lower--and forage quality higher--with the March planting. The three-step recipe specifically applies to alfalfa grown for pasture or mixed grass hay.
U.S. Regional Pasture Research Lab, University Park, PA
Robert A. Byers, (814) 863-0941

Plant buds, tissue culture, and certain types of pollen might be preserved in liquid nitrogen at -320°F. Currently, such germplasm survives freezing no better than a water-filled glass jar; both break, allowing leaks when thawed. ARS and Colorado State University scientists will investigate safe ways to preserve plant genetic material for future breeding needs. RJR Nabisco, Inc., pledged $375,000 to CSU to do the research for 3 years at the ARS seed lab. Seeds of wheat and most other major crops can be stored safely in liquid nitrogen, but some seed is injured by ice crystals that burst plant cells, which bear genes that dictate traits such as disease resistance. In tests, small pieces of plant tissue will be exposed to selected chemical compounds to find which ones will stop the crystals from forming.
National Seed Storage Lab, Fort Collins, CO
Eric E. Roos, (303) 484-0402

Despite the sexual incompatibility between many wild and cultivated potatoes, scientists can now tap genetic reservoirs in both the nucleus and the surrounding cytoplasm in cells of wild potato plants. They can identify economically desirable genes in wild spuds, moving the genes into potatoes by using somatic hybridization. That means fusing together protoplasts--cells stripped of walls--of wild and cultivated varieties and growing back whole plants. Some surviving somatic hybrids, scientists recently found, had genes in their chlor-

oplasts (bodies in the cytoplasm) that were identical to genes in chloroplasts of the wild parent. The hybrids can pass on these chloroplast genes sexually; the eventual result could be cultivated potato varieties with such desirable charateristics as more efficient photosynthesis and better disease resistance.
Plant Disease Resistance Research, Madison, WI
John P. Helgeson, (608) 262-0649

Proso millet is giving farmers an extra cash crop every 6 years in the central Great Plains. This highly nutritious small grain needs only 6 inches of water to produce seed, while winter wheat requires more than 9 inches. Ordinarily, farmers in western Kansas and Nebraska and eastern Colorado grow wheat every other year, leaving fields fallow during the off-years. That adds up to three wheat crops and 3 idle years every 6 years. But researchers found that the less thirsty millet can be planted the year after the wheat harvest; the soil still has enough moisture for the millet. Fields are left fallow the following year--only twice instead of three times over each 6-year planting schedule.
Central Great Plains Experiment Station, Akron, CO
R.L. Anderson, (303) 345-2259

The inverse relationship between fiber strength and yield in cotton has been severed with the release of PD-3, a new cotton variety developed in cooperation with Clemson University. In the past, when cotton was bred for greater fiber strength, yield dropped. But fiber strength in PD-3 is almost on a par with Acala, one of the strongest cotton varieties available, and yields of the new variety have rated satisfactory to excellent in trials in much of the Southeast. PD-3 produced over 35% more lint than Acala SJ-5 in the 1981, 1983, and 1985 Regional High Quality tests. Foundation seed is available to breeders through the South Carolina Foundation Seed and Crop Improvement Association at Clemson.
Cotton Production Research, Florence, SC
Thomas W. Culp, (803) 669-6664

Farmers who grow sweetpotatoes have a better chance for a successful harvest with five new pest-resistant varieties developed by ARS researchers. Sweetpotatoes have traditionally been vulnerable to many insect and disease problems because few effective pesticides are available to protect the crop. The new varieties have proven resistant to 16 highly destructive insects, nematodes, and diseases. Resisto, Regal, Southern Delite, and Excel are orange-fleshed varieties, while Sumor is a white-fleshed sweetpotato. All five varieties have been released to commercial breeders.
U.S. Vegetable Lab, Charleston, SC
Alfred Jones, (803) 556-0840

Genes have been found that code for resistance to leaf rust, the most widely destructive rust disease of wheat in the United States and probably in the world. The most economical way to control leaf rust is by breeding resistant varieties. Resistance, however, often lasts only a few years before new races of the disease appear that can overcome that resistance. Long-lasting resistance could prevent severe leaf rust epidemics and save wheat growers millions of dollars, or about 15% of their annual loss, in the all-too-frequent years when rust is severe. ARS scientists have found a unique type of longer lasting resistance called slow-rusting resistance. Studies show that each of three varieties used in breeding wheats with the new resistance has two or three genes that are different from those in the other two varieties. Identifying these genes will help scientists to understand slow rusting and develop varieties with longer lasting resistance.
Wheat Genetics, Quality, Physiology and Disease Lab, Pullman, WA
Roland F. Line, (509) 335-3755

Six new mildew-resistant crape myrtles have been released from the U.S. National Arboretum. Named for American Indian tribes, (Apalachee, Comanche, Lipan, Osage, Sioux, and Yuma) all have dark-green summer foliage and bright autumn hues. From June to September, flowers bloom in a range of new colors from light and dark lavender to light, dark, and coral pink. They have mottled bark with colors that vary throughout the year, from near-white to light brown and sandalwood to gray-brown, chestnut, and mahogany. The new varieties grow to a height of less than 16 feet--between that of the 35-foot and 5-foot varieties. They may be grown as small trees and shrub borders or planted in large containers for lawns and parks. The varieties are winter-hardy as far north as Washington, D.C.
U.S. National Arboretum, Washington, DC
Donald E. Egolf, (202) 475-4862

Virus Diseases of Small Fruits is the title of the new Agricultural Handbook Number 631. Crops covered are strawberries, blueberries and cranberries, currants and gooseberries, and blackberries and raspberries. This 277-page handbook, compiled by international authorities, includes discussions of the history, geographic distribution, importance, symptoms, transmission, cause, detection, and control of virus and viruslike diseases attacking these crops.
Horticultural Crop Research Lab, Corvallis, OR
R.H. Converse, (503) 757-4544

Two potato varieties and a wild relative that resist brown rot have been identified by ARS scientists. Brown rot, a bacterial wilt, is the major limiting factor in potato production in warm, humid regions, including the coastal plain area of the southeastern United States. The rot-resistant selections should prove a valuable germplasm reservoir for the development of a commercial wilt-tolerant potato.
Coastal Plain Experiment Station, Tifton, GA
Casimir A. Jaworski, (912) 386-3355

Yellow soybean leaves--symptoms of chlorosis--will be only a bad memory for farmers who plant any of several new varieties of soybeans due on the market in 2 years. Chlorosis, caused by iron deficiency, robs yields and can kill plants. The new varieties will come from plants with significantly more chlorosis resistance than any other soybean lines.

Iowa State University breeders selected the plants with a lab-screening technique improved by an ARS scientist who discovered that calcium bicarbonate in soil causes chlorosis by keeping roots from taking up enough iron. To screen for chlorosis, breeders grew seedlings in solutions with low levels of iron and high levels of bicarbonate. This is a much more accurate method than field-testing to select for resistance.
Soil-Microbial Systems Lab,
Beltsville, MD
Rufus L. Chaney, (301) 344-3324

Future varieties of sugarbeets should be better equipped to withstand cold temperatures. That improvement would be welcome in most beet-growing areas because cool weather often slows early plant growth, which can cut yields by 25%. After four cycles of selecting sugarbeet pollen that best survived cold temperatures, scientists pollinated plants that were growing in near-freezing rooms and achieved a slight increase in cold tolerance. Scientists are now increasing the level of stress to find beets even more tolerant of cold weather.
Sugarbeet Production Research,
Fort Collins, CO
Richard J. Hecker, (303) 482-7717

Virus diseases in potatoes can be detected faster and more accurately by an improved ELISA test. ARS scientists shortened the standard ELISA (enzyme-linked immunosorbent assay) and increased its sensitivity so that smaller quantities of viruses can be spotted. Use of the new test is expected to further reduce potato spoilage losses caused by viruses. Beet western yellows, potato leafroll, and potato viruses M, S, X, and Y can be detected in 2 hours compared to the 2 days for the standard ELISA. A potato seed certification agency has already adopted the new method for mass potato virus testing.
Vegetable and Forage Crop Production,
Prosser, WA
Peter E. Thomas, (509) 786-3454

The best treatment for wireworms, major pests of potatoes grown in the Northwest, is to broadcast the insecticide fonofos before planting for 2 years at 4 pounds of active ingredient per acre. Insecticide recommendations were previously based on estimates of the numbers of these insects found in soil samples taken before planting. But most potato growers say it is too costly to test for wireworms. As a result, they are not sure their treatments will provide adequate, lasting control. Applying fonofos as recommended ensures effective control, plus eventual elimination of control measures, in the shortest time at least cost. Although the insecticide may be more expensive than other treatments, the cost is offset by the greater effectiveness of fonofos and by the fact that the treatment will not have to be repeated.
Yakima Agricultural Research Lab,
Yakima, WA
Harold H. Toba, (509) 575-5981

████████████████

Soil, Water & Air

Hairy vetch, an annual legume, is a good winter cover crop for spring-planted grains in the Northern Plains: it supplies nitrogen and may reduce nitrate pollution of groundwater. A 6-year study showed that vetch fixes nitrogen more rapidly than perennial legumes. It eliminates the need to apply nitrogen fertilizer to continuous dryland corn because growing it is equivalent to applying 50 to 60 pounds of fertilizer nitrogen. Vetch also uses up the residual soluble nitrogen left over by the corn crop. For nitrates to accumulate in groundwater, soluble nitrogen must be present when water leaches through soil to the groundwater below. Legumes like vetch also provide ground cover to reduce erosion and improve soil tilth and productivity.
Soil and Water Conservation Research,
Lincoln, NE
James F. Power, (402) 472-1484

With some plumbing pipes, plastic boxes, and simple electronic equipment, an ARS engineer has built high-tech sensors that

measure groundwater. One set of these sensors gives a series of water pressure readings that can be mapped to show groundwater flow direction. Much of the precipitation enters soil at higher elevations and resurfaces at lower elevations. Another set of sensors detects this resurfacing groundwater as it flows through a specially designed detector system. The equipment is now operating on a farm in Pennsylvania Dutch country. The data shows that groundwater can resurface over much of the near-stream area before it enters a stream. Because of this, farmers may need wider buffer zones around streams than previously recommended.
Northeast Watershed Research Center, University Park, PA
J.R. Hoover, (814) 865-2048

Pesticide concentrations in groundwater in many parts of the country may be less a problem under typical farming conditions than first thought. That's the conclusion from a 2-year sampling of 20 wells in a diversfied small family farm area in central Pennsylvania. Of nine pesticides tested for, only three were found, and these at extremely low concentrations. The nation's most widely used weed-killer, alachlor, was not present. Traces of atrazine, a herbicide popular with corn farmers, showed up in most wells, however, despite the fact that the chemical is used relatively sparingly in the watershed tested.
Northeast Watershed Research Lab, University Park, PA
Harry B. Pionke, (814) 865-2048

Natural bacteria living in some types of soil can help clean groundwater contaminated by nitrate. The product of nitrogen compounds in fertilizer, animal waste, and other sources can sometimes leach through the soil, polluting groundwater. But some bacteria can change nitrate into nitrous oxide or dinitrogen gases that harmlessly disperse. In cooperation with the U.S. Geological Survey, ARS scientists conducted tests that showed this occurring in a sandy-clay aquifer, an underground geological formation holding useful amounts of groundwater, in the Coastal Plains of

Georgia. Scientists are looking for ways to boost bacteria's usefulness as a way to reduce groundwater pollution.
Southeast Watershed Research Lab, Tifton, GA
Richard Lowrance, (912) 386-3514

Computer model estimates show that within 100 years, U.S. soil productivity could decrease by 2.3%--the equivalent of taking 8.9 million acres of cropland out of production. To meet the requirements of the Soil and Water Conservation Act of 1977, that USDA gather and maintain data on the status of agricultural land, ARS scientists developed two models to simulate interactions of soil, climate, and plant management. One model, EPIC (Erosion-Productivity Calculator), developed in 1985, estimates the effect of erosion on productivity and fertilizer requirements. The other, EPIS (Erosion-Productivity Simulator), processes and analyzes the output from EPIC. Estimates from EPIC show that if currently used cropping patterns and tillage practices, including conservation tillage, are continued for 100 years, soil loss by water will exceed about 5 tons per acre on 127 million acres, with a similar loss from wind erosion on 64 million acres. The model also estimates that annual fertility requirements will increase by 817 million pounds of nitrogen, 676 million pounds of phosphate, and 10,778 million pounds of lime. The scientists suspect that further studies will show these productivity loss estimates to be on the low side.
Natural Resources Systems Research, Temple, TX
Jimmy R. Williams, (817) 770-6508

A computer model that predicts chemical movement in soils can also calculate how fast nuclear fallout from some future disaster would contaminate groundwater supplies. Preliminary results with the model OPUS indicate that soil type is a main factor that determines how much and how fast radioactive material moves. Sandy soils would act like a sieve, while heavier soils, like clays, would hold

13

such materials longer and keep them out of underground water.
Hydro-Ecosystems Research, Fort Collins, CO
Roger E. Smith, (303) 221-0578

Evapotranspiration (ET), or water lost by evaporation from the soil surface and by transpiration from plant leaves, must be accurately evaluated in order to manage scarce water resources. ARS scientists determined evapotranspiration over agricultural fields and natural desert vegetation using both remote sensing and traditional ground-based meteorological measurements. Reflectance and surface temperature measurements made from aircraft were combined with ground-based data of solar radiation, air temperature, humidity, and windspeed to yield instantaneous, or "snapshot" values of ET. Using this technique, water managers can now assess water loss from vegetated and nonvegetated areas to make rational decisions on the wise use of water on agricultural fields, rangeland, and watersheds. The method works best over cropland.
U.S. Water Conservation Lab, Phoenix, AZ
Robert J. Reginato, (602) 261-4356

Crops can be grown with irrigation waters that contain boron, a naturally occuring chemical in some western soils, but too much can seriously reduce both quality and quantity of agricultural products. Scientists have determined the boron tolerance of 20 high-value crops to stay ahead of potential problems in the future. So far, they have found cauliflower and broccoli are among the most boron-tolerant; green and wax beans are the least tolerant. As more fresh water is diverted from agricultural to urban use, farmers may have to irrigate with water currently not used because of its high boron content.
U.S. Salinity Lab, Riverside, CA
Leland E. Francois, (714) 369-4835

Animal Production & Protection

Lambing sheep can be made less chancy with a test that is currently used to tell whether cows are pregnant. The new procedure will allow scientists to predict single or multiple births of sheep with 70% accuracy. It can also more accurately pinpoint where and when fetal loss is occurring and how to prevent it. ARS scientists, in cooperation with scientists from the University of Idaho, recently adapted for ewes a reliable blood test to measure pregnancy-specific protein. The test, called a radioimmunoassay, showed that pregnant ewes have a measurable blood level of the protein as early as 21 days after becoming pregnant. With this information, sheep producers can rebreed ewes or sell them to reduce feed costs.
U.S. Sheep Experiment Station, Dubois, ID
John N. Stellflug, (208) 374-5306

A pig's intestines can sometimes serve as a potent barrier to roundworms, a discovery that could lead to a vaccine for the parasites. ARS scientists found that mast cells—body cells like those in mammals' respiratory system that cause wheezing allergic reactions—also play a key role in a pig's immunity to roundworms. Worms in a pig's gut cause a rapid buildup of mast cells that can trigger a hypersensitive allergic response. The work could lead to a vaccine that would clear pigs of roundworms before they do tissue damage, and reduce need for drug treatments. Over 15 species of parasitic roundworms, some up to a foot long, cost U.S. swine farmers hundreds of millions of dollars yearly.
Helminthic Diseases Lab, Beltsville, MD
Joseph F. Urban, (301) 344-2195

Cows on western rangeland can lose up to 130 pounds (or more than 10% of their body weight) after just 2 weeks of harsh winter weather. That was one finding in ongoing studies to help ranchers graze cattle to get maximum returns on their herds. Studies so far show as temperatures plummet to -40°F and winds pick up to 15 miles per hour, cows graze only 2.9

hours each day; at 32°F above they graze 9.3 hours each day. That translates to about a 30-minute reduction in grazing time for each 5-degree drop in temperature. Also, younger and smaller cows graze less at colder temperatures than do older and larger cows.
Fort Keogh Livestock and Range Research, Miles City, MT
Don C. Adams, (406) 232-4970

Just about the only way to keep cattle from eating larkspur--the number one livestock killer on western intermountain range--is to keep herds away from infested land until after the larkspur flowers and their poisons are at a lower level. What makes larkspur such a menace is that cattle find it palatable, and scientists have learned they find it even more palatable than ever after summer thunderstorms. The result is higher-than-normal rates of cattle deaths during the summer storm season. The scientists are studying various options ranchers can use to reduce the risk of larkspur poisoning, including spraying the plant with herbicides and grazing sheep before the cattle, since sheep are not affected by the poisons.
Poisonous Plant Research Lab, Logan, UT

Improved genetics in livestock has led to faster growing beef cattle, but more calves die at birth because they are too big to pass through their mother's pelvis. Scientists found that 51% of calf deaths at birth result from this but are puzzled by what causes the other 49%. So far, in studying the effect of hormones and breed differences on calf deaths, they found that an abnormal balance before calving of hormones that control pregnancy and birth (estrogen and progesterone) can increase calving difficulties. Also, the Brahman breed seems better able to control calf growth in the uterus and thus have fewer calving difficulties. Continued research may show that the control is related to hormones, or perhaps to some mechanism in the cow's body that regulates the amount of nutrients passed to the fetus.
Fort Keogh Livestock and Range Research, Miles City, MT
Robert A. Bellows, (406) 232-4970

There's new help for veterinarians in selecting the best drugs for cows with mastitis. Scientists tested 65 drugs to check for adverse effects on white blood cells, which fight off many kinds of infections. Mastitis is a disease of the udder with a $2 billion annual cost to U.S. dairy farmers. Lab-cultured white blood cells were treated with the drugs, as were the udders of healthy cows. Scientists rated the drugs best that killed the smallest percentage of white blood cells.
Milk Secretion and Mastitis Lab, Beltsville, MD
Max J. Paape, (301) 344-2302

Animal breeders can benefit from a laser that researchers are using to study white blood cells in dairy cattle. Aided by the laser, scientists hope to identify cattle whose neutrophils--a type of white blood cell--are powerful enemies of mastitis, a bacterial disease of udders. A cow's immune system sends neutrophils to swallow and destroy bacteria and other foreign invaders. In tests, scientists mark bacteria with fluorescent dye and "feed" them to neutrophils. After incubation, the mixture is zapped with a laser beam, causing bacteria to fluoresce. Special sensors "read" the fluorescence to determine the number of bacteria engulfed as well as missed by neutrophils and those present in individual neutrophils. Older systems for making these counts have been slower and less accurate. Mastitis costs U.S. dairy farmers $2 billion annually.
Milk Secretion and Mastitis Lab, Beltsville, MD
Max J. Paape, (301) 344-2302

Toxoplasma parasites, well-known to infect humans, sheep, goats, and cats, have been found to persist in pigs. The discovery of resting-stage cysts of Toxoplasma góndii in swine could broaden the understanding of the single-cell parasite's role in disease transmission. The parasite causes abortions in sheep. Pregnant women who get toxoplasmosis give birth to approximately 3,300 infected infants each year in the United States. ARS scientists, working toward a vaccine

for sheep, found that T. gondii cysts remained alive in edible tissues of sows up to 865 days after infection, or practically the life of a pig. Three days of freezing killed most of the cysts in commercial cuts of pork. (Thorough cooking will kill the rest.)
Protozoan Diseases Lab, Beltsville, MD
Jitender P. Dubey, (301) 344-2128

Simple housekeeping chores around barns and feedlots can get rid of up to 80% of stable fly populations by reducing breeding sites. ARS researchers identified the major launching pads for these pesky, biting insects that torment livestock. Best advice for farmers and livestock workers: cover feed storage facilities; eliminate standing water pockets; and practice better sanitation. Flies reduce feeding efficiency and weight gains in cattle because they annoy the animals at mealtime. They also prompt nuisance suits against farmers by neighbors. Researchers found that occasionally leveling feedlots and maintaining a clean livestock environment also help reduce stable fly populations.
Midwest Livestock Insects Research, Lincoln, NE
Conrad B. Gilbertson, (402) 437-5267

Dairy farmers may soon be able to predict their cows' milk-production capabilities more accurately because of the latest computer technology. In recent tests with a "super-class" computer having one billion bytes of memory, scientists simultaneously evaluated more than 10 million cows and bulls going back nearly 10 generations. This allows consideration of the genetic contributions of all ancestors and progeny—female and male—in predicting the breeding values of today's stock. Data from the system will be available beginning next year.
Animal Improvement Lab, Beltsville, MD
George R. Wiggans, (301) 344-2334

Injecting cows with a hormonal form of vitamin D before calving reduces the incidence of milk fever, which costs the dairy industry $150 million a year. Milk fever, a metabolic disorder of dairy cows, can occur when lactation causes a sudden drop in levels of blood calcium. Milk fever weakens a cow and makes her susceptible to other ailments such as uterine infections and mastitis—an infection of the udder. In severe cases, cows lapse into comas and die if not treated. In tests, however, only 29% of cows injected with the hormone—fluorinated 1, 25-dihydroxyvitamin D3—developed the disease; 85% of the untreated cows got sick. The hormone stimulates a rise in blood calcium, preventing milk fever. An injection was given 7 days before the expected calving date and every 7 days thereafter until birth. Scientists are working on an implantable, slow-release system to deliver the synthetic hormone to the cow's blood stream.
National Animal Disease Center, Ames, IA
Jesse P. Goff, (515) 239-8343

Many farmers may be wasting money and labor applying bacterial inoculants to preserve stored hay against molds and subsequent quality losses. When commercially available Lactobacillus bacteria are applied to high-moisture hay, its quality and appearance stayed the same or deteriorated compared with untreated hay. Propionic acid, a chemical treatment, is recommended for hay. Researchers are looking for an alternative that is cheaper and less corrosive to equipment.
Dairy Forage Research, East Lansing, MI
C. Alan Rotz, (517) 353-1758

WW-Iron Master Old World bluestem, a livestock forage released in 1987, is more productive on iron-deficient soils than any currently available bluestem. The new grass variety is well adapted for 10 million acres of iron-deficient soils in the Southern Plains. It also has higher crude protein content and higher average digestibility than other bluestems, making it valuable for beef production as well as for erosion control on marginal, iron-deficient farmland. WW-Iron Master was jointly developed by ARS and USDA's Soil Conservation Service.
Southern Plains Range Research Station, Woodward, OK
Chester L. Dewald, (405) 256-7449

Scientific Information Systems

Tiny electric current leaks in farm buildings can now be tracked down while the power is on--thus eliminating a lot of guesswork and unnecessary replacement of electrical parts and wires. A new procedure requires little more than a digital voltmeter and a few simple calculations to evaluate the quality of electrical connections and to determine whether the proper gauge wiring has been used. Safe, inexpensive, and accurate, the procedure may save some folks a lot of headaches: faulty connections and undersized wiring are the two major causes of "stray" or "tingle" voltages in livestock housing facilities. Such leaks--which can affect animal behavior and reproduction--have been the basis of several successful lawsuits brought by livestock and poultry producers against rural power suppliers.
Soil and Water Conservation Research, Lincoln, NE
Laverne E. Stetson, (402) 472-2945

Leather production standards might be tightened through use of lasers that reveal how collagen fibers are structured in cattle hides and other animal skins. Collagen fiber structures are critical to the strength of the leather, but changes in their alignment beneath the surface of the skin have been too difficult and time-consuming to monitor during the production process. An analytical technique called small angle light scattering (SALS)--long used in labs for examining molecular structures in plastics--has now been modified and automated to handle fibrous networks quickly in hides. The SALS systems beams a laser thorough a thin section of hide, rotates a photocell around the axis of the beam to measure light scatter caused by collagen fibers, and provides a printout of the scatter pattern. The pattern shows how the fibers are oriented with respect to one another.
Animal Biomaterials Research, Eastern Regional Research Center, Philadelphia, PA
Paul L. Kronick, (215) 233-6506

In 1906 cattle fever cost the industry $130 million in loss, and experts believe a similar outbreak today would cost producers and consumers billions. While ticks that spread cattle fever have been eradicated from most of the United States, occasional infestations still occur, especially in southern Texas. ARS researchers have developed a computer model based on the biology and ecology of the cattle fever tick, carrier of the fever. The model simulates the life cycle of the tick on and off its host, predicting survival against a range of factors including temperature, rainfall, humidity, and pesticide dipping schedules. The model also enables researchers to predict where infestations of the tick might occur, so appropriate control measures can be taken.
Insects Affecting Man and Animals Lab, Gainesville, FL
Lynita Cooksey, (904) 374-5853

Off-farm damages to water quality can be reduced with little or no effect on farm income. Using a central Pennsylvania dairy farm as an example, ARS water quality scientists and economists with USDA's Economic Research Service pioneered the merging of an economics model with an ARS model called CREAMS (Chemicals, Runoff, and Erosion from Agricultural Management Systems). The combined models showed that dairy farmers who grow corn could--just by changing their tillage practices--cut by about half their losses of soil and manure nutrients in surface runoff. The same procedure can be used to assess practices elsewhere.
Northeast Watershed Research Center, University Park, PA
Harry B. Pionke (814) 865-2048

Notorious international plant diseases are about to be "booked"--logged into new computer files, that is. The World Plant Pathogen Database will provide critical biological information on any plant disease threatening any country's major crops. The database, which can be updated as needed, should improve early warnings of disease outbreaks and speed decisions on importing and quarantining plants and germplasm. Diskettes contain-

ing the database will soon be available free of charge to regulatory officials and scientists in cooperating countries. Foreign Disease-Weed Science Research Frederick, MD
Matthew H. Royer, (301) 663-7344

A computer program for predicting the watering needs of crops is available in a new version that is easier for farmers, consultants, and county agents to use. Weather information supplied by a local radio station or newspaper provides enough data for the program, called SCHED. Users can also enter on-farm weather data they collect themselves. ARS researchers released version 1.0 about 2 years ago after 15 years of research and development.
Irrigation and Drainage Research,
Fort Collins, CO
Harold R. Duke, (303) 491-8230

Scientists and consultants have developed an extremely detailed yet flexible computer model for predicting how tillage, fertilizer, and crop residues interact over time. It's possible for the model, called Nitrogen-Tillage-Residue-Management (NTRM), to predict the consequences of raising up to 20 different crops for the next 100 years or more. A simpler model has been developed for farmers to calculate the best practices to follow on their land to save soil from erosion and to conserve fertilizer and thus reduce the possibility of contaminating surface and groundwater. Great Plains Systems Research,
Fort Collins, CO
Marvin J. Shaffer, (303) 484-8777

Satellites can survey waste disposal sites and help investigate the environmental impact of landfills. Recent tests showed that high resolution images from the French satellite SPOT are good enough to identify recently exposed soils, disturbed and reclaimed land, new ponds, and other ground cover changes that normally accompany landfill development. The SPOT images are judged by ARS researchers to be more cost-effective than high altitude aerial photography for county or regional monitoring programs.
Remote Sensing Research Lab,
Beltsville, MD
Galen Hart, (301) 344-2822

A mathematical procedure widely used in economics and engineering has been modified for use in plant breeding and genetics. With "linear optimization," breeders can now objectively rate the importance of various genetic traits. While many experienced breeders intuitively know which plants and combinations of genetic traits they want to use, they are often at a loss to specify how each trait individually affects the selection process. Quantifying and comparing values of different traits could improve the management of breeding operations and help breeders convey knowledge to other scientists, farmers, and commercial firms.
Wheat and Sorghum Research, Lincoln, NE
Blaine E. Johnson, (402) 472-1562

Human Nutrition

Sugar junkies, beware! Another study shows that too much sugar can lift your cholesterol and fat levels as well as your spirits. The culprit is fructose, which accounts for half the sugar in table sugar (sucrose) and more than half in high-fructose corn sweeteners. When combined with a diet high in saturated fat and cholesterol, fructose significantly increased several danger signs for coronary artery disease in 21 men. The men consumed diets containing 20% fructose--about twice the level in an average diet--and 20% starch. On the high-fructose diet, the men had significant increases in blood levels of total cholesterol, LDL (the "bad" cholesterol-carrying particle), and total triglycerides. As expected, the high-fructose diet caused the greatest increase in the 10 men who normally overreact to dietary sugar. Between 9% and 17% of the U.S. population is sugar sensitive--a condition thought to precede diabetes.
Carbohydrate Nutrition Lab, Beltsville Human Nutrition Research Center,
Beltsville, MD
Daniel J. Scholfield, (301) 344-2385

Sluggish enzymes may explain why alcohol hits older people quicker and harder than young people. In a study of old and young inebriated rats, some of the enzyme systems that dispose of ethanol and its toxic byproduct--acetaldehyde--were less active in the old rats. Forty percent of the old rats died from a large dose of alcohol, while all the young rats survived. Scientists have attributed the difference in sensitivity to the fact that older animals (and people) have less body water, increasing their alcohol concentration. However, these findings suggest that delayed alcohol elimination also contributes to acute and chronic toxicity of alcohol in the elderly.
Human Nutrition Research Center on Aging at Tufts, Boston, MA
Robert M. Russell, (617) 556-3335

Vitamin E supplements may help promote heart disease rather than prevent it, as some researchers have suggested. Two recent studies found that the vitamin has an adverse effect on cholesterol-carrying lipoproteins--both the low-density (LDL) and high-density (HDL) types. It causes them to become more rigid. By contrast, a healthful, low-fat diet has the opposite effect: it makes both lipoproteins more fluid. This could mean that more cholesterol is deposited in the arteries by rigid LDL and less is removed by rigid HDL. Large daily doses of E (600 international units) reduced LDL fluidity in women (no men were in this study). In a second study, moderate daily doses (30 and 100 i.u.) reduced HDL fluidity in women but not in men. Women taking 100 i.u. had lower levels of the beneficial HDL after 6 weeks.
Lipid Nutrition Lab, Beltsville Human Nutrition Research Center, Beltsville, MD
Elliott Berlin, (301) 344-2297

Summarizing many years of research and experience, a top ARS nutritionist told a food safety and nutrition conference recently that the best way to get all of the nutrients one needs is to eat a balanced variety of foods in moderation and to avoid dietary fads, pill-popping, and focusing on a single nutrient. To get fish oil--high in omega-3 fatty acids that may help slow hardening of the arteries--eat fish, he said. Good sources: cod, mackerel, bluefish, swordfish, and salmon. A good source of calcium, important for bone building, is low-fat milk. He added that there is no such thing as an anticancer or an anti-heart-disease diet as such. Nutrition is but one factor that influences disease, he said, adding that genetic or environmental factors can also have a substantial impact.
Beltsville Human Nutrition Research Lab, Beltsville, MD
Walter Mertz, (301) 344-2157

Breast-fed infants take in fewer calories and grow at a different rate than published national norms used by pediatricians nationwide, suggesting the norms need revising. The evidence stems from several independent and ARS studies of nursing infants, including a recent study of 45 infants from birth to 8 months of age. Their calorie intake slipped from 100% of the Recommended Dietary Allowance during their first month to 80% by their fourth month and remained at that level after solid foods were introduced. Growth rate reflected calorie intake. During their first 3 months, the infants grew 5% to 10% faster than projected by the National Center for Health Statistics growth standards, then dropped 3% to 4% a month. By the eighth month, these infants were about 17% below their starting level on the growth curve. Current RDA and growth standards are based on older data from predominantly formula-fed infant populations. This, plus the fact that today's formulas are more like mother's milk, suggests the need for a fresh look at the norms.
Children's Nutrition Research Center, Houston, TX
Janice E. Stuff/Cutberto Garza, (713) 799-6178/6004

Families in diet studies should find it easy to use a new computerized system that tracks exactly what they eat. Volunteers in two pilot tests of the experimental system needed little training to operate the portable computer and computer-linked components intended for use in the home kitchen. These include

19

an electronic scale that weighs food automatically and a bar code reader and catalog for recording the foods in each meal or snack. Nutrition studies designed to detect unhealthy trends in the American diet involve thousands of pieces of data; computerization will speed up and simplify analyzing and tabulating this information.
Western Human Nutrition Research Center, San Francisco, CA
M.J. Kretsch, (415) 556-6225

Determining whether the human body has enough vitamin B_6 is now faster and easier. A newly automated test, based on well-known chemical interactions between vitamin B_6 and red blood cell enzymes (alanine aminotransferase and aspartate aminotrasferase), requires only a few drops of blood to check the activity level of the two enzymes before and after B_6 is added to the sample. The vitamin must be present for the enzymes to function. The increase in enzyme activity accurately indicates an individual's B_6 status. The improved procedure is simple to run and can analyze up to 100 samples a day with an automated chemistry analyzer, an instrument found in most labs. Most likely candidates for vitamin B_6 deficiency are females over the age of 15 and elderly men. Severe deficiency can result in skin disorders, nausea, vomiting, and central nervous system problems.

Biochemistry Research, Western Human Nutrition Research Center, San Francisco, CA
James H. Skala, (415) 556-5954

Lactoengineering could become common practice for mothers nursing very low-birthweight infants. In the first attempt to manipulate breastmilk composition by changing the mother's diet, scientists tailored its fat content to the special needs of infants under 3-1/2 pounds. These infants have difficulty absorbing long-chain fatty acids (having 16 or more carbon units) common in the milk of mothers on a typical diet. When 10 mothers switched to a diet very low in fat and high in carbohydrates (80% of total calories compared with 45% in a typical diet), their breastmilk contained more medium-chain fatty acids. Since these have only 10 to 14 carbon units, they are more readily absorbed by very low-birthweight infants. Further studies will assess the benefits to infants.
Children's Nutrition Research Center at Baylor, Houston, TX
Richard J. Schanler, (713) 799-4297

Unanswered questions about folate, including an RDA for the elderly, will be easier to resolve with a vastly improved analysis for the vitamin. While most vitamins have a few biologically active forms, folate (a.k.a. folic acid or folacin) comes in 40 to 50 slightly different chemical entities, each having a different function in the body. To identify these forms in food or tissue, scientists now use bacterial assays that take 2 to 3 weeks and give poor measurements. The new chemical analysis, using standard lab equipment, takes less than 3 hours and gives accurate measurements of all forms of folate. The two-stage process first removes up to 97% of the folates in a food or blood sample then separates the individual forms in a high-performance liquid chromatograph. Folate deficiency is the most common vitamin deficiency in this country and affects about 30% of pregnant women.
Human Nutrition Research Center on Aging at Tufts, Boston, MA
Jacob Selhub, (617) 556-3191

⊕U.S GOVERNMENT PRINTING OFFICE·1988-201-020-60590/ARS

Quarterly Report
of Selected Research Projects

United States
Department of
Agriculture

Agricultural
Research
Service

April 1 to June 30, 1988

CONTENTS

DROUGHT-RELATED RESEARCH

An ARS-developed grass and a new machine to harvest its chaffy seed are helping control erosion and boost forage productivity on more than 1 million acres in dry areas of Oklahoma, Texas and New Mexico. WW-Spar bluestem grass, released in 1982, was selected for drought tolerance, forage production and winter hardiness from among 800 Old World bluestem specimens. WW-Spar stayed green longer and produced forage longer under drought conditions than the other bluestems tested. The harvester, the Woodward Flail-Vac Seed Stripper, was developed by a rancher with ARS help. It uses a revolutionary process to harvest the chaffy bluestem seed. About 500 have been sold commercially, making it possible to speed supplies of WW-Spar and other chaffy grass seed to growers. Much

Note: One or more scientists familiar with each research project are listed for further information. If the scientists are unavailable, others at the same telephone number may also be familiar with the work.

Items marked with the word PATENT are being patented by ARS. For more information contact Ann Whitehead, National Patent Program, Bldg. 005, Rm. 401, Beltsville Agricultural Research Center, Beltsville, MD 20705, (301) 344-2786.

of the acreage in WW-Spar is enrolled in USDA's Conservation Reserve Program. Southern Plains Range Research Station, Woodward, OK
C.L. Dewald, (405) 256-7449

The carbon in a wheat plant may be a tipoff on how well it can withstand drought. Scientists are now examining the ratio of two different natural forms of carbon, C_{12} and C_{13}, in winter wheat. They are also using infrared thermal "guns," gas-measuring equipment and portable chambers to measure plant response to drought. They hope to identify wheats with superior resistance that could be used to improve plant varieties.
Great Plains Systems Research, Fort Collins, CO
Jack A. Morgan, (303) 491-8224

A new drought-tolerant breeding line of white clover, Brown Loam Synthetic No. 2, was released by ARS and the Mississippi Agriculture and Forestry Experiment Station in 1987. At Mississippi State, the new white clover had greater forage production and persistence and less peanut stunt virus than two standard varieties, Regal and Tillman. Tests at more than 10 locations are now evaluating the new line's potential throughout the Southeast.
Forage Research Unit, Mississippi State, MS
G.A. Pederson, (601) 323-2230, ext. 186

Sorghums from drought-stressed areas of sub-Sahara West Africa may lead to improved U.S. varieties. Recent tests make scientists suspect that the African sorghums have more of a natural chemical that enables them to withstand drying

(cont. on pg. 18)

SOIL, WATER, & AIR

Surface-mined land in the Northern Great Plains can be reclaimed more economically by planting cool-season grasses alone. Federal law requires the land to be revegetated with species that have seasonal use similar to the native plants. In the Northern Plains, the native prairie is a mix of cool- and warm-season grasses. In recent studies, however, cattle grazing on reclaimed land planted mainly to smooth bromegrass and alfalfa thrived as well as animals grazing on native prairie or on reclaimed land planted with warm-season grasses. Seed cost for the mixture of cool-season grass and alfalfa is about one-third that for the warm-season grasses. The mix is also easier to sow and establish.
Forage and Range Research, Mandan, ND
Lenat Hoffman, (701) 663-6445

Hardwood swamps control water pollution by trapping and recycling nutrients washed from farmland. Such swamps flank intermittent streams from Georgia to Maryland and are found throughout most of the United States. In the Little River watershed near Tifton, GA, scientists found that swamps filtered out about 90% of nitrogen washed from the land. Some was intercepted by tree roots in the swamps; some was converted from its nitrate form to nitrogen gas by microbes in the carbon-rich soil under the trees. Also, tree roots kept half the phosphorus out of streams. The hardwoods thrive on the two nutrients. Proper management of these hardwood forests--including periodic selective tree harvesting--will maintain or increase their pollution-control function.
Southeast Watershed Research Lab, Tifton, GA
Richard Lowrance, (912) 386-3514

Laser beams are being used to chart the flight and clock the velocity of pesticide droplets. It's part of an effort by researchers to eventually help pesticide equipment operators better control the amount of chemical sprayed on crops--for environmental safety and cost effectiveness. These intersecting beams, generated by a laser-spectrometer, can measure a droplet as tiny as 1 micrometer. Cooperating with ARS on the project is the Laboratory for Pest Control Application Technology, a cooperative program that also includes Ohio State University and the Ohio R&D Center. Applications Technology Research, Wooster, OH
Ross D. Brazee, (216) 263-3870

Water that flows into furrows from openings in irrigation pipelines laid on sloping land can be slowed to an even flow, reducing the chances of erosion. Water pressure builds up in downhill lines; the velocity is so high that soil washes off the upper ends of the fields where the water strikes the soil surface. But ARS engineers found that this excess pressure can be controlled by inserting into the pipeline low-cost, energy-dissipating orifices and butterfly disks, which could be manufactured commercially using ARS designs.
Snake River Conservation Research Center, Kimberly, ID
Allan S. Humpherys, (208) 423-5582

Increasing water depth in groundwater recharge basins can actually reduce, rather than promote, desirable infiltration of water. Fine-textured soil particles settle at the bottom of these basins to form a slowly permeable lining. From time to time, the basins must be drained and dried to remove this lining. Attempts to increase infiltration by increasing water depth often fail because the additional weight and pressure of the deeper water compacts the lining even more, which further reduces infiltration rates. Municipalities and others planning such basins can avoid problems by conducting preliminary tests using small basins to determine optimum water depth for effective recharge at specific sites.
U.S. Water Conservation Lab, Phoenix, AZ
Herman Bouwer, (602) 261-4356

A new method for sampling well water can provide better, more representative samples of underground pools of water,

enabling improved assessment of ground-water contamination. Surface waters may enter the well from faulty well construction, or the well casing may cause significant chemical changes in the well water. In the new method, a manifold monitoring device continuously measures chemicals such as nitrate or dissolved oxygen. When the concentration of these chemicals stabilizes at prescribed levels, the device signals that water is being pumped from the underground aquifer and it's time to sample.
Watershed Research, University Park, PA
H.B. Pionke/J.B. Urban, (814) 865-2048

Rain or irrigation after a popular herbicide is sprayed on the soil can stunt the growth of peanuts. Metolachlor is widely used to control yellow nut-sedge, one of peanut's most troublesome weeds. In 3 years of field tests, seedling growth and fruiting were delayed when researchers irrigated soon after applying the chemical. This was the first time metolachlor's interaction with irrigation has been demonstrated. To lessen injury, growers should take greater care to distribute the herbicide more evenly into the soil, especially when irrigation is required for crop establishment.
Nematodes, Weeds and Crops Research, Tifton, GA
John Cardina, (912) 386-3172

Changing tillage practices and vehicle traffic over clay soils could help farmers advance their planting dates and increase corn yields. By planting corn on raised beds of soil--called ridge tillage--and restricting farm equipment traffic over fields to predetermined lanes, scientists believe farmers can restrict soil compaction, reduce damage to the soil structure and minimize depletion of organic matter. Following these practices advanced planting dates an average of 12 days and doubled yields on test plots of Hoytville silty clay that was severely compacted previously by conventional tillage.
Soil Drainage Research, Columbus, OH
Norman R. Fausey, (614) 292-9806

CROP PRODUCTION & PROTECTION

Two new varieties of disease-resistant, soft white winter wheat--bred from weed-like parents--will be available to farmers this fall. Madsen and Hyak are the first U.S. varieties of soft white winter wheat to resist infection by strawbreaker foot rot, the most devastating soilborne disease of wheat in the Pacific Northwest. Over 175 million bushels or 90% of the soft white winter wheat produced in Washington, Oregon and Idaho each year is exported to Japan, Korea, Egypt, India and other countries. There the wheat is milled into flour used in baking oriental noodles, pastries, cakes and cookies. If uncontrolled, the disease could wipe out 50% to 60% of the crop. Madsen and Hyak also resist three other major wheat diseases--stripe, leaf rust and stem rust. Farmers are currently using costly fungicides on about a million acres to control strawbreaker. The new varieties could help lower farmers' production costs $15 to $30 an acre.
Wheat Genetics, Quality, Physiology and Disease Research, Pullman, WA
Robert E. Allan, (509) 335-3632

Salinas 88, a new iceberg lettuce, is expected on the market by 1989. ARS scientists developed the summer variety for California's Salinas Valley and adjacent Santa Maria Valley. Together these areas produce 80% of the nation's June-through-September lettuce harvest, worth an estimated $400 million. Salinas 88 is resistant to lettuce mosaic virus, a costly disease that broke out recently in the Salinas Valley and infected one-third to one-half of the lettuce fields there.
Vegetable Production Research, Salinas, CA,
Edward J. Ryder, (408) 755-2860

Using ARS technology, a Colorado firm is mass-producing a grasshopper-killing parasite, Nosema locustae, and marketing it as "NoloBait." Evans BioControl of Broomfield, CO, puts dormant protozoa spores on bran flakes. The flakes attract grasshoppers. The parasite

attacks the pest's fat cells and depletes its energy stores, killing 50% to 60% of the pests in 3 to 4 weeks. It is then passed along in two ways. First, sick females protect eggs they lay with a casing that newly emerging grasshoppers must chew through to hatch--but the casing is infected with the spores. Next, the cannibalistic grasshoppers ingest the spores from these dead grasshoppers. The technology is part of an effort aimed at avoiding the $400 million annual damage caused by grasshoppers. ARS scientists saw the parasite's potential as a biocontrol. After proving its effectiveness, they developed the production and storage methods now used by Evans BioControl.
Range Insect Control Research Lab, Bozeman, MT
John Henry, (406) 994-3051

In a related project, ARS and Evans BioControl are teaming up to field-test a grasshopper virus. ARS will supply to the Colorado firm entomopox virus and technology to produce it. The firm will produce it and mix it with Nosema locustae, and test the two controls together on 10,000 acres in the West. Farmers generally want faster action than the 3 to 4 weeks it takes to kill grasshoppers using only N. locustae. So the scientists theorize that the entomopox virus could knock down the worst of a grasshopper infestation in the short term and then let the N. locustae take over for the long run. Evans BioControl has agreed to share their data with the ARS scientists.
Range Insect Control Research Lab, Bozeman, MT
Doug Streett, (406) 994-6439

Russian wheat aphids, which threaten 60 million acres of grain fields in 14 states, are themselves threatened by a new research program resulting from a redirection of $800,000 this year. Despite the application of $17.2 million in pesticides, this newly imported pest damaged $36 million worth of wheat, barley, oats and rye last year. First confirmed in Texas 2 years ago, the aphid hitched a ride on the wind to Arizona, Colorado, Idaho, Kansas, Montana,

Nebraska, New Mexico, Oklahoma, Oregon, South Dakota, Utah, Washington and Wyoming. Research at four locations will focus on resistant varieties, biological controls, pesticide screening, basic research on the aphid's life cycle, and computer models for devising integrated pest management strategies.
National Program Staff, Beltsville, MD
Richard S. Soper, (301) 344-3930

A microscopic worm--called a nematode-- could benefit farmers and gardeners by acting as a biological control for corn rootworms, one of the most serious pests of corn. Many nematodes victimize plants, but ARS scientists have found a few species that attack only insects. One in particular--Steinernema feltiae-- infects rootworm larvae in the soil and releases bacteria that kill them. In field studies to date, bacteria-toting nematodes have reduced root damage by only 11%. But scientists hope further research will lead to protection equal to that from chemical insecticides. Corn producers annually spend nearly $350 million on chemicals to battle the rootworm.
Northern Grain Insects Research, Brookings, SD
Jan Jackson, (605) 693-5205

Tiny worms that inject lethal bacteria into Japanese beetles are being developed by commercial companies, thanks in part to ARS research. On research plots, Heterohabditis nematodes immediately killed 60% of beetle larvae in the soil and within a month built up enough of a nematode population to kill 90%. They even survived an Ohio winter to kill 90% of larvae again the following year. Japanese beetle larvae eat grass roots, while adults feed on many plants; their favorites are roses, grapes and corn. Available chemicals don't work well on the beetle larvae; soil organisms break the compounds down. Found in every state east of the Mississippi River, the beetles cost homeowners, golf courses and parks almost $500 million a year. Researchers found that the tiny nematode worms should be distributed through an insecticide sprayer in rain or at night, when the sun's ultraviolet rays are

4

weakest. Companies are selling the nematodes on a small scale and continue improving shipping and storage methods. ARS scientists continue tests, including one on a golf course, to see how many worms are needed per square foot. Horticultural Insect Research Lab, Wooster, OH
Michael Klein, (216) 263-3896

For safer and better control of European corn borers--pests that cost farmers $400 million a year in damage and control costs--farmers may one day plant corn seed pretreated with insecticide. Commercial companies are interested in treating seed with thiodicarb to spread pesticide throughout the plant's leaves and stalks. ARS scientists pretreated different strains of corn with the pesticide; some gave better control than others. The good ones--A623H+, A641H+ and CM105--are lines available to commercial breeders. Pretreating these strains gave 75% to 80% control, compared to 70% with spraying. Tests continue to see how weather and other factors will affect these results. Thiodicarb has not yet been approved for commercial use by the Environmental Protection Agency as a seed treatment to control European corn borers.
Corn Insects Lab, Ankeny, IA
Edwin C. Berry, (515) 964-6664

Ragweed and pigweed--pests that allergy sufferers and farmers despise--may get a chance to redeem themselves. Planting either weed near a bell pepper plot as a decoy "crop" will help to protect peppers from the destructive leafminer insect, an important pest in south Texas that can cut harvests by at least 30%. Normally, pepper plants are a favorite breeding and feeding spot for these insects. But researchers have discovered that leafminers actually favor ragweed or pigweed plants over the pepper plants. A patch of either weed seems to divert the insect's attention. Bell pepper growers who are allergic to these weeds can reduce the plot's attractiveness to the insects by clearing it of all weeds.
Subtropical Cotton Insects Research, Weslaco, TX
Laurence D. Chandler, (512) 968-6739

Northern Plains wheat farmers may soon have a solution to a weed-control dilemma. Wild oats, one of the worst weed pests there, can reduce spring wheat yields by 30% or more. Equally bad, yields of some wheat varieties are reduced just as much by a herbicide widely used to control the weed. Now scientists have found that tolerance to difenzoquat herbicide is simply inherited and can be bred easily into new wheat varieties. Difenzoquat does not reduce yields of tolerant wheat. The researchers say that crop plants bred for triazine tolerance undergo metabolic changes that reduce yield. Breeding wheat for difenzoquat tolerance may give farmers more choices both for wheat varieties and for herbicides.
Plant Science Research, St. Paul, MN
Robert H. Busch, (612) 625-1975

The common cocklebur weed could become less of a pest in soybean fields if its aggressiveness could be understood and modified. It now causes more soybean yield reduction per weed than any other weed. In field studies, scientists proved that the weed's "pushy" shoots are its main weapons--unlike other weeds, which more often interfere with soybean growth from the roots. Cocklebur's leafy canopy blocks sunlight and crowds out soybeans, reducing yield by up to 24%. In one trial, crowding alone cut yields 15%. The weed can grow 4 feet tall and is one of the most serious pests of soybeans, corn and sorghum.
Crop Protection Research, Urbana, IL
Edward W. Stoller, (217) 333-9654

Sweetpotatoes release a group of chemicals that can suppress weeds, scientists found. They took a sweetpotato that ARS originally released to resist insects, diseases and nematodes and tested extracts from its skin against weeds. In tests, one group of chemicals--called phenolics--was especially active at suppressing germination of eight weeds: velvetleaf, proso millet, morningglory, goosegrass, black nightshade, pigweed, cassia and eclipta. Scientists foresee three benefits from the research. Breed-

ers could develop new weed-resistant varieties in much less time by selecting plants with high levels of these chemicals instead of having to grow and test multiple strains of plants. The crop could also be genetically engineered to produce phenolics continuously. And chemical companies could develop synthetic phenolics for new pesticides. The researchers are also testing the effects of phenolics on bacteria and nematodes.
U.S. Vegetable Lab, Charleston, SC
Joseph Peterson, (803) 556-0840

Insects from Argentina and Paraguay look like promising candidates to control mesquite on U.S. rangeland. A weevil and several beetle species eat mesquite seed, and a leaftier moth eats the foliage. Scientists hope these biocontrols can help reduce enormous stands of mesquite in the Southwest. The weed annually costs the livestock industry $250 to $500 million in beef production, controls and "theft" of soil water. Field tests indicate that biocontrols could cut mesquite density as much as 70%, pushing it back to levels of the early 1800's. Researchers will first examine the effectiveness of the seed-eating insects before determining if the leaftier or other candidates will be needed.
Grassland, Soil and Water Research, Temple, TX
C.J. DeLoach, (817) 770-6500

A new herbicide also shows promise for controlling honey mesquite and other rangeland weeds without getting into groundwater. When sprayed on a 1-acre test plot in Texas, the herbicide, clopyralid, did not show up in water wells within the test area or on adjacent land, despite above-normal rainfall during nearly 6 months of sampling. Scientists also say clopyralid did what two commonly used herbicides, 2,4,5-T and triclopyr, didn't do: wipe out a stand of mesquite with better than 70% effectiveness. The herbicide can also control Canada thistle, musk thistle, spotted knapweed and huisache. Honey mesquite infests more than 55 million acres in the southwestern United States, crowding out forage for

livestock and puncturing truck and tractor tires with its thorns.
Grassland Protection Research, College Station, TX
Rodney W. Bovey, (409) 260-9238

A hot water bath before planting may help sugarcanes clean up their act. Treating three commercial varieties of seed canes with 131°F water three times in 3 days freed half to three-quarters of infected stalks from sugarcane mosaic and ratoon stunting disease. Mosaic, caused by a virus, and ratoon stunting disease, caused by a bacterium, are two of the most important diseases plaguing the American sugarcane industry.
Sugarcane Research, Houma, LA
Gerd T. Benda, (504) 872-5042

Chemical sprays have been found that will partially overcome iron deficiency in apple and pear trees, which causes fruit loss in some areas of the Pacific Northwest. The chlorosis is most serious where orchards are planted in highly alkaline soils, especially when these soils are over-irrigated and poorly drained. Several iron compounds were tested in sprays on trees; most resulted in greener leaves and improved tree vigor. Some, however, left burn marks on the fruit. Most promising so far: fertilizer sprays containing iron lignosulfonate compounds. When applied at low concentrations, these compounds reduce chlorosis by 40% without marking the fruit.
Tree Fruit Research Lab, Wenatchee, WA
J. Thomas Raese, (509) 662-4317

Although little is known about hollow heart, an abnormal cavity in pea seeds, it can now be detected at an early stage. If conditions are wet and cold, these abnormal seeds develop into stunted plants with reduced yields. But ARS scientists can get an advance warning of the defect. They used a commercially available electronic seed analyzer to detect and estimate the severity of hollow heat in small samples of seeds. Using this sampling method, the scientists found that as much as 75% of a

large seed lot may contain hollow heart. Such an early alert could help seed producers avoid serious yield losses. Irrigated Agriculture Research and Extension Center, Prosser, WA
John M. Kraft, (509) 786-3454

Soybeans and other legumes will provide a more complete source of protein when a corn gene for sulfur storage can be bioengineered into the crops. Legumes are usually very low in sulfur-containing essential amino acids. As a start, scientists have inserted corn's sulfur-storage gene into tobacco cells and have grown back plants with high levels of sulfur and sulfur-containing substances. Legume varieties with high-sulfur amino acid can be developed only after scientists can regenerate seed-bearing soybeans and other plants from bioengineered cells. Meanwhile, the achievement with tobacco--as a model--helped scientists polish gene-inserting techniques.
Plant Molecular Genetics Lab, Beltsville, MD
Eliot M. Herman, (301) 344-3258

Spinach leaves and mouse-ear cress are providing scientists with clues that bring them closer to genetically engineering many crops for improved photosynthesis. ARS researchers have isolated and cloned a gene responsible for the enzyme, rubisco activase. This enzyme helps plants adjust to changes in light intensity during the first step in photosynthesis--converting atmospheric carbon dioxide to sugar. Now scientists can transfer modified versions of the cloned gene into chloroplasts (part of the plant cell that contains chlorophyll) to see which versions work best in different environments.
Photosynthesis Research, Urbana, IL
William L. Ogren, (217) 244-3082

In this age of biotechnology, does tissue culture mean better? Scientists say yes. They compared nutrient concentrations in apple leaves regenerated from lab-cultured cell tissue with leaves of the same varieties grown from buds grafted onto seedlings and root stock. Results

from the 3-year study showed that the leaves of tissue-cultured trees contained more calcium. These trees also took up nutrients more efficiently. Further study is needed to see if more leaf calcium means more fruit calcium. Advantages of tissue culture include lower production costs, tree uniformity for easier management and shorter time to planting.
Fruit Lab, Beltsville, MD
Ronald F. Korcak, (301) 344-4650.
Appalachian Fruit Research, Kearneysville, WV
Stephen S. Miller, (304) 725-3451

New tissue culture techniques allow scientists to regenerate numerous plants from one seed of a stone fruit like the European plum, peach and sour cherry. Using thidiazuron--a cotton defoliant that can regulate growth--scientists can now regenerate as many as 15 to 20 plants from one seed's cotyledon. This is the part of the embryo that stores food. With the new method, rooted plants are ready for the greenhouse in just 90 to 100 days, and only two growth media are needed. Current culture methods using the embryo take up to twice the time and require four growth media. ARS and Cornell University researchers, while working with stone fruits (Prunus), discovered that the new method also regenerates soybean plants more efficiently and rapidly than current methods. The cotyledon method can lead to new soybean varieties (including those genetically engineered) and improved Prunus rootstock.
Appalachian Fruit Research Station, Kearneysville, WV
Ralph Scorza, (304) 725-3451

Keeping potato plant shoot tips in the dark, a new tissue culture method, may make them healthier and cheaper to grow. The new method, likely to be adopted by other potato breeders, researchers, and seed producers, could help lower costs to potato growers and provide better quality, more competitive varieties in the marketplace. Currently, cultures of disease-free clones (or mother plants) are grown in light and then cut into

pieces and transferred to fresh nutrients several times a year. With the new method, clones are stored in a refrigerator at 50°F, where a culture medium high in sugars and plant hormones induces small disease-free cuttings of these clones to form tiny tubers. These microtubers can be stored up to 2 years and replanted with 95% success, saving the cost of transferring the plants to new culture media every 3 or 4 months. The technique has already reduced the cost of breeding potatoes in the lab where about 400 clones are maintained as microtuber-forming cultures.
Irrigated Agriculture Research and Extension Center, Prosser, WA
Charles R. Brown, (509) 786-3454

Heating or pre-soaking Pensacola bahiagrass seed could solve its germination problems. Used extensively on millions of acres of roadsides, recreation areas and pastures in the South and other tropical and semitropical areas, Pensacola bahiagrass has a reputation of being slow to germinate and difficult to establish. The germination problem stems from its thick seed coat, which makes the seed vulnerable longer to erosion, drought and predators. But heating the seeds to 122°F or soaking them in water before planting softens the coat so seeds sprout faster. Commercial seed producers will likely find the heat treatment more convenient, since it's easier to package heat-treated seed for retail customers.
Plant Stress and Protection Research, Gainesville, FL
Sherlie H. West, (904) 392-1821

Why do some muskmelon varieties resist fungal disease while others don't? It may be because resistant varieties have more of a sugar called galactose in cell walls. In preliminary studies, scientists grew the fungus Myrothecium roridum on three sugars--arabinose, glucose and galactose--found in muskmelon cell walls. The fungus grew well on the first two but was inhibited by galactose. Scientists are using this information in breeding muskmelons with higher galactose levels to fight decay.
Horticultural Crops Quality Lab, Beltsville, MD
Harold E. Moline, (301) 344-3128

ANIMAL PRODUCTION & PROTECTION

Combining the use of warm-season and cool-season grass pastures can keep cattle in the Northeast grazing lustily and gaining weight from April until December. Profit potentials from these mixed pasturing systems exceed those where only cool-season grasses are grazed, since cattle raisers must limit herd size to the pastures' carrying capacity in July and August. Summer heat sharply limits the growth of Kentucky bluegrass and orchardgrass. Warm-season grasses, such as switchgrass and big bluestem, make their best growth, however, at temperatures between 90°F to 100°F. Rotating between warm-season and cool-season pastures to allow new growth can boost grass production 4 to 10 times over that of exclusive cool-season pastures, and cattle can gain 2 to 2.5 pounds per day. Fertilizer requirements for warm-season grasses are only one-third to one-half those of cool-season grasses.
U.S. Regional Pasture Research Lab, University Park, PA
Gerald A. Jung, (814) 963-0948

Burning off the competing grasses before planting clover for cattle grazing could boost the clover's overall output. Clover can be difficult to get started because its seedlings don't compete well with certain grasses already in place. But clover offers beef and dairy producers many pluses. It has a higher crude protein content, can be grazed when grass is not usually available, and has the ability to use nitrogen from the atmosphere. Tests comparing clover's output showed a 38% stand where competing grasses had been burned first. By contrast, only 16% of the clover seed sprouted when the grass was simply clipped before planting clover. But there's nothing magic about burning, scientists say; the key to clover's success lies in completely suppressing the vegetative competition.
Forage Research Lab, Starkville, MS
Geoff Brink, (601) 232-2230

8

A friend of yesteryear's roaming buffalo could become an ally of cattle and dairy producers if a new research strategy works. The friend is a parasitic wasp that kills stable and house flies by laying its eggs inside pupae--the last fly stage before adulthood. The wasp, Muscidifurax zaraptor, did fine on America's vast unpeopled plains where fly pupae were found in fields and pastures. But today, with cattle confined to smaller areas, the parasite isn't doing as good a job locating the feedlots where concentrations of fly pupae are found. So scientists will mass-rear thousands of wasps by placing 50,000 freeze-killed fly pupae into a feedlot next to 5,000 wasp pupae. About 17 days after the emerging wasps lay eggs in the fly pupae, a new generation of wasps will be patrolling the lot in force. The scientists hope the scheme will cut the number of pesky flies and let farmers reduce their use of insecticides.
Midwest Livestock Insects Research, Lincoln, NE
James J. Petersen, (402) 437-5267

To help pig breeders produce leaner porkers, scientists can now harmlessly predict a pig's genetic tendency toward obesity. Cultures of fat cells from rats developed faster when "fed" serum from genetically obese fetuses and young pigs than they did when given serum from lean pigs. Now the scientists plan to identify serum factors such as hormones, proteins or other substances, to explain the test results.
Animal Physiology Research Lab, Athens, GA
Gary J. Hausman, (404) 546-3224

A milk enzyme may offer a faster method for detecting mastitis in dairy cows. A serious disease of the udder, mastitis costs dairy farmers $2 billion annually. An enzyme--N-acetyl-B-D-glucosaminidase (NAGase)--is present in all milk. But in tests on normal and mastitis-infected dairy cows, infected milk had significantly larger amounts of the enzyme. The conventional U.S. test used to detect mastitis consists of counting "somatic cells"--white blood cells and some epi-thelial cells (lining the udder)--in milk. The test for the enzyme NAGase can be automated--but even run manually, it can accurately handle thousands more samples faster and would be ideal for milk-processing plants.
Milk Secretion and Mastitis Lab, Beltsville, MD
Robert H. Miller, (301) 344 2330

The first U.S. "naked" oats, named Pennuda, may benefit both millers of breakfast oatmeal and processors of feeds. Pennuda oat grain is virtually hull-less, a feature millers could exploit to cut transportation and dehulling costs. The hull-less grain is also higher in both protein and digestible energy, thus highly desirable in rations for such monogastric (one-stomached) animals as poultry and swine. Pennuda is a high-yielding variety with short stalks that resist lodging, or falling down. It has been released, and foundation seed (a generation before that which farmers plant) should be available for the 1989 planting season.
U.S. Regional Pasture Research Lab, University Park, PA
Richard R. Hill Jr., (814) 863-0939

NEW & IMPROVED PRODUCTS

Glasnost, or openness, should reap rewards for cooperating U.S. and Soviet scientists, but it spells trouble for hitchhiking insect pests. Scientists from the two countries conducted a joint study last winter confirming that phosphine gas, if properly circulated through wheat transported aboard ship, kills insects that may infest the grain. The study was done on 2.6 million bushels of U.S. wheat shipped from Galveston, TX, to the Soviet Union last December. As a result, the Soviets will use the procedure for U.S. wheat shipments of more than 40,000 tons and may use it for similar shipments of corn.
Stored-Product Insects Research and Development Lab, Savannah, GA
Robert Davis, (912) 233-7981

Homeowners battling imported flying cockroaches now have a weapon available to turn these pests belly up without endangering pets and wildlife. A toxic bait that kills nearly 100% of Asian cockroaches in a few days has been registered for use against them, thanks to ARS and two private firms. Southern Mill Creek Products contacted agency scientists for advice on controlling this imported pest. The scientists recommended modifying an existing product to get something on the market quickly. The firm's bait for mole crickets was chosen, and agency scientists tested it with volunteer help from Lady Bugs Pest Control. The new bait is easily distributed with a fertilizer spreader.
Insects Affecting Man and Animals Research Laboratory, Gainesville, FL
Richard J. Brenner, (904) 374-5937

Even though salt has been used since antiquity to preserve food, few studies have been done to identify how it inhibits bacteria from contaminating food. Now preliminary studies with Escherichia coli, a bacterium commonly found in the human intestinal tract, are shedding light on this phenomenon. Scientists found that salt, or sodium chloride, forces E. coli to waste energy as it rids itself of the toxic sodium ions. This means the bacterium has less energy to take in and use the nutrients it needs to grow to proportions that would cause illness. This provides new information for scientists and the food-processing industry in efforts to prevent contamination of foods.
Microbial Food Safety, Eastern Regional Research Center, Philadelphia, PA
James L. Smith/Robert L. Buchanan, (215) 233-6520

Eliminating salmonella bacteria from fresh poultry is high on the priority list of both the poultry industry and government inspectors. Carcasses are now washed in poultry processing plants before they are chilled. But ARS scientists, using a special microscope, have found that salmonella bacteria are difficult to wash off poultry because these bacteria hide themselves in the ridges and crevices of the skin. To make things more difficult, these ridges become more pronounced when the carcass is immersed in water, sheltering the bacteria that much more. Washing the carcasses with salt water removed only a small percentage of the salmonella bacteria. Research is continuing, however, to find new ways to eliminate salmonella contamination of processed poultry.
Poultry Meat Quality and Safety Research, Richard B. Russell Research Center, Athens, GA
Huda S. Lillard, (404) 546-3567

Growers of asparagus are wary about importing the asparagus aphid to non-infested growing areas. These aphids can severely reduce stands and yields of the crop. The aphids hitch rides on asparagus foliage as well as on spears shipped for fresh-market sales. An ARS study shows that aphids on spears can be eliminated by use of very low levels of irradiation at room temperature. The asparagus could be treated while being prepared for storage or shipment with no risk to workers or consumers. This is the first study on the use of irradiation against aphids on food crops.
Yakima Agricultural Research Lab, Yakima, WA
J. Eric Halfhill, (509) 575-5982.

Why do some citrus varieties show varying degrees of resistance to citrus scab? Scientists now think it's because they contain differing levels of phototoxins-- natural chemicals that kill scab organisms in sunlight. ARS and Florida International University scientists tested two mandarin orange varieties (Robinson and Fremont) and a lemon root stock for susceptibility to the disease. Robinson was resistant to the scab fungus, Elsinoe fawcettii, but rough lemon and Fremont were susceptible. In tests with healthy plants, the scientists discovered Robinson contained the highest levels of three phototoxins, called coumarins, present in all three citrus. Knowing that these chemicals are present in healthy plants and probably function as anti-infection agents, scientists now need to determine

their role after a pathogen has infected the plants.
U.S. Horticulture Research Lab, Orlando, FL
Stanley Nemec, Jr., (305) 897-7344

Mom was right when she said don't put tomatoes in the refrigerator, and now there's new evidence to prove it. A new procedure for measuring amounts of key flavor chemicals in tomatoes has shown that storing tomatoes in the refrigerator lowers the amount of a flavor component called (Z)-3-hexenal. With the help of taste panels, scientists had earlier identified this chemical as a key ingredient in fresh tomato aroma. But until now, no one had been able to measure the exact amount of (Z)-3-hexenal or other flavor components because of chemical changes that occur when tomatoes are cut open. ARS researchers developed a better method to analyze precisely the amounts of natural chemicals that give fresh tomatoes their flavor. Breeders developing tastier tomatoes can use the test to evaluate the flavor components in new varieties.
Food Quality Research, Western Regional Research Center, Albany, CA
Ronald G. Buttery, (415) 559-5667

To make a good loaf of bread, bakers need wheat containing certain glutenins--the natural proteins that give dough its strength and elasticity. Preparing samples to chemically screen different wheat strains for desired glutenins is a painstaking, all-day task. But a new method takes less than an hour. Chemists have found that dimethyl sulfoxide purifies glutenins by dissolving away nonglutenin protein and starch. Then the glutenins can be dissolved in other chemicals and identified by a high-tech method called reversed-phase, high-performance liquid chromatography.
Plant Protein Research, Northern Regional Research Center, Peoria, IL
Jerold A. Bietz, (309) 685-4011 ext. 594

Sugar-snap cookies are traditionally made with flour from soft wheat. Now scientists have found that sugar snaps can

also be made from the flour of hard wheats if a commercial enzyme preparation made from papaya is added to the dough. Traditionally, hard winter and hard spring wheat flours have been known as bread wheats because of their higher content of glutens--the proteins that help bread rise. Using hard wheat flour for cookie dough usually results in smaller cookies. But adding the papaya enzyme preparation to the dough let the cookies turn out as large as those made from soft wheat flour. The discovery gives the baking industry more flexibility in choosing wheat flours and may open a new market for hard wheat growers from South Dakota to Texas.
Soft Wheat Quality Lab, Wooster, OH
Charles S. Gaines, (216) 263-3891

When it comes to flavor, U.S. peanuts fare better in world markets than those grown by three competing countries-- China, Argentina and Malawi. That was the preliminary finding after the first year of a joint ARS/industry study. An agency flavor panel said U.S. peanuts had the highest intensity of roasted peanut and other positive flavors--and less bitterness and other off-flavors. Chemical analysis of the peanuts supported the panel's findings. Agency scientists and the U.S. peanut industry plan more studies over the next 2 years to confirm these findings--as part of an overall strategy to increase U.S. peanut exports.
Food Flavor Quality Research, Southern Regional Research Center, New Orleans, LA
John Vercellotti, (504) 286-4421

New products often come from old research. This year, for example, Heinz USA began selling partially defatted roasted peanuts nationwide under the Weight Watchers label. The process for making the peanuts is based on technology agency scientists developed more than 20 years ago. They found a chemical-free way to remove some of the fat from raw peanuts by using a press, which squeezes out about 50% of the oil. Raw peanuts don't crumble like roasted ones and regain their shape. After they are

11

squeezed, the peanuts are moistened with hot water before being roasted in oil for 5 minutes. Water steaming out of the peanut prevents oil from reentering. The result: a crunchy peanut with about 50% less fat than normal peanuts. Besides Heinz, Paul's Peanuts sells partially defatted peanuts based on this technology.
Food and Feed Processing Research, Southern Regional Research Center, New Orleans, LA
Joseph Pominski, (504) 286-4338

Chinese chestnuts have about the same amounts of nutritious proteins as American chestnuts. That's good news for consumers as well as for American growers who are replacing American trees with Chinese species resistant to chestnut blight disease, which virtually wiped out chestnut trees in the eastern United States in the early 20th century. In a cooperative study, the first of its kind for chestnuts, ARS and USDA's Human Nutrition Information Service found no significant differences between the two chestnut species in essential amino acids, the main components of proteins.
Horticultural Crops Quality, Richard B. Russell Center, Athens, GA
Filmore I. Meredith, (404) 546-3150

Nutmeg and mace may one day be used not only as cooking spices, but as natural controls for insects that infest stored wheat and other cereal grains. In lab studies, oil extracts of these spices—from the fruit of the evergreen tree Myristica fragrans—killed 10% to 20% of two beetle pests and 30% to 40% of rice weevils at doses of 30 micrograms per insect. And the extracts, sprayed on wheat at concentrations of 2,000 parts per million, repelled rice weevils for up to 4 months. Natural controls such as these are needed as insects become more resistant to malathion and other synthetic chemicals.
Stored-Product Insects Research and Development Lab, Savannah, GA
Helen C.F. Su, (912) 233-7981

Grapes fumigated with sulfur dioxide are protected from Botrytis rot, but dosages of the fumigant must be adjusted according to the kind of box the fruit is packed in. Results from ARS experiments with Thompson Seedless, Ribier and Emperor grapes show packers and shippers how to tailor dosages for today's polystyrene foam and fiberboard cartons, which absorb different amounts of the fumigant. Until now, fumigation was based on storing grapes in traditional wooden boxes (which are no longer used commercially in the United States for shipping) or in wood-kraft-veneer boxes. Precision application of the fumigant helps keep sulfite residues below the legal limit of 10 parts per million. That limit protects consumers who are allergic to sulfites, yet also saves grapes from rot while they're in cold storage. Grapes that receive too little fumigant will decay, while those that get too much may be damaged by the chemical.
Horticultural Crops Research Lab, Protection and Quarantine Unit, Fresno, CA
C.M. Harris, (209) 453-3000

The bacterial disease fire blight kills fruit tree plant tissue leaving branches looking as if they'd been burned. A study by ARS scientists showed no Erwinia amylovora bacteria that cause the blight were found inside or outside 755 apples harvested from blighted trees. Based on this study, the scientists believe Washington State apples pose no threat to countries where fire blight is absent. Such studies are designed to help Pacific Northwest apple growers overcome import restrictions imposed on U.S. fruits in countries like Japan, which limit apple imports to prevent diseases from entering their country.
Tree Fruit Research Lab, Wenatchee, WA
Rodney G. Roberts, (509) 662-4317

Researchers have found a plantain variety, Lacknau, that is resistant to the corn weevil—possibly setting the stage for the natural control of a pest that costs banana and plantain growers millions of dollars each year. Plantains are large first cousins of the banana that have become increasingly popular

with consumers. Imports of plantains rose from about 85,000 metric tons in 1983 to almost 123,000 metric tons in 1987. Without pesticides, Lacknau plantains in recent tests suffered 77% less damage per plant while yielding 30% more fruit than Maricongo, the commonly raised commercial variety. And in taste tests, 59% of a taste panel chose fried Lacknau slices over Maricongo. However, 90% of the same panel preferred Maricongo chips (prepared like potato chips) to those of Lacknau.
Tropical Crops and Germplasm Research, Mayaguez, PR
Heber Irizarry, (809) 834-2435

Answers to some of the marketing problems caused by broken kernels of corn may not be far off. Researchers studying how to minimize damage to six common yellow dent corn types discovered that low-temperature drying--under 180°F--makes kernels much less likely to break or develop stress cracks that increase the chances of breakage. Scientists also discovered that some varieties of corn tend to tolerate poor handling and harvesting damage better than others. They are now focusing on crossing harder flint corn varieties with yellow dent corns that have softer characteristics to develop corn that resists damage while yielding well.
Food Physical Chemistry Research, Peoria, IL
A.J. Peplinski, (309) 685-4011

Lemont, a rice variety developed by ARS scientists in cooperation with Texas A&M researchers, has had an economic impact of over $3 billion in Texas, Louisiana, Arkansas and Mississippi between 1983 (when the variety was released) and 1987. The cultivar, one of the first semidwarf varieties of rice developed for the southern U.S. rice-growing region, has lowered production costs in that region from $12.43 per hundred pounds in 1983 to $8.20 in 1987. Because the semidwarf variety is very high yielding, has excellent quality and resists lodging (falling over in high winds), Lemont has become one of the major rice cultivars grown in the United States.
Rice Research, Beaumont, TX
Charles N. Bollich, (409) 752-2741

A fly leg in your soup: the restaurant-goer's worst fear. To help prevent that from happening, the Food and Drug Administration asked ARS to find out how far fly parts scatter when house flies are caught in electrocuting traps. To be safe, wall-mounted traps should be 6 feet away from food areas, studies show, while ceiling-hung traps should be 10 feet away. These recommendations are safe even if there is a 5-mph breeze--such as that from a strong fan--blowing through the kitchen. The four major manufacturers of industrial restaurant fly traps, which cooperated by supplying them for the studies, can now use the data to recommend to restaurants which trap to buy and where to put it. In addition, state health inspectors can use the new FDA recommendation to make sure restaurants have traps a "healthy" distance from food.
Livestock Insects Lab, Beltsville, MD
Lawrence Pickens, (301) 344-2974

HUMAN NUTRITION

Dietary iron may do more than prevent tired blood; it may also quell chattering teeth. A new study indicates that a person's ability to regulate or maintain body temperature in the cold may depend on his or her daily intake of iron. And these changes in metabolism occur before a person becomes anemic. In the study, six healthy young women consumed less than one-third the Recommended Dietary Allowance of iron for 80 days. Afterwards, when exposed to a cool temperature, they not only generated less body heat but also lost more body heat than they did after a 114-day period of replenishing their iron stores with supplements. More than half of the American women between ages 11 and 50 consume less than the recommended iron intake. This could explain why these women may be more affected by cold temperatures.
Grand Forks Human Nutrition Research Center, Grand Forks, ND
Henry C. Lukaski, (701) 795-8429

. . . And low copper or iron could be the culprit if you're sleeping more and enjoying it less. The findings of five controlled studies on trace element nutrition are the first to link body stores of trace elements with sleep behavior. Women in the studies answered eight questions each morning about how long and how well they slept. Their responses were correlated with dietary intake and blood plasma levels of the element in question. Of seven elements studied, copper, iron and aluminum most strongly altered sleep patterns. Low copper intake (0.8 milligram/day) prompted the most sleep problems, followed by low iron intake (5 milligrams/day). In both cases, sleep time increased and its quality decreased. The findings are from long-term intakes and don't mean that a copper or iron supplement will act as a sleeping pill. High doses of the non-essential element aluminum--common with regular use of antacids--decreased sleep quality only. The findings with calcium, magnesium, manganese and zinc were less conclusive and will be studied further. Grand Forks Human Nutrition Research Center, Grand Forks, ND
James G. Penland, (701) 795-8471

Older women can maintain healthy bones through endurance exercise despite the fact that the exercise makes them leaner and reduces circulating estrogen--two factors that normally increase risk of osteoporosis. A recent study compared 15 women between 55 and 70 years of age, who had been running at least 10 miles per week for 2 or more years, with 18 sedentary women of the same age range. The runners averaged 20 pounds lighter and 5% less body fat than the sedentary women even though they consumed more calories. And the runners had lower blood levels of estrone--the primary circulating form of estrogen in postmenopausal women. But bone density was the same for both groups, meaning the runners had greater bone mineral content for their weight. None of the runners began running until after menopause; and their level of exercise before menopause was about the same as the sedentary group's, indicating they didn't start with more bone mass. Human Nutrition Research Center on Aging at Tufts, Boston, MA
William Evans, (617) 556-3076

Senior citizens who get their vitamin A at the drug counter, rather than from fruits and vegetables, may be building up toxic levels. A recent study found that prolonged daily use of supplements containing retinyl esters--the pure form of A used in multivitamins--could lead to low-level toxicity. Although retinyl esters are not toxic themselves, once in the blood they can be converted into free retinol, which is toxic. In a survey of 562 men and women over 60, half reported taking supplements, mostly as multi-vitamin/multimineral preparations. Five participants who had taken the preparations daily for more than 5 years had retinyl ester levels two to three times normal. And four of the five had early signs of liver damage, a signal of chronic toxicity. Their daily dosage ranged from as little as the Recommended Dietary Allowance for vitamin A (5,000 IU's) to four times the RDA. Younger people apparently don't have the same buildup of retinyl esters, the researchers found. This suggests that elderly Americans should get their vitamin A from fruits and vegetables rich in beta carotene--a nontoxic source. These include carrots, squash, tomatoes, dark-green leafy vegetables, peaches and apricots. Human Nutrition Research Center on Aging at Tufts, Boston, MA
Stephen Krasinski, (617) 956-5864

Vitamin C supplements may someday be prescribed for mild hypertension if recent findings hold up under more intensive research. An extra gram (1,000 mg) of vitamin C each day for 6 weeks significantly reduced blood sodium levels and sodium-to-potassium ratios in 12 men and women with mildly elevated blood pressure. These changes did not occur in eight men and women with normal blood pressure. Although the human body keeps a tight rein on blood sodium levels, they frequently run at the high end of normal in hypertensive people. The vitamin C supplements also lowered systolic pressure in the hypertensives but did not affect diastolic pressure--the one that concerns doctors most. ARS cooperated with researchers from Alcorn State University (Mississippi) in this carefully controlled study. The findings

corroborate an earlier report indicating vitamin C might be effective against borderline hypertension.
Carbohydrate Nutrition Lab, Beltsville Human Nutrition Research Center, Beltsville, MD
David L. Trout, (301) 344-2386

The old maxim, "You are what you eat," is proving truer than ever. It appears that dietary fat harbors more than extra calories; it also has a tendency to turn into body fat. In the first human study of its kind, 28 women consumed a high-fat diet (40% fat) for 4 months, then switched to a low-fat diet (20% fat) with the same number of calories for 4 more months. Carbohydrates replaced fat calories in the low-fat diet. The women's fat-to-lean ratio was assessed at the end of each period. After the low-fat period, they averaged 1% less body fat even though their weight remained constant. Although these findings are the first to confirm this effect in people, they agree with results of similar studies in animals. Cutting dietary fat helps to trim body fat in two ways-- by reducing the tendency to deposit fat as well as calories--not to mention other health benefits.
Energy and Protein Nutrition Lab, Beltsville Human Nutrition Research Center, Beltsville, MD
Joan M. Conway, (301) 344-2977

Large doses of vitamin C don't reduce copper levels in people the way they reportedly do in laboratory animals. Eight women got daily vitamin C supplements containing 25 times the Recommended Dietary Allowance (1.5 grams) while consuming two diets--one low and one adequate in copper. With one exception, the supplements did not significantly affect copper retention or commonly measured indices of copper metabolism during either diet. They did depress the activity of a copper-containing enzyme, ceruloplasmin, as noted in a previous human study, but scientists don't know how this might affect the body.
Grand Forks Human Nutriton Research Center, Grand Forks, ND
David Milne, (701) 795-8424

Sound waves are helping scientists accurately measure infants' fat vs. lean tissue as they grow. The new, harmless method will enable researchers to determine how breastmilk or formula affects an infant's body composition and what a normal growth pattern looks like. Comparable to underwater weighing in adults, the method is based on an established physical principle that the resonant frequency of a chamber is inversely proportional to its volume. That is, the less air space in the chamber, the higher the resonant frequency. Researchers measure the frequency of sound from an empty acrylic box, then place an infant inside and measure the change in this frequency. The difference is used to calculate the infant's volume, which, together with body weight, is used to calculate body fat. The researchers have also adopted a more sophisticated equation to calculate body fat than is typically used for adults, because infants' body composition changes as they grow.
Children's Nutrition Research Center at Baylor, Houston, TX
Hwai-Ping Sheng, (713) 799-6013

Dietary fiber is touted as a preventive of heart disease, diabetes, obesity and possibly some forms of cancer. But it causes real headaches for chemists who have to measure it in foods. Now a simplified version of the method adopted by the Association of Official Analytical Chemists for determining dietary fiber gets rid of a lot of the fuss and muss but yields comparable results. Chemists will be able to analyze more samples with half the personal attention and at half the cost. The method could help speed up fiber information on foods if validated in further tests now being arranged by USDA's Human Nutrition Information Service, which publishes comprehensive food composition tables known as Agriculture Handbook 8. The simplified method also appears to be better than the official U.S. method for distinguishing between soluble and insoluble fiber--an important point since different types of fiber reportedly have different health benefits. HNIS will eventually list both fiber types in Agriculture Handbook 8.

15

Nutrient Composition Lab, Beltsville
Human Nutrition Research Center,
Beltsville, MD
Betty Li, (301) 344-2466

Diabetics--who have twice the rate of
heart disease as nondiabetics--may not
benefit from taking fish oil, which is
being sold in capsules to help prevent
heart disease. People with uncontrolled
type II (mature-onset) diabetes have high
blood triglyceride levels, which is also
a risk factor for heart disease. In
studies with nondiabetic animals and
people, fish oil rapidly lowered blood
triglycerides. Does it have the same
effect on diabetics? Not when scientists
tested it in an obese strain of rats that
has all the symptoms of human type II
diabetes. After 4 weeks on a diet containing menhaden oil (from the Atlantic
herring), the rats' blood triglyceride,
glucose and insulin levels were just as
high as those who got corn oil instead.

Lipid Nutrition Lab, Beltsville Human
Nutrition Research Center, Beltsville,
MD
Norberta Schoene, (301) 344-2388

A high calcium intake plus whole grains
at mealtime can actually subtract iron
from the body. These and earlier findings indicate that taking a large calcium
supplement at or close to a meal could
reduce iron stores, particularly in many
women who don't consume enough iron.
Whole grains contain phytate--a constituent of bran that can bind to minerals in
the intestine and carry them out in the
stool. And animal studies have indicated
that calcium enhances this phytate-
mineral binding. While phytate levels in
most American diets don't significantly
reduce mineral absorption, will calcium
supplements tip the balance? Nine men
ate meals containing nearly twice the
average intake of phytate together with
three levels of calcium in food and
supplements. Calcium levels of 600 and
1,100 milligrams did not increase iron or
zinc in the stool. But 1,600 milligrams
of calcium significantly increased stool
iron levels and slightly increased stool

zinc. The Recommended Dietary Allowance
for calcium is 800 milligrams, but a
consensus panel at the National Institutes of Health suggests an intake of
1,500 milligrams for postmenopausal
women. Such a dose taken with high-fiber
meals could reduce the bioavailability of
iron.

Vitamin and Mineral Lab, Beltsville Human
Nutrition Research Center,
Beltsville, MD
Eugene Morris, (301) 344-2282

A major improvement in analyzing foods
for zinc, copper and other trace elements
should mean more comprehensive and more
accurate food labeling in the future.
With a new ultrasonic mixing technique, a
chemist can prepare a slurry of a finely
ground food sample (or other biological
sample) in minutes--instead of the hours
or days it now takes to digest the sample
completely for analysis. And the new
sample preparation has been designed to
fit into a fully automated system for
routine analyses of trace elements.
Because it cuts out most of the steps and
reagents now used, there is far less
chance of human error or contamination by
trace elements ever present in the testing laboratory. (PATENT)

Nutrient Composition Lab, Beltsville
Human Nutrition Research Center,
Beltsville, MD
Nancy Miller-Ihli, (301) 344-2252

Scientific Information Systems

Wheat Wiz, a new computer program, helps
farmers compare over 180 varieties of
hard red winter wheat to select the ones
that are best for them. Important traits
such as winter hardiness, maturity,
height, color, yield, and insect and
disease resistance are described for each
variety. When asked to recommend varieties having particular traits, the
computer program takes into account the
farmer's geographical location, farming
methods, and past problems with crop
pests and diseases. Although the
database in Wheat Wiz applies
specifically to Kansas, the program--

which can be run on most personal computers—could be useful to farmers and growers elsewhere, as well as to researchers, extension specialists, consultants and teachers. Wheat Wiz diskettes are available from Kansas State University.
Wheat Genetics Research, Manhattan, KS
Thomas S. Cox, (913) 532-7260

Different plant species use sunlight at different rates. Even within species, this rate varies according to the location and conditions the plant is growing in. But in building computer models to simulate plant growth, many scientists assume a rate for a species based on data from only one location and set of conditions. Now, more precise rates are available for five grain species. ARS scientists analyzed data from several countries to compare a crop's growth of biomass—dry plant matter—to the amount of sunlight its leaves intercepted. Of the five species tested, they found that corn is the most efficient user of sunlight. Compared to it, average rates of growth per sunlight unit were 62% for rice, 64% for sunflowers, 79% for wheat and 82% for sorghum. Knowing these rates should help modelers simulate growth and yield more accurately.
Natural Resources Systems Research, Temple, TX
James R. Kiniry, (817) 770-6506

Farm ponds, lakes and reservoirs may be slowing down the Earth's buildup of carbon dioxide in the atmosphere. Sediment samples from 58 small agricultural reservoirs throughout the country show these water bodies are a missing "sink" in the carbon cycle. Carbon dioxide goes into the air from burning fossil fuels; plants take in CO_2 and gradually release it back into the air when they die and decay. But some carbon in decaying plant material is carried away with eroded soil to bodies of water. The study shows it's trapped there and won't be re-released to the air for a very long time. Researchers estimate that 4% to 6% of the total carbon originally released each year to the atmosphere by burning fuel ends up in reservoirs after being taken up by plants. Understanding the carbon cycle is essential to creating computer models that will predict crop yields in a high-CO_2 world.
Hydrology Lab, Beltsville, MD
rry C. Ritchie, (301) 344-1717

Low-cost soil phosphorus tests which are widely used to measure plant available phosphorus for producing crops can now be used to estimate the phosphorus content that promotes algae and aquatic weed growth in lakes. The prediction and management of both phosphorus fertilization and erosion to control the premature aging and algae production in receiving lakes requires knowing what portion of the phosphorus in field runoff is algae-available. Unfortunately, direct laboratory measurements of algae-available phosphorus are much too time consuming and expensive to be practical. ARS and the Penn State College of Agriculture jointly developed the relationships and correlations needed to make these estimates, using 27 soils from 19 eastern and central states.
Northeast Watershed Research Lab, University Park, PA
Harry B. Pionke, (814) 865-2048

Aerial photographs and satellite images can be used to more accurately estimate forage production on rangelands. The technique being tested is aimed at helping rangeland resource managers like those in USDA's Soil Conservation Service interpret aerial imagery. In a recent study of six important forage grasses, a spectroradiometer was used to vertically measure light reflected from plant canopies. Results showed certain light wavelengths could be used to identify the amount of ground covered and water content by individual grass species, as well as the height and yield of the forage. The technique works best when grasses are in early growth stages.
Remote Sensing Research, Weslaco, TX
James H. Everitt, (512) 968-5533

Drought-Related Research (continued)

out. They soaked seed of U.S. and African sorghums in the chemical, abscisic acid, and grew seedlings in the greenhouse. Then they deprived the seedlings of water. Of the African sorghums, 42% from the treated group and 36% from an untreated group survived, compared to only 25% and 7%, respectively, of the U.S. sorghum seedlings. In other experiments, water-stressed seedlings were transplanted outdoors; they were then given enough water to avoid stress. Result: both the U.S. and African plants grown from seed soaked in abscisic acid outyielded those from untreated seed. Researchers are now trying to determine if the African sorghums have a naturally higher accumulation of abscisic acid during early growth.
Wheat and Sorghum Research, Lincoln, NE
Charles Y. Sullivan, (402) 472-3058

In the United States, about 65% of the peanuts grown are not irrigated, so peanut harvests are very susceptible to drought damage. Scientists are evaluating peanut cultivars, breeding lines and exotic germplasm, including commercial varieties grown in Africa and India. Attributes being studied include root density and length and the ability to maintain plant hydration, as well as other traits that can help the crop better tolerate drought. Once promising genotypes are identified, they can be developed by breeders into new, more drought-tolerant varieties.
Plant Science and Water Conservation Lab, Stillwater, OK
Darold L. Ketring, (405) 624-4361

Some potato varieties, like Nooksack, developed by ARS, tolerate drought better than the popular Russet Burbank. Under dry conditions, the meaty, tasty Nooksack produced as much as 60% U.S. No. 1 potatoes, whereas Russet Burbank only reached 40%.
Irrigated Agriculture and Extension Center, Prosser, WA
David E. Miller, (509) 786-3454

Researchers have found more drought-tolerant strains of rhizobia. These microorganisms on roots of soybeans and other legumes allow the plants to take in nitrogen from the air. The drought-tolerant strains can survive longer in dry soils and apparently lend to their soybean host the ability to go longer without water. While researchers don't yet have drought-tolerant rhizobia ready for commercial use, they expect drought resistance to be part of evaluations of new rhizobia strains. The current selection method is based on nitrogen accumulation and yield potential.
Coastal Plains Soil and Water Conservation Research Lab, Florence, SC
Patrick Hunt, (803) 669-5203

Scientists have found a single recessive gene, tr, that substantially increases drought tolerance in pearl millet, a crop grown as a forage in the United States and as a grain in many arid Third World countries. The gene's physical expression—leaves with a thick, shiny wax cuticle or "skin" and without tiny surface hairs—helps the plant conserve moisture. Under drought conditions, pearl millet with these traits had forage yields as much as 25% higher than equivalent varieties without the traits. With adequate water, yields were similar. Drought tolerance conferred by the tr gene could be a major plus in areas where pearl millet is a grain crop. Yield increases are offset when the crop is grown for forage because the waxy cuticle makes leaves less digestible. Future improvements in genetic engineering may allow the tr gene to be introduced into other grain crops, improving their drought tolerance.
Coastal Plain Experiment Station, Tifton GA,
Glenn W. Burton, (912) 386-3353.

Qua

Quarterly Report
of Selected Research Projects

United States
Department of
Agriculture

Agricultural
Research
Service

July 1 to September 30, 1988

Contents

Human Nutrition

Can megadoses of vitamin E recharge the immune system of older people? Preliminary results of a study of 34 men and women over age 60 indicate yes. Compared to those who got a placebo, the volunteers who took huge daily doses of vitamin E for 30 days showed a significant improvement in two measurements of immune response analyzed so far. If test results continue to be positive, it could mean better protection against infections for older Americans who are most susceptible. The daily dose of vitamin E in this study was 800 international units. That's 53 and 67 times the Recommended Dietary Allowance for men and women, respectively. Further research is needed to tell if a lower dose might be as effective.
Human Nutrition Research Center on Aging at Tufts, Boston, MA
Simin N. Meydani, (617) 556-3129

Note: One or more scientists familiar with each research project are listed for further information. If the scientists are unavailable, others at the same telephone number may also be familiar with the work.

Items marked with the word PATENT are being patented by ARS. For more information contact Ann Whitehead, National Patent Program, Bldg. 005, Rm. 401, Beltsville Agricultural Research Center, Beltsville, MD 20705, (301) 344-2786.

A low-fat diet won't necessarily lower cholesterol in women before menopause. A study by National Cancer Institute and ARS scientists indicates that healthy, pre-menopausal women with low cholesterol levels may not reduce their chance of heart disease by replacing dietary fat with carbohydrates. But they might benefit from replacing saturated with unsaturated fat. In the study, 31 women between 20 and 40 years of age had an insignificant drop in total cholesterol after eating a low-fat diet (20 percent fat) for four months. (They had very low cholesterol to begin with.) In fact, because of the extra carbohydrates in the low-fat diet, their blood triglycerides went up an average 32 percent compared to levels during the high-fat (40 percent) portion of the study. However, the type of fat in their diets made a difference in the type of cholesterol that was reduced--which has been observed in other studies. Women whose ratio of polyunsaturated-to-saturated fat intake was balanced one-to-one lost the "bad" LDL cholesterol, which is good. Those who got three times more saturated fat lost significantly more "good" HDL cholesterol and had a greater rise in triglycerides, which is not good.
Lipid Nutrition Lab, Beltsville Human Nutrition Research Center, Beltsville, MD
Joseph T. Judd, (301) 344-2014

.. And a high-fiber diet may not help ward off heart disease or diabetes in men unless they reduce their saturated fat and cholesterol intakes at the same time. Twelve healthy men alternated between a high- and low-fiber intake while eating a typical high-fat, high-cholesterol diet for 12 weeks. Fiber intake differed fivefold from twice the typical American intake (25 grams) to less than half (5 g). But the men had an insignificant drop in blood cholesterol due to the extra fiber and no change in triglyceride or uric acid levels (both indicators of risk of heart disease) or in fasting blood glucose levels (a measure of risk of diabetes). On the plus side, the high-fiber diet did not appear to rob the body of essential trace minerals, even though it also contained high levels of oxalic acid--a component of spinach and a few other foods known to block mineral absorption. Plasma levels of zinc, copper, calcium and magnesium remained the same or increased throughout the study. Only phosphorus levels dipped, but that was due to the oxalic acid, not to the extra fiber.
Carbohydrate Nutrition Lab, Beltsville Human Nutrition Research Center, Beltsville, MD
Daniel Scholfield, (301) 344-2385

It takes more than copper deficiency to provoke symptoms of heart disease and cause sudden death of animals that don't get the mineral in their feed. Seven years of studies point to a three-way interaction: the dire consequences of copper deficiency occur only to male animals and only when their feed contains substantial amounts of fructose. (Fructose accounts for half the sugar in table sugar and in high-fructose corn sweeteners.) Male animals on such a diet accumulate at least twice as much sorbitol--an alcohol byproduct of sugar metabolism--in their tissues as do females or males who get starch instead of fructose. Sorbitol has the ability to bind copper, potentially making the animals even more deficient. Why male animals accumulate sorbitol and females don't is not known. The alcohol is known to accumulate in certain tissues of diabetics--even those who use insulin to control blood sugar levels--causing inevitable damage to eyes, nerves and kidneys. The findings indicate an urgent need to answer the many unknowns about how the human body metabolizes carbohydrates, particularly fructose.
Carbohydrate and Vitamin and Mineral Nutrition Labs, Beltsville Human Nutrition Research Center, Beltsville, MD
Meira Fields, (301) 344-2417

To protect their infants, pregnant and nursing women may want to go easy on sodas and processed foods containing high-fructose corn sweeteners or table sugar (sucrose), which is half fructose. It's well established that this sugar aggravates copper deficiency in animals. Recent studies with pregnant and lactating rats show that a very high fructose intake can cause deficiency in developing pups even when their mothers' copper intake is adequate. Such a diet, containing 62 percent fructose--about 5 times the level in a typical American diet--reduced the copper in mothers' milk by 33 percent compared to a diet containing starch instead of fructose. The pups of mothers on the high-fructose diet averaged 50 percent less copper in the liver, the organ that stores copper and regulates circulating levels. And male pups had only half as much copper in their livers as female pups. If the mothers' diets were also copper-deficient, none of the pups survived. The findings with rats suggest that more research is needed on the interaction between fructose and copper and its potential impact on pregnant and nursing women.
Carbohydrate and Vitamin and Mineral Nutrition Labs, Beltsville Human Nutrition Research Center, Beltsville, MD
Meira Fields, (301) 344-2417

Mother's milk can help very premature infants get a head start. And scientists are close to overcoming the biggest hurdle--getting enough calcium and phosphorus in the breast milk in a form the infants can absorb. A shortage of these minerals could slow growth, impair healing of chronic lung diseases and lead to bone malformations. They want to tube-feed mother's milk rather than commercial formula from birth because breast milk contains immune factors that can help these highly susceptible premies fight infections. It's also more digestible. But like commercial formula, it has to be fortified with the extra protein, calories and minerals that very low-birth-weight infants need for normal growth and development. So far, these infants have absorbed more calcium and phosphorus from the breast-milk formula than from the two commercial products for premies tested. (There are only five such products on the market.)
Children's Nutrition Research Center, Houston, TX
Richard Schanler, (713) 799-4297

Very premature infants who are breastfed after leaving the hospital are likely to have a lower bone mineral content than those who get a commercial formula, a study shows. But the researchers believe this risk does not outweigh the benefits of breastfeeding. In a year-long followup of infants born 10 to 13 weeks before term, those fed mother's milk after being released from the hospital had a significantly slower rate of bone mineralization than those fed a cow-milk-based formula. The findings suggest that mother's milk may need to be fortified with extra minerals for a longer period. There was no difference in body weight or length or head circumference between the two groups, indicating that the premies grow equally well on breast milk or formula. Pediatricians should periodically check the mineral status of breastfed premies through standard lab tests.
Children's Nutrition Research Center, Houston, TX
Richard Schanler, (713) 798-7176

The recommended daily intake of copper may be higher than necessary, if results from a 3-month study of 11 healthy young men prove true for other Americans. At different times, volunteers ate diets that were either at, below, or more than twice the recommended "safe and adequate range" of 2 to 3 milligrams of copper per day. When they received less than half of the currently recommended level they had the highest rate of copper absorption and the least losses and never depleted their body's supply of the mineral. At the higher intake level--more than twice the recommended amount--they had a very low absorption rate and high losses. At the currently recommended level, absorption and losses were midway between the other findings, indicating the body can adapt to a range of intake levels. This suggests that Americans probably get enough copper through their diet, even though the typical intake is about half the amount now believed adequate.
Biochemistry Research, Western Human Nutrition Research Center, San Francisco, CA
Judith R. Turnlund, (415) 556-5953

Body fat can be estimated in black Americans using the same equations developed from studies of white populations, a study shows, even though blacks carry their fat somewhat differently. The difference, however, may explain why blacks are at higher risk for diabetes and heart disease. Contrary to our earlier report, comparisons of 179 black and white volunteers with two of the most common methods for estimating body fat--skinfold thickness and bioelectrical impedance--show there is no need to factor race into the equations for estimating body fat. Skinfold measurements also showed: blacks carried more of their external fat above the waist, and black women had more fat on their backs and less on their upper arms and thighs than white women. It is well established that people who deposit fat in their upper trunk are at higher risk for developing diabetes, high blood pressure and atherosclerosis than those who deposit fat in their hips and thighs.
Energy and Protein Nutrition Lab, Beltsville Human Nutrition Research Center, Beltsville, MD
Joan Conway, (301) 344-2977

Being obese does not necessarily increase the risk of iron deficiency, according to studies with mice. The findings suggest that obese people who eat a well-balanced diet don't need iron supplements. Genetically obese mice absorbed and retained about twice as much iron from test meals as their lean littermates. However, the mineral was distributed differently in the obese animals: iron levels were higher in blood and fat pads and lower in muscle and bone compared with the lean animals. The extra iron absorbed by the obese animals was apparently used to make hemoglobin for their larger volume of blood.
Vitamin and Mineral Lab, Beltsville Human Nutrition Research Center, Beltsville, MD
Mark L. Failla, (301) 344-2148

It's well known that some foods can interact with drugs to alter the effect of the medication. Now research shows that the same thing can happen with a trace element. In this case, the trace element was selenium, for which the body's daily requirement is only about one-fiftieth of a milligram. Collaborating with the Chinese Academy of Preventive Medicine in Beijing, the National Institutes of Health and the Food and Drug Administration, ARS scientists found that a deficiency in selenium magnified the growth inhibiting side effects of the anticancer drug adriamycin, when tested in rats. Those results suggest that a person's selenium status should be checked before adriamycin is used in chemotherapy.
Vitamin and Mineral Nutrition Lab, Beltsville Human Nutrition Center, Beltsville, MD
Orville Levander, (301) 344-2504

New and Improved Products

Tired of ironing cotton clothes? Agency scientists have developed new technology to make cotton fabrics as wrinkle resistant as permanent press blend fabrics. The researchers are patenting a group of chemicals that produce permanent press, 100-percent cotton fabrics that dry smooth even after 65 washings. And there are other advantages: the fabrics are about 20 percent stronger than current ones, creases can be taken out or put in with a hot iron (difficult with current materials) and the new fabrics don't contain formaldehyde, which can irritate the skin and eyes. It will

take several years, however, before consumers find these items on clothing store racks. That's because the chemicals are not available commercially at cost-effective prices. But companies are working to do this, and several textile mills are interested in the new process. (PATENT)
Textile Finishing Chemistry, Southern Regional Research Center, New Orleans, LA
Clark M. Welch, (504) 286-4272

Kenaf studies are resuming at ARS. In the 1960's and 1970's, agency researchers demonstrated that fiber from the plant makes good pulp for newsprint and other paper products. Since the late 1970's, industry interest has blossomed after test runs of kenaf newsprint at several large newspapers. Now, new studies at Lane, OK, and Weslaco, TX, will focus on better meeting kenaf's nutrient and water requirements and on improving its resistance to nematodes and insects. Researchers will also identify the best methods of harvesting and storing the plant, which can grow 15 to 18 feet in less than four months and yield 7 to 12 tons of dry fiber per acre. Besides paper products, kenaf fiber can be turned into rope, carpet backing, roofing felt, fire logs and cattle feed.
Oil Chemical Research, Northern Regional Research Center, Peoria, IL
Marvin O. Bagby, (309) 685-4011

Cornstarch, rice straw, wheat straw and corn stalks can be turned into two widely used industrial chemicals, using a process developed by ARS researchers. Glycolic and oxalic acids are used in processes to dye textiles, tan leather, clean metal and for other applications. They are typically derived from fossil fuels such as petroleum, but farm sources of starch or cellulose can be added to sodium hydroxide solution, then heated under pressure to yield a liquid with surprisingly high amounts of these two chemicals. An increase in the price of oil, or a shortage, might make the process economical. Other promising applications include the use of farm-derived glycolic acid to produce antifreeze (ethylene glycol) and to make biodegradable plastic products. (PATENT)
Processing and Conversion Research, Western Regional Research Center, Albany, CA
John M. Krochta, (415) 559-5860

A small tree native to the northeastern United States may someday join the war on garden pests. Extracts from the bark of the paw paw tree have proved effective in control tests against Mexican bean beetles, melon and pea aphids, striped cucumber beetles, two spotted spider mites, blowfly larvae and cabbage loopers. ARS scientists, working with Purdue University researchers, discovered the bark yields natural pesticides that killed up to 100 percent of the bean beetles and blowfly larvae and at least 50 percent of the aphids and spider mites at various concentrations. In tests on beetles and aphids, the paw paw pesticides equaled or exceeded control by pyrethrin and rotenone, two widely used natural insecticides. Further testing is ahead to verify results and improve yield from the bark. (PATENT)
Bioactive Constituents Research, Northern Regional Research Center, Peoria, IL
Richard G. Powell, (309) 685-4011

Do you long for a TV dinner with tastier meat than the standard fare? If so, a team of agency "WOF Busters" may have found the answer. WOF, for warmed-over flavor, occurs when oxygen breaks down fats vital to fresh meaty taste. Sometimes termed "cardboardy" or "painty," WOF can develop when uncured meats are reheated. This includes the precooked, frozen meat in TV dinners, as well as that familiar leftover, the family meatloaf. But in lab studies, scientists found that adding just two-hundredths of an ounce of certain proteins to two pounds of ground beef blocked the warmed-over flavor for up to five days. Scientists made this additive by chemically treating chitin, a substance common in shells of lobsters, crabs and other shellfish. These chitin substances bond to iron, preventing it from speeding up fat breakdown. Scientists say there is commercial interest in their process which may work in other meats, poultry and fish. (PATENT)
Food Flavor Quality Research, Southern Regional Research Center, New Orleans, LA
John R. Vercellotti, (504) 286-4421

Pesticides and antibiotics can now be monitored in meat and meat byproducts without harmful chemical solvents. The technology, refined by ARS scientists, relies on heated and pressurized gases such as carbon dioxide to extract chemical residues from meat products. Gas, compressed and made to act as a fluid, flows through the meat to dissolve fat and chemicals in the fat. This separates fat

from the meat product. The food industry has used the technology for several years to decaffeinate coffee, extract hops for flavoring beer and perform other food-processing tasks. Removing pesticides with supercritical extraction could minimize the use of chemical solvents in research and eliminate the problem of disposing of solvent wastes.
Food Physical Chemistry, Northern Regional Research Center, Peoria, IL
Jerry King, (309) 685-4011

Cheesemakers can use a new chemical test to see if their cheeses are properly aged and ready to sell. No routine scientific measure had been suitable for cheeses that develop their characteristic flavor, texture and aroma during ripening. But the new test reveals the breakdown of casein, a milk protein, into small fragments--a normal change that properly cured cheeses undergo as they age. The amount of casein breakdown that has occurred is measured by a purple color that changes in intensity as cheese ages. Commercial dairies could automate the procedure and use it to check such cheeses as cheddar, feta, Monterey Jack, Teleme and Gouda.
Food Safety Research, Western Regional Research Center, Albany, CA
Mendel Friedman, (415) 559-5642

Improving the quality of the 3.6-billion-pound U.S. **peanut crop** may be possible with new tests that agency scientists are evaluating for possible use in the **federal peanut grading system.** The tests could help inspectors remove from the food chain peanuts contaminated with aflatoxin, which is produced by certain fungi. Peanut inspectors now visually examine peanut samples for the presence of the toxin-producing fungi, which can infect drought-stressed peanuts and make them unsafe to eat. The new tests measure aflatoxin directly, letting inspectors know whether aflatoxin levels exceed acceptable limits. In lab studies, one of the new tests was 96 percent accurate, compared to 53 percent for visual inspection.
National Peanut Research Lab, Dawson, GA
Richard J. Cole, (912) 995-4441

A large, firm, high quality peach that ripens uniformly is being released by researchers. The new peach can be mechanically harvested and does not discolor when exposed to air, which makes it desirable for home canning. Appropriately named Bounty, it is very productive, particularly in

areas with dry soil like eastern Texas, and scores "excellent" in taste tests. Researchers recommend planting as a midseason, fresh-market peach in the south central, mid-atlantic, and eastern U.S. Trees, which will be available through commercial nurseries in 1989, should bear fruit about four years after propagation.
Appalachian Fruit Research Station, Kearneysville, WV
Ralph Scorza, (304) 725-3451

Attractive, square plastic boxes could be just the thing for packaging apples for sales in vending machines and 24-hour convenience stores. ARS scientists who tested the commercially manufactured see-through containers found they reduced bruising up to 60 percent. The scientists also found the boxed apples keep better if refrigerated or kept on ice.
Tree Fruit Research Lab, Wenatchee, WA
Stephen R. Drake, (509) 662-4317

Mothballs and the soil fungus *Streptomyces avermitilis* have at least one thing in common: they protect woolen clothing from insects. The fungus produces a chemical called avermectin that in lab studies protected woolen fabric from damaging moths and beetles for up to five years. In the studies, scientists soaked the fabric in a solution of water and avermectin for 15 minutes and then exposed the fabric to insect pests. The result: the chemical killed webbing clothes moths and furniture carpet beetle larvae and repelled black carpet beetle larvae. Scientists say avermectin, now used as a drug to kill worms in animals, is relatively nontoxic to the skin and has potential to be a new mothproofing spray.
Stored-Product Insects Research and Development Lab, Savannah, GA
Roy E. Bry, (912) 233-7981

How do disease-causing bacteria and fungi invade plants? Scientists have taken a step toward answering this question by studying *Pseudomonas marginalis*, a bacterium that rots bell peppers, spinach, lettuce and other vegetables and fruits. Researchers have isolated three key carbohydrates secreted by *P. marginalis* that may help the organism survive on the plant and cause rotting. Once scientists

determine how these carbohydrates work, they will look for enzymes to counteract them. The long-term goal: to improve a plant's self-defenses by genetically engineering these enzymes into the plants to help them ward off disease-causing organisms.
Plant Science Research, Eastern Regional Research Center, Philadelphia, PA
Stanley F. Osman/William F. Fett, (215) 233-6419/6418

Soybean proteins for the first time can be easily extracted, separated and identified. This is important news for processors and breeders since protein content is a key factor in determining price and the best potential uses for soybeans--from animal feed to cooking oil. Protein content also indicates how well the soybean holds up in storage, regardless of intended use. The new wrinkle is a technique called high performance liquid chromatography (HPLC), which until now was used only on cereal grains. HPLC also lets scientists "fingerprint" soybean varieties based on differences in protein--which also wasn't possible before. The method is quick and simple and can be fully automated.
Soil Drainage Research, Columbus, OH
Tara T. Van Toai, (614) 292-9806

"Suspended animation" roughly describes plant cells after they've been soaked in a natural growth regulator that also inhibits animal tumor growth. Scientists found that camptothecin, a chemical produced by a tree found in China, inhibits the growth of fescue grass and controls potato sprouting. Camptothecin appears to work in a unique way--by blocking production of a plant enzyme that regulates the genetic material, DNA, formed in a plant. This, in turn, shuts down cell growth and puts the plant in a kind of "suspended animation." Camptothecin is being studied by the National Cancer Institute as a possible anticancer compound because of its ability to control animal tumor growth. It also has the potential to become a new type of plant growth regulator.
Plant Hormone Lab, Beltsville, MD
J. George Buta, (301) 344-3598

Plant biochemists and biotechnologists have a new tool to help them study how plant root cells take in nutrients from the soil. For the first time scientists isolated and purified an enzyme, cytochrome c oxidase, from corn roots. Until now, this enzyme--known to help plants take in nutrients--has been difficult to study because methods to extract it usually destroyed its ability to function. With a new extraction method, however, the enzyme maintains 91 percent of its activity.
Macromolecular and Cell Structure Research, Eastern Regional Research Center, Philadelphia, PA
Nicholas Parris, (215) 233-6453

Biological Control

Natural chemicals produced by fungi can biologically control corn earworms and fall armyworms as effectively as commercial insecticides. But more research is needed before the fungi can be commercially available to farmers. Larvae of both insects were fed compounds from several fungi, primarily in the genus *Penicillium*. Two of the compounds tested--penitrem A and roseotoxin B--were found to be most effective. Fall armyworms fed 25 parts per million penitrem A grew to just half the size of larvae on a control diet. Corn earworms reacted similarly to 25 parts per billion. Roseotoxin B fed at 25 ppm killed all the fall armyworms and more than 30 percent of the corn earworms within two days. Researchers will now try to determine why the compounds are so effective and which sites of biologcal activity are affected in a larva's body. (PATENT)
Mycotoxin Research, Northern Regional Research Center, Peoria, IL
Patrick F. Dowd, (309) 685-4011

A seed-eating insect and a group of hitchhiking fungi may give farmers a dual biological weapon against velvetleaf, a serious weed in row crops such as soybeans, corn and cotton. The insect--*Niesthrea louisianica*--feeds on immature seeds of velvetleaf. The fungi, mostly from the genera *Fusarium* and *Alternaria*, ride on the insect's stomach, back and legs to mop up the remains. Only about five percent of the seeds attacked by the duo are able to

germinate. No danger is posed to crops since the insect eats only the seeds of velvetleaf and two other weeds--prickly sida and spurred anoda. Additional tests will try to find fungi that are even more effective than those currently teamed with the insect. Researchers hope the insect/fungus combination will someday be available for commercial use.
Crop Production Research, Columbia, MO
Robert J. Kremer, (314) 875-5357

A setback for biological control means good news for the Indianmeal moth--but only for now. A major pest of grain, many processed cereals and other food products, these moths have been building up resistance to the bacterium *Bacillus thuringiensis* (BT), the first biological insecticide approved for stored grain. For years the presumption was that the insect could not build up resistance to the spore-crystal protein complex in BT. Early studies had seemed to confirm this. But now, researchers have discovered that the capacity for resistance to doses of BT that kill most of the mealworms can be widespread within only a few genera-tions of Indian-meal moth strains. More work is on tap to overcome the resistance by determining how it overcomes the BT toxin and whether it occurs with other strains of BT.
U.S. Grain Marketing Research Lab, Manhattan, KS
William H. McGaughey, (913) 776-2705

A delicate fly from Greece is being recruited in the West to stop the spread of yellow starthistle--a weed that pokes hikers, poisons horses and discourages cattle from grazing. The fly, *Chaetorellia australis*, helps keep the weed under control in Greece by feeding on starthistle's developing seeds. ARS researchers in California reared almost 200 flies from larvae living inside starthistle plants collected by agency colleagues in Greece. This year, the insects were set free in a thistle-infested horse pasture near the San Francisco Bay area. It was the first time the fly was released in North America. Additional releases with larger numbers of flies are planned for next year not only in California but also in Idaho, Oregon and Washington, where yellow starthistle is also a problem.
Biological Control of Weeds, Western Regional Research Center, Albany, CA
Charles E. Turner, (415) 559-5975
Biological Control of Weeds, Thessaloniki, Greece
Rouhollah Sobhian, 30-31-473-272
Regional Plant Introduction Station, Pullman, WA
Stephen L. Clement, (509) 335-3572

Insects from South America and the Middle East may help solve brush problems on Southwestern rangeland. Found from California to Texas, brush such as snakeweed and mesquite serves useful purposes, providing emergency grazing, wildlife habitat and in the case of mesquite and saltcedar, ornamental plantings for southwestern yards. But brush also competes with more desirable grass for water and nutrients. Chemical controls are too costly where many acres of land are needed to provide enough grazing for a single cow. Scientists are seeking biological controls such as insects or fungi to fight the brush. South America was picked as a good place to look for natural enemies of brush there that resembles southwestern U.S. species. Saltcedar, which hogs the choicest land next to streams, was intro-duced as an ornamental from the Middle East. Scientists in Texas are already testing imported insects that might be used to suppress rangeland brush to workable levels.
Grassland, Soil and Water Research Lab, Temple, TX
C. Jack DeLoach Jr., (817) 770-6537

Helpful worms known as beneficial nematodes can be dried out, stored, shipped to where they're needed, then re-activated by adding water. It's a new technique developed by an ARS scientist and colleagues at Biosys, a California biotechnology company. Nearly invisible, beneficial nematodes such as *Steinernema feltiae* are natural enemies of home, garden and farm pests, but the expense and problems of storing and shipping them have prevented their wider use as a biological control. They must be mass-reared to get enough of them to be effective. Large numbers can be dried by a technique using osmotic desiccation, a natural process in which water in the worms is pulled out. Benefi-cial nematodes are harmless to humans, pets, birds and plants. (PATENT)
Commodity Protection and Quarantine Insect Research, Fresno, CA
James E. Lindegren, (209) 453-3023

A nematode variety named "kapow" has proven to be a powerful natural enemy of the Mediterranean, melon and oriental fruit flies. These fruit fly species thrive in the Hawaiian Islands and pose a continuing threat to mainland agriculture. Several extremely costly eradication programs have been carried out in Southern California to eliminate hitch-hiking fruit flies. In recent experiments in Hawaii, the microscopic, almost invisible nematodes killed from 89 to 97 percent of the fly larvae when sprayed on the ground with water at the rate of 500 nematodes per fruit-fly larva.

Steinernema feltiae nematodes of the kapow variety move faster than other nematodes in pushing their way through natural openings in larvae to kill them with a special bacterium.
Commodity Protection and Quarantine Insect Research, Fresno, CA
James E. Lindegren, (209) 453-3023

An insect once given a bum wrap for damaging pecans may now be a hero in disguise. *Plagioganthus repletus,* one of the leaf bugs that feed on plants, are now known to prefer dining on three species of pesticide-resistant aphids, the real culprits behind pecan damage. Damage by these aphids and costs for aphicides amounted to $10 million in losses for growers during 1986. To get the jump on aphids during early spring, *P. repletus* hatch from overwintering eggs just ahead of their aphid prey. But pesticide sprays by growers during April and May, when *P. repletus* first appear, kill the wrong insects. Simply not spraying during this period allows *P. repletus* to naturally control aphids on their own. This adds up to more money in the pockets of pecan growers.
Southeastern Fruit and Tree Nut Research Lab, Byron, GA
W.L. Tedders, (404) 238-0421

Chemicals inside leafy spurge may bring scientists closer to eventually controlling this unruly weed infesting the northern Great Plains. Researchers want to use three newly discovered chemicals to match American spurges with their European counterparts. This match is important in identifying and importing European insects such as the flea beetle to the United States for control of the leafy spurge. These imported insects must be placed on spurge plants that closely match the variety of spurge they attack in their homeland. Matching plants merely by the way they look has not worked; comparing the chemicals in the spurges may be the answer. Such chemotaxonomy has already proven successful in helping distinguish different varieties of sunflower and other plants that are similar in appearance yet differ chemically .
Plant Protection Research, Western Regional Research Center, Albany, CA
Gary D. Manners, (415) 559-5813

In the meantime, a North American ant is an unwelcome ally to leafy spurge. Worker ants of the species *Formica obscuripes* tote spurge seeds to their nests where the seeds can escape hungry predators and grow. What attracts the ants is a soft, cream-colored little package, called an elaiosome, that is attached to the weed seeds. The ants eat only the elaiosome, rich in fat and protein, not the seed. Until now, this alliance of ants and plants was not known to occur between a native ant and a foreign weed (leafy spurge originates from Europe and Asia). New experiments will show if the alliance occurs with other foreign weeds that have successfully invaded the United States, such as thistles and scotch broom. Seeds of these plants appear to attract ants.
Rangeland Insect Lab, Bozeman, MT
Robert W. Pemberton, (406) 994-4890

Blackfaced leafhoppers use a "helper" to earn their notoriety for spreading one of the nation's most serious viral diseases of corn. Researchers found that maize chlorotic dwarf virus disease did not infect corn after it was fed on by leafhoppers that had been exposed only to purified virus of a potent strain. However, corn did become infected with the potent strain if the leafhoppers had stopped enroute and picked up an as yet unidentified helper from corn infected with a mild strain. The findings are a step toward understanding how viruses and insects interact and may lead to new strategies for biological control of the disease.
Corn and Soybean Research, Wooster, OH
Roy E. Gingery, (216) 263-3836

Scientific Information Systems

Our GRIN is getting bigger all the time. The Germplasm Resources Information Network now profiles the genetic stuff of 360,000 plant varieties--more than four times as many as when it came on line in 1984. Developed and managed by ARS, the computer network helps scientists and plant breeders determine which seeds they need and where to get them by serving as a centralized inventory for germplasm collections throughout the United States. Recent additions to GRIN's database include collections representing 1,300 varieties of rice and 2,500 varieties of flax. Next to come: pecan collections maintained in Brownwood, TX, and thousands of landscape and garden plants at the U.S. National Arboretum in Washington, D.C. New procedures for making the network more user friendly are being developed and should be in place by 1989.
GRIN Database Management, Beltsville, MD
Jimmy D. Mowder, (301) 344-3318

America's most wanted 235 farm and public health pests are now posted in a computerized database. The North American Immigrant Arthropod Database, NAIAD, systematically distinguishes native insects and mites from those that have immigrated here. Without their normal parasites and diseases to stop them, immigrant arthropods often become serious pests of U.S. crops. The NAIAD is the first single-source reference for scientists to locate names, host range and traits of these unwanted aliens that destroy about 5 to 6 percent of U.S. crops. Although most are less dreadful than gypsy moths or fire ants, their proper and swift identification is essential to developing biological controls and to keeping effective USDA pest exclusion programs at U.S. ports of entry.
Systematic Entomology Lab, Beltsville, MD
Lloyd V. Knutson, (301) 344-3182

TEXCIM, a computer model developed to predict the seasonal onslaught of cotton bollworms in Texas, also turns out to be accurate in South Carolina. The bollworm, which U.S. growers spent $215 million to control last year, is most attracted to well-watered and well-fertilized cotton plants. But TEXCIM, short for Texas Cotton-Insect Model, can predict when the insects will be in the field laying eggs. That information can help growers reduce insect damage by simply delaying irrigating and fertilizing until the peak infestation passes. Researchers had expected TEXCIM to need modifications for South Carolina, but it didn't. This turn of events lets them move faster to integrate TEXCIM into COMAX, the master cotton computer model. COMAX (Cotton Management Expert) was also developed by ARS and is being widely tested by growers throughout the South. Currently, it can create irrigation and fertilizing schedules. With the addition of TEXCIM, it will also be able to take insect pest infestations into account.
Cotton Production Research, Florence, SC
W.M. Thomas, (803) 669-6664

Some TV-watchers are called couch potatoes, but real spuds resemble all people--they take in oxygen and release carbon dioxide, moisture and heat. When potatoes are piled in storage, this breathing process can create excessive heat and moisture that lowers tuber quality. Ventilation can eliminate much of the problem, but storage operators need to choose the right airduct system. ARS scientists are helping by developing a personal computer program to assess the performance of different types of common airducts. The program considers numerous factors, such as the uniformity of air discharge from ducts and a duct's distance from a fan. Researchers are expanding the program to examine airflow in the entire ventilation system for stored potatoes.
Red River Valley Potato Research Lab,
East Grand Forks, MN
Lewis A. Schaper, (218) 773-2473

Close encounters of the video kind could provide the raw data for a computerized system to inspect and grade corn in grain elevators. Researchers are now running preliminary tests on the color video component of this new system. Images of the kernels are broken into thousands of tiny rectangular picture elements (pixels) arranged in a grid. These are scanned by the computer and converted into numerical values corresponding to each pixel's color. Certain colors can signify damage caused by insects, molds, heat, drying operations and other factors related to the corn's transportation and storage. Even when perfected, video grading won't replace human inspectors but the electronic technology could make the inspectors' evaluations more consistent and objective.
U.S. Grain Marketing Research Lab, Manhattan, KS
James L. Steele, (913) 776-2727

Cheese producers could benefit from some recent discoveries about the molecular structure of caseins, the major group of proteins found in milk. Ever since caseins were first studied nearly 60 years ago, scientists have been unsure about their collective molecular structure and interaction with water. The result has been a continual and costly measure of unpredictability in the production of cheese and certain dry-milk products. Now, through a unique combination of lab techniques called small-angle X-ray scattering and NMR (nuclear magnetic resonance), scientists have finally mapped that structure and determined how it traps water in a way that enables caseins to be clotted through enzyme activity. Such clotting is critical to cheesemaking, and understanding the molecular dynamics behind it will help food technologists develop more effective and reliable processing methods.
Macromolecular and Cell Structure Research Lab, Philadelphia, PA
Thomas F. Kumosinski, (215) 233-6475

Crop Production and Protection

Most modern soybean varieties take longer than older varieties to fill their pods with beans. This trait is an unintended consequence of past breeding that focused on yield, but today's breeders are purposely selecting for it. As a result, tomorrow's soybeans could produce higher yields and more efficiently use sunlight, soil fertility and moisture. After crossing two soybean varieties, researchers selected 19 experimental breeding lines based on the flowering and maturity dates, to shorten or lengthen pod-filling periods. In a two-year test, the best early-blooming line with a long pod-filling time outyielded by 10 bushels per acre the best late-blooming line with a short pod-filling time. It also yielded more than the best yielding parent variety, Williams, by six bushels, or 15 percent.
Plant Physiology and Genetics Research, Urbana, IL
Randall L. Nelson, (217) 244-4346

Breeding winter wheat with improved resistance to leaf rust involves many challenges. One is to prevent surprise epidemics caused by spores of new rust races that were carried into a wheat region by the wind. Another challenge is breeding wheat to prevent early spring epidemics caused by locally produced spores that survive winter. These epidemics strike almost every year but are less severe in resistant wheats and after harsh winters. In three recent harsh winters, leaf rust trimmed yields of hard red winter wheat in nursery plots by less than 2 percent. But in 1986, one of the mildest winters of the 1980's, rust cut yields by 9 percent. The higher losses underscore the importance of not only breeding resistant varieties, but also planting them late enough to avoid buildup of local rust spores in the fall.
Plant Science and Entomology, Manhattan, KS
Merle G. Eversmeyer, (913) 532-6168

Some commercial spring wheat varieties can have leaf temperatures that are 2-1/2 to 4-1/2 degrees F warmer than others. When plants have plenty of water, those varieties that maintained warmer temperatures lost less water through their leaves than their cooler cousins. Leaf temperature differences don't affect yield if plants get enough water. During drought, however, scientists say the warmest varieties had a 25 percent yield reduction while the coolest plants--which lost more moisture--had a yield reduction of 55 percent.
U.S. Water Conservation Lab, Phoenix, AZ
Paul J. Pinter, Jr., (602) 261-4356

Scientists have discovered a key to helping plants cope with heat. They found that plant enzymes operate only within narrow temperature ranges called thermal kinetic windows. Enzymes--of which there are thousands in each plant cell--are catalysts for life processes such as making and breaking down proteins. Scientists removed two drought-related enzymes from five plant species and measured the enzymes' activity at various plant temperatures. The tests showed enzymes functioned best within a temperature "window" that varied by species: 62 to 73 degrees F for wheat, 77 to 88 degrees for corn, 73 to 90 degrees for cotton, 50 to 63 degrees for spinach and 93 to 100 degrees for cucumbers. Field tests are continuing, and other enzymes will be studied. Transferring one plant's genes for controlling an enzyme's temperature response into other plants may change those plants' thermal kinetic windows. That could lead to new crop varieties that grow better at warmer--or cooler--temperatures than they do now.
Cropping Systems Research Lab, Lubbock, TX
Jerry L. Hatfield, (806) 746-5353

Cotton is the clothing of choice in hot weather, but now there's evidence the plant itself can "keep its cool." Researchers found that even as air temperatures rise as high as 90 degrees F, a cotton plant can keep its own temperature in the low-to-mid 80's. The discovery may help breeders develop crops adapted to specific climates. In the study, when soil water was adequate and humidity was low, cotton plants gave off just enough water for leaves to stay cool. Many plant-growth enzymes turn off at high temperatures—an ability that may allow these enzymes to keep working. With cotton as a model, researchers plan to develop a plant with a root system large enough to absorb the water needed to fight high temperatures but not so large that it wastes water and plant nutrients.
Plant Stress and Water Conservation Research,
Lubbock, TX
James R. Mahan, (806) 746-5353

A group of special proteins that corn plants produce at times of drought or salty conditions could hold the key to eventually developing plants that can better withstand such adverse conditions. Studies in the lab have shown that when clusters of corn cells are subjected to too much salt or too little water, the cells will manufacture three proteins not found in other cells free of such stresses. Likewise, when corn seedlings were deprived of water, they reacted by synthesizing two other proteins that were not produced by their well-watered counterparts. Those two proteins rapidly disappeared when the tiny plants were watered. A plant's genes instruct it when to produce these proteins. If these genes can be isolated, scientists hope to use biotechnology to genetically engineer more tolerant varieties of corn as well as transfer these tolerance genes into other plants.
Sugarcane Physiology, Aiea, HI
Subbanaidu Ramagopal, (808) 487-5561

Genetically improving the processes by which citrus plants take in carbon dioxide (CO_2) from the air may produce drought-resistant varieties. Plants absorb CO_2 during photosynthesis—the process by which they convert chemical energy to food. ARS scientists found that when Sweet Valencia orange trees were deprived of water, they took up less CO_2 and had less enzyme activity—and produced less sucrose, starch and soluble proteins. The research also reiterated the need for well-designed and efficient irrigation in citrus orchards.
Horticultural Research Lab, Orlando, FL
Joseph C. Vu, (407) 897-7354

Nectarine growers in California sold a half-million dollars worth of the fresh fruit to Japan this summer, partly a result of ARS research. Until now, Japan had banned U.S.-grown nectarines because of concern that the codling moth might enter the country via imported fruit. The Japanese dropped this long-standing trade barrier in June by approving fumigation procedures developed by ARS scientists. The researchers found that the fumigant methyl bromide, applied in moderate doses (48 grams per cubic meter) for 2 hours at about about 70 degrees F, would kill any codling moth eggs or larvae that might be hiding inside the fruit. American growers use the fumigant also to treat cherries and unshelled walnuts destined for Japan. Most of the U.S. nectarine crop, worth about $65.5 million in 1987, comes from California orchards. California nectarine growers funded part of the research.
Horticultural Crops Research Lab, Fresno, CA
Patrick V. Vail, (209) 453-3000

Sowing the genes of wild oats into commercial varieties could lead to bioengineered or conventionally bred oats that resist disease, insects and pesticides and have other good traits. That's because scientists have bred new oat lines with all the maternally inherited genes from wild oat cytoplasm—the cell region outside the nucleus. This is important because today's oat varieties lack adequate genetic diversity in the cytoplasm; in corn this problem spurred a 1971 epidemic of Southern corn leaf blight. Now the scientists are checking the new oat lines for desirable traits conferred by cytoplasmic genes. These lines produced as much grain as the high-yielding paternal ancestors from which they got most of their nuclear genes.
Plant Science Research, St. Paul, MN
Howard W. Rines, (612) 625-5220

Sunflowers are gaining a new lease on life through selective breeding of wild and cultivated varieties. New strains are being developed that will resist powdery mildew and two of the most damaging diseases that attack sunflowers—downy mildew and rust. Through a new tissue-culturing method, scientists are making faster progress in screening sunflowers for desired traits. And a new method for producing male-sterile breeding lines is speeding development of new genetically diverse hybrids. Another

newly developed method--this one for doubling chromosomes in pollen cells of some hybrid sunflowers--may make them compatible for breeding with other sunflowers--further broadening their genetic diversity.
Oilseeds Research, Fargo, ND
Jerry F. Miller, (701) 239-1321
Thomas J. Gulya, (701) 237-8901
Chao-Chien Jan, (701) 237-7544

Wild potatoes may hold the answer to combating verticillium wilt, the most devastating field disease of potatoes in the Pacific Northwest. Wilt can reduce the yield of some potato varieties as much as 50 percent. ARS scientists have identified a few wild potato species, related to the common potato, that have excellent resistance to verticillium wilt. Of nearly 70 wild species tested, four have shown more resistance to the disease than the cultivated potato. These four are native to Bolivia and northwestern Argentina. Potato breeders will use these species to breed improved wilt resistance into new potato varieties.
Small Grains and Potato Germplasm Research,
Aberdeen, ID
Dennis Corsini, (208) 397-4181

Four advanced breeding lines of green peas are flourishing in the Pacific Northwest where their counterparts had been devastated by bean leaf roll virus only 8 years ago. Development of immunity to this major disease in such a short time is a landmark achievement in breeding crops for resistance to viral diseases. The bean leaf roll virus belongs to a group of viruses called luteoviruses, which are probably the most destructive in the world. Prior to 1980, bean leaf roll virus was unknown in the Pacific Northwest. That year it devastated thousands of acres of green pea fields in southern Idaho, where more than half of the nation's pea seeds are grown. By 1987, an ARS scientist monitoring the progress of private breeders determined that they had succeeded in transferring to peas an immunity to the bean leaf roll virus. No virus was found in the advanced breeding lines although they were growing in the same area where virus-susceptible varieties were being killed by the disease.
Horticultural Crops Research Lab, Corvallis, OR
Richard O. Hampton, (503) 754-3451

Scientists have found a staining process that marks root-lesion nematodes faster, cutting the time it takes to evaluate alfalfa for resistance to these little pests. This microscopic worm feeds in the roots and nitrogen-fixing nodules of alfalfa plants, making stands unproductive, particularly in the northern and northeastern U.S. Researchers for years have counted the number of nematodes in the roots by shaking them in water for 7 days, then counting the worms found in the water. Now, by staining the worms within the roots and examining the roots under a microscope, researchers are able to estimate nematode numbers in alfalfa plants in just 1 hour.
Plant Science Research, St. Paul, MN
Judy A. Thies, (612) 625-8240

A treasure of wild beet seeds buried on greenhouse shelves for half a century can soon help protect the $750 million U.S. sugarbeet crop. When *Rhizomania*, a devastating root disease, was discovered in 1983 in the nation's leading sugarbeet state, California, scientists turned to European wild beets collected by ARS plant breeder George H. Coons from 1925 to 1935. They found that Coons' beets, unlike most modern varieties, are resistant to the virus-caused disease. And new experimental beets with genes bred from the wild plants now show resistance--good news for beet farmers in 13 states who can get $600 to $1,000 per acre for the crop. *Rhizomania*, carried by a fungus in the soil, tends to be spread by harvesting operations.
Sugarbeet Research Lab, Fargo, ND
Devon L. Doney, (701) 237-8151

Slow-growing sugarcane produces more sugar than fast-growing varieties. Growers have traditionally preferred fast-growing sugarcane varieties, even though they tend to have lower sugar concentrations. It was believed the more vigorous canes competed better against weeds. But researchers have found the slow-growing varieties compete as successfully against short or prostrate weeds and often yield more sugar per ton of cane, which makes the cane more attractive to processors. In addition, researchers found weed control needs to be most intense during the second ratoon crop--subsequent harvest sprouted from the original root--of sugarcane. That contrasts with traditional management practices of concentrating weed control in the first year crop and using less and less during the two subsequent ratoon crops.
Sugarcane Field Station, Canal Point, FL
Barry Glaz, (407) 924-5227

12

A shot that kills gypsy moths? For areas where aerial or ground spraying is impossible or undesired, scientists have tried injecting systemic insecticides directly into oak trees to discourage gypsy moth caterpillars. Tree sap dispersed the chemicals, acephate and methamidophos, which were injected or implanted just after budburst. During the three-year study at four locations in Maryland and Pennsylvania, no treated tree was seriously defoliated by gypsy moths. Implantation cartridges of powdered acephate to control the gypsy moth have been registered with the Environmental Protection Agency, while injection units of liquid acephate are awaiting EPA approval.
Insect Chemical Ecology Lab, Beltsville, MD
Ralph E. Webb, (301) 344-4562

Tiny, virus-carrying whiteflies--blamed for last winter's sky-high lettuce prices--can now be tracked faster and easier than ever before. ARS researchers and an Israeli colleague have adapted a hand-held, mini vacuum cleaner to harmlessly suck up the gnat-sized sweetpotato whiteflies, which spread infectious yellows virus in lettuce fields. Insects are vacuumed into a small plastic jar then taken to the lab so researchers can estimate how many are carrying the infectious virus and how fast it is building up in weeds and crops. Researchers count whiteflies on weed samples to focus costly control measures only on those weed species that the whiteflies prefer. Previously, scientists used a much heavier backpack vacuum.
U.S. Agricultural Research Station, Salinas, CA
O. Reily Dawson/Raymond Perry, (408) 755-2825

As lilac and honeysuckle start to bloom, they can help forecast when to treat threatening grasshopper populations on ranches and farms. The key is warm weather--which these ornamental plants and the destructive insects both react to. Grasshoppers go through five growth stages. Scientists found the peak of the third stage occurs about 35 days after lilac begins flowering or red berries begin to appear on honeysuckle. If sufficient numbers of immature grasshoppers are found in fields at this time, landowners have about two to three weeks advance notice to control the hoppers before they grow into destructive adults. Scientists are now developing ways to pinpoint the peaks of all five grasshopper stages, based on temperatures.
Rangeland Insects Lab, Bozeman, MT
William P. Kemp, (406) 994-3344

Male-female ratios among insects might differ according to species, and these differences could be important to pest management programs. Recent studies of the tobacco budworm and cotton bollworm--two of agriculture's most destructive pests--show an even split for the budworm and a 55/45 male-female ratio in the bollworm. Furthermore, the rate at which these insects emerge as moths depends on the crop they were feeding on as caterpillars. Females of both species come out first on all crops, beating the males by as much as 72 hours. However, their emergence patterns and total moth populations differ by crop. This type of data, when more fully developed, will make insect population predictions more accurate, and that should make pest control strategies more efficient through more accurate estimates of potential insect damage and better timing of pesticide applications.
Southern Field Crops Insect Management Lab, Stoneville, MS
Jane L. Hayes, (601) 686-2311

Red rice, a weed that lowers the value of the rice crop, appears to have met its match in a chemical that does not kill it, but blocks its reproduction. A single red rice plant can spew out as many as 1,500 seeds. Just 4 percent of the weed seed in rice can cut the crop's value by 15 cents a bushel. But two applications of the herbicide fluazifop have been found to slash red rice seed output from 1,829 a yard to zero. Farmers have traditionally battled red rice by planting alternate crops such as soybeans between rice crops and treating the weed with chemicals that the alternate crops can withstand. However, other chemicals have offered only 80 to 90 percent control. Fluazifop, federally approved for soybeans, does not kill the red rice weed, which will die anyway at the end of the growing season. But fluazifop does eliminate the seeds that form the foundation for the next year's crop of weeds.
Rice Research Center, Stuttgart, AR
Roy J. Smith Jr., (501) 673-2661

Farmers may soon be able to apply herbicide and fertilizer with a single "pill." Using existing technology that encapsulates the herbicide chemicals in starch, researchers have now enclosed both a herbicide and a fertilizer inside a single layer of starch. Esters of 2,4-D-- widely used for weed control--were mixed with gelatinized

starch and wrapped around pellets of urea fertilizer. Tests using the experimental product show it reduces the evaporation of herbicide chemicals and may cut back on the number of applications of chemicals farmers need to apply to their fields. This would increase safety for farmers and others handling the chemicals.
Plant Polymer Research, Northern Regional Research Center, Peoria, IL
Baruch S. Shasha, (309) 685-4011

Frustrated ranchers may have an alternative when it's not practical to use herbicide sprays and mechanical treatments to control range weeds and brush near homes or crops. A carpeted roller, developed and tested by ARS researchers, can be mounted on the front of a farm tractor. The 6.5-feet-wide by 10-inch diameter roller "wipes" weeds with herbicide as the tractor pushes it along. In experiments, certain roller-applied herbicides killed as much as 90 percent of brushy plants like mesquite within 6 weeks of application. Researchers found the roller method also uses less herbicide than other methods of application. Carpeting with a thick, medium length nap works best.
Grassland Protection Research, Temple, TX Herman S. Mayeux, Jr., (817) 770-6500

Important news for nurserymen: promptly removing plant debris from greenhouses will prevent leafminer insects from reinfesting plants. The results can mean happier customers and lower costs for replacing damaged plants. Researchers picked chrysanthemum leaves infected with leafminer eggs and stored them under warm, high-humidity conditions. As many adults developed from the detached leaves as from leaves left on infected plants. Adult pests developed even when the leaves dried out. The leafminer, *Liriomyza trifolii*, is a serious international pest of flower and vegetable crops.
Florist and Nursery Crops Lab, Beltsville, MD
Hiram G. Larew, (301) 344-4560

Horticultural oils may be a new, important alternative for greenhouse pest management. Although used as insecticides and miticides in orchards, lawns and on greenhouse-grown hardy shrubs, until now oils have not been used in the greenhouse on flower and vegetable crops. In tests,

Sunspray 6E--a petroleum-based horticultural spray--proved poisonous to greenhouse whiteflies, leafminers, two-spotted mites, and green peach aphids without damaging plants. Plants sprayed with the oil repelled these insect pests, for which there are no effective controls. Insects and mites seem unable to develop resistance to oils, which are not toxic to humans or animals. Sunspray 6E is available commercially from a firm in Philadelphia, PA.
Florist and Nursery Crops Lab, Beltsville, MD
Hiram G. Larew, (301) 344-4560

New, no-mess crabapple trees are the first to combine strong disease resistance with beauty and low maintenance. Adirondack, one of two new resistant trees, has a narrow, upright shape suitable for crowded streets or urban yards. Both Adirondack and Narragansett, the other new variety, have snow-white blossoms. Their fruit is less than one-half inch in diameter, small enough so that cleanup is not necessary. Also, the fallen fruit will not kill the lawn or attract bees like the larger-fruited types. In field trials for 10 years in several states, Adirondack resisted the four leading diseases of crabapples. Narragansett resisted three and was highly tolerant of the fourth. Commercial nurserymen, gardeners and landscape architects consider the crabapple one of the most versatile and widely cultivated small landscape trees throughout the northern United States and southern Canada.
U.S. National Arboretum, Washington, DC
Donald R. Egolf, (202) 475-4862

Three new roses-of-Sharon, bearing names of Greek goddesses, raise the flowering shrub above its weedy place among landscape plants. All three new *Hibiscus syriancus* varieties are nearly sterile and produce no seed, unlike other roses-of-Sharon that drop troublesome seed. Aphrodite bears dark pink flowers with red "hearts," or centers, from June through September. The others are Diana with large, pure white flowers; and Helene with white flowers that have bright red centers. They join Minerva with lavendar flowers that was introduced last year. All four plants produce bell-shaped flowers up to one-third larger than standard types and bloom longer.
U.S. National Arboretum, Washington, DC
Donald R. Egolf, (202) 475-4862

14

Animal Production and Protection

When can scientists know if a gene they insert in an animal embryo takes hold? Up to now, they've had to wait until the animal is born to get the answer from a standard test. A new gene-copying system, successful in mice but designed for future use in cattle, will save them a long wait--a cow's approximately 230 day gestation period. Five to seven days after injecting a new gene, they will split the embryo into identical twins. One twin embryo will be used for the gene-copying technique, in which as few as 25 of its cells are mixed with an enzyme, polymerase. If the injected gene is present, polymerase makes a million or more copies--enough for the standard test to determine the gene's presence. If the result is positive, scientists will implant the other twin in a surrogate animal mother. The new copying system could save money and time while assuring scientists that their gene engineering tests are on track.
Reproduction Lab, Beltsville, MD
Donna King, (301) 344-1500

Cattle, like humans, inherit the ability to resist disease from their parents. Researchers are developing blood tests to identify groups of cattle genes associated with disease resistance that can be used as genetic markers. These gene markers may lead to improved disease resistance in future U.S. cattle breeds, thereby reducing annual veterinary bills and animal losses in the millions of dollars. If researchers can identify the specific genes for disease resistance that are associated with the markers, it may be possible to insert these genes into cattle embryos. The markers will also aid breeders in selecting disease-resistant cattle.
U.S. Meat Animal Research Center, Clay Center, NE
Roger T. Stone, (402) 762-4166

Cows may hold the key to a measure of relief for some AIDS patients. Certain AIDS patients have been found to be infected with a one-cell internal parasite, *Cryptosporidium*, that also infects animals. The parasite--found in contaminated food or water--causes severe diarrhea in humans. It does not produce AIDS in animals or humans. Scientists have obtained a chemical called transfer factor from the lymph nodes of parasite-infected cows. When weekly oral doses were given to AIDS patients at New York University Medical School, 75 percent of them stopped having diarrhea. In most cases, by the third week, the treatment produced an immune response to the parasite in the patient's body. Patients had no ill effects. Scientists think the product somehow reactivates immunity-producing cells that have been "turned off" by AIDS. Oddly, transfer factor doesn't give newborn calves much protection against Cryptosporidium, since a mature immune system is needed for the material to be effective.
Animal Parasite Research Lab, Auburn, AL
Phillip H. Klesius, (205) 887-3741

Transgenic chickens that can resist avian leukosis virus have been bred by ARS scientists--paving the way to potential savings for U.S. egg producers of $50 to $100 million a year. Transgenic means genes are transferred from one species to another--in this case from a weak strain of this virus to chickens. The virus cannot infect humans, but in chickens it can reduce egg production and quality. In hundreds of attempts to get virus genes to "take," scientists squirted virus through the eggshell near the day-old embryo and then hatched the egg. Transgenic chickens bred from a second-generation descendant of one of these embryos resisted lab and field strains of the avian leukosis virus in tests lasting 40 weeks. Ordinarily, the virus commands chicken cells to make more virus particles. But cells in the resistant birds make only the virus "envelope," or empty virus shell. With more research, virus genes may become "locomotives" for transporting "freight trains" of other beneficial genes so that chickens could resist other diseases, grow faster on less feed or lay larger, higher quality eggs.
Regional Poultry Research Lab, East Lansing, MI
Lyman B. Crittenden, (517) 337-6828

Calves can develop stomach ulcers. Unlike humans, calves get their ulcers from licking and swallowing hair. Scientists who conducted autopsies on nearly 900 calves that died over 15 years in Montana learned at least one percent were killed by hair balls. The massaging action in the last part of the calf's stomach, the abomasum, forms the hair into sandpaper-rough balls that can wear through the stomach lining. Why calves eat hair is unknown, but studies suggest a lack of copper in diets may be one cause. Additional research is continuing in Nebraska, Wyoming and Montana.
Fort Keogh Livestock and Range, Miles City, MT
Robert A. Bellows, (406) 232-4970

15

A commonly used deworming drug administered to calves in three doses at just the right time cuts infection by a potentially deadly parasite by more than 60 percent. ARS scientists believe the treatment may stimulate immunity in calves to medium brown stomachworms (*Ostertagia*). These parasites damage stomach tissue, disrupting protein digestion and causing malnourishment in cattle despite a sound diet. Older cattle can develop immunity to the parasites, usually after two grazing seasons on wormy pastures, but a heavy infection can kill a calf. Scientists fed calves 200,000 *Ostertagia* larvae, followed nine days later by treatment with fenbendazole at the standard rate of 2.3 milligrams for every pound of the calf's weight. The drug application was aptly timed to catch the worms just before they became adults. After undergoing this infection-treatment routine three times, the calves had 60 percent fewer worms than untreated calves.
Helminthic Diseases Lab, Beltsville, MD
Louis C. Gasbarre, (301) 344-2509

Low-fat, tender lamb can be produced by feeding ram lambs a high forage diet. A 5-year ARS study shows that marketing lamb meat from young rams, rather than from castrated rams (called wethers), could benefit consumers and farmers. Most lamb meat comes from wethers, which are tender but high in total fat and saturated fat. However, young rams fed a test diet of mostly alfalfa forage were 54 percent leaner than wethers. The rams produced rib-eye chops with 22 percent less total fat and nearly double the polyunsaturated-to-saturated fat ratios than wethers on the same diet. The ram meat is not as tender as that from wethers, but current research may solve that problem soon. The farmer could benefit too, because forage-fed rams grow about 15 percent faster and use feed about 15 percent more efficiently than wethers.
Meat Science Lab, Beltsville, MD
Morse Solomon, (301) 344-1713

All neutrophils are not created equal. Researchers have discovered these white blood cells that engulf and kill foreign intruders come in four types--at least in cows. The finding, the first of its kind in any animal, could lead to the breeding of more disease-resistant cattle. It may also explain long-noted differences in the ability of these white blood cells to move to an infection site and kill invading bacteria. To separate the four types of neutrophils, scientists tested cow blood samples with custom-designed proteins called monoclonal antibodies. These antibodies are like guided missiles and "home in" on only the targets they are programmed for. The antibody test could be used to identify cows with active neutrophils; those cows in turn become the parents of more disease-resistant breeds.
Milk Secretion and Mastitis Lab, Beltsville, MD
Max J. Paape, (301) 344-2302

Honey bees are master chefs when making their daily meals. Bee bread is made by mixing just the right proportions of more than 200 microorganisms--molds, yeasts and bacteria--that an ARS scientist has identified for the first time. Now she hopes to learn the bees' complex recipe to find ways to make an inexpensive, nutritious artificial feed for bees, which pollinate $20 billion of crops annually. Bees may need extra food in the spring, especially if the winter is colder than normal or if their hives become diseased.
Carl Hayden Bee Research Center, Tucson, AZ
Martha Gilliam, (602) 629-6380

Soil, Water and Air

Southwestern farmers struggling to meet conservation compliance regulations may want to consider a fall planting of spring barley as a cover crop. The barley will grow well, even where the soil has little moisture, until killed by December frost. The surface residue shields the soil from wind erosion from December through May, the period when wind erosion is highest. In the spring, cotton or sorghum can be planted directly into the residue, which also serves as a herbicide-free way to reduce weeds.
Wind Erosion and New Crops Research, Big Spring, TX
T. Bilbro, (915) 263-0293

Farmland is being crushed under the weight of vehicles with axle loads at least twice as heavy as those of trucks on the nation's superhighways. The price is paid at harvest time--lower yields due to soil compaction. ARS computer calculations can show farmers how high this price will be so

they can decide on the tradeoff between lower yields and quicker harvests. For example, corn farmers typically follow their harvesting combines (18 to 20 tons per axle) with tractor-pulled wagons (40 tons per axle). The combines can store about 200 bushels of corn, so unloading continuously into the 1,200-bushel-capacity wagons eliminates the need to interrupt harvesting. But field data fed into a computer model showed that the soil could grow another 17 bushels of corn an acre if farmers left the wagons at field edges and unloaded combines at the end of each round. That's worth about $34 an acre. The computer program being developed will allow Extension Service specialists to calculate the compaction effects of different equipment sizes and combinations and balance them against harvest delays.
North Central Soil Conservation Research Lab, Morris, MN
Ward B. Voorhees, (612) 589-3411

When tractors and other heavy farm equipment travel only in designated lanes in fields of alfalfa hay, yields improve. A 4-year experiment in California shows that such fields yielded 10 percent more hay than plots where the traffic was unrestricted, which is typical for most fields. Heavy harvesting equipment moves through alfalfa fields as often as every 30 to 45 days during the growing season, compacting the soil and squashing pores that would otherwise hold air and water that roots need. Compaction also causes water to infiltrate soil more slowly. The longer each alfalfa plant is surrounded by standing water, the more susceptible it becomes to disease. On plots with restricted traffic, irrigation water moved through the soil 25 percent faster than through soil in fields with normal traffic.
U.S. Cotton Research Station, Shafter, CA
Lyle M. Carter/Burl D. Meek/Eric A. Rechel,
(805) 746-6391

A new device for tractor-drawn planting equipment could boost yields and help farmers manage their crops more effectively. With the ARS invention--called an interactive depth and downpressure control system--seeds can be automatically planted at the same depth regardless of variations in soil height or density. Such uniformity can increase germination and seedling emergence rates because seeds planted too near the surface dry out and seeds buried too deeply won't emerge. Uniform seed depths could also save time and money in pesticide applications and improve harvest quality, because the crops are more likely to grow and mature at the same rate. (PATENT)
Grassland, Soil and Water Research Lab, Temple, TX
John E. Morrison, (817) 770-6507

Russet Burbank potato plants root more deeply when compacted soil is broken up, or subsoiled, at planting time. Deeper rooting allows potato roots to contact a larger volume of water and avoid the water stress that occurs between irrigations. On plots left alone, (without subsoiling hard layers), only 22 percent of the tubers were U.S. No. 1. Subsoiling increased this percentage to 59, indicating the sensitivity of Russet Burbank to water stress, especially in sandy soils, which retain low amounts of water. Benefits from subsoiling should last several years if farmers cut down on the number of trips they make over their fields with heavy equipment which recompacts the soil.
Irrigated Agriculture Research and Extension Center,
Prosser, WA
David E. Miller, (509) 786-3454

Snow can provide a warm blanket to help winter wheat survive the previously fatal winters in northeast Montana, North Dakota and the prairie provinces of Canada. These areas traditionally grow spring wheat because the cold winters usually kill winter wheat planted in fallow fields. Finding a way to grow winter wheat in harsh climates means an alternative crop that earns farmers more money. Winter wheat spreads the workload because it's planted in the fall and harvested earlier than spring wheat. The key to success with winter wheat in extremely cold areas is to drill the seed into unplowed fields, directly into standing stubble left after harvesting a spring-planted cereal crop. The stubble traps blowing snow that insulates the soil around the base of plants, maintaining enough warmth to keep the plants alive. Trapped snow also provides more snowmelt to replenish soil moisture. In tests, the 4-year average winter wheat yield was 45 bushels per acre when winter wheat was planted in 10-inch-high spring wheat stubble. Nearby spring wheat grown conventionally yielded only 37 bushels per acre.
Northern Great Plains Research Lab, Mandan, ND
A.L. Black, (701) 663-6445

While evaluating the moisture requirements of wheat on an hour-by-hour basis, researchers found that irrigation water may need to be supplied in smaller, more frequent doses to maximize plant growth and yield. Plants grow the most during the sunniest periods of partly cloudy days. They also require the most water during these sunny periods--just when evaporation is highest. Even as little as 15 minutes without enough water may cut into plant growth. More data are needed before explicit changes in irrigation schedules can be recommended.
Coastal Plains Soil and Water Conservation Research Lab, Florence, SC
Edward Sadler, (803) 669-5203

Cotton plants yield more fiber and use irrigation water more efficiently if water is piped underground directly to plant roots instead of applied to the soil surface. A two-year experiment with two cotton varieties in California showed the yield difference. On plots irrigated underground, plants produced from 51 to 64 percent more fiber than plants watered at frequent intervals on the surface. Water from the soil surface drains down through the soil towards the water table. But in some Californian soils the water table is shallow and saline and the salty water from the lower soil levels moves up into the root zone. This upward movement must be avoided to prevent yield loss from excess salt. Subsurface irrigations applied daily or several times a day reduce the amount of saline water near the roots because they continually flush the soil. It becomes economically feasible to use this type of irrigation when the cost to treat this salty drainage water is greater than $70/acre foot (an acre of land covered by one foot of water). In the experiment, underground watering was computer controlled, but growers who use simpler subsurface drip systems also should expect to see comparable yield increases, scientists say. And some chemicals normally sprayed onto plants or onto the ground can instead be delivered directly and more safely into the soil through the buried pipes.
Water Management Lab, Fresno, CA
Claude J. Phene, (209) 453-3100

Qua

Quarterly Report
of Selected Research Projects

United States
Department of
Agriculture

∂ℛ𝒮 Agricultural
Research
Service

October 1 to December 31, 1988

Contents

Animal Production and Protection

Cattle can graze safely under 500,000-volt power lines, according to a 3-year study in Oregon. Scientists regularly monitored 200 cows, 100 grazing directly under the powerful direct current line and the other 100 within 1,500 feet of it. Each month the cows were weighed, and their activity was recorded every 15 minutes for 24 hours. No significant differences were found in the body weights of cattle or in the number of calves born. Further, they showed no signs of nervousness, discomfort or loss of production. The Bonneville Power Administration and nine other U.S. and Canadian power companies funded the $1.7-million field study.
Range and Meadow Forage Management, Burns, OR
David C. Ganskopp, (503) 573-2064

Note: One or more scientists familiar with each research project are listed for further information. If the scientists are unavailable, others at the same telephone number may also be familiar with the work.

Items marked with the word PATENT are being patented by ARS. For more information contact Ann Whitehead, National Patent Program, Bldg. 005, Rm. 401, Beltsville Agricultural Research Center, Beltsville, MD 20705, (301) 344-2786.

Drummond rattlebush, coffeeweed and bladderpod are three weeds with at least one thing in common: Poisonous seeds. Researchers have developed a procedure using mass spectrometry to quickly analyze and estimate the amount and type of poisonous compound in those seeds. If eaten, they can be fatal to chickens, cattle and sheep and may cause illness in children. The seeds are often found on roadsides and in abandoned pastures near the Atlantic and Gulf coasts from North Carolina to Texas. Information about the poison in the seeds, provided by the new procedure, can help physicians, veterinarians and toxicologists.
Bioactive Constituents Research, Northern Regional Research Center, Peoria, IL
Richard G. Powell, (309) 685-4011

A little bit of bacteria goes a long way toward protecting Florida cattle whose owners want to make use of a tropical forage called leucaena. Used as forage for cattle, goats and sheep in many tropical areas of the world, leucaena is a tree-type legume. But it contains a toxic amino acid that is converted in the fore-stomach into a chemical compound called 3,4-DHP. This compound can cause animals to grow poorly, lose their hair and develop goiters, although symptoms disappear in a few weeks if the animals stop eating the legume. However, studies have shown that some ruminants can eat leucaena because of bacteria in their fore-stomach that break down 3,4-DHP. Hereford cattle in Florida inoculated with the bacteria were able to safely graze leucaena. And the bacteria thrived in the Herefords' stomachs through the winter when no leucaena was being eaten. Scientists say cattle producers would need to inoculate only a few head with the bacteria, since they spread rapidly through the herd, possibly by contact between animals or through the environment by organisms shed in the manure. Armed with this insurance, cattle producers could put leucaena to work in forage plans for subtropical Florida.
Beef Cattle Research, Brooksville, FL
Andrew C. Hammond, (904) 796-3385

While Brahman cattle can outgain their English cousins grazing on summer fescue, they apparently pay a price in reproductive efficiency. A toxin in summer fescue causes "summer slump," which raises the animal's body temperature. As a result, cattle eat less. In grazing tests on summer fescue, Brahman heifers outgained Aberdeen Angus heifers by half a pound per head per day. But subsequent tests showed only 78 percent of the Brahmans became pregnant while grazing on summer fescue, compared with 90 percent of the Angus. Scientists think Brahman-based animals headed for market may be a good way to utilize summer fescue, but developing replacement heifers requires other forage.

South Central Family Farm Research, Booneville, AR
Michael A. Brown, (501) 675-3834

Cattle and ticks infected with the blood disease anaplasmosis can now be diagnosed by detecting the parasite's DNA (genetic material). The test, which could ultimately save U.S. cattlemen about $100 million annually, is very specific and has greater sensitivity than other techniques currently in use. Carried by ticks, anaplasmosis infects the red blood cells of cattle worldwide, resulting in anemia. Controlling the disease has been difficult, since no techniques exist to quickly or reliably identify chronically infected cattle or infected ticks. Since DNA of a given species is unique, parasite DNA that researchers label with a radioactive tracer can be used to probe or test samples for the presence of the disease.

Animal Diseases Research, Pullman, WA
Willard L. Goff, (509) 335-3179

Improved "communications" between a cow's uterus and her fertilized egg could result in bigger profits for livestock producers. Studies indicate that if a fertilized egg does not send the proper chemical signals to stimulate the correct endometrial response, it may also fail to attach itself to the uterus. A large percentage of embryonic deaths of cattle may result from this failure to communicate. Researchers say the cows may lose their offspring in the first 30 days of pregnancy, prompting producers to think those cows have failed to conceive. Work is under way to identify how the egg signals the uterus; scientists think this signal may be a protein. They hope to enhance or prolong this chemical message to help ensure more successful cattle pregnancies.

Forage and Livestock Research, El Reno, OK
William A. Phillips, (405) 262-5291

Pregnant heifers may abort anytime during pregnancy if they are vaccinated with a live or modified live virus for IBR—the infectious bovine respiratory disease that's also known as red nose. ARS scientists tested eight heifers by vaccinating them with one of four strains of live IBR virus just 2 weeks after breeding. Half of them aborted. Research is under way to develop a safer vaccine. In the meantime, the scientists recommend vaccinating heifers from 4 to 10 months-old—well before they reach breeding age.

Virology Cattle Research, National Animal Disease Center, Ames, IA
Janice M. Miller, (515) 239-8349

Testosterone, the male sex hormone, can turn bull calves into aggressive, troublesome rogues. That's the main reason for castrating animals bound for the feedlot. Researchers are testing a more humane alternative to conventional castration methods, which may cause shock, hemorrhage and infection. The new experimental method is to vaccinate young calves with a brain hormone chemically reacted with another protein. The vaccination makes the animals sterile and docile by decreasing their testosterone levels. The resulting sterility from this procedure is potentially reversible. Researchers believe this procedure would be acceptable to both consumers and meat packers.

U.S. Meat Animal Research Center, Clay Center, NE
Bruce D. Schanbacher, (402) 762-4100

A computer-based system could make quick work of beef-carcass grading and relieve much of the tedium and subjective judgments experienced by human graders. With the new system, meat graders would concentrate on verbally describing and measuring carcass characteristics, instead of subjectively assessing how well a carcass conforms to standard grading criteria. The new computerized system takes less than 20 seconds per carcass. A major component of the new system—a voice recognition subsystem— "hears" the grader's words. Another component— the knowledge-based subsystem—compares this information with the official U.S. Meat Grading Standards and awards a grade such as Prime, Choice or Select to the carcass and determines its yield grade. A printout explains the grades given. Another advantage would emerge if and when official standards are changed: The computer could be quickly updated with the new standards without costly, time-consuming retraining of human graders. The system was tested on more than 300 beef carcasses of varying characteristics. (PATENT)

U.S. Meat Animal Research Center, Clay Center, NE
Y.R. Chen, (402) 762-4100

Chemicals added to feed to prevent caking could also help keep aflatoxin out of cows' milk. Aflatoxin is a natural toxin produced by molds on grain. Scientists found adding hydrated-sodium calcium aluminosilicate, or HSCAS, to chicken feed would protect the birds against the toxin's residue by tying up the aflatoxin so that it passes harmlessly through the birds' intestinal tract. Since alfatoxin in cattle feed can produce residues in milk, researchers wondered if HSCAS would have the same effect on dairy cows. Federal regulations prohibit more than 0.5 part per billion of aflatoxin in milk. Researchers fed three dairy cows feed containing 100 parts per billion of aflatoxin plus 1 percent HSCAS. Aflatoxin levels in the cow's milk dropped: from 0.65 ppb to 0.27 in one, from 1.1 to 0.449 in the second, and from 1.4 to 0.65 in the third.

Mycotoxin Research Lab, College Station, TX
Roger B. Harvey, (409) 260-9259

Up to 50,000 adult biting midges can now be reared each week for scientists who need these disease-carriers for research on **bluetongue disease** of cattle, sheep and wildlife. Bluetongue costs U.S. livestock producers about $125 million yearly in lost exports to countries that do not have the disease. A new rearing system developed by ARS scientists automatically maintains the ideal light and temperature to provide a constant supply of *Culicoides variipennis* midges. The technique also saves labor and floor space. Scientists say their new system could give researchers rearing other insects an easier way to keep enough insects on hand to continue their research programs full time.

Arthropod-borne Animal Diseases Research,
Laramie, WY
Gregg J. Hunt, (307) 721-0314

Help is closer for producers of sheep and dairy goats that develop lesions when they are vaccinated for pseudotuberculosis. Researchers are now closer to a vaccine that won't inflame the animals' skin around the inoculation site. Healthy lambs were vaccinated with a synthetic compound, muramyl dipeptide, that was added to the current vaccine. No inflammation occurred, and the animals were able to resist infection. In 1987, $250,000 worth of sheep and lamb carcasses were condemned by meat inspectors because of pseudotuberculosis lesions. Next, researchers will test the compound on animals with field infections of the disease.

National Animal Disease Center, Ames, IA
Kim Brogden, (515) 239-8287

St. Croix sheep could boost profits for some sheep producers. Imported into the United States from the Caribbean, this breed of sheep has hair rather than wool. This hair, which is unusable, is shed naturally without having to be sheared. For sheep producers located long and costly distances from profitable wool markets, this would eliminate what can be an expensive, annual burden for shearing other breeds and sending the wool to market. In addition, the St. Croix sheep producer three lamb crops rather than two in a 24-month cycle, and the breed frequently produces a higher percentage of twins. St. Croix sheep also seem to be more resistant to parasites that plague Southern sheep production. Scientists are studying the breed to see how it might fit into a grazing plan with cattle to make the most of available forages.

South Central Family Farm Research, Booneville, AR
Michael A. Brown, (501) 675-3834

Prolactin, a hormone produced naturally by ewes, appears to affect barberpole worm's timing for infecting lambs on pasture. *Haemonchus contortus,* called the barberpole worm because of its striped barberpole appearance, is an internal parasite of ruminants and considered the number one parasite in U.S. sheep. The worms rupture the animal's stomach lining and feed on its blood, causing anemia and sometimes death. It is believed that barberpole worms become dormant in a ewe's tissue during pregnancy until just before she gives birth. The worms then develop into adults and produce large numbers of eggs to be dumped on the pasture when highly vulnerable lambs are most likely to be grazing there. Giving an infected ewe daily doses of prolactin, one of the hormones triggered in gestation and giving birth, can cause female barberpole worms in the animal to double their egg production to 6,000 a day.

3

Scientists are studying whether prolactin affects the worms directly or instead impairs the ewe's immune system. They hope to develop a drug that would disrupt the relationship between prolactin and parasite egg production.
Helminthic Diseases Lab, Beltsville, MD
Michael W. Fleming, (301) 344-1759

The poultry disease ascites may be a classic case of nature's inability to keep up with technology. Also known as waterbelly, ascites is increasingly plaguing the U.S. broiler industry. Death rates average 4 to 5 percent of affected flocks and can go as high as 50 percent. But even those birds that survive don't grow as well as their healthy cousins and are condemned at slaughter because of internal damage caused by the disease. Scientists believe the problem is oxygen deprivation—that the birds are growing faster than their cardiopulmonary systems can deliver the oxygen that their bodies need. Studies found that broilers housed in high-altitude chambers for 5 weeks had 6 times more ascites than those grown under normal conditions. Also, at 6-weeks old, the broilers raised with the least amount of oxygen available weighed about 19 ounces less than the control group. The solution may be breeding poultry lines in which the cardiovascular system grows more rapidly or has a greater oxygen-carrying capability.
Mycotoxin Research, College Station, TX
Donald A. Witzel, (409) 260-9420

Adipsin, a protein that controls the size of fat cells, has finally been detected in chickens. The discovery could ultimately lead to lower feed costs for broiler producers and leaner, meatier chicken for consumers. Modern broiler chickens have been bred to grow faster than their ancestors, but this growth has resulted at least a 100 percent increase in fat over the bird of 30 years ago. Basically, this increase in fat is attributable to an increase in fat cell size more than to an increase in number of fat cells. Having now detected adipsin in the chickens' fat cells, ARS scientists are working on genetic probes to determine which genes control its production and whether that production will respond to genetic engineering or drugs.
Poultry Research Lab, Georgetown, DE
Teresa L. Blalock, (302) 856-0046

A fish called mahimahi is an excellent candidate for fish-farming; it spawns readily in captivity, grows rapidly and commands a good price because of its delicate flavor. But it is also susceptible to vibriosis, a stress-related bacterial disease. Humans are not affected, but symptoms in fish include loss of appetite, fin erosion and skin ulcers. Scientists had a rare opportunity to study the symptoms in captive mahimahi when the disease broke out in half a dozen young fish living in tanks at Hawaii's Oceanic Institute. They also monitored effects of antibiotics used to treat the fish. Some were cured by adding nifurpirinol to the tanks and oxytetracycline to the feed. New studies should provide other information farmers can use to keep hand-reared fish free of vibriosis and other diseases caused by crowding, handling and other stresses fish don't normally encounter in their natural homes.
Tropical Aquaculture Research, The Oceanic Institute, Makapuu Point, Waimanalo, HI
Brad R. LeaMaster, USDA-ARS/Anthony C. Ostrowski, Oceanic Institute, (808) 259-7951

Scientific Information Systems

Farmers could fertilize several crops more economically next year because researchers have given an old concept a new job. The concept, called degree days, allows farmers to finally get a practical answer to the question: "When can I stop or cut down on nitrogen fertilizer because the growing crop will start getting it from the buried residues of the last crop?" Degree days, the sum of daily temperatures over a period of time, have long been used for estimating crop growth and development. But in a new approach, they are used to tell how long it takes each season for soil microbes to break down buried plant residue enough to release its nitrogen. If farmers know precisely when this will happen, they can avoid adding excess nitrogen. With corn residue, the interval between burial and release is 2,000 to 2,400 degree days (centigrade). Researchers have developed degree-day figures for residues of corn, potatoes and white lupin, and have others in the works. The only equipment the farmer needs is a thermometer that records minimum and maximum temperatures, commercially available for $50 to $100.
New England Plant, Soil and Water Research Lab, Orono, ME
C. Wayne Honeycutt, (207) 581-3266

Work is under way on a new "farmers' almanac," one that can look decades into the future, rather than merely weeks or months. ALMANAC is a computer program that fine-tunes the prediction process begun with EPIC, the Erosion-Productivity Impact Calculator. EPIC simulates natural processes on the land to show the long-term impact of farmers' choices of crops, as well as cultivation, irrigation and fertilization techniques. Using information compiled on weather and soil types across the United States, EPIC can predict annual crop yields over the years, water runoff, soil erosion, loss of nitrogen fertilizer to percolation down through the soil, and the condition of the soil and water at any time of the year. All the farmer needs to supply is management details, such as when and what he'll plant. ALMANAC will offer even more information than EPIC, concentrating in greater detail on a farm manager's decisions affecting the soil. EPIC's users within USDA now routinely check how the land will look 50 or 100 years from now. With ALMANAC, they can look as far as 1,000 years into the future; scientists expect to have it ready for use within 2 to 3 years.

Grassland, Soil and Water Research Lab, Temple, TX
Jimmy R. Williams, (817) 770-6500

Second-guessing *Salmonella* is just one of the goals of a computer program being developed by ARS to forecast the growth of food-poisoning bacteria. The program could be used by the nation's food processors to predict how rapidly any one of six bacteria could grow in their products. When the model is finished, processors will be able to type in data about the temperature at which they will process their product, the product's pH, salt and nitrite levels and whether the processing is done with or without oxygen. In return, they'll get a graph that calculates levels for *Listeria monocytogenes* and *Aeromonas hydrophila,* both of which can grow at refrigerated temperatures; *Salmonella typhimurium* and *Staphylococcus aureus,* the two major causes of food poisoning in the United States; *Clostridium botulinum,* which causes botulism, and *Shigella flexneri,* a pathogen that still poses many unanswered questions for scientists. More organisms may be added to the model in the future.

Microbial Food Safety, Eastern Regional
Research Center, Philadelphia, PA
Robert L. Buchanan, (215) 233-6620

Consumers of the future will be treated to milk and cheese from a more efficient U.S. dairy herd. That's due to a new computer model for evaluating the cows' ability to pass on high milk-production capability to their offspring. Called the Animal Model, the new system takes into account more details on each animal's relatives and traces back its pedigree as far as possible. The system is designed to give farmers a more scientific basis for management decisions such as which cows and calves to keep in the herd and which bulls to use for breeding. Under the previous system, called the Modified Contemporary Comparison, milk production records of a cow's offspring were not considered when evaluating the cow. Also, in evaluating bulls, neither their sons nor the genetic impact of their mate on their daughters was considered. The Animal Model is possible because supercomputers can handle the mountain of production information accumulated for more than 15 million cows over 30 years in a nationwide dairy herd improvement program.

Animal Improvement Programs Lab, Beltsville, MD
George R. Wiggans, (301) 344-2334

Silage-making can be improved by a computer program that ARS scientists have developed to predict the quality changes and losses in silage under various management practices, including the speed at which a silo is filled. The computer model integrated much of what is known about making silage, in part to help farmers predict feed quality so as to determine the proper diet for livestock. Different types, sizes and combinations of silos can also be compared, which will help farmers make money-saving decisions when buying a silo. The computer program is part of a larger dairy model that farmers can obtain by contacting the researcher and sending a floppy disk for copying.

U.S. Dairy Forage Research Center, East Lansing, MI
C. Alan Rotz, (517) 353-1758

Younger generations get blamed for many problems, and southwestern corn borers are no different than others. But a new computer model may spell the end for these highly destructive youngsters. These corn pests cause an annual loss of 1 percent of the nation's corn; 4 percent in the High Plains of Texas alone. The best time to apply insecticides to kill these pests is when second-generation corn borer eggs and young larvae first appear on plants. But knowing the exact time to spray has been a problem, especially since the larvae hide in corn ears, behind leaf sheaths and in stalks. A computer model, called Southwestern Corn Borer Model, designed by ARS scientists in collaboration with Texas A&M scientists, can predict when thousands of first generation moths will emerge to lay their eggs on flowering corn plants. Field tests have confirmed the accuracy of the model; around 60 percent of predicted emergence dates were within 2 days of the actual dates. Farmers and extension agents can use the model to develop pest management programs targeted for the corn borer when they're needed most.

Crop Science Research Lab, Mississippi State, MS
Frank M. Davis, (601) 323-2230

Meanwhile, corn growers on Virginia's Coastal Plains. could increase yields by using DRAINMOD, a new computer model, to design below-ground systems for controlled irrigation and drainage. Simulations on DRAIN-MOD have shown that for best distribution of irrigation water in cornfields, underground pipes should be spaced about 35 percent closer than is the usual practice for drainage only. Narrowing the spacing between pipes from the conventional 44 to 28 inches in Myatt fine sandy loam soil improves distribution of irrigation water and provides better drainage, two reasons for the higher yields.

Peanut Production Diseases and Harvesting Lab,
Suffolk, VA
Farrin S. Wright, (804) 657-6403

Computer programs can be found for almost everything; they've even got one to study controls for a kind of mosquito that infests flooded ricefields in the South. The dark ricefield mosquito is being studied using an ARS-developed computer model called PCSIM, for *Psorophora columbiae* Simulation. It was designed to help scientists figure out scenarios for various control practices. One encouraging result so far: Treating cattle with insecticides such as permethrin, or removing them from ricefields, can suppress adult mosquitoes and larvae from spring through fall. PCSIM also showed that tilling rice fields or applying insecticides provides only temporary relief. Field trials of the model results are being conducted in southeastern Louisiana.

Insects Affecting Man and Animals Research Lab,
Gainesville, FL
Dana A. Focks/Roy E. McLaughlin,
(904) 374-5976/5975

New and Improved Products

Natural enzymes from fungi could replace the use of ethylene gas as a method of ripening green tomatoes. While ethylene gas works well for ripening mature green tomatoes, immature ones, although they turn red, stay hard and unripe. But when scientists applied fungal enzymes to immature and mature green tomatoes, they softened as they reddened, providing a more uniform, quality product. That's because the enzymes break down cell walls and induce tomatoes to produce their own ethylene—usually faster than with artificial gas exposure.

Plant Physiology Research Lab, Athens, GA
Elizabeth A. Baldwin, (404) 546-3544

Body lice and the diseases they can transmit—typhus and relapsing fevers—are common problems faced by U.S. troops stationed in other countries. The fevers caused by lice, although not fatal, can be debilitating because they cause severe headache, fever and muscle aches. ARS, in cooperation with the Armed Forces Pest Management Board and the Department of Defense, originally developed military clothing with the insecticide permethrin impregnated in the fabric to protect soldiers against ticks and mosquitoes. Recently, this technique was tested against body lice in a cooperative study with the Uniformed Services University of the Health Sciences in Bethesda, Maryland. The result: 100 percent of lice were killed within 2 hours when exposed to insecticide-impregnated patches—even after the patches had been washed 20 times. It is expected that permethrin-treated cloth will provide long-term protection from lice and louse-borne diseases.

Insects Affecting Man and Animals Research Lab,
Gainesville, FL
Carl Schreck, (904) 374-5930

Fruit that tastes like a baked cinnamon apple dessert? Yes. Southern Florida's sugar apple and its relative, the atemoya, may become new additions to supermarket produce sections throughout the country. These tropical fruits, genus *Annona*, have had limited market potential because of their perishability. Current research with seedlings from Brazil could improve the sugar apple's 3- to 4-day shelf life. The atemoya—produced from the sugar apple and the *Annona cherimola*, a South American species from the Andes—is even more promising. Scientists found that hybrids produced from the sugar apple and cherimoyas from Australia and Israel may increase shelf life up to 10 to 14 days.

Subtropical Horticulture Research, Miami, FL
Robert J. Knight, (305) 238-3357

A new time- and labor-saving way to grow shiitake mushrooms may provide an added source of income for small farmers. Instead of drilling 15 to 20 holes in freshly cut oak logs, scientists smear the log ends with a mixture of grain and spawn (starter culture of the fungus *Lentinus edodes*). Tightly covering the ends of the logs with aluminum foil preserves needed moisture and eliminates contamination by other microorganisms, which could slow down mushroom production. Left outside and uncovered, which reduces insect and green mold damage, inoculated logs can produce mushrooms within 2 months and keep producing for up to about 6 years. The valuable and exotic shiitake is second only to the common white button. mushroom in annual cultivation worldwide.

Vegetable Lab, Beltsville, MD
William W. Cantelo, (301) 344-3380

Consumers are closer to getting themselves into a fine pickle—one with about half the salt. That's because Milwaukee-based Chr. Hansen's Laboratory, under an agreement between ARS and Pickles International, has been licensed to grow commercial quantities of two new ARS-developed bacterial strains for fermenting cucumbers. ARS researchers identified, selected and chemically mutated the new strains of *Lactobacillus plantarum* to help prevent pickle bloat. Bloat, caused by pockets of carbon dioxide gas, destroys the crunchiness required for premium pickles, but the new strains don't produce CO_2. To allow the gas to escape, now picklemakers use open-topped tanks. But leaving the top open requires using a lot of salt to prevent contamination by rain water and foreign material. With the new strains, picklemakers could use closed top tanks and less salt. (PATENT)

Food Science Research Lab, Raleigh, NC
Henry P. Fleming, (919) 737-2979

New polymers with industrial uses and a natural, noncaloric sweetener may eventually result from the study of polysaccharides—a long chain of sugar molecules—made by a bacterium found in the gastrointestinal tract of ruminant animals. Many of these polysaccharides contain the sugar L-altrose—patented as a noncaloric sweetener, but until now only available at high cost as a lab-produced speciality chemical. ARS scientists have recently agreed to work cooperatively with a private firm to see if these polysaccharides have novel properties that would make them commercially valuable. Polysaccharides are already extensively used in textiles, adhesives, paper, paint, drugs, detergents and foods and to recover oil from low-producing wells. (PATENT)

Fermentation Biochemistry, Northern Regional Research Center, Peoria, IL
Robert J. Stack, (309) 685-4011, ext. 339

Gins that specialize in processing the longer-than-normal fiber of Pima cotton could be run twice as fast if operated by computers. Pima's longer fibers must be removed from cotton seed by a slower, gentler gin than that used for shorter fibered, regular cotton. Engineers have worked out a computer program to operate a small gin five times faster without damaging cotton fibers. The program relies on information supplied by sensors on the gin. Pima cotton is fashioned into more luxurious cloth because of its longer fibers. Currently, U.S. production of Pima is less than one-tenth that of regular cotton because Pima is a specialty cotton that is grown only in New Mexico, Texas and Arizona.

Southwestern Cotton Ginning Research Lab, Mesilla Park, NM
Ed Hughs, (505) 526-6381

Market potatoes quickly and you may sidestep the effects of purple top, a disease that causes dark-colored potato chips. Scientists have found that purple top—transmitted by infected aster leafhoppers—does not immediately create the chemical changes that ruin a potato. It can take up to 4 months for the disease to cause sugars to develop within the stored potato, which results in dark, low-quality chips. By shipping infected potatoes to processing plants within 4 months of harvest, product quality remains high. Researchers will now try to develop a uniform test for early detection of purple top—which does not affect humans or animals.

Potato Research Lab, East Grand Forks, MN
Paul H. Orr, (218) 773-2473

Calcium is known for building stronger bones, but now it's also credited with making sturdier strawberries. In a 3-year study, calcium was applied to growing Cardinal and Fern variety strawberries. Scientists had hoped the calcium would make the berries firmer; instead, it enabled berries to better withstand storage. On some test plots, the calcium was worked into the soil, while elsewhere it was sprayed directly on the berry plants or delivered via drip-irrigation systems. After berries from treated plants were stored at 70 degrees F for 3 days to accelerate decay, they had 5 to 8 percent less decay, regardless of the way the calcium had been applied.

South Central Family Farm Research, Booneville, AR
Donald J. Makus, (501) 675-3834

What do cattle and carpets have in common? Both could count on kenaf for support, scientists say. Kenaf is a plant that can grow 15 to 18 feet in 5 to 6 months. While it's primarily being tested as a home-grown source of newsprint, it may also provide feed for cattle and fiber for carpet backing, and its fibers can be used for rope, roof felt and fire logs. Until now, the top 2 to 3 feet of the plant have been lopped off in harvest and left in the field to rot. But researchers believe this leafy portion of the plant may make good cattle forage. Kenaf leaves are very digestible and have a feed value similar to alfalfa's. Cattle producers could get several tons of forage per acre from kenaf and help cut the herd's protein costs. Sheep readily devour kenaf tops, and studies are underway to determine the plant's suitability as hay or silage for cattle as well.

Forage and Livestock Research, El Reno, OK
William A. Phillips, (405) 262-5291

Keeping with the consumer trend toward "natural" food products, researchers are working on a new, 100-percent fruit juice drink. The drink, a blend of passion fruit and orange juices, scored better with taste test panels when the amount of orange juice exceeded the amount of passion fruit juice. Passion fruit has a full-bodied, tangy flavor that tends to be more popular when mixed with another juice. Abundant in Australia and Brazil, passion fruit is rarely consumed as a fresh fruit because of its many seeds. Researchers plan other all-natural tropical fruit juice blends, including ones with mango, for the health-conscious consumer.

Citrus and Subtropical Products Lab, Winter Haven, FL
Philip E. Shaw, (813) 293-4133

Alfalfa declines in yield and number of plants after 4 or 5 years in the same field. That's because alfalfa is auto-toxic—it poisons itself. Scientists believe the toxin helps alfalfa defend itself against insects, fungi and competition from other plants, but a slow buildup of the toxin in the soil eventually takes its own toll. Researchers have now isolated the compound medicarpin from alfalfa roots as one of the culprit chemicals in the toxin. In lab tests, alfalfa seedling growth was reduced by 40 percent for 72 hours after being dipped in a medicarpin solution. The compound also delayed seed germination for 4 hours and seedling growth for 48 hours. In soil containing no medicarpin, seedling emergence was 16 percent greater than in soil with the compound. Next, researchers will try to determine how much medicarpin is produced by different varieties of alfalfa while testing the compound as a potential, natural biodegradable herbicide for various weeds.

Bioactive Constituents Research, Northern Regional
Research Center, Peoria, IL
David L. Dornbos, Jr., (309) 685-4011

A creature feared in the days of wooden ships harbors a bacterium that researchers hope will someday help improve animal nutrition. The marine shipworm, the scourge of wooden ships, carries the as-yet-unnamed bacterium for one reason: It converts atmospheric nitrogen and cellulose into protein that helps the shipworm grow on its diet of wood. But researchers have found the bacterium may also be useful in converting agricultural residues into more nutritious animal feed. The bacterium grows well on wheat straw and corn stover, changing the waste plant material into more valuable protein. How the bacterium accomplishes this and its commercial application to corn residues will be subjects of future research.

Plant Polymer Research, Northern Regional
Research Center, Peoria, IL
Richard V. Greene, (309) 685-4011

Ten newly discovered natural substances might hold the key to removing the bitter taste from navel orange juice and some other winter citrus fruits. These chemicals, which ARS researchers have named "limonoid glucosides," are found in maturing citrus fruit. They are formed from two bitter parent compounds, nomilin and limonin, and contain a sugar molecule, glucose. Studies show they are only slightly bitter, as compared to their intensely bitter parent chemicals. Boosting production of the glucosides in citrus cells might eliminate bitterness and increase the market value of navel oranges and several other winter citrus— including some varieties of grapefruit, lemon and tangerine. Bitterness compounds form several hours after navel orange juice is extracted. That means only limited amounts of this juice can be added to frozen orange juice and other juice products, costing California navel orange growers an estimated $6 to $8 million a year.

Fruit and Vegetable Chemistry Research Lab, Pasadena, CA
S. Hasegawa/Z. Herman/R.D. Bennett, (818) 796-0239

Air heated to 117 degrees F will kill fruit flies trying to piggyback their way into the United States inside freshly picked papaya. Melon, Mediterranean and oriental fruit flies are snuffed out without damaging the taste or texture of other papayas in the shipment. Growers in tropical climates such as Hawaii may be able to use the process to also treat atemoya, mango and other exotic tropical fruits and vegetables to open new export markets. Hawaiian growers sold $11 million of fresh and processed papaya to Japanese, Canadian and mainland U.S. markets in 1987. USDA's Animal and Plant Health Inspection Service is now in the process of incorporating this treatment into its regulations for papaya shipped from Hawaii. These regulations guard against fruit fly outbreaks on the mainland. Commercially grown papaya is carefully checked before it leaves Hawaii to guard against consumers finding a fruit fly-damaged papaya in the supermarket.

Tropical Fruit and Vegetable Research Lab, Hilo, HI
John W. Armstrong, (808) 959-9138

Soil, Water and Air

TV news from the underground? A mini-camera is giving scientists a live-action look at crop roots. They are learning the effects of water- and soil-conserving tillage techniques on crop roots and ultimately on crop harvests. The camera, originally a medical tool for surgical explorations of the human body, is attached to a long metal shaft. The shaft is lowered into a clear rigid tube inserted in cropland. The viewer then sees crop roots on a television monitor. Unfortunately, the rigid tube causes visibility problems from water condensation and soil smearing. It also compacts soil and changes root growth near the tube. Now, scientists are having some success by sealing a plastic bag over the tube. When air is pumped between the tube and the plastic, the pressure keeps the plastic tight against the soil, eliminating gaps that make it harder to see the roots. Yet the bag is flexible enough to avoid most disturbance to soil.

Northern Great Plains Research Lab, Mandan, ND
Stephen D. Merrill, (701) 663-6445

Like a dehydration process, soil freezing sucks water from underlying soil, ultimately affecting crop growth, erosion and water pollution. Studies, now in their seventh winter, have shown that this redistribution of soil water can last well into spring planting time. In cool, humid climates, water that accumulates this way in the upper 2 feet of soil can promote quicker seed germination and earlier growth. It may also provide an extra reservoir against drought. In warmer, drier climates to the west and south, however, the sun may evaporate water drawn up to the top 4 inches of a bare-plowed field. Fall-through-spring cycles of freezing and thawing can open up a badly compacted soil. But these cycles also make good soil more erodible, increasing runoff and the potential for runoff-related pollution by fertilizers and pesticides. The cycles also influence the effectiveness of various tillage methods and the timing of spring planting. Researchers are now developing a computer model for freeze-and-thaw cycles. To account for winter's effects, it will be merged with USDA models predicting soil erosion and water pollution.

North Central Soil Conservation Research Lab, Morris, MN
George R. Benoit, (612) 589-3411

Private firms are marketing ARS-developed computer programs aimed at reducing farm demand for electricity to operate irrigation sprinklers. The computer programs help farmers to not only pay lower utility bills, but also increase crop yields even though watering is reduced. One farmer near Yuma, CO, boosted his corn yield by 25 percent and reduced the number of times he had to visit his fields from twice a day to only eight times a month. Scientists originally worked out the programs to schedule irrigation and shut off pumps selectively on huge center-pivot sprinklers when electric power suppliers were facing potential brown-outs; cooperating irrigators following these schedules paid lower rates.

Irrigation and Drainage Research, Fort Collins, CO
Dale F. Heermann, (303) 491-8229

Artificial pools in streambeds can prevent downstream erosion and make better fishing holes than naturally occurring pools. Steel or concrete barriers, called low-drop grade structures, were placed in some streams in Mississippi's Yazoo River Basin. Studies showed the barriers keep the fast-flowing water from cutting river channels too deep, eroding streambeds and depositing soil or gravel at the mouth of the stream. Even though the pools that form just downstream from the barriers are similar in size to natural pools, they are less apt to cause erosion. They also provide stable channels and supplies of food and oxygen for fish. While scientists collected more fish and a greater number of species from the natural pools, the synthetic pools yielded about 11 percent more fish of harvestable size. The Yazoo River Basin makes up the Demonstration Erosion Control Project (DEC), set up in 1984 by the U.S. Army Corps of Engineers and USDA's Soil Conservation Service to find ways to control erosion, sedimentation and flooding. ARS engineers designed the barriers.

Sedimentation Lab, Oxford, MS
C.M. Cooper/S.S. Knight, (601) 232-2900

Cows now graze where little or no vegetation once grew on more than 15,000 acres of reclaimed strip-mined land in the northern Great Plains. The reclaimed plains are being transformed into lush rangeland that produces more forage than nearby undisturbed land. All known reclamation efforts had failed on this bentonite-mined land. But scientists found that sawdust, wood chips and tree bark plus nitrogen fertilizer aided plant growth best. Reclamation is now three-fourths done; 5,000 more acres will be reclaimed by 1990. This same technology is now being evaluated for use on bauxite-mined land in Australia.

High Plains Grasslands Research, Cheyenne, WY
Gerald E. Schuman, (307) 772-2433

Switchgrass and big bluestem, warm-season forages usually grown in the West, **have an extraordinary tolerance for extremely acid soils** common to mined areas of the Northeast. These perennial grasses grow well enough in very acid mine soil, without any added dressings of lime, that the land could be used for grazing or wildlife habitat. The grasses tolerate the low levels of soil nutrients and high levels of aluminum and would also help control soil erosion during reclamation of mined land.

U.S. Regional Pasture Research Lab,
University Park, PA
Gerald A. Jung, (814) 963-0948

Too much aluminum in acid soil, scientists now know, prevents enzymes in corn root membranes from doing what they are supposed to do—letting nutrients into the plant. But when roots get normal amounts of oxygen (from the soil) and glucose (from photosynthesis), the aluminum is trapped in the walls of root cells. Adding calcium lime to the soil, a recommended practice, can reduce but not completely stop aluminum's harmful effect. Scientists found about these mechanisms using nuclear magnetic resonance spectroscopy (NMR), which can examine plant root activity in living tissue as it happens. This new information could be used to genetically engineer aluminum-resistant crops and improve management practices on acid soils.

Plant and Soil Biophysics Research, Eastern Regional Research Center, Philadelphia, PA
Shu-I Tu/Philip E. Pfeffer, (215) 233-6611/6469

Yecorra Rojo ranks first in tests of wheat varieties that tolerate acid soils. Of eight wheat varieties studied, it can best withstand dry periods and take up nutrients from these low-pH soils. Acid soils prevent crop roots from taking up needed nutrients and water from subsurface soil layers. Planting this wheat variety could lower the cost of liming soil to raise its pH. To find the more acid-tolerant wheat, scientists tested the eight varieties by measuring root length and ability to absorb water. Yecorra Rojo grew the longest roots and extracted about three times more water from an acid subsoil than the variety most sensitive to acid soil. Titan, another variety, came in second.

Appalachian Soil and Water Conservation Lab, Beckley, WV
R.J. Wright/V.C. Baligar, (304) 252-6426
Tropical Agricultural Research Station, Mayaguez, PR
Kenneth D. Ritchey, (809) 834-2435

Wheat plants lose up to 4 percent of the nitrogen fertilizer they take up from the soil—a loss 10 times greater than earlier tests had indicated. A very sensitive new lab technique detected the loss, most of which occurs when grain is formed. Its discovery will help environmental scientists better predict the consequences of human activity on our atmosphere. To make reliable predictions, scientists need to calculate precise amounts of all natural and manufactured gases that cover the globe—and knowing how much gas is given off by plants becomes essential. Also, researchers would like to breed future plant varieties that are more efficient in retaining nitrogen because that determines how much protein plants contain.

Irrigation and Drainage Research, Fort Collins, CO
William A. O'Deen, (303) 482-5733

Ozone may be a bigger enemy than acid rain to loblolly pine trees in the Southeast. Data from a preliminary 2-year pilot study of three loblolly pine families showed that ozone levels of 2.25 and 3 times more than the average level in the air (about 2 parts per million) suppressed trunk diameter growth as much as 19 percent and height growth by as much as 12 percent. Pine needles also matured and dropped off faster under high ozone conditions. Acid rain, on the other hand, even at 100 times more acid than the average for the area, did not suppress pine growth during the pilot study. Effects from acid rain may show up when the trees are followed for a longer period of time.

Air Quality-Plant Growth and Development Lab, Raleigh, NC
W.W. Heck, (919) 737-3311

Crop Production and Protection

Why do some plant varieties have greater natural pest-resistance than others? To answer that question, a research team chemically analyzed juice from the green parts of resistant corn and cotton plants. They found that the resistant cotton plants have more natural bug toxin than susceptible varieties. The resistant corn has more fiber but less protein and sugar than susceptible corn and also differs in amino acid content, factors which may account for pest resistance. The research could have three payoffs. First, genetic engineers could duplicate and insert genes for these traits to develop new commercial varieties. Second, if scientists find varieties within species that have more than one kind of resistance, they could combine these traits for a double whammy against pests. Finally, they could screen new plants for resistance in the lab by looking for chemical traits instead of having to actually grow the crop to see if insects attack—cutting screening time substantially.

Crops Research Lab, Mississippi State, MS
Paul Hedin/Frank Davis/W. Paul Williams,
(601) 325-2311

To help guard against the Russian wheat aphid, grain farmers should avoid planting certain grasses—especially cool-season species. Researchers can provide some timely advice to farmers wishing to return highly erodible cropland to soil-protecting grasses and trees. First found in Texas in 1986, the aphid now inhabits 15 western states. It devastates wheat and barley but also dines on a smorgasbord of cool- and warm-season grasses and weeds. In the greenhouse, researchers tested how the aphid fared on 124 plant species. It survived on all cool-season grasses, except Mediterranean ricegrass, and on about half the warm-season grasses. None of the 27 legumes or 17 native forbs played host to the insect. Some of the warm-season grasses that resist aphid damage include switchgrass, little and big bluestems, several lovegrasses, sacatons, bermudagrass and indiangrass. The resistant cool-season grasses are reed canarygrass, Kentucky bluegrass, red top and pubescent wheatgrass.

Wheat and Other Cereal Crops Research, Plant Science Research Lab, Stillwater, OK
S. Dean Kindler, (405) 624-4189

Meanwhile, Turkish wasps are being studied as a potential new weapon in the battle against the Russian wheat aphid, which cost Northwest farmers about $100 million in chemical control in 1988. To see how the wasps survive and reproduce, ARS and Washington State University scientists released three species into a caged area covering aphid-infested grass. The wasps lay their eggs in the bodies of immature aphids. Hatching wasp larvae feed on the aphids, killing them. Adult wasps eventually emerge and look for other aphids to parasitize. Only a millimeter or two in length, the wasps are natural enemies of the Russian wheat aphid in its native habitat in southwestern Asia.

Plant Germplasm Introduction and Testing, Pullman, WA
Stephen L. Clement, (509) 335-1502
European Parasite Lab, Behoust, France
Raymond F. Moore, (301) 344-2605

Stabilizing or increasing the growth of winter wheat is the goal of many wheat breeding programs in the Pacific Northwest. Dusty, a soft white winter wheat developed by the ARS in cooperation with Washington State University, was released to wheat producers. The new variety produces more grain per acre than present commercial winter wheat varieties and is very resistant to the cereal diseases common bunt and stripe rust. Dusty should help stabilize production and make it possible for northwestern wheat growers to produce grain more economically.

Wheat Genetics, Quality, Physiology.and Disease Research, Pullman, WA
Clarence J. Peterson, (509) 335-3632

An exotic Japanese soybean has been found with extraordinary resistance to drought. Under extreme water stress, this soybean yields up to 25 percent more than some of the best yielding varieties grown in the Southeast. Two mechanisms give the soybean its drought tolerance: A much deeper root system and an unusual process called osmotic adjustment. In this process, various compounds such as salts and sugars accumulate in the leaves. This increases levels of organic acids, which in turn promote water retention and prevent wilting. The deep root system, besides delivering water to the plant more efficiently, allows it to tolerate high levels of aluminum in the soil. The next steps by ARS scientists: Pinpoint which of the chemical changes due to osmotic adjustment are most important to the plant's drought tolerance and then transfer this trait to high-yielding farm varieties.

Soybean and Nitrogen Fixation Research Lab, Raleigh, NC
Richard Wilson/Thomas E. Carter, Jr., (919) 737-3171

"Flower power" has new meaning for soybean breeders. Most soybean plants are both male and female so they are . self-pollinating. But soybeans that only function as females can now be readily identified by their white flowers. That could be time-saving news for breeders wanting to produce hybrids through insect pollination rather than tedious hand pollination. The discovery came when scientists located at least one useful marker genes in a new soybean line. Such genes make an organism express a readily detected trait—such as white instead of purple flowers—that in itself may not be valuable. Markers are useful if associated with other genes that do affect important traits. And in the new line, the white-flower marker is on the same chromosome as a gene or genes that make the plant male-sterile. The male sterility came about by an unexpected mutation, which the marker enables breeders to exploit. It means that white-flowered plants will nearly always produce hybrid seed when insects fertilize them with pollen carried from purple-flowered plants. Until now, none of the five male-sterile mutations discovered since 1971 was closely linked to marker genes. Researchers are now working to link other marker genes to important measurable traits.

Cereal and Soybean Improvement, Ames, IA
Reid G. Palmer, (515) 294-7378

A newly discovered plant enzyme may, through genetic engineering, lead to soybeans and other crops that will be more efficient at photosynthesis—converting atmospheric carbon dioxide to sugars. ARS scientists discovered the enzyme, carboxyarabinitol-1-phosphatase in spinach and tobacco leaves. In these plants, the enzyme starts working at sunup. It splits a phosphate compound produced by leaves at night to block the activity of rubisco, an essential enzyme in the first step of photosynthesis. Without the newly discovered enzyme, rubisco wouldn't switch on after sunrise. One idea being explored is whether the new enzyme could be altered to start work at lower light intensities—earlier in the morning or under heavy cloud cover.

Tobacco and Forage Research, Lexington, KY
Michael E. Salvucci, (606) 257-2683

Cantaloupes grown in soil treated with mycorrhizal fungi can overcome infestations of tiny worms that chew on the roots. Greenhouse experiments show that the fungus attaches to cantaloupe roots—in effect, lengthening them—and promotes their uptake of soil nutrients. This counteracts the harm done by the worms, called **nematodes**. Nematodes cause U.S cantaloupe growers to lose as much as 20 percent of their crop. Inoculating the soil with mycorrhizal fungi could reduce that figure considerably.
Plant Health and Stress Physiology Lab, Weslaco, TX
Charles M. Heald, Jr., (512) 968-7546

Walnut trees of the future may be able to rely on borrowed genes to ward off damaging insects and diseases, now that scientists have transferred a foreign gene into walnut embryos. Some experimental embryos—the beginnings of the familiar nutmeat—took up the gene and have produced plants that also contain the active gene. Since this marker gene—not useful in walnut trees—proved that a gene can be taken up and work, subsequent embryo experiments will use other useful genes to confer traits such as resistance to codling moth. Such transfers of genes into embryos may be the best technique yet for moving valuable traits into walnuts, pecans, almonds, grapes, cherries and peaches.
Crops Pathology and Genetics Research, Davis, CA
Gale H. McGranahan, (916) 752-0113

Tiny hairs that ooze a gluelike substance are what give the pecan tree Pawnee its resistant edge against aphids. Since these pests reproduce so quickly—yellow aphids, for example, produce about 15 generations per year with 40 to 60 young in each generation—they are difficult to control and require frequent spraying. But scientists noticed much smaller aphid populations on Pawnee and found that small hairs on stems and leaves secrete a thick fluid. The aphids' little legs get stuck on this glue and they die from exhaustion. Scientists breeding for aphid resistance in pecans trees can simply look for this trait instead of having to grow rows of trees and check to see which have the fewest aphids.
Pecan Genetics and Improvement, Brownwood, TX
Tommy Thompson, (915) 646-0593

An Asiatic-type citrus canker strain has been identified at two sites in commercial citrus groves in Manatee County, Florida. The disease, caused by the bacterium *Xanthomonas campestris* pathovar *citri*, appeared as lesions on leaves, stems and fruit on more than 800 trees in an 80-acre grove. If controlled, canker usually doesn't kill the tree, but it makes fruit less attractive for sale and causes severely infected fruit to drop prematurely. Control methods are available. While citrus canker disease can be eradicated by destroying infected trees, a new method based on defoliation is being evaluated. Now that the bacterial disease has been identified, the Animal and Plant Health Inspection Service will determine the next step—some type of control strategy.
National Program Staff, Beltsville, MD
Edwin L. Civerolo, (301) 344-3915

Red maples that resist potato leafhoppers have been identified for the first time. This landscape tree, which is grown from Minnesota to Florida, must currently be protected from leafhoppers by chemical pesticides. Now scientists have found a method to breed and select for resistance to these pests, which distort and stunt trees in nurseries. In tests with over 3,000 red maples from all over the country, trees that came from the far north had the most resistance and showed the least injury when exposed to the leafhoppers.
U.S. National Arboretum, Washington, DC
Alden Townsend, (202) 475-4848

Home and truck gardeners can look forward to a new beefsteak tomato—just released to breeders—that is shapely, tasty, extra firm and resistant to several diseases. Many beefsteak tomatoes are prone to cracking and bruising and lack the smooth, globe shape of the new variety. Along with crack and bruise resistance, the yet unnamed tomato resists *Fusarium* and *Verticillium* wilt diseases that afflict tomatoes in the East. Tasters informally rated the new variety at least as flavorful as existing beefsteak types.
Plant Genetics and Germplasm Institute, Beltsville, MD
Allan K. Stoner, (301) 344-3235

Specially treated faba beans grown alongside fertilized oats can increase the yield and nutritional value of forage for Alaskan dairy cattle. The combination of faba beans (a legume) with oats (a grain) as a forage may be a first for Alaskan agriculture. Scientists alternated the bean and oat seeds in paired rows. Bean seed was inoculated with nitrogen-fixing *Rhizobia* bacteria, which helped the beans fix over 50 pounds per acre of nitrogen for their own use. This added nitrogen increased protein levels in the faba beans—and therefore in the oat/faba bean forage. By selectively adding nitrogen fertilizer, the scientists tripled oat yields, even though the oats were unable to use the nitrogen fixed by the faba beans. There's a hitch, however. Faba bean seed is costly in Alaska because it must be imported from Canada and Washington. ARS researchers are working with University of Alaska scientists to produce faba bean seed within Alaska.

Subarctic Agricultural Research, Fairbanks, AK
Verlan L. Cochran, (907) 474-7652

A salt bath or bed of gelatin may be the newest and best way to gently release a pollen cell's contents—intact. Using the bath or gelatin may avoid the damage that scientists suspect results when other tactics are used to release cell contents (protoplast) from leaf, stem and root cells. Researchers expect that pollen protoplasts freed by the new methods can be nurtured into healthy plantlets. If so, this could simplify plant breeders' search for superior plants with useful new genes. The pollen plantlets would contain only the genetic material of one parent—the male. Plantlets produced from leaf, stem or root protoplast, in contrast, contain genes of both parents. Other possible applications of the research: Genetic engineers might be able to infuse bath-extracted protoplasts with useful new genes. Or, they might be able to use them in protoplast fusion, a technique that makes it possible to produce new hybrids by fusing protoplasts of plant species that don't breed with each other in nature. The saline bath safely pops protoplast out from the protective walls of green bean pollen cells. The gelatin technique shatters the cell wall to release protoplasts of green peppers, tomatoes, lima beans, cucumbers, zucchini, soybeans and black-eyed peas. *(PATENT)*

Plant Development-Quality Research, Western Regional Research Center, Albany, CA
Merle L. Weaver, (415) 559-5760

Whorls of hairs found on the young, emerging roots of big sagebrush (*Artemesia tridentata*) help these desirable native range plants germinate. ARS scientists discovered that the hairs on the seedlings help anchor the seed to the soil surface, ensuring that the root tip will penetrate the soil to help the plant survive on hot, dry desert range. Improved varieties of the shrub might be bred with more root hairs. Big sagebrush can be planted to reclaim areas disturbed by surface strip mining or to establish or restore wildlife habitats.

Landscape Ecology of Rangelands Research, Reno, NV
James A. Young, (702) 784-6057

Insect Research

The world's tiniest bar codes, miniature versions of those found on most supermarket packages, are helping scientists keep track of honey bees. Only one-tenth of an inch wide, these codes are glued to the hairs on bees' backs so laser scanners at the entrances to hives can record their comings and goings. Such information will help scientists spot superior bees that are healthier and more productive. The new technique is less time-consuming than previous tagging techniques and requires much less handling of the bees, which upsets their normal behavior and has flawed some research findings.

Carl Hayden Bee Research Center, Tucson, AZ
Stephen L. Buchmann, (602) 629-6327

Hanging plastic strips impregnated with fluvalinate in beehives kills more than 90 percent of varroa mites infesting the honey bees within a week. This information is the result of cooperative work between scientists at ARS, USDA's Animal and Plant Health Inspection Service (APHIS) and Zoecon, the company that manufactures the pesticide strips. Fluvalinate, a chemical currently registered for use on mites in ornamental and crop plants, also kills the blood-sucking bee pest without hurting bees. APHIS has received emergency registration from the Environmental Protection Agency to use the plastic-impregnated fluvalinate strips to detect and control the varroa mite in colonies of honey bees. Varroa mites were first found in Wisconsin in 1987 and have been found in 17 other states—including Florida, Georgia, South Carolina, Mississippi, Minnesota, Michigan, Illinois, Indiana, Ohio, Pennsylvania, New York,

Massachusetts, Maine, Washington, North and South Dakota and Nebraska—causing major problems for bee-keepers and farmers who rely on honey bees for pollinating a wide range of crops.

Beneficial Insects Lab, Beltsville, MD
H. Shimanuki, (301) 344-2205

Steroids have been splashed across a lot of sports pages recently. Believe it or not, insects also use steroids. Insects, unlike mammals, are incapable of synthesizing sterols and need dietary cholesterol or plant sterols to produce cells and tissues and reproduce normally. Tobacco hornworms—a good model for studying how insects function—use cholesterol to make steroids such as the molting hormones for their normal growth. ARS scientists have also discovered that insects use cholesterol to produce pregnenediol, a compound structurally related to steroid hormones found in mammals. The exact function of the steroid, found on the insects' eggs, is unknown. Entomologists think it might deter predators or protect the eggs from harmful bacteria or fungi. Knowing just how the steroid works could lead to better ways of controlling insects.

Insect and Nematode Hormone Lab, Beltsville, MD
Malcolm J. Thompson/James E. Oliver, (301) 344-2389

A friendly wasp, *Uga menoni*, might someday help stop the Mexican bean beetle—a major pest of soybeans and green beans on the East Coast. ARS scientists in Korea collected the tiny wasp for release in Maryland and Delaware by U.S.-based colleagues during the summer of 1988. The wasp is harmless to humans. If it survives the winter, scientists hope it will increase in number so as to curb the bean beetle. ARS researchers tried once before to establish the helpful wasp on the East Coast, but only one made it through the winter. Female wasps lay a single egg inside the bean beetle's bright yellow, wormlike larva. The egg develops into a larva that feeds on the bean beetle larva, then pupates, later emerging as an adult wasp.

Asian Parasite Lab, Seoul, Korea
Phone: 82-02-963-6561
David K. Reed (Stillwater, OK), (405) 624-4407
Beneficial Insects Research Lab, Newark, DE
Paul W. Schaefer, (302) 731-7330

The sex perfume of a tiny wasp is being formulated in ARS labs. Scientists have begun reproducing two components of the sex pheromone of *Microplitis croceipes*, a wasp that can provide 85 to 90 percent **control of tobacco budworms and cotton bollworms.** If produced on a large scale, the pheromone could entice the tiny wasps to stay in farmers' fields or be used in traps to count wasp numbers. Such a head count of wasps would tell a farmer when not to spray pesticides. These two pests devour $1 billion in cotton, corn, soybeans, tobacco, tomatoes and other vegetables each year—despite the $250 million a year worth of insecticides applied to crops.

Southern Field Crop Insect Management Lab, Stoneville, MS
Gary Elzen, (601) 686-2311

Entomologists are trying to reproduce a natural chemical that keeps female corn earworm moths from mating again. Male moths transfer this chemical to females when they mate. Found in the female's blood for up to 2 hours after mating, this "mating factor" both prevents a female from producing a sex attractant called a pheromone and halts her desire for and receptivity to other males. Scientists determined that even if sperm does not enter the female, the mating factor will still be transferred. Once it is identified and a suitable method of applying it to insects in the field is developed, the chemical could be an environmentally sound way to control a pest that costs farmers about $2 billion a year.

Insect Chemical Ecology Lab, Beltsville, MD
Ashok Raina, (301) 344-4396

Even the despised corn rootworm must eat. Now, a new "burger" diet for this insect pest saves time for scientists who need to raise hundreds of thousands of rootworms for research studies. The new food is a firm patty that sticks to the bottom of the insects' diet container. It's meant to replace the dry, granular diet that is standard fare for adult rootworms in lab tests—and that spills easily during shipping and routine tests. Rootworm beetles fed the new diet laid as many eggs as those on the dry diet. There was also no difference in egg viability—the number of live eggs. The new diet is nutritious and easy to make and allows for quick cleanup of cages.

Grain Insects Research Lab, Brookings, SD
Terry F. Branson, (605) 693-5208

Black cutworms, a serious pest in the Corn Belt, are creatures of habit. And corn farmers can now turn that habit to their advantage. Researchers have found that adult black cutworm moths begin their northward migration from Texas following the first southerly winds of spring. The insects take to the air for three or four nights of flight, during which time they mature sexually. Upon arrival in the Midwest, they mate immediately and females lay their eggs. By catching early-arriving adult cutworms in pheromone traps in cornfields—an event that can be forecast by extension agents using an Iowa State University-ARS computer model—farmers can pinpoint the best time to start applying insecticides to protect their crops.

Corn Insects Research, Ankeny, IA
William B. Showers, (515) 964-6664

By destroying cotton stalks immediately after harvest, farmers can reduce by as much as 80 percent the amount of pesticides they use the following season to kill boll weevils. As a result, a new Texas law mandates the destruction of cotton stalks to help suppress the boll weevil in that state. In tests, farmers destroying cotton stalks applied pesticides only 3 to 4 times the next season; on untouched cottonfields, 15 to 18 applications were needed. Boll weevils use cotton stalks for food and shelter over winter, producing a whole new population the following year to infest the next crop. The new law can be enforced with aerial infrared photography for about a half cent per acre using a system developed by the scientists.

Subtropical Agricultural Research Lab, Weslaco, TX
K.R. Summy, (512) 968-6739

Not all flies are pests; most are relatively inconspicuous but important elements of ecosystems, and some are even beneficial. Two newly identified species may be useful as biological controls against disease-carrying snails. Sciomyzid flies prey on fresh-water snails, some of which serve as hosts to flatworms that cause parasitic diseases in cattle and humans. One disease, schistosomiasis—the second most serious parasitic disease in humans—can cause fever or damage to various organs, especially the liver. Another disease, fascioliasis, causes liver inflammation in cattle and sheep—as well as fever, diarrhea and jaundice in humans. Found worldwide, flatworms are more prevalent in tropical rural communities where water hygiene is minimal. Because of this, scientists are intrigued by the potential of sciomyzidae flies to reduce snail populations. Scientists plan to "model" the effect of such snail suppression on the

transmission of flatworm parasites to humans and livestock. These studies may lead to the development of a practical technology for alleviating these serious diseases.

Biological Control of Weeds Lab-Europe, Rome, Italy
Lloyd V. Knutson, Phone: 011-39-6-648-0140

Screwworm flies are more abundant in forests than in livestock pastures, experts have discovered. Trapping flies to monitor the effectiveness of controls has been concentrated in pastures where livestock graze. But in a recent study geared to extension of the screwworm eradication program into Central America, scientists found an abundance of screwworm flies in forests even though few livestock were there for the flies to parasitize. In Mexico, Belize, Guatemala and Costa Rica, hundreds of adult female flies were captured, tagged and released and later recaptured. Flies that were released in forests tended to stay there; those released in pastures tended to migrate into the forests—and researchers aren't sure why. One explanation is that before the Spanish introduced cattle to Central America in the early 1500's, the flies probably infested deer, tapir, agouti (a large rodent) and other mammals believed to have been common in the forests. These animals were also susceptible to bites from vampire bats, and the flies could have exploited the wounds as egg-laying sites.

Screwworm Research,
Tuxtla Guiterreza, Chiapas, Mexico
Donald B. Thomas, Phone: 011-52-961-33550

Human Nutrition

Can a person be overweight—and not be fat? Determining obesity with weight-to-height tables was found to be about as accurate as skinfold measurements—and that's not very accurate. For example, muscular athletes such as weightlifters and football players could easily score overweight despite their low body fat. Searching for a simple yet accurate way to predict obesity and its related diseases, scientists compared the weight-height tables with standard methods for estimating body fat content in 593 men and women. About 30 percent of those rated "overweight" based on the tables were in the normal range for body fat levels. And 11 percent of the women and 18 percent of the men who scored "obese" didn't have excessive body fat. A problem is that scientists have not yet defined obesity as it relates to disease: Is it overweight or, as some recent studies indicate, overfat or distribution of body fat? While science grapples with that question, ARS researchers are looking for a body measurement, such as waist or hip girth, that can be plugged into weight-height indices to give health and fitness practitioners a more accurate estimate.

Grand Forks Human Nutrition Research Center, Grand Forks, ND
William A. Siders, (701) 795-8430

Runners, cyclists and other very active men need about 60 percent more protein than current dietary recommendations, a study shows. But there's little reason for concern because all western diets supply more than enough protein, even vegetarian diets that include milk and eggs. This is the first study to show that physically active men, both young and middle-aged, need more protein than sedentary men. The current U.S. and World Health Organization recommended daily protein intake—0.8 gram per kilogram of body weight—is based on studies of sedentary men and was not thought to differ for active men. Based on the 12 very active men in this study—half in their twenties and half in their fifties—an average of 1.25 g, or about 60 percent more protein, would be the recommended intake for athletes. USDA food consumption data indicate that men in this age range already average at least 70 percent more protein than the Recommended Dietary Allowance. Athletes who maintain their weights are getting enough protein. Only those who continually diet, such as dancers, gymnasts and wrestlers, may be getting less than they need.

Human Nutrition Research Center on Aging at Tufts, Boston, MA
Carol Meredith, now in California at (916) 386-2836

Women don't have to be anemic to have tired blood. A recent study found that women have less energy available during a workout and tire faster when their iron stores are low. After 11 healthy young women consumed a low-iron diet for three months, they used less oxygen during hard exercise, burned fewer calories and accumulated considerably more lactate, which causes that "lead in the legs" feeling. According to their hemoglobin and hematocrit levels, two measures of iron associated with red blood cells, the women were in the low-normal range for iron after the low-iron diet. But their indicator of stored iron—serum ferritin—had dropped dramatically to one-fifth the starting

level. As exercise progresses, the body normally switches from burning all glucose (anaerobic exercise) to burning a mixture of glucose and fat (aerobic exercise). But it takes more oxygen to burn fat, so the women continued to burn mostly glucose. And that's not as fuel efficient.

Grand Forks Human Nutrition Research Center, Grand Forks, ND
Henry C. Lukaski, (701) 795-8464

Building more bone during the formative years is the best insurance against osteoporosis later in life. Studies with aged female rats show that neither extra calcium—above the recommended amount—nor the activated form of vitamin D, reduces bone loss in the aging. In one study, a diet containing nearly twice the recommended calcium intake (for rats) did not affect the rate of bone turnover in 2-year-old female rats but increased bone formation in young female rats. In another study, the use of activated vitamin D to preserve skeletal integrity was compared in two groups of old rats—those with no ovaries and others with intact ovaries. In the rats without ovaries, the activated vitamin did not prevent bone loss. But it improved bone mineral content in the rats with intact ovaries, indicating that ovarian hormones are critical in bone metabolism. The active (hormonal) form of vitamin D has been tested in this country as a treatment for osteoporosis in the past, but its use has become controversial because a considerable body of evidence indicates it might promote the disease.

Vitamin and Mineral Lab, Beltsville Human Nutrition Research Center, Beltsville, MD
James C. Smith, (301) 344-2022

A healthy, low-fat regimen that included poultry, fish, lean beef and pork, dairy products and eggs **improved blood pressure and cholesterol levels** in a study of 12 men, ages 35 to 65. Their blood pressure was lowered an average of 10 percent, and cholesterol levels an average of 20 percent. In the low-fat meals, fat contributed only 25 percent of the day's total calories. Among the servings were about 4 ounces of lean meats, low-fat cheeses, skim milk and margarine. The recent study was one of a series on the role of nutrition in lowering risk of heart disease.

Biochemistry Research, Western Human Nutrition Research Center, San Francisco, CA
Rita M. Dougherty, (415) 556-0132

Remember how cod-liver oil made you gag? Animal studies are now showing that fish oil may actually prevent loss of appetite during an inflammatory illness or injury. In a series of studies with rats, scientists found what causes people with chronic infections or cancer to lose appetite and thus weight. A substance secreted by activated immune cells apparently boosts production of prostaglandin E_2—a hormonelike chemical—which caused the rats to eat less. However, when the animals were fed fish oil for several weeks before being injected with the immune cell substance (interleukin-1), the oil reduced their production of E_2 and maintained their food intake. If substantiated in human studies planned at the University of California, fish oil supplements would be a simple and safe intervention for patients experiencing, or expected to experience, loss of appetite and weight.

Human Nutrition Research Center on Aging at Tufts, Boston, MA
Simin N. Meydani, (617) 556-3129

Linseed oil from flax might help the immune system fight infection, if results from a study of rabbits prove true for humans. For that 5-month experiment, rabbits ate feed rich in either linseed, safflower, soybean or menhaden (fish) oil. Compared to the other three oils, linseed proved the best in three tests of how the immune system responds to attack, including one that measures proliferation of infection-fighting white blood cells in culture dishes. A study with human volunteers is planned for 1989. However, researchers caution against people treating themselves with doses of linseed oil; in the United States, it's made into industrial products and has not been approved by the Food and Drug Administration for human consumption.

Biochemistry Research, Western Human Nutrition Research Center, San Francisco, CA
Darshan S. Kelley/Gary J. Nelson, (415) 556-4381

As men age, they don't lose the ability to absorb and metabolize vitamin B6—allaying the concern of some nutritionists that older men were either not absorbing enough of the vitamin from diets or were not able to use what they got as efficiently. The body's ability to absorb and use this water soluble vitamin is critical to hemoglobin formation, protein synthesis and other major metabolic functions. A study showed that 65- to 75-year-old men

maintained their ability to absorb B6 and convert it to the active form as well as two younger groups, which were 45 to 55 and 25 to 35 years old. And 3-day diet records indicate no significant difference in intake among the groups. The study did find evidence that the vitamin is broken down faster in older men, which may account for their having lower plasma levels than their juniors. Further research is needed to determine how much vitamin B6 is needed by both senior men and women.

Vitamin and Mineral Lab, Beltsville Human Nutrition Research Center, Beltsville, MD
Robert D. Reynolds, (301) 344-2459

Should mothers who depend on insulin to control juvenile (type I) diabetes nurse their infants? Preliminary findings suggest there's no reason not to—if the infant is healthy and the mother feels good. Analyses of the breast milk from five insulin-dependent mothers found almost no difference in levels of protein, carbohydrate, fat, energy and essential minerals compared with the milk of nondiabetic mothers. And there was no difference in immune factors. Only glucose and sodium were significantly elevated in the diabetics' milk, but the increases were not large enough to affect the infant.

Children's Nutrition Research Center, Houston, TX
Nancy F. Butte, (713) 798-7000

Some citrus fruits contain a chemical that may help prevent cancer, if results from a study of mice prove true for humans. A University of Minnesota researcher, collaborating with an ARS scientist, found that nomilin—one compound that causes bitterness in some citrus juices—helped prevent cancerous tumors from forming in the stomachs of 28 percent of the mice that were fed a potent carcinogen. Apparently, nomilin can more than triple the normal activity of an important detoxifying enzyme, glutathione S-transferase. More research is needed to find out if nomilin and the nomilin-derived compounds, known as nomilin glucosides, have anticarcinogenic effects in humans, and if nomilin's bitterness can be removed without removing its potential benefits.

Fruit and Vegetable Chemistry Lab, Pasadena, CA
Shin Hasegawa, (818) 796-0239
University of Minnesota, Gray Freshwater Biological Institute, Navarre, MN
Luke K.T. Lam, (612) 471-0013

Qua

Quarterly Report
of Selected Research Projects

United States
Department of
Agriculture

 Agricultural
Research
Service

January 1 to March 31, 1989

Contents

Soil, Water and Air

A new fertilizer applicator invented by ARS and Iowa State University scientists may help farmers produce no-till corn more efficiently, conserve fertilizer and reduce nitrogen pollution of lakes and streams. The point-injector applicator, made by a firm in Iowa, pumps a solution of ammonium nitrate and urea through rolling spokes that penetrate about 4 inches into the soil. Putting fertilizer near the roots, instead of on the surface, keeps rainstorms from washing it away. And the point-injector treats roots gently, unlike conventional applicators that "knife" fertilizer into the soil. With the new applicator, farmers can apply nitrogen according to plant needs several times during the growing season. This will reduce nutrient losses from evaporation and chemical breakdown of nitrogen. In a 2-year test, researchers injected fertilizer into soil at a rate of 156 pounds of nitrogen per acre. Yields averaged about 7 bushels per acre higher than when the same amount of nitrogen was knifed in deep bands beside the corn rows.

Soil and Water Conservation Research, Ames, IA
Thomas S. Colvin, (515) 294-5724

Note: One or more scientists familiar with each research project are listed for further information. If the scientists are unavailable, others at the same telephone number may also be familiar with the work.

Items marked with the word PATENT are being patented by ARS. For more information contact Ann Whitehead, National Patent Program, Bldg. 005, Rm. 401, Beltsville Agricultural Research Center, Beltsville, MD 20705, (301) 344-2786.

An acre can yield 6,500 pounds of sorghum if farmers irrigate before planting seed. But the market price for the crop may not offset the cost of this early irrigation. A better payoff: Rely on rainfall to start the crop. Yields are 10 percent lower, but irrigation costs are about 45 percent less, which offsets the lower yield. The extra grain produced with preplant-irrigation can cost as much as $7.85 per 100 pounds, according to scientists. A 4-year study of continuous grain sorghum showed that rainfall-started crops used only 14 inches of irrigation water that cost $56 per acre compared with 25 inches at $100 per acre with preplant-irrigated fields. With both methods, plants were irrigated from 2 to 4 times during the summer, depending on rainfall. One potential setback: Dependence on rainfall could delay planting up to a month.

USDA Conservation and Production Research Lab, Bushland, TX
Ron Allen/Jack Musick, (806) 378-5725

Nitrogen that is symbiotically fixed in nodules on roots of alfalfa and other legumes is a potential source of high nitrate concentrations in drinking water from wells. When alfalfa is killed by plowing or herbicides, nitrogen-containing roots and nodules decompose. Natural decay processes can release as much as 350 pounds/acre into the soil over a 24-month period, and rainfall or irrigation can leach this nitrate into groundwater—a major source of drinking water. When crops that require high levels of nitrogen, such as corn or cereals, are grown following alfalfa or other legumes, a significant portion of this nitrate can be absorbed by the growing crops. This reduces the need to apply fertilizer and lowers the quantity of nitrates available for leaching into groundwater. Thus, crop rotation management is an important factor in controlling nitrate in groundwater. In addition, farmers can save $50 to $80 an acre in fertilizer costs.

Snake River Conservation Research Center, Kimberly, ID
David L. Carter, (208) 423-5582

Farmers can reduce soil erosion and maintain crop yields with fewer chemicals—and less cost—by turning to an equation model developed and modified by ARS researchers. Soil erosion and the movement of soil-attached phosphorus can be accurately predicted using the model. The equation can help farmers choose management practices that will improve water quality and reduce soil erosion. Available through extension agents, the as-yet-unnamed model should help interested farmers slow chemical transport in surface runoff, thereby reducing the cost of treating crops and soil.
Watershed Research Lab, Durant, OK
Andrew N Sharpley, (405) 924-5066

Western water-supply forecasts can now be made any time—instead of once a month—from January through summer runoff. That means watershed managers, farmers and ranchers can get continuous data, which has been lacking in earlier forecasts. Water-supply forecasts are usually made using traditional statistical procedures based on monthly snowfall measurements. These traditional forecasts estimate total water volume for the season and are available only near the first of each month from January on. ARS scientists have developed computer models they've combined with techniques for continuously measuring snowfall in the field to produce forecasts whenever needed. Timely forecasts would make it easier for ranchers and farmers to stay alert to available water supplies.
Northwest Watershed Research Center, Boise, ID
Keith N. Cooley, (208) 334-1363

A chemical that regulates plant growth may also help crops fend off the ravages of air pollution. Red clover is very sensitive to ozone, which inhibits photosynthesis. But a single dose of 500 parts per million of ethylenediurea, or EDU, applied as a soil drench for 48 hours in the lab significantly reduced the plant's sensitivity to the pollutant. Studies must still be done to establish EDU's effectiveness in field applications on ozone-sensitive crops. American farmers lose about $3 billion a year from crops damaged by air pollution. Reducing just one of the pollutants, ozone, by 10 percent could save farmers an estimated $808 million in 1982 dollars.
Climate Stress, Beltsville, MD
Edward H. Lee, (301) 344-3143

New and Improved Products

Since government and industry joined hands in research under the Federal Technology Transfer Act of 1986, ARS has signed about 60 research and development agreements with private firms. Another 30 agreements are currently under negotiation. Most of the agreements to transfer technology from the lab into practical use involve research combating disease in plants and animals. Other agreements include developing new products and refining existing plant and animal production practices, which provide the farmer a greater financial return and the consumer an improved product. A sampling of the signed agreements includes research for new vaccines to help curb *Salmonella* in poultry, development of a method to curb cockroach infestation, development of a new source of rubber from plants and a disease-detection kit for plant viruses. All agreements with private firms are consistent with ARS' program plan for agricultural research. The new authority to cooperate with the private sector is demonstrating that technologies can be rapidly developed and proprietary interests preserved to spur industry participation.
Office of Cooperative Interactions, Beltsville, MD
Richard M. Parry, (301) 344-2734

A sugar produced naturally by a Mediterranean plant could reduce the chances of *Salmonella* bacteria contaminating poultry. D-mannose, produced by the *Fraxinus ornus* plant, reduces by at least 90 percent the ability of *Salmonella typhimurium* bacteria to settle in broilers' intestines. The bacteria pass harmlessly from the birds' bodies. Scientists dosed 120 broiler chicks with 100 million *Salmonella* bacteria when they were 3 days old and then gave half the chicks 2.5 percent D-mannose in their drinking water for 10 days. At 50 days of age, the time when broilers typically go to market, only one of the 60 birds that received the D-mannose had *Salmonella* bacteria, while 6 of the birds on plain water were infected. Studies in which larger groups of birds received mannose treatment, but were examined earlier than 50 days of age, showed equally significant reductions in *Salmonella*. Humans can get salmonellosis by eating improperly prepared chicken that is contaminated by the bacteria; symptoms include nausea, vomiting and diarrhea. D-mannose is available commercially in the United States, and a sister compound, mannitol, has been used for many years as a stabilizer and preservative in pharmaceutical products.

Veterinary Toxicology Research, College Station, TX
John R. DeLoach, (409) 260-9484

A high-tech microphone can tell grain operators when insects are most active inside stored grain. The microphone is part of a durable acoustic system that can detect the feeding sounds—amplified up to 75,000 times—of the lesser grain borer, rice weevil and Angoumois grain moth. This information can cut costs for farmers and grain operators by telling them—with no need for grain samples—when insecticidal fumigants should be used to do the most good. Researchers found the acoustic system to be less costly and more reliable than conventional detection methods, such as grain sifting and measuring insect-produced carbon dioxide. Someday, an acoustic system could be automated to monitor several grain bins from a single central location.

U.S. Grain Marketing Research Lab, Manhattan, KS
David W. Hagstrum, (913) 776-2718

American and overseas bakers buying soft white winter wheat have become very quality conscious because of competition among wheat-exporting nations. ARS scientists are fine-tuning ways to evaluate the quality of major varieties grown in the Pacific Northwest. This research is the first to show differences in the milling and baking qualities of four varieties—Stephens, Lewjain, Daws and Nugaines. Over a 3-year period, the scientists evaluated the varieties at various storage facilities, using seven traditional quality criteria. Two tests were the most reliable and essential measurements. One test was for the percentage of flour yield—that portion of the grain that can actually be milled into flour. Another was cookie diameter. Bakers striving for uniform cookies need to know how much a given amount of cookie dough of a particular flour variety spreads during baking. Although the quality of all four varieties was generally acceptable, Stephens ranked highest.

Wheat Genetics, Quality, Physiology and Disease Resistance, Pullman, WA
Robert E. Allan, (509) 335-3632

Infant formulas, diet shakes and other soy-based products can be easily and accurately checked by two new tests for traces of natural compounds known as protease inhibitors. If they aren't stopped by heat or chemical treatment, these compounds block helpful enzymes the body needs to digest incoming protein. Food processors can use the new monoclonal antibody tests to make sure their products are free of or contain only low levels of the inhibitors. One test reveals levels of the Kunitz-type inhibitor, the other screens for the Bowman-Birk type. Other prospective users of the new tests include researchers who want to develop soybean varieties low in both types of inhibitors and scientists who are investigating whether the inhibitors can fight cancer. (PATENT)

Food Safety Research, Western Regional Research Center, Albany, CA
D.L. Brandon/A.H. Bates/M. Friedman, (415) 559-5783

Beta III, a carrot rich in beta carotene, is now receiving high marks for flavor and good growth in diverse geographical settings. This carrot, developed by ARS scientists, provides hope for improved nutrition—eye health and disease resistance—throughout the world. Beta III is three to five times richer than most other carrots in beta carotene. Favorable reports have come from agricultural scientists in 15 of 16 developing countries who received generous amounts of free seeds from a U.S. company. A square foot of land typically produces slightly more than a dozen of the new carrots, enough to meet an adult's vitamin A needs for about a month. Globally, vitamin A deficiency has been pegged as one of the most common dietary problems, ranking behind total energy and protein deficiencies. In the United States, more than 40 percent of Hispanics, 20 percent of blacks and 10 percent of Caucasians may consume less vitamin A than they need. Carrots, which now account for about 14 percent of the vitamin A in U.S. diets, may contribute increasing amounts as scientists learn more about carotene absorption and try to keep on improving carrot eating quality and carotene content.

Vegetable Crops Research, Madison, WI
Phillip W. Simon, (608) 262-1248

Minced fish may someday partially replace ground meat in certain cured meat products, if researchers can resolve concerns over compounds that might be formed in the products. Some meat processors want to add fish to cut costs, increase nutritional quality and improve binding and gel characteristics. Adding just 5 percent minced fish to meat franks alone would boost by about 45 million pounds the demand for fish. But there's a hitch to this gastronomic marriage. Nitrite must be used in cured meats to prevent botulism and give these products their pink color and characteristic flavor. Fish are especially high in chemical compounds called amines. Nitrite can combine with amines during processing to form nitrosamines, some of which are potent carcinogens. Since the nitrosamines found are in very low concentrations, researchers are studying variables such as the species of fish used, the age of the fish before processing and its time in frozen storage to see how these affect the level of nitrosamines in the product. The USDA's Food Safety and Inspection Service has already approved a nugget product that combines meat and processed minced fish.

Food Safety Research, Philadelphia, PA
Walter J. Fiddler, (215) 233-6502

Citrus growers in south Florida and coastal areas may get bigger harvests and healthier trees from a new rootstock. Just released to nurseries after 14 years of tests in Florida, Sun Chu Sha is a Chinese citrus rootstock that thrives in Florida's flatwoods. Not only does it efficiently use the small amount of magnesium available from the soil, but Sun Chu Sha also resists citrus blight, citrus tristeza virus and *Phytophthora* foot rot, which plague citrus groves in this area. The rootstock also did well in Texas where soil conditions are similar.

U.S. Horticultural Research Lab, Orlando, FL
Donald J. Hutchison, (407) 897-7343

Melons that look and smell ripe at the supermarket are often picked too soon to be sweet. To solve this problem, ARS engineers have developed a device that uses light rays to measure just how sweet melons like honeydew, watermelon and cantaloupe are. The breadbox-size device can monitor sweetness in melons by measuring the amount of near-infrared light the fruit absorbs. The more infrared absorbed, the sweeter the fruit. Unripe melons with only 6 percent sugar can sweeten in just a few days on the vine to an ideal sugar content of 11 percent. Besides helping farmers pinpoint when a melon is ripe for picking, the meter should make it easier for wholesalers and retailers to identify vine-ripened fruit. Someday consumers may have purse-size sweetness meters to take to the produce market. So far, the meter also works for onions and papayas. Peaches and nectarines will be tested next.

Field and Horticultural Crops Research, Athens, GA
Gerald Dull, (404) 546-3320

Ever bite into a crisp-looking apple only to get a mouth full of mush? Fruit researchers are working to remedy that. With a technique called spectrophotometry, they can now detect invisible bruises on apples. This method breaks down a light beam into its individual colors, or wavelengths. In a cooperative effort between ARS and Cornell University, researchers bruised apples and directed a beam of light to different parts of the fruit. Damaged areas showed lower light reflectance, indicating the bruised areas absorbed the light. Undamaged sections reflected more light, characteristic of a healthy apple. Packinghouses could use this technique along with equipment they now use for color sorting.

Appalachian Fruit Research Station, Kearneysville, WV
Bruce L. Upchurch, (304) 725-3451

A new viburnum named Eskimo will be available commercially next year to satisfy the demand of those home gardeners who want a dwarf ornamental plant that blooms profusely and is resistant to bacterial leaf spot. Most viburnums grow too large and vigorously for home landscaping, but scientists at ARS' National Arboretum developed this new dwarf variety to grow slowly under partial-to-full sunlight in heavy loam soil with an adequate moisture supply. It has glossy, dark, semi-evergreen foliage, and is ideal for landscaping, hedging or mass-planting. After 3 or 4 years, it produces an abundance of snowball-like flowers in early May.

U.S. National Arboretum, Washington, DC
Don Egolf, (202) 475-4850

Sunflower seeds have twice as much iron as raisins, as much calcium as whole milk and all the protein of beef, without any cholesterol. (That's on a pound-for-pound, dry weight basis). And now there are three tasty new ways to eat them: Sour cream and onion flavored, honey roasted or a roasted and salted/raisin blend. The new taste treats are part of a sampler of three North Dakota crops in a package to celebrate the state's centennial. The National Sunflower Association and Sigco Sun Products of Wahpeton, N. Dak., have packaged the sampler with seven different sunflower, soybean and wheat snacks. ARS researchers developed the sunflower products. This research has given new life to the active sunflower industry in the United States and renewed vigor to export markets in Europe, the Middle East and Asia. According to the National Sunflower Association, in 1988 over 80 percent of the nation's sunflower crop was exported, either as oil or seed, bringing in $204 million.

Oilseeds Research, Fargo, ND
Jerry F. Miller, (701) 239-1321

A new, longer lasting lure for trapping the Mediterranean fruit fly (medfly) may become an important defensive weapon for California, Arizona, Texas, Florida and other states susceptible to invasion by this destructive insect. Agricultural agents in those states monitor thousands of traps equipped with a lure to detect incoming medflies before their populations have a chance to build. The medfly can infest more than 250 different fruits and vegetables and can easily cost millions of dollars to eradicate. Called Ceralure, after the medfly's scientific name *(Ceratitis capitata)*, the new formula lasts at least 2 to 3 times longer than Trimedlure, the most widely used medfly bait. That could mean impressive labor savings for states such as California, which runs 30,000 medfly traps. (PATENT)

Insect Chemical Ecology Lab, Beltsville, MD
Terrence P. McGovern, (301) 344-2138
Fruit Fly Biology and Control, Hilo, HI
Roy T. Cunningham, (808) 959-9138

Scientific Information Systems

Certain farmer's decisions—such as when, where and how much to seed and fertilize—are based on the weather. But weather station records may not fit a farmer's local needs. ARS hydrologists have developed a computer software package called Weather Wizard that can fine-tune records for a specific northwestern farm. It will provide rainfall, temperature and degree-day information for any specified time between 2 weeks and 1 year. Weather Wizard can generate 30-year weather records for any of 18 weather stations in northeastern Oregon and Washington. It can also interpolate information from the three stations nearest to a particular farm to get local data. The program is being developed in cooperation with Oregon State University Extension Service and is now available. To order, request OSUES Special Report 831, September 1988.

Columbia Plateau Conservation Research Center,
Pendleton, OR
John F. Zuzel, (503) 276-3811

Grasshopper populations can be kept in check with insecticides and biological controls. But because both methods are relatively expensive in relation to the value of rangeland grass, ranchers have been reluctant to apply them until grasshoppers have already inflicted costly damage. Other ranchers use control measures when not really needed. Now a computer program will help ranchers decide what to do if grasshoppers appear on their rangeland. The easy-to-use program selects appropriate ways to control the insects. It also provides ranchers with profit or loss estimates for any action, including doing nothing.

Rangeland Insects Lab, Bozeman, MT
James S. Berry, (406) 994-6403

For a select group of Holstein calves in Alabama, lunchtime isn't just grazing in a pasture. It's also a time to supply data for a computer model, still in its early stages, that could predict when cattle parasites are likely to be most numerous on pastures. The calves are part of a study begun in August 1987. Each month, two parasite-free calves are put on selected pastures for 30 days, then checked for internal parasites. The findings give researchers a good idea of which parasites appear on those pastures and when they'll probably pop up. These data will be combined with weather data to try to predict parasite development at different locations and times. Farmers could use the program to schedule grazing to avoid pastures when parasites are likely to peak. Although the study is being done in Alabama, researchers say the program could also be adapted to serve farmers in Georgia, North and South Carolina, Mississippi, Louisiana and Florida.

Animal Parasite Research, Auburn, AL
Daniel E. Snyder, (205) 887-3741

A robot that doesn't mind monotonous, backbreaking work could one day help automate the labor-intensive raising, shipping and transplanting of vegetable and tree seedlings into fields, nurseries and greenhouses. Researchers have designed and filed for a patent on the first component of a robotic transplanting system that could work at least four times faster than human-dependent systems, with each row in the machine processing and planting 180 to 240 seedlings per minute vs. a typical 40 by hand. The device, which could be mounted on today's farm machinery, removes seedlings from shipping containers and plants them one at a time into rows of a field. When complete, the system could plant seeds, automatically cull unusable seedlings and empty containers in which seeds did not germinate and transfer the rest from growing trays to shipping containers from which they can be transplanted into the fields. If the automated system is completed and becomes widely used in the industry, it could eventually reduce costs to less than one-half that of hand labor, open up major new markets and help the U.S. horticultural industry to be competitive on a global basis. (PATENT)

Crop Systems Research, Tifton, GA
Harold L. Brewer, (912) 386-3666

Crop Production and Protection

Naturally occurring delicate wax crystals on the surface of weed plants' leaves could help destroy the weeds at a fraction of current herbicide costs. Farmers have traditionally applied herbicides against weeds such as johnsongrass in as much as 20 gallons of water per acre. But studies showing that much less water would work just as well led scientists to wonder if the water was needed at all. The answer appears to be "no." Instead, farmers can get more action from their herbicides by blending them with another important ingredient—an oil concentrate composed mainly of paraffinic oil. That's where the wax crystals come into play. They start forming on the weed's leaves within 3 to 5 days after the weed emerges. These crystals pull the herbicide-laden oil across the leaf top. Using herbicides and oil, researchers controlled up to 90 percent of targeted weeds with only one quart per acre.

Southern Weed Science Lab, Stoneville, MS
Chester G. McWhorter, (601) 686-2311

A magnifying glass saved a farmer $40,000 one season in fertilizer not used because of what he saw on wheat seedheads that were only one-eighth inch long. The farmer is one of a growing number taking advantage of growth data collected by ARS scientists on spring wheat yields. Their data showed that yields could be estimated early in the growing season by calculations using total number of plants and the number of seedheads per acre, kernels per seedhead and kernel weight. An extension agent at North Dakota State University, using ARS data, found a way to simplify the calculations for immediate use by area farmers. Assuming each plant would have three seedheads and the crop would be sown at a certain density, the maximum possible

yield can be estimated by counting the grain-bearing spikelets on each seedhead and multiplying the average number by three. The simplified calculation works so well for spring wheat that farmers are rapidly using the technique to calculate fertilizer needs. The count can be done when the plants have about five or six leaves on the main stem, which indicates a growth stage when all spikelets have been formed, usually 30 to 35 days after emergence. Besides saving fertilizer, the formula lessens the potential amount of excess nitrogen available to pollute streams, lakes or groundwater.

Soil, Water and Crop Management Research, Mandan, ND
A.B. Frank/A. Bauer, (701) 663-6445

A bean called Blackhawk—the first completely anthracnose-resistant black bean available in the United States—will soon be on the market for farmers and home gardeners. A joint release by ARS and Michigan State University, the bean is also resistant to all strains of bean common mosaic virus and is highly resistant to the indigenous races of rust to Michigan. The bean is expected to play a vital role in preventing the spread of anthracnose, a seed-borne pathogen now threatening certain varieties of navy beans in Michigan. The bean also figures in future export markets, particularly Mexico, where black bean consumption is high.

Crops and Entomology Research, East Lansing, MI
Alfred W. Saettler, (517) 353-0860

A preliminary gene map, showing the position of 36 genes, is now available for lentils, a beanlike crop valued at more than $10 million a year. Soups and side dishes with lentils are very high in protein, fiber and lysine (an essential amino acid.) As more lentil genes are identified, the new gene map will become a valuable tool to transfer useful genes into lentils to improve their germplasm and varieties. Manipulating gene-linked traits could result in higher yielding, virus-resistant plants that grow larger, more uniform seeds that resist splitting. About 80 percent of the lentil crop—grown mostly in the Pacific Northwest—is exported to Venezuela, Spain, the Middle East, Egypt, Italy and Germany.

Grain Legume Genetics and Physiology Research, Pullman, WA
Frederick J. Muehlbauer, (509) 335-9521

Tracking disease in sugar beets with a piece of medical equipment may aid in the nondestructive and long-term study of the plant's roots, a first for sugar beet research. Methods used to study structure and development changes within the roots normally require cutting and chemically analyzing the roots, which makes impossible later study of root development. But ARS scientists, in cooperation with Michigan State University, have found that an imaging technique—proton nuclear magnetic resonance (NMR)—can give good results with no root destruction. Using NMR, researchers examined healthy and fungal-infected sugar beet roots. The healthy roots showed high-contrast images of the inner root structure, including the varying concentrations of sucrose. Images of infected roots showed dark areas at the front of the advancing infection, which were not associated with healthy roots.

Crops and Entomology Research, East Lansing, MI
John M. Halloin, (517) 355-3443

Sugar beets piled up and awaiting processing are kept alive by the breathing of their cells. But this takes energy from the beets' own sugars. Each year about 250,000 tons of beet sugar is lost—mostly breathed away—from 9 million tons of sugar beets before they are processed. Another major sugar loss comes from fungal attack. Now scientists have bred sugar beet germplasm that plant breeders can use to develop commercial varieties that breathe lightly while resisting three of the most prevalent storage rot fungi.

Sugarbeet Research, Northern Crop Science Lab, Fargo, ND
Larry G. Campbell, (701) 239-1357

Potato breeders can now develop commercial varieties that are much more resistant to the potato leafhopper, a pest that, without pesticides, can cut yields by more than half in the East and North. Controlling the leafhopper currently requires extensive use of pesticides. ARS researchers selected parent stock from potatoes that showed the best natural resistance to the pest in successive generations. After 7 generations of selection, plants from the improved germplasm had 45 percent less leafhopper damage than plants from the original, unselected stock. A commercial variety from this stock would allow the use of less pesticide.

Vegetable Lab, Beltsville, MD
Lind L. Sanford, (301) 344-2901

Plant pathologists have discovered a new, devastating disease that attacks pecans. First observed among mature fruits of major pecan varieties in central Georgia in September 1988, it caused yield losses of 50 percent or more and reduced nut quality. Named phytophthora shuck and kernel rot, this disease rots the pecan shuck in 4 to 6 days. Caramel-colored areas of rot cover over 25 percent of the surface of the kernels. Scientists think this disease, caused by the fungus *Phytophthora cactorum*, is moved from orchard soil to pecan trees by stinkbugs or pecan weevils in early August. Splashing raindrops spread the fungus, which is a water mold. Looking for controls, scientists found the fungicides dodine and triphenyl tin hydroxide, commonly used for disease control in pecans, were effective against the disease. Timing and application rates of the fungicides will be determined next season.

Southeastern Fruit and Tree Nut Research Lab, Byron, GA
Charles C. Reilly, (912) 956-5656

Sampling soil before planting cantaloupes could determine their success. Researchers studying the fungus *Macrophomina phasolina* have found that just a little of the fungus in soil could spell trouble for growers. The fungus causes vine decline, a disease that rarely appears before plant maturity. Vines may begin to yellow about 10 days before the harvest period begins. The leaves gradually die, exposing melons to sunburn and premature ripening. Losses as high as 50 percent have been noted in isolated cases, and losses of 10 percent are common. Soil sampling is the only preventive measure available to growers. Samples should be tested specifically for the fungus.

South Central Agricultural Research Lab, Lane, OK
Benny D. Bruton, (405) 889-7395

The cryptic case of the dying cranberries has been cracked by an ARS researcher. He fingered the culprit: A previously unknown fungus, now named *Synchronoblastia crypta*, that represents a new genus. *S. crypta*, it turns out, has often been responsible for dead patches in hundreds of cranberry bogs. These dead patches were previously blamed entirely on standing water. The fungus, a close relative of fungi that attack rhododendrons and blueberries, is one of two root pathogens of cranberries. It was first found in Massachusetts, where it was isolated in more than 200 bogs (3,100 acres of the states's 12,000 producing acres) and caused an estimated 5 percent decrease in the

$91.5-million crop for 1986-87. Losses in some bogs reached 25 percent. The fungus has now also been identified in bogs in New Jersey. With identification of the pathogen, control measures have been devised including better bog drainage, addition of sand to promote drainage, extra fertilizer on fringes of dead spots, and the granting of emergency use of the fungicide metalaxyl.

Mycology and Nematology Lab, Beltsville, MD
F.A. Uecker, (301) 344-2270

A box trap and a newly synthesized pheromone may help farmers in North and South Carolina cut their pesticide war on pickleworms almost in half. The pheromone is used to attract adult pickleworm moths to 3-foot-square net boxes in cucumber fields. The pest migrates north with the spring to lay eggs in cucumber fields, and the hatched larvae then eat their way into the young cucumbers. Moths appearing in the traps would signal cucumber growers when pesticides are needed. Currently, growers begin spraying as soon as night-time temperatures reach 60 degrees—a critical "temperature path"—that the moths follow north. Growers then spray weekly throughout the moth's 6- to 7-week season. They pursue the pickleworm with such vigilance because pickle packers will refuse a truckload of cucumbers if they spot even a single pickleworm hole. Preliminary tests show that growers could get the same protection with about half as much spraying and the pheromone traps as with the conventional calendar-spraying approach.

U.S. Vegetable Lab, Charleston, SC
Kent D Elsey, (803) 556-0840

Demonstration plots of kenaf are beginning to produce base figures on crop yield—data essential to improving varieties of the plant and its quality. Kenaf harvested from five 5-acre plots in Oklahoma yielded about 6 tons per acre of dry stalks—the part of the plant that is pulped into newsprint. The demonstration yields reflected below-normal rainfall of last year's drought; only one plot was irrigated. Formal studies are under way to expand this yield research and focus on plant density, dry matter production, fiber quality and yield response to water.

South Central Agricultural Research Lab, Lane, OK
Charles L. Webber III, (405) 889-7395

Genetic engineering can now make a fungus cell pathogenic. This achievement allows researchers to study disease production and sexual development in certain fungal strains, studies that were previously impossible using naturally occurring fungal strains. Usually, these strains must fuse cells of opposite mating types before they can attack plants, since unmated cells cannot cause disease. ARS scientists working with the fungus that causes corn smut successfully introduced a cloned gene made up of one mating type into a cell of the opposite type. The result: A pathogenic cell that still lacks other genetic information it would normally have gotten from the cell of the second mating type. Researchers hope the results will be applicable to a broad range of important plant pathogens such as rust fungi and other smut fungi as they study how a pathogen is formed and how it can be prevented.

Plant Disease Resistance, Madison, WI
Sally A. Leong, (608) 262-5309

Animal Production and Protection

An important clue in the mystery of where *Salmonella* infection enters the cattle marketing chain may have been uncovered. A check of blood and fecal samples from 200 beef cattle showed that 1.5 percent of the animals were shedding *Salmonella* bacteria in their feces as they were being moved from farm to feedlot, but 8 percent of the cattle were shedding the bacteria about a month later, when they left the feedlot. However, scientists believe infection is actually occurring earlier in the marketing chain, at the sale barn where they were first sold off the farm. Cattle can be infected with *Salmonella* for 2 to 3 months and not shed bacteria in their feces until they are stressed. None of the cattle in the study were shedding the bacteria in their feces on the farm or at the sale barn. Five types of *Salmonella* known to infect humans were found in the animals, but the scientists stressed that if the meat is properly handled and cooked, the bacteria are killed and cannot harm consumers.

Veterinary Toxicology and Entomology Research Lab,
College Station, TX
Don E. Corrier, (409) 260-9342

Federal and state agencies are cooperating in an unusual project to try to solve a problem that costs cattle producers an estimated $200 million each year. The problem: Cattle that eat grass or grass hay infected by a certain fungus fail to gain weight during the summer and also develop reproductive problems. The fungus, *(Acremonium coenophialum)*, is an endophyte, meaning it lives inside the grass. While the endophyte helps the grass tolerate insects and drought, it's also responsible for production losses in cattle. ARS scientists in Peoria, Ill., will study the toxin in endophyte-infected Kentucky 31 tall fescue hay grown at a state correctional center in Vienna, Ill. The inmates will prepare ethanol extracts from 36,000 pounds of fescue seed and 15,000 pounds of fescue hay. Toxic materials isolated from the extract will be used in feeding trials intended to overcome production problems in cattle eating tall fescue. The trials will be conducted by ARS's Veterinary Toxicology Research Lab in College Station, Tex,. and several other institutions.

Bioactive Constituents, Northern Regional Research Center, Peoria, IL
Richard G. Powell, (309) 685-4011, ext. 595

Chicken farmers might get an effective weapon against a pest that destroys the insulation in poultry houses. The lesser mealworm, larval form of the darkling beetle, burrows into insulation of high-rise caged layer and broiler houses. In 5-week tests with 600 chickens, researchers got almost 100 percent control of mealworms and adult beetles using ivermectin, a compound registered to control many parasites in cattle, swine, horses and dogs. The ivermectin was mixed into the chickens' feed at the rate of 2 parts per million. The mealworm and the beetle don't infect chickens, but they thrive on spilled feed. The U.S. Food and Drug Administration would have to approve the new use of the compound. So far, researchers have found no ivermectin residues in chicken livers, which means there probably would be none in the meat. (PATENT)

Livestock Insects Lab, Beltsville, MD
Richard W. Miller, (301) 344-2478

Fish farmers are hoping a hormone called DHT will do the trick in producing all male catfish. Their aim: Make the most of the finding that male catfish grow faster than females, because even a small advantage could mean big bucks to producers in one of the nation's fastest growing agricultural endeavors. Research has shown that many species of young fish will change from female into males when treated with male hormones, but catfish so far have been a puzzling exception to the rule. However, scientists are now trying dihydrotestosterone, or DHT, considered one of the strongest masculinizing agents. Daily doses of DHT have been added to the fishes' water at various levels as they grew from eggs through sac-fry, swim-up fry and beyond. If DHT does the trick in turning catfish into males, the scientists anticipate little trouble in getting approval from the U.S. Food and Drug Administration because DHT is a naturally occurring hormone in humans.

Catfish Genetics Research, Stoneville, MS
Gary J. Carmichael, (601) 686-2987

Veterinarians searching for a bluetongue vaccine have succeeded in developing the first cell line from *Culicoides variipennis*—the insect that carries the disease virus among animals in North America. Cell lines are collections of cells that can be reproduced in the lab and are vital to scientists' experiments. Scientists have often been hampered in their search for vaccines against insect-spread viral disease because they lack enough insects (such as *C. variipennis*), animals or viruses for their research. But the new cell line might lead to a vaccine or a diagnostic test to identify disease-free cattle. The presence of bluetongue virus in U.S. cattle and sheep has led to international barriers to exports, costing as much as $125 million in lost sales each year.

Arthropodborne Animal Diseases Research Lab, Laramie, WY
Sally J. Wechsler, (307) 721-0316

Frustrated Southwestern ranchers losing the battle with snakeweed may soon have some help from foreign allies. Argentine weevils—brown, long-snouted insects with chewing mouthparts—are being field-tested in parts of New Mexico and Texas. The weevil, *Heilipodus ventralis*, destroys snakeweed by clipping its leaves and buds and tunneling down inside its stems. In its native Argentina, the weevil is not known to damage any major crops. Snakeweed is a major weed that causes $70 to $140 million in losses annually to the cattle industry. Eating it makes cattle and other livestock ill, and a small amount can cause abortions in cattle. The weed also competes with forage plants and is expensive to control by herbicide and mechanical treatments. Researchers hope the insect can reduce the amount of snakeweed in the Southwest, eventually saving ranchers more than $35 million a year. The release of the weevils represents one of the first efforts to biologically control a native U.S. plant with a foreign insect. Most biocontrols are aimed at species that invaded the United States from elsewhere.

Grassland, Soil and Water Research, Temple, TX
C. Jack DeLoach, (817) 770-6520

Human Nutrition

Thousands of Americans may not be getting enough vitamin A, while many others may be getting too much through daily supplements. But a new test may make it faster and easier to find out who needs more of this essential nutrient. Most healthy people store 90 to 95 percent of their vitamin A (retinol) supply in their liver. Taking a liver sample is painful, so blood tests have been used to measure the amount of a special protein that binds to vitamin A. In the new test, high performance liquid chromatography, a standard lab procedure, distinguishes between how much of this special protein acts independently (free) and how much is bound to another protein. Earlier tests couldn't distinguish the two forms—a drawback because some researchers think the free form is a better indicator of vitamin A stored in the liver. Retinol-binding protein moves the vitamin from the liver to other tissues where it's needed for good vision, growth and reproduction. To ensure a safe and adequate intake, eat the foods rich in the vitamin or its precursor, beta carotene.

Liver, dark green vegetables and brightly colored vegetables such as tomatoes, carrots and squash are the best sources.

Biochemistry Research, Western Human Nutrition
Research Center, San Francisco, CA
Betty J. Burri, (415) 556-6016

If athletic rats are any indication, human athletes may be able to endure a little longer and compete a little better with a little more chromium in their bodies. Marathoners and other long-distance athletes prepare for competition by eating a high-carbohydrate diet to stockpile all the glycogen—the storage form of glucose—their muscle tissue will hold. But how fast the glycogen disappears during competition may determine who finishes first—or who finishes at all. Rats fed adequate chromium for 5 weeks lost significantly less muscle glycogen during strenuous exercise than those fed a low-chromium diet. The average chromium intake for U.S. men is two-thirds the minimum currently thought to be adequate. U.S. women average only half the minimum. Good sources of chromium are fortified breakfast cereals, cheese, liver, whole wheat, beef, beer and wine.

Vitamin and Mineral Nutrition Lab, Beltsville Human
Nutrition Research Center, Beltsville, MD
Richard A. Anderson, (301) 344-2091

Nature appears to be watching out for you, judging from findings on how the body deals with certain types of cholesterol products. Cholesterol oxides are chemical compounds that can form in any food with cholesterol when the cholesterol meets air at high temperatures, such as in frying and some forms of processing. Among the 60 to 80 known cholesterol oxides, the alpha-epoxide and the beta-epoxide have been reported to be carcinogenic in animal experiments. But ARS studies with simulated gastric juices indicate that both the alpha-epoxide and beta-epoxide break down rapidly in the human stomach, changing into other noncarcinogenic cholesterol oxides.

Food Safety, Eastern Regional Research Center,
Philadelphia, PA
Gerhard Maerker, (215) 233-6446

More evidence that boron could be essential for optimal health surfaced recently in a study with older men and women. Using an electroencephalograph (EEG), one researcher found striking differences in brain wave patterns between periods of low and adequate boron intake—0.23 vs. 3 milligrams per day—suggesting the volunteers were less alert when their boron intake was low. Another researcher found signs that boron depletion reduces copper status. Copper is thought to be important in preventing heart disease as well as bone and joint disorders.

Grand Forks Human Nutrition Research Center,
Grand Forks, ND
James G. Penland, (701) 795-8471
Forrest H. Nielsen, (701) 795-8456

Plan on nursing your baby after delivery? You'll be happy to know that a few of those extra pounds you gained during pregnancy will help your baby thrive. Recent findings show that stored body fat contributes about 60 percent of the fat in breast milk, and milk fat is the infant's major source of energy. The mother's diet contributes about 30 percent of breast milk fat; the breast synthesizes the rest. These estimates agree with findings from large animals. In the unique study, three nursing mothers consumed saturated and mono- and polyunsaturated fatty acids labeled with a harmless, nonradioactive isotope of hydrogen so that researchers could follow their fat metabolism all the way through milk production. Since a nursing mother puts out about 20 grams of fat in breast milk each day, researchers estimate each pound of body fat supplies enough fat for 3 to 4 weeks.

Children's Nutrition Research Center, Houston, TX
David L. Hachey, (713) 798-7000

Breast-fed infants are more fuel-efficient than formula-fed infants—burning significantly fewer calories when they sleep. In a study of 40 healthy infants, the 20 who were breast-fed expended 5 percent less energy per day than the 20 formula-fed infants at one month of age and about 12 percent less by 4 months. The difference was in their sleeping, or basal, metabolic rates, not in their activity levels, according to the first 24-hour measurement of energy expenditure in healthy infants. The findings partly explain why breast-fed infants get by on about 20 percent fewer calories than formula-fed infants by the fourth month.

They also grew more slowly, as seen in other studies. This study is part of ongoing research to redefine the energy requirements of rapidly growing infants. The current Recommended Dietary Allowance was derived from calorie intakes of predominantly formula-fed infants and is substantially higher than the intakes of breast-fed infants. Based on the study's findings, mother's milk provides adequate energy during the first 4 months. Formula-fed infants funnel some of their excess calories into growth and burn the rest.

Children's Nutrition Research Center, Houston, TX
Nancy Butte, (713) 798-7000

One-month-old infants can't absorb cereal—or so the experts thought—because they don't produce the main starch-digesting enzyme until they're 4 to 6 months old. New findings show they can digest cereal at one month, but that doesn't mean they should get it. The 10 infants studied absorbed an average 88 percent of the rice cereal mixed with their formula—one tablespoon per ounce. But they didn't retain any more calories or protein from the cereal-formula mixture than they got from formula alone. The extra nutrients passed out in the stool, suggesting there's no nutritional benefit to feeding cereal to very young infants. Also, the cereal may reduce absorption of needed minerals. The American Academy of Pediatrics recommends not introducing cereals before 4 to 6 months of age unless the infant frequently spits up liquid formula. Mothers often start feeding cereal earlier, however, to help infants sleep through the night. The findings so far support the current recommendations.

Children's Nutrition Research Center, Houston, TX
Robert J. Shulman, (713) 798-7000

From breath samples alone, scientists at an ARS center in Houston, Tex., were able to identify which infants would have difficulty absorbing glucose sugar—the basic unit of cereals and all other complex carbohydrates. And they determined the degree of malabsorption. The Houston center is a world leader in developing and using harmless, non-radioactive isotopes for nutrition research. With partial funding from the National Institutes of Health, the Houston scientists collaborated with researchers in Brazil, France and East Germany to study glucose absorption in infants from each country. They found that infants with chronic diarrhea lost most of their ability to absorb glucose, whereas severely malnourished infants without diarrhea handled glucose almost as well as healthy infants. All 17 of the study infants had been given a solution of glucose enriched with a naturally occurring variant of carbon, which was later measured in the carbon dioxide they exhaled. In a related study, the researchers are investigating the use of locally available cereals as nutritional supplements for infants who can't absorb lactose, or milk sugar, during acute gastroenteritis.

Children's Nutrition Research Center, Houston, TX
Carlos Lifschitz, (713) 798-7000

Folic acid supplements—often prescribed during pregnancy—can interfere with zinc absorption when body zinc stores are low. And they can reduce the body's ability to mobilize stored zinc during stress, such as strenuous exercise, according to a series of ARS studies of men and women. Supplements of the vitamin (also called folacin or folate) that contain 400 micrograms or more could cause problems for vegetarians who eat fewer zinc-rich foods and for pregnant women. Low zinc status in mothers is linked to low birthweights of their infants. Among its many functions, zinc is involved in protein synthesis—crucial in a developing fetus—and in immune function. Cooperative studies with scientists at Wright State University in Dayton, Ohio, and Tulane University in New Orleans found that women with the highest blood levels of folic acid and the lowest levels of zinc had the most infections during and after delivery. The findings suggest that obstetricians prescribe a zinc supplement along with a folic acid supplement. Ironically, people need zinc to absorb folic acid from foods.

Grand Forks Human Nutrition Research Center, Grand Forks, ND
David B. Milne, (701) 795-8464

Even drug-resistant malarial parasites didn't take hold in mice fed a diet enriched with fish oil and deficient in vitamin E. Fatty acids from the fish oil may be incorporated into either the parasite's membranes or membranes of the host's red blood cells. But without any vitamin E to protect membrane integrity, the organism self-destructs. Mice who were started on this diet 1 to 4 weeks before being infected with a large dose of parasites were free of them 3 to 4 weeks after infection. If people respond similarly, the dietary approach developed by ARS and University of Miami researchers holds promise for prevention and treatment of this recalcitrant disease. Far from being subdued, malaria is back with a vengeance. The latest estimate is that nearly 300 million people in Africa, Latin America, Asia and the Pacific are infected. Malaria claims the lives of one quarter of African children under the age of 4.

Vitamin and Mineral Nutrition Lab, Beltsville Human Nutrition Research Center, Beltsville, MD
Orville A. Levander, (301) 344-2504
Center for Tropical Parasitic Diseases, University of Miami, Miami, FL
Arba L. Ager, Jr., (305) 284-7330

☆U S Government Printing Office : 1989 - 241-788/80667

Qua

Quarterly Report
of Selected Research Projects

United States
Department of
Agriculture

Agricultural
Research
Service

April 1 to June 30, 1989

*If you want to continue receiving this publication, please
fill out and return the enclosed postcard within 30 days.*

Contents

Human Nutrition

Healthy nursing mothers in a recent study provided the
same total fat and cholesterol for their infants regardless of
how much fat they ate or how much milk they produced.
Fat accounts for about half the calories in breast milk and is
the nursing infant's major source of energy for the first few
months. Although preliminary, the findings indicate that the
breast controls its total fat output more closely than its sugar
or protein output, contrary to current thinking. When the 11
mothers switched from a high-fat (40 percent) to a very low-
fat (10 percent) diet, the percentages of fat and cholesterol in
their milk dropped slightly. But their daily milk volume
increased to keep total fat and cholesterol the same. The
mothers who were selected for the study naturally produced

Note: One or more scientists familiar with each
research project are listed for further information.
If the scientists are unavailable, others at the same
telephone number may also be familiar with the
work.

Items marked with the word PATENT are being
patented by ARS. For more information contact
Ann Whitehead, National Patent Program, Bldg.
005, Rm. 401, Beltsville Agricultural Research
Center, Beltsville, MD 20705, (301) 344-2786.

either low-fat milk (less than 3 percent fat) or high-fat milk
(more than 4 percent fat). Breast milk normally has 3.5
percent fat—about the same as most cow's milk—but can
range from 1.5 to 6 percent for reasons unknown. Regardless of diet, the "low-fat-milk" group produced 50 percent
more milk by volume containing the same total fat as the
"high-fat-milk" group. But the "low-fat" milk contained
more lactose and protein—about 30 percent more calories
worth—making it more nutritious.
*Children's Nutrition Research Center, Houston, TX
David L. Hachey, (713) 798-7000*

**A large, Grade A egg actually has about 22 percent less
cholesterol** than previously thought, according to results of
a nationwide study by USDA and the egg industry. On the
average, cholesterol measured 213 milligrams per egg
instead of the 274 mg last published by USDA in 1976.
The analyses were done on egg composites representing
over 60 percent of the nation's egg production. The
cholesterol values were monitored throughout the study
against an egg-cholesterol standard recently certified by
the National Institute of Standards and Technology
(formerly the National Bureau of Standards). The change
in the cholesterol content is the result of improved analytical methods as well as careful quality control. Other
factors that may have had an impact include changes in
poultry feeding and management practices. The updated
data will be included in a 1989 supplement to Agriculture
Handbook 8: Composition of Foods—used widely by
nutritionists, other health professionals and food
scientists—that will be released later this year by USDA's
Human Nutrition Information Service.
*Nutrient Composition Lab, Beltsville Human Nutrition
Research Center, Beltsville, MD
Gary Beecher/Joanne Holden, (301) 344-2356*

Eggs aren't the only food having less cholesterol than
previously thought. A whole day's meals may be lower.
ARS scientists analyzed the cholesterol contents of
samples of 60 days of meals, not of individual foods, by
the most accurate method available—gas-liquid chromatography (GLC)—and by an older colorimetric
method—the Zak method. Such colorimetric methods are
now known to give erroneously high values because they
measure all plant and animal sterols, not just cholesterol.

Scientists also estimated cholesterol content of the daily 60 menus using the USDA food composition tables, where the values are often obtained by colorimetric as well as GLC analyses. GLC analysis yielded the lowest values, while the colorimetric method yielded the highest. Estimates from the USDA food tables fell in between. These findings indicate that cholesterol values in the food tables need to be reviewed and updated. But they should not be construed to justify increasing cholesterol intake.

Lipid Nutrition Lab, Beltsville Human Nutrition Research Center, Beltsville, MD
Beverly Clevidence, (301) 344-2430

Scientists are now closer to learning how fish oils may protect against cardiovascular disease or reduce the pain of rheumatoid arthritis or migraine headaches. A highly sensitive test for measuring the body's production of E prostaglandins can also help shed light on the chemistry behind other diet-or drug-induced physiological changes. The E prostaglandins are hormone-like substances known to reduce blood pressure, to depress the activity of natural killer cells and to congregate wherever there is inflammation. They also may play a role in the nervous system and possibly in tumor formation. The test, which is conducted on a small urine sample, measures a metabolite of E prostaglandins with a variability (standard deviation) of less than 1 percent.

Lipid Nutrition Lab, Beltsville Human Nutrition Research Center, Beltsville, MD
Aldo Ferretti, (301) 344-2171

Dietary surveys and recent animal studies increasingly support the theory that too little copper may be at the root of heart disease. Ten dietary surveys indicate that 35 percent of Americans consume half or less of the current suggested 2-milligram copper intake. Recent ARS studies suggest the requirement may be lower. Nevertheless, nearly 50 similarities between copper-deficient animals and people with coronary heart disease have now been observed. Two new studies show that taking in too little copper and too much salt aggravates kidney failure, and adding stress raises blood pressure. Rats fed a copper-deficient diet and 10 times as much salt as they require—quite common in human diets—lost all kidney function. The animals getting adequate copper were able to excrete the extra salt and retain fluid, which is important in maintaining normal blood pressure. In a second study, rats fed a copper-deficient diet and exposed to stress—confinement in a small cage for 45 minutes each day—developed higher blood pressure than the animals subjected to only one or none of the conditions. In both studies, survival rates of the doubly stressed animals were dramatically reduced.

Grand Forks Human Nutrition Research Center, Grand Forks, ND
Leslie M. Klevay, (701) 795-8454

Diets high in simple sugars can drain your body of chromium—an essential element for regulating blood sugar levels. And few of us get enough chromium, which helps keep insulin levels in check by making the hormone more efficient at processing dietary glucose. A study of 20 men and women indicates that the more insulin we secrete to handle sugars from a meal, the more chromium we use and lose, because used chromium is excreted in the urine. And when body chromium is in short supply, we secrete more insulin. Chronically high insulin levels—an early warning sign for adult-onset diabetes—may be due to low body stores of chromium. The study showed that the biggest rise in insulin levels and, consequently, the greatest loss of chromium result from eating glucose followed shortly by fructose—the two most common sugars in our diets. It's more important to conserve body chromium than to replace it because few foods provide more than 10 to 15 percent of the minimum suggested intake—50 micrograms (millionths of a gram) per day. A few breakfast cereals provide more than 25 percent; General Mills' Total provides about 60 percent. Beer and wine are also good sources.

Vitamin and Mineral Nutrition Lab, Beltsville Human Nutrition Research Center, Beltsville, MD
Richard A. Anderson, (301) 344-2091

Don't put too much stock in a single test for mineral levels. A study of 10 women found that blood tests for five essential elements—calcium, magnesium, iron, copper and zinc—differed up to 10 percent over time due to normal biological variation. And the five women who were eating a controlled diet showed about as much variability over the 5-month study as those who selected their own foods. Analytical variance could add another 10 percent difference to test values. Such variability is well known in clinical tests. Physicians would be wise to run a second analysis several weeks later before prescribing mineral supplements. If the second value falls within 10 percent of the first, it's likely to be a real value. If not, wait and do a third test.

Grand Forks Human Nutrition Research Center, Grand Forks, ND
Sandra K. Gallagher, (701) 795-8494

Adding buckwheat to our diets—not just to pancakes—could help us cut calories and keep blood sugar at optimal levels, preliminary findings show. Buckwheat grain is digested more slowly than other carbohydrates. So a meal containing buckwheat leaves us feeling full longer, curbing the urge to snack or gorge at the next meal. Studies now show that its slow uptake also has the potential to prevent adult-onset diabetes and to improve glucose tolerance in those who have developed the disease. The studies were done in Korea—where buckwheat is a dietary staple—by a visiting scientist from the University of Oklahoma.
Carbohydrate Nutrition Lab, Beltsville Human Nutrition Research Center, Beltsville, MD
Eunsook T. Koh, (301) 344-2385

Rice bran—the thin brown layer that's milled off in processing the familiar white rice kernel—may prove to be a powerful cholesterol-fighter. Hamsters fed fiber-rich rice bran plus a high dose of pure cholesterol had cholesterol levels similar to hamsters fed cholesterol plus oat bran, another fiber source. Both groups' cholesterol levels were significantly lower than those of hamsters fed cholesterol plus cellulose, a fiber generally shown to have no cholesterol-lowering effects. To more rigorously test rice bran's beneficial effects, further ARS studies with hamsters are planned for this year. Products containing rice bran include brown rice, several snack foods and a topping made of light, naturally sweet bran flakes. ARS scientists have expanded bran's use in nutritious new foods by developing a process that stops bran's rich oil from turning rancid. Because of this natural deterioration, rice bran has been used primarily as a high protein ingredient in animal feed. An added benefit: In countries where rice is a staple, the process makes it more practical and economical to extract rice oil for refining into salad or cooking oil.
Food Quality Research, Western Regional Research Center, Albany, CA
Talwinder Kahlon, (415) 559-5665/Antoinette Betschart, (415) 559-5656/R.M. Saunders, (415) 559-5664

Soil, Water and Air

Wheat farmers on the Northern Great Plains could earn 68 percent more profit by planting a crop each year instead of every other year. Farmers in the region traditionally have left idle, or fallow, their fields for a year, then seeded wheat. Such a sequence allows extra time for the soil to soak up moisture for the next crop. Soil scientists, who recently completed an economic analysis of more than 20 years of research on a field in northeastern Montana, say annual cropping is safe and profitable. Studies show fallowing isn't necessary when farming practices such as grass barriers and reduced tillage are used to conserve water and guard against soil erosion. If a long drought is expected, however, farmers should remain flexible and consider fallowing.
Northern Plains Soil and Water Research Center, Sidney, MT
Kris Aase, (406) 482-2020

Common chickweed, though a bane to winter wheat, may be good for continuous no-till soybeans. Soybean plants leave almost no plant residue when harvested. But in a 3-year study, University of Missouri and ARS scientists found that chickweed, left as a "living mulch" on soybean plots, reduced annual soil erosion by 87 percent and nitrate losses by 77 percent. During early spring when frequent rains and most runoff occur in the Midwest, chickweed provided a protective canopy over the soil before other weeds or soybeans could do so. Other living mulches, including legumes that enrich the soil with nitrogen, may be killed by herbicides to keep them from competing with soybeans for nutrients and moisture. But chickweed naturally dies after maturing and reseeding itself just before soybean planting-time. It reappears just at the right time to provide a fall mulch. A potential problem: The early spring growth of chickweed may dry out the soil enough to decrease yields. Through fine-tuning of living mulch management, researchers hope to produce good crop yields while conserving valuable soil nutrients and reducing water pollution.
Cropping System and Water Quality Research, Columbia, MO
Eugene Alberts, (314) 882-1144
Cereal Genetics Research, Columbia, MO
Paul Beuselinck, (314) 882-6406

Farmers might someday partition their irrigated fields into smaller segments to reduce the risk of fertilizers and pesticides being leached into groundwater. This would also cut water waste without reducing crop yields. Field experiments showed that farmers could divide their fields by soil type so flood and furrow irrigation water soaks evenly into soil root zones. Scientists measured a 7-fold difference in water infiltration across a field. Some irrigators now apply water over large fields until soil with the least permeability is soaked. Meanwhile, other areas of the field—with sandy soils—have absorbed so much water that the excess goes below the reach of roots. If irrigation water is scarce, crop yields can be reduced by 30 percent in areas where little water infiltrated the soil.

U.S. Water Conservation Lab, Phoenix, AZ
Dan B. Jaynes, (602) 261-4356

Plants that "eat" selenium could help prevent too much of this potentially toxic mineral from ending up in food and water. After testing 200 plants already known to have a liking for selenium, an ARS plant nutritionist has pinpointed the best of the lot—wild mustard from Pakistan. It is a yellow-flowered plant similar to mustard that grows wild throughout the West. If the Pakistani mustard does as well in field tests as it did in greenhouse experiments, five mustard crops a year could remove up to 50 percent of the soluble selenium in the top 12 inches of soil. In humans, extremes in selenium can lead to health problems: Too little can lead to the weakening of the heart and too much to severe liver and kidney damage.

Water Management Research Lab, Fresno, CA
Gary S. Banuelos, (209) 453-3115

Animal Production and Protection

Salmonella colonization in broiler chicks can be blocked for just pennies per bird by adding lactose, or milk sugar, to the birds' drinking water. Scientists added 2.5 percent lactose to the drinking water of 1-day-old chicks. Two days later, the chicks each were given an oral dose of 100 million *Salmonella typhimurium* bacteria. The scientists also dosed other chicks with the bacteria, but did not give them lactose. When the chicks were 10 days old, 53 percent of the chicks given lactose were still colonized with *Salmonella* bacteria. All of the chicks that did not receive lactose were still colonized with *Salmonella*. The lactose-treated chicks that still had *Salmonella* had 99.9 percent less *Salmonella* bacteria in their bodies than the chicks not given lactose. Although studies to date have been conducted only under lab conditions, they offer hope for reducing the incidence of *Salmonella* in commercially grown poultry. The lactose treatment could cost as little as 2 cents per bird over the 10-day treatment period. Humans can contract *Salmonella* infection from eating contaminated meat, resulting in diarrhea, vomiting and/or nausea. But proper handling, kitchen sanitation and cooking of poultry kills the bacteria and eliminates the health threat to humans.

Veterinary Toxicology Research, College Station, TX
John DeLoach, (409) 260-9484

Leaner chickens could be the result of using a new device, called a pycnometer, developed by an ARS scientist working with a collaborator at Virginia Polytechnic Institute. The machine, about the size of a desk, takes only 30 seconds to determine the bird's volume by recording the amount of air it displaces from a cylinder. Scientists can then determine the density of a chicken by dividing its weight by its volume. This is the first time these measurements have been obtained from live birds. Scientists hope to get leaner chickens by using density of the birds as a marker in breeding trials. In practice, a producer would put breeding age chickens through the machine. Those that match a preset standard for density would be mated to produce leaner chickens, probably over a number of generations. The new pycnometer is based on the same principles as an earlier one that measured the volume of inanimate objects such as seeds and grain.

Poultry Research, Georgetown, DE
Vernon A. Garwood, (302) 856-0046
Virginia Polytechnic Institute, Blacksburg, VA
Kenneth C. Diehl, (703) 961-7937

A health-threatening problem among grazing cattle may be caused by rising soil temperatures. Grass tetany, a condition that can kill cattle, occurs as temperatures rise and grasses put on sudden spurts of spring growth. Scientists have found that grass tetany poses a threat to grazing animals where the grass contains more than 2.2 parts of potassium for every part of magnesium and calcium combined. Ranchers may want to keep a watchful eye when temperatures rise quickly and either move their cattle off suspect pastures of lush spring grasses such as fescue and small grains, or offer them a magnesium-calcium feed supplement.

U.S. Plant, Soil and Nutrition Research, Ithaca, NY
David L. Grunes, (607) 255-3003

Animal scientists are now using ultrasound to study the development of unborn calves and lambs whose mothers eat poisonous plants. Using sonograms—a harmless way to see and measure fetal activity and development—ARS scientists have been studying what happens to a fetus when its mother eats such range weeds as lupine, poison-hemlock, tree tobacco or locoweed. Research shows that the first three plants reduce movement of the fetus in the uterus by producing anesthetic-like toxins. If the fetus is prevented from moving freely, it won't develop and grow normally. Sonograms have also shown that when pregnant cows or ewes eat locoweed, fetal heart rate and strength of contractions are reduced. Ranchers can prevent poisoning by not grazing livestock on ranges containing these plants, but this is not always feasible. Other measures include altering breeding schedules so that livestock graze these plants only intermittently or when they are least toxic or when the fetus is least susceptible.

Poisonous Plant Research Lab, Logan, UT
Kip E. Panter, (801) 752-2941

In feeding trials with 20 Holstein cows, researchers found that fish meal can be a more economical protein source than soybean meal when fed with large amounts of high quality alfalfa silage. Cows fed a fish meal protein diet produced 3 pounds more milk daily than those fed soybean meal, the "usual" protein supplement fed to U.S. dairy herds. The cows fed 3 percent fish meal protein in their dry matter ate as much of the total mixed ration as those fed soybean meal. Unlike soybean meal protein, fish meal protein resists breakdown by bacteria living in the rumen, the first part of a cow's four-part stomach. Substituting fish meal for soybean meal will help cows make better nutritional use of their total feed.

U.S. Dairy Forage Research Center, Madison, WI
Glen A. Broderick, (608) 263-6824

Does it matter to catfish how long their pond water is recirculated? ARS researchers don't think so, which could mean long-term savings for fish farmers. In an attempt to increase production and maintain water quality, channel catfish were grown in ponds—some of which were recirculated continuously and the others for 12 hours a day. The continuously recirculating ponds produced an average of 710 pounds of fish, while those with 12-hour recirculation averaged 789 pounds. Fish biologists conclude that while recirculating water—which increases oxygen supplies—is vital to production and quality, half-day pumping is just as effective and more economical for fish farmers than continuous pumping.

Genetics and Production Research, Lane, OK
Wendell J. Lorio, (405) 384-5390

A bacterium deadly to catfish may actually help save fish farmers from regularly finding their "crop" belly up in the ponds. *Edwardsiella ictaluri*, a mud-dwelling bacterium, is suspected of causing up to 40 percent of all catfish diseases in the southeastern U.S. The catfish death toll in an *Edwardsiella*-infected pond can hit 50 percent. Fish . farmers traditionally have fought back by using feed dosed with antibiotics. But medicated feed is more expensive and farmers have had no way of determining whether their fish were really at risk until the fish began dying and the bacterium was found in their bodies. Researchers have found that a protein from the bacterium can be mixed with blood from a representative sample of fish to determine if a pond's fish are truly infected and need medicated feed. The protein may be ready for commercial testing as early as next year and might someday form the basis for a vaccine against *Edwardsiella ictaluri* attacks.

Animal Parasite Research, Auburn, AL
Phillip H. Klesius, (205) 887-3741

Insect and Weed Research

A sequence of herbicide treatments to control Canada thistle may pay handsome dividends to Northern Plains farmers. In North Dakota alone, this weed reduces yields of spring wheat by several million bushels each year. The sequence of herbicide treatments is the most effective control yet found. In a 3-year study, scientists applied glyphosate to thick stands of thistles in the fall and then applied bromoxynil plus MCPA (methyl chlorophenoxy-acetic acid) on wheat crops each spring. By the third fall, thistle numbers were reduced from about 30 to 1 per square yard. It only takes two Canada thistles per square yard to reduce grain yields up to 15 percent. All three herbicides are approved by the Environmental Protection Agency.
Cropping System and Water Quality Research, Columbia, MO
William W. Donald, (314) 882-6404

Alternatives to chemical pesticides will get a boost now that ARS and Russian scientists are working together to find, test and exchange biological controls. In May, scientists began exploring Moldavia, the Ukraine and the northern Caucasus for beneficial insects and microbes to thwart the Russian wheat aphid. The aphid cost U.S. wheat and barley growers about $123 million in 1988. First found in the United States in Texas in 1986, it has spread to 15 states and Canada. When the aphid begins sucking sap from a wheat or barley leaf, the leaf rolls around it, protecting it from insecticides and large predatory insects. This summer, five ARS researchers and one from the University of Idaho are scheduled to tour Russia in search of biocontrols for the aphids as well as grasshoppers and two serious U.S. range weeds, leafy spurge and knapweed.
National Program Staff, Beltsville, MD
Richard S. Soper, (301) 344-3930

Researchers are preparing to roll out a new weapon from Australia to beat back this year's crop of pesky grasshoppers. Grasshoppers gobble up about 23 percent of all forage suitable for grazing in 17 western states, at an annual cost of about $400 million. Earlier attempts to battle the pests with biocontrols turned up *Entomophaga grylli*, a naturally occurring soil fungus. Found throughout the United States, the fungus penetrates the grasshopper's body with enzymes that dissolve the body cuticle. Then the fungus grows inside the insect, attacking body tissue and reserve fat supplies until the grasshopper dies. However, grasshoppers love to bask in the sun, raising their internal body temperatures to levels that kill the *E. grylli* at work inside them. Scientists are hopeful that another member of the *Entomophaga* family, this one from Australia, will be able to withstand the basking bugs' high body temperatures. The Australian pathogen appears especially promising because it kills more grasshopper types than *E. grylli*. Plans are to introduce the Australian fungus on the American range this summer.
Plant Protection Research, Ithaca, NY
Raymond I. Carruthers, (607) 255-2456

Perking up the corn borer's appetite for *Bacillus thuringiensis* (Bt) may just be the ticket to its destruction. Cornstarch granules containing pathogens such as Bt provide effective controls for the hungry larvae—if they eat the granules. But many will not oblige because the taste of the starch is unappealing. ARS researchers found that when wheat germ or amino acids were incorporated into the starch granules, the larvae not only ate the granules but preferred them over healthy corn foliage. Several feeding products were tested. The most effective was the commercial product COAX, which was developed by ARS scientists for another moth species. Tests showed, in general, that starch granules containing Bt and a feeding stimulant, such as 5 percent COAX, will help farmers control corn borer larvae more effectively than granules that contain only Bt.
Bioactive Constituents Research, Northern Regional Research Center, Peoria, IL
Robert J. Bartelt, (309) 685-4011

Corn growers can reduce black cutworm damage and maintain yields by removing field weeds at least 8 days before planting corn. ARS researchers, in cooperation with Iowa State University and the University of Illinois, found that the female cutworm moth—*Agrotis ipsilon*—lays eggs in weedy fields before they are planted to corn. Newly hatched larvae feed on the weed seedlings, and are half- to full-grown by the time the corn plants emerge.
Corn Insects Research, Ankeny, IA
William B. Showers, (515) 964-6664

More practical pheromone traps could be in store to catch moths that plague soybeans. The male velvetbean caterpillar moth costs southern soybean growers $10 million yearly in losses and chemicals to control it. Since it doesn't survive winter temperatures in much of the United States, entomologists are trying to learn more about its reproduction and annual migration from Mexico and the Caribbean Basin into soybean-growing areas. So far, researchers have found that a pheromone—or sex attractant—of the velvetbean caterpillar moth contains two chemicals, C20 (eicosatriene) and C21 (heneicosatriene). In field studies, the greatest number of male moths flew around the cone-type traps that emitted a 78 to 22 ratio of C20 to C21. And the most effective release rate was about 10 nanograms (ten-billionths of a gram) of the pheromone per hour. Scientists can use this information to catch moths, research their overwintering habits and study the moths' migration patterns in order to develop control programs for this pest. Three species of grass loopers—pests of pasture grasses—were also attracted to the velvetbean caterpillar moth's pheromone, but they preferred the traps containing only the C21 chemical.

Behavioral Ecology and Reproduction Research, Gainesville, FL
John R. Mclaughlin, (904) 374-5795

The first outdoor test of cotton plants genetically engineered to kill harmful caterpillars is now underway at an ARS lab. If the plants control tobacco budworm and cotton bollworm—and pass other tests—farmers could gain a way of controlling these pests with little or no chemical insecticide. That could lower costs, increase profits and help the environment. Scientists at Agracetus, a private firm, engineered and greenhouse-tested the experimental cotton. They inserted a gene from a natural bacterium, *Bacillus thuringiensis* (Bt) into the cotton's chromosome. The Bt gene produces a toxin that interferes with caterpillars' digestion. Bt has been sold as a biological control for nearly 30 years in this country. It does not harm people, the environment or beneficial insects. The firm asked ARS to run the tests because of the agency's 30 years of expertise at breeding pest-resistant cotton varieties.

Crop Science Research Lab, Mississippi State, MS
Johnie N. Jenkins, (601) 323-2230

A newly discovered pheromone that attracts male driedfruit beetles may someday save California fig growers and the dried-fruit industry millions of dollars annually. Entomologists, working with a wind tunnel and hundreds of beetles, tested the pheromone's effectiveness in attracting both sexes to baited traps. In one test, 62 males and 80 females responded to the bait. Studies indicate that a commercial trap containing the pheromone and another substance, such as the scent given off by fermenting fruit, could attract beetles away from the fields. Besides figs and dried fruit such as raisins and prunes, the insects feed on nuts, peanuts, rice, peaches, strawberries and other fresh fruit.

Bioactive Constituents/Mycotoxin Research, Northern Regional Research Center, Peoria, IL
Robert J. Bartelt/Patrick F. Dowd, (309) 685-4011

Petunias—a distant relative of the tomato—contain natural insecticides that apparently help the plant fend off the destructive tomato fruitworm *(Heliothis zea)*. ARS chemists have discovered in petunia leaves and stems natural chemicals that confer this resistance. When fed to fruitworms in lab tests, the chemicals—named petuniolides and petuniasterones—killed young tomato fruitworm larvae and stunted the growth of older worms. Studies of two other tomato relatives, cape gooseberry and tomatillo, suggest that chemicals in these plants also may defend them from the fruitworm. Tools of modern biotechnology, such as protoplast fusion and microinjection, may make it possible for scientists to transfer natural resistance into tomatoes from its relatives. Similarly, other crops such as potato, corn, cotton and soybean that the tomato fruitworm attacks might be protected.

Plant Protection Research, Western Regional Research Center, Albany, CA
Carl A. Elliger/Anthony C. Waiss, Jr., (415) 559-5821/20

A wilt-fighting fungus from the ARS has teamed up with a beetle-fighting wasp to cut pesticide needs in a pilot biological control project. For 5 years, tiny, nonstinging *Edovum puttleri* wasps that ARS entomologists imported from South America have stifled Colorado potato beetles for several New Jersey eggplant growers. The growers now need to apply insecticide only twice instead of as many as 15 times. The wasp eggs are "time bombs" laid inside beetle eggs. When the wasp eggs hatch, wasp larvae gobble up the beetle eggs. This year, growers in the project are also testing an ARS strain of *Talaromyces flavus* fungus against *Verticillium* wilt. The wilt, which clogs plants' water passageways, attacks about 150 plant species. But field tests have shown that *T. flavus* can reduce wilt in eggplant by as much as 75 percent, reducing the need for a fumigant by 75 percent. Scientists at Rutgers University ran the pilot project with support from the state and USDA.

Biocontrol of Plant Diseases Lab, Beltsville, MD
Deborah Fravel, (301) 344-3653

A termite that homeowners don't have to worry about? Yes! It's a new species of drywood termite from south Florida. Instead of damaging structural timber or agricultural crops, the newly identified species, *Neotermes luykxi*, does its part to replenish Nature by recycling nutrients contained in wood or forest litter. Since it needs a lot of moisture, it has only been found in the dead wood of Black Mangrove trees, which grow in swamps. It can be distinguished from its closest relative, *N. jouteli*, only by the slight differences in size and various body structures. ARS entomologists examined these body characteristics to develop an identification key with detailed illustrations. Using this key, other insect scientists now can correctly differentiate these termites from those that damage manmade wooden structures. Since each harmful termite species requires a different control method, a quick way to differentiate between them and the non-pest termites is essential.

Systematic Entomology Lab, Washington, DC
David A. Nickle, (202) 382-8982

A recently found hydrilla that grows faster than other varieties of this pesky aquatic weed poses a new threat to northeastern U.S. waterways. Unlike the familiar variety which has only female flowers, the new hydrilla has both male and female flowers that can function at the same time. Called monoecious plants, they can reproduce sexually, mixing the female and male genes to form more adaptable weeds. To grow new plants, hydrilla produces tubers in the soil. Usually tubers are produced in winter because the weed needs long, dark nights to form them, as is the case with the dioecious (female only) hydrilla. But the new monoecious hydrilla can form tubers during summer. This assures its survival in areas with a shorter growing season, such as in the northern U.S. The researchers found that monoecious weeds took half the time—only 4 weeks—to produce 5 to 7 times more tubers than the dioecious weed. Understanding the growth characteristics and biology of this new form of hydrilla is essential to develop controls.

Aquatic Weed Control Research, Fort Lauderdale, FL
Thai K. Van, (305) 475-0541

Crop Production and Protection

The quality of light, or the amount of each color in white light, appears to play a major role in determining whether a plant puts more energy into growing roots or shoots. More blue in light directs soybean plants to grow more roots, while little or no blue causes a plant to put more resources into leaves and stems. This concept, that blue light might be a controlling factor, adds a new dimension to the previous belief that a plant directs its resources into either shoots or roots, based primarily on a balance of total light, available water and nutrients. After 86 days, soybean plants grown under fluorescent light with blue in it had 16 percent of their dry matter in roots. Plants getting no blue light had only 8 percent of their dry matter in roots. Ultimately, scientists may be able to genetically engineer new lines of photosensitive plants to put more or less energy into roots or shoots.

Photobiology Lab, Beltsville, MD
Steven J. Britz, (301) 344-3607

A particularly troublesome type of soybean cyst nematode may be about to meet its match in Cordell, a new soybean variety. Soybean cyst nematodes infest as much as 70 percent of the soybean acreage in the Mid-South and southeastern U.S. The pest penetrates the roots of soybean plants, reducing yields as much as 40 percent. As new types of soybean cyst nematodes have appeared, plant breeders have developed new soybean varieties specifically resistant to those nematodes. Cordell is the first commercial variety with resistance to Race 5 nematodes, an increasing problem. In 2 years of tests on fields infested with Race 5 soybean cyst nematodes, Cordell soybeans yielded 33.4 and 38.9 bushels per acre—9.5 more than Bedford variety soybeans and 6.3 more than Forrest soybeans. Cordell grows best in Virginia, North Carolina, Tennessee, southern Missouri, Arkansas, northern Mississippi, Alabama and part of South Carolina, and should be available to farmers in 1990.
Nematology Research, Jackson, TN
Lawrence D. Young, (901) 424-1643

Checking for cereal aphids—and knowing when to treat the grain crop—has never been simpler, cheaper or more accurate. ARS researchers developed a method for inspecting grain tillers, or stems, for cereal aphids. It can be done by untrained personnel, requires minimal labor and provides accurate results. The method involves checking between 25 and 100 small grain tillers for the presence or absence of aphids. After each tiller is inspected, results are compared with graphs or tables that contain upper and lower limits of infestation. Prepared in cooperation with South Dakota State University, the tables tell when to treat for cereal aphids, saving a farmer the time and expense of treating when few aphids are present. The tables will be soon be available through county extension agents.
Northern Grain Insects Research Lab, Brookings, SD
Norman C. Elliott, (605) 693-5212

Nematodes have the dubious distinction of being the most serious pest of sugar beets grown in the western U.S. These microscopic worms spend the summer feasting on delicate root hairs which sugar beets depend on for healthy growth. Crop rotation effectively controls nematodes. But many growers don't have enough land to rotate, so they combine short rotations (only 1- to 3-years long) with chemical treatments. Scientists compared the effectiveness of three

chemical treatments—1,3-D (a gaseous soil fumigant that destroys nematode eggs before sugar beets are planted) and aldicarb and terbufos (two chemicals that destroy the nematode after it hatches). The fumigant 1,3-D provided the best control, aldicarb the second best. All three chemicals are registered for use on sugar beets by the Environmental Protection Agency.
Forage and Range Research, Logan, UT
Gerald D. Griffin, (801) 750-3066

Sunflower farmers expecting severe thunderstorms soon may have fewer worries about winds knocking down their crops and reducing yields. ARS and North Dakota State University scientists have developed seven new sunflower breeding lines which produce short and strong hybrids that can stand up to winds. Not quite three-fourths the normal sunflower height, these experimental hybrids produced equal or higher yields than their conventional cousins in North Dakota tests. Hybrid sunflower seeds were also higher in oil, averaging 48.1 percent vs. 44.5 percent. These results resembled parallel tests of these breeding lines in Australia and Yugoslavia. Seed companies now are breeding their own experimental hybrids by crossing the 7 sunflower pollen sources—called restorer lines—with cytoplasmic male sterile lines. Such hybrids grow over a wider geographic area than where sunflowers now grow. For example, on highly fertilized soil that gets average rainfall in North Dakota's Red River Valley where corn and soybeans are the dominant row crops, the new short sunflower hybrids have yielded up to 3,000 pounds per acre (about 20 percent more than taller sunflowers).
Oilseeds Research, Fargo, ND
Jerry F. Miller, (701) 239-1321

Genes coated on tiny tungsten particles can be propelled into plant cells. It's a new high-speed biotechnology technique for engineering genes such as those for disease resistance into plants. High-speed "microprojectiles" were used to shoot sample genes into tobacco—a plant that has long been used as a research model. This is one of the first examples of using particle-gun technology to transfer foreign genes into cells of a "higher" plant that can then be nurtured into tiny plantlets with the gene actively working inside. ARS scientists now want to use the particle-bombardment process to get crops such as corn to accept new genes.
Plant Gene Expression Center, Albany, CA
Theodore M. Klein, (415) 559-5923

Scientists are tracking genes in corn to increase its resistance to the European corn borer, a pest that costs farmers $400 million a year in losses and control efforts. Locating specific genes in corn may help researchers map resistance to this insect pest that also attacks beans, potatoes and other vegetables. By marking the genes on specific chromosomes, researchers can track which genes are passed from corn plants to their offspring. In a cooperative ARS-Iowa State University study, scientists will attempt to isolate insect-resistance genes. They will cross highly-resistant corn lines with highly-susceptible lines. Genes that are passed to the next generation of corn will be studied for their resistance or susceptibility to corn borers. Eventually, researchers hope to manipulate the resistant genes to give future generations of corn greater resistance to the insect.

Corn Insects Research, Ankeny, IA
Wilbur D. Guthrie, (515) 964-6664

Fire blight, a disease caused by the bacterium *Erwinia amylovora*, strikes apple and pear trees in this country—a finding that could have implications for U.S. exports. Some countries where the disease does not occur have banned imports of these fruit from the United States. Six varieties of mature apples were harvested from blighted trees at three locations in Washington State. They were rigorously tested for the presence of the bacterium on external and internal tissues. Bacteria were not found on or in any of the 755 tested apples. This suggests that mature apples, even when harvested from trees with fire blight-infected foliage, are unlikely to transmit the bacterium.

Tree Fruit Research Lab, Wenatchee, WA
Rodney G. Roberts, (509) 662-4317

When an insecticide fails to control an insect pest, a grower may think the insect has become resistant to the pesticide. This sometimes may be true, but in many cases the pesticide was not applied properly. ARS scientists evaluated 29 applications of azinphosmethyl sprayed on apple trees in commercial orchards to control damage caused by codling moths. Only 43 percent of these applications provided enough pesticide to totally control the moth. The study demonstrates that it's more difficult to apply pesticides to orchards than many people realize. Growers should take more care in calculating application rates and in

properly using, calibrating and maintaining spray equipment. If this is done, scientists say, more effective and reliable insect control can be achieved.

Yakima Agricultural Research Lab, Yakima, WA
Charles R. Sell, (509) 575-5967

Southeastern peach growers should irrigate their trees after harvest to reduce stress and vulnerability of orchards to peach tree fungal gummosis. Most growers do not irrigate after the fruit is picked, between May and August. But, in a greenhouse study, scientists found the disease was worse when drought stress was imposed than when trees were irrigated daily. The disease causes decline in peach tree vigor in Georgia, South Carolina, Alabama, Mississippi, Louisiana and Florida orchards. First reported in Fort Valley, Ga., in 1966, the disease is caused by the fungus *Botryosphaeria dothidea* and is believed to be spread by spores carried in splashing water or wind-driven rain. There is no known control for fungal gummosis, but ARS is conducting field studies on irrigation and chemical control.

Southeastern Fruit and Tree Nut Research Lab,
Byron, GA
P. Lawrence Pusey, (912) 956-5656

Hawthorn lace bugs reproduce three times a year, not once, as previously reported. This discovery may help gardeners control this serious pest of ornamentals. It attacks 32 species of the Rosaceae family, including roses, American hawthorn, pyracantha, cotoneaster and sometimes apples. By spraying registered pesticides in early to mid-May, growers and homeowners can control emerging adults and possibly eliminate generations two and three. No parasites or predators are known to be effective against the bug. This, plus its longevity and the female lace bug's high egg-laying capacity, increase the pest's potential threat to ornamentals.

Florist and Nursery Crops Lab, Beltsville, MD
John W. Neal, (301) 344-4559

Could anemia be the cure for what ails many crop plants? Certain microbes snuggle up to roots and infect the plants with diseases that cost farmers roughly $4 billion dollars a year. But farmers and gardeners might someday make bad microbes anemic—depriving them of iron by using beneficial bacteria. The key: Iron-hoarding compounds, called siderophores, produced by nearly all bacteria and fungi. But there are no reliable methods for studying siderophores in their natural state or determining why they sometimes do and sometimes don't help control disease organisms. Now, however, researchers have taken a small but important step forward. They devised the first monoclonal antibody, or custom-built protein, that can bind to siderophores so they can be measured. Further research and an effective delivery system—such as seeds coated with iron-greedy beneficial bacteria—are needed before growers can make widespread use of siderophores to protect their crops.

Soil Microbial Systems Lab, Beltsville, MD
Jeffrey S. Buyer, (301) 344-3436

Iron starvation, however, may not be a magic bullet against take-all, one of the most damaging fungal diseases of wheat in the Pacific Northwest. Scientists initially thought that increasing the amount of siderophores produced by beneficial bacteria on the roots would starve the fungus for iron and reduce its killing effect. But new studies suggest that iron starvation alone is not enough to thwart the fungi, even in soils already low in iron. Several years ago, ARS researchers discovered that a bacterial strain, *Pseudomonas fluorescens* 2-79, suppresses take-all. The 2-79 strain produces an antibiotic—as well as siderophores. The new studies show that it's the antibiotic that takes the lead in fighting the fungus.

Root Diseases and Biological Control, Pullman, WA
Linda S. Thomashow, (509) 335-0930

New and Improved Products

A new wool protectant developed by an ARS scientist protects wool garments from moths and beetles longer than moth balls and doesn't leave an odor. The protectant is made from avermectin, an anti-parasitic agent produced by the soil fungus *Streptomyces avermitilis*. Tests have shown that a single application of avermectin protects garments from moth and beetle damage for at least 5 years. The new wool protectant also has survived washing, dry cleaning, excessive heat and light tests for durability. Avermectin was originally developed as a medicine to prevent internal parasites in animals. The new wool protectant kills webbing clothes moth and black carpet beetle larvae, while repelling furniture carpet beetle larvae—the primary enemies of wool clothing. Two U.S. companies are considering marketing the new protectant. Avermectin wool protectant can be applied to a garment in manufacturing or developed for household use.

Environmental and Special Problems Research, Savannah, GA
Roy Bry, (912) 233-7981

Listening to sounds emitted when treated leather is stretched can determine its texture, strength, softness and appearance. ARS scientists are using a research method—acoustic emission spectroscopy—that measures acoustic impulses discharged from leather. The technique has been used in the plastic and metal industries since the late 1960s to measure durability of objects like underground gasoline tanks. ARS scientists are applying that same principle to leather as demand increases for more diverse lines of leather products for clothing, furniture and automobile seats. As leather is stretched and fibers separate, scientists hear small popping sounds. When the sounds get louder, they know that fibers are breaking. The acoustical method can evaluate when and how much lubricant should be applied to leather to soften it. Workers now feel the fabric with their hands to determine how much lubricant to add. Acoustic emission spectroscopy isn't currently in industrial use, but could end the current subjective measurement of leather.

Hides, Leather and Wool Research, Philadelphia, PA
Paul Kronick, (215) 233-6585

The fungus *Trichoderma harzianum* has been found to produce a compound that inhibits the growth of *Aspergillus flavus*, one of the two fungi that produce aflatoxin, a contaminant of corn, cotton and peanuts. In lab tests, a 1:40 dilution of 6-pentyl-pyrone (6PP) created a one-half inch circle in which *A. flavus* did not grow, even when heavily seeded, showing the compound's promise as an agent to fight aflatoxin contamination. While 6PP has so far been tested only in the lab, it eventually might be sprayed on crops and stored products to cut back the growth of *A. flavus* and reduce or eliminate aflatoxin.
Plant Physiology Research Lab, Athens, GA
Hank Cutler, (404) 546-3378

By altering or removing genes from the fungi that produce aflatoxin, scientists may prevent these fungi from making the toxin, which has been found to be carcinogenic. Genes in two soil fungi—*Aspergillus flavus* and *A. parasiticus*—determine the presence of enzymes that produce aflatoxin. ARS research has identified two of these enzymes that aflatoxin needs in the late stages of its growth. Once these genes are located, scientists can either remove them from the fungus or determine what causes the gene to send signals to these enzymes. Scientists could also make a fungus without the gene that controls release of the aflatoxin-producing enzyme.
Food and Feed Safety Research, New Orleans, LA
Thomas E. Cleveland, (504) 286-4200

Stored rice may one day be free of munching pests without the use of insecticides. Researchers have begun breeding a variety that naturally resists insects that attack rice in storage. Millions of dollars are spent annually fighting these infestations, and experts estimate there is still a 5- to 10-percent loss of stored rice each year. After screening several thousand varieties of rice in the USDA World Collection, three were selected as showing potential for resistance to the Angoumois grain moth, lesser grain borer, rice weevil, red flour beetle, and several *Cryptolestes* species. Interbreeding these varieties, all originating in Asia, for just three to five generations has already resulted in a rice that is far less suitable as a host for stored-rice-attacking insects, reducing insect infestation by 90 percent.

The rice's resistance seems to come from having a hull that maintains its integrity rather than some biochemical difference. Researchers are adding a cross with high-yielding commercial varieties to create elite germplasm with both excellent yield and storage-insect resistance.
Rice Research, Beaumont, TX
Robert R. Cogburn, (409) 752-5221

A newly released orange hybrid is expected to help Florida growers and processors reduce U.S. dependence on imported juice. Juice from Ambersweet, the new orange hybrid, exceeds Federal color standards for Grade A juice. It can be mixed with other domestic orange juices that don't quite make the grade. This should help processors who must now import and store juice to mix with Hamlin and other orange varieties. Ambersweet, which matures earlier than most other varieties, is also ideal for the fresh market. Test-grown in two areas of Florida since 1974, it should be available from commercial nurseries within a year. U.S. orange juice imports totaled about $535 million in 1987-88, mostly from Brazil.
U.S. Horticultural Research Lab, Orlando, FL
C. Jack Hearn, (407) 897-7339

Muskmelons will keep a week longer if producers dip the fruit in a hot bath and cover it with a shrink-film wrap. ARS researchers sterilized the outside of the melons by bathing them for 3 minutes at 134 degrees F. The melons were then wrapped in a breathable polymer that was sealed by heat. The dual treatment controlled decay, slowed moisture loss and maintained quality for 20 days, an increase of 7 days over melons not treated and wrapped. Plant physiologists also discovered that gamma irradiation—successfully used with other fruits as a non-chemical treatment to maintain quality—caused a decrease in muskmelon quality and did not control decay.
Plant Health and Stress Physiology Research, Weslaco, TX
Gene E. Lester, (512) 969-2511

A friendly bacterium that helps stop mold-causing fungi on apples and pears has yielded a clue about its makeup. Researchers have discovered a new derivative of the bacterium's powerful natural antibiotic, pyrrolnitrin. Golden Delicious apples were punctured, exposed to three common rot-causing organisms and then treated with the new derivative—a phenylpyrrole. The compound completely stopped one fungus and reduced the other two by 80 percent each. By substituting a different broth for growing the bacterium, *Pseudomonas cepacia*, researchers increased yield of pyrrolnitrin by 50 times. Because it helps stop blue mold and gray mold in fruit, the bacterium might be used as a safe, effective alternative to fungicides to stop fruit from spoiling.

Process Biotechnology Research, Western Regional Research Center, Albany, CA
J.N. Roitman/N.E. Mahoney/M.E. Benson,
(415) 559-5971
Appalachian Fruit Research Station,
Kearneysville, WV
Wojciech J. Janisiewicz, (304) 725-3451

An "eat-it-all" melon could be as handy a snack as an apple. Imagine a melon with an edible rind but no core or seeds left to throw away in a single serving size. As part of the project to create such a snack melon, two disease-resistant, cantaloupe-like melons with smooth skin and firm flesh like an apple's have been developed. The more attractive of the two has a bright-yellow rind, pink flesh and excellent quality, although the fruit is still too large to eat as a snack like an apple. The other has high yields with 6 to 15 grapefruit-size melons per plant, but the sweet flesh is an unattractive off-white color. Bringing the size of each melon down to peach- or plum-size is not expected to be difficult, but breeding in seedlessness probably will be. Also planned is breeding for longer shelf life with an eye toward being able to market the melon in vending machines, such as those that currently offer apples and oranges. The finished variety, at least 2 or 3 years away, will almost certainly be some type of hybrid.

U.S. Vegetable Lab, Charleston, SC
Perry E. Nugent, (803) 556-0840

Dusting or bathing sugar beets with lime (calcium hydroxide) can yield 10 to 20 percent more sugar beet pulp. The pulp is used as a high-fiber additive in foods and as an ingredient in feed for dairy cattle. Liming strengthens pulp cell walls, and researchers believe it prevents a pulp component—soluble pectins—from dissolving. With conventional processing, some pulp is lost when those same pectins dissolve. Processors can also expect more than a 10-percent savings in energy costs. That's because pulp from limed beets is easier to squeeze and so contains significantly less moisture when it enters energy-hogging pulp dryers. U.S. sugar beet processors produced about 3.7 million tons of sugar, worth about $2 billion, from the 1988 sugar beet crop.

Process Chemistry and Engineering Research,
Western Regional Research Center, Albany, CA
Attila E. Pavlath, (415) 559-5620

Sugar beets of the future will pack improved resistance to the crop's two most damaging diseases. Scientists have turned over beet germplasm to plant breeders who are working to incorporate that resistance into commercial varieties. Two of the new lines resist cercospora leaf spot, and another two resist rhizoctonia root rot. These fungal diseases cost beet growers $50 million in lost sugar every year. Fungicidal controls for *Cercospora* can cost up to $200 per acre; there is no chemical control for *Rhizoctonia*.

Sugarbeet Production Research, Fort Collins, CO
Richard J. Hecker, (303) 482-7717

A conveyor that uses jets of air to move peppers reduces the number of peppers lost to injury during mechanical harvesting. Unlike a conventional belt conveyor, which can cause fruit to fall to the ground, the ARS design features a continuous flow of air through tiny horizontal slots in the conveyor surface. In design tests, the air passing through the carefully positioned slots moved the peppers in the desired direction. Different air velocities were used, ranging from 30 to 38 meters per second measured at the slots. The design can handle most types of peppers, including jalapeno, hot banana and large bell peppers. In addition to harvesting, the conveyor is designed to remove light trash, primarily leaves and small branches. Two commercial firms have adopted the design.

Fruit and Vegetable Harvesting Research,
East Lansing, MI
Dale E. Marshall, (517) 353-5201

It's light and bubbly, and tastes a little like champagne. But it's not champagne, it's muscadine grape juice. And now that scientists have developed new planting and growing practices, it may become more plentiful. Working with the Mississippi Agriculture and Forestry Experiment Stations at Starkville and Crystal Springs, Miss., ARS researchers have developed management practices that increase yield and fruit quality without chemicals and with less labor. These new practices could produce a commercial crop in the third year—2 years faster than currently possible. A muscadine juice-processing plant was recently completed in Mississippi, with a satellite plant in North Carolina. Muscadines grow wild in the South and were the first American grapes to be cultivated. Part-time farmers in the Southeastern U.S. and those looking for an alternative crop are showing increased interest in the muscadine.

Small Fruit Research Station, Poplarville, MS
William C. Olien, (601) 795-8751

The star-shaped, Florida-grown carambola has a brighter future since ARS scientists developed a cold storage treatment for the exotic fruit to kill mature larvae of the Caribbean fruit fly, *Anastrepha suspensa*. Carambolas subjected to 34 degrees F for 15 days proved pest free and showed little or no damage to fruit quality. The fruit remained marketable 7 days after removal from cold storage. Taste was not affected. Because there currently are no quarantine treatments approved for carambolas infested with the pest, marketability to citrus states has been restricted. The treatment should open up new domestic and possible foreign markets for the Florida fruit industry. Currently 1 million pounds of carambola is produced annually. Within a few years, production is expected to rise to about 10 million.

Subtropical Horticulture Research Station, Miami, FL
Walter P. Gould, (305) 238-9321

The pili nut, with its tasty, light-cream colored kernel, might someday become as popular in the United States as the macadamia, another exotic tropical nut species. A prominent macadamia nut breeder estimates that pili nuts have the same potential that the macadamia had in Hawaii 30 years ago. Today, Hawaii's macadamias have a farm value of $36 million. At the tropical crops repository in Hilo, Hawaii, researchers will soon collect and preserve pili specimens for use by breeders and researchers worldwide. In related work aimed at developing pili's commercial potential, the scientists are nurturing seedlings from almost

100 recently acquired seeds of a pili relative, Chinese olive *(Canarium album)*. This olive may contain genes that are not found in pili but may be of value to that species. Chinese scientists provided the olive seeds for the Hawaii collection.

National Clonal Germplasm Repository for Tropical and Subtropical Fruit and Nut Crops, Hilo, HI
Francis T.P. Zee, (808) 959-5833

A plump little pineapple that's bright red on the outside might someday be marketed as a decorative centerpiece for buffets or salad bars. And techniques of modern biotechnology might enable genetic engineers to eventually improve this exotic pineapple's flavor, making it sweet enough to eat. Only about half the size of the familiar yellow pineapple, the mini-pineapple "Saigon Red" is one of more than 160 specimens donated by a Hawaii pineapple company to the ARS-University of Hawaii tropical crops repository in Hilo, Hawaii. Within the collection may be genes that pineapple breeders seek for such valuable traits as flavor and resistance to cold or disease. Saigon Red and more than half of the other pineapple specimens are now being maintained as tissue culture plantlets. They take up less space in the lab than field-grown plants, yet preserve their genetic makeup and can be easily shipped worldwide to scientists or to breeders who are developing improved commercial pineapple varieties.

National Clonal Germplasm Repository for Tropical and Subtropical Fruit and Nut Crops, Hilo, HI
Francis T.P. Zee, (808) 959-5833

New jobs and added income for central Illinois residents will be the result of an ARS patent for making a no-calorie, high-fiber flour from corn fiber. Mt. Pulaski Products, Mt. Pulaski, Ill., has been licensed to use the ARS-patented process that softens the fibrous parts of corn cobs and other cereal crops so they can be made into flour. The flour is made by using a dilute solution of hydrogen peroxide to break down the lignin, or woody substance, in plant materials. The flour can boost the fiber content of breads, cake mixes, pancakes, doughnuts, crackers and other prepared foods without affecting taste or adding calories. Scientists worked on the process for over 4 years before patenting the procedure in 1988. Mt. Pulaski Products expects to sell the flour to companies that want to produce fiber-rich baked goods. (PATENT)

Biopolymer Research, Northern Regional Research Center, Peoria, IL
J. Michael Gould, (309) 685-4011

Scientific Information Systems

Western ranchers and range managers are closer to using a computer model to accurately predict snowmelt runoff and its affect on soil erosion. Since field studies are time consuming and expensive and cannot be conducted at every location where data is needed, managers are using mathematical models instead. ARS scientists evaluated the ability of the computer model SPUR (Simulation of Production and Utilization of Rangelands) to predict the amount of snowmelt runoff on sagebrush rangeland. The study compared predicted runoff to observed runoff from five small subwatersheds on the Reynolds Creek Experimental Watershed in southwestern Idaho. Results indicate the model adequately predicts runoff from areas with a relatively uniform snow cover, but does poorly on watersheds where runoff comes from a few isolated snowdrifts. The scientists will be examining other models and methods of describing variations in runoff.

Northwest Watershed Research Center, Boise, ID
Bradford P. Wilcox/Keith R. Cooley, (208) 334-1363

A new computer spreadsheet could reduce the risk of raising livestock on rangelands. Weather, forage production and livestock prices vary unpredictably from year to year. In addition, there is always the chance that imperfect management decisions will cause damage to rangeland plants and soils. For example, if cattle producers use the same stocking rate—the number of acres per grazing animal—every year, they may get high average returns over several years. But they risk losing money in years when forage production is poor—and sacrifice higher returns in years when it's good. Adjusting the stocking rate annually to the amount of forage produced and current livestock prices is more profitable and less risky, even if the producer somewhat misjudges forage production and prices. By relating the amount of forage per animal to weight gain, the new software guides the producer in adjusting stocking rates. The scientists also found that stocking for maximum short-term profits and minimum short-term risk is not likely to cause long-term damage to rangelands.

High Plains Grasslands Research Station,
Cheyenne, WY
Richard H. Hart, (307) 772-2433

Farmers could earn up to $25 more an acre by counting the number of weed seeds in their soil. Fifteen Colorado corn farmers are testing on weeds a rule long used in insect control—don't spray unless pest counts indicate yield loss will be great enough to justify the expense. Farmers can enter weed seed numbers into a home computer using software that does the financial calculations. ARS scientists developed the computer model in cooperation with an economist from Colorado State University. The Corn/Weed Bioeconomic Model forecasts crop losses, in dollars, based on weed seed numbers and other information. The computer "knows" the price of herbicides and the probable selling price of corn as well as the estimated yield. The scientists plan to refine this model to handle crop rotations that include corn, pinto beans, barley and sugar beets.

Sugarbeet Production Research, Fort Collins, CO
Edward E. Schweizer, (303) 482-7717
Colorado State University, Fort Collins, CO
Donald W. Lybecker, (303) 491-5496

An ARS-developed computer model is helping plan an attack against the southern cattle tick. The tick carries the pathogen that causes cattle fever, which once nearly devastated the U.S. cattle industry. These ticks are tough, and all U.S. cattle breeds are susceptible. To prevent any reintroduction of the ticks at the U.S.-Mexico border, a new strategy is being tried on the island of St. Croix. Cattle fever is widespread in the Caribbean, including the U.S. Virgin Islands and Puerto Rico, as well as in Mexico. Researchers have crossbred two species of ticks—*Boophilus annulatus* and *Boophilus microplus*—both known to cause babesiosis, or cattle fever. The males of this match are sterile, and the females pass along this sterility to their young. The computer model—BCTSIM for *Boophilus* Cattle Tick Simulation—was fed data on the number of free-living ticks in the test plots. This was matched with simulated environment and weather conditions, so the computer could predict the number of hybrids needed to overwhelm the native population. Based on the findings, 10 hybrid larvae would need to be released for every free-living female tick to overwhelm the native insects.

Insects Affecting Man and Animals, Gainesville, FL
Daniel G. Haile, (904) 374-5928

⋆U S Government Printing Office 1989 · 241-788/80946

6503
Que

Quarterly Report
of Selected Research Projects

United States
Department of
Agriculture

 Agricultural
Research
Service

July 1 to September 31, 1989

Contents

Insect and Weed Research

A long-forgotten fungus ruined spring for gypsy moth caterpillars in much of the northeast this year. By devouring the pest's insides, the fungus changed caterpillars into "mummies"—sometimes thousands on a single tree—in seven states. First seen in Connecticut, the phenomenon surprised scientists because no similar outbreak of gypsy moth fungi had ever been seen in the United States. Now the identity and curious origin of the fungus have been uncovered by ARS researchers. The fungus is *Entomophaga maimaiga*, imported from Japan 80 years ago. It was thought to have died without a trace in field tests against the moth near Boston in 1910 and 1911. In 1984, ARS imported and field-tested the same species, again to no avail. But the "old" fungus—unnoticed—slowly spread for 78 years, blooming in last spring's unusually cool and rainy weather. Researchers say if it is, in fact, adapted to North America's climate, it could turn into a potent biological control agent.
Plant Protection Research, Ithaca, NY
Richard A. Humber, (607) 255-1276

Note: One or more scientists familiar with each research project are listed for further information. If the scientists are unavailable, others at the same telephone number may also be familiar with the work.

Items marked with the word PATENT are being patented by ARS. For more information contact Ann Whitehead, National Patent Program, Bldg. 005, Rm. 401, Beltsville Agricultural Research Center, Beltsville, MD 20705, (301) 344-2786.

An Argentinian protozoan, *Thelhania solenopsdae*, could be an answer to controlling menacing fire ants found in the southeastern U.S. A year-long ARS study in Argentina is examining the protozoan's ability to control fire ant populations in pastures resembling those of such states as Texas and central Florida. While seeking moisture and nutrients, the small but voracious fire ants inflict painful welts to humans and animals and damage many crops. This protozoan thrives only within the fire ant—infecting the fat of workers' bodies and the ovaries of queens. To successfully eliminate a colony using *T. solenopsdae*, scientists must further study how the disease affects total colonies. If the study confirms the protozoan's effectiveness in controlling fire ant populations, it could be imported to the United States without worry of harming other beneficial insects.
Insects Affecting Man and Animals Research Lab, Gainesville, FL
Richard S. Patterson, (904) 374-5910

And on the home front... House-fly pupae may also help control bothersome fire ants without harming beneficial ants. Present control methods of feeding fire ants corn-grits mixed with the toxins hydramethylnon and fenoxy-carb end up wiping out all species of ants. The fly pupae, soaked in toxins, are attractive mostly to prowling fire ants which carry the pupae back to the colony as food. ARS studies have shown the toxin-laced fly pupae is as effective as the corn-grit mixture, albeit more expensive. The fly pupae can be freezer-stored at 23 degrees F for up to a year or longer before scattering them on fire ant hunting grounds. Scientists are now investigating ways in which the fly-pupae can be cheaply mass-produced and effectively combined with the two toxins.
Insects Affecting Man and Animals Research Lab, Gainesville, FL
David Williams, (904) 374-5982

The much maligned March fly is really beneficial, though some turf farmers may not know it. ARS scientists studying the biology and feeding habits of the flies found that they eat only dead organic matter—such as straw and dried-up grass roots—thus recycling unwanted residues. The flies got a bad reputation in 1977 and 1984, when the larvae became so numerous they inadvertently damaged delicate grass seedlings as they burrowed through the soil. This destroyed commercial stands of Oregon-grown grass seed that is normally shipped around the world to be planted for turf and forage. Because severe outbreaks cannot be predicted, the researchers recommend farmers plant early in the fall to obtain well-established plants that can withstand the burrowing larvae. Growers should not spray insecticides on their fields to kill the larvae.

National Forage Seed Production Research Center, Corvallis, OR
James A. Kamm, (503) 757-4365

Insect attractants last longer in traps if first encapsulated in starch granules. ARS researchers found this to be the case while studying corn rootworms. Granular-coated attractants were equally alluring to the insects as plain attractants, which are volatile and evaporate quickly. A 59-day field test, done in cooperation with the University of Nebraska, showed that rootworms were most attracted to an encapsulated mixture of several rather than single attractants. Western, northern and southern corn rootworms were more attracted to the encapsulated attractants at certain times, such as before and after corn flowering. Encapsulated attractants may save farmers money and play an important role in the development of environmentally sound pest management practices.

Plant Polymer Research, Northern Regional Research Center, Peoria, IL
Donald Trimnell, (309) 685-4011

Lesser cornstalk borers may be doomed if scientists can speed up the rate at which a fungus, *Beauveria bassiana*, kills these soil-dwelling insects. Over 60 crops are targets of this pest, including peanuts, corn, sorghum, soybeans and peas, and its damage can run into millions of dollars annually. Entomologists so far have learned that, in dry areas, the fungus spores are more effective if the soil is inoculated when the crop is planted, or just before the seeds sprout. The fungus kills the borers by getting into their cuticles and spreading into their bloodstream, but the delayed death of the insect only occurs after considerable damage has been done to plants. *B. bassiana* is also being tested on other soil insects such as the pecan weevil, as well as on the corn earworm, fall armyworm and European corn borer.

Insect Biology and Population Management Research Lab, Tifton, GA
Robert E. Lynch, (912) 382-6904

No parasites have been known to live their entire lives on one insect host—until now. A new nematode, *Noctuidonema guyanense*, attacks only the adult stage of fall armyworm and closely related *Noctuidae* moths. These pests attack crops in southern states including vegetables and all field crops such as corn, cotton, soybeans and sorghum. The nematode, found by ARS entomologists first in French Guiana and later in Florida, is the first occurrence of an "obligatory" parasitic nematode that attacks certain adult moths. Most nematodes attack the immature stages of their insect hosts and more than one host. The nematode also attacks six moth species found in Florida—including two *Spodoptera* armyworms and two grassy armyworms. The new nematode is no threat to beneficial insects. Its biology and effect on the armyworm moth need further testing to see if it could be an effective natural enemy of adult moths by limiting their migrations and population buildup.

Insect Biology and Population Management Research Lab, Tifton, GA
Charlie E. Rogers, (912) 387-2331

Two "lost colonies" of beneficial flies that attack the notorious weed yellow starthistle have been found—one in California and another in Oregon. Until now, scientists thought the quarter-inch long gall flies, *Urophora sirunaseva*, had died out shortly after ARS scientists released them at thistle-infested sites in 1984 and 1985. Agency colleagues in Greece originally collected and shipped the beneficial insects to the United States to help stop starthistle's spread. The weed poisons horses, pokes hikers with its needle-like thorns, deters cattle from grazing and crowds out desirable forage. In its larval (worm-like) stage, the gall fly eats starthistle flowerheads that would otherwise develop into seeds. This prevents the weed from reproducing. The plant forms small, garlic-shaped galls, apparently in response to this attack. But the insect simply uses the galls as a convenient home while transforming into adult flies. Encouraged by the endurance of these early colonies, scientists plan to import more gall flies next year for release in western states plagued by the fast-spreading weed.

Biocontrol of Weeds Lab, Western Regional Research Center, Albany, CA
Charles E. Turner, (415) 559-5975
Biocontrol of Weeds Lab, Thessaloniki, Greece
Rouhollah Sobhian, 011-3031-473-272

Two beneficial wasps will be mass reared in a joint project by ARS and Ciba-Geigy Corp. to see if they can be used as a biological control of destructive insects. The two wasp species, *Trichograma minutum* and *T pretiosum*, parasitize eggs of over 200 insects, including the codling moth and European corn borer. The cooperative effort will focus on inexpensively rearing the insect on an artificial diet and automating the rearing process. Currently, *Trichograma* are reared on insect eggs or expensive lab diets combining insect blood, cow's milk and chicken egg yolk; both diets are labor intensive. New discoveries or inventions made solely by ARS or Ciba-Geigy will be owned separately by the inventors. Joint inventions will share ownership.

Biological Control of Pests Research, Weslaco, TX
William C. Nettles, Jr., (512) 968-7546

The Mexican fruit fly, a pest of citrus, can be detected earlier if monitoring traps are placed on the right spot on trees. Early detection through trapping leads to faster and less expensive control of the flies. ARS researchers found that placing traps 3 to 6 feet above the ground on the north side of trees resulted in more flies captured per trap than in other locations. Researchers speculate that the north side of the trees shield the flies from direct sunshine and prevailing winds. The traps—baited with yeast hydrolysate, the standard chemical bait—captured an average of 18 flies compared to 1 fly in traps placed just above ground level or near tree tops in a 9-month study of more than 100 traps. Mexican fruit flies pose a serious threat to growers in citrus-growing regions of the United States. Wherever the insects are detected, eradication or fruit disinfestation treatment is required at a substantial cost to government agencies and industry. In 1988, for example, that cost exceeded $1 million in Texas alone.

Subtropical Crop Insects Research, Weslaco, TX
David C. Robacker, (512) 565-2647

Soil, Water and Air

Ryegrass and cereal rye are about four times more efficient than legumes in recycling nitrogen fertilizer, keeping it from leaching into groundwater. That's the finding of scientists taking a rare look at how much fertilizer is recycled by winter cover crops. A 2-year ARS study of nitrogen fertilizer recycling was done on a University of Maryland research farm using a form of nitrogen called N^{-15} as a tracer. The N^{-15} tracer/fertilizer was applied soon after corn planting each May. Each fall, the amount of leftover nitrogen was measured down to 2 feet in the soil. Then cover crops of cereal rye, ryegrass, hairy vetch and crimson clover were planted. After spring harvest, the crops were analyzed for N^{-15}. Cereal rye and ryegrass each took in about 40 percent of the leftover nitrogen. Hairy vetch and crimson clover legumes each used only about 10 percent.

Environmental Chemistry Lab, Beltsville, MD
Jack Meisinger, (301) 344-3276

Without trees and plants to stabilize them, streambanks erode, clogging downstream water reservoirs, reducing fish populations and blocking hydroelectric dams. ARS researchers are using a rhizotron—a high-tech, below-ground periscope—to study how the roots of willow trees and grasses control erosion and sedimentation, especially in the spring when melting snows cause heavy streamflow. Optical fibers in the instrument light its sidewalls, enabling scientists to observe the exact point at which roots grow the most, a process not observable from above ground. Until the root systems have grown enough to stabilize a streambank, livestock grazing should be controlled to give willow and grasses the best opportunity to grow. The study is being conducted along the banks of a tributary of the Feather River in northern California.

Landscape Ecology of Rangelands Research, Reno, NV
Tony J. Svejcar, (702) 784-6057

Friendly soil microorganisms known as mycorrhizal fungi may help plants survive on manganese-laden soils. Lands left barren after mining and some farmland in the southern United States are high in this mineral. In preliminary greenhouse experiments, soybean seedlings with roots "colonized" by the helpful fungi shrugged off manganese toxicity. But seedlings without the soil microorganism took up toxic amounts of the mineral. Their lower leaves yellowed and died and the upper leaves became wrinkled and developed unhealthy red veins. The finding confirms similar reports of the fungi's ability to help protect plants from toxic effects of other heavy metals like zinc and cadmium. Through repeated screening of new generations of fungi, strains could be developed that offer even better protection to plants.

Plant Development and Productivity Research,
Western Regional Research Center, Albany, CA
Raymond L. Franson, (415) 559-5724

Packing the soil after seeding clover will improve germination and increase production by making better use of soil moisture. Using a 50-hp tractor, scientists criss-crossed fields after seeding clover in November. The result: 2.4 times more plants were established, producing 1,750 more pounds of clover per acre in spite of a dry autumn. Repeated trips across fields with a tractor often result in undesirable compacting of the soil. But in the case of the coarse, light-textured soils of the Coastal Plains, packing the seed beds with a medium-sized tractor helps the ground retain water. The technique was also proven effective with bermudagrass earlier this decade. Not only do adequate levels of soil moisture improve clover yields, this legume plant also helps protect soil from erosion and returns more nitrogen to the land for use by subsequent crops.

Coastal Plain Experiment Station, Tifton, GA
Roger N. Gates, (912) 386-3175

Adding a little clay to the surface of sandy soils can help landowners prevent damaging wind erosion and reestablish vegetation where it's been blown away in a storm. It's also much less expensive than treating sandy soils with a chemical soil stabilizer. To test this approach, scientists mixed small amounts of bentonite clay with sand and subjected it to 31-mile-per-hour winds in a wind tunnel. These abrasive gusts were 30 times more damaging to untreated sandy soil than the clay-sand mixture. Preventing wind erosion on sandy soils is a worldwide challenge. This new technique may be economical in many countries where deposits of clay can be found near erosion-prone soils to improve soil structure enough to support profitable plant growth.

Wind Erosion Research, Manhattan, KS
Edward L Skidmore, (913) 532-6726

Crop Production and Protection

Using less nitrogen fertilizer could be good for food as well as water quality. Overfertilizing greenhouse pots slashed vitamin C levels in green beans, swiss chard and kale. It's not the form of nitrogen that matters—i.e., synthetic, manure or compost—but the amount of nitrogen. A loss of vitamin C in leafy greens could also lower the amount of iron available to consumers since vitamin C enhances the body's ability to use iron. (A cup of cooked kale has as much vitamin C and more iron than a cup of orange juice made from concentrate.) Researchers will next grow kale, collard greens, spinach and other greens with low applications of nitrogen fertilizer to see if iron availability is affected. If it is, to confirm the results of the greenhouse experiments, further research will be conducted with animals or people and large-scale field experiments. In another study, different nitrogen fertilization levels are being tested on high-carotene carrots to check effects on beta-carotene, which can be used to produce vitamin A in the human body.

Soil-Microbial Systems Lab, Beltsville, MD
Sharon B. Hornick, (301) 344-3327

A suicidal pea plant could give scientists clues to increasing the iron in American crops. Discovered in studies begun in 1985, the pea plant, dubbed E107, is a mutant and doesn't know when to stop taking up iron from the soil. It eventually accumulates enough of the element to kill itself. Normal plants have mechanisms for taking up iron from the soil, but they shut down those processes when they get

enough iron to satisfy their needs. Scientists are studying the differences between the mutant and normal pea plants to help find ways to increase the useful iron content of edible parts of crop plants.

U.S. Plant, Soil and Nutrition Lab, Ithaca, NY
Ross M Welch, (607) 255-5434

A yeast found in the stomach of the cigarette beetle can detoxify farm chemicals and natural toxins, rendering them safe. ARS entomologists found the yeast produces an enzyme that neutralizes insecticides, plant toxins and fungal toxins. The enzyme breaks down or changes the chemical structure of the toxin. Lab tests showed the yeast produced increased levels of detoxifying enzymes when exposed to certain toxins, such as the plant toxin flavone. Cigarette beetles, a pest of stored products, provide the yeast with a safe home. In turn, the yeast supplies the insect with vitamins and nutrients. Because the yeast neutralizes toxins, it also allows the beetle to feed on a wider range of plant materials. The researchers expect to test the yeast—grown independently of the insect—against aflatoxin in future studies. (PATENT)

Mycotoxin Research, Northern Regional Research Center, Peoria, IL
Patrick F. Dowd/Samuel K. Shen, (309) 685-4011

Peach orchards in danger of being devastated by certain nematodes may possibly be reclaimed by planting wheat. The ring nematode, *Criconemella xenoplax*, which causes a disease known as "peach tree short life" in Southeastern orchards, feeds off a tree's nutrients, causing it to be more susceptible to cold injury and eventual death. Scientists discovered that when Stacy, a winter wheat variety, was planted in infested peach orchards and greenhouse tests, the nematodes mysteriously disappeared. Experiments are now being run to investigate the possibility that wheat is a biocontrol form of poison to nematodes. If so, rotating land previously planted to peaches with wheat, before new trees are planted, may prove to be an alternative control method for this nematode in orchards suffering from peach tree short life.

Southern Fruit and Tree Nut Research Lab, Byron, GA
A.P. Nyczepir, (912) 956-5656

Growing cotton in 30-inch-wide rows instead of the traditional 40 inches increased yields about 15 percent and shortened maturity 6 to 7 days. ARS researchers found that cotton grown in 30-inch rows also produced fewer short fibers and less trash such as leaves and stems, both of which reduce quality and contribute to waste. During a 5-year test, higher yields from 30-inch rows ranged from 8 to 25 percent. A comparison of bale quality in 1988 revealed that

4

94 percent of the 30-inch-row cotton graded premium, compared with 80 percent for 40-inch row cotton. Growing the crop in 30-inch rows also enables farmers to double-crop by planting soybeans, corn or grain sorghum in the space between rows

Conservation and Production Systems Research, Weslaco, TX
Marvin D. Heilman, (512) 969-2511

Semi-dwarf rice varieties have a better chance of sprouting if seed is treated with gibberellic acid, a growth regulator. Semi-dwarf varieties such as Lemont are popular with farmers because the shorter stalks are stiffer and less likely to dump the grain on the ground. But if semi-dwarf seed is planted even a quarter-inch too deep, the rice might never emerge from the soil. As the seed germinates, its first parts—the mesocotyl and coleoptile—are too short to push through the soil's surface. Scientists have found that a 5-minute bath in a growth regulator called GA3 gives semi-dwarfs enough growth to push them up even taller than conventional rice varieties, at least until the plants are 6 to 8 inches tall. After this early growth spurt gets them safely above ground, the semi-dwarf characteristic prevails, and the mature plants are no taller than they would have been without GA3 treatment. At least one chemical company is considering the cost-effectiveness of offering a commercial rice seed treatment of gibberellic acid.

Rice Production and Weed Control Research, Stuttgart, AR
Robert H. Dilday, (501) 673-2661

Soil bacteria that cost soybean farmers money may be humbled one day. More than 60 percent of the U.S. soybean crop relies on commonly occurring bacterial strains, classified as serogroup 123, to capture nitrogen from the air and fix it in the roots as free fertilizer. Bacteria compete fiercely for a home on soybean roots and serogroup 123 strains of *Bradyrhizobium japonicum* usually win the race at the expense of other bacteria such as strain USDA 110. This is unfortunate for farmers because strain 110 delivers more nitrogen to developing pods. ARS scientists may change all that. They discovered soybean breeding lines that reject serogroup 123 strains and found three soybean genes that seem to be responsible for this rejection. They have also found genetic material in USDA 110 that influences one of the new soybean lines to favor it. The scientists have applied for a patent outlining a two-pronged approach that could boost profits for a crop worth almost $11 billion annually. (PATENT)

Nitrogen Fixation and Soybean Genetics Lab, Beltsville, MD
Michael J Sadowsky/Perry B. Cregan/Harold H. Keyser, (301) 344-1723

A small red lentil, relished for its taste in Turkey and Egypt, could become a cash crop for some Pacific Northwest farmers. ARS scientists have documented good yields of the lentils when grown in fields that usually would be left fallow after a winter wheat crop. Red lentils appear to be better adapted to drier areas of the Palouse region of Washington state than the large yellow lentils commonly grown in eastern Washington and northern Idaho. Growers can skip using nitrogen fertilizer for the crop since red lentils, about half the size and weight of the yellow lentils, fix their own nitrogen in the soil. Red lentil seed is expected to be available for the 1990 crop season. These lentils are preferred in about 75 percent of the world market, principally in Pakistan and parts of the Middle East.

Grain Legume Genetics and Physiology Research, Pullman, WA
Frederick J. Muehlbauer, (509) 335-9521

Scientific Information Systems

The type of weeds found in farmers' fields can help those farmers decide when and how to fight back. For example, researchers calculate that it takes three bearded sprangletop weeds to cause as much loss of rice yield as a single barnyardgrass weed. The researchers studied the impact of these and six other major weeds—broadleaf signalgrass, eclipta, northern jointvetch, hemp sesbania, red rice and ducksalad—on both conventional and semi-dwarf varieties of rice. Yield losses from each of these weeds are being worked into a computer model that rice farmers can someday use to assess their weed problems and plot the most cost-effective strategy for dealing with them. Farmers would supply only information on the variety of rice they're growing and an estimate of the number and type of weeds per square foot in their fields. A working model may be available next year.

Rice Production and Weed Control Research, Stuttgart, AR
Roy J. Smith Jr., (501) 673-2661

Sealing herbicides in cornstarch capsules for slow release often requires less chemical to control weeds for an extended time. Reducing the amount of chemical applied can lower by 60 to 90 percent chemicals lost by leaching below the root zone of a sandy soil, according to computer simulations. This would decrease the threat to groundwater. Simulations of what happens to 14 encapsulated herbicides applied at corn planting time each year for 50 years were made possible by a new adaptation of the ARS main groundwater leaching model, GLEAMS (Groundwater

Loading Effects of Agricultural Management Systems). The simulations demonstrate how GLEAMS can be used to evaluate the environmental impact of encapsulating various herbicides and other chemicals used by farmers. Several major pesticides have been encapsulated using a USDA-patented technique and are ready for commercial introduction. The technique is now being tested on insecticides, fungicides, nematocides, herbicides and fertilizer.

Southeast Watershed Research Lab, Tifton, GA
Walter G. Knisel, (912) 386-3290

Predicting the number of pigs to which a sow will give birth has always been a guessing game. But a computer model now being tested by ARS scientists may replace this guesswork. Ultimately, the model could be used to select sows that will give birth to, and wean larger, healthy litters. So far, the model has shown that litter size depends on a combination of factors, including genetics, nutrition and hormonal influences. The model bases its predictions on data about ovulation rate, embryo survival and uterine capacity—i.e., the maximum number of embryos a sow can carry to birth. One prediction: One more embryo—gained by improving nutrition or by superovulation—will not increase a sow's litter size if her uterine capacity is limited. If that capacity were enlarged, that additional egg would increase average litter size by about three-fourths of a pig.

U.S. Meat Animal Research Center, Clay Center, NE
Gary Bennett, (402) 762-4254

Animal Production and Protection

"Good" bacteria can be injected into incubating eggs to prevent *Salmonella* organisms from getting a toe-hold in the intestinal tract of baby chicks and later causing contamination of poultry with this food-poisoning organism. About 2 million cases of *Salmonella* food poisoning in humans are reported each year. Many are attributed to contaminated poultry products. USDA estimates these food poisonings cost $1.2 billion annually in lost wages, decreased employee productivity, medical expenses, industry production losses and destruction of contaminated foods. ARS scientists are patenting this injection method, which can be used on any type of bird including chicken, turkey, duck, goose, quail and pheasant. The process works best when the "good" bacteria are injected into a fertile egg's air cell. This allows the injected bacteria to develop inside the chick's digestive tract before it hatches, preventing *Salmonella* organisms from attaching themselves to the intestinal walls and multiplying to dangerous levels. (PATENT)

Poultry Microbiological Safety Research, Athens, GA
Nelson A Cox Jr /Joseph S. Bailey, (404) 546-3531

A **disease-causing bacterium** known as *Leptospira bratislava* is one of several possible causes being studied of the mysterious stillbirths, abortions and pre-weaning deaths of pigs that began in the Midwest a year ago. The bacterium causes the disease leptospirosis, which produces reproductive problems in swine. But until now, bratislava has only been known to affect pigs in Europe. Its linkage to the U.S. outbreak came under scrutiny after scientists isolated bratislava from stillborn and weak baby pigs in an infected Iowa swine herd. Bratislava has been identified in at least 17 herds in Iowa and Indiana. Other possible causes of the mysterious outbreaks being studied by ARS scientists include viral infections and moldy corn.

National Animal Disease Center, Ames, IA
Carole A. Bolin, (515) 239-8325

In their annual war against horn flies, cattle producers may soon draw yet another weapon from an arsenal that has included sprays, dust bags, ear tags and pills. ARS researchers designed neckbands that slowly release organophosphates, insecticides to which the pests have no resistance. A polymerized plastic reservoir holds the insecticide inside the neckband. The device-within-a-device releases just the right amount for fly control. The stakes are high. Annually, horn flies cost U.S. cattle producers more than $700 million in reduced weight gains and milk production. In addition to the horn fly, organophosphates are effective against face flies, mange mites, and the Gulf Coast, Lone Star, and southern cattle ticks. (PATENT)

U.S. Livestock Insects Research Lab, Kerrville, TX
J. Allen Miller, (512) 257-3566

Zapping plants with laser beams could make forage more digestible for livestock. Lab tests showed switchgrass, a warm-season grass, hit by laser beams was 11 percent more digestible. Tall fescue, a cool-season grass, hit with the laser was 14 percent more digestible. Previous research showed that improving forage digestibility by just 3 percent can increase livestock weight gains 25 to 35 percent. If lasers become as common as calculators, farmers someday may replace energy-consuming grinders with lasers. (PATENT)

Animal Physiology and Nutrition Research,
Columbia, MO
James R. Forwood, (314) 875-5357

A South American peanut plant could help produce steaks, roasts and burgers from Gulf Coast cattle at a lower cost. In preliminary findings from the first year of a 3-year study, hay from rhizoma peanut forage was compared in cattle feeding trials with a feed supplement typically fed to wintering cattle. Cow weights tended to be higher—950 pounds versus 911 pounds—at 12 weeks with the feed supplement, but there was no difference at other times during the trials. The hay from rhizoma peanut has about 13 percent crude protein, compared with tropical grass hays such as bahiagrass, which can have as little as 6 percent protein. In addition, the peanut is a legume, so it can transform atmospheric nitrogen to forms the plant can use, thereby reducing fertilizer needs. Rhizoma peanut can grow in well-drained soils along the Gulf Coast and as far north as the coastal areas of North Carolina.

Subtropical Agricultural Research, Brooksville, FL
Andrew C. Hammond, (904) 796-3385

A forage grass from New Zealand proved remarkably resistant during the 1988 drought in central Pennsylvania. In field plots at the ARS pasture research lab, Matua bromegrass remained green and growing into December, long after other grasses shriveled or stopped their growth because of the drought. In fact, its steady growth permitted six cuttings from June through November, raising the possibility that its use could extend the fall grazing season. And in tests last spring, grown in strips alongside other grasses, this cool-season grass was preferred by dairy cattle over other forage grasses tested. They ate the Matua first, down to a stubble of only 2 to 3 inches. The other grasses were eaten only after the Matua was too short for cows to graze.

U.S. Regional Pasture Research Lab,
University Park, PA
Gerald A. Jung, (814) 863-0948

Higher levels of protein and energy may be obtained from some crop residues when they are treated with previously unknown bacteria that simultaneously fix atmospheric nitrogen and break down cellulose. In a 10-week feeding trial, crayfish fed bacteria-treated wheat straw gained about 50 percent more weight than crayfish fed untreated wheat straw. Scientists think that treated crop residues such as wheat straw, rice straw and beet pulp may also raise feed value for farm animals. Of 194 bacteria discovered since 1985, 30 appear to be new strains or species of the genus *Bacillus*. The remainder do not fit any known classification and researchers are planning to classify additional strains. (PATENT)

Biopolymer Research, Northern Regional
Research Center, Peoria, IL
J. Michael Gould, (309) 685-4011

Human Nutrition

Here's more proof that combining exercise with a reducing diet boosts weight loss. Moderately overweight women who cut calories and exercised during a 3-1/2 month study lost about 2-1/2 pounds a week. Other volunteers who exercised but didn't diet lost about 1 pound a week. The 10 participants in the study were 23 to 50 pounds overweight. Each woman logged a rigorous workout 6 days a week on a treadmill or exercise bike. Everyone's fitness level improved equally. But the dieters burned more fat while they exercised than non-dieters. Although the dieters received 50 percent fewer calories than they would have otherwise needed to maintain their weight, they were still able to keep up their daily workout. Other results of the experiment, now being analyzed, may pinpoint biochemical or physiological changes that accurately predict important shifts in the body's fat-and-lean makeup.

Body Composition and Energy Metabolism Research,
Western Human Nutrition Research Center,
San Francisco, CA
Nancy L. Keim, (415) 556-5800

Women who exercise so rigorously that they stop menstruating may have less protection against heart disease than those who continue to menstruate. Researchers analyzed the blood of 25 runners—9 of whom had stopped menstruating—and 36 sedentary women for indicators of heart disease risk. All runners scored 20 percent lower than sedentary women in an indicator of the artery-clogging LDL cholesterol. But other risk factors were about the same between the runners who had stopped menstruating and the sedentary women. Only the menstruating runners scored lower in total cholesterol and triglycerides and higher in indicators of the artery-cleansing HDL cholesterol and the important HDL/LDL ratio. The findings indicate that some benefits of strenuous exercise can be reversed if women fail to produce enough estrogen to maintain normal menstruation.

Human Nutrition Research Center on Aging at Tufts,
Boston, MA
Stefania Lamon-Fava, (617) 556-3100

If your muscles are sore several days after heavy exercise and you can't grin and bear it, be careful what pain reliever you take. New evidence suggests that aspirin and aspirinlike compounds could interfere with muscle repair and thus prolong the soreness. For the first time, scientists have found increased levels of interleukin-1 (IL-1)—a protein that promotes inflammation—in damaged muscle tissue well after blood levels have returned to normal. The protein was present in the thigh muscles of four men 5 days after they ran downhill for 45 minutes—a highly damaging exercise for the untrained person. This is strong evidence that IL-1stimulates the repair process, which involves the production of hormone-like substances called prostaglandins. But aspirin blocks prostaglandin synthesis and so does ibuprofen to a lesser degree. Acetaminophen does not.

Human Nutrition Research Center on Aging at Tufts, Boston, MA
William J. Evans, (617) 556-3076

A sophisticated device for measuring bodyfat is proving to be especially useful for middle aged and elderly women suffering bone loss. Known as TOBEC (for "total body electrical conductivity"), the instrument may be superior to the longtime standard technique—underwater weighing—for accurately checking body composition. These measurements determine how much of a person's body is lean and how much is fat. Many nutritionists and physicians now say bodyfat measures are a better indication of overall health than body weights dictated by the widely used height-weight tables. When weighed underwater, postmenopausal women, who lose at least 1 percent of their bone mass each year between ages 50 to 65, will show up as less lean than they actually are because underwater weighing does not accurately compensate for the effects of the loss of bone. Although a second test—a bone scan usually done by photon absorptiometry—will correct the measurement, TOBEC quickly provides an accurate reading in one step, not two.

Body Composition and Energy Metabolism Research, Western Human Nutrition Research Center, San Francisco, CA
Marta Van Loan, (415) 556-5729

Older people who enjoy a daily cocktail or glass of wine or beer are probably not replacing nutritious food with "empty" alcohol calories—though too much can be harmful. In a study of 586 nonalcoholic Bostonians over the age of 60, researchers found that the senior citizens' food intake remained constant when they consumed alcoholic beverages. Their caloric intake increased in proportion to their alcohol intake. Moreover, those who had at least one drink per week had substantial increases in the beneficial HDL cholesterol: 8 percent for the group consuming one to six drinks per week and 16 percent for those consuming one or more drinks per day. This latter group, however, also had elevated levels of two enzymes that indicate liver damage, suggesting that a daily drink may be hard on the aging liver.

Human Nutrition Research Center on Aging at Tufts, Boston, MA
Paul F. Jacques, (617) 556-3322

Megadoses of vitamins and minerals don't improve the performance of children with Down Syndrome as was reported elsewhere several years ago. In a collaborative study with pediatricians at the University of Illinois Medical Center, an ARS scientist evaluated the vitamin and mineral levels of 50 such children before, during and after 8 months of supplementation. Half the children got a megavitamin-mineral preparation (up to 10 times the Recommended Dietary Allowances); the other half got a placebo. Except for a few who tested low in zinc, the children began the study with adequate levels of the five vitamins and two minerals studied. And 8 months of megadoses did not improve their nutritional status compared with the placebo group. Nor did the two groups differ in physical development, health, or tests of mental proficiency.

Grand Forks Human Nutrition Research Center, Grand Forks, ND
David B. Milne, (701) 795-8424
University of Illinois Medical Center, Chicago, IL
Parvin Justice, (312) 996-5725

The popular food preservative TBHQ reduces the damage caused by copper deficiency in rats and may be protecting people whose copper intake is less than adequate. Young rats fed a copper-deficient diet develop enlarged hearts two to three times heavier than normal. And they develop severe anemia with about half the normal number of red blood cells. When TBHQ was fed to copper-deficient rats at the same levels found in human food, it significantly reduced both heart size and anemia. TBHQ is an antioxidant that is replacing the chemically related preservatives BHT and BHA in many foods. DMSO, another antioxidant not approved for human use, also protected the animals but at much higher doses. Copper-deficient diets produce the most severe effects in very young animals, suggesting that children may benefit most from food preservatives.

Grand Forks Human Nutrition Research Center, Grand Forks, ND
Jack T. Saari/W. Thomas Johnson, (701) 795-8499/8411

Beef is rich in the essential element zinc and is thought to supply as much as half the zinc in the U.S. diet, despite new findings. The studies show that when beef is eaten as part of a meal—as it usually is—the body absorbs about one-third less zinc than previously thought. Nevertheless, meals containing 7.5 ounces of beef still supplied between 1.1 and 2.2 milligrams of available zinc. That's between half and all of what the body needs each day.

Grand Forks Human Nutrition Research Center, Grand Forks, ND
Phyllis E. Johnson, (701) 795-8416

Thin layers of skin pigment cells basking under a sun lamp or soaking in a warm bath are helping scientists learn how sunlight triggers the tanning process. Such information should eventually lead to treatments for irregular pigmentation as well as to sunless tanning. A tan is the skin's major defense against ultraviolet-induced cancer, but cells are inevitably damaged to some degree in the course of getting a sun tan. So far the scientists have learned that sunlight directly stimulates the pigment cells, or melanocytes, to mimic the tanning process. So does "bath water" taken from culture dishes housing the skin cells we continually shed (keratinocytes), indicating that they secrete a stimulatory substance. And a chemical "messenger" common in many types of cells causes the pigment cells to produce much more of the tanning pigment.

Human Nutrition Research Center on Aging at Tufts, Boston, MA
Philip R Gordon/Barbara A. Gilchrest, (617) 556-3144/3141

Disappearance of the thymus gland in middle age may play a role in the aging of skin as well as the decline of the immune system, a preliminary study shows. The gland, which normally atrophies completely in the middle years, is where immune cells, particularly T cells, mature to their functional stage. Recent research has uncovered several links between the immune system and the skin. Now, an ARS study shows that cells from the outer layer of skin, keratinocytes, grow and divide more rapidly in a culture dish when an extract from calf thymus is added to the growth media. But cells from young donors responded to the extract better than cells from older donors and continued to respond at doses that were toxic to the "older people's" cells. This indicates that skin cells lose their sensitivity to thymus secretions after the gland disappears and suggests it may be partially responsible for skin maintenance. The study was also funded by the French research group, Moet-Hennessy Recherche.

Human Nutrition Research Center on Aging, at Tufts, Boston, MA
Betzabe Stanulis-Praeger (retired), (906) 482-0142/ Barabara A. Gilchrest, (617) 556-3141

New and Improved Products

Sliced apples, pears or peaches may look appetizing longer if dipped in a new bath. Scientists found that a zinc chloride solution delays unsightly browning of these fruits when they are sliced, bagged and refrigerated A zinc chloride that's approved for human consumption would need to be used for the bath. Browning is caused by a polyphenol oxidase enzyme that is released from cells when fruit is sliced or chopped. The treatment's effectiveness varies with the type of fruit used. Experiments show it may fend off browning of presliced, bagged and refrigerated fruit from several days up to 10 weeks or more. (PATENT)

Process Chemistry and Engineering, Western Regional Research Center, Albany, CA
Harold R. Bolin, (415) 559-5863

Two techniques will nearly double the post-harvest life of zucchini squash and other horticultural products. Using the first technique, temperature preconditioning, squash is kept at 59 degrees F for 2 days before being stored at 41 degrees F. The second method is intermittent warming, or heating the squash every 48 hours at 68 degrees F for 1 day. Both methods preserve freshness and prevent chilling injury—characterized by pitting on the zucchini's surface. Because post-harvest life is increased from 8 to about 16 days, the squash can now be stored longer, cutting retail store losses from spoiled produce. Fruits such as watermelon, grapefruit, lemons and nectarines can also be preconditioned or warmed to reduce chilling injury.

Horticultural Crops Quality Lab, Beltsville, MD
Chien Yi Wang/George F. Kramer, (301) 344-3128

Edible coatings made from milk could keep cut-up fresh fruits and vegetables colorful, flavorful and nutritious longer than before. When fully developed, the films would not alter the taste or texture of the foods they protect, and would meet the needs of consumers who like fresh produce but don't want to spend time in the kitchen washing, slicing, peeling, pitting and paring. In tests, a nearly invisible coating that includes milk's major protein—casein—kept small pieces of sliced and peeled apple fresh-looking for 2 to 3 days. Unprotected pieces shriveled and turned brown in just a few hours. A small amount of vitamin C can be added to the coating to further reduce browning. ARS scientists now want to tighten the molecular structure of the protein to block water's escape, yield a thinner film and increase protection to 15 to 20 days. This work may take about 2 years. Other edible films could also be made from the protein in soybean, corn or wheat.

Western Regional Research Center, Albany, CA
Attila E. Pavlath, (415) 559-5620
University of California, Davis, CA
John M. Krochta, (916) 752-2164

An apple's condition at the checkout counter is partly determined by how it was shipped, how far it traveled, by what route and how it was packaged. An ARS study conducted with two packinghouses, two distribution centers and six retail stores found that Golden Delicious apples were least damaged when packed in foam cellmaster cartons, regardless of distance traveled. The study used an electronic apple to record the duration, time and magnitude of impacts during travel over eight distances. In each case, cellmaster-protected apples fared better than bagmaster cartons or traymaster cartons. Rough roads and railroad crossings added to the average amount of damage to apples. The study's results can be used by shippers to select packing materials, transportation distances and routes that will help maintain top apple quality.

Fruit and Vegetable Harvesting Research,
East Lansing, MI
Galen K. Brown, (517) 353-5185

Covering green asparagus with a 4-mil-thick, 14-inch-tall opaque plastic drape before the spears emerge from the soil results in white spears rather than green ones. This difference can more than double the prices paid at the market. Using the covers is less labor-intesive than methods used to grow it in Eastern Europe and Asia, chief sources of white asparagus in the United States. White asparagus results from lack of light that inhibits the development of chloroplasts, which produce the chlorophyll that gives plants their green color. In field tests, black plastic covers boosted the number of spears emerging during the first 3 weeks of harvest. Also, trimmed spears grown under cover weigh more than their open-air cousins. The covers protected the spears against cold temperatures indirectly by slowing down the change in sugars, a sort of anti-freeze, into more complex carbohydrates. More than 50 percent of spears grown under cover survived a freeze that killed uncovered spears. Another payoff: Researchers say the white asparagus has a more delicate flavor.

South Central Family Farms Research, Booneville, AR
Donald J. Makus, (501) 675-3834

New peanut varieties released to Southern Plains farmers in recent years are increasing their profits and expanding food production in protein-deficient developing countries. Pronto and Spanco, two early maturing spanish-type varieties, produce 20 percent more peanuts than other varieties, adding some $7.1 million annually to the incomes of Texas and Oklahoma farmers. A genetically similar variety has been adapted to the Sudan, Africa, and other areas with short, dry growing seasons. A fourth variety, Okrun, was grown commercially by Oklahoma farmers for the first time this year, and should increase farm profits even more. In a 6-year test, field plots of Okrun yielded 5.7 percent more peanuts than plots of Florunner, the state's most popular variety. Had Okrun been grown instead of Florunner, the farm value of the state's peanuts in 1988 would have increased by $1.4 million.

Peanut Research, Stillwater, OK
Donald J. Banks, (405) 624-4121

Aflatoxin contamination of peanuts before harvest might be prevented if the peanut's natural defense is lengthened. ARS researchers found that drought stress stops production of phytoalexins, compounds believed to be part of the peanut's natural defense against aflatoxin. Scientists have found a link between moisture inside a peanut kernel and production of these compounds. When moisture in a peanut kernel drops below a specific level, the phytoalexin-based resistance breaks down and the fungi *Aspergillus flavus* and *A. parasiticus* can then produce aflatoxin. Aflatoxin is a natural poison that is carcinogenic to some animals, and therefore, its presence in foods is regulated by the Food and Drug Administration. High soil temperatures accompanied by drought can break down a peanut's natural defense sooner. Scientists will be looking at various peanut varieties that are not considered desirable by the $3 billion per year peanut industry to see if they have genetic traits needed to extend the natural defense.

National Peanut Research Lab, Dawson, GA
Joe W. Dorner, (912) 995-4481

New varieties of a plum and nectarine—both bred to resist fruit diseases in the Southeast—have been introduced by ARS and are now available from nurseries. Rubysweet is a freestone, Japanese-type plum bearing fruit about 2 inches in diameter that has firm, high quality, blood-red flesh. Bred for the humid climates, it resists southeastern plum diseases except leafscald. Researchers recommend interplanting Rubysweet with other plums to ensure cross pollination. Roseprincess is a larger, firmer and more attractive nectarine than other white-fleshed varieties. Tart and flavorful, it, too, is a freestone fruit.

Southeastern Fruit and Tree Nut Research Lab,
Byron, GA
William R. Okie, (912) 956-5656

Picking peaches when they are ripe doesn't necessarily mean they must be eaten soon before they spoil. Instead, they can go into cold storage. The Cresthaven variety represents peaches best suited for shipping and most often sold in stores. Currently, most shipped peaches are picked before they reach full maturity. ARS scientists found that by cooling mature fruit properly and holding it at 32 degrees F during shipping from harvest to sale, the shelf life increases up to 4 weeks. The information allows growers to harvest peaches when they are mature. These results indicate that it is possible to hold some varieties, such as Cresthaven, long enough for export shipment to overseas markets. ARS plans to study effects on peach quality and shelf life when different varieties of peaches are stored at temperatures higher than 32 degrees F.

Food Quality Evaluation Research, Athens, GA
James A. Robertson, (404) 546-3318

The severity of a major citrus disease can be detected faster with a new test. Until now, it's taken 3 to 12 months for orchard owners to confirm the severity of citrus tristeza virus (CTV). Now, it can be done in as little as 4 hours. Scientists have produced a monoclonal antibody that reacts to strains of CTV that cause stem-pitting and tree decline. This antibody, now being patented, can identify severe strains of the virus in budwood sources and can be used to monitor the aphid spread of the disease in the field. It isn't reactive to mild strains of this disease. Scientists at the University of California and the University of Florida assisted in this research. (PATENT)

Subtropical Plant Pathology, U.S. Horticultural Research Lab, Orlando, FL
Stephen M. Garnsey/Thomas A. Permar, (407) 897-7341

American raw wool could become more attractive to the textile industry thanks to a new bleaching method developed by ARS scientists. Some American raw wool has a high degree of urine stain—one of the reasons for the bleaching process. By changing the chemistry currently used for bleaching, scientists found the number of baths commonly used to whiten U.S. wool can be cut from two to one. The single-bleach method could lower manufacturing costs and improve profits for American sheep producers, who usually breed sheep primarily for meat. Imported wool comes primarily from sheep bred specifically for finer textured wool. Researchers are currently working on ways to bleach black hairs that appear in American wool but have been bred out of imported wool. (PATENT)

Hides, Leather and Wool Research, Philadelphia, PA
Mustafa Arifoglu/William Marmer, (215) 233-6585

Two natural chemicals released by algae give freshwater fish a musty and muddy taste and also affect the flavor of drinking water. ARS scientists are studying ways to stop algae from making the chemicals—geosmin and 2-methyliso-borneal. Freshwater fish absorb the chemicals through their gills Within 2 hours, the chemicals deposit in fat tissues resulting in an off-flavor. Even if fish are moved to algae-free water or "purge ponds," it takes at least 2 weeks to flush the two chemicals from fatty tissue. Fish farmers can't simply kill algae to correct an off-flavor problem because as algae die more of the chemicals are released into the water. The research also has sparked interest from water-utility officials worldwide. ARS has received water samples for testing from Japan to Norway and from various U.S. states. ARS researchers are developing tools for test kits to monitor chemical levels in drinking water. Early detection and treatment are essential to providing good-tasting drinking water and ponds.

Food Flavor Quality Research Lab, New Orleans, LA
Peter Johnsen, (504) 286-4200

New studies show that low-tar cigarettes may be more polluting to the environment than to the smoker, and are more polluting than high-tar cigarettes. Using the Ames test of mutagenicity, ARS scientists compared the smoke from 15 low-tar brands (those ranging from 1 to 10 milligrams of tar) with smoke from a nonfiltered high-tar brand (23 mg. of tar). Filtered smoke from the low-tar cigarettes was about 20 to 30 percent less mutagenic than the inhaled smoke from the high-tar cigarette. But smoke from the lighted end (sidestream smoke) was 20 to 30 percent more mutagenic. Chemical analysis showed that compounds that amplify the activity of carcinogens, such as catechols and phenols, were generally as high in the sidestream smoke of the low-tar cigarettes as in the high-tar smoke. The brands with the lowest tar values had the least potent sidestream smoke, based on both the Ames test and chemical analyses.

Tobacco Quality and Safety Research, Athens, GA
O.T. Chortyk, (404) 546-3424

RBANA-CHAMPAIGN

Quarterly Report
of Selected Research Projects

United States
Department of
Agriculture

Agricultural
Research
Service

October 1 to December 31, 1989

Contents

Crop Production and Protection

Russian wheat aphids are giving some Western farmers another headache. These pests can create drought-like damage to cereal crops such as barley and wheat, even with ample soil moisture around the roots. Tests show that barley plants damaged by the insects could not take up enough water to survive, nor could they adjust to lack of water. Healthy plants deprived of water normally respond by regulating their intake according to available moisture. Two plant compounds, glycinebetaine and proline, help the plant regulate water intake. But, researchers found that in aphid-damaged barley the levels of both compounds were low, preventing the plants from adjusting to water stress. When an aphid feeds on a plant, it injects it with a toxin that researchers suspect may interfere with production of the compounds. More experiments are planned.
Northern Grain Insects Research Lab, Brookings, SD
Walter E. Riedell, (605) 693-5207

Note: One or more scientists familiar with each research project are listed for further information. If the scientists are unavailable, others at the same telephone number may also be familiar with the work.

Items marked with the word PATENT are being patented by ARS. For more information contact Ann Whitehead, National Patent Program, Bldg. 005, Rm. 401, Beltsville Agricultural Research Center, Beltsville, MD 20705, (301) 344-2786.

Sunn hemp could have a role in controlling leafy spurge, a noxious weed that has taken over millions of acres in Minnesota, Montana, Nebraska, Idaho and the Dakotas. The weed, originally from eastern Europe, has no natural enemies in the United States. While testing naturally produced plant toxins as alternatives to synthetic pesticides, ARS scientists found that two sunn hemp seeds, planted in a small pot of leafy spurge, reduced the weed's growth by 63 percent. And an extract of the seeds reduced growth by 54 percent. Researchers are currently identifying the toxic compound in the seeds. Sunn hemp, a legume that grows in the United States, makes a good forage. It could be planted in stands of leafy spurge, or extracts from the seeds could be sprayed on the weed. Either method should be an effective part of an integrated program to manage the weed.
Foreign Disease-Weed Science Research Lab, Frederick, MD
Gerald Leather, (301) 663-7132

A special protein found in one of the world's worst weeds could lead to new weapons in the farmer's battle to protect crops. Goosegrass, which infests virtually every major crop in the southeastern United States, traditionally has been controlled with grass-killing herbicides called dinitroanilines. But a goosegrass variety surfaced in 1984 that is 10,000 times more resistant to these herbicides. The difference apparently is a new form of a vital plant protein called tubulin. Tubulin makes up the plant's microtubules, the structures that actually move chromosomes in cell division and plant growth. In lab experiments, tubulin was isolated from resistant and non-resistant goosegrass and treated with dinitroanilines. Tubulin from the resistant goosegrass still produced normal microtubules, indicating its capability of growth even in the face of herbicide treatments, while the susceptible goosegrass' tubulin produced almost none. Researchers hope to locate the gene responsible for production of this hardy tubulin. That would open the way to genetically engineering it into important crops such as corn, barley, wheat and sorghum that are now too sensitive to allow use of dinitroanilines to control grassy weeds.
Herbicide Interactions in Plants and Soils, Stoneville, MS
Kevin C. Vaughn, (601) 686-2311

A weed that resists atrazine by rapidly detoxifying the herbicide is helping scientists learn more about this process and how it might be manipulated to create herbicide-resistant crops. This resistance mechanism makes one strain of the velvetleaf weed 10 times more resistant to atrazine than a normal strain. The resistant velvetleaf strain produces high levels of glutathione S-transferase (GST), a protein that renders the herbicide ineffective. Researchers found that a change in a single gene is responsible for this resistance. They are continuing their study to learn more about how the level of this herbicide-detoxifying protein is regulated in plants and how this knowledge could be used to develop herbicide- resistant crops without sacrificing yield.

Plant Science Research St. Paul, MN
John W. Gronwald, (612) 625-8186

It was scientific serendipity—a happy accident—but the results may pay off for farmers: The first finding that rice plants naturally ward off the worst weeds in that crop. At first, researchers were testing rice varieties for tolerance to agricultural chemicals. Then they noted that ducksalad, a weed growing in the test plots, snuggled up to some rice varieties but gave others a wide berth. In some instances, the weed stayed as much as 8 inches away from the rice. Subsequent testing of 5,000 rice varieties for this anti-weed ability, called allelopathy, turned up 191 varieties that could repel ducksalad, 132 that fend off redstem and 6 that looked promising for resistance to broadleaf signalgrass, all troublesome weeds in rice fields. Fifteen varieties naturally repelled both ducksalad and redstem. The secret apparently is chemicals that the rice varieties put into the soil to discourage unwanted neighbors. A dozen alleopathic rice varieties have already been crossed with commercial varieties in hopes of finding a commercially appealing rice plant that comes equipped with built-in defenses against weeds.

Rice Production and Weed Control Research,
Stuttgart, AR
Robert H. Dilday, (501) 673-2661

Jasmine 85—a new long grain rice that smells of jasmine as it cooks—could provide a substitute for the 10,000 tons of specialty "aromatic" rices annually imported into the United States at premium prices. When produced under Texas growing conditions, the new rice has an aroma and flavor at least equal to that of the premium Basmati rices of India and Pakistan or the Fragrant rices of Thailand. It is more pleasing to some Asian groups than standard U.S. long grain rice. Jasmine 85 was originally bred in the Philippines, but ARS scientists developed the protocol for growing the rice under Texas conditions. Eventually, there could be a market for as much as 30,000 to 50,000 acres of this specialty rice.

Rice Research Station, Beaumont, TX
Charles Bollich, (409) 752-5221

Triticale—a wheat-rye hybrid—is grown on about 3 million acres throughout the world. Even on some of the poorer croplands, it produces up to 30 percent more grain than does wheat. Recent genetic studies by ARS scientists have uncovered some genes in certain wheat varieties that could improve the ability of these triticales to withstand high levels of acid and aluminum found in about 86 million acres worldwide. Some of these genes are on the same chromosome as those associated with good quality bread. But other genes from wheat tend to reduce the ability of genes from rye to tolerate aluminum. Learning which genes from one crop species affect the expression of genes from another species will help plant geneticists make better use of genetic engineering to adapt plants to various soils. That, in turn, will give farmers practical alternatives to fertilizing, irrigating or otherwise modifying soils to meet crop requirements.

Cereal Genetics Research, Columbia, MO
J. Perry Gustafson, (314) 882-7318

Root rot diseases in Pacific Northwest grain fields need careful attention, since fungicides used to control some infestations may make wheat and barley more susceptible to others. For example, take-all, *Pythium* root rot and *Rhizoctonia* root rot—three root diseases caused by soil-dwelling fungi—are frequently found in the same wheat and barley fields. ARS researchers found that applying one fungicide at seeding time specifically to control *Pythium* would significantly increase yields. But where *Pythium* and *Rhizoctonia* fungi occur together, use of a fungicide that is specific for *Pythium* results in greater damage caused by *Rhizoctonia*. Likewise, experimental fungicides aimed only at *Rhizoctonia* did not protect crops from *Pythium* damage when both fungi infest the same fields, and controls specific for take-all did not increase yields when *Pythium* and *Rhizoctonia* were present. Additional research is needed to determine what combinations of microbial or fungicidal seed treatments, cultural practices and plant resistance work best when more than one root disease exists in this region's grain fields.
(PATENT)

Root Disease and Biological Control Research,
Pullman, WA
R. James Cook, (509) 335-3722

Parasitic nematodes may be effective biocontrols against white grubs in sugar cane, according to preliminary experiments. Currently no chemical control is available for white grubs, pests that can cause losses as high as 39 percent of the sugar cane field. Under lab conditions, the nematodes killed 80 to 100 percent of white grubs. Yet to be worked out for effective control in the field: the number of nematodes per application and the timing of applications. A 3-year pilot study will begin developing such information this year. Results from preliminary lab experiments also indicate that these same nematodes may also control sugar cane borers, even killing young borer larvae inside the cane. Studies are currently underway to test effectiveness against the borers in the field. The most effective insectide for sugar cane borers in Florida was recently taken off the market.

Sugar Cane Production Lab, Canal Point, FL
Omelio Sosa, Jr., (407) 924-5227

Human Nutrition

The reason why so many dieters lose the first few pounds quickly, but then can't lose the rest, is because their calorie intake isn't decreasing along with their weight. That is the first finding from two weight-loss studies of volunteers in the Beltsville room calorimeter. Study results don't support the currently popular premise that people's metabolism slows down in response to fewer calories. ARS scientists assessed the number of calories 28 overweight men burned before, during and after they cut their caloric intake by 25 or 50 percent. While dieting, the men burned fewer calories, but no less than would be expected from reducing the amount of food they had to digest, absorb, convert and store from daily meals. And most of the drop occurred on the first day of the weight-loss diets—too soon to be attributed to an energy-saving loss in metabolic rate.

Energy and Protein Nutrition Lab, Beltsville Human
Nutrition Research Center, Beltsville, MD
William V. Rumpler, (301) 344-4360

Vitamin D's Recommended Dietary Allowance may be too low to protect older women from losing bone calcium during late winter, when reserves are lowest. Without direct sunlight, the skin makes little or no vitamin D, which helps the body to absorb calcium. And when not enough of the vitamin is supplied by food or supplements, the body may "borrow" calcium from the bones to maintain a constant blood level. In a study of 333 women past menopause, those who consumed at least 10 percent more vitamin than the RDA of 200 international units did not have the seasonal see-saw of hormones that regulate blood calcium levels. The women's vitamin D levels hit their lowest in late winter and early spring. At the same time, levels of the hormone thought to pull calcium from the bones were at their highest. The women averaged 58 years of age and were all healthy Caucasians—the group most prone to develop osteoporosis. The findings suggest that older people and those with absorption difficulties or

diseases that affect vitamin and mineral levels would need even more vitamin D. But further studies are needed before a specific level can be recommended.

Human Nutrition Research Center on Aging at Tufts,
Boston, MA
Elizabeth Krall, (617) 556-3069

"Tired blood" sufferers take note: Adding a serving of vitamin C-rich foods to each meal can help you absorb more iron from plant foods. Many women have difficulty getting enough iron in their diets, despite a recently lowered RDA for the mineral. And cutting back on red meat consumption increases their problem. A recent study of 11 borderline anemic women showed that adding vitamin C to each meal significantly improved their absorption of iron from breads, cereals and other plant sources throughout 5-1/2 weeks of supplementation. The supplemented group showed significant improvement in several indicators of iron status compared with those who got a placebo instead. Scientists note it's preferable to add vitamin C through foods. Tomatoes, cantaloupe, broccoli, potatoes and the cabbage family are nearly as rich in the vitamin as citrus.

Grand Forks Human Nutrition Research Center,
Grand Forks, ND
Janet R. Hunt, (701) 795-8323

Older people who smoke, in addition to being at greater risk for several diseases, are generally not as well nourished as those who don't. The finding is from a comparison of the nutritional status of 746 men and women between the ages of 62 and 100. The 87 who smoked had significantly lower blood levels of vitamin C, riboflavin, magnesium and vitamin A and related carotenoids than the 659 who didn't smoke. Their choice of less nutritious foods, not the amount of food consumed, accounted for most of the difference. Smokers ate about the same number of calories as nonsmokers of the same age and sex. For reasons unknown, blood calcium levels were higher in the smokers—even though they consumed less of the mineral.

Human Nutrition Research Center on Aging at Tufts,
Boston, MA
Sandra I. Sulsky, (617) 556-3323

An organic acid that occurs naturally in strawberries and apples may reduce the risk of some forms of cancer. In animal and human tissue, medical researchers found that ellagic acid in purified form reduced the incidence of cancer caused by some carcinogenic chemicals. ARS scientists are testing different strawberry and apple varieties to study the genetics associated with the production of ellagic acid in fruit. They're hoping to breed varieties high in the acid— but have not yet determined how much would be needed in diets to be effective against cancer.

Fruit Lab, Beltsville, MD
John L. Maas, (301) 344-3572

While a glass of milk a day can go a long way toward preventing osteoporosis, preliminary findings indicate that, in certain people, it may increase the risk of developing cataracts. Infants who have a rare genetic disorder that prevents them from metabolizing a component of milk sugar develop cataracts early in life if fed milk. These infants are lacking enzymes necessary to metabolize the sugar galactose. Now, an epidemiological study of 112 people between 40 and 70 years old suggests that enzyme levels can influence a person's risk of developing cataracts later in life. Those whose levels of galactokinase were at the low end of the normal range had four times as many cataracts as those having average levels and above, even if they had consumed as little as one cup (8 oz.) of milk a day. But those in the low-enzyme group who had not consumed milk or other sources of galactose, such as yogurt, cheese or ice cream, had about the same cataract incidence as the group with higher levels. No one should stop drinking milk, however, until the findings are confirmed in other studies.

Human Nutrition Research Center on Aging at Tufts, Boston, MA
Paul F. Jacques, (617) 556-3322

Researchers have found a clue as to why mice and rats retain a stronger immune system when their food intake is dramatically restricted throughout life. Knowing how food restriction works means scientists can look for practical alternatives to improve older people's ability to fight infection and nip would-be cancers in the bud. Allowing mice to eat only 80 percent of their normal caloric intake after weaning significantly reduced their synthesis of prostaglandin E_2. This hormone-like compound is known to suppress function of the immune system, so suppressing it helps to boost immunity. Other less stringent dietary modifications, such as increasing vitamin E intake, can also reduce PGE_2 levels. Researchers expect that food restriction causes other changes in body chemistry besides a drop in this compound. But the finding is a beginning.

Human Nutrition Research Center on Aging at Tufts, Boston, MA
Simin Nikbin Meydani, (617) 556-3129

Manufacturers of fish oil capsules add extra vitamin E to prevent this highly unstable oil from going rancid on the shelf. But is it enough to prevent the oil from oxidizing in the body? Apparently not, according to a study of 25 women who took 6 capsules a day for 3 months. Levels of lipid peroxides—the damaging byproducts of oxidation—increased 30 percent in the women who were in their mid-20's and 50 percent in women in their early 60's, even though their vitamin E levels were significantly higher. This could spell trouble since these peroxides can damage cellular structures, including DNA. The fish oil capsules

contained 1 milligram (mg) of vitamin E per gram of oil. According to earlier analyses, the amount of vitamin E in 13 brands of fish oil capsules on the market today ranges from 0.6 mg to 2.2 mg. It now appears these levels may not be sufficient to protect users from cellular damage.

Human Nutrition Research Center on Aging at Tufts, Boston, MA
Mohsen Meydani, (617) 556-3126

The popular sunscreen PABA is helping scientists who are studying diet and weight problems monitor the calorie consumption of research volunteers. Experience has shown that volunteers in diet studies often have difficulty overeating day after day. But, since every morsel must be eaten and every drop of urine collected so as to account for every calorie, scientists were looking for a way to monitor a group of men who would be required to eat an extra 1,000 calories a day—one-third their normal consumption. PABA, once thought to be part of the B vitamin complex, is harmless when eaten. When added to food, the scientists found that 99 percent of its components will appear in the urine within 8 hours. If less than 93 percent of its components are recovered, it means a volunteer cheated by not eating all his food or collecting all his urine. So far, the PABA test has disqualified 3 of 26 volunteers in one study. The use of PABA could have wider applications in other nutrition studies, particularly in monitoring the food intake of anorexic or bolemic patients.

Human Nutrition Research Center on Aging at Tufts, Boston, MA
Susan Roberts/Frank D. Morrow, (617) 556-3227/3166

New and Improved Products

Yellow corn mash can be used not only to fuel a car but also to help get rid of cockroaches. Corn mash from producing ethanol and a water-absorbent gel are key ingredients in a new toxic bait that attracts and kills at least 15 species of cockroaches. Invented by ARS scientists, the bait, called Insect Control System, also works against grasshoppers, crickets and fire ants. The corn mash and the gel keep the bait aromatic and moist under high temperatures and dry conditions when a cockroach's metabolism increases, making it hungry and thirsty. Cockroaches are especially turned on by a moist bait. A microencapsulated toxin inside the bait kills the insect. While corn mash lures these insects, it doesn't attract mammals. Even with dry food and water available, research shows that cockroaches find the new bait more appealing. (PATENT)

Insects Affecting Man and Animals Research Lab, Gainesville, FL
Richard J. Brenner, (904) 374-5937

A **worthless byproduct of sugar processing** might turn out to be worth big bucks. This byproduct, known as levan, is a natural gum made by the soil microorganism *Bacillus polymxa* to protect the bacteria from harmful invasion. It also can be used by the bacteria as a food reservoir. ARS scientists are patenting a way to rapidly produce levan. It can be used in printing, cosmetics and sweetners, as a thickener and possibly to maintain the blood volume of a patient suffering severe loss of blood. Levan is found in certain plants, such as sugar beets, and in sugar-processing factories. Scientists found that growing *B. polyxma* on a sucrose solution produced three times as much levan and in a purer form than at least 28 other levan-producing microorganisms tested on the solution. ARS and Sugar Processing Research Inc., in New Orleans, began working 2 years ago on ways to diversify the sugar industry to find other valuable products besides sugarcane. San Diego-based Kelco Co., a division of Merck Co., Inc., of Rahway, NJ, has a research and development agreement with ARS to commercialize the levan-production technique. (PATENT)

Food and Feed Processing Research, New Orleans, LA
Youn W. Han, (504) 286-4228

Storage conditions make a big difference in the stability and flavor quality of soybean, sunflower and canola oils. In a continuing series of tests aimed at determining what causes flavor and stability differences in edible vegetable oils, ARS scientists found that soybean oil retained a desirable bland flavor better than canola and sunflower oils when they were rapidly aged with or without a preservative in darkness at 140 degrees F. In the same study, they found that under fluorescent lighting, sunflower and canola oils resisted flavor deterioration better than soy oil if citric acid was added at concentrations of 100 parts per million. On the other hand, flavor is least stable in canola oil without citric acid. Citric acid is a natural preservative that is normally included in edible vegetable oils. The scientists found that 100 ppm of citric acid does not change flavor but does slow the development of strong flavors caused by trace minerals that occur naturally in these oils. Soybean oil comprises about 80 percent of the vegetable oil market in the United States.

Vegetable Oil Research, Northern Regional Research Center, Peoria, IL
Kathleen A. Warner, (309) 685-4011, Ext. 584

Fresh fruits and vegetables that are less likely to spoil in shipping and storage may eventually result from a recent advance in genetic engineering. Much produce harvested in the United States is lost due to overripening, and ethylene (a ripening hormone formed naturally by the plants) is blamed for much of that waste. Now, scientists have isolated and cloned a gene which plants must have in order to make ACC synthase—an enzyme needed in one of the final steps

leading to the plant's production of ethylene. Armed with this new knowledge, biotechnological researchers can zero in on stopping the ACC synthase enzyme and thus thwart ethylene formation—a goal that may take another 5 to 10 years to achieve. (PATENT)

USDA-University of California Plant Gene Expression Center, Albany, CA
Athanasios Theologis, (415) 559-5911

Some watermelons have a longer shelf life if they're refrigerated during storage and shipment. That's increasingly important because of the trend towards importing smaller variety watermelons from Central and South America and the Caribbean Islands. Consumption of the large-size, domestically-produced watermelons—which are not usually refrigerated during domestic transit—has decreased because of smaller families, handling problems and higher prices for melons sliced in retail stores. ARS researchers stored four varieties of icebox (small) watermelons for up to 5 weeks at varying temperatures. After two seasons of tests, Minilee and Mickeylee retained freshness and quality longer than other varieties tested. The Minilee was less susceptible to chilling injury at lower storage temperatures and had the least amount of decay. And both the Minilee and Mickylee melons retained their firmness and taste.

U.S. Horticultural Lab, Orlando, FL
Roy E. McDonald, (407) 897-7326
European Marketing Research Center, Rotterdam, The Netherlands
Lawrence A. Risse, 011-31-10-4765233

Eight natural aroma chemicals are responsible for the rich, fruity flavor of high-quality tomato paste, scientists have now learned. They focused on aroma-imparting chemicals because how something smells often dictates how it will taste. One volatile, beta-damascenone, was so potent that aroma panelists could detect it at less than one part per 100 billion—the equivalent of a pinch of salt in 1,000 tons of potato chips. Critical chemicals were identified by a sensory panel of volunteers and studies using sophisticated lab tests and computers. Processors of tomato paste can use the new findings to check flavor quality and possibly enhance flavor by modifying factory procedures such as the methods of heating tomatoes. The research should also help genetic engineers and tomato breeders develop better tasting tomatoes for processing.

Food Quality Research, Western Regional Research Center, Albany, CA
Ronald G Buttery, (415) 559-5667

Animal Production and Protection

Farmers can reap a **five-to-one return** on the dollar—in more digestible hay—by using a special hay-making machine developed by ARS scientists. The machine, reported earlier, shreds the forage crop, presses it into a mat and lays the mat on the field to dry. In 4 to 6 hours, the shredded mat is dry enough to use, a process that once took 3 to 4 days. Now researchers have determined the economic value of the machine lies not only in the speed of harvest but in the quality of the forage fed to livestock. The hay has more digestible fiber than forage cut and dried with conventional methods because leaves and stems are mixed together and dry quickly and uniformly. With conventional forage machines baled leaves dry faster than stems and sometimes shatter, resulting in lost harvest. Researchers found that sheep could digest 15 percent more of the quality quick-dry forage. Tests are planned to see if this forage will increase milk production in high-producing dairy cows. (PATENT)

U.S. Dairy Forage Research Center, East Lansing, MI
C. Alan Rotz, (517) 353-1758

A yet unnamed microorganism may help pork producers save money on feed. About 50 percent of a producer's total production costs is spent on food. *Clostridium longisporum*, a bacterium found in the American buffalo, could indirectly play a role in reducing these costs. Feeding *C longisporum* to pigs stimulated the production of a new microorganism, until now not found in pigs. The new organism better degrades fiber in pigs fed corn and soybeans. Metabolic studies will be done to determine how much energy the pig derives from this organism. If the fiber-degrading activity in pigs is increased, producers may be able to switch to less expensive feeds, such as feed grains from ethanol production.

Nutrition Research, U.S. Meat Animal Research Center, Clay Center, NE
Vincent H. Varel, (402) 762-4207

"Shipping fever" or bacterial pneumonia, the most common cause of contagious respiratory infection in cattle, may be the result of too much of a good thing. Certain chemicals are normally released in short surges by a cow's adrenal gland and are important in the animal's energy balance. But when cattle are stressed for long periods, such as by lengthy rides to sale barns or feedlots, these chemicals, called glucocorticoids, flow in a continuous stream. They attach to receptors on cells throughout the animal's body. The glucocorticoid surplus is believed to depress the animal's natural immune system, allowing infections to set

in. To prevent this, scientists hope to block or mask cells' receptors with some other compound so glucocorticoids cannot attach. One such anti-glucocorticoid, melengestrol acetate or MGA, seems effective at dampening the adrenal gland's ability to release the chemicals. Cattle dosed with another anti-glucocorticoid, progesterone, showed a normal immune response even when stressed. Researchers hope to fine-tune anti-glucocorticoids for possible future use as treatment to counteract the health-threatening effects of stress on livestock.

Forage and Livestock Research, El Reno, OK
Brian J. Hughes, (405) 262-5291

Why animals continue to lose weight after being cured of some disease has intrigued scientists for years. Now, experimental studies have shown that some hormones, including one called cachectin, might cause the weight loss. Such hormones are released by the body in response to an infection. Swine serum thought to contain cachectin was collected from pigs infected with the parasite *Sarcocystis suicanis*. When tissue cultures of rat fat cells were inoculated with this serum, the number of cells was drastically reduced. Inoculations of cachectin produced the same result in other cultures. Scientists speculate that similar reactions occur in animals following an infection. Further studies may lead to methods for controlling the production of cachectin and related hormones. This could prevent weight loss and poor growth that occurs in the wake of many infections of livestock.

Animal Physiology Research Lab, Athens, GA
Gary J. Hausman, (404) 546-3224

Look to turnips if you are a sheep producer searching for a better source of winter grazing than wheat. Scientists have found that turnips will support twice as many sheep as comparable wheat acreage because they yield almost double the amount of dry matter per acre. Equally important, the sheep gained weight well, going first for the leaves, then the top of the turnip and finally nibbling into the heart of the root. Costs of planting turnips as a forage crop are about the same as wheat. Now in the fourth year of feeding trials, researchers have found Purpletop is the best turnip for sheep forage (it's also a familiar table variety). Further, turnips planted in late September and early October were ready for grazing by the end of October. And the vegetable offers crude protein levels of 16 to 20 percent and total digestible nutrients of 80 percent—putting them on par with grain. Turnips also can take the cold; they'll survive light freezes easily and still provide food for the animal.

Forage and Livestock Research Lab, El Reno, OK
Steven P. Hart, (405) 262-5291

367 8/97 22
39270

Planting a new, low-alkaloid variety of reed canarygrass with alfalfa—instead of smooth bromegrass or orchardgrass—may provide a superior forage for cattle and sheep grazed on alfalfa pastures. Livestock grazed on alfalfa bloat easily, and may die, because of the excessive buildup of gas in the rumen. Planting grass with the alfalfa reduces this risk, but too much grass in a pasture decreases the amount of digestible forage the animals consume. Smooth bromegrass and orchardgrass have been preferred by cattle and sheep because they don't like the taste of ordinary canarygrass and eat it sparingly. Using an experimental low-alkaloid canarygrass, MN-76, ARS scientists were able to produce a nearly ideal proportion of alfalfa and grass in a Minnesota study. When harvested 3 times annually, the mixture was 34 percent canarygrass by the third year. In contrast, stands of smooth bromegrass declined, failing to consistently provide a desired mix. And the orchardgrass crowded out the alfalfa, reducing the legume to only one-third of the mix.

Plant Science Research, St. Paul, MN
Gordon C. Marten, now at (301) 344-3078

Sainfoin could become the legume of the future for Oklahoma cattlemen looking for a legume that tolerates dry conditions but doesn't cause bloat. Sainfoin offers many of the same qualities as alfalfa, including crude protein levels of 15 to 20 percent. But unlike alfalfa and other legumes used for grazing, sainfoin does not cause bloat. Sainfoin grows well in the West, but performs poorly in the acidic soils of the East. Though sainfoin yields only 70 to 80 percent as much forage as alfalfa, it could fill an important niche in grazing schedules from March to May where winter wheat grazing has ended but warm-season grasses are not yet ready. Further test plantings are scheduled to see if this legume's potential lives up to scientists' expectations.

Forage and Livestock Research Lab, El Reno, OK
Danny P. Mowrey, (405) 262-5291

Soil, Water and Air

Switching tillage systems this fall could cut machinery costs and add profit next year for corn and soybean farmers cultivating nearly level soils in the central Cornbelt. A farmer can leave the residue of the 1990 crop on the surface and—in the fall—build 1991's seedbeds as low, narrow ridges. It's a practice called ridge tillage—the ridges peek above the residue, letting in sunlight and allowing excess moisture to drain off slowly. Ridging is done by a sub-

soiler-bedder. Conventional tillage—chisel plowing the soybean residue and moldboard plowing the corn residue—has been used less and less, especially on erosion-prone soils. To compare ridge and conventional tillage systems, scientists grew corn and soybeans in a 2-year rotation on Flanagan silt loam soil. Their computer analysis showed machinery costs for ridge tilling 1,000 acres was about $59 per acre. But the per acre cost for the conventional system was $67. Yields were about the same, so the $8 difference translates to clear profit.

Crop Protection Research, Urbana, IL
John W. Hummel, (217) 333-0808

Agricultural chemicals have less chance of reaching groundwater when farmers use a computer model to help them decide whether and how to apply chemicals through irrigation sprinklers. Farmers can irrigate, fertilize and apply pesticides all at the same time in a technique called chemigation. It often allows farmers to split a chemical application over two or more irrigations. ARS has modified its groundwater computer model, called GLEAMS (Groundwater Loading Effects of Agricultural Management Systems), to evaluate the technique. Computerized simulations with ten major herbicides and one nematicide were reasonably close to actual field observations. A typical example: Chemigation reduced by about 40 percent the average annual amount of the nematicide fenamiphos that leached below the root zone. It also reduced by about a third the average annual amount of two toxic byproducts leached below the crop roots. With conventional spraying, farmers usually apply more chemical to be sure enough stays in the upper soil for the desired length of time. Splitting the applications in chemigation allows farmers to acheive the same goal while reducing both individual and total doses.

Southeast Watershed Research Lab, Tifton, GA
Ralph A Leonard, (912) 386-3290

An experimental chemical called V53482 may open the door to no-till farming of rice. No-till helps reduce soil erosion because farmers plant seed directly into the residue of preceding crops, rather than plowing under the stubble and weeds and exposing the soil to rain and wind. No-till has not been feasible for rice farmers because no chemicals were available to rapidly and economically eliminate winter weeds without plowing or leaving a residue that could damage the next rice crop. In test plots, researchers have found that a mixture of V53482, a chemical developed in Japan, and glyphosate, already registered for use on rice fields before planting, delivers a double whammy to weeds The experimental chemical, when mixed with glyphosate, provides "burndown" of winter weeds such as horseweed

and annual bluegrass before planting. The V53482 also provides residual control, even on weeds that germinate after
rice has been seeded. V53482 is highly selective, so it
won't harm the rice plants. It has performed well at rates as
low as 15 grams of active ingredient per acre. More tests on
the chemical are planned.

Rice Production and Weed Control Research,
Stuttgart, AR
Roy J. Smith, Jr., (501) 673-2661

By changing land-clearing techniques, Alaskan farmers
could save money on phosphorus and nitrogen fertilizers
during the first 5 years after clearing forested acreages.
Current practices remove 8 to 10 inches of organic material
from forested areas, leaving a thinner layer of topsoil.
While this retained layer is rich in organic phosphorus and
nitrogen, it is low in the inorganic form of these nutrients—
which is what plants use. Cooperative studies by ARS and
University of Alaska scientists have shown that most of the
organic phosphorus is converted to the inorganic forms
through microbial process during the first 5 years after the
land is cleared. But the conversion of nitrogen occurs much
slower. Even so, these conversions provide only half the
phosphorus and nitrogen needed to grow barley economically, meaning that Alaskan farmers have to purchase costly
supplemental fertilizers. Similar tests on the conversion of
phosphorus and nitrogen in the organic layer that now gets
removed showed that these nutrients are readily converted
into the inorganic form through microbial activity—and thus
would be a valuable resource if more of it was left during
the land-clearing operations.

Subarctic Agricultural Research, Fairbanks, AK
Verlan Cochran/Elena Sparrow, (907) 474-7652

Federal agencies have begun testing the new Water
Erosion Prediction Project (WEPP) computer model
developed by ARS. By 1995, Soil Conservation Service
field personnel will use WEPP software to help farmers
devise individual plans to reduce soil erosion to acceptable
levels. The Forest Service and Bureau of Land Management
will use it to plan ways to control erosion on forest and
range lands those agencies administer. WEPP will largely
replace the Universal Soil Loss Equation (USLE), which
has been used since the 1950's. WEPP can estimate losses
for any period of time, from a single storm to several years.
ARS will work with the agencies to complete two additional
versions of the model for use on larger areas.

National Soil Erosion Research Lab, West Lafayette, IN
John M Laflen, (317) 494-8673

Scientific Information Systems

Acid rain damage to forests and grasslands could soon be
spotted in its earliest stages by aircraft and satellites
equipped with the latest remote sensing technology. Until
now, scientists have been unable to accurately measure the
light reflected from tiny leaf structures such as conifer
needles and thin blades of grass. ARS researchers have
developed new standards for interpreting super-high resolution images on this type of vegetation. Scientists can then
analyze the data for signs of plant stress from acid rain and
other environmental hazards.

Remote Sensing Research Lab, Beltsville, MD
Craig S. Daughtry, (301) 344-2822

How firm do these apples sound? Scientists are developing a way to rapidly measure the firmness and maturity of
apples based on their absorption of low-frequency sound
waves. Firmness and maturity are important considerations
in regulations covering the shipping and marketing of fresh
fruit. At present, the apple industry uses a relatively slow
procedure that measures the pressure needed to penetrate
sample apples to a specified depth. With the new method,
each apple is exposed to either a physical thump or momen-
tary "click" sound as it passes by a tiny speaker. Corresponding measurements of sound coming through the apple
reveal how firm and mature it is. Once fully automated,
this approach could be used to test around five apples per
second, as compared to two apples per minute under the old
method. (PATENT)

Instrumentation and Sensing Lab, Beltsville, MD
Judith A. Abbot/Henry A. Affeldt, (301) 344-3650

*U.S.GOVERNMENT PRINTING OFFICE.1990-262-866 20234/ARS